HD 5650 OXF

THE OXFORD HANDBOOK OF

PARTICIPATION IN ORGANIZATIONS

THE OXFORD HANDBOOK OF

PARTICIPATION IN ORGANIZATIONS

Edited by

ADRIAN WILKINSON

PAUL J. GOLLAN

MICK MARCHINGTON

and

DAVID LEWIN

OXFORD
UNIVERSITY PRESS

Great Clarendon Street, Oxford OX2 6DP
Oxford University Press is a department of the University of Oxford.
It furthers the University's objective of excellence in research, scholarship,
and education by publishing worldwide in
Oxford New York

Auckland Cape Town Dar es Salaam Hong Kong Karachi
Kuala Lumpur Madrid Melbourne Mexico City Nairobi
New Delhi Shanghai Taipei Toronto
With offices in

Argentina Austria Brazil Chile Czech Republic France Greece
Guatemala Hungary Italy Japan Poland Portugal Singapore
South Korea Switzerland Thailand Turkey Ukraine Vietnam

Oxford is a registered trade mark of Oxford University Press
in the UK and in certain other countries

Published in the United States
by Oxford University Press Inc., New York

© Oxford University Press 2010

British Library Cataloguing in Publication Data
Data available

Library of Congress Cataloging in Publication Data
Data available

Typeset by SPI Publishing Services, Pondicherry, India
Printed in Great Britain
on acid-free paper by
CPI Antony Rowe, Chippenham, Wiltshire

ISBN 978–0–19–920726–8

1 3 5 7 9 10 8 6 4 2

ACKNOWLEDGEMENTS

Thanks to our editor David Musson and Matthew Derbyshire for their patience and advice along the way.

Contents

PART I INTRODUCTION

PART II PERSPECTIVES

PART III FORMS OF PARTICIPATION IN PRACTICE

PART IV PROCESSES AND OUTCOMES

PART V POLICY AND COMPARATIVE ISSUES

List of Figures

List of Tables

About the Contributors

The Editors

Professor Adrian Wilkinson

Adrian Wilkinson is Professor of Employment Relations at Griffith University and Director of the Centre for Work, Organization, and Wellbeing. He is also a Visiting Professor at Loughborough University Business School. His books include *Making Quality Critical* (1995), *Managing Quality and Human Resource* (1997), *Managing through TQM: Theory and Practice* (1998), *Understanding Work and Employment: Industrial Relations in Transition* (2003), *Human Resource Management at Work* (2008), *Contemporary Human Resource Management* (2009), and the *Sage Handbook of Human Resource Management* (2009). He has written over 100 articles in refereed journals and many book chapters. He is a Fellow and Accredited Examiner of the Chartered Institute of Personnel and Development. He is chief editor of the *International Journal of Management Reviews* and associate editor of the *Human Resource Management Journal*.

Associate Professor Paul J. Gollan

Paul J. Gollan is currently an Associate Professor at the Department of Business, Division of Economic and Financial Studies, Macquarie University. He is also Associate Fellow in the Employment Relations and Organizational Behaviour Group in the Department of Management, and Research Associate at the London School of Economics. He is also a Fellow of the Labour-Management Studies Foundation at Macquarie University which is jointly hosted by the Division of Economic and Financial Studies and the Macquarie Graduate School of Management (MGSM).

Paul has authored, co-authored, and co-edited a number of books in the fields of human resources and industrial relations including *Employee Relations in the Press* (1997) and *Models of Employee Participation in a Changing Global Environment—Diversity and Interaction* (2001). His latest book *Employee Representation in Non-Union Firms* was published in 2007. Another book, *Strategic Human Resource Management: A Critical Review* is due for release in 2009. He is a co-editor of *Advances in Industrial and Labor Relations* and consulting editor for the *International Journal of Management Reviews*.

Professor Mick Marchington

Mick Marchington has been Professor of Human Resource Management at what is now Manchester Business School, University of Manchester since 1995, having joined the University in the late 1980s. Prior to that, he worked at the Universities of Aston and Central Lancashire. He moved into HRM after gaining a first class honours degree in Chemical Engineering and indeed much of his work has been in that sector. While being at Manchester he has also been a Visiting Professor at the Universities of Sydney, Auckland, and Paris. During his employment at Manchester, he has occupied a wide range of managerial roles, including Dean of Management Studies and Divisional Research Co-ordinator. He is currently the fortieth Anniversary Visiting Fellow at the Institute for Employment Studies.

He has published widely on HRM, including twenty books and monographs, and nearly 150 book chapters and papers in refereed journals. He is also editor of the *Human Resource Management Journal*, one of the leading journals in the area, and he has been joint chair of the HRM Study Group of the International Industrial Relations Association since 2003. He has been active in the CIPD since the late 1980s, as Chief Examiner until 2002 and as Chief Moderator, Standards up to 2008. He is a Chartered Companion of the CIPD, the highest grade of membership available.

Professor David Lewin

David Lewin is the author of many published works on such topics as human resource strategy, human resource management practices and business performance, workplace and organizational dispute resolution, and compensation and reward systems, including executive compensation and public sector pay practices.

Professor Lewin's recent books include *Human Resource Management: An Economic Approach*, *The Human Resource Management Handbook*, and *Advances in Industrial and Labor Relations*. He is presently working on two new books, *Conflict Management in the Modern Corporation* and *The Dual Theory of Human Resources and Business Performance*. Professor Lewin serves on the editorial boards of *Industrial and Labor Relations Review*, *Industrial Relations*, and *California Management Review*, is a Fellow of the National Academy of Human Resources, a member of the board of directors of K-Swiss, and a Director of the Law and Economics Consulting Group (LECG). Professor Lewin has consulted widely with business, government, and voluntary organizations in the United States and abroad, and serves as an employment litigation expert. He is also Faculty Director of the UCLA Anderson School's Advanced Program in Human Resource Management, Young Presidents' Organization (YPO) Management Seminar, and Strategic Leadership Institute (SLI).

THE CONTRIBUTORS

Peter Ackers Professor of Industrial Relations and Labour History, Loughborough University.

Robin Archer Lecturer in Political Sociology, The University of London.

Nicola Balnave Senior Lecturer, University of Western Sydney.

Peter Berg Associate Professor of Labour and Industrial Relations, Michigan State University.

Richard N. Block Professor of Labour and Industrial Relations, Michigan State University.

Peter Boxall Professor of Human Resource Management, The University of Auckland.

Alex Bryson Research Director, London School of Economics.

John W. Budd Professor, Department of Human Resources and Industrial Relations, University of Minnesota.

Almudena Cañibano Ph.D. student, LSE.

Tony Dundon Lecturer in Human Resource Management, National University of Ireland, Galway.

Carola Frege Reader in Employment Relations, London School of Economics.

Gregor Gall Professor of Industrial Relations, University of Hetfordshire.

John Godard Professor of Management, University of Manitoba.

Paul J. Gollan Associate Professor, Macquarie University, Sydney.

Rafael Gomez Lecturer in Marketing, The London School of Economics and Political Science.

Howard Gospel Professor of Management, Kings College, London.

Rebecca Gumbrell-McCormick Lecturer in Management, University of London.

Richard Hyman Professor of Industrial Relations, The London School of Economics and Political Science.

Eric Kaarsemaker Lecturer in Human Resource Management, University of York.

Bruce E. Kaufman Professor of Economics, Georgia State University.

Ian Kessler University Reader in Employment Relations, University of Oxford.

Russell D. Lansbury Professor of Work and Organisational Studies, The University of Sydney.

David Lewin Professor of Management, Human Resources, and Organizational Behaviour, University of California.

Miguel Martinez Lucio Professor of International Human Resource Management, University of Manchester.

Mick Marchington Professor of Human Resource Management, The University of Manchester.

Raymond Markey Professor of Employment Relations, Auckland University of Technology.

David Marsden Chair in Industrial Relations, The London School of Economics and Political Science.

Glenn Patmore Senior Lecturer, The University of Melbourne.

Greg Patmore Professor of Business and Labour History, University of Sydney.

Andrew Pendleton Professor of Human Resource Management, University of York.

Erik Poutsma Associate Professor of Employee Relations, Radboud University Nijmegen.

John Purcell Research Professor—Industrial Relations, The University of Warwick.

Daphne G. Taras Professor of Industrial Relations, University of Calgary.

Andrew R. Timming Lecturer in International and Comparative HRM, The University of Manchester.

Nick Wailes Associate Professor, The University of Sydney.

Adrian Wilkinson Director of the Centre for Work, Organization, and Wellbeing, Griffith University, Brisbane.

Paul Willman Professor of Management, The London School of Economics and Political Science.

Geoffrey Wood Professor of Human Resource Management, University of Sheffield.

Stephen Wood Professor of Employment Relations, University of Sheffield.

Stefan Zagelmeyer Professor of Human Resource Management, International University of Applied Sciences Bad Honnef-Bonn, Germany.

PART I

INTRODUCTION

CHAPTER 1

CONCEPTUALIZING EMPLOYEE PARTICIPATION IN ORGANIZATIONS

ADRIAN WILKINSON

PAUL J. GOLLAN

MICK MARCHINGTON

DAVID LEWIN

INTRODUCTION

THE concept of employee participation is common to many different discipline areas in the social sciences. In terms of the classic texts on the topic, there are books which relate participation to politics and question the real form of that involvement (Pateman, 1970), that examine the relationship between participation and satisfaction (Blumberg, 1968), and that link participation to notions of industrial citizenship (Clegg, 1960; Webb and Webb, 1902). The pioneering work of the Tavistock Institute (Heller et al., 1998) or the Swedish experiments in work design (Berggren, 1993) constitute yet more perspectives on the subject. Despite often using the same terminology, it is also clear that the meaning and form that participation can take varies considerably depending on the discipline. On the one hand, it could relate to trade union representation through joint consultative committees and collective bargaining, to worker cooperatives or to legislation designed to provide channels for employee representatives to engage in some form of joint decision making with employers. On the other hand, and at a different level, it could encompass myriad mechanisms that employers introduce in order to provide information to their staff or to offer them the chance to engage in joint problem-solving groups or use their skills/discretion at work via job enrichment programmes.

One of the problems in trying to develop any analysis of participation is that there is potentially limited overlap between these different disciplinary traditions, and scholars from diverse traditions may know relatively little of the research that has been done elsewhere. Accordingly in Part 2 of the book, a number of the more significant disciplinary areas are analysed in greater depth in order to ensure that readers gain a better appreciation of what participation means from these quite different contextual perspectives. To some extent this is reflected in the different terms used to describe the subject. For example, while the notion of industrial democracy clearly draws on the traditions of political science, and representative participation and collective bargaining emerge from the industrial relations and law literatures, employee involvement and engagement are more likely to have their roots in human resource management where the focus tends to be on the role of workers as individuals and their relationships with line managers (Wilkinson and Fay, 2009). While some of the disciplines are more interested in processes, economics tends to look more closely at outcomes and the distribution of resources that flow from participation.

Not only is there a range of different traditions contributing to the research and literature on the subject, there is also an extremely diverse set of practices that congregate under the banner of participation. Part 3 of the book examines the range of forms that participation can take in practice, and the way in which it meets objectives that are set for it, either by employers, trade unions, individual workers, or indeed the state. This requires us to understand the meaning of the terms used in the literature in order to classify these diverse forms, so as to make sure readers are not confusing one form with another.

Following Marchington and Wilkinson (2005), participation can be differentiated into: direct communication; upward problem solving; representative participation; and financial participation. The first two of these are essentially direct and individually focused, often operating through face-to-face interactions between supervisors/first line managers and their staff. Some take the form of verbal participation, while others are based on written information or suggestions. The third form is quite different and revolves around the role that employee or trade union representatives play in discussions between managers and the workforce, via mechanisms, such as joint consultation, worker directors, or even collective bargaining. These particular schemes raise major issues about the distribution of power and influence within organizations, and in some cases—unlike direct participation for the most part—is part of the legislative framework of the country in which the employing organization is located. The final form we consider in the second part of the book is financial participation, whereby employees have a monetary stake or benefit from their work, via profit sharing or employee share ownership. In one sense this is a little different from participation based on information, consultation, and joint decision making because employees might be encouraged to participate precisely because there is the expectation that their work efforts might ultimately be rewarded by additional benefits. Of course these forms of participation also raise questions about how the financial benefits are allocated, who makes decisions about their distribution, and what happens if the organization suffers a loss rather than making a profit.

Although this is sometimes overlooked in studies, participation practices do not take place in a vacuum without some clearly defined purpose. As the HR manager of a firm well known for its innovative approach to employee engagement once told one of the authors, 'We are here to manufacture high quality products at a profit not to practise participation.' Consequently Part 4 of the book moves on to examine some of the processes and outcomes associated with participation. A key question is who gains what from being involved. In most developed countries management are the key drivers of participation so it is likely they will expect to see some advantage from investing in what critics might see as an expensive waste of time. Evidence suggests that senior managers are not likely to persevere with participation if it does not meet their goals, either in the short or the long term, and that the benefits must be seen to outweigh the costs for it to survive. Yet, as versions of high commitment HRM have some form of participation as a centre-piece of their models, it seems to be accepted that rather than being seen as a zero sum concept where one party's gains come at the expense of the other, participation might lead to a larger cake to be shared among workers and employers. On the other hand, some critics of participation would argue that it is only a fig leaf behind which the worse excesses of capitalism can hide. Under this scenario, the real purpose of participation schemes, especially those aimed at individual workers, is to increase work intensification and con employees into accepting management ideas that may not necessarily be in their best interests. This might be supplemented by a drive to engage in non-union forms of participation as well.

Depending on the societal regime within which participation takes place, the benefits might be seen in different ways. So, for example, in a liberal market economy participation is likely to be measured in terms of profit and shareholder value at the organizational level and in customer service, product quality, and staff retention at the workplace level. Issues to do with worker commitment, job satisfaction, and alignment with organizational goals are often the proxies used to measure the success of participation but in themselves these may tell us little about the impact of particular schemes on bottom-line success. In coordinated market economies, the focus is more likely to be longer term and more widely defined in terms of a range of stakeholder interests: government; employers; trade unions; and workers. The time-scale over which returns are expected is also longer, and the focus—for the most part—is on peak level institutions and forms of participation that are representative in nature. In other words, in these situations the expectation is more likely to be of mutual gains, either at the level of the individual employing organization or more broadly in terms of citizenship and long-term social cohesion.

This theme is also woven through the final parts of the book. In Part 5, contributors focus on issues beyond the individual workplace, and on the role that employee participation plays in societies more generally. We know from the studies that have been published over time that participation can take diverse forms in different countries given the role of the state and institutional frameworks in shaping the environment in which it operates. If legislation is extensive, then participation will be present—at least in structural terms—in all organizations above a certain size within that country. It could be argued that this, therefore, provides a safety net and a structure around which other forms of participation can develop, and in most cases that has been assumed to happen. However, there is also the possibility that the presence of formal structures could also hamper the growth, sustainability, and contribution of more informal participation practices, and it is also likely that at least some employers might try to find ways around the requirement to involve their employees. For example, given the growth in subcontracting, employers might seek to avoid some of their responsibilities by shifting work to other organizations, either in the same country or even overseas where the same level of regulations do not exist. This raises major questions about ethics, public policy, and corporate governance, issues that are explored in chapters later in the book.

Discussion about comparative and societal issues provides a valuable lens through which to examine the extent to which product and labour markets can determine the forms that participation takes in practice. In Anglo-Saxon economies, where the amount of legislation governing participation is limited and employers have a fair degree of choice in what practices to implement, it is easy to assume that markets are very important. The financial turmoil that commenced in 2008–2009 shows how influential they can be. However, in countries where legislation is more extensive and there is a stronger state commitment to long-term financial stability, the power of product markets is likely to be constrained and there is a greater chance that higher-level forms of participation will survive. Similarly, in developing countries, labour market expectations may shape participation depending on educational and training opportunities for the population as a whole or on the way in which cultural traditions promote acceptance of or challenge to management decisions.

Having introduced the broad ideas behind the book and its overall shape, we can now turn to examine the forces that shape participation and the ways in which it can be defined. In the next section we examine the dynamics of participation in practice, illustrating how different forms have come to prominence at different periods in recent history. We also look at how these specific practices might interact with one another. Following this we review the ways in which participation can be defined. We believe firmly that the concept of participation needs to be broken down into its constituent parts so as to allow a sharper analytical edge when investigating the range of forms that it can take in practice and comparing different perspectives on the topic. In the final section of this chapter, we introduce briefly the rest of the book.

THE DYNAMICS OF EMPLOYEE PARTICIPATION IN CONTEXT

Although much of the research has focused on particular forms of participation, it is also important to note how these forms vary over time, and how they interact with each other. It is clear that new forms of employee participation have emerged during different periods, sometimes replacing and at other times coexisting with prior forms of participation. The political and economic environment has been a key influence on the emergence and spread of particular forms of employee participation, especially in developed economies. During the 1970s, for example, the idea of power sharing through broad industrial democracy and narrower representative participation through trade unions took hold. The subsequent decline in union membership and changes in public policy during the 1980s and 1990s combined to move industrial democracy off the domestic agenda of most advanced economies. In its place came a more managerially-oriented set of practices under the banner of employee involvement (EI), where the focus was at workplace level and the outcomes were more explicitly measured in terms of what employers might gain from these arrangements (Marchington et al., 1992). During the late 1990s and early part of this century, however, the potential impact of the Information and Consultation Directive on industrial democracy in the United Kingdom led to renewed debate about employee participation in organizations (Gollan and Wilkinson, 2007; Gospel and Willman, 2003).

This British example is by no means an isolated one because the last twenty years have witnessed growing interest in employee participation, specifically in employee involvement. Recent EI initiatives have been largely management sponsored, therefore, and not surprisingly, such initiatives reflect management's dominant concerns about employee motivation and commitment to organizational objectives. Given there has been no legislative framework behind these developments, the take-up of

EI is voluntary and heavily reliant on senior management at each workplace and the expectations of workers and managers at local level. Although evidence shows that direct EI has become much more important across Europe (Kessler et al., 2004), this has been because it fits with the times. Any attempt to legislate would be opposed by employers, and indeed it is hard to see what its role might be, given that direct participation and EI rely on flexible arrangements which suit particular workplaces and competitive pressures. These EI initiatives have focused on direct participation by small groups of employees in workplace level information sharing and decision making rather than on employee input into higher-level decision making. For whatever else can be said about it, such direct employee participation in workplace level decision making is fundamentally different from earlier notions of industrial democracy and representative participation (Marchington and Wilkinson, 2005).

A major factor shaping employee participation in private sector organizations is increasing product market competition. The public sector has also been subjected to increasing competition, as reflected in numerous deregulation and privatization actions on the part of governments and in the rise of the idea of the citizen–taxpayer as a 'customer' of the government. In both sectors, increased competition has led to a barrage of new employee participation initiatives. Shifts in the structure of employment away from manufacturing toward services have also impacted concepts, forms, uses, and scope of employee participation as well as the employment relationship, per se. (Wilkinson et al., 2007). In particular, both private and public sector employers have substantially increased their use of contracted or outsourced employees. In these situations, where the employer is 'elusive' and there is no simple, traditional employer–employee relationship, it becomes more difficult to devise and implement appropriate systems of employee participation (Marchington et al., 2005).

While each of the aforementioned factors is important in shaping the environment within which direct employee participation operates, it is also necessary to examine how macro-level factors interact with developments at the organizational level—where business decisions are made—to influence employee participation. Notable here is the influence of 'ideas brokers'—consultants and popular management writers—who offer their particular interpretations of the changing global marketplace and who advocate normative recipes for responding to such change. To illustrate, organizations are encouraged to be flexible, innovative, and responsive in dealing with newly intensified global competition, rather than seek economies of scale through more conventional mass production (Piore and Sabel, 1983). A related line of reasoning argues that the knowledge economy provides enhanced impetus for employee involvement in decision making, which is claimed to be a positive development for employers *and* employees (Scarborough, 2003). Assessing such arguments, Poole et al. (2000: 497) observe that 'increased competition and concerns about economic performance have made the achievement of "rights-based" employee participation more remote whilst encouraging the development of EI as a route to better "market performance"'.

These various arguments and prescriptions appear to have clear implications for the management of employee participation in organizations. Among these implications are that hierarchy and compliant rule following are inappropriate for employees who are expected to work beyond contract and exercise their initiative. As Walton (1985: 76) put it, managers have now 'begun to see that workers respond best—and most creatively—not when they are tightly controlled by management, placed in narrowly defined jobs, and treated like an unwelcome necessity, but instead when they are given broader responsibilities, encouraged to contribute, and helped to take satisfaction from their work'. The contrast here is between a 'high control' and a 'high commitment' work environment, with employee participation constituting a 'best fit' with the latter environment (Wright and Gardner, 2003). A high commitment-type work system is intended to improve employee relations and increase organizational performance through substantive communication and consultation between management and employees. As part of this approach, jobs are designed broadly and combine planning with implementation, individual responsibilities are expected to change as conditions change, and teams rather than individuals are the organizational unit accountable for performance. In addition, differences in status are minimized, with control and lateral coordination based on shared goals and expectations. There is thus an alignment of interests with expertise, rather than formal position or title, in determining influence and power. Similarly, US-based 'best practice' human resource management (HRM) research emphasizes the importance of employee participation by drawing on an array of sophisticated statistical evidence to document systematic links between high involvement-type HRM and organizational performance (Becker and Huselid, 2009; Huselid, 1995). Comparable findings and conclusions have been reached by British researchers (Patterson et al., 1998; Wood, 1999).

Several studies have found that many new employee participation initiatives lack sufficient structure and scope (Gollan, 2007; Gollan and Markey, 2001; Kessler et al., 2000). This research also concludes that an integrated approach to employee participation in which such participation is accompanied by related initiatives in employment security, selective employee hiring, variable compensation, extensive training, and information sharing with employees is most likely to lead to higher levels of organizational performance (Dundon and Gollan, 2007; EPOC Research Group, 1997; Gibbons and Woock, 2007; Guest and Peccei, 1998). In other words, a 'bundled' or 'packaged' approach to employee participation (and HRM more broadly) is preferable to narrow, one-dimensional employee participation initiatives (Ichniowski et al., 1997; MacDuffie, 1995; Marchington and Wilkinson, 2008; Wood and De Menezes, 1998).

A wide variety of labels has been attached to these newer employee participation initiatives: high-performance work design (Buchanan, 1987), lean production (Womack, et al., 1990), voice (Lewin, 2005b), high-involvement work systems (Edwards and Wright, 2001), teamworking (Mueller, 1994), self-managed teams

(Pfeffer, 1998), and employee engagement (Emmott, 2007). Despite (or perhaps because of) these labelling differences, there is a notable tendency for employee participation initiatives to be viewed solely in a positive light and therefore to ignore the more contested and mundane aspects of such participation. Many would argue that, rather than leading to autonomy and self-management, employee participation may lead to work intensification, increased stress levels, and redundancies (Ramsay et al., 2000). There is also a tendency for employee participation researchers to ignore industries, firms, and types of work in which low involvement rather than high-involvement HRM practices predominate (Lewin, 2002, 2005b, 2008).

THE MEANINGS OF EMPLOYEE PARTICIPATION

Whether labelled employee participation, high-involvement HRM, voice or any other of the aforementioned descriptors, each of these is a somewhat elastic term with a considerably wide range of definitions rather than a single uniform definition (Bar-Haim, 2002; Budd, 2004; Marchington and Wilkinson, 2005; Poole, 1986; Wilkinson 1998, 2008). Indeed, the definitions may be as broad and all-inclusive as 'any form of delegation to or consultation with employees,' or as narrow as a 'formal, ongoing structure of direct communications, such as through a team briefing' (Gallie et al., 2001: 7). Stated differently, the extant literature has often treated different forms of participation as if they were synonymous, and there has not been sufficient distinction between the different forms that employee participation in decision making can take. As Heller et al. (1998: 15) observe in this regard:

Definitions of participation abound. Some authors insist that participation must be a group process, involving groups of employees and their boss; others stress delegation, the process by which the *individual* employee is given greater freedom to make decisions on his or her own. Some restrict the term 'participation' to formal institutions, such as works councils; other definitions embrace 'informal participation', the day-to-day relations between supervisors and subordinates in which subordinates are allowed substantial input into work decisions. Finally, there are those who stress participation as a *process* and those who are concerned with participation as a *result*.

Consequently, it is difficult to make precise comparisons about employee participation initiatives and changes over time in such initiatives, which also means that caution must be exercised in generalizing about employee participation when different practices (and outcomes) are being compared (Wilkinson et al., 1997).

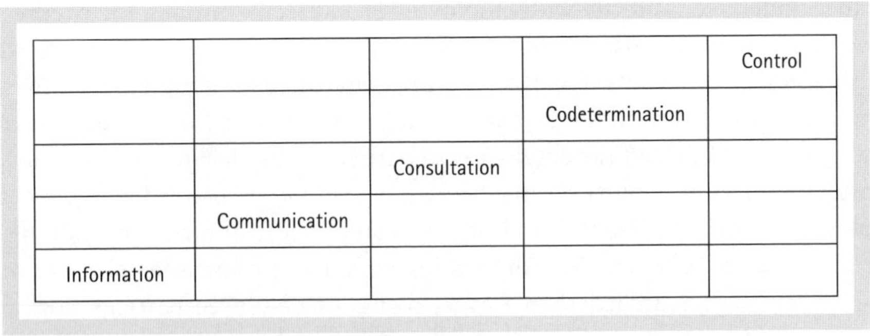

				Control
			Codetermination	
		Consultation		
	Communication			
Information				

Figure 1.1 The escalator of participation

It is helpful if the terms can be deconstructed according to degree, form, level, and range of subject matter (Marchington and Wilkinson, 2005). Taking the first of these, **degree** indicates the extent to which employees are able to influence decisions about various aspects of management—whether they are simply informed of changes, consulted, or actually make decisions. The escalator of participation (see Figure 1.1) illustrates this; it implies a progression upwards rather than simply a move from zero participation to workers control. Second, there is the **level** at which participation takes place; task, departmental, establishment, or corporate HQ. Clearly there are likely to be major differences in the nature of participation at these different levels, and in the type of people who are actually involved in the process. But it is not a simple matter of correlating degree and level; it is just as feasible that high-level participation might be little more than an information passing exercise as that workplace level involvement could lead to control over decisions about work organization. The **range** of subject matter is the third dimension, ranging from the relatively trivial—such as the quality of canteen food—to more strategic concerns relating, for example, to investment strategies. Fourth, there is the **form** that participation takes. Indirect participation is where employees are involved through their representatives, usually elected from the wider group. Financial participation relates to schemes, such as profit sharing or gain sharing, whereby employees participate directly in the commercial success or failure of the organization, usually linking a proportion of financial reward to corporate or establishment performance. Face-to-face or written communications between managers and subordinates that involves individuals rather than representatives is often referred to as 'on-line' participation (Appelbaum and Batt, 1995), where workers make decisions as part of their daily job responsibilities as distinct from 'off-line' participation where workers make suggestions through a formal scheme.

From our perspective, employee participation encompasses the range of mechanisms used to involve the workforce in decisions at all levels of the organization, whether undertaken directly with employees or indirectly through their represen-tatives. Information and consultation are two main components of this process. Information in this context means the provision of data about the business—regarding workplace issues or more strategic matters—to employees or their representatives, which allows employees to participate in dialogue with employers. Consultation in this context means the exchange of views between employers and employees or their representatives but which stops short of formal bargaining, so that final responsibility for decision making remains with management. Although less likely to be researched than formal forms of employee participation, it is important not to forget that informal participation—between first line managers and their staff, and within teams—is vitally important to provide some of the glue that holds together more formal practices and helps to make them work (March-ington and Suter, 2008).

A key theme that has emerged from organizational behaviour-based research on employee participation is the importance of such initiatives to achieving successful organizational change. Particular attention is given to creating and developing an organizational culture that provides a foundation for successful organizational change—foundation building that may require a considerable investment of man-agement time and resources (O'Reilly, 2008). Where there is a lack of formal participative (or representative) structures, such as in the growing non-unionized sector, stronger emphasis is placed on management's ability to implement change processes. Research also shows that many organizations do not involve employees in organizational change initiatives until the later stages of change, that is, after management has designed an organizational change initiative and determined how it will be implemented (Gollan, 2007; Millward et al., 2000; Terry, 1999; Tushman and O'Reilly, 1996).

Several studies have also identified managerial attitudes as key to the existence of highly-developed employee participation practices (Fenton-O'Creevey et al., 1998; Kessler et al., 2000; Millward et al., 2000; Wilkinson et al., 2004; Wood and Albanese, 1995; Wood and De Menezes, 1998). They suggest that underpinning such practices is a relationship based on a high level of trust between management and employees. In such circumstances, management assumes that employees can be trusted to make important workplace decisions that will result in positive outcomes (e.g., increased productivity), and employees assume that management can be trusted to share with employees the rewards emanating from those out-comes (e.g., a gain sharing payment)—in other words, mutual gains (Lewin, 2008). In order to make more substantive workplace decisions and to enhance the likelihood that trust-based employee participation initiatives will work well, employees must be given the opportunity to develop the requisite knowledge, skills, and abilities (Coyle-Shapiro et al., 2002). It is also necessary for management to sustain its support for a particular employee participation initiative, and not modify or abandon that initiative when market conditions change or a portion of management turns over. Otherwise, and as considerable research has shown, employee trust in management can dissipate quickly (Bruno and Jordan, 1999; Frost, 1998; Horvath and Svyantek, 1998).

While business imperatives generally, and supportive management in particular, may lead to enhanced employee participation initiatives (Wilkinson et al., 1998), these are hardly the only 'drivers' in this regard. A substantial literature that also supports such initiatives is rooted in concepts of industrial citizenship, worker rights, and organizational democracy (Harrison and Freeman, 2004). Indeed, these concepts are grounded in even more fundamental notions of free speech and human dignity for which supporting arguments are often expressed in political, moral, and religious terms. To illustrate, consider these examples:

Managers are the dinosaurs of our modern organizational ecology. The Age of Management is finally coming to close ... Autocracy, hierarchy, bureaucracy and management are gradually being replaced by democracy, heterarchy, collaboration and self-managing teams.

(Cloke and Goldsmith, 2002)

Organizational democracy is frequently associated with increased employee involvement and satisfaction, higher levels of innovation, increased stakeholder commitment, and, ultimately, enhanced organizational performance. However, democratic processes can also absorb significant time and other organizational resources and bog down decisions, which may lead to reduced efficiency. In the end, we conclude that although the economic arguments for organizational democracy may be mixed, increased stakeholder participation in value creation and organizational governance can benefit both society and corporations. In fact, the corporation itself may be envisioned as a system of self-governance and the voluntary cooperation of stakeholders.   (Harrison and Freeman, 2004: 49)

Another strand of the employee participation literature focuses centrally on the role played by trade unions, not only as a vehicle for representative democracy at the industry or organizational level, where the emphasis is on increasing liberty on the job, but for political democracy as well (Voos, 2004). This dual focus was made manifest in the recent (2008) US presidential election and continues to the moment as unionists and would-be union members seek to replace formal union representation elections with Canadian-style authorization card-determined union membership and representation.

THE BOOK: APPROACH AND STRUCTURE

In this book, leading perspectives on employee participation, including those briefly summarized above, will be analysed, discussed, and assessed with the aim of identifying key challenges associated with employee participation in practice.

The book is organized into five parts and contains twenty-five chapters. We have managed to bring together a group of leading scholars from around the world in order to ensure that the book is not just based upon experiences in any one country. These authors bring a variety of disciplinary perspectives, empirical research and case examples to bear on the topic of employee participation in organizations.

Part 2 features five chapters that provide, respectively, HRM, industrial relations, legal, political science, and economics perspectives on employee participation. Despite drawing on different theoretical traditions and country examples, it is also apparent that there is rather more overlap—at least in terms of the practices examined—than at first sight might have been expected. Peter Boxall and John Purcell develop ideas that have appeared in previous work on what they term 'analytical HRM' to examine the notion of employee voice. Analytical HRM eschews the ideas of best practice HRM, instead focusing on the sorts of choices that appear before management (and to a lesser extent, workers) in building and sustaining viable versions of voice and participation. One of the key outcomes therefore is that participation can take quite different forms depending on the factors shaping HRM, and unlike some of the more critical accounts of HRM (Bolton and Houlihan, 2007) they consider representative participation to be a potentially core feature of voice just like direct employee involvement. Unlike the other perspectives, however, Boxall and Purcell devote much more space to talking about high-involvement work systems and the benefits these might offer to employers whose objectives can best be furthered if employees are allowed considerable discretion at work.

Peter Ackers' chapter starts out by considering the view that employee participation at work should centre exclusively on collective bargaining and other attempts to create industrial democracy at the workplace. He counterpoises the ideas propagated by the utopian socialists and the industrial relations realists, arguing that in Britain they effectively 'fought themselves to a standstill which lead to the silent triumph, by default, of EI'. Rather than deal with the issues merely from a contemporary perspective, Ackers examines six different historical examples of how key British industrial relations scholars have approached the topic of employee participation. His conclusion is somewhat pessimistic, at least from the standpoint of participation, in that he argues that future research is likely to be more mundane and dull than in the past because it is now centred on everyday workplace realities rather than the big struggles of the past.

The law chapter has been written by Glenn Patmore, who has focused almost entirely on the role that legislation can play in indirect or representative participation. This review considers the legal framework in three separate jurisdictions; the EU, Australia, and the USA, and it examines legal intervention in the areas of information, consultation, and representation. Among other things he raises questions about whether or not the law automatically acts as a support for the development of participation, and in the case of Australia notes how joint consultation is flourishing compared with other mechanisms. He concludes that its success undoubtedly owes a lot to the legislation, and much the same conclusion is reached from experiences in the EU where the law has braced and/or stabilized representative participation. By contrast a voluntarist regime, while not preventing some organizations from investing in participation, does run the considerable risk of contributing to a workplace culture of unilateralism.

Miguel Martinez Lucio has contributed the political science chapter, and this draws from a wide range of sources both at the macro and micro levels of debate. He commences by focusing on the role of the state in terms of organizations and individuals and with Marxist accounts of work and participation, and with what is often seen as the inevitable subjugation of labour. But, rather than restricting his analysis to the macro framework he chooses to link Marxist accounts with more recent developments in labour process theory that have concentrated on workplace issues, often from a sociological perspective. He notes a continuing tension between forces for cooperation and conflict, and dismisses simplistic notions that workers (and trade unions) automatically lose out if they choose to engage with management. He suggests that rather than seeing cooperation as nothing more than a route to incorporation, it can also offer opportunities for workers and trade unions to occupy new spaces for confrontation. To do otherwise would be to regard them as cultural dupes, always outwitted by management, and to see currently popular forms of participation—such as teamwork—as totally controlled by management for their own objectives. As analysts such as Burawoy (1979) make abundantly clear, workers can also play games to beat the system.

The final chapter in Part 2 examines economics and participation. In this chapter, David Marsden and Almudena Cañibano take a wide-ranging view of the topic, and choose not to focus narrowly on issues to do with supply and demand. They draw upon literatures that are also common to sociology and psychology—such as the alienation at work material—and on notions of exit, voice, and loyalty, on frontiers of control, and even population ecology—to argue that participation needs to be investigated for its impact on both performance and employee well-being. In terms of the alienation literature, for example, the case for participation is effectively made in the negative: workers who are alienated from work are likely to be unproductive, so therefore some form of participation is of value. The authors argue that the contribution of economic approaches to participation within organizations lies in their focus on the difficulties of coordination under conditions of uncertainty and limited information where actors are subject to bounded rationality in that their activities are mostly goal-oriented. They suggest the question arises as to how different models of the employment relationship help to solve the resulting problems of coordination, and in so far as their solutions build on arrangements that endure over time, how these can be best adapted to changing needs.

Part 3 reviews a range of forms of participation in practice. This contains eight chapters dealing, respectively, with direct participation, collective bargaining, other processes of collective voice, non-union forms of employee representation, works councils, worker directors and worker ownership/cooperatives, employee share ownership, and financial participation. Adrian Wilkinson and Tony Dundon review developments in direct participation over the last twenty-five years showing how schemes have been influenced by different political, economic, and legal climates and how fads and fashions have played a key role. But they also suggest that it is the orientation of management which may be more important than the specific scheme. They suggest that practices may have become more embedded as management have learnt from the limitation of the shallow depths of participation in the 1980s and 1990s. While it is too grand to talk of participative architecture, they do see some attempts to integrate participation. The challenges that lie ahead are how such a dynamic will be played out in practice, and how multiple schemes for participation can be embedded.

Richard Block and Peter Berg look at the role of independent representatives, such as unions and works councils. As they point out, these forms of representation are generally part of a legal structure that sets the context for participation. The rights of labour unions, works councils, the bargaining process, and labour agreements may be defined by law as in the United States and Germany or left in the hands of the parties themselves to resolve as in the United Kingdom. They compare and contrast collective bargaining in the United States and Europe, and show how the basis for collective bargaining in the former has been the removal of barriers to economic efficiency caused by disputes over union recognition in contrast to that in Europe which gives more weight to worker rights.

Paul Gollan examines employer strategies towards non-union collective voice. He suggests that when employer-initiated voice arrangements are established they create employee expectations about outcomes. If these expectations are not realized, a widening of the gap between expectation and achievement leads to lack of trust and disenchantment in management leading to instrumental collectivism. This could manifest itself in either the peaceful pursuit of desired outcomes through mutual gains, such as union recognition by the employer and/or employer–employee partnership, or through union readiness for action against an employer based on a conflict of interests and a 'win' and 'lose' strategy. He argues that the old dichotomy of a union versus non-union channels of voice is likely to prove inadequate in shaping future representation arrangements.

Raymond Markey, Greg Patmore, and Nikki Balnave assess the role of employee representatives on the boards of companies and producer cooperatives. Employee participation in decision making can be seen via employee representatives sitting alongside shareholder representatives on the boards of public companies and state-owned enterprises; and producer cooperatives in which the workers own the organization. Producer cooperatives are also likely to have employee representation on their boards, but as they point out the two forms of participation differ fundamentally. In the case of the former, employee representation on the boards of public companies and state-owned enterprises constitutes employee participation as employees, whereas producer cooperatives owned by the employees constitutes participation as owners. They observe that consequently the motivational bases for each approach differ, even when the structures may be similar.

Bruce Kaufman and Daphne Taras analyse indirect participation through forms of non-union employee representation (NER). They note that NER has been practiced in industry for over a hundred years but with considerable diversity and variation both across countries and over time. As they observe, this is a subject of much controversy but NER's importance appears to be increasing. Non-union forms of employee representation are one method for implementing employee participation in organizations and are both a complement and a substitute for other methods, such as direct forms of participation and other forms of indirect participation via trade unions.

Rebecca Gumbrell-McCormick and Richard Hyman review experience with works councils as a form of participation. They focus on countries with generalized systems of representation where participation structures exist largely independently of management wishes and not with those where representative bodies may be established voluntarily through localized management (or union) initiatives. Using this definition, works councils are largely confined to continental Western Europe, and they explain why this is the case looking at six European countries: Germany, the Netherlands, Belgium, France, Italy, and Sweden. As they explain, works councils are engaged in a difficult balancing act with employees, unions, and management which is made more precarious as a result of changes in work organization, corporate ownership, and the global economy.

Eric Kaarsemaker, Andrew Pendleton, and Erik Poutsma take-up the issue of employee share ownership and show how governments in North America, Europe, Australasia, and Asia have promoted various forms of employee share ownership. In theory, employee ownership provides employees with additional rights to those normally expected by employees and these could bring about changes in employee attitudes and behaviour, which may affect company-level outcomes, such as productivity and financial performance. However, they conclude that most share ownership plans do not appear to transform the employment relationship. Of course this should not be surprising as the amount of equity passing to employees is usually small, and those involved do not expect that share ownership will transform the way their company is run. But they do argue there is evidence to suggest that share ownership does have favourable effects on company and workplace performance.

In the final chapter in Part 3, Ian Kessler focuses on financial participation more generally. This is defined as a mechanism by which employees are provided with a stake in the performance or ownership of an organization. This stake is reflected in remunerative arrangements, typically in the form of a payment linked to a corporate outcome measure or to an allocation of shares in the company. It directly involves workers in corporate financial performance with a payout, but also provides the basis for employee involvement in organizational decision making. He reviews the character, use, and consequences of financial participation, and in so doing explores the contributions made by these different research communities to our understanding. Much research on financial participation has focused on the consequences of schemes, in particular on whether and how it has impacted on employee attitudes and behaviours as well as on organizational performance.

In Part 4, the book shifts to examine the processes and outcomes of participation. It contains four chapters dealing, respectively, with labour union responses to participation, the shift from union to non-union voice, high-involvement management and performance, and employee voice and mutual gains.

Gregor Gall examines how labour unions have sought 'participation' in an attempt to gain the organizational and institutional means to protect and advance their members' interests. Participation would on the surface represent a movement towards achieving greater workers' control or codetermination at the workplace. But, as Gall observes, the majority of systems of participation originated from employers with almost all the remainder derived from initiatives by the state. The problem for unions is that while they want forms of workers' control, as the weaker party to the employment relationship they face a dilemma which makes them unsure whether entering participation will strengthen or weaken their ability to prosecute their members' interests. This raises concerns about whether avenues of participation facilitate or undermine collective bargaining.

Alex Bryson, Rafael Gomez, and Paul Willman look at the nature of workplace voice and its determinants in Britain since the early 1980s focusing on implications for debates about worker participation, labour relations, human resource management, and organizational behaviour. Their approach draws on insights from consumer theory, industrial organization and transaction cost economics and explores the conditions under which employee voice mechanisms emerge inside the workplace. They show that union collective representation has been replaced by non-union voice in new workplaces and, where union voice persists in older workplaces, it has been supplemented by non-union voice.

The chapter by Stephen Wood on high-involvement management and performance provides a more nuanced picture regarding the link between worker participation and individual performance. As Wood suggests, while worker participation can provide an opportunity for workers to influence events it is also assumed that it will not only provide greater procedural justice but fairer substantive outcomes and thus have an impact on individual and organizational performance. However, Wood suggests that studies of the association between job satisfaction and individual performance may be weak and may be contingent on the type of job undertaken. In addition, the link between participation and performance at individual and organizational levels may not necessarily be positive.

The chapter by David Lewin explores employee participation and mutual gains. He argues that the theory and research on mutual gains has focused largely on employee exercise of voice in unionized settings featuring collective bargaining between representatives of management and labour. These typically lead to formal written agreements (i.e., contracts) that contain grievance procedures. This chapter by contrast focuses on employee voice in non-union enterprises addressing a central question, 'Do mutual gains to employer and employee result from non-union employees' exercise of voice?' Lewin suggest that a substantial majority had a formal arrangement of voice through alternative dispute resolution (ADR) mechanisms, were used by employees, and were considered by senior executives as beneficial for the business. Lewin concludes that implication of these findings is that employee voice can be exercised outside of a collective context, and that analysis of mutual gains should include both collective and individual forms of participation.

In Part 5, attention turns toward comparative and societal issues which are addressed in the final eight chapters. These deal respectively, with participation across organizational and national boundaries, public policy and employee participation, corporate governance and employee participation, cross-national variation in representation rights and work governance, employee participation in developing and emerging countries, international and comparative perspectives on employee participation, and freedom, democracy and capitalism through the lens of ethics and employee participation.

Mick Marchington and Andrew Timming's chapter investigates employee participation across organizational boundaries. They suggest that the recent growth of inter-organizational contracting, whether in the form of a public–private partnerships, joint ventures, agency work, or outsourced production, poses a significant threat to the traditional conception of employment relations as a contract between a single employer and an employee. Those workers employed by the weaker party to a commercial contract have less scope for both direct and indirect participation as compared to core employees in a traditional employment relationship. They go on to suggest that non-citizen workers, as Marchington and Timming define them, face a set of unparalleled obstacles to participation that effectively dampens their ability to influence decision making and have their 'say', a situation that is only likely to worsen as globalization becomes yet more pervasive.

The chapter by John Budd and Stefan Zagelmeyer highlights a number of issues around public policy and the role of employee participation. They state that employee participation is frequently seen within the private sector context in voluntary terms; that is, employers that believe it is in their self-interest to provide vehicles for employee participation will do so; others will not. However, the authors argue that employee participation can reach far beyond competitiveness and profitability and also shape the psychological and economic well-being of individuals, the physical and emotional health of a community's families, and the quality of a country's democracy. As a consequence employee participation has important implications for public policy through governmental regulation of the employment relationship.

Corporate governance and the role of participation are examined in the chapter by Howard Gospel and Andrew Pendleton. The authors analyse the role and extent of employee participation in the main areas of corporate governance differences between countries. They provide an overview of the main practitioner and academic perspectives on governance, highlighting differences in the role accorded to employees. To ascertain the potential for employee participation they go on to identify the main elements of corporate governance systems—the involvement of owners, the role of governing boards, information flows and transparency, the remuneration of managers, and the market for corporate control. The chapter outlines how employee participation and representation may impact on various aspects of 'mainstream' corporate governance, such as executive pay, even where there is little direct role. The authors argue that if corporate governance is defined in broader terms than the conventional way found in most policy discussions, the role for labour should be greater.

Carola Frege and John Godard explore cross-national variation in representation rights and governance at work. In particular they address the reasons for the considerable cross-national diversity in both the institutional context of the employment relationship and the way in which conflicts are resolved given this diversity. They address various explanations that have or can be advanced to explain this variation and why it persists. The authors argue that attempts to prescribe or alter representation rights are not likely to succeed unless they take into account not just the broader institutional environments within which these rights are (or are not) embedded, but also historically rooted institutional norms and traditions.

Employee participation in developing and emerging countries is examined by Geoffrey Wood. Wood argues that outside a few 'islands' of economic activity, characterized by sophisticated production paradigms, the levels of participation and involvement encountered in the developing world are generally low. He goes on to state that while Fordist practices are widespread in these economies, unions have been unable to limit the wholesale abandonment of pluralist employment relations polices under increasing forces of global forces. Wood argues that in the informal sector networks are built around the usage of labour on an open-ended basis. These are generally outside of formal labour law and great power imbalances between employers and employees exist with the concentration of power under management control which has resulted in many cases of labour repression. However, in some developing societies, such as South Africa, greater higher-value-added production practices based on longer-term productivity and equity have created opportunities for employees to have a voice in firms, increasing fairness and creating greater corporate sustainability.

Nick Wailes and Russell Lansbury apply the varieties of capitalism (VofC) framework to evaluate international and comparative perspectives of employee participation. They attempt to modify and extend the VoC approach to account for both within country diversity and the role that international factors play in shaping national patterns of participation. They highlight two main limitations of existing VoC theory. First, the VoC framework makes it difficult to explain diversity in participation practices *within* national systems. Second, the VoC approach does not account for developments in participation which are international in origin. They argue that VoC analysis should adopt a less deterministic view of the role institutions play in shaping social action, to focus more on the role of agency and interests, and suggest the need to explore the interconnections between countries in more detail. The authors apply this modified VoC framework to examine the extent to which it can explain recent developments in the United Kingdom and Germany.

The final chapter in this *Handbook*, highlights the role of freedom, democracy, and capitalism in ethics and employee participation. Robin Archer suggests that the idea of individual freedom or individual liberty has provided a basic ethical reference point against which the legitimacy of social and political institutions has been judged. He outlines an argument for democracy being based on individuals being free only to the extent that their choices govern (or determine) their actions. He then seeks to show that it applies not just to political institutions but also to many other kinds of associations and, in particular, to economic enterprises. He argues that the same basic ethical commitments that lead us to promote political democracy should lead us to promote economic democracy in terms of a system in which enterprises operate in a market economy but are governed by those who work for them.

Overall not only do these chapters provide readers with a wide range of theoretical and empirical insights into employee participation, they connect such participation to broader issues and influences of organizational and political change. As such, we intend the book to be a leading reference work and to thereby provide a benchmark against which students and scholars of employee participation can assess its contribution in the future.

References

Applebaum, E. and Batt, R. (1995) 'Worker Participation in Diverse Settings: Does the Form Affect the Outcome, and if so, Who Benefits?', *British Journal of Industrial Relations*, 33(3): 353–78.

Bar-Haim, A. (2002) *Participation Programs in Work Organizations: Past, Present, and Scenarios for the Future*. London: Quorum Books.

Becker, B. and Huselid, M. (2009) 'Strategic Human Resources Management: Where Do We Go From Here?', in A. Wilkinson, N. Bacon, T. Redman, and S. Snell, (eds), *The Sage Handbook of Human Resource Management*. London: Sage Publishing.

BERGGREN, C. (1993) *The Volvo Experience: Alternatives to Lean Production in the Swedish Auto Industry*. Basingstoke: Macmillan.

BLUMBERG, P. (1968) *Industrial Democracy: The Sociology of Participation*. London: Constable.

BOLTON, S. and HOULIHAN, M. (2007) *Searching for the Human in Human Resource Management: Theory, Practice and Workplace Contexts*. London: Palgrave Macmillan.

BRUNO, R. and JORDAN, L. (1999) 'From High Hopes to Disillusionment: The Evolution of Worker Attitudes at Mitsubishi Motors', in D. Lewin, and B. Kaufman, (eds), *Advances in Industrial and Labour Relations* 9: 153–82, Stamford: JAI Press.

BUCHANAN, D. (1987) 'Job Enrichment is Dead: Long Live High Performance Work Design', *Personnel Management*, May: 40–43.

BUDD, J. (2004) *Employment with a Human Face*. Ithaca: Cornell University Press.

BURAWOY, M. (1979) *Manufacturing Consent: Changes in the Labor Process under Monopoly Capitalism*. Chicago: University of Chicago Press.

CLEGG, H. (1960) *A New Approach to Industrial Democracy*. Oxford: Blackwell.

CLOKE, K. and GOLDSMITH, J. (2002) *The End of Management and the Rise of Organisational Democracy*. New York: Jossey-Bass.

COYLE-SHAPIRO, J., MORROW, P., RICHARDSON, R., and DUNN, S. (2002) 'Using Profit Sharing to Enhance Employee Attitudes: A Longitudinal Examination of the Effects of Trust and Commitment', *Human Resource Management*, 41(winter): 423–39.

DUNDON, T. and GOLLAN, P. J. (2007) 'Re-conceptualizing Voice in the Non-Union Workplace', *International Journal of Human Resource Management*, 18(7): 1182–98.

EDWARDS, P. and WRIGHT, M. (2001) 'High-involvement Work Systems and Performance Outcomes', *International Journal of Human Resource Management*, 12(4): 568–85.

EMMOTT, M. (2007) 'Hear me Now.' *People Management*, p. 38.

EPOC Research Group (1997) 'New Forms of Work Organisation: Can Europe Realise its Potential?' *European Foundation for the Improvement of Living and Working Conditions*, Dublin.

FENTON-O'CREEVEY, M., WOOD, S., and CALLEROT, E. (1998) 'Employee Involvement within European Multinationals', *European Works Council Study Group*, Stage 1 Research Report, July.

FROST, A. (1998) 'Variation in Labor-Management Collaboration over the Redesign of Work: Impacts on Work Organization and Outcomes', in D. Lewin, and B. Kaufman, (eds), *Advances in Industrial and Labour Relations*. Stamford: JAI Press, 8: 89–117.

GALLIE, D., FELSTED, A., and GREEN, F. (2001) 'Changing Patterns of Employee Involvement', *ESRC SKOPE Working Paper*.

GIBBONS, J. and WOOCK, C. (2007) *Evidence-Based Human Resources: A Primer and Summary of Current Literature*. New York: The Conference Board.

GOLLAN, P. J. (2007) *Employee Representation in Non-Union Firms*. London: Sage Publications.

——and MARKEY, R. (2001) 'Conclusions: Models of Diversity and Interaction', in R. Markey, P. J. Gollan, A. Chouraqui, A. Hodgkinson, and V. Veersma, (eds), *Models of Employee Participation in a Changing Global Environment: Diversity and Interaction*. Ashgate: Aldershot.

——and WILKINSON, A. (2007) 'Developments in Information and Consultation', *The International Journal of Human Resource Management*, 18(7): 1133–45.

GOSPEL, H. and WILLMAN, P. (2003) 'High Performance Workplaces: The Role of Employee Involvement in a Modern Economy', Evidence of the EU Directive Establishing a General Framework for Informing and Consulting Employees, *Centre for Economic Performance*, London.

GUEST, D. and PECCEI, R. (1998) *The Partnership Company: Benchmarks for the Future*, *Involvement and Participation Association*. London: IPA.

HARRISON, G. and FREEMAN, R. (2004) 'Democracy in and Around Organizations', *The Academy of Management Journal*, 18(3): 49–53.

HELLER, F., PUSIĆ, E., STRAUSS, G., and WILPERT, B. (1998) *Organizational Participation, Myth and Reality*. Oxford: Oxford University Press.

HORVATH, W. L. II and SVYANTEK, D. J. (1998) 'Participative Management in Union Settings: Lessons from Saturn. Advances in Industrial and Labour Relations', in D. Lewin, and B. E. Kaufman, (eds), *Advances in Industrial and Labour Relations*. Stamford: JAI Press, 8: 119–38.

HUSELID, M. (1995) 'The Impact of Human Resource Management Practices on Turnover, Production and Corporate Financial Performance', *Academy of Management Journal*, 38(3): 635–72.

ICHNIOWSKI, C., SHAW, K., and PRENNUSHI, G. (1997) 'The Effects of Human Resource Management Practices on Productivity: A Study of Steel Finishing Lines', *American Economic Review*, 87(3): 291–313.

KESSLER, I., JENNINGS, R., and UNDY, R. (2000) *A Comparative Study of Employee Communication and Consultation in Private Sector Companies: Final Report*. Templeton College: University of Oxford.

——UNDY, R., and HERON, P. (2004) 'Employee Perspectives on Communication and Consultation: Findings from a Cross-National Survey', *International Journal of Human Resource Management*, 15(3): 512–532.

LEWIN, D. (2002) *HRM and Business Performance Research: Empiricism in Search of Theory*. Paper Presented at the 62nd Annual Meeting, Academy of Management, Denver, CO, August, 33 pp.

——(2005a) 'The Dual Theory of Human Resource Management and Business Performance: Lessons for HR Executives', in M. Losey, S. Meisinger, and D. Ulrich, (eds), *The Future of Human Resource Management*, pp. 285–92. Hoboken, NJ: Wiley.

——(2005b) 'Unionism and Employment Conflict Resolution: Rethinking Collective Voice and its Consequences', *Journal of Labor Research*, 26(2): 209–39.

——(2008) *Employee Voice and Mutual Gains*. Proceedings of the 60th Annual Meeting, Labor and Employment Relations Association. Champaign, IL: LERA, 61–83.

——and DOTAN, H. (2009) *The Triple Theory of Human Resources and Business Performance*. UCLA Anderson School of Management, Working Paper, 43 pp.

MACDUFFIE, J. P. (1995) 'Human Resource Bundles and Manufacturing Performance: Organizational Logic and Flexible Production Systems in the World Auto Industry', *Industrial and Labor Relations Review*, 48(2): 197–221.

MARCHINGTON, M., GOODMAN, J., WILKINSON, A., and ACKERS, P. (1992) 'New Developments in Employee Involvement', *Employment Department Research*, Series no 2.

——GRIMSHAW, D., RUBERY J., and WILLMOTT, H. (eds) (2005) *Fragmenting Work: Blurring Organizational Boundaries and Disordering Hierarchies*. Oxford: Oxford University Press.

MARCHINGTON, M. and SUTER, J. (2008) *Informal employee voice: filling the gaps or reinforcing the status quo?* Paper presented to the Academy of Management conference, Anaheim, August.

—— and WILKINSON, A. (2005) 'Direct Participation and Involvement', in S. Bach (ed.), *Personnel Management in Britain* (4th edition). Oxford: Blackwell.

—— and WILKINSON, A. (2008) *Human Resource Management at Work*, 4th edition. London: CIPD.

MILLWARD, N., BRYSON, A., and FORTH, J. (2000) *All Change at Work?* London: Routledge.

MUELLER, F. (1994) 'Teams Between Hierarchy and Commitment: Change Strategies and their Internal Environment, *Journal of Management Studies*, 31(3): 383–403.

O'REILLY, C. A. (2008) 'CMR Classics: Corporations, Culture and Commitment: Motivation and Social Control in Organizations', *California Management Review*, 50(2): 85–101.

PATEMAN, C. (1970) *Participation and Democratic Theory*. Cambridge: CUP.

PATTERSON, M., WEST, M., HAWTHORN, R., and NICKELL, S. (1998) 'Impact of People Management Practices on Business Performance Issues', *People Management*, 22, Wimbledon: Institute of Personnel and Development.

PFEFFER, J. (1998) *The Human Equation: Building Profits by Putting People First*. Boston: Harvard Business School Press.

PIORE, M. and SABEL, C. (1983) *The Second Industrial Divide*. New York: Basic Books.

Poole, M. (1986) *Towards a New Industrial Democracy: Workers Participation in Industry*. London: Routledge.

—— LANSBURY, R., and WAILES, N. (2000) 'A Comparative Analysis of Developments in Industrial Democracy', *Industrial Relations*, 40(3): 490–525.

RAMSAY, H., SCHOLARIOS, D., and HARLEY, B. (2000) 'Employees and High-Performance Work Systems: Treating Inside the Black Box', *British Journal of Industrial Relations*, 38(4): 501–31.

SCARBOROUGH, H. (2003) 'Knowledge Management', in D. Holman, T. Wall, C. Clegg, P. Sparrow, and A. Howard (eds), *The New Workplace: A Guide to the Human Impact of Modern Working Practices*. Chichester: John Wiley.

TERRY, M. (1999) 'Systems of Collective Representation in Non-Union Firms in the UK', *Industrial Relations Journal*, 30(1): 16–30.

TUSHMAN, M. L. and O'REILLY, C. A. (1996) 'Ambidextrous Organizations: Managing Evolutionary and Revolutionary Change', *California Management Review*, 38(4): 8–30.

VOOS, P. (2004) *Democracy and Industrial Relations*. IRRA Presidential Address.

WALTON, R. (1985) 'From Control to Commitment in the Workplace', *Harvard Business Review*, March–April: 77–84.

WEBB, S. and WEBB, B. (1902) *Industrial Democracy*. London: Longmans Green.

WILKINSON, A. (1998) Empowerment theory and practice *Personnal Review*, 27(1): 40–56.

—— (2008) 'Empowerment', in S. Clegg and J. Bailey (eds), *Encyclopedia of Organizational Studies*, pp. 441–2, London: Sage.

—— Dundon, T., and GRUGULIS, I. (2007) 'Information but not Consultation: Exploring Employee Involvement in SMEs', *International Journal of Human Resource Management*, 18(7): 1279–97.

—— GODFREY, G., and MARCHINGTON, M. (1997) 'Bouquets, Brickbats and Blinkers: Total Quality Management and Employee Involvement', *Organization Studies*, 18(5): 799–820.

—— MARCHINGTON, M., and ACKERS, P. (2004) 'Changing Patterns of Employee Voice', *Journal of Industrial Relations*, 46(3): 298–322.

——REDMAN, T., SNAPE, E., and MARCHINGTON, M. (1998) *Managing with TQM: Theory and Practice.* London: Macmillan.

WOMACK, J., JONES, D., and ROOS, D. (1990) *The Machine that Changed the World The Story of Lean Production.* New York: Harper Perennial.

WOOD, S. (1999) Human Resource Management and Performance, *International Journal of Management Reviews,* 1(4): 367–413.

——and ALBANESE, M. (1995) 'Can we Speak of High Commitment Management on the Shop Floor?' *Journal of Management Studies,* 36(2): 215–47.

——and DE MENEZES, L. (1998) High Commitment in the UK: Evidence from the Workplace Industrial Relations Survey, and Employees' Manpower and Skills Practices Survey', *Human Relations,* 512(4): 485–515.

WRIGHT, P. M. and GARDNER, T. M. (2003) 'The Human Resource-Firm Performance Relationship: Methodological and Theoretical Challenges', in D. Holman, T. D. Wall, C. Clegg, P. Sparrow, and A. Howard, (eds), *The New Workplace: People Technology, and Organisation.* Sussex: Wiley.

PART II

PERSPECTIVES

CHAPTER 2

AN HRM PERSPECTIVE ON EMPLOYEE PARTICIPATION

PETER BOXALL

JOHN PURCELL

INTRODUCTION

SINCE the 1980s, human resource management (HRM) has become the most widely recognized term in the Anglophone world referring to the activities of management in organizing work and managing people to achieve organizational ends. The term is not restricted to organizations in the Anglo-American sphere: it is popular in the Francophone and Hispanic worlds and is growing in the Arabian world, among others.[1] HRM is an inevitable process that accompanies the growth of organizations (Watson, 2005). It is central to entrepreneurial and managerial activity and occurs whether or not HR specialists are employed to assist in the process. It can certainly be reformed and renewed as organizations change but it is not something that can ever be 'restructured' out of organizations unless everyone is laid off—but then the organization itself will die.

As a field of practice, HRM exhibits great diversity across occupations, hierarchical levels, workplaces, firms, industries, cultures, and societies. Differentiation in HRM within and across organizations is a widely noted phenomenon (Jackson and Schuler, 1995; Lepak and Snell, 2007; Pinfield and Berner, 1994). The need to manage employee voice has long been recognized as an important aspect of the HRM process (Beer et al., 1984). Like other dimensions of labour management, there is significant diversity in the ways in which employers seek to foster and respond to employee voice: styles adopted range from highly cooperative 'partnership' models of labour management through to highly unitarist philosophies of workforce governance, with various blends in between (Dundon and Gollan, 2007; Purcell and Ahlstrand, 1994).

Given its inescapable role in the management of all but the very smallest organizations, HRM is also an academic phenomenon. It is a central feature of the curricula of business schools around the world and a major sphere of research, drawing on a wide range of academic traditions. Theorists in HRM draw concepts and theories from the companion disciplines of Organizational Behaviour, Strategic Management, and Industrial Relations and, like colleagues in these fields, draw from deeper academic wells in social science, including Psychology, Sociology, Economics, and Political Studies. HRM itself can be subdivided into three domains: Micro HRM, Strategic HRM, and International HRM (Boxall et al., 2007b). Micro HRM is concerned with practices within the sub-functions of HRM, drawing on long traditions of studies on such aspects as selection, appraisal, and pay. Strategic HRM and International HRM are both more systemic or macro in their outlook. Strategic HRM is concerned with how HR practices cluster into HR systems, and with the relationships between HR strategy and the organization's internal and external contexts and its performance outcomes. International HRM focuses on HRM in companies operating across national boundaries and shows a particular concern with the interplay between corporate integration and local adaptation. This diversity in HRM—in practice and in theory—gives us a major problem if we are asked to describe *an HRM perspective* on employee participation. As management researchers, our response to this challenge is to emphasize the value of taking an 'analytical approach' to HRM. The goal of this chapter is to explain what this means and to explore what such an approach can offer to the analysis of employee participation.

ANALYTICAL HRM AND EMPLOYEE VOICE

Boxall et al. (2007b) use the notion of 'analytical HRM' to emphasize that the fundamental mission of the discipline of HRM is not to propagate claims about 'best practice' in 'excellent companies'. While this remains a feature of much popular writing for managers, it does not provide a credible basis for management research and education. The role of analytical HRM is to identify *what* managers do in HRM, *how* they go about it, to understand *why* they do it, and consider *who* benefits from these actions. Analytical HRM privileges research and explanation over prescription. Its primary task is to gather empirical data and build theory in order to account for what management tries to achieve and the way management actually behaves in organizing work and managing people across diverse contexts.

The weaknesses of a decontextualized propagation of 'best practices' in the management literature were identified by Legge (1978) in her critique of what was then known as Personnel Management. She showed how Personnel Management textbooks commonly failed to analyse the goals of management and to recognize differences in the interests of managers and workers. She also criticized the personnel textbooks for failing to examine the way in which their favourite prescriptions worked well in some contexts but not in others. This argument has been reinforced by similar critiques of best practice prescriptions in the HRM literature (Marchington and Grugulis, 2000), by major reviews of the relationships between contextual variables and HR practices (Jackson and Schuler, 1995), and by studies of the social embeddedness of HR systems (Gooderham et al., 1999). The international growth of academic interest in HRM has strongly emphasized the way in which models of HRM vary across cultures and reflect the impact of different employment laws and societal institutions, often making explicit key differences with US managerial mindsets (Aycan, 2005; Brewster, 1999; Paauwe and Boselie, 2003). To quote the technical language of methodology, 'moderators' are important in our understanding of HRM: although all organizations benefit from a soundly managed process of HRM, specific HR practices vary in their relevance and effectiveness under different conditions. Further, what are seemingly the same practices can be interpreted in quite different ways across cultures. Those who take an analytical approach to HRM are therefore sceptical about claims that particular clusters of HR practices, such as the lists offered in the works of the US writer, Jeffery Pfeffer (1994, 1998), can have value across economic and social contexts (Marchington and Grugulis, 2000).

Building on the way analytical HRM seeks to understand the complex goals and diverse contexts of HRM, an important trend is the construction of models of *how* HRM processes work, models that lay out the intervening variables or 'mediators' involved. One driver of this trend in analysis stems from the literature on strategic HRM with its slew of studies on the links between HRM and organizational performance. This literature frequently draws on the 'resource-based view' of the firm, which argues that hard to imitate human resources can be sources of sustained competitive advantage. To make this perspective truly useful, however, we need to show *how* HRM helps create valuable and rare organizational capabilities (Boxall and Purcell, 2008). A second driver stems from the basic realization that in any model of HRM, outcomes are better when desired HR practices are effectively enacted by line managers and foster the kind of employee attitudes and behaviours required (Guest, 2002; Purcell et al., 2003). This means that notions such as organizational culture, psychological contracting, and social exchange, which have been important in the companion discipline of Organizational Behaviour, are now being integrated into models of the process of HRM. HR researchers increasingly investigate the way in which HR policies and practices affect employee attitudes and behaviours, such as trust in management, perceived organizational support, job satisfaction, discretionary job behaviour, and organizational commitment (Guest, 2007; Macky and Boxall, 2007).

This brings us to a final point about analytical HRM: the approach lays a more credible basis for assessing outcomes in work and employment. This is obvious in terms of the growth of studies on the HRM performance link but, in the light of what we have said about the mediating role of employee attitudes and behaviour, it is not simply about outcomes sought by shareholders or by their imperfect agents, managers. HRM research is increasingly taking on board the question of mutuality (Guest, 2002, 2007; Peel and Boxall, 2005), examining the extent to which employer and worker outcomes are mutually satisfying and, thus, more sustainable in our societies over the long run.

Employee Voice Through the Lens of Analytical HRM

On this basis, we can consider what an analytical approach to HRM might offer to the study of 'employee participation'. To the uninitiated, this must seem a rather absurd term: surely every employee participates in their organization by virtue of being employed in it. Taking a job in an organization is a decision to participate in it using one's skills and experience. What academics are really getting at when they talk of 'employee participation' is the *degree* of influence or voice employees have in decisions about their work, their employment conditions, and the management of their organization. Because most organizations are managed rather than constituted as democracies, and employment law upholds the right of managers to give 'lawful and reasonable orders', there is always an issue around how much say employees have in how they do their jobs and in how the organization is run. But we must be talking about matters of degree because even in highly controlling work environments, such as assembly lines, individuals still need to exercise some discretion in how they do their work (Bendix, 1956). The act of employing means that managers are forced, in effect, to trust workers to some extent.

Our preference is to analyse the degree of 'employee voice'. We understand employee voice as incorporating representative or indirect forms of voice and various forms of participation that facilitate direct employee involvement in work-related decisions. Representation thus traverses both union and non-union institutions while participation includes a range of activities in which managers engage workers in work-related decisions, either on the job or off it. The focus of these forms of voice varies enormously: from those which are clearly focused on organizational power sharing, such as collective bargaining, through those which involve ownership, such as employee share ownership plans, through to those which are focused on work tasks within departments and jobs. The range of practices that can fit within these categories is illustrated in Table 2.1 (Boxall and Purcell, 2008).

A note of caution is, however, needed. While it is common to draw a distinction between representation of employee interests and employee participation in management, there can be considerable overlap between representation and participation. Managers, for example, may design consultative structures with non-threatening participation in mind—to communicate with employee representatives and enhance employee support for management proposals—but to stop well short of negotiation of interests (Gollan and Wilkinson, 2007). On the other hand, what may start life as a top-down, 'tell and sell' channel may grow into a forum which employees make more interactive, one in which they raise *their* concerns and management learns to listen and respond. It is thus more realistic to see representation and participation as having something of a permeable and dynamic boundary (Freeman et al., 2007a).

Table 2.1 Types of employee voice

	Power–centred	Ownership–centred	Task–centred
Indirect involvement	- Worker Directors - Works' Councils/ Employee Forums/ Joint Consultative Commitees (JCCs) - Collective bargaining - Joint Partnership Committees	- ESOP (Employee Share Ownership Plans) where shares are held by trustees directly elected by employees - Worker Cooperatives	- Employee representatives meeting local/ department management
Direct involvement	- Attitude surveys - Newsletters/ email/intranet - 'Town hall' meetings	- Share option (purchase schemes) giving employees 'votes' as shareholders	- Job enrichment (voice in how the job is done) - Semi-autonomous teams - Team briefing - Problem-solving groups (quality circles/Kaizen team, continuous improvement group) - Suggestion schemes

Source: Adapted from Boxall and Purcell, 2008: 151.

Having described the relevant terminology, we now offer our analysis. In the next section, we describe what we know about trends in employee voice practices and the larger organizational patterns of which they form a part: we look at what managers are doing and how they are going about it. Our focus is mainly on the Anglo-American world but we inevitably make some comparisons with practices outside the Anglophone sphere to illustrate what is distinctive. The subsequent section then discusses what an analytical approach has to say about why these trends are happening: what seem to be management's goals or underpinning motives? Following this section, we offer a discussion of what our analysis implies about how outcomes might be improved for the parties in the field of employee voice, and then conclude the chapter.

THE *WHAT* AND *HOW* OF CONTEMPORARY WORKPLACE VOICE

We must first of all situate management's actions within the context of historically-shaped voice practices. In the big picture, the most commonly noted trend is the declining significance of employee representation through trade unionism and collective bargaining, something which is most apparent in Anglophone, liberal market economies. Boxall, Freeman, and Haynes' (2007a) summary of trends in union representation across the Anglo-American world is shown in Table 2.2. They note that 'outside the public sector, unions are no longer the "default" option for worker voice in any (Anglophone) country' (Boxall et al., 2007a: 207). Only in Ireland is private sector union density above 20 per cent but Ireland experienced the largest fall in private sector union density among the six countries surveyed in the nine years to 2003 (17 percentage points). Ireland's 'social partnership' model of trade unionism, which operates at the level of national politics, has failed to stem the decline of employee support for unions at the workplace.

It is fair to say that most private sector workers in the Anglo-American world are now relatively indifferent to what unions offer, preferring direct over union forms of voice (Boxall et al., 2007a). Direct dealing with management over training and career issues and a philosophy of self-reliance in the labour market have grown. In Canada, for example, six out of ten workers prefer direct over collective forms of voice (Campolieti et al., 2007: 58). Workers increasingly believe that unions cannot usefully mediate job design and career development issues. In Australia, for example, two-thirds of non-union workers believe that a union would make no difference to them personally (Teicher et al., 2007: 133). Even

Table 2.2 Trends in union density across the Anglo–American world

	USA	Canada	Britain	Ireland	Australia	NZ
Union Density, 2004	12.5 per cent	30.4 per cent	28.8 per cent	34.6 per cent	22.7 per cent	21.1 per cent
Density trend in the private sector: 1995–2004 (% of private sector employees)	Fell from 10.4 per cent to 7.9 per cent	Fell from 22.2 per cent to 18.0 per cent	Fell from 21.6 per cent to 17.2 per cent	Fell from 45 per cent to 28.2 per cent (2003)	Fell from 25.1 per cent to 16.8 per cent	Fell from 19.8 per cent (1996) to 12 per cent

Source: Boxall et al., 2007a: 208.

among those who express a strong desire to join a union, over a third thinks a union would make no difference to them personally.

While union density in the private sector has fallen, trade unionism in the Anglo-American world is increasingly dominated by the public sector unions. The public sector is characterized by tensions over wage levels and work pressures and an ongoing clash between professional work cultures, on the one hand, and managerial ideologies and bureaucracy, on the other (Bach and Kessler, 2007; Boxall and Purcell, 2008). Budget constraints have been applied while client demands, as in public education and health, have risen, fuelling employee discontent with the wage–work bargain. This discontent has been readily organized by public sector unions which have the advantage of operating on much larger worksites and in much larger organizations than is true, on average, in the private sector.

Has the realm of employee voice receded with the decline of trade unionism? Has management decided that voice can be dispensed with as an area of HR practice? The answer is a resounding 'no'. As Willman, Bryson, and Gomez (2007: 1321) put it, the decline of trade unionism does not mean employers have lost 'their appetite' for employee voice. The key change is in the *how* of employee voice: direct types of employee voice have grown since the 1980s across the industrialized world. In the UK, forms of communication between management and employees are widely used with 91 per cent of workplaces having face-to-face meetings, 83 per cent using some form of downward communication, like an intranet (34%) or communication chains (sometimes called cascade briefing) (64%), and written two-way communication methods like email or suggestion schemes evident in two-thirds of workplaces (Kersley et al., 2006: 135). Team working is also widespread in Britain (in 72% of workplaces) although in only half of these establishments are all employees in teams. The pattern of increasing use by management of direct forms of employee involvement is repeated both in other

Anglophone countries (Boxall et al., 2007a) and in continental Europe (Poutsma et al., 2006).

More formalized forms of direct employee involvement are, of course, much more likely in large enterprises (Kersley et al., 2006). Does this mean that small firms are some kind of realm where workers have very little influence because managers go about their work with a high degree of autocracy? The empirical data does not suggest this at all. In small firms, worker satisfaction with their influence on the job and with the quality of management communication is typically higher (Forth et al., 2006; Macky and Boxall, 2007). In small firms, there is likely to be much more personal face-to-face contact between management and workers, something which fades rapidly when the workplace gets above forty to fifty employees. Even in financially vulnerable firms operating in highly competitive markets, critical workers, such as chefs in small restaurants, have some bargaining power which means the employer often takes their voice into account and makes concessions to accommodate their interests (Edwards and Ram, 2006).

To be sure, less critical workers in small firms are less likely to get management consideration but this rather forcibly makes the point that big firms tend to be more impersonal, bureaucratic, and rule driven. The social and power distance between the managed and top decision makers is much greater and individual voices are much more muted. Formal types of participation can therefore be imagined as antidotes to these tendencies, but it must be doubted how successful they can be in large organizations unless managers at various levels give support and bring them to life (Boxall and Purcell, 2008). A key variant in formal voice is always in the extent to which it is 'embedded': applied extensively across the workforce of a large organization and regularly practised (Cox et al., 2006). Purcell and Hutchison's (2007) study of the British retail organization, Selfridges, is a case in point. It underlines the value of senior management taking a much greater interest in the selection, development, support, and motivation of front line managers so that they, in turn, are more responsive to the needs of the employees they manage. Better management of managers sets in train a positive process that enhances the attitudes and behaviours of the employees dealing directly with customers and, thus, leads on to such important organizational outcomes as enhanced customer satisfaction and higher sales.

What, then, do we know about the sort of indirect or representative schemes, such as works councils or joint consultative committees (JCCs), which can be important in larger organizations? In most of continental Europe, the legal require-ment for works councils ensures that such forms of indirect voice are widespread, but not universal. In the USA, they are virtually unheard of but there is evidence of significant growth in the other Anglophone countries in recent years (Boxall et al., 2007a). In the UK, the most recent WERS[2] survey provides comprehensive data on joint consultative committees (Kersley et al., 2006: 126–32). As expected, these are unusual in small firms (and small firms make up a growing proportion of British firms (Kersley et al., 2006: 19), but two-thirds of workplaces with 100–199 workers have JCCs, either at the workplace itself or through access to one at a higher corporate level. This figure rises to 72 per cent in respect of workplaces with between 200 and 500 workers and 82 per cent in workplaces with 500 or more employees. Indeed, there is some evidence that in these larger companies the use of JCCs might be spreading. The employers' body, the Confederation of British Industry (CBI), recorded a 10 per cent growth in 'permanent information and consultation bodies' in their annual employment survey in 2006 (IRS Employment Review 856, October 2006: 7). One of the most significant features of British JCCs is their composition: overall, in 2004, 11 per cent of JCCs were composed exclusively of union representatives, 67 per cent of them were non-union, and a further 22 per cent were mixed with both union and non-union representatives sitting alongside each other in discussions with management (Kersley et al., 2006: 131).

What these statistics cannot tell is quite what is meant by consultation. It is well known, for example, that if management wish to render consultation an empty process they can easily do so with JCCs' agenda being restricted to 'tea and toilets'. Meaningful consultations, which the UK's Involvement and Participation Association calls 'option-based consultation' requires employee representatives to have a right to express their views on issues before final decisions are taken. To be effective, they need a lot of information from within, and outside, the company, time to draw up proposals, an opportunity to present them, and time for the proposals to be treated seriously by management. In practice, this type of consultation is quite rare since, as we discuss below, it impinges uncomfortably on management autonomy. Consultation which involves information sharing and is discursive, yet non-threatening to managerial interests, is the preferred style of many managements in the Anglo-American world (Hall et al., 2007).

The picture in the Anglo-American world, then, is that management's preference has been to foster direct forms of employee influence. With the exception of the USA, employee-centered, indirect forms of employee voice, such as joint consultative committees, have also gained greater traction in the management of large organizations. These are typically used to enhance levels of communication and consultation, and have a greater universality about them by covering all employees rather than only union members. They can operate either alongside or instead of trade unions. In the UK, in fact, dual or hybrid channels of voice have become far more common over the last twenty years than union only voice regimes (Willman et al., 2007: 1321). British unionized employers have developed a model of employee voice which widens the engagement with employees, both in the sense of opening voice opportunities up to a greater range of employees and in the sense of expanding what is discussed. Dual voice systems may be enabling them to handle distributive or conflictual issues through the union channel while handling integrative or cooperative issues more effectively through the more broadly-based consultative channel. This may explain why productivity outcomes are better in dual voice systems than in union only regimes (Charlwood and Terry, 2007; Purcell and Georgiadis, 2007).

A key contrast within the Anglo-American world is, therefore, between the USA and everyone else: the ability to have complementary union and non-union voice is possible outside the USA but is effectively banned there. What we observe outside the USA is a much greater evolution in indirect forms of employee voice and much more open attitudes towards alternative voice regimes (Boxall et al., 2007a). While some industrial relations commentators still have difficulty accepting that non-union representative voice can deliver valuable outcomes for employees, the evidence is that employees are generally very positive about contemporary consultative channels (Boxall et al., 2007a: 216). This should not be surprising: the Anglo-American workforce shows a strong preference, if at all possible, for working cooperatively with management.

Our analysis of voice trends has so far talked about specific voice practices. This is very much a micro level of analysis: it is important but runs the risk that we miss the wood for the trees. In Strategic HRM, an analytical approach involves trying to get an overview of change in the HR systems in which employers situate their voice practices. HR systems are clusters of work and employment practices oriented to a particular group of employees (Boxall and Purcell, 2008). Large organizations typically have one type of HR system for managers and another for their main group of production or operations workers. Where professionals, technical specialists, and administrative support staff are employed, it is also commonplace to have distinctive HR models for these groups. While there are typically overlaps across HR systems, their voice dimensions have usually been differentiated: managers and highly-skilled professionals have historically enjoyed greater influence in their jobs and in organizational decision making than those in operating roles.

A key development challenging, or diminishing, these divisions has been the growth of high involvement work systems for production workers. HIWSs, also known as high performance work systems (HPWSs), aim to increase employee involvement in task-related decision making ('empowerment') and enhance the skills and incentives that enable and motivate them to take advantage of this greater empowerment (Appelbaum et al., 2000). Serious management interest in HIWSs stems from the rise of Japanese high-quality production systems in the 1970s and 1980s, including such techniques as quality circles, just in time inventory and delivery, and flexible, team-based production (Boxall and Purcell, 2008). This interest forms part of a major change in production systems in those parts of Western manufacturing, such as steel making and car manufacture, where the deskilling of production work and demarcation among trades took a strong hold as mass production developed in the early twentieth century. In these manufacturing contexts, the need to adopt Japanese-style lean manufacturing principles in order to survive has led to change towards a high-involvement model incorporating greater decision making autonomy on the job, as well as off it in quality circles or other types of problem-solving groups or employee forums (MacDuffie, 1995). Along with the Japanese quality challenge, a key environmental stimulant of change towards HIWSs in manufacturing over the last twenty years has been the advent of advanced manufacturing technology (Challis et al., 2005). This includes such technologies as robotics, computer-aided design (CAD), computer numerical control (CNC) machine tools, and electronic data interchange (EDI) systems, all of which depend for their effectiveness on astute and timely decision making by workers.

While interest in HIWSs sprang from manufacturing, it is not simply a manufacturing issue. There are similar developments in the service sector. High-skill, high-involvement systems of managing people are naturally common in professional services because such workers need to exercise high levels of skill and judgement but they are also becoming important in those service industries which are able to segment customer needs (Boxall, 2003). In the hotel industry, for example, luxury hotel operators can improve revenue and customer retention through HR systems that empower front line employees to personalize service (Haynes and Fryer, 2000). They therefore have an interest in investing in the employee development and voice practices that will support a high-quality competitive strategy in this industry. Such investments in employees, however, are less common at the low price end of the hotel industry where customers want a cheap bed 'without frills', as recently illustrated in a study of Chinese hotels of different quality ratings (Sun et al., 2007).

The implementation of HIWSs for core operating staff is part of what Kelley (2000) calls the growth of the 'participatory bureaucracy'. The participatory bureaucracy is characteristic of capital intensive or high-tech manufacturing firms seeking to respond to high-quality competition through a process of differentiation which builds higher skills, stronger learning, and greater innovation. It is also a feature of large service firms, such as hotels, banks, and rest homes, trying to differentiate their offerings to meet the more demanding requirements of more lucrative market segments (Boxall, 2003). More participatory bureaucracies have also developed, to some extent, in those parts of the public sector where governments and unions have developed labour management 'partnerships' (Bach and Kessler, 2007). It is fair to say, however, that the rhetoric is often more powerful than the reality in the public sector, which remains prone to high conflict levels due to struggles over budget constraints and the escalation of managerial controls.

There is, however, a second, and competing, trend in the big picture: the growth of what we might call the 'flexible bureaucracy' (Boxall and Purcell, 2008). We use this term to recognize what Grimshaw, Marchington, Willmott, and Rubery (2005) describe as a growth of fragmentation in large organizations. The flexible bureaucracy combines an inner core of salaried managerial and specialist staff, whose own contracts have often been heightened in terms of performance expectations and rewards, with outsourced HR systems. The outsourced models adopted can include any number of types, including those which foster high levels of involvement but do so with lower cost workers or those which simply send work offshore into environments with low levels of employee voice and much lighter levels of employment regulation (Cooke, 2007). Where trade unions exist, they may extract relatively high wage levels for slimmer workforces in the developed countries but cannot protect jobs against rounds of restructuring (Konzelmann et al., 2004). The flexible bureaucracy is common among multinationals responding to heightened cost pressures in their international markets, service firms in deregulated, cost conscious industries (e.g. airlines, telecommunications) and public sector organizations which have been required to adopt a greater emphasis on financial control (Bach and Kessler, 2007).

Trends in employee voice can therefore be interpreted in terms of the larger picture of how management is trying to cope with the problem of change. Management responses are diverse, reflecting different assessments of how flexibility is best served in the particular markets in which they are engaged. The fact that large organizations—both in the private and in the public sectors—may be characterized by developments in one quarter which are participatory and developments in another quarter which are disempowering to the employee groups downsized or outsourced is a feature of our times.

THE *WHY* QUESTION: MANAGEMENT'S MOTIVES IN EMPLOYEE VOICE

Our overview of trends in employee voice has started to explore the reasons for the patterns we see. We turn now to focus more closely on the *why* behind the *what* and *how*: on the goals or motives that underlie management's voice strategies. Understanding management's goals and how these vary across contexts is a fundamental priority in analytical HRM and helps us to interpret employer behaviour in respect of employee voice. An analytical framework for interpreting employer goals is shown in Figure 2.1 (Boxall and Purcell, 2008). The basic premise in this framework is that employers pursue a mix of economic and socio-political goals which are subject to strategic tensions. This mix of motives affects employer attitudes to voice regimes.

The fundamental economic goal of employers is concerned with cost-effectiveness (Boxall, 2007; Godard and Delaney, 2000; Osterman, 1987). Cost-effective management of labour is a critical aspect of making a firm viable and how it is tackled depends greatly on the technological characteristics and economic structure of the

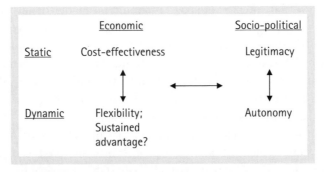

Figure 2.1 The goals of HRM

Source: Boxall and Purcell, 2008: 20.

industry concerned (Batt and Doellgast, 2005; Blauner, 1964). There are, for example, major differences in what is invested in employees between high-tech or capital-intensive manufacturing, on the one hand, and labour-intensive, low-tech manufacturing, on the other. Investments in expensive high-involvement work systems are commonplace in the former because they enhance productivity and improve the possibilities for product and process innovation. Research on advanced manufacturing technology, referred to in our review of trends, shows that such technologies reach more of their potential when production workers' jobs are redesigned to enable them to enhance the operating performance of these technologies. Studies by Wall et al. (1990, 1992), for example, show how work redesign and training that enables production operators to solve technical problems as they occur, reduces reliance on the need to call in specialist technicians for problem solving and thereby enhances productivity. The productivity benefits come from quicker response to these problems and thus lower machine downtime. In the longer run, productivity improvements also come from more effective use of the capacity of operators for learning: employees who enjoy greater empowerment learn more about the reasons why faults occur in the first place and find ways to reduce their incidence.

The converse of this argument is that investments in HIWSs are unlikely to be cost effective in low-tech, labour-intensive manufacturing which makes little use of AMT. Much of the apparel and toy manufacturing being conducted in China, for example, works very cost effectively on classical management principles of labour specialization without much worker empowerment and in a context of much less demanding labour regulation (Cooke, 2004). Firms in labour-intensive manufacturing are increasingly offshoring their plants to lower cost countries.

Similarly, in services, there are major differences in employee involvement, remuneration, and development opportunities between knowledge-intensive services, on the one hand, and low margin, mass services, on the other (Boxall, 2003). In general, HIWSs are less likely in mass services where customers are price conscious and willing to engage in self-service to help keep prices low. Where, however, customers are prepared to pay a premium for higher-quality services, there is often potential for a pay-off from higher investments in employee involvement and retention to ensure better service. This is evident, for example, in Hunter's (2000) study of US rest homes which reveals greater HR investments in training, pay, career structures, and staffing levels in firms that target higher-value niches.

Securing cost-effective management of labour is thus a primary concern of all employers and accounts for major variation in their HR strategies—including the voice elements—across industries and across the market segments within them. Cost-effective management of labour helps a firm to survive the economic short run when conditions in its industry are relatively stable. Survival beyond the short run, however, requires a degree of managerial attention to a second goal domain: organizational flexibility. In those firms in which managers see participatory styles of management as essential to long-run flexibility, we can expect to see attempts to create and maintain higher levels of employee involvement. This may, in fact, form part of a strategy to build sustained competitive advantage through differentiation in the quality of the firm's human and social capital (Boxall and Purcell, 2008). Where, however, change is likely to bring instability in product markets or major challenges from low-cost producers, management is likely to weaken its longer-term commitments to employees (Marchington, 2007), fuelling the growth of the type of 'flexible bureaucracy' referred to above. In liberal market economies, then, it is very unlikely that managers will all subscribe to the view that HIWSs and extensive voice practices are in the long-term interest of their firms.

We cannot, however, solely account for management attitudes to voice practices through economic reasoning. The goals of HRM are not purely economic: they are also socio-political (Boxall, 2007). Firms are embedded in societies, which make claims on the behaviour of employers. This means that social legitimacy is also a key goal for many employers, at least to the extent of compliance with their responsibilities under employment law (Boxall and Purcell, 2008; Lees, 1997). The larger firms, in particular, are affected by employment regulation and by prevailing social views on what sort of voice practices are appropriate. Multinationals are increasingly under scrutiny, not only in their rich country operations but in terms of the way they and their contractors employ labour in the Third World (Boxall and Purcell, 2008). Use of illegal migrant workers and non-compliance with the minimum wage are practices that can survive in small firms outside the public gaze (Edwards and Ram, 2006) but are much less likely to characterize firms which are 'household names'. A more demanding model of employment citizenship, incorporating initiatives in work–life balance and employee support, is characteristic of a range of the more prominent firms, including those wishing to be perceived as 'employers of choice' (Boxall and Purcell, 2008).

The need for social legitimacy, as an end in itself, is thus an explanation for why we tend to see certain similar patterns in employee voice across the larger organizations in particular societies and contrasts with organizations in other societies. There are major differences between voice practices in the Anglo-American liberal market economies, where voice regulation is less extensive, and those in the 'social partnership' societies of Western Europe where union power is much more institutionalized (Freeman et al., 2007; Marchington, 2007; Paauwe and Boselie, 2003, 2007).

As with economic goals, where we see both attempts to stabilize cost-effectiveness in the short run and attempts to build some capacity for change if firms are to survive into the long run, the socio-political goals of HRM have a dynamic dimension (Boxall, 2007). As time goes by, management exhibits a fundamental desire to enhance its autonomy or power to act in the governance of the workplace (Bendix, 1956). Gospel (1973) refers to management as having a less openly acknowledged 'security objective' alongside the profit (cost-effectiveness) motive, a goal to maximize managerial control over an uncertain environment including threats to its power from work groups and trade unions. Thus, while management is generally concerned about social legitimacy, at least to the extent of legal compliance in societies where there is a risk of legal enforcement or public rebuke, and sometimes well beyond this, we also observe management playing a longer run political game. The natural tendency of management is to act, over time, to enhance its room to manoeuvre. This is evident in the way multinational firms tend to favour investment in countries with less demanding labour market regulations (Cooke 2001, 2007). It is evident at industry and societal levels, in the tendency of employer federations to lobby, over time, for greater freedom to manage and to resist new employment regulations seen to be diminishing managerial prerogative.

The autonomy motive helps to explain why the forms of voice that management has fostered over recent years, as unions have declined, are very largely those which are either direct between management and employee or those which foster non-union representative voice. Management clearly intends that these forms of voice will either lift productivity without challenging managerial power or provide consensus around the implementation of major workforce decisions.[3] On the other hand, the need to make labour cost effective in its specific product market means that managers will act to restrain their own autonomy when the benefits of enhancing employee autonomy outweigh the costs. Where productivity or service quality are highly sensitive to employee discretionary judgement and employee commitment levels, as in high-tech manufacturing and knowledge-intensive services, management is much more likely to set out to empower workers through high-involvement work systems, as we have noted. Such a process, however, does not necessarily proceed without political contestation within the management layers of large organizations. Batt (2004: 206–7) provides a vivid illustration of this point where a successful initiative introducing self-managing teams, measured in terms of economic benefits, was abandoned because 'the voluntary cooperation of supervisors and middle managers was not forthcoming'. In this particular case, front line managers felt threatened by self-managing teams. In the ensuing managerial politics, the cost of pushing through worker voice in the form or autonomous teams, even though it had great benefits, was too high when opposed by them. Such an illustration reinforces the point that the management of employee voice can be as much about politics within management, as it is about economic rationality.

How can Voice Outcomes be Improved for Firms and Workers?

This brings us naturally to the question of how voice outcomes might be improved for firms and workers. Such a question involves looking at the converging and diverging interests of these parties. Our argument here is framed in terms of underpinning principles rather than 'best practices' (Boxall and Purcell, 2008). It is not appropriate, as indicated in our discussion of the analytical approach to HRM, to consider particular voice practices, or even sets of practices, as 'cure-alls'.

The first principle that we see in the data is that it is in *both* management and worker interests for managers to continue to expand direct forms of voice. That management is, in general, politically comfortable with this, and sees productivity advantages, has been indicated in our review of the what, how, and why of management behaviour but there is also a powerful congruence with worker interests. In Anglo-American workplaces, workers have generally been responding positively to the direct voice opportunities developed by management because they typically like to increase their control over their working environment (Boxall et al., 2007a; Harley et al., 2007; Macky and Boxall, 2007). The empowerment that comes with greater involvement in decision making is generally appealing to workers providing it is not accompanied by work intensification (Macky and Boxall, 2008). There is something motivating and affirming when a worker's direct managers listen and act on his or her ideas that cannot be replicated by indirect, more distal forms of voice (Purcell and Georgiardis, 2007). The extension of direct voice is a principle that can be applied across all sizes of organizations but it does require cost-effective application to continue to work in the interests of firms. There are many situations in which management will decide it is not cost effective to go as far as full-blown high-involvement work systems because the costs of increased train-ing and performance incentives are not going to deliver an adequate payback (Cappelli and Neumark, 2001; Way, 2002).

The second principle we see in the data is that the larger organizations also have something to gain from expanding indirect voice to improve communication, solve problems jointly, and harness cooperative energies in areas such as training, career development, and work design. Again, there is a congruence with worker interests, particularly when employee representatives are drawn from the total workforce: adopting an inclusive approach is more in touch with the current cultural climate or *zeitgeist*. This more comprehensive, more universal approach to representative voice can sit alongside union voice, creating a more effective kind of dual voice, as British employers have shown (Charlwood and Terry, 2007; Purcell and Georgiadis, 2007). In large organizations which are non-unionized, it is also in employer and employee interests to institute representative voice although this option is not legally available under the inflexible regime of employment law that prevails in the USA (Boxall et al., 2007a).

There are, however, ways in which voice regimes can be improved which will not be introduced without management opposition. This is due to the ongoing prevalence of union representation gaps. Surveys across the Anglo-American world find that around one in three workers in non-union firms would be likely to vote for a union (Boxall et al., 2007a). Some of this support is soft or hypothetical, and does not materialize when workers are actually faced with a real union choice, but much of it does reflect an objective need for better voice. The workers who express frustrated demand for unionism are often young or on low incomes and are disproportionately located in workplaces with large numbers of problems. Their employers are unlikely to invite unions in to represent them and, for their part, unions face difficulties organizing or even locating these workplaces. Because the natural tendency of management is to avoid restraints on its own power, providing better voice opportunities to these workers is more likely to come from government interventions that extend requirements for representative forms of voice. An enlightened approach to such regulation, however, would be to empower worker choice as to the form this voice takes, allowing for both union and non-union forms of representation. It is the failure to enable the direct parties to make sensible, local arrangements which has so constrained the evolution of employee voice in the United States, restricting the capacity of firms and workers to experiment with more cooperative styles of engagement (Boxall et al., 2007a).

CONCLUSIONS

Analytical HRM aims to identify *what* managers do, examine *how* they go about it, understand *why* they do it, and assess *who* benefits from it. It privileges research and explanation over prescription. This chapter has applied an analytical HRM approach to the study of contemporary patterns of employee representation and participation. Rather than ditching employee voice as trade unionism and collective bargaining have receded, management has fostered major changes in how employee voice is expressed. Direct forms of voice have multiplied throughout the Anglo-American world. Outside the USA, indirect forms of voice have become more diverse: in large firms, management has used a more flexible regulatory framework to foster dual or hybrid systems in unionized environments and, to some extent, non-union representative regimes outside them. The motives behind managerial behaviour are both economic and socio-political. Managers tend to be most comfortable with voice practices that improve economic outcomes, primarily to do with cost-effectiveness, while also preserving as much management autonomy or power as possible. On the other hand, managers of firms, particularly the larger firms, need to have regard to social legitimacy, both in their domestic and in their international operations. Legal compliance is a baseline goal for many firms and some aspire to a level of employment citizenship which goes well beyond this.

In terms of the larger HR systems and organizational patterns in which voice practices are embedded, there are two important trends. In some situations, such as high-tech manufacturing and knowledge-intensive services, where managers see them as cost-effective, and in which managerial politics are supportive, there has been a growth of high-involvement work systems. HIWSs not only enlarge worker voice but make costly-investments in employee skills and performance incentives. This means these systems are typically not economic in labour-intensive industries where firms face tough, low-cost competition and are unable to develop a barrier to such competition through differentiation. The prognosis for employee voice is therefore one in which diversity in management behaviour will continue. While we anticipate that direct voice practices will remain broadly appealing to management and workers, the growth of full-blown, high-involvement work systems is likely to be much spottier, depending very much on management's assessment of the global economics of the industries in which they are competing. In those situations where worker demand for union representation is frustrated, management is unlikely to reform voluntarily: social regulation will be needed. However, it will stand a much better chance of succeeding if it allows managers and workers to make flexible choices in the forms that representative voice can take.

NOTES

1. For the Arabian Society of Human Resource Management, see http://www.ashrm.com/about/
2. This is the UK's *Workplace Employment Relations Survey*. Five surveys have been conducted over the last twenty-six years. They are comprehensive, representative assessments of employee and managerial opinion and financial performance in British workplaces. Arguably, they provide the UK with much better data on the state of its workplace relations than any other country in the world.
3. Within the EU, labour law establishes that in business transfers and major redundancy programmes employee representatives must be consulted for the duration of the change programme.

REFERENCES

APPELBAUM, E., BAILEY, T., BERG, P., and KALLEBERG, A. (2000) *Manufacturing* Advantage: why High-Performance Systems Pay off. Ithaca, NY: ILR Press.

AYCAN, Z. (2005) 'The Interplay between Cultural and Institutional/Structural Contingencies in Human Resource Management Practices', *International Journal of Human Resource Management*, 16(7): 1083–119.

BACH, S. and KESSLER, I. (2007) 'Human Resource Management and the New Public Management', in P. Boxall, J. Purcell, and P. Wright (eds), *The Oxford Handbook of Human Resource Management*. Oxford: Oxford University Press.

BATT, R. (2004) 'Who Benefits from Teams? Comparing Workers, Supervisors, and Managers', *Industrial Relations*, 43(1): 183–212.

—— and DOELLGAST, V. (2005) 'Groups, Teams, and the Division of Labor', in S. Ackroyd, R. Batt, P. Thompson, and P. Tolbert (eds), *The Oxford Handbook of Work and Organization*. Oxford: Oxford University Press.

BEER, M., SPECTOR, B., LAWRENCE, P., QUINN MILLS, D., and WALTON, R. (1984) *Managing Human Assets*. New York: Free Press.

BENDIX, R. (1956) *Work and Authority in Industry*. Berkeley, CA: UCLA Press.

BLAUNER, R. (1964) *Alienation and Freedom: The Factory Worker and His Industry*. Chicago, IL: University of Chicago Press.

BOXALL, P. (2003) 'HR Strategy and Competitive Advantage in the Service Sector', *Human Resource Management Journal*, 13(3): 5–20.

—— (2007) 'The Goals of HRM', in P. Boxall, J. Purcell, and P. Wright (eds), *The Oxford Handbook of Human Resource Management*. Oxford: Oxford University Press.

—— FREEMAN, R., and HAYNES, P. (2007a) 'Conclusion: What Workers Say in the Anglo-American World', in R. Freeman, P. Boxall, and P. Haynes (eds), *What Workers Say: Employee Voice in the Anglo-American World*. Ithaca, NY: Cornell University Press.

—— and PURCELL, J. (2008) *Strategy and Human Resource Management*. Basingstoke and New York: Palgrave Macmillan.

—— PURCELL, J., and WRIGHT, P. (2007b) 'Human Resource Management: Scope, Analysis, and Significance', in P. Boxall, J. Purcell, and P. Wright (eds), *The Oxford Handbook of Human Resource Management*. Oxford: Oxford University Press.

BREWSTER, C. (1999) 'Different Paradigms in Strategic HRM: Questions Raised by Comparative Research', in P. Wright, L. Dyer, J. Boudreau, and G. Milkovich (eds), *Research in Personnel and Human Resource Management (Supplement 4: Strategic Human Resources Management in the Twenty-First Century)*. Stamford, CT: JAI Press.

CAMPOLIETI, M., GOMEZ, R., and GUNDERSON, M. (2007) 'Say What? Employee Voice in Canada', in R. Freeman, P. Boxall, and P. Haynes (eds), *What Workers Say: Employee Voice in the Anglo-American Workplace*. Ithaca, NY: Cornell University Press.

CAPPELLI, P. and NEUMARK, D. (2001) 'Do "High Performance" Work Practices Improve Establishment Level Outcomes?' *Industrial and Labor Relations Review*, 54(4): 737–76.

CHALLIS, D., SAMSON, D., and LAWSON, B. (2005) 'Impact of Technological, Organizational and Human Resource Investments on Employee and Manufacturing Performance: Australian and New Zealand Evidence', *International Journal of Production Research*, 43(1): 81–107.

CHARLWOOD, A. and TERRY, M. (2007) '21-Century Models of Employee Representation: Structures, Processes and Outcomes', *Industrial Relations Journal*, 38(4): 320–37.

COOKE, F. L. (2004) 'Foreign Firms in China: Modelling HRM in a Toy Manufacturing Corporation', *Human Resource Management Journal*, 14(3): 31–52.

COOKE, W. N. (2001) 'The Effects of Labor Costs and Workplace Constraints on Foreign Direct Investment among Highly Industrialised Countries', *International Journal of Human Resource Management*, 12(5): 697–716.

——(2007) 'Multinational Companies and Global Human Resource Strategy', in P. Boxall, J. Purcell, and P. Wright (eds), *The Oxford Handbook of Human Resource Management*. Oxford: Oxford University Press.

COX, A., ZAGELMEYER, S., and MARCHINGTON, M. (2006) 'Embedding Employee Involvement and Participation at Work', *Human Resource Management Journal*, 16(3): 250–67.

DUNDON, T. and GOLLAN, P. (2007) 'Re-conceptualizing Voice in the Non-Union Workplace', *International Journal of Human Resource Management*, 18(7): 1182–98.

EDWARDS, P. and RAM, M. (2006) 'Surviving on the Margins of the Economy: Working Relationships in Small, Low-Wage Firms', *Journal of Management Studies*, 43(4): 895–916.

FORTH, J., BEWLEY, H., and BRYSON, A. (2006) *Small and Medium-Sized Enterprises: Findings from the 2004 Workplace Employment Relations Survey*. London: Department of Trade and Industry.

FREEMAN, R., BOXALL, P., and HAYNES, P. (2007) 'Introduction: The Anglo-American Economies and Employee Voice', in R. Freeman, P. Boxall, and P. Haynes (eds), *What Workers Say: Employee Voice in the Anglo-American Workplace*. Ithaca, NY: Cornell University Press.

GODARD, J. and DELANEY, J. (2000) 'Reflections on the "High Performance" Paradigm's Implications for Industrial Relations as a Field', *Industrial and Labor Relations Review*, 15(3): 482–502.

GOLLAN, P. and WILKINSON, A. (2007) 'Contemporary Developments in Information and Consultation', *International Journal of Human Resource Management*, 18(7): 1133–44.

GOODERHAM, P., NORDHAUG, O., and RINGDAL, K. (1999) 'Institutional and Rational Determinants of Organizational Practices: Human Resource Management in European Firms', *Administrative Science Quarterly*, 44: 507–31.

GOSPEL, H. (1973) 'An Approach to a Theory of the Firm in Industrial Relations', *British Journal of Industrial Relations*, 11(2): 211–28.

GRIMSHAW, D., MARCHINGTON, M., WILLMOTT, H., and RUBERY, J. (2005) 'Introduction: Fragmenting Work Across Organizational Boundaries', in M. Marchington, D. Grimshaw, J. Rubery, and H. Willmott (eds), *Fragmenting Work: Blurring Organizational Boundaries and Disordering Hierarchies*. Oxford: Oxford University Press.

GUEST, D. (2002) 'Human Resource Management, Corporate Performance and Employee Well-Being: Building the Worker into HRM', *Journal of Industrial Relations*, 44(3): 335–58.

—— (2007) 'HRM and the Worker: Towards a New Psychological Contract?' in P. Boxall, J. Purcell, and P. Wright (eds), *The Oxford Handbook of Human Resource Management*. Oxford: Oxford University Press.

HALL, M., HUTCHINSON, S., PARKER, J., PURCELL, J., and TERRY, M. (2007) 'Implementation of Information and Consultation: Early Experiences', *Employment Relations Research Series no. 88*. London: Department for Business, Enterprise and Regulatory Reform.

HARLEY, B., ALLEN, B., and SARGENT, L. (2007) 'High Performance Work Systems and Employee Experience of Work in the Service Sector: The Case of Aged Care', *British Journal of Industrial Relations*, 45(3): 607–33.

HAYNES, P. and FRYER, G. (2000) 'Human Resources, Service Quality and Performance: A Case Study', *International Journal of Contemporary Hospitality Management*, 12(4): 240–48.

HUNTER, L. (2000) 'What Determines Job Quality in Nursing Homes?' *Industrial and Labor Relations Review*, 53(3): 463–81.

JACKSON, S. and SCHULER, R. (1995) 'Understanding Human Resource Management in the Context of Organizations and their Environments', *Annual Review of Psychology*, 46: 237–64.

KELLEY, M. (2000) 'The Participatory Bureaucracy: A Structural Explanation for the Effects of Group-Based Employee Participation Programs on Productivity in the Machined Products Sector', in C. Ichniowski, D. Levine, C. Olson, and G. Strauss (eds), *The American Workplace: Skills, Compensation and Employee Involvement*. Cambridge: Cambridge University Press.

KERSLEY, B., ALPIN, C., FORTH, J., BRYSON, A., BEWLEY, H., DIX, G., and OXENBRIDGE, S. (2006) *Inside the Workplace: Findings from the 2004 Workplace Employment Relations Survey*. London: Routledge.

KONZELMANN, S., FORRANT, R., and WILKINSON, F. (2004) 'Work Systems, Corporate Strategy and Global Markets: Creative Shop Floors or "A Barge Mentality"?' *Industrial Relations Journal*, 35(3): 216–32.

LEES, S. (1997) 'HRM and the Legitimacy Market', *International Journal of Human Resource Management*, 8(3): 226–43.

LEGGE, K. (1978) *Power, Innovation, and Problem-Solving in Personnel Management*. London: McGraw-Hill.

LEPAK, D. and SNELL, S. (2007) 'Employment Sub-Systems and the "HR Architecture" ', in P. Boxall, J. Purcell, and P. Wright (eds), *The Oxford Handbook of Human Resource Management*. Oxford: Oxford University Press.

MACDUFFIE, J. (1995) 'Human Resource Bundles and Manufacturing Performance: Organizational Logic and Flexible Production Systems in the World Auto Industry', *Industrial and Labor Relations Review*, 48(2): 197–221.

MACKY, K. and BOXALL, P. (2007) 'The Relationship Between High-Performance Work Practices and Employee Attitudes: An Investigation of Additive and Interaction Effects', *International Journal of Human Resource Management*, 18(4): 537–67.

MACKY, K. and BOXALL, P. (2008) 'High-Involvement Work Processes, Work Intensification and Employee Well-Being: A Study of New Zealand Worker Experiences', *Asia Pacific Journal of Human Resources*, 46(1): 38–55.

MARCHINGTON, M. (2007) 'Employee Voice Systems', in P. Boxall, J. Purcell, and P. Wright (eds), *The Oxford Handbook of Human Resource Management*. Oxford: Oxford University Press.

—— and GRUGULIS, I. (2000) ' "Best practice" Human Resource Management: Perfect Opportunity or Dangerous Illusion?', *International Journal of Human Resource Management*, 11(6) 1104–24.

OSTERMAN, P. (1987) 'Choice of Employment Systems in Internal Labor Markets', *Industrial Relations*, 26(1): 46–67.

PAAUWE, J. and BOSELIE, P. (2003) 'Challenging "Strategic HRM" and the Relevance of the Institutional Setting', *Human Resource Management Journal*, 13(3): 56–70.

—— —— (2007) 'Human Resource Management and Societal Embeddedness', in P. Boxall, J. Purcell, and P. Wnght (eds), *The Oxford Handbook of Human Resource Management*. Oxford: Oxford University Press.

PEEL, S. and BOXALL, P. (2005) 'When is Contracting Preferable to Employment? An Exploration of Management *and* Worker Perspectives', *Journal of Management Studies*, 42(8): 1675–97.

PFEFFER, J. (1994) *Competitive Advantage Through People*. Boston, MA: Harvard Business School Press.

—— (1998) *The Human Equation: Building Profits by Putting People First*. Boston, MA: Harvard Business School Press.

PINFIELD, L. and BERNER, M. (1994) 'Employment Systems: Toward a Coherent Conceptualisation of Internal Labour Markets', *Research in Personnel and Human Resources Management*, 12: 41–78.

POUTSMA, E., LIGTHART, P., and VEERSMA, U. (2006) 'The Diffusion of Calculative and Collaborative HRM Practices in European Firms', *Industrial Relations*, 45(4): 513–46.

PURCELL, J. and AHLSTRAND, B. (1994) *Human Resource Management in the Multidivisional Company*. Oxford: Oxford University Press.

—— and GEORGIADIS, K. (2007) 'Why Should Employers Bother with Worker Voice?' in R. Freeman, P. Boxall, and P. Haynes (eds), *What Workers Say: Employee Voice in the Anglo-American Workplace*. Ithaca, NY: Cornell University Press.

—— and HUTCHINSON, S. (2007) 'Front-Line Managers as Agents in the HRM-Performance Causal Chain: Theory, Analysis and Evidence', *Human Resource Management Journal*, 17(1): 3–20.

—— KINNIE, N., HUTCHINSON, S., RAYTON, B., and SWART, J. (2003) *Understanding the People and Performance Link: Unlocking the Black Box*. London: CIPD.

SUN, L-Y., ARYEE, S., and LAW, K. (2007) 'High-Performance Human Resource Practices, Citizenship Behaviour, and Organizational Performance: A Relational Perspective', *Academy of Management Journal*, 50(3): 558–77.

TEICHER, J., HOLLAND, P., PYMAN, A., and COOPER, B. (2007) 'Australian Workers: Finding their Voice?' in R. Freeman, P. Boxall, and P. Haynes (eds), *What Workers Say: Employee Voice in the Anglo-American Workplace*. Ithaca, NY: Cornell University Press.

WALL, T., CORBETT, M., MARTIN, R., CLEGG, C., and JACKSON, P. (1990) 'Advanced Manufacturing Technology, Work Design and Performance: A Change Study', *Journal of Applied Psychology*, 75(6): 691–97.

WALL, T., JACKSON, P., and DAVIDS, K. (1992) 'Operator Work Design and Robotics System Performance', *Journal of Applied Psychology*, 77(3): 353–62.

WATSON, T. (2005) 'Organizations, Strategies and Human Resourcing', in J. Leopold, L. Harris, and T. Watson (eds), *The Strategic Managing of Human Resources*. Harlow: Pearson Education.

WAY, S. (2002) 'High Performance Work Systems and Intermediate Indicators of Firm Performance within the US Small Business Sector', *Journal of Management*, 28(6): 765–85.

WILLMAN, P., BRYSON, A., and GOMEZ, R. (2007) 'The Long Goodbye: New Establishments and the Fall of Union Voice in Britain', *International Journal of Human Resource Management*, 18(7): 1318–34.

CHAPTER 3

AN INDUSTRIAL RELATIONS PERSPECTIVE ON EMPLOYEE PARTICIPATION

PETER ACKERS

If we look back to the days of James Morrison [an early socialist] and then re-examine our own times, it is true that we shall find some people who have learnt nothing since 1833, and still repeat old words or deeds as if nothing has changed'

(Coates and Topham, 1970: xxv)

INTRODUCTION: BRITISH IR PERSPECTIVES—SIX HISTORICAL INSTANCES

INDUSTRIAL Relations (IR) has two historical meanings. In one usage, the term describes public policy and the employment *practices* of employers and unions. But

IR also refers to a specific *academic perspective*, centred on certain normative and theoretical principles. Since the latter discipline or field has been highly policy orientated, and at times has both shaped public policy and organizational practice and been shaped by them, it is easy to conflate the two (Ackers and Wilkinson, 2008). As Kaufman (2004) has argued, it is instructive to trace this historical interplay of 'events' and 'ideas'. Thus, the varying approaches of academic IR to organizational participation have tended to respond to policy and practice developments in the real world of a given society. Intellectuals have not simply echoed these, but have elaborated their own novel theories of participation in response to them. Moreover, participation theorists have rarely been purely pragmatic in their response and instead have drawn on wider ideologies, which have shaped their proposals for reforming the employment relationship.

Over the twentieth century, Anglo-American IR writers constructed a powerful realist, pluralist conventional wisdom that participation should centre exclusively on collective bargaining with unions, which they termed joint regulation; an approach that reflected the mainstream preference of their own, highly pragmatic working-class movements. At first sight, therefore, academic IR appears to hold a common outlook on participation and a disciplinary story of ever increasing influence, followed by precipitate decline. Kaufman (2004, 2008) has conducted a persuasive post-mortem on the rise and fall of American academic IR, identifying a rigid and narrow view of participation as the chronic disease that is killing the patient. Accordingly, John Commons and the early Institutional Labour Economists took a catholic view of the employment relationship: favouring the growth of unions and collective bargaining, but also valuing progressive non-union companies and the sort of participation programmes—profit sharing, consultation committees, teamwork—that later would be associated with human relations. This is the trend that I term managerial participation, because it is driven by management, though it may also have substantial benefits for employees.

With the strongly pro-union ideology of Roosevelt's 1930s New Deal, however, American IR turned its back on this tradition. A strong hostility to non-union forms of employee representation was coupled with an exclusive focus on unions and collective bargaining. Managerial proponents of personnel management and human relations were eased out of the then powerful American academic IR community. Jacoby's (1997) parallel history of the American welfare capitalism in practice has documented how this preference of the labour movement and its academic IR sympathisers for arms-length collective bargaining and scientific management, not only deprived workers of more humanistic forms of work, but also hampered productivity in the unionized sector—once large non-union organizations came back into their own from the 1950s onwards. In short, the American IR community shunned other non-union forms of participation for decades and then suffered the consequences, both in the university and the workplace, once management practice and social science debate moved elsewhere.

There are some similarities in the British experience, discussed below, but only some. As I have argued elsewhere, there are also important differences (Ackers, 2005). American unions went into decline in the 1960s, now cover only a small fraction of the workforce, and have dragged down academic IR with them. The same danger is apparent in Britain. Recently, Terry (2004) declared 'the end of joint regulation', the mainline that pluralist IR thought has travelled for almost a century (see also Purcell, 1993). However, the decline of unions and collective bargaining only began in 1979 and coverage still extends to a substantial, if shrinking, section of the workforce. In addition, British IR academics remain a strong force in the new field of human resource management (HRM), including research on participation, and work closely with other critical European social scientists.

A second, crucial characteristic of the British academic IR tradition also distinguishes it from America and connects it to continental European and global experience—from France to India—especially in the area of participation. This is the historical dialogue with Marxism and associated socialist ideas about workers control. The relative absence of this debate makes the historical experience of American IR exceptional and particular. For whereas the Americans produced a cohesive, highly institutionalized academic IR tradition from the 1920s onwards, centred largely on public policy problem solving, British IR thought was formed in a more open and fluid intellectual arena, and engaged in fundamental European debates about the nature of capitalist society as well as pragmatic policy responses to national problems. All the thinkers discussed here reflect this wider socialist and social democratic debate and, among them, only Clegg could be defined in narrow terms as an IR specialist. For British IR barely existed as an institutionalized, academic field—with university courses and departments—before the emergence of the Oxford School in the 1950s (Ackers and Wilkinson, 2003, 2005). This different ideological context made for a much more hotly contested debate about organizational participation, which continues to this day.

My chapter traces the argument between the British theorists of mainstream IR *realism* and their *utopian* 'workers control' protagonists.[1] In the background, outside the mainstream IR community, runs a third, largely forgotten, widely despised, *managerial* or unitarist view of organizational participation, as practiced on an ad hoc basis by a deviant group of British employers over the years and theorized by the human relations school from the 1940s onwards (Fox, 1966). My approach here is highly selective and illustrative, rather than comprehensive. I have chosen six historical examples of British IR (broadly defined) approaches to organizational participation, which demonstrate the long and recurring intellectual dispute between radical utopians and pluralist realists.

We commence with the cooperative co-partnership movement, which carried Robert Owen's workplace micro-utopia into the twentieth century. Next, Beatrice and later Sidney Webb responded with a blistering social science critique and in *Industrial Democracy* (1897) founded the Anglo-American IR realist tradition.

Until the 1980s, all subsequent IR debates about participation were a response to them. G. D. H Cole developed Guild Socialism, an influential macro-utopian riposte, during the first half of the century. After that, in the social democratic 1950s, came Hugh Clegg, a key figure in modern British IR, who reformulated Webbian realism with the explicit normative proposition that the best and only true form of industrial democracy was collective bargaining by unions. From 1968, however, there was a New Left return to utopian enthusiasms with the Institute of Workers Control, led by Ken Coates and Tony Topham, who rejected the Webbs and Clegg and revived Cole.

The chapter concludes with some research that I have been involved with over recent decades—as part of the Marchington et al. team—to illustrate how far even IR realists have shifted off the old collective bargaining axis. This cannot speak for all the many recent studies of organizational participation, but it does indicate how the mainstream academic mentality has changed. I argue that, by 1979, British utopians and realists had fought themselves to a standstill, leading to the silent triumph, by default, of Employee Involvement (EI). This predominantly managerial perspective, shaped by human relations and deviant company practice, had laid in wait for much of last the century. For the past three decades, however, popular management theory has projected EI as a managerial utopia of the *neo-unitarist* business organization; a happy team of committed employees led by charismatic managers (Ackers, 1994). At the more down to earth level of everyday business practice, EI techniques are now the only channel for employee voice in most British organizations. In this light, the old IR realism has begun to seem increasingly utopian, as its pluralist normative vision of organizations jointly regulated by unions has become detached from the social science reality of a largely non-union workforce regulated by employers and the law (Ackers and Wilkinson, 2008). *Neo-pluralist* IR has been left with the task of analysing this new workplace reality, while holding firm to the social science scepticism and concern for employees of the old realism (Ackers, 2002). The research by Marchington et al. is just one illustration of the more measured, less normatively ambitious, contemporary realist approach to participation.

Little Utopias: Christian Socialists and Worker Cooperatives in the Nineteenth Century[2]

As a historian of British cooperation has observed: 'It is a strange fact that most of the promoters of the Consumer Cooperative Movement were, during the second half of the last century, more concerned with the role of workers than that of consumers' (Burchall, 1994: 102; see also Backstrom, 1974). Although the Christian Socialists were middle-class idealists, they constructed their workers' control utopia in response to real changes in British society. In particular, there was the early growth of the British cooperative and labour movement and the disillusionment of male skilled workers with mass production and deskilling in industries, such as hosiery and footwear (Fox, 1958). These were practical, moderate, small-scale experiments in the spirit of Robert Owen, leading to a minor but resilient movement of worker cooperatives. Producer cooperation had been an integral part of the original British cooperative ideal, yet as consumer cooperation grew to become a major national economic and social force, a sharp ideological divide emerged between those 'idealists' who championed a democracy of producers and the 'practical' advocates of a democracy of consumers. Supporters of cooperative workers control argued that workers should be given sovereignty and control within the productive sphere, as well as the first call on profits. Employee participation would engender good workplace relations, and, hence, contribute to higher business efficiency.

The first attempt to put this ideal into practice created the short-lived, self-governing workshops of the 1850s. The second wave of producer cooperation in the 1860s and 1870s embraced a wider range of investors—including retail cooperatives, the two national societies, unions, individual Christian Socialists and workers—and exhibited a more diverse stakeholder pattern of ownership and control. Most of these also failed, but the need to marry worker participation with external investment funds and consumer cooperative links created the germ of the *cooperative co-partnership* idea. The Co-operative Productive Federation (CPF) was founded in 1882, in direct response to the defeat of the worker participation ideal within the mainstream consumer cooperative movement. The Labour Co-partnership Association (LCA), founded two years later, in 1884, held a broader and looser propaganda brief to spread the gospel of copartnership in industry, not only through producer cooperatives, but also through more managerial worker shareholdings and bonus schemes in conventional, capitalist business organizations. Again, this plotted a participation road 'not taken' by mainstream British academic IR.

Although each member of the CPF had its own constitutional peculiarities, the basic model was as follows (Burchall, 1994: 102–7). All members or shareholders had one vote, no matter how much share capital they held, and elected the management committee. Represented on this were members employed by the society, individual members not so employed, and other cooperative societies. No member had any right to employment, though in practice societies endeavoured to employ as many members as was commercially possible. The general manager was appointed by the management committee which exercised a stronger oversight than a normal company board of directors. Net profits were devoted first to a 5 per cent dividend on shares, followed by some further division between workers, customers, shareholders, educational, and providential funds. Usually workers could not take their share of the profits in cash until they had accumulated the requisite sum in the shares of the society.

Thus, while co-partnership did not amount to a straightforward workers' control, this model did depart radically from the conventional business organization, by offering the workers a substantial share in profits, at least a place on the board, and, in many versions, majority control. Such schemes remained marginal to the national cooperative movement, let alone the mainstream capitalist world of work. They are interesting today as the embodiment of a utopian idea, found, for instance, in the Leicester Equity and Anchor shoemaking worker cooperatives; the latter with its own cooperative 'garden suburb' (Ackers, 2000). This practical dream of a non-capitalist workplace, owned and controlled by its workers, was to become—under the influence of Marxist socialism—ever grander and more remote from everyday organizational life.

REALISM: THE WEBBS AND *INDUSTRIAL DEMOCRACY* (1897)

Industrial Democracy is widely regarded as the foundation text of Anglo-American IR and the ultimate source of the realist view that strong unions and collective bargaining represent the royal road to participation. One obvious stimulus was the rise of the modern, mass trade union movement, after the 1889 'New Unionism' strikes of unskilled workers in the docks and gasworks. Earlier, the Webbs had identified consumer cooperation as the key industrial institution for the permeation of Fabian socialist ideas, while Labour had yet to emerge as a potential national political party. But, by 1897, they had recognized the new potential of the unions as a force in British society. Their classic study is also significant because it bridges prescription and description, or normative theory and social science research and analysis. The Preface includes a substantial discussion of sociological methods. This became a central feature of the realist approach, which was concerned to ground discussions about the future of participation in a critical, empirical understanding of current industry developments.

The arguments of *Industrial Democracy*, however, also rested on Beatrice's earlier, withering social science critique of workers' control in the cooperative movement (Potter, 1895). Her realist response to these utopian ideas sets the tone for the modern British IR debate over participation. In their later joint work, the Webbs contended that producer cooperation was a form of selfish 'individualism', to which they counterposed the more expansive social vision of 'federal' consumer cooperation. Worker-controlled societies were doomed to fail, either as businesses or as 'democracies of producers' (Webb and Webb, 1921: 463–8). Workers' control would interfere unduly with efficient, professional management, undermine work discipline and thus render the business inefficient; or succeed only in creating closet semi-capitalist societies, which pursued their own selfish interest at the expense of other workers. The Webbs thus furnished academic IR with some of the standard arguments that have been deployed against 'isolated' forms of workers cooperation ever since. Their dismissive view of direct participation has resurfaced in two versions: the realist IR view that the only feasible form of participation is representative collective bargaining; and the big utopian claim that the only feasible alternative to managerial pseudo participation is the annexation of the entire capitalist system under workers' control.

To their credit, the Webbs did pioneer an empirical social science analysis in their studies of both unions and cooperatives as channels for participation. Beatrice's 'ruthlessly logical' (Burchall, 1994: 106) analysis of the CPF statistics for 1890 was later complimented by a longitudinal comparison of the Cooperative Union returns for 1890 and 1913 (Webb and Webb, 1921). Here they tried to gauge the level of participation according to the proportion of the management committee that were employees and then labelled the producer cooperatives as self-governing, partially autonomous or dependent on the stores. Jones (1976: 43–5) argues that the 'Webbs' ideological stance impaired their objectivity and that as a result their data were misleading and inadequate'. Cooperatives under workers' control were hard to isolate in the statistics—demonstrating the limitations of this method—while 'success' was hard to define and measure. According to Jones, far from bring 'ill-adapted to survive' (Potter, 1895: 156), cooperative co-partnerships outlasted private businesses of a comparable size. Harrison (2000: 163, 177) also observes that the Webbs' attitude to worker cooperatives was partly a product of their ideological architecture or 'the tripartite conception of labour movement'. Hence, it suited their emerging political strategy to see cooperation as the *consumer* arm of the movement, with unions as the *producer* arms and, later, the Labour Party as the *political* arm. Producer co-operatives muddied the water. Moreover, while Beatrice 'recognized the moral excellence of collective self-help ... Her opposition to co-operative production depended upon convictions about the efficient organization of business and not upon hostility to self-management as such. Democratic collectives might replace capitalists; but she denied that they could dispense with the services of professional experts.' Behind the veil of social science realism lay some strong normative assumptions.

Industrial Democracy (1897) synthesized the earlier critiques of worker cooperatives and trade union 'primitive' direct democracy into the definitive statement on the role of unions as representative bodies in the new industrial order (see also Webb and Webb, 1894). As the title suggests, the Webbs saw union representation as the basis for a new constitutional order in industry that complemented political democracy and countered the power of employers. However, they were not concerned with workplace authority relations per se and their vision of participation made three rather conservative realist assumptions. First, they saw industrial democracy primarily in macro economic, instrumental terms, as a form of countervailing labour power that would reduce inequality of outcomes and poverty in society. Second, they saw collective bargaining as a useful vehicle for the correction of economic imbalances, precisely because, unlike direct workers' control, it did not interfere with the managerial decision making of the experts who would replace the old style capitalists in their new collectivist social order. Finally, their limited interest in the process of participation was reflected in the priority they gave to legal regulation over joint regulation. If the state could abolish poverty and promote national efficiency in pursuit of the utilitarian goal of the happiness of the greatest number, the precise nature of organizational participation was a largely secondary issue.

Big Utopia: GDH Cole and Guild Socialism between the Two World Wars[3]

The period just before and during the Great War (1914–1918) saw a new movement of events and ideas. A pre-war strike wave, a wartime shop stewards' movement led by radical socialists, a union programme like The Miners Next Step, and ideas of a big strike against capitalism and industrial unionism—all these turned the attention of radical socialists away from parliamentary reform and towards revolutionary Syndicalism (Wright, 1979). This was the movement of a small minority within the trade union movement, but it caught the imagination of one young socialist intellectual, G. D. H. Cole. Cole, among others, developed in response a new blueprint for workers' control within a putative Guild Socialist society. Although these ideas now appear eccentric, Cole became *the* central intellectual figure of the interwar British left, as Oxford Professor of Social and Political Theory. He was never formally an IR academic—since such a role and discipline barely existed in the interwar years—but all his work centred on the labour movement and after the war he became a crucial personal link between the Webbs and Clegg (Ackers, 2007).

Cole was a peculiarly English socialist, who was never in step with orthodox Marxism or Communism. But his Guild Socialist ideas swam in the Marxist socialist currents of the time; even if, then as later, not all radicals shared the enthusiasm for workers' control. During the interwar years there was a widespread belief on the political left that capitalism was in terminal crisis and that the main task was not to reform and moderate it, but to design an entirely new social order (Pimlott, 1977). Hence most of Cole's writing centred on how worker participation could be incorporated into a future system of universal public ownership. For this reason, he challenged the model of nationalization as a centralized bureaucracy directed by experts, favoured by Soviet central planners, the Webbs, and the future architect of the Labour Party's policy, Herbert Morrison. It is characteristic of Cole's idealistic approach that he preferred to construct grand utopian plans for the reconstruction of all industry, rather than subject existing form of participation to rigorous, empirical social science analysis—as the Webbs had begun to.

'Cole's early political outlook and activity was above all else a response to the Fabian tradition of socialist collectivism' (Wright, 1979: 13–14). In response, he took inspiration from the older tradition of explicitly utopian socialism. 'Nourished by [William] Morris, Cole was a romantic, poet, dreamer, excited by the new labour militancy and determined to give it a theory of industrial control.' The Syndicalist leaders of these revolts talked of workers taking collective control of industry, ideally through a general strike, and then running it themselves in a socialist society. To Cole, these trends appeared as a vibrant popular alternative to the elite state social engineering of the Webbs, to their emphasis on distribution rather than production, and to the prosaic collective bargaining championed in *Industrial Democracy*. 'Yet syndicalism itself was flawed by its refusal to recognize the necessity of a cooperative relationship between the state and the industrial associations in a socialist society' (Wright, 1979: 24). Therefore, through Guild Socialism, Cole set about reconciling the role of the state, unions (and later consumer organizations) in the plan for a fully socialist society. What cooperative co-partnership had attempted on a micro scale within the organization, Cole projected as a macro-level plan for the society of the future.

In Cole's first major work, *The World of Labour* (1913: 61) he argued that 'the whole question of the control of industry is not economic but ethical'. Accordingly: 'Self-expression implied a share in control, in turn implying a conception of industrial democracy which challenged the assumptions of traditional parliamentary democracy' (Wright, 1979: 28). For the Webbs, industrial democracy meant extending the coverage of representative democracy through the state and unions, at the expense of the capitalist market; for Cole, by contrast, it meant direct workers' control in industry. While the Webbs had seen the main function of unions as collective bargaining, Cole foresaw a more dramatic double role. First, they were to be militant organizations to fight for better wages and conditions—a standard Marxist perspective. Second, they were to be proto-guilds, preparing for future control of industry in a socialist society.

Self-Government in Industry (1917), Cole's earliest full statement of Guild Socialism, centred on a post-capitalist reconciliation of the different functions of the state as the representative of citizens and consumers, and the unions or guilds as the representative of producer groups. Later on, he developed still more elaborate structures for the direct representation of consumer interests. Throughout Cole tried to balance the principle of workers' control of industry against the need for the state to express the common interest and safeguards to prevent customers suffering at the hands of producers. In this respect, he reversed the Webbs' line of argument that prioritized the needs of the state or community and customers over the needs of workers. And whereas the Webbs were concerned with industrial democracy, mainly as a means for a fairer and more efficient distribution of wealth and income, Cole was concerned with 'democracy as process' (Wright, 1979: 58)—an end in itself.

Cole's subsequent thinking on participation vacillated between utopian first principles and more pragmatic responses to the practical policies of employers and trade unions. During the later 1920s, for instance, when the labour movement called out for more practical, short-term approaches to participation, under capitalism, he was prepared to countenance forms of industrial cooperation like the Mond–Turner talks and to entertain ideas about unions improving efficiency (Wright, 1979). This said, while the ideas of Guild Socialism were influenced by trade union strategies, Cole's version was a comprehensive map of the future; a castle in the air that bore little relationship to what was happening on the ground. Although he became a key figure in the development of British social science, and wrote widely on the history of the labour movement, Cole made little attempt to ground his vision of participation in the real world of organizational life.

Hence, there was always a large, unspannable gap between the Guild Socialist utopia and the sort of managerial or realist union policies that were happening in actual British business organizations; or for that matter, the authoritarian and slave labour regimes practised in 'socialist' Russia. Cole sought to provide a strategy for the labour movement only in the very grand sense of displaying how unions—as, in his view, anti-capitalist working-class organizations—could transform themselves into part of the structure of the new socialist society. In this respect, Cole established the fundamentally utopian view of workers' control advocates that participation can only exist in its purest socialist form or not at all.

More Realism: Clegg and Industrial Democracy as Collective Bargaining in the 1950s[4]

The 1945 Labour Government introduced a major programme of social democratic reconstruction, including the nationalization of major industries, such as rail and coal, and the creation of the modern welfare state. During the Second World War, the unions had played a central role under the influential Minister of Labour, Ernest Bevin, former leader of the Transport and General Workers' Union. This had also been a period of experiment in forms of organizational participation, with the establishment of powerful Joint Production Committees in many factories, through which management consulted with workers about how to increase output for the war effort. Labour's plans to nationalize large parts of the economy raised questions about what forms organizational participation should take, linked to wider discussions about the spread of collective bargaining in a new era of full employment (Kynaston, 2008).

During the 1950s, Hugh Clegg developed a sustained critique of workers' control and the ideas of Cole—an early mentor at Nuffield College, Oxford—on the central themes of nationalization and industrial democracy. Using both theoretical arguments about the nature of democracy and empirical evidence about the efficacy of different organizational approaches, he established the central assumption of post-war, realist British IR that joint regulation—not public ownership or workers' control—was the key to organizational participation. Clegg's ideas developed over a decade and began with the post-war debate about participation in the newly nationalized industries. The dominant labour movement view, associated with Herbert Morrison and heavily influenced by the Webbs, was that these industries should be administered by boards of experts in the public interest, with worker participation confined to collective bargaining and joint consultation. Clegg's (1950a) Fabian pamphlet endorsed this broad approach and argued that more direct involvement by unions in management could undermine their role as independent representative bodies and, thus, damage real industrial democracy. Clegg's (1950b) in-depth empirical study of one industry, London Transport, which had already been under public ownership since 1933, was sceptical of the claims of both public ownership and managerial joint consultation to improve the employment relationship, and argued again that effective collective bargaining was far more crucial.

Clegg's *Industrial Democracy and Nationalization* (1951) linked these empirical observations to a political theory, by tracing the historical evolution of the theory and practice of the socialist idea of industrial democracy through Marx, Bakunin, William Morris, Syndicalism, Guild Socialism, Whitley Councils, and Joint Production Committees. Clegg noted the practical hostility of unions to many of these participation schemes, and deliberately associated the threat to free trade unions from both utopian and managerial schemes: 'Workshop representation in this form bears a close resemblance to company unionism or to profit–sharing schemes, which are anti-trade union devices of industrial paternalism' (Clegg 1951: 8). He argued that post-war social democrats rejected the old Syndicalist idea of industrial democracy replacing political democracy in a socialist society. Drawing on the recent experience of Communism *and* Fascism, he rooted this new realist view of democracy in the danger of concentrated power and the importance of opposition in any large-scale social system, be it a nation state or a business organization. Totalitarianism was rooted in utopian conceptions of active participation, so democracy should be interpreted relatively passively, by stressing the fundamental independence of unions from the state and management. This political analogy led Clegg to his famous conclusion: 'The trade union is thus industry's opposition—an opposition which can never become a government' (Clegg, 1951: 22).

Clegg's *A New Approach to Industrial Democracy* (1960) presented the most sophisticated, fully developed, and influential version of this thesis. 'A New Theory of Democracy' emerged from both the negative experience of totalitarianism and a more realistic political appraisal of the strengths of Western democratic societies, such as Britain and the United States. Central to the latter were the numerous pressure groups, of which unions were the most important. Such groups organized countervailing power against major concentrations of power in society. Recognition of this led to 'three principles of industrial democracy'. 'The first is that trade unions must be independent both of the state and of management. The second is that only the unions can represent the industrial interests of workers. The third is that the ownership of industry is irrelevant to good industrial relations' (p. 21). In this way, Clegg's realist approach rejected both utopian and managerial alternatives, for the same reason, proclaiming: 'A practical and empirical creed, the creed of democracy achieved, of trade unionism which has arrived ... The new theories are both pessimistic and traditional. They are rooted in distrust—distrust of power. They argue that the political and industrial institutions of stable democracies already approach the best that can be realized. They return to traditions of liberal thought which preceded the rise of socialism' (Clegg, 1960: 29).

Understood in these terms, the true goal of industrial democracy was to protect workers against concentrations of power, whether in the state or industry. What later became known as 'unitarism' was simply a micro-level manifestation inside the business organization of the macro-level totalitarian threat (Fox, 1966). On this basis, the new pluralist IR could depict Communism and managerial human relations as almost ideological cousins. Despite the claims of Elton Mayo and early industrial sociology, Clegg was highly sceptical too of claims that participation would improve efficiency, reduce conflict or increase job satisfaction. In his view, there was little evidence to support this, while his case for industrial democracy rested on political principles alone. In particular, he found no evidence that managerial joint consultation had contributed to high productivity or low strike rates. Indeed, 'joint consultation could be written off as an effective instrument of industrial democracy', though it 'may serve the purposes of personnel management' as one communications option among others (Clegg, 1960: 91–3). To conclude, 'there is no effective alternative to collective bargaining as a means of protecting the interests and rights of workers' (p. 113). Clegg's last word on 'Industrial Democracy' (1976, Chapter 7) maintained this position, while allowing some scope for joint consultation or worker directors as 'supplements' to collective bargaining.

Clegg's writing on industrial democracy builds on the Webbs' realist analysis of unions and collective bargaining as a representative system, while absorbing Cole's pluralist, non-instrumental emphasis on the autonomy of work groups—or at least trade unions—from the general interest of society and the state. He does so by stripping away the socialist emphasis on public ownership and drawing on the latest realist democratic political theory of Schumpeter and Dahl. Pateman (1970: 71–2) argues that Clegg's analogy between democracy in politics and industry is invalid, since management is permanently in office, and unaccountable to anyone except, formally, to shareholders and the state. More tellingly, she attacks Clegg's claim that it is impossible for workers to share directly in management, exposing a blind spot in IR's exclusively representative understanding of organizational participation.

Clegg (1960) was well aware of Trist's human relations work and sometimes used the term 'direct participation', but he could not accommodate this within his theory of industrial democracy. In places, he caricatured direct participation, in the spirit of the Webbs, as a particularist return to craft values of 'self-govern-ment' of very limited application. Anything less was merely a management communications device. Clegg's industrial democracy was a representative dem-ocracy, a passive democracy as far as ordinary employees were concerned: about committees, procedures, and agreements. As Poole (1986: 132–3) points out, Clegg issued the warning that 'workers' participation in management was not only irrelevant to the question of industrial democracy but could actually be harmful to workers' interests and to the extension of "democratic" social relationships in industry'—as anything that weakened unions would be. This meant that, as far as organizational participation was concerned, realist IR put all its eggs in one basket.

Big Utopia Again: Coates and Topham and Workers' Control in the 1970s

The combination of 1960s student revolt and widespread industrial conflict led to a renaissance of radical New Left socialism among intellectuals that left an important residue in British academic IR. The virtues of stable joint regulation, or 'Clegg's anodyne variant of the theory of "opposition" as the keystone of democracy' (Coates and Topham, 1970: 350) was attacked, with a renewed emphasis on worker self-activity designed, once more, to replace capitalism with socialism.

This perspective found a strong voice in the Institute of Workers' Control, led by two adult education academics, Ken Coates and Tony Topham. Like the Webbs and Cole before, they were significant figures in the British IR tradition—of which adult education was a central component—without ever being employed by an IR department. In addition, they were part of a much wider radical ferment that fostered an enduring British strand of Marxist IR, centred on Hyman's (1975) influential text. Ideas of workers' control that had appeared wildly utopian and archaic in the 1950s and would again in the 1980s, became for a time a hot topic. As Wright (1979: 1) noted: 'In recent years, however, the renewal of interest in issues of organizational size, democratic participation and self-management has occasioned a rediscovery of Cole and his concerns.'

Workers' Control (Coates and Topham, 1970) was a reprint of the 1968 collection, *Industrial Democracy.* The titles indicate a new take on old themes and the extracts included stretch from early Syndicalism, through Cole and Clegg to the latest statements of left-wing intellectuals and militant trade unions. The tone of the book and the movement was not objective social science analysis, but committed political advocacy. 'It is not an orthodox academic source book, since the idea for it was first conceived in the process of our active participation in the trade union agitation for an extension of industrial democracy which has developed in the last few years.' The declared point was to use past and present union experiences to inform 'the present-day search for viable socialist policies' (Coates and Topham, 1970: xvii). In this respect, workers' control, was part and parcel of the New Left Marxist backlash against post-war affluence, social democracy, and welfare capitalism: a militant call for unions to seize more and more control over workplace conditions from management and to resist government attempts 'to emasculate trade union power' (Coates and Topham, 1970: xv).

Where this approach differed most dramatically from Clegg was in rejecting private ownership and the market, along with stable collective bargaining as a moderate, peaceable mechanism for joint regulation. Where this recalled Cole was by distinguishing between the struggle for *workers' control* under capitalism, as a central motor of the transition to socialism, and *self-management* as the means of managing a publicly-owned economy under socialism (Coates and Topham, 1970: 363). Moreover, in contrast to many other Marxists and industrial militants, who focused on economic struggles to undermine capitalism, notably strikes for higher wages; the workers' control movement, like Morris, Cole, and the early Marx, stressed the alienation of the capitalist division of labour and the need to target issues of control rather than distribution. For them, the cause célèbre was the factory occupation, like the Upper Clyde Shipbuilders sit-in of 1971, rather than the mere strike (Coates, 1981).

Workers' control was more of a political state of mind than a concrete strategy for organizational participation. However, it deserves our attention for a number of reasons. To begin with, workers' control cut with the grain of growing industrial relations conflict and provided a political rationale for militant trade unionism and the breakdown of Clegg's stable social democratic system of collective bargaining. Further—and again like Cole in the 1920s—workers' control by the late 1970s had to come down from the mountain and address the real, practical concerns of labour. These included factory closures, redundancy, and worker occupations, on the one hand; and worker directors in nationalized industries, on the other (Coates, 1981; Coates and Topham, 1970, 1977). 'The transition to socialism in Britain is not necessarily a matter of decades', opined Coates and Topham (1970: 439), but they were aware that it might take a while. And so with Cole, they believed that the process would be hastened, if they discussed the shape of workers' control in the new society to come.

This led to the vexed question of at what point, if any, should unions cooperate with company management? At first, the answer to 'the current rhetoric about "participation" by workers in management' had been obvious. 'Formulas which provide for minority of "worker directors" on the Boards of public or private industry, accountable to the Board and not to the industries' workers, have a historical continuity with the former discredited device of joint consultation' (Coates and Topham, 1970: 438). The 1977 Bullock Royal Commission on Industrial Democracy, with its proposal of parity for employees and shareholders on a tripartite board, with unions nominating the employee representatives, posed more of a conundrum. Was this another instance of incorporation or a step on the road to workers' control under socialism? Coates and Topham's (1977) writing began to moderate its political tone.

Yet, at the end of the day, Workers' Control, like Guild Socialism before, remained wedded to the big utopian solution, however long it took to get there: 'Our industrial democracy must be bold enough to declare war on money and death to the market' (Coates and Topham, 1970: 441). By raising the demand to replace capitalism and arguing that, short of this, any form of participation was a hoax, Workers' Control rejected a priori all forms of managerial participation or partnership between management and trade unions. Thus even utopian communities or producer cooperatives within capitalism were excluded from their edited collection on similar, if still stronger, grounds to the Webbs: they would either become capitalist or undemocratic, they could not be both. 'The lesson which Socialism learnt about all this was a very simple one: that piecemeal reform of a rapacious market system by contracting out was impossible', due to the 'totalizing appreciation of the anatomy of the capitalist market, and of the nature of the political State which grew up within its precincts' (Coates and Topham, 1970: xxx, xxxiv). Above all else, they excluded 'employers' placebos and surrogate forms of industrial democracy', such as human relations in toto, joint consultation, and 'successive strategies for the incorporation of trade unionists into capitalist and neo-capitalist organizational structures ... co-determination schemes, profit-sharing schemes, suggestion schemes, and similar stratagems great and small' (pp. xxxvii–xxxviii).

New Realism: Marchington et al. and Employee Involvement since the 1980s[5]

The election of the right-wing Thatcher Conservative Government in 1979 ushered in a period of socio-economic change as dramatic as that which had spawned the modern labour movement a century earlier. Indeed, the major impact on IR institutions was to halt and then reverse the 'forward march of labour' (Hobsbawm, 1981), as union power went into dramatic and sustained decline. At the same time, Britain made a rapid transition to a post-industrial service economy, with only about 15 per cent of employees in manufacturing today. Naturally such fundamental political and socio-economic change opened up new choices for management in the area of organizational participation. In these changed circumstances, the 1970s workers' control movement faded away, while the realist panacea of collective bargaining began to seem increasingly utopian. Now the managerial approach to organizational participation—as practiced in apparently maverick organizations like IBM, John Lewis, and other welfare capitalist or paternalist businesses and advocated by the human relations school—could no longer be ignored. Indeed, in the diluted form of *Employee Involvement* (EI), this quickly became the new mainstream management practice, which IR realists were forced to take seriously and subject to empirical analysis.

The rise of EI went against the grain of a century of both pluralist and radical IR analysis. As we have seen, managerial participation—team working, profit sharing, joint consultation, and various communications techniques—was actively resisted by all the IR theorists discussed above. Radical and pluralist alike, they had long dismissed pseudo or 'phantom' participation that gave no real power to workers and only served to undermine either unions or work group militancy or real workers' control (Ramsay, 1980). Alan Fox's (1966) influential distinction between unitarism and pluralism had poured scorn on management efforts to develop team spirit in the workplace. On the radical wing, writing by Hyman (1975) and Ramsay (1977) cemented this distaste for human relations and all associated forms of participation.

Few academic IR radicals today discuss the type of new social order that might replace capitalism, let alone champion workers' control; but unlike Cole or Coates and Topham, they do conduct detailed empirical studies into the realities of organizational participation. Atzeni and Ghigliani (2007) is a rare recent instance of an empirical study of workers' control itself. More generally, though, the radical antipathy to all extant, capitalist forms of workplace participation or cooperation has not abated—as the publicity for some new research indicates. '*The Realities of Partnership at Work* finds evidence of work intensification, increased stress and more job insecurity where partnership has been introduced in the workplace ... [and] suggests that partnership is a utopian Third Way project designed to suppress and deny workplace conflict ... Government and employer efforts to use workplace consensus as a vehicle for productivity growth inevitably exacerbate the tensions between worker and employer interest, making prospects for mutual gains illusory' (Upchurch et al., 2008 see Johnstone, 2007 and Johnstone et al., 2009 for a different interpretation of partnership).

Contemporary pluralists expect less of organizational participation and therefore tend to see it in shades of grey; saving the darker shades for truly authoritarian societies. In this spirit, Marchington et al. (1992) began the first major realist IR study of the new EI in Britain. We found many companies experimenting with four main EI techniques (excluding collective bargaining): *representative participation*, including joint consultation and Japanese-style company councils; *downward communications*, including team briefing, employee financial reports, and other media; *financial EI*, including Employee Share Ownership Plans and profit sharing/ bonus schemes; and *upward problem solving*, including suggestion schemes, quality circles, and Total Quality Management. Only a few of these techniques were entirely new to British industry, though the last three types had gained in prominence in the 1980s. As for the context and process of EI, management motives had shifted away from narrow concerns with IR and labour control to wanting to involve employees in meeting the challenge of quality control and customer care in an era of intensified global competition. Popular management concepts, like quality circles or TQM, were a poor guide to the great diversity that existed in practice; with schemes under the same name doing entirely different things, while schemes with the different names were often quite close in their design and purpose. Our stress on the contextual 'meaning' of participation highlighted the unique value of comparative case study research that explored the full organizational context and operation of EI (Marchington et al., 1994).

EI initiatives frequently came in waves, driven both by the internal dynamics and external context of the organization (including factors such as changing state policy and product markets). Management often had a short attention span, however, with the result that popular management fads, consultants, 'impression management', and individual careers also drove new initiatives. Consequently, many schemes withered on the vine (Marchington et al., 1993). As a result, the impact of the new EI on employee commitment was relatively modest. It was not the 'culture change' panacea that popular management writers like Tom Peters (1987) had advocated, mainly because it did not give employees enough say to dramatically change their commitment to the organization. But nor was EI entirely 'phantom participation', as Ramsay's radical analysis (1977, 1980; Ackers et al., 1992) had argued. Rather it was a package of new management techniques that often made a valuable if modest contribution to improving communications and participation in the company. Many established companies had evolved two channels of communication: the traditional channel through the trade union; and the new

EI channel. While there were inevitable tensions between these, we also rejected the view that all EI was primarily a means of bypassing trade unions and suggested there was scope for a more complimentary relationship.

The public policy context of participation changed significantly again in 1997, the centenary of *Industrial Democracy*, with the end of two decades of Conservative rule and the consequent engagement of Britain with European Social Policy. However, this policy change was not comparable to 1979. New Labour was sympathetic to unions and while it did not repeal the Conservative legislation controlling industrial action, it did introduce the National Minimum Wage and Statutory Trade Union recognition. The scheme that best illustrated Labour's new approach to participation was the Partnership Fund that gave grants for collaborative projects between management and trade unions. New Labour was also highly sympathetic to the business case for efficiency and competitiveness and to the existing EI techniques that were associated with the British revival of enterprise in the 1980s and 1990s. In effect, the main direction of Labour's policy on participation was to encourage *social partnership* (Ackers and Payne, 1998), or a fusion of the dualism that existed in many organizations under the two channels approach, by unions becoming closer to and more cooperative with management and employers becoming less antagonistic to trade unions. A good example of this was the partnership agreement at the supermarket chain, Tesco, the largest private sector unionized organization in Britain. This merged bargaining and consultation channels into one integrated consultation system for the discussion of wages, conditions, and wider company policies.

In *Management Choice and Employee Voice*, Marchington et al. (2001) returned to comparative case study research at eighteen organizations, with a subsample of seven companies from the original 1989 study to assess developments over the interim. This time the focus was on managers' perspectives on employee voice, which embraced both collective bargaining and three of the main forms of EI, but excluded financial participation. We found that the change in government or 'regime' had occasioned a new mood towards both state regulation and unions among companies, with several adopting the language of 'partnership' in response to the government conception of 'best practice'. New forms of state regulation, rather than simply constricting management choice, actually stimulated new participation initiatives. Moreover, EI had been normalized and was no longer a novelty, so that a new generation of managers took EI for granted and were using it in a more confident, integrated, and strategic way, often combining communications and problem solving.

Although overt hostility towards unions per se—as fostered by previous Conservative Governments—had abated, managers were still uncomfortable with those forms of participation, such as European Works Councils, that stressed employee rights, and hostile to any discussion of grievances or conflict through participation channels—or any slide back into adversarial collective bargaining. For managers, employee voice through unions or EI was only valuable in so far as it 'added value' to the business organization. The message for trade unions might well be 'partnership or bust'. Employers have a clear strategic choice, especially in the private sector, with considerable room for manoeuvre. In several cases they had already thought about possible non-union alternatives should partnership fail to deliver effective workforce cooperation. For trade unions this is a double bind, since managers would turn away from unions not only if they were too strong and adversarial, but also if they were too weak and became unrepresentative of the workforce. Hence there was the danger of both management and employee support for the union ebbing away.

I would argue that the Marchington et al. research is firmly in the sceptical, empirical tradition of British IR realism; and retains a concern with employee well-being as well as organizational and national efficiency. Even so, current pluralist IR research on organizational participation has lost the overt normative mission and optimism of previous generations of IR realists, such as the Webbs and Clegg. In theoretical terms, Marchington et al. have directly challenged both Ramsay's pessimistic radicalism and prescriptive managerial readings (Ackers et al., 1992). In the first instance, we rejected the rather conspiratorial view that EI is mainly about defeating and marginalizing unions, by pointing out that management has many other goals than labour control; especially during a period of intensified competition in local and global product markets when issues like quality and customer care are paramount in employers' minds. Once again, we saw the importance of context and meaning, with local management customizing their approach to EI and unions to local realities, rather than dancing to one tune orchestrated by the New Right or the Confederation of British Industry (Dundon et al., 2004).

In effect, research like Marchington et al. has cut the British IR participation debate down to size, in an era where utopians are more likely to be found among pop management writers than socialist revolutionaries (Ackers, 1994). Our implicit assumption is that no version of participation should be regarded as a definitive solution to the problems of capitalist society and the employment relationship. Rather, EI incorporates a range of useful techniques that are used much more seriously by some organizations than others. And the very different size, shape and context of organizations in their product and labour markets have shaped their approach to participation. All this questions the 'validity' of human relations inspired attempts to prove and measure the contribution of EI to business performance, in a decontextualized, generic way (Marchington et al., 1994). Not only do a great variety of factors shape output and profitability; but often the causal chain flows in the opposite direction with successful businesses finding it easy to involve and motivate employees even with weak participation structures. Ultimately, however, management will only get out of participation what it puts in. And the biggest obstacle to winning greater employee commitment is that most new forms of EI concede only limited power to ordinary employees, compared to both their rhetoric and to older forms of collective bargaining. There are few signs that this had changed, outside a few of the stronger partnership agreements (Johnstone, 2007).

SOME FINAL THOUGHTS

This review of British IR thinking about organizational participation suggests a number of lessons for the future. One is that big utopian blueprints for some future frictionless social system based on workers' control are as futile as overblown pop management rhetoric about 'empowerment' in the contemporary capitalist workplace. At the same time, a dogmatic realism that settles on one technique or institution for all time—such as unions and collective bargaining—is liable to cramp the potential of both employees and the business organization. Indeed, excessive fears of 'incorporation' and manipulation by management may stand in the way of better employee well-being and greater partnership in the employment relationship, which also contribute to the general prosperity and welfare of society. There are worse ordeals for employees than a little human relations or EI, while the alternative of an arms length adversarial relationship between management and workers, coupled to low discretion scientific management, often led to fruitless conflict, mutual suspicion, and poor job satisfaction.

The main problem for contemporary radical IR is that—shorn of a big utopian vision of organizational participation—it has become a rebellion without a cause: left to demonstrate, relentlessly, the intrinsic futility of all attempts to improve worker participation in the contemporary workplace, without indicating any practical alternative. There is more than a touch of Dickensian melodrama to the radical picture of the average contemporary business organization. Management appears much more oppressive than it really is, in order to sustain the dream of a future working life without these problems. Then again, spelling out the alternative has its own pitfalls. Both Guild Socialism and Workers' Control were envisaged as democratic socialist alternatives to authoritarian Soviet Communism. Yet neither socialist theory explained convincingly how centralized state ownership and direct workplace democracy could be reconciled.

For IR pluralists the problem is rather different. British IR realism has been closely linked to social democracy, which, with Clegg, renounced the big socialist dream in the 1950s and sought instead to reform and regulate capitalist market society. However, the specific IR mechanism for doing so, collective bargaining, is now in crisis and there is a struggle to find new and alternative channels for organizational participation. There is an attendant fear that without trade unions, pluralism will simply collapse into unitarism. In my view, moderate idealism and a concern with adequate employee voice in organizations can outlive the slow death of joint regulation. Moreover, the enduring virtue of searching out the facts of organizational participation is as germane as ever. The old realists wore heavy normative blinkers. Now that their perspective is no longer tenable, either as normative vision or as social science, there is scope to conduct academic research that is broad-minded enough to assess each set of participation techniques—managerial or otherwise—on its merits.

Perhaps little utopias merit some re-evaluation. After a century haunted by over-optimistic solutions to social problems gone wrong, there is a case for what Popper (1995) termed piecemeal social engineering: little participation schemes tried out on a case-by-case basis for as long as they work. They offer an outlet for idealism and enthusiasm denied by a realist appraisal of conventional EI. The 2008 Banking Crisis has revealed some of the antisocial limitations of completely unfettered capitalism, reviving old social democratic arguments for both regulation of the employment relationship and the coexistence of alternative, cooperative, or mutual forms of work organization. In an age of footloose global capital, such organizations might strengthen and anchor local communities and civil society (Ackers, 2002). They might also offer novel participative opportunities for those who self-select to work and live differently; rather than attempting to conscript entire populations into a high participation utopia. These alternatives might still include small-scale economic experiments, like worker cooperatives, for those who choose to work to a different drum.

As an aspiration, organizational participation is worth striving for, but it is not the holy grail of business success and it is not a new Heaven and new Earth. At best, it may enhance the lives of working people by giving them some 'voice', while making the business more efficient—both highly worthwhile contributions to society. In the social sciences, however, practical utility and intellectual stimulation only rarely coincide. I can still recall the excitement of Workers' Control and idealism and strong ideologies often breed stirring debates. Without the utopian challenge, IR research on organizational participation in the future will be much more mundane and dull than in the past. As things stand, it is not clear that it will ever again hold the centre ground of large-scale intellectual debates about the future of civilization.

NOTES

1. I use the term 'utopian' quite differently to many Marxists (Engels, 1968). For some it is utopian to believe in piecemeal forms of participation within capitalism, but realistic to anticipate the collapse of capitalism and its replacement by a socialist system that abolishes clash conflict and injustice. In my terminology, 'realists' work with the grain of existing capitalist society, trying to reform it, while 'utopians' try to construct an entirely

new social system, either within the individual workplace (little or micro-utopians) or across the entire social system (big or macro-utopians).
2. This section draws widely on Burchall, (1994).
3. Wright (1979) is main general source for this section and I draw on him widely: see also the Cole extracts in Coates and Topham (1970).
4. This section is condensed and revised version of Ackers (2007).
5. This section is a condensed and revised version of Ackers et al. (2006).

References

ACKERS, P. (1994) 'Back to Basics: Industrial Relations and the Enterprise Culture', *Employee Relations*, 16(8): 32–47.

—— (2000) 'Taylor, John Thomas/ Special Note: The Churches of Christ as a Labour Sect', *Dictionary of Labour Biography*, pp. 195–206. Basingstoke: Macmillan.

—— (2002) 'Reframing Employment Relations: The Case for Neo-Pluralism', *Industrial Relations Journal*, 33(1): 2–19.

—— (2005) 'Between the Devil and the Deep Blue Sea: Global History, the British Tradition, and the European Renaissance', *Comparative Labor Law & Policy Journal*, 27(1): 93–104.

—— (2007) 'Collective Bargaining as Industrial Democracy: Hugh Clegg and the Political Foundations of British Industrial Relations Pluralism', *British Journal of Industrial Relations*, March, 45(1): 77–101.

—— MARCHINGTON, M., WILKINSON, A., and GOODMAN, J. (1992) 'The Use of Cycles? Explaining Employee Involvement in the 1990s', *Industrial Relations Journal*, 23(4): 268–83.

—— —— —— and DUNDON, T. (2001) 'Partnership and Voice, With or Without Trade Unions: Changing UK Management Approaches to Organisational Participation', in M. Stuart and M. M. Lucio (eds), *Partnership and Modernisation in Employment Relations*. London: Routledge.

—— —— —— —— (2006) 'Employee Participation in Britain: From Collective Bargaining and Industrial Democracy to Employee Involvement and Social Partnership—Two Decades of Manchester/ Loughborough Research', *Decision* Indian Institute of Management, Calcutta, January-June, 33(1): 75–88.

—— and PAYNE, J. (1998) 'British Trade Unions and Social Partnership: Rhetoric, Reality and Strategy', *The International Journal of Human Resource Management*, June, 9(3): 529–50.

—— and WILKINSON, A. (2003) 'The British Industrial Relations Tradition—Formation, Breakdown, Salvage', in P. Ackers and A. Wilkinson (eds), *Understanding Work and Employment: Industrial Relations in Transition*. Oxford: Oxford University Press.

—— —— (2005) 'The British Industrial Relations Paradigm: A Critical Outline and Prognosis', *Journal of Industrial Relations*, December, 47(4): 443–56.

—— —— (2008) 'Industrial Relations and the Social Sciences', in P. Blyton, N. Bacon, J. Fiorito, and H. Heery, (eds), *The Sage Handbook of Industrial Relations*. London: Sage.

ATZENI, M. and Ghigliani, P. (2007) 'Labour Process and Decision-Making in Factories under Workers Self-Management: Empirical Evidence from Argentina', *Work Employment and Society*, 21(4): 653–71.

BACKSTROM, P. N. (1974) *Christian Socialism and Co-operation in Victorian England.* London: Croom Helm.

BURCHALL, P. (1994) *Co-op: The People's Business* Manchester: Manchester University Press.

CLEGG, H. A. (1950a) *Labour in Nationalised Industry: Interim Report of a Fabian Research Group.* London: Fabian Publications.

—— (1950b) *Labour Relations in London Transport.* Oxford: Blackwell.

—— (1951) *Industrial Democracy and Nationalization: A Study Prepared for the Fabian Society.* Oxford: Blackwell.

—— (1960) *A New Approach to Industrial Democracy.* Oxford: Blackwell.

—— (1976) *Trade Unionism under Collective Bargaining: A Theory based on Comparisons of Six Countries.* Oxford: Blackwell.

COATES, K. (1981) *Work-ins, Sit-ins and Industrial Democracy.* Nottingham: Spokesman.

—— and Topham, T. (eds) (1970) *Workers' Control.* London: Panther.

———— (1977) *The Shop Stewards Guide to the Bullock Report.* Nottingham: Spokesman.

COLE, G. D. H. (1913) *The World of Labour.* London: Bell and Sons.

—— (1917) *Self-Government in Industry.* London: Bell and Sons.

DUNDON, T., WILKINSON, A. J., MARCHINGTON, M., and ACKERS, P. (2004) 'The Meanings and Purpose of Employee Voice', *The International Journal of Human Resource Management,* September, 156: 1149–70.

ENGELS, F. (1968, [1892]) *Socialism: Utopian and Scientific.* Moscow: Progress.

FOX, A. (1958) *A History of the National Union of Boot and Shoes Workers, 1874–1957.* Oxford: Blackwell.

—— (1966) 'Sociology and Industrial Relations', Research Paper 3, Royal Commission on Trade Unions and Employers Associations. London: HMSO.

HARRISON, R. J. (2000) *The Life and Times of Sidney and Beatrice Webb, 1858–1905: The Formative Years.* London: Palgrave.

HOBSBAWM, E. J. (ed.) (1981) *The Forward March of Labour Halted.* London: Verso.

HYMAN, R. (1975) *Industrial Relations: A Marxist Introduction.* Basingstoke: Macmillan.

JACOBY, S. M. (1997) *Modern Manors: Welfare Capitalism since the New Deal.* Princeton, NJ: Princeton University Press.

JOHNSTONE, S. (2007) 'Partnership in UK Financial Services: Achieving Efficiency, Equity and Voice?', Ph.D. Thesis, Loughborough University.

ACKERS, P. and WILKINSON, A. (2009) 'The British Partnership Phenomenon: a ten year review. *Human Resource Management Journal,* July, 19(3): 260–79.

JONES, D. C. (1976) *British Producer Co-operatives,* in K. Coates (ed.), *The New Worker Co-operatives.* Nottingham: Spokesman.

KAUFMAN, B. (2004) *The Global Evolution of Industrial Relations.* ILO: Geneva.

—— (2008) 'Paradigms in Industrial Relations: Original, Modern and Versions In-Between', *British Journal of Industrial Relations,* 46(2): 314–39.

KYNASTON, D. (2008) *Austerity Britain, 1945–51.* London: Bloomsbury.

MARCHINGTON, M., GOODMAN, J., WILKINSON, A., and ACKERS, P. (1992) *New Developments in Employee Involvement,* Employment Department, UK, Research series. London: HMSO.

—— (1994) 'Understanding the Meaning of Participation: Views from the Workplace', *Human Relations*, 47(8): 867–94.

—— and DUNDON, T. (2001) *Management Choice and Employee Voice*, CIPD Report, September.

WILKINSON, A., ACKERS P., and GOODMAN, J. (1993) 'The Influence of Managerial Relations on Waves of Employee Involvement', *British Journal of Industrial Relations*. 31(4): 553–77.

PATEMAN, C. (1970) *Participation and Democratic Theory*. Cambridge: Cambridge University Press.

PETERS, T. (1987) *Thriving on Chaos*. London: Macmillan.

PIMLOTT, B. (1977) *Labour and the Left in the 1930s*. Cambridge: Cambridge University Press.

POOLE, M. (1986) *Towards a New Industrial Democracy: Workers' Participation in Industry*. London: Routledge and Kegan.

POPPER, K. (1995 edition) *The Open Society and its Enemies*. London: Routledge.

POTTER, B. (1895) *The Co-operative Movement in Great Britain*. London: Swan Sonneneschein.

PURCELL, J. (1993) 'The End of Institutional Industrial Relations', *Political Quarterly*, 64(1): 6–23.

RAMSAY, H. (1977) 'Cycles of control: worker participation in sociological and historical perspective', *Sociology* 11: 479–506.

—— (1980) 'Phantom Participation: Patterns of Power and Conflict', *Industrial Relations Journal*, 11(3): 46–59.

TERRY, M. (2004) 'Can Partnership Reverse the Decline of British Trade Unions?' *Work, Employment and Society*, 17(3): 450–72.

UPCHURCH, M., DANFORD, A., TAILBY, S., RICHARDSON, M. (2008) *The Realities of Partnership at Work*. Basingstoke: Palgrave Macmillan.

WEBB, S. and WEBB, B. (1894) *The History of Trade Unionism*. London: Longmans, Green and Co.

———— (1897) *Industrial Democracy*. London: Longmans, Green and Co.

———— (1921) *The Consumers' Co-operative Movement*. London: Longmans, Green and Co.

WRIGHT, A. W. (1979) *GDH Cole and Socialist Democracy*. Oxford: Oxford University Press.

CHAPTER 4

A LEGAL PERSPECTIVE ON EMPLOYEE PARTICIPATION*

GLENN PATMORE

INTRODUCTION

IN Western countries, employee participation in workplace decision making is regulated by the law. Legally prescribed rules, and voluntary and customary standards (norms) operate side by side in a system of regulation (Fudge, 2008: 3). Different forms of regulation may coexist, but one form often dominates; and this may change over time (Fudge, 2008: 3). There are typically three types of regulation (Fudge, 2008: 4; Lee, 2004: 31).

First, there is market-based regulation, through agreements between employees and employers at the individual or enterprise level. Such agreements typically govern forms of direct participation by employees in the organization of work, such as face-to-face consultation with a manager, participating in a workplace team with other employees or attending a plant or company-wide meeting. Voluntary agreements may regulate indirect participation in workplace decision making, by providing for representative participation schemes, for instance.

The second form of regulation is negotiated collective agreements at the plant and industrial level. Trade unions have traditionally acted as the representative of employees who collectively negotiate with employers over pay and working conditions.

Third, there is regulation by state-initiated intervention via statutes or Acts of parliament. Laws may specify conditions of employment that apply throughout the labour market. Legislation often protects employees against the power imbalance that is inherent in the employment relationship. For example, anti-discrimination law may protect the participation of disadvantaged groups, such as women and people with disabilities, in the labour market.

Governance structured by various forms of regulation is central to employee participation in complex human structures like companies. Employee voice is important for the governance of the workplace, the efficiency of enterprise, and the development and enhancement of employee interests (Kaufman et al., 2000: 260; Rogers and Streeck, 1995: 3–5).

This chapter examines a specific aspect of regulation: that covering indirect participation at the workplace through employee committees. The purpose of these committees is to provide representative consultation or structured communication between employee representatives and management (Rogers and Streeck, 1995: 3–5). This form of participation is regulated through voluntary and collective agreements as well as through legislation.

There is a legal spectrum of regulation of representative consultation. At one end of the spectrum, representative councils are legally required or supported 'through collective agreement or legislation giving the entire workforce of a plant or enterprise some form of institutionalized voice in relation to management' (Rogers and Streeck, 1995: 10). Such bodies, known as works councils, exist in Europe. Works councils provide employees with a general right of consultation and representation. Employees are generally elected to a committee which must be consulted by management about important workplace decisions on such topics as redundancies, transfers of the business, investment in the company, and threats to employment. Works councils are well-established workplace institutions in Western continental EU countries.

Towards the middle of the spectrum are consultative councils. These may be voluntarily established by management to improve communication between themselves and labour (Rogers and Streeck, 1995: 10). In Australia, these sorts of arrangements exist in the form of joint consultative committees, which are 'formal ongoing consultative committees, comprised of managers and representatives of employees' (Marchington, 1992: 533).

At the other end of the spectrum are laws that prohibit councils formed by employers or government from forestalling or undoing unionization (Rogers and Streeck, 1995: 10). Such a legal prohibition exists in the United States.

Each of these schemes of regulation will be explored in this chapter, to highlight the range of legal relationships that exist between labour and management. My purpose is to show that these different forms of regulation are not simply directives issued by workplace authorities but rather have a profound impact on the relations among the industrial parties. The diversity of these legal arrangements illuminates our understanding of the role law plays in relationships between managers and representatives. Each of these modes of regulation has problems, particularly concerning their practical operation, and these problems seem to reduce the role of the employee voice. The focus of my analysis will be on the regulation that institutionalizes consultation through workplace representatives. At the same time, though to a lesser extent, attention will be given to the important relationships between employee representatives, managers, and trade unions.

This chapter will describe the spectrum of legal regulation, from legal rights, through voluntary entitlements to prohibitions. A brief history of each jurisdiction's legal arrangements, and the legal and practical operation of its laws, will be examined. It will be shown that the law has had both intended and unintended consequences, and that these have both advanced and defeated its purposes in various jurisdictions.

THE EUROPEAN UNION

There has been a long tradition of legally requiring management to inform and consult employee representatives in European firms, but the EU has adopted a gradualist approach to mandating employee participation. There remains some uncertainty about the entitlements of employees, though, because of the terms of the EU laws themselves and because of their impact on industrial relations practice in Europe. One challenge arises because of the difficulty of transposing EU directives into the domestic law of Member States and the potential conflict over the interpretation of that transposition.

Making Representative Consultation Universal

The EU began issuing Directives requiring laws for workplace consultation over specific situations: such as redundancies in 1975 (CRD, 1975, amended 1998), and over mergers in 1977 (TUBD, 1977, amended 1998). It promulgated general rules for information and consultation in large multinational companies in 1994 and 1997 (EWCD, 1994, 1997).

In March 2002, the EU went further and adopted a Directive establishing a general framework for improving participation rights of employees in large nationally-based enterprises (hereafter 'ICED 2002'). The Directive applies to all undertakings with more than fifty employees or establishments with more than twenty employees (ICED 2002: arts. 3(1)(a) and (b)). It is estimated that the ICED 2002 would cover about 60 per cent of employees within the EU (Burns, 2000). In the United Kingdom, it is estimated that three-quarters of the labour force would be covered—the Directive came into full implementation in 2007 (Gospel and Willman, 2003).

The Directive seeks to comprehensively set down an employment standard throughout Europe, which may be conveniently described as 'universalism' (Ahlering and Deakin, 2005). EU legislation is the 'traditional instrument' of EU social policy used to set standards when existing member state laws are unclear, insufficient, or not uniform, and to support the common market (Quintin, 2003: 5). EU legislation for participation was required because 'in practice ... no common minimum rules applied to European companies for timely and appropriate information and consultation' (Quintin, 2003: 5). By setting a minimum standard, the law lessens competition between firms over information and consultation arrangements. It creates a baseline standard which contributes to a single or universalist regulatory environment (Streeck, 1995: 340). As a result, many of these minimum standards take effect as a form of 'social rights'.

These 'social rights' exist in the EU labour market in tiers of regulation, at the supranational, nation state, and firm levels. Supranational and nation state laws set employment standards in the labour market, and provide for corporate governance and worker participation at the level of the firm (Ahlering and Deakin, 2005).

Supranational Law

The ICED 2002 is a public legal statement which proclaims a pan-European right to representative consultation. The Directive's minimum standards impose a general legal obligation on management to inform and consult employee representatives in national enterprises (Commission of the European Communities, 2006: 102).

Article 2 defines one of the most important employees' entitlements as representative consultation. Information and consultation are to occur between the employer and employee representatives. The following definitions are specified:

Information' means 'transmission by the employer to the employees' representatives of data.   (ICED 2002: art. 2(f))

Consultation' means 'an exchange of views and establishment of dialogue between the employees' representatives and the employer.   (ICED 2002: art. 2(g))

There are two distinct kinds of entitlement: a right and a freedom. Article 4 provides the right for employee representatives to be informed and consulted, and specifies the level, timing, procedure, and topics for information and consultation.

The topics are:

- information on the future development of the enterprise's activities and its economic situation (ICED 2002: art. 4(2)(a));
- information and consultation about employment, particularly where there is a threat to employment within the business (ICED 2002: art. 4(2)(b)); and
- information and consultation, with a view to reaching an agreement on issues of substantial change in work organization or contractual relations, especially issues directly affecting job security, such as collective redundancies and business transfers (ICED 2002: art. 4(2)(c)).

Article 4 imposes on management an obligation to inform (ICED 2002: art. 4.3), consult (ICED 2002: art. 4.4), engage in reasoned dialogue and seek to reach agreement over change in work organization or contractual relations (ICED 2002: arts. 4(c) and 4(d)). It also requires the level and timing of information and consultation to be at the appropriate level of management (ICED 2002: arts. 4.3 and 4.4).

Three rights for employee representatives are provided for in Article 4: the right to be a recipient of information, an adviser and a negotiator:

- the right to information allows for an informed view;
- the right to consultation allows representatives to counsel, advise, and warn; and
- the right to negotiate provides for a form of power-sharing between management and representatives.

The gravamen of Article 4 is the protection of employee interests, particularly regarding risks to employment. Employee voice is to be achieved through dialogue and representation. Article 4 is therefore intended to enhance employee rights, and to increase employee involvement over a range of enterprise issues (Gollan and Wilkinson, 2007: 1146).

The rights in Article 4 are without prejudice to any provisions and/or practices in force in Member States that are more favourable to employees (ICED 2002: art. 4 (1); recital 18). It is assumed that more favourable provisions would include practices and laws which provide for increased representation. Article 4 is therefore not meant to alter more favourable laws and practices.

Article 4 is a right, norm, and minimum employment standard. As a right, the Article provides an enforceable entitlement to employee representatives. As an employment standard it provides a public benchmark according to which conduct can be scrutinized and checked. As a norm, it influences the behaviour and conduct of the industrial parties.

Article 5 provides a freedom: for management and labour to negotiate an alternative form of representative consultation to the right given in Article 4. Article 5 states:

Member States may entrust management and labour at the appropriate level, including at undertaking or establishment level, with defining freely and at any time through negotiated agreement the practical arrangements for informing and consulting employees.

The UK regulations, for instance, permit such voluntary agreements. Article 5 provides for a negotiated agreement that assumes a process of representation by labour to management. Arguably this article does not permit labour and management to agree to abandon the process of representative consultation itself in reaching an agreement.

While Article 5 grants a freedom to labour and management to negotiate the practical arrangements for informing and consulting employees it does not empower them to define the meaning of these terms. Article 5 is subject to Articles 1 and 2. Article 1 states that the employer and the employees' representatives shall work in a spirit of cooperation when defining or implementing practical arrangements for information and consultation. Article 2 defines 'information' and 'consultation' to be between management and employee representatives. While the process of negotiation to establish employee information and consultation assumes employee representation it does not explicitly require it. However, the definition of the information and consultation procedure itself uses mandatory language, 'means', in defining 'information' and 'consultation' (see also ICED 2002: recital 23). Thus in all Member States a procedure must be established whereby representatives must be informed and consulted.

Management and labour may depart from the topics, timetable, and procedure to be applied in Article 4; this is expressly permitted by Article 5. This potentially lowers the levels of protection provided by the Directive, to the extent that Article 4 does not operate as a default rule. Any departure from the minimum standards set in Article 4 means that there will no longer be common standards. But the Directive does place some limits on negotiated agreements: the arrangements in Article 5 do not, after all, allow employers to avoid or defer their legal obligations to inform or consult.

The Directive also permits direct forms of communication between employees and management, where 'employees "represent" themselves without any intermediation' (Davies and Kilpatrick, 2004: 134).

Recital 16 provides that the Directive is 'without prejudice to those systems which provide for the direct involvement of employees'. Thus systems of direct communication are not prejudiced by the Directive. However, this protective clause is qualified by a proviso: 'as long as employees are always free to exercise the right to be informed and consulted through their representatives'. Accordingly, employees' freedom to seek representative consultation remains, whether or not systems of direct communication are being used.

Questions have arisen over whether or not direct forms of communication in fact satisfy the requirements in the Directive. Some have suggested that direct communication might simply take the form of an email (Davies and Kilpatrick, 2004: 134). Critics of this view have pointed out that email communication seems a barely adequate structure to address issues of organizational change and redundancies (Davies and Kilpatrick, 2004: 134). The Directive may place some limits on the email option. It requires that Member States provide arrangements for informing and consulting employees that are practical (ICED 2002: arts. 4 and 5) and effective (ICED 2002: art. 1(2)). While email communication may be a practical tool for conveying information, it may not be effective, as it strains the meaning of genuine 'consultation'.

However, one difficulty in assessing this option is that neither 'effective' nor 'practical' is defined by the ICED. The interpretation of these terms may well be determined in litigation, as is envisaged by Article 8, which requires Member States to ensure that adequate administrative or judicial procedures are available to enable the obligations derived from the Directive to be enforced.

It remains to be seen whether in countries like the United Kingdom, where negotiated information and consultation arrangements are permitted under Article 5, these terms will be defined by the parties purely by their agreement, or determined according to an objective standard in a court of law. In the United Kingdom there are numerous legal uncertainties about the content of negotiated agreements and about whether or not direct forms of communication will satisfy the Directive. Concerns have been expressed that negotiated agreements may give rise to more individualized arrangements through direct communication rather than promoting collective employee rights envisaged by Article 4 (Gollan and Wilkinson, 2007: 1151).

The freedom given in Article 5 entitles labour and management to negotiate their own employment standards in the absence of externally imposed restraints. In other words, employment standards are fixed by the parties themselves. Voluntary agreements mean that negotiated standards apply for the duration of the agreement. The freedom is granted and limited by the law: some limits imposed on the negotiations may be enforced and cannot be abandoned.

Overall, the Directive preserves representative consultation, or a right to negotiate about the adoption of arrangements for representative consultation. Article 4 does not alter more favourable employee rights that exist in Member States.

National Laws and Practice

While EU Directives do not form part of Member States' national laws, they must be defined and implemented by the national legislatures (Lingemann et al., 2003: 6; see ICED 2002: art. 1). This is achieved through giving a domestic legal basis to the employee rights and freedom in the ICED 2002. The legal obligations imposed on management by the Directive will therefore in effect continue to be found in a 'patchwork' of different forms of laws in EU Member States (including collective agreements and legislation) (Industrial Relations in Europe, 2006: 77).

According to the Directive, the rights and freedoms contained in the Directive must be integrated into existing laws and practices of employee representation

(ICED 2002: art. 2(e)). This has important implications for the Directive's application:

- Information and consultation rights are typically conferred by Member States' laws on union representatives or works councils; there are many variations in the way these rights are exercised.
- Information and consultation rights in Member States' laws are designed to complement rather than substitute for trade union rights (Industrial Relations in Europe, 2006: 88–9).
- Employee representatives within many EU countries enjoyed most or all of the information and consultation rights under Article 4 before the promulgation of the Directive.
- Information and consultation procedures in Member States are typically triggered by a request of a certain number of employees or union members, and are not automatically imposed on management.

Thus, compliance with the Directive may be satisfied by existing laws or may require new laws. In any event, a legal representative consultation employment standard is now to be found in all Member States' laws. In other words, no option remains for Member States to adopt a purely voluntary standard.

Overall, employees—wherever they are in Europe, and whether they are bound by legislation or collective agreements, or represented by trade unions or works councils—are at least entitled to initiate or enjoy similar rights of representative consultation in all companies operating within the EU (Industrial Relations in Europe, 2006: 11).

Modernizing the EU Labour Market

The role of law in supporting information and consultation procedures may be better understood in light of the EU Commission's objectives. The European Commission's aim in encouraging representative consultation is to develop a framework for the modernization of the organization of work. It seems, though, that there will be different qualities of information and consultation procedures in different Member States (Gollan and Wilkinson, 2007: 1146).

In those states where legally-based representative consultation has been established for a long time, one recent report noted: 'Cumulating evidence from north-western Europe shows that a well functioning employee representation system can play an important role in the modernisation and performance of a workplace' (Industrial Relations in Europe, 2006: 102). In states where non-statutory systems did not exist previously, such as the United Kingdom and Ireland and some Eastern European countries, it might take much longer for a framework for the modernization of the performance and organization of work to be developed.

A July 2005 survey provides a snapshot of employees' knowledge of UK Information and Consultation Regulations (CHA, 2005). The survey of 1,002 employees below director level found that only 12 per cent of employees had been informed of the Directive's requirements by their employer, only 6 per cent had been told about these requirements from their trade union,[1] and only 13 per cent were aware that the requirements gave them a right to ask their employer about the future of their organization (CHA 2005: 4–5).

Ignorance of the provisions is certainly not conducive to their adoption. Workplace cultures that have not previously had such legal arrangements and practices implemented through law may be resistant to change. It may be that unions are uncertain about supporting consultative bodies. Employers may be ambivalent or hostile to them (Cox et al., 2006: 262). These possible problems may in part explain why according to the survey trade unions and employers have not started to initiate the process of establishing representative consultation.

Overall, the right to establish representative consultation recognized in the ICED is aimed at modernizing the EU labour market. This right is intended to support a pan-European employment standard. Importantly this builds on existing rights enshrined in national laws. Many Member States' laws already comply with the ICED requirements, and consequently little, if any, amendment is required. This ensures constancy in arrangements for representative consultation, which, in turn, provides stability and predictability of workplace institutions for employers, unions, and employees (Rogers and Streeck, 1995: 20–21). However, in countries where there is not an established legislative tradition of supporting works councils or union representation the status quo of diminished representation may continue, due to an entrenched workplace culture. The challenge in these countries may be to address through new laws, the conservatism of the parties to change by striking a new political bargain over legally required representative arrangements (Rogers and Streeck, 1995: 20–21).

AUSTRALIA

Australia has taken two distinct approaches to regulation of representative consultation. Legislatures and industrial tribunals partially mandated representative consultation in the later part of the twentieth century. At other times the legislature has adopted a voluntarist approach, leaving it up to management and labour to work out their own agreements for consultation. The two approaches have important implications for the practice and development of consultation in Australia today.

Unlike the governments of the United States and many European countries, Australian Governments have engaged in significant legislative changes to existing industrial relations laws over the past two decades. The zest for reform has been regardless of changes in political majorities. Governments of both political persuasions, Labor and Conservative, have been motivated by the need to change economic and organizational conditions to meet the challenges of globalization. The most profound change was a shift of Australia's industrial relations system from one in which wage fixing was conducted centrally by a national tribunal to a system based on enterprise bargaining. The shift to enterprise bargaining is supported by organized labour and capital. Charting the history of legal regulation in Australia reveals the reasons and policy agendas of both Conservative and Labor Governments. But political and ideological differences exist, for example, over joint consultation.

The History of Legal Regulation of Information and Consultation in Australia

The role of law in promoting consultation between labour and management has evolved over time. Traditionally, industrial tribunals, supported by the courts, treated managerial prerogative as sacrosanct in areas outside a narrow conception of 'industrial issues' (essentially wages and hours) (Markey, 1987). Other matters, such as productivity, technological change, and redundancy issues were therefore effectively excluded from the jurisdiction of industrial relations tribunals in Australia (Markey, 1987).

Legal support was provided for information sharing and consultation over a limited range of topics for a short period of time. Consultation procedures were required over proposed redundancies and other workplace changes in the late 1980s, and over 'efficiency and productivity' in the early 1990s. These procedures were made conditions of employment through orders of state and federal centralized tribunals. Such orders are known as arbitrated awards. The federal body was known as the Australian Conciliation and Arbitration Commission, and is now referred to as the Australian Industrial Relations Commission (AIRC). The spread of joint consultative committees between employee representatives and management, set up to deal with issues of 'efficiency and productivity', was a result of the National Wage Case of April 1991 (Combet, 2003).

In the early 1990s, the Keating Government introduced legislative provisions which mandated a consultative process for issues concerning changes to the organization or performance of work. These provisions established a mechanism for employee consultation, and went a significant distance beyond the terms of the enterprise bargaining process itself. The legislation, which facilitated enterprise bargaining, required that enterprise bargaining agreements establish 'a process for the parties to the agreement to consult each other about matters involving changes to the organization or performance of work in any place of work to which the agreement relates' unless 'the parties have agreed that it is not appropriate for an agreement to provide' such a process[2] (Campling and Gollan, 1999).

Underlying the Keating Government's approach to consultation was a view of enterprise bargaining that was deeply committed to consultation as a means of providing sustainable economic reform (Brown, 1992, see Australia, House of Representatives: 3794; Cook, 1992a: 2518, see Australia Senate). The government promoted enterprise bargaining that encouraged 'an effective partnership at work and a highly skilled, adaptable, and committed workforce' (Sherry, 1992b: 3580, see Australia Senate).

However, these Keating Government initiatives to promote efficiency and productivity were removed by the Conservative Federal Government after it won office in 1996 (*Workplace Relations Act 1996* (Cth), s. 89A; *Re Award Simplification Decision* (1997) 75 IR 72).[3] While the Conservative Howard Government supported enterprise bargaining, it opposed the enforcement of employee participation by legislation (Liberal-National Party Coalition 1996). It argued that the Keating Government's 'complex consultation provisions' were unnecessary because of the general requirement that certified agreements under the *Workplace Relations Act 1996* (Cth) (determining wages and conditions) would be required to be genuinely endorsed by a majority of employees at the workplace' (Mitchell et al., 1997: 198). Subsequent legislation by the Howard Government also removed the requirement to use consultative mechanisms to deal with proposed redundancies, productivity and other workplace changes from the awards system (see *The Workplace Relations Act 1996* (Cth); the *Workplace Relations Amendment (Work Choices) Act 2005* (Cth)).

After the Howard Government's electoral victory in 2004, it introduced further dramatic changes to Australian labour law in its *Work Choices Act 2005* (Cth). The effect of the Act was to consolidate 'voluntary bargaining between the parties in the interests of "co operative workplace relations"' (Jones and Mitchell, 2006: 9; *Workplace Relations Act 1996* (Cth) s. 3). The Act reduced the influence of collectively determined working conditions by reducing the influence of trade unions, and diminished worker entitlements under awards (s. 513 of the *Workplace Relations Act 1996* (Cth), as amended in 2005).

Thus the Howard Government legislation simply allowed the establishment of consultative committees through agreement at the workplace level.[4] The Howard Government regarded workplace representation in the same way it did other workplace institutions; it preferred voluntaristic arrangements.

In 2007, the Conservative Government lost the federal election to the Australian Labor Party (ALP), partly due to its 'radical' industrial relations agenda. The new government's emphasis on creating minimum workplace standards and recognizing an enhanced role for trade unions suggests a 'protectionist' approach, quite a contrast to the more voluntarist, 'free market approach' of the Liberal Party. However, the Rudd Government appears to have adopted a narrow definition of participation in the workplace, seeming to focus on persons' *access* to the workforce rather than on dialogue between employer and employees.[5]

The policies of the Labor Government do, however, address in a modest way the concept of consultation at work. The new government has introduced new award conditions. Section 576J(1)(j) includes 'procedures for consultation, representation and dispute settlement' as a term which may be included in a 'modern award'.

The ALP policy also refers to the concept of democracy in the workplace (in conjunction with freedom of association) (Rudd and Gillard, 2007: 12). It appears, though, that the new government's approach (like the old) simply permits volun-tarist representative consultation through workplace agreement making and reinstates an award right to representative consultation that was removed by the Howard Government. There is no suggestion that the ALP will create legislative support for a new system of workplace participation and consultation. No mention is made of joint consultation or works councils in government documentation.

Overall, the Rudd Labor Government's approach to reforming the Howard Government's Work Choices legislation appears to be fairly modest in comparison with the attitudes to workplace reform in the European Union. The focus in Australia is on bargaining for wages and narrowly defined conditions (such as pay, entitlements, etc.), rather than on facilitating, through law, an ongoing dia-logue between employers and employees at the workplace.

Legally Supported Joint Consultation in Australia

The role of law in supporting joint consultation may be better understood in light of empirical data. There are only a small number of studies about joint consulta-tive committees in Australia. The Australian Workplace Industrial Relations Surveys in the 1990s showed an increase in the number of joint consultative committees of employers and employees from 14 per cent of surveyed workplaces in 1991 to 33 per cent in 1996. The ADAM database maintained by the Workplace Research Centre, at the University of Sydney,[6] indicates that from 1991 to 2003 there was 'a steady rise in the number of consultative committees provided for in [registered] Federal agreements ... reaching a height of close to 58 per cent in 1999 and declining thereafter' to 33.3 per cent in 2003 (Forsyth et al., 2006: 12).[7] These surveys seem at first to indicate a correlation between legislative support and increase in joint consultation. However, interestingly, the statistics also show that the number of joint consultative committees continued to increase even when legislative support had been removed by the Conservative Government in 1996. Even so, later their numbers ultimately declined. It seems that the link between laws supporting voluntary joint consultative initiatives and their effects are not straightforward, and perhaps that their impact is delayed (Forsyth et al., 2006: 29).

The Keating Government's support of such committees nonetheless apparently brought the parties together to craft suitable arrangements. Some of the representatives were appointed by the unions, others were elected by the employers. Some forms of representative consultation included information, consultation, and co-decision making. In practice, employers, trade unions, and employee representatives were able to work cooperatively to draft these arrangements. However, the Keating provisions have been criticized, on the grounds that the procedures they sought to establish did not 'prescribe the means (structure or processes) through which such consultation was to occur' (Mitchell et al., 1997: 203). The provisions were vague, it was said, and failed to give any guidance on the frequency or make-up of this 'process' (Mitchell et al., 1997: 204). In sum, the Keating Government's approach provided an impetus but not a suitable structure for joint consultation in Australia.

The Voluntarist Approach to Joint Consultation

Purely voluntarist joint consultation was ushered in by the Howard Government's removal of the Keating Government's initiative. The new Rudd Labor Government's decision not to reconsider this issue defers to purely voluntarist arrangements, leaving it to employees and employers to work out their own agreements. It is unclear from government documentation as to why it has chosen this course of action and whether it is likely to continue along this path into the future. Nonetheless, this paradigm has resulted in a decline in representative consultation in Australia. What then are the possible reasons for the decline in representative consultation, and what kind of joint consultation exists in a voluntaristic system?

First, one might well expect diminished workplace representation if there is no legal support for it. Employees and employers may be reluctant to establish such bodies because of the difficulty in setting up and structuring a joint consultative committee. Second, in an unregulated environment, representative consultation may be seen as a challenge to the inviolable principle of managerial prerogative. Trade unions may fear that unregulated representative consultation may interfere with their legitimate activities and that workplace organizations will be used as union substitutes.

Workplace representation remains at risk of leading a precarious existence if it is not supported by the law. Employers may fear that workplace committees will be used for bargaining over the distribution of company earnings (Rogers and Streeck, 1995: 16). Unions may need legal protection to organize, and employees may require legal protection to exercise the managerial prerogative (Rogers and Streeck, 1995: 21). All these, taken together, indicate that legal intervention for workplace representation is desirable, because it would protect the interests of both employers and employees.

Widespread employee representation seems impossible for employers and unions to achieve without the assistance of a legal framework. Trade unions are not able to achieve widespread representative consultation on their own because they do not have the power to establish a continuing general right to information and consult-ation for all employees. Union density was 20.3 per cent for all employees in 2006.[8] Non-union employees also have an interest in the right to be informed and consulted in their workplaces.

Employers have not created widespread schemes of representative consultation. Under today's voluntaristic approach, representative consultation in Australia can only be based on an employer's (enlightened) self-interest or sense of obligation (Streeck, 1995: 339), because the institutionalization of workplace representation has been left to them. Once an employer has created a joint consultative commit-tee, he or she may equally demand or bring about the committee's disbandment (Streeck and Vitols, 1995: 278). Employer-based 'voluntarism' is an insecure basis for joint consultation because it gives employers, rather than employee represen-tatives, the right to establish joint consultation committees and more control over the committee's agenda (Streeck and Vitols, 1995: 278). Under the doctrine of managerial prerogative, employees have to obey the reasonable commands of their employer at common law.

While these reasons might explain the decline in joint consultation committees in Australia, the quality of existing information and consultation committees can be discerned from survey data. Although paternalistic councils apparently exist, (Gollan, 2006: 268, 282) 'union and nonunion voice practices do not [generally] operate as substitutes in Australia' (Teiocher et al., 2007: 126, 136). Teiocher et al. have found that '[u]nion presence is positively associated with the presence of several non-union voice arrangements in Australia' (Teiocher et al., 2007: 138). Therefore non-union arrangements complement rather than compete with union voice (Teiocher et al., 2007: 138). In addition, employer-initiated consultative committees offer positive forums for ongoing dialogue and cooperative work relations in the workplace. However, multiple channels of voice (union, non-union, and direct) have greater benefits for employee job control and job rewards (Teiocher et al., 2007: 139).

Overall, joint consultation is flourishing where there are multiple channels of voice in Australian workplaces. However, without legal support, representative consultation may not flourish, and there is a risk that its effectiveness may be undermined in the long term (Streeck and Vitols, 1995: 277). Workplace represen-tation institutions increased under the Keating Labor Government's policy of legal support, then decreased under the Howard Government's conservative voluntaristic policies. It remains to be seen whether the current Labor Government will take an interest in the issue, or leave the voluntarist approach as the dominant one. In any event, legal intervention has promoted the growth of representative consultation in Australian workplaces.

THE UNITED STATES

The regulation of representative consultation in the United States contrasts starkly with the other two jurisdictions. There has been a long history of schemes of non-union representation in North America, but schemes of non-union representative consultation are today mostly prohibited by federal laws. These laws were passed in the 1930s, and were born out of intense conflict between management and trade unions. Employee representation diminished dramatically under this legislation, and the law continues to have a profound impact on corporate governance in the United States.

The History

The United States has never required non-union worker representation (Rogers, 1995: 389). But such schemes did exist in US enterprises in the nineteenth and twentieth centuries. 'U.S. shop committees', for instance, 'date back to 1833' (Rogers, 1995: 390). Employee representation committees or plans were encouraged by the US Government during the First World War (Gorman and Finkin, 2004: 257). Many employer-initiated committees folded during the Great Depression, but others were more long lasting (Gorman and Finkin, 2004: 257; Rogers, 1995: 391). Some of these schemes formed part of 'welfare capitalism' and had benefits for employees at the workplace (Gorman and Finkin, 2004: 257).[9]

In the 1930s there was a growth of company unions, given impetus by the *National Industrial Recovery Act* in 1933, which required employee representation.[10] Company unions, though, had one very significant disadvantage: while these unions, and other employee representation plans, purported to provide representation for employees, employer domination and control of them meant that they were widely seen as shams (Senator Wagner, quoted in *Electromation Inc.* 1992, NLRB, 309, enf'd, 35 F.3d 1148 (7th Cir, 1994), 992–3 (*Electromation*); Estlund, 2007: 597; Rogers, 1995: 392). Accordingly, in the mid-1930s, federal legislation was passed to prohibit employee representation plans and company unions; that prohibition continues today.

The Current Law

The *National Labor Relations (Wagner) Act 1935* ('NLRA') (NLRA s. 8; Gorman and Finkin, 2004: 257; Patmore, 2003: 178–86; Taras and Kaufman, 2006: 516), as amended by the *Labor Management Relations (Taft-Hartley) Act 1947*, prohibits unfair labour practices. These provisions are enforced through judicial-type proceedings administered by the National Labor Relations Board (NLRB) (Gorman and Finkin, 2004: 6).

Section 8(a) makes it an unfair labour practice for an employer to dominate or interfere with the formation or administration or contribute financial or other support to a labour organization (*EI du Pont de Nemours & Co*, 311 NLRB 893 (1993), 895–6 (*du Pont*); *Electromation*: 995–6). A 'labor organization' is defined in s. 2(5) as:

any organization of any kind, or any agency or employee representation committee or plan, in which employees participate and which exists for the purpose, in whole or in part, of dealing with employers concerning grievances, labor disputes, wages, rates of pay, hours of employment, or conditions of work.

The NLRB has been faithful to the legislative intent of the NLRA, which was to exclude company unions and employee representation plans from American workplaces but to permit some forms of representation. Two key steps have informed the analysis of the NLRB.

First, the Act restricts the activities of company unions and employee representation plans by defining them as labour organizations and then prohibiting employer domination, interference, or support of them as an unfair labour practice. Each statutory definition—'labour organization' and 'unfair labour practice'—is interpreted broadly by the NLRB.

In *Electromation* the NLRB defined a labour organization in s. 2(5) to cover:

(1) an organization in which employees participate; [and]
(2) that exists, at least in part, for purposes of 'dealing with' the employer; and
(3) where these dealings involve the prohibited subject areas of 'conditions of employment'.

The term 'dealing with' has been interpreted to exclude a wide range of bilateral mechanisms between management and employees. In *du Pont* the NLRB explained:

[t]hat 'bilateral mechanism' ordinarily entails a pattern or practice in which a group of employees, over time, makes proposals to management, management responds to these proposals by acceptance or rejection by word or deed, and compromise is not required. If the evidence establishes such a pattern or practice, or that the group exists for a purpose of following such a pattern or practice, the element of dealing is present.[11]

In sum, a bilateral mechanism includes a pattern or practice of bargaining, negotiation, or consultation between employees and management.

The prohibition of bilateral communication is limited to the subjects listed in s. 2 (5), which include the traditional topics of collective bargaining: conditions of work, grievances, labour disputes, hours of employment. These subjects have been interpreted broadly. The following topics discussed by non-union employee representatives have been held to fall within the meaning of s. 5(2): bonuses, no smoking policies, raises, incentive awards for safety, and workers' recreation and fitness (Gorman and Finkin, 2004: 258–62).

For there to be an unfair labour practice, an employee representation or participation scheme must fall within the definition of a labour organization in s. 2 (5), and the practice must violate the s. 8(a)(2) prohibition regarding employer 'domination'. 'Domination' and 'interference' include the appearance of employer control over the formation or administration of a labour organization (*du Pont*: 895–6; *Electromation*: 995–6). But a violation does not require hostility towards a union, or a specific intention to exclude a labour organization (*Electromation*: 996–7). Financial support to the committee or other forms of lesser assistance, such as paying employees for missed work time as a result of attending the employer's committee meetings (*Electromation*: 997–8) are also prohibited by s. 8(a)(2). Overall, s. 8(a)(2) prohibits employer activity that establishes or is conducive to the operating of a non-independent labour organization.

Second, the Wagner Act provides the means to establish independent labour organizations: these are trade unions, not company unions, or employee representation plans. The Act protects the rights of employees to self-organization, to form, join, and assist trade unions, to collectively bargain and engage in other concerted activities (NLRA (1935): s. 7). It also provides exclusive union bargaining rights over rates of pay, wages, hours of employment, and other working conditions (NLRA (1935) s. 9(a)). The purpose of the Act was to create independent trade unions free of management interference. Trade union independence was guaranteed by trade union representatives being chosen by employees through secret ballot elections (Rogers, 1995: 95; Weiler, 1993). Exclusivity—cutting out other bargaining organizations—provided a guarantee of a single collective voice (Rogers, 1995: 399). The purpose of the Act was to promote independent labour organizations that would help deliver growth in real incomes as well as productivity and act as a 'countervailing power' to 'otherwise overwhelming business domination' (Rogers, 1995: 376).

Various provisions in the Act would almost certainly be infringed by the kind of works council of employee representatives that is common in Europe. Such a council would satisfy the definitional elements of s. 2(5). A committee or group that is representational in nature clearly meets the criterion of 'employees participate in' (*Electromation*: 994; Kaufman et al., 2000: 263). Also, a representative committee would be dealing with management, and would constitute a bilateral mechanism, assuming that the purpose of the committee was to deal with conditions of employment (such as incentives for health and safety issues, or the use of a new technology) (Rogers, 1995: 377). In addition, a works council would be likely to be in violation of the s. 8(a)(2) prohibition on domination or support of a labour organization if the employer specified the purposes and powers of a committee, funded that committee, provided meeting rooms, or paid employees for missed work time at council meetings, or appointed some managers to the committee (Kaufman et al., 2000: 264; Rogers, 1995: 377). Such a committee would also likely contravene the exclusive union bargaining rights over rates of pay, wages, hours of employment, and other working conditions. A works council would infringe the prohibition even where there was no finding of hostility towards unions or exclusion of union activity.[12]

Employee Representation in the American Workplace

Overall, the Act rules out a 'wide swath of potentially valuable forms of employee involvement' (Estlund 2007: 597). Estlund argues that the Act makes it unlawful for 'employers to sponsor or support institutionalized forms of give-and-take, consultation, cooperation, or negotiation' which are not conducted with a trade union (Estlund, 2007: 597). Rogers points out that 'for at least some non-union employers, this imposes a legal restraint on desired innovations in worker partici-pation and "empowerment" in workplace governance' (Rogers, 1995: 377). Thus, non-union employers and their employees are legally restricted in the design, support, and topics covered by employee representation committees because of the NLRA.

However, the sanctions for breach of the prohibition are largely regarded as ineffective. Only limited sanctions are available; the most typical is a 'cease and desist' order (Kaufman et al., 2000: 278). As the NLRB is an administrative body, it cannot provide judicial relief such as compensatory or punitive damages (Estlund, 2007: 598). Estlund explains that 'as things stand, employers can treat the small and confined risk of an unfair labor practice charge as a minor cost of doing business' (Estlund, 2007: 599). The scope of the prohibition is broad but it is limited in its effectiveness.

Unilateralism in US Firms

The broader impact of the Act on corporate governance in the United States today is that it has permitted the diminishing of employee representation. Trade union representation has been severely curtailed by employers despite the legislative support provided in the NLRA, and there is a legal prohibition on most forms of non-union representative consultation.

Unilateral communication on employment conditions flourishes in US work-places: decisions are made by management without the advice or involvement of employee representatives (Wever, 1995: 139). Managerial responsibility and auton-omy is maximized at senior, middle, and junior management levels. Also, it is individualized, thus minimizing hierarchy (Wever, 1995: 139). Input from individ-ual or certain groups of employees may be welcomed and encouraged, but the ultimate decision rests with management.

US labour law permits unilateral communications about employment condi-tions. The NLRA requires that workers be represented by 'an organization wholly independent of employer influence or not at all' (Summers, 1987: 338). Most US employers have chosen no representation. They have found ways to use labour laws and other tools to reduce trade union presence in their companies. Anti-union employers are in part motivated by the higher costs that union membership entails—in wages and, more particularly, in conditions, such as health care and pension plans (Rogers, 1995). These benefits are provided by the firm, not the individual or the state, as occurs in some other Western countries.

US labour law scholars have pointed out that most US trade unions are denied their right to organize and collectively bargain on behalf of workers (Rogers, 1995: 376–7; Summers, 1987: 336). Employer opposition threatens the existence of trade unions in US workplaces and in public life. The decline in union density has also, of course, reduced their political impact(Rogers, 1995: 394).[13]

But there are some employers who do deal with independent labour organizations. In those firms, managers and trade unions may agree to establish a union management information and consultation committee through the process of collective bargaining. While there are some of these Labour–Management Cooperation Committees in unionized workplaces in the United States,[14] trade unions cover a very small percentage of US workplaces. Today, only 7.5 per cent of US employees in the private sector are represented by a trade union (Bureau of Labor Statistics, 2008).[15] Thus, 92.5 per cent of private sector workers are not represented by a union, have no union worker representative and no right to participation in their union.

For non-union employers, a decision to establish and support an employee representation committee discussing working conditions would be unlawful under the NLRA. However, there is a proviso to the prohibition in s. 8(a)(2) that stipulates that 'subject to rules and regulations made and published by the Board pursuant to Section 6, an employer shall not be prohibited from permitting employees to confer with him [sic] during working hours without loss of time or pay' (NLRA: s. 8(a)(2)). But this too is limited.

Gorman and Finkin note that the 'proviso makes it clear that adjustment of grievances by an employee group while drawing pay does not constitute illegal "financial support" of that group by the employer' (Gorman and Finkin, 2004: 258). Only very limited forms of non-union employee involvement are legally permitted—ad hoc mechanisms or ongoing mechanisms focusing exclusively on productivity, efficiency, and quality, for instance. Thus conversations about productivity or quality issues may take place between management and groups of employees. Managers may certainly provide information to their employees; employees may provide information to their managers; managers may meet with employee representatives to discuss quality or efficiency issues. Thus, employee committees which are mere 'communication devices'—used for topics other than employment conditions—are protected under the Act (*Electromation*: 997).

There is little empirical data about the spread and significance of joint consultation procedures in the United States. Lipset and Meltz in 2000 found in their
survey that coverage of such schemes amounted to 20 per cent for firms without
unions (Lipset and Meltz, 2000: 226). Richard Freeman and Joel Rogers reported in
1999 that over a third of the workplaces they surveyed had an established employee
participation committee that discussed problems with management on a regular
basis (Freeman and Rogers, 1999: 92). Both Freeman and Rogers and Lipset and
Meltz found that a large proportion of non-unionized committees regularly discuss
issues such as wages and benefits—this was an unexpected result, because this type
of interaction is prohibited by s. 2(5), 8(a)(2) of the Wagner Act (Taras and
Kaufmann, 2006: 516). Thus, many committees operate in the shadow of illegality
(Lobel, 2006: 1547).

Where schemes of representative consultation are operated, legally or illegally,
ultimately, they can be terminated by a unilateral decision of management.[16]
Unilateral communication on employment conditions has become the default
choice, an inexorable choice, for the vast majority of US private sector employers.
Yet it is not simply an economic preference; it has been forged through US labour law.

Reforming Unlawful Representative Consultation

Reformers were active in the mid-1990s, when 'the Teamwork for Employees and
Managers Bill' (TEAM Bill) was passed. Its aim was to loosen the ban on employer-
sponsored employee representation plans. The TEAM Bill would have permitted
employee committees to 'discuss "matters of mutual interest"', including terms
and conditions of employment, 'as long as the committees [did] not take on the
role of bargaining agent for employees' (Estlund, 2007: 595; Kaufman et al., 2000:
260, 283).[17] The Bill passed both houses of Congress but was ultimately vetoed by
President Clinton (Estlund, 2007: 595; Lobel, 2001: 158). It was opposed because of
concerns that it would be a form of 'subtle employer coercion and [would place]
additional weapons in employers' already sizable arsenal of anti-union tactics'
(Estlund, 2007: 595; see also Kaufman et al., 2000: 260) It appears that the TEAM
Bill provided insufficient protection for legitimate trade union activity. The spectre
of US labour history and unhappy management union relations forestalled the
success of the reform.

There are at least two possibilities for reform now. It may be that a limited
amendment to the NLRA permitting a wider variety of representative consultation
schemes in US firms will spur the development of representative consultation. But
such a reform would need to be seen as a fair and acceptable accommodation of the
interests of labour and capital (see, for example, Kaufman et al., 2000: 283–5).
Alternatively, more far-reaching reform may be necessary to address the problems inherent in the overall NLRA scheme. To even allow participatory

schemes, it would be necessary, in the words of Charles Hecksher, to '[turn] the Wagner Act upside down' (Hecksher, 1988: 254–6).

To go further and address the challenge of unilateralism may require a rethinking of the whole scheme of labour relations law in the United States. It would require consideration of the totality of economic and social pressures on US firms as well as the appropriateness of the legal arrangements.

In sum, the protective prohibition in the United States limits the capacity for representative consultation to be used to avoid trade union activity. Yet it has placed some forms of representative consultation in the realm of illegality which would otherwise be regarded as legitimate. Given the previous experience, it will take patience, skill, and effort to reform the NLRA to address the fundamental problems of employee representation.

Conclusion

In each jurisdiction committees of managers and employees exist. Ultimately, there is a common underlying legislative purpose in each jurisdiction of framing and facilitating consultation. The law provides a framework that crafts the engagement among managers and employee representatives. However, the constitution, operation and effectiveness of these committees will vary according to a legal spectrum of representative consultation.

Examining the legal spectrum illustrates the diversity of regulatory regimes governing relationships between managers and employee representatives. Legislatures have adopted a number of responses to the role of representation in advancing structured communication in larger organizations. As we have seen, they range from a right to a voluntary entitlement to a prohibition on representative consultation. Each of these modes of regulation reflects different purposes, entitlements, and problems involved with various employee participation schemes and highlights the role of law as a form of social regulation.

The legal right to representative consultation in the ICED is now implemented in Member States' laws and is a form of universalist regulation. Through the institutionalizing of employee rights in national industrial laws and practice the EU Directive may develop a value consensus for representative consultation. Common assumptions have been forged by a long history of works council legislation in many Western European countries. However, where new legislative schemes have been enacted it will be a challenge to fill the gap between the law in the statutes and the law in action in the workplace. It may take some time for representative consultation procedures to be widely accepted by labour and capital in some Member States. In the end, successful implementation may depend upon both legislative direction and the perceived legitimacy of these processes in the workplaces of the European Union. Even so, the option adopted by a small number of Member States for individualized negotiated agreements provided for in Article 5, may have a centrifugal force that erodes the ICED's universalist aspirations, by displacing the minimum standards in Article 4.

As in Europe, the purpose of legally supported representative consultation in Australia in the 1980s and 1990s was to promote cooperative communication between labour and capital. The right to representative consultation covered a more limited range of topics than in Europe, yet these laws correlated with an increase in the number of joint consultative committees in Australian workplaces. Management and labour, in negotiating workplace agreements, had to consider whether such committees would be appropriate in their workplace. Their acceptance depended upon the extent to which the industrial parties agreed to their adoption. Arguably, their adoption depended upon their perceived legitimacy and effectiveness as communication devices within the workplace. However, the lack of legislative direction as to structure which hampered their implementation was one practical problem. Another, the removal of legislative support has been associated with a decline in the number of joint consultative committees in Australia.

In Australia, the policy of voluntarism has left it to employees and employers to work out their own agreements. Voluntarism protects managerial prerogative because it leaves representative participation in the grasp and the release of those whose hands wield authority. Voluntarism provides maximum choice for management over the initiation and structure of representative consultation arrangements. Representative schemes have been initiated by management to enhance communication about productivity and flexibility; these schemes may also in part redress the imbalance of power inherent in the employment relationship. One problem is that voluntary bodies are less reliable than legislatively supported schemes because they can be terminated at the will of the employer. Yet union voice generally operates in a complementary way with joint consultative committees. The legislative trend has been to move away from collective representation to individual representation at least until the election of the Rudd Labor Government.

In the United States, a culture of workplace unilateralism has developed, in which management operates without the advice of workplace representatives about employment conditions. This was not the expected outcome of the NLRA, it was intended to promote collective bargaining between management and independent labour organizations. The prohibition in the NLRA on employee representation plans or company unions, for example, was supposed to limit employer domination and control of employee labour organizations.

Yet labour laws must be seen in their practical operation if we are to discern their regulatory effects. Legal prohibitions act to constrain choices which are seen as socially or economically undesirable. However, employers' choices may be structured by the law in unexpected ways. The NLRA's ban on bilateral mechanisms, which prevents employers from dealing with a non-union employee representation plan, contributes to unilateral communications. In addition, under the NLRA, management is given a choice: to negotiate with an independent labour organization or not at all. Many employers have chosen the latter option.

While the prohibition on employee representation plans has reduced the number of employer non-union schemes, it has not removed them entirely. This is because the sanctions in the NLRA are weak. The NLRA was intended to limit the activities of powerful employers for the good of the employees and the economy, and to provide a means of adjusting and reconciling conflicting interests (Rogers, 1995). But the Act seems no longer to be serving this purpose. Rather, the NLRA is now supported by powerful employers because it is used to guard their interests. Other employers are hampered in their development of genuine non-union employee representation schemes. Some forms of representative consultation now operate in the realm of illegality. Yet many of these employee involvement schemes are no longer regarded as sham forms of representation, rather they are seen as a legitimate voice in workplace decision making (Kaufman et al., 2000: 260, 279–81). Trade unions are caught in a dilemma: the law has supported their interests but played a role in perpetuating their decline.

Overall, the function of legal intervention is to brace or stabilize employment relations. The inherent inequality in the employment relationship whereby employees must obey the reasonable commands of their employer remains a feature of Western IR systems. Experience in Australia and the EU highlights the fact that legal support is needed if representative consultation is to spread throughout an economy. Voluntarist representative consultation will continue to be driven by economic and social pressures, which means its adoption could be spurred at some times and in some enterprises, and deterred in others. The legal prohibition in the United States hinders harmful and helpful schemes of representation alike. The prohibition on employer workplace representation schemes there contributes to a workplace culture of unilateralism.

NOTES

* The information in this chapter is current as of December 2008.
1. Please note that the survey did not reveal the coverage of unions of surveyed employees. This information would have been useful to assess the effectiveness of trade unions in providing information about the Information and Consultation Regulations.
2. See the Keating Labor Government's *Industrial Relations Reform Act 1993* (Cth) ss. 170MC(1)(d) and 170NC(1)(f).
3. The Howard Government introduced these legislative changes to limit or remove consultation mechanisms introduced by the operation of the TCR case and the National Wage case.

4. Provisions establishing joint consultative committees are not matters that must not be included in a workplace agreement, namely falling under the 'prohibited content' prescribed by *Workplace Relations Act 1996* (Cth) s. 356 and the *Workplace Relations Regulations 1996* (Cth) 8.4–8.7.

5. '[W]orkforce participation' in government documentation refers to the need to maximize inclusion and participation in the workforce per se (Gillard and Wong, 2007: 3–4; Rudd and Gillard, 2007: 12).

6. Formerly known as Australian Centre for Industrial Relations Research and Training (ACIRRT).

7. The Australian Worker Representation and Participation Survey (AWRPS) (2004) conducted in 2003–2004 reported a higher figure of 38.9 per cent of companies with committees of employees (Teiocher et al., 2007: 137).

8. ABS, *Employee Earnings, Benefits and Trade Union Membership*, 6310.0, August 2006: 35. Union density refers to the proportion of the workforce organized in trade unions, ABS, *Employee Earnings, Benefits and Trade Union Membership*, 6310.0, August 2006: 35.

9. Welfare capitalism meant social benefits were 'administered through attachment to the workplace rather than the state' (Lobel, 2006: 1548).

10. The enactment of the *National Industrial Recovery Act* in 1933, s. 7(a) of which required employee representation, resulted in employer-established 'company unions' being widely created (Gorman and Finkin, 2004: 257; see also Rogers, 1995: 391).

11. *EI du Pont de Nemours & Co* 1993, NLRB, 311, 894. The concept of 'dealing' does not require that the two sides seek to compromise their differences. It involves only a bilateral mechanism between two parties.

12. For a review of the relevant case law see Gorman and Finkin, 2004: 257–76.

13. Lobel notes that 'Both Stone and Hogler view the decline of unionism as a complex development, which should be linked to both the changes in market production and the inadequacies of the legal regime' (Lobel, 2006: 1544).

14. See Lobel, 2001: 152.

15. Under the *Wagner Act* trade union membership of non-agricultural employees reached 33.2 per cent in 1955 (Summers, 1987: 336).

16. Legal employee involvement schemes appear to be widespread but 1992 data indicates that employee participation in these schemes appears to be low and often terminated at the will of management (Lawler et al., 1992: 30).

17. *Teamwork for Employees and Managers Act* of 1995, H.R. 743, 104th Cong. (1996).

References

AHLERING, B. and DEAKIN, S. (2005) 'Labour Regulation, Corporate Governance and Legal Origin: A Case of Institutional Complementarity?' Working Paper no. 72/2006, University of Cambridge.

Australia, House of Representatives (1992) *Debates* (R. Brown, MP Charlton, Minister for Land Transport, government) http://parlinfoweb.aph.gov.au at 24 June 1992.

Australia, Senate (1992a) *Debates* (P. F. Cook, Senator for Western Australia, Minister for Industrial Relations, government) http://parlinfoweb.aph.gov.au at 7 May 1992.

Australia, Senate (1992b) *Debates* (N. Sherry, Senator for Western Australia, Minister for Industrial Relations, government) http://parlinfoweb.aph.gov.au at 24 November 1993.

Australian Bureau of Statistics (2001) *6310.0 Employee Earnings, Benefits and Trade Union Membership*, Canberra.

—— (2002) Cat. no. *6310.0 Employee Earnings, Benefits and Trade Union Membership*, Canberra.

—— (2004) Cat. no. *6105.0 Australian Labour Market Statistics, Benefits and Trade Union Membership*, Canberra.

—— (2006a) Cat. no. *6310.0 Employee Earnings, Benefits and Trade Union Membership*, Canberra.

—— (2006b) Cat. no. *6303.0 Employee Earnings and Hours, 6303.0*, Canberra, reissued 24 April 2007.

Australian Centre for Industrial Relations Research and Training (ACIRRT) (2003) 'Australian Centre for Industrial Relations Research and Training', retrieved 1 April 2007 from http://www.acirrt.com/research/default.htm. Now Workplace Research Centre, University of Sydney, http://www.wrc.org.au// at 24 April 2008.

BROWN, M. and AINSWORTH, S. (2000) 'A Review and Integration of Research on Employee Participation in Australia 1983–1999', Working Paper no. 18, Centre for Employment and Labour Relations Law, Melbourne Law School.

Bureau of Labor Statistics (2008) *Union Members in 2007*, Press Release USDL 08-0092 (25 January 2008), retrieved 11 April 2008 from http://www.bls.gov/news.release/union2.nro.htm.

BURNS, P. (2000) 'The Silent Stakeholders: Reforming Workforce Consultation Law', Policy Paper, London: The Industrial Society.

CALLUS, R., MOREHEAD, A., CULLY, M., and BUCHANAN, J. (1991) *Industrial Relations at Work: The Australian Workplace Industrial Relations Survey*, Commonwealth Department of Industrial Relations. Canberra: Australian Government Publishing Service.

CAMPLING, J. and GOLLAN, P. (1999) *Bargained Out: Negotiating Without Unions in Australia.* Sydney: The Federation Press.

CHA (2005) *A Little More Conversation: Employee Communications Approaches and Their Impact.* London: CHA.

COLLINS, H. (2003a) 'Partnership at Work', Paper presented at the Melbourne Law School, 12 March 2003.

—— (2003b) 'The Evolving Direction of European Labour Law: Social Inclusion, Competitiveness and Citizenship', Paper presented at the Annual Labour Law Conference: Rethinking the Law of Work: Perspectives on the Future Shape of Employment Regulation, 4 April 2003, Sydney.

COMBET, G. (2003) 'Employee Consultation in an Australian Context: The Works Council Debate and Trade Unions', in P. Gollan and G. Patmore (eds), *Partnership at Work: The Challenge of Employee Democracy, Labor Essays 2003*, pp. 165–77. Sydney: Pluto Press.

Commission of the European Communities, 'Industrial Relations in Europe 2006' (Commission Staff Working Document no. SEC (2006) 1499).

COX, A., MARCHINGTON, M., and ZAGELMEYER, S. (2006) 'Embedding Employee Involvement and Participation at Work', *Human Resource Management Journal*, 16(3): 250–67.

DAVIES, P. and KILPATRICK, C. (2004) 'UK Worker Representation after Single Channel', *Industrial Law Journal*, 33(2): 121–51.

DAVIS, E. and LANSBURY, R. (1999) 'Consultation and Employee Participation in Australian Workplaces: 1986–1995', in E. Davis and R. Lansbury (eds) *Managing Together: Consultation and Participation in the Workplace*, pp. 1–24. Melbourne: Longman.

Department of Employment and Industrial Relations (DEIR) (1986) 'Industrial Democracy and Employee Participation: A Policy Discussion Paper'. Canberra: Australian Government Publishing Service.

Department of Employment and Workplace Relations (2005) 'WageNet', retrieved 6 February 2008 from http://www.wagenet.gov.au/WageNet/Search/Search.asp? Render=All.

ESTLUND, C. (2007) 'The Ossification of American Labor Law and the Decline of Self-Governance in the Workplace', *Journal of Labor Research*, 28(4): 591–608.

European Commission (1998) 'Commission Adopts a Proposal for a Directive on Information and Consultation of Employees', 11 November, Brussels (IP/98/981).

European Parliament and Council (CRD) (1975) 'On the Approximation of the Laws of the Member States relating to Collective Redundancies', Council Directive 75/129, 1975 OJ (L 48).

—— (TUBD) (1977) 'On the Approximation of the Laws of the Member States relating to the Safeguarding of Employees' Rights in the Event of Transfers of Undertakings, Businesses or Parts of Undertakings or Businesses', Council Directive 77/187, 1977 OJ (L 61).

—— (EWCD) (1994) 'European Works Council', Council Directive 94/45, 1994 OJ (L 254).

—— (1997) 'European Works Council', Council Directive 97/74, 1998 OJ (L 010).

FORSYTH, A., KORMAN, S., and MARSHALL, S. (2006) 'Joint Consultative Committees in Australia: An Empirical Update', Paper presented at the 3rd Australian Labour Law Association National Conference, Brisbane, 22–23 September 2006.

FREEMAN, R. and ROGERS, J. (1999) *What Workers Want*. Ithaca, NY: ILR Press.

FUDGE, J. (2008) 'Working-time Regimes, Flexibility, and Work–Life Balance: Gender Equality and Families', Paper presented at Melbourne Law School, Melbourne, 18 February 2008.

GILLARD, J. and WONG, P. (2007) *An Australian Social Inclusion Agenda*. Retrieved 2 June 2009 from http://www.alp.org.au/download/now/071122_social_inclusion.pdf.

GOLLAN, P.(2006) 'Representation at Suncorp—What do the Employees Want?', *Human Resource Management Journal* 16(3): 268–86.

—— MARKEY, R., and ROSS, I. (2001) 'Additional Forms of Employee Representation in Australia', ACIRRT, Working Paper no. 64, University of Sydney.

—— and PATMORE, G. (2003) *Partnership at Work: The Challenge of Employee Democracy, Labor Essays 2003*. Sydney: Pluto Press.

—— and WILKINSON, A. (2007) 'Implications of the EU Information and Consultation Directive and the Regulations in the UK—Prospects for the Future of Employee Representation', *International Journal of Human Resource Management*, 18(7): 1145–8.

GORMAN, M. and FINKIN, M. (2004) 'Employer Domination and Support of Unions', in *Basic Text on Labor Law: Unionization and Collective Bargaining, Hornbook Series*. St Paul: West Publishing.

GOSPEL, H. and WILLMAN, P. (2003) 'The Coming of Workplace Information Sharing and Consultation: What It Means for Employee Representation in Britain', *Perspectives on Work*, 7(1): 38.

HECKSCHER, C. (1988) *The New Unionism: Employee Involvement in the Changing Corporation.* New York: Basic Books.

JONES, M. and MITCHELL, R. (2006) 'Legal Origin, Legal Families and the Regulation of Labour in Australia', Paper presented at the Workshop: Corporate Governance and the Management of Labour: Australian Perspectives, 8 December 2006, Melbourne.

KAUFMAN, B. E., LEWIN, D., and FOSSUM, J. A. (2000) 'Nonunion Employee Involvement and Participation Programs: The Role of Employee Representation and the Impact of the NLRA', in B. E. Kaufman and D. G. Taras (eds), *Non-union Employee Representation: History, Contemporary Practice, and Policy.* Armonk: M. E. Sharpe.

LAWER, E., MOHRMAN, S., and LEDFORD, G. (1992) *Employee Involvement and Total Quality Management: Practices and Results in Fortune 1000 Companies.* San Francisco: Jossey-Bass.

LEE, S. (2004) 'Working-Hour Gaps: Trends and Issues', in Jon C. Messenger (ed.), *Working Time and Workers' Preferences in Industrialized Countries: Finding the Balance,* pp. 29–59. New York: Routledge.

Liberal-National Party Coalition (1996) 'Better Pay for Better Work', The Coalition Industrial Relations Policy, Canberra.

LINGEMANN, S., VON STEINAU-STEINRUECK, R., and MENGEL, A. (2003) *Employment and Labour Law in Germany.* München: Beck'sche CH Verlagsbuchhandlung Oscar Beck.

LIPSET, S. M. and MELTZ, N. M. (2000) 'Estimates of Nonunion Employee Representation in the United States and Canada: How Different Are the Two Countries?' in B. E. Kaufman and D. G. Taras (eds), *Nonunion Employee Representation: History, Contemporary Practice, and Policy.* Armonk, NY: M. E. Sharpe.

LOBEL, O. (2001) 'Agency and Coercion in Labor and Employment Relations: Four Dimensions of Power in Shifting Patterns of Work Fall', *University of Pennsylvania Journal of Labor and Employment Law,* 121(4): 121–94.

—— (2006) 'The Four Pillars of Work Law', *Michigan Law Review,* 104(6): 1539–58.

MARCHINGTON, M. (1992) 'Surveying the Practice of Joint Consultation in Australia', *Journal of Industrial Relations,* 34(3): 530–49.

MARKEY, R. (1987) 'Neo-Corporatism and Technological Change in Australia: An International Perspective', *New Technology, Work and Employment,* 2(2): 142–53.

MITCHELL, R., NAUGHTON, R., and SORENSEN, R. (1997) 'The Law and Employee Participation—Evidence from the Federal Enterprise Agreements Process', *Journal of Industrial Relations,* 39(2): 196–217.

MOREHEAD, A., STEELE, M., ALEXANDER, M., STEPHEN, K., and DUFFIN, L. (1997) *Change at Work: The 1995 Australian Workplace Industrial Relations Survey.* Melbourne: Addison Wesley Longman.

PATMORE, G. (2003) 'Employer Responses to Workplace Democracy: A North American Perspective', in P. J. Gollan and G. Patmore (eds), *Partnership at Work: The Challenge of Employee Democracy: Labor Essays.* Sydney: Pluto Press.

QUINTIN, O. (2003) 'High Performance Workplaces: Information and Consultation Rights for UK Workers' Conference', presented at a conference organized by the TUC, 17 January 2003, London, retrieved 24 April from http://ec.europa.eu/employment_social/speeches/2003/oq170103_en.pdf.

ROGERS, J. (1995) 'United States: Lessons from Abroad and Home', in J. Rogers and W. Streeck (eds), *Works Councils: Consultation, Representation, and Cooperation in Industrial Relations.* Chicago: University of Chicago Press.

ROGERS, J. and STREECK, W. (eds) (1995) *Works Councils: Consultation, Representation, and Cooperation in Industrial Relations*. Chicago: University of Chicago Press.

RUDD, K. and GILLARD, J. (2007) 'Forward with Fairness—Labor's Plan for Fairer and More Productive Australian Workplaces' retrieved 18 April 2008 from http://www.alp.org.au/media/0407/spel00280.php.

STONE, K. V. W. (2004) *From Widgets to Digits: Employment Regulation for the Changing Workplace*. Cambridge: Cambridge University Press.

STREECK, W. (1995) 'Works Councils in Western Europe: From Consultation to Participation', in J. Rogers and W. Streeck (eds), *Works Councils: Consultation, Representation, and Co-Operation in Industrial Relations*. Chicago: University of Chicago Press.

——and VITOLS, S. (1995) 'The European Community between Mandatory Consultation and Voluntary Information', in J. Rogers and W. Streeck (eds), *Works Council: Consultation, Representation, and Cooperation in Industrial Relations*. Chicago: University of Chicago Press.

SUMMERS, S. (1987) 'An American Perspective of the German Worker Participation Model', *Comparative Labor Law Journal*, 8: 333–56.

TARAS, G. and KAUFMAN, B. (2006) 'Non-Union Employee Representation in North America: Diversity, Controversy and Uncertain Future', *Industrial Relations Journal*, 37 (5): 513–42.

TEIOCHER, J., HOLLAND, P., PYMAN, A., and COOPER, B. (2007) 'Australian Workers: Finding their Voice?' in R. Freeman, P. Boxall, and P. Haynes, *What Workers Say: Employee Voice in The Anglo American Workplace*. Ithaca, NY: Cornell University Press.

WEILER, P. (1993) 'Governing the Workplace: Employee Representation in the Eyes of the Law', in B. Kaufman and M. Kleiner (eds), *Employee Representation: Alternatives and Future Directions*, pp. 81–104. Wisconsin: Industrial Relations Research Association.

WEVER, K. (1995) *Negotiating Competitiveness: Employment Relations and Organizational Innovation in Germany and the United States*. Boston: Harvard Business School Press.

Worker Representation and Participation Survey (WRPS) (1999) In R. B. Freeman and J. Rogers (eds) *What Workers Want*. Ithaca, NY: ILR Press.

Cases and Legislation

Corporations Law Amendment (Employee Entitlements) Act 2000.

Crown Cork & Seal Co v NLRB, 36 F 3d 1130 (2001).

EI du Pont de Nemours & Co, 311 NLRB 893 (1993).

Electromation, Inc., 309 NLRB 990 (1992).

European Parliament and Council (CRD) (1975) 'On the Approximation of the Laws of the Member States Relating to Collective Redundancies', Council Directive 75/129, 1975 OJ (L 48).

——(TUBD) (1977) 'On the Approximation of the Laws of the Member States relating to the Safeguarding of Employees' Rights in the Event of Transfers of Undertakings, Businesses or Parts of Undertakings or Businesses', Council Directive 77/187, 1977 OJ (L 61).

——(EWCD) (1994) 'European Works Council', Council Directive 94/45, 1994 OJ (L 254).

——(EWCD) (1997) 'European Works Council', Council Directive 97/74, 1998 OJ (L 010).

——(ICED) (2002) 'A General Framework for Informing and Consulting Employees', Council Directive 2002/14/EC, 2002 OJ (L 080).

Industrial Relations Act 1988 (Cth).

Industrial Relations Amendment Act 1993 (Cth).

Industrial Relations Reform Act 1993 (Cth).

National Industrial Recovery Act, 15 USC 703 (1933).

National Wage Case (1991) 36 IR 120.

NLRB v Cabot Carbon Co, 360 US 203 (1959).

North American Van Lines Inc., 288 N.L.R.B. 38 (1988).

Re Award Simplification Decision (1997) 75 IR 272 ('Re Award Simplification Decision').

Re Review of Wage Fixing Principles (1993) 50 IR 285.

Redundancy Case (2004) 129 IR 155 ('Redundancy Test Case 2004').

Review of Wage Fixing Principles (1994) 55 IR 144.

Termination, Change and Redundancy Case (1984) 26 AILR 256; (1984) 294 CAR 175; (1984) 8 IR 34 ('TCR Case 1984').

—— (1985) 27 AILR 1; (1984) 295 CAR 673; (1984) 9 IR 115 ('TCR Case 1985').

The Information and Consultation of Employees Regulations (2004) UK Statutory Instrument 2004, 3426.

The Labor Management Relations (Taft-Hartley) Act 1947 (US) 29 USC §§ 141–197 (2000).

The National Labor Relations (Wagner) Act 1935 (US) 29 USC §§ 151–169 (2000) ('NLRA').

The Transnational Information and Consultation of Employees Regulations (1999) UK Statutory Instrument 1999, 3323.

Workplace Relations Act 1996 (Cth).

Workplace Relations and Other Legislation Amendment Bill 1996 (Cth).

Workplace Relations Amendment (Work Choices) Act 2005 (Cth).

CHAPTER 5

....

LABOUR PROCESS AND MARXIST PERSPECTIVES ON EMPLOYEE PARTICIPATION*

....

MIGUEL MARTINEZ LUCIO

INTRODUCTION

....

THE question of participation is of increasing interest in discussions within organizations and the academy. It is argued that the future workplace and the 'enlightened organization' must consist of a culture and practice of participation as a vital characteristic of its portfolio of practices. There are various imperatives contributing to the development of participation. It is seen as an essential ingredient of the way organizations may harness employee creativity and commitment for the cause of economic success. Increasingly, management texts and gurus suggest that successful organizations are those that 'involve', 'empower', and 'listen' (Collins, 1998: 34–65). This allows for innovation and knowledge to emerge from a

* I would like to thank Paul Stewart and David Turner for reading this piece and providing comments.

workforce and for their expertise to be harnessed. Second, participation facilitates a sense of belonging among workers. It responds to a sense of justice in that one is addressed less as an employee and more as part of the organization, as a stakeholder. The rising levels of social expectations require a new concordat between management and workers: a new awareness of the centrality of dialogue (Stuart and Martínez Lucio, 2005). Third, the role of participation is critical in terms of legitimacy. Increasingly a legitimate management decision making process is seen to require a sense of fairness and openness. Participation allows management to be seen as justified and reasonable in its actions.

However, there hangs over the rhetoric and fascination with participation within management agendas a serious amount of concern and cynicism. This is nothing new and reflects anxiety about the vagaries of participation within academic circles and among various practitioners. Participation is a term that is deemed to be both ambivalent and politically-oriented at the same time. Many empirical studies of a quantitative and qualitative nature have, in relation to the experience in the United Kingdom, for example, questioned the cohesiveness and extent of new forms of participation within the modern workplace (Marchington and Wilkinson, 2000). It is seen as being a questionable development in the current economic and social context: it also is seen as an essential subject of debate given its potential manipulation within a society based on managerial prescription. Within this critical vein of thought the Marxist and Labour Process traditions of thinking are pivotal. They are not the sole or dominant part of such critical currents, but they are in broad terms a significant contribution to the way participation is understood in more sober and critical terms.

This chapter aims to outline how an apparently positive feature of organizational life can also be considered a focus of concern. The chapter starts with an outline of some of the variations in Marxist and Labour Process debates, along with discussion in those debates within political science that have had most impact on discussions in industrial relations especially the debate on corporatism. It then moves to a discussion of critical accounts of the broad notion of participation within capitalist economies at various levels. It explains why forms of worker participation are both the subject of political demands by various constituencies, yet are also a cause of concern in the way they have evolved. The chapter will outline the contribution of critical debates in the form of Marxist and Labour Process debates, and show how they provide an essential component and reality check within relevant discussions, especially within business schools. Finally, the paper outlines some of the challenges facing critical and, in particular, Marxist and Labour Process approaches to the debates on participation.

The chapter argues that we must develop an understanding of participation that is aware of the different vectors and dimensions in terms of its formation. We must reflect in terms of the levels and regulation of participation and not just isolate it as an institution which happens to have various varieties and dynamics. It is also essential for an understanding of the dynamics and dialectics of participation that we note the tensions in terms of vectors of analysis, such as the question of worker incorporation through indirect representation into capitalist interests, symbolic and cultural forms of participation, direct modes of participation that are workplace centred, and more individualized modes of participation. Across these new spaces we see conflicts and tensions emerge that suggest that participation is a contested space.

CRITICAL AND MARXIST POSITIONS: THE AUTONOMY OF PARTICIPATION

It is easy to stereotype Marxist and Labour Process approaches to debates on work and in particular debates on participation. Yet before we can start any discussion we need to understand the way Marxist approaches to understanding work have evolved. The work of Karl Marx in the nineteenth century was concerned with explaining the development of capitalism and its internal and inherent contradictions. Marx focused, among other things, on the exploitative dimension of employment relations within a capitalist context. At the heart of his work was a careful dissection of the capitalist system with its reliance on market relations, the extension of the market to employment relations, and the extraction of surplus value from the working class (Marx, 2000: 372–568). His studies introduced a range of insights into the way we understand how workers are exploited in a system where they have to sell their labour and where they become alienated within the production process and society. Marx wrote at a time when worker participation in political, social, economic, and cultural terms within capitalism was limited, even if their economic contribution was vital to the development of the economy. This meant that Marx never really engaged with broader issues of the state (Jessop, 1990), the regulation of employment conditions, and trade unionism in a consistent manner as they were in their infancy in Europe and the USA at that time. The institutions of capitalist society in terms of legislation, state agencies, and regulatory structures within employment (and presumably modes of worker involvement) were seen as having very little autonomy from the interests and control of the dominant and capitalist classes, and they were viewed with great distrust, partly because of their undeveloped nature. One can speak of his approach being a more pessimist view of the ability of trade unions and worker forms of representation to recraft the priorities of capitalists (Hyman, 1971). It should, however, be noted that in analysing Marx's legacy, much depends on the specific texts that are examined.

In fact, the concept of labour relations or industrial relations was not part of Marx's terminology (Müller-Jentsch, 2004: 5). Workers—in very general terms—were not always seen to be challenging the nature of decision making and control systems within the employment relationship without some form of external political guidance. On the other hand, the argument was that challenges did not need to be politically articulated, given the strong and obvious impact of work intensification within a capitalist system. Hence Lenin (1961) oscillated between a defence of trade union action as a form of class struggle and the need to lead it through a political elite in order for it to be more robust in its critique of the system of capitalist relations as a whole.

Marxists in the twentieth century were more concerned with the fact that such arguments could not always explain the way institutions managed exploitation and legitimated it over a longer time frame. Moreover, it became apparent that systems of regulation and the way rules and relations were established within capitalist societies began to mediate the experience and role of workers. Regulation was the outcome of worker struggles as capitalists accommodated to worker responses and framed the nature of worker participation (see the discussion on collective bargaining later). Given this, many began to realize that the political level and the organizational processes within a capitalist society could be more subtle and discreet, especially in liberal democratic contexts. Hence, Lenin (1917) as a political theorist and revolutionary in the early twentieth century spoke of the role of the political in terms of the state as an actor in mobilizing on behalf of capitalist interests. Yet the extent to which capitalist institutions and political institutions within capitalism could be open to participation was questioned by proponents of various Marxist and neo-Marxist traditions, such as the Frankfurt school. A broad school of thought, some of its main proponents, such as Marcuse (1964), argued that consumerism and wage-related struggles merely incorporated further the working class into the socio-economic system. In effect, be it through coercion or through consensus, capitalist organizations and their political allies could mould working class demands and depoliticize them; and, in the case of industrial relations, collective bargaining and various forms of 'worker participation' were seen as strategic vehicles for doing this. In fact, there was also concern within the Frankfurt school that much of the problem was the Socialist and Leninist engagement with ideas of scientific management and Taylorist forms of worker control (see Traub, 1978 on these ideas in Lenin).

Antonio Gramsci, as a Communist leader and thinker who wrote much of his work in prison during the 1920s and 1930s under the Italian fascist dictatorship, was concerned with the ideological dimension of capitalism and the way interests among workers were accommodated and represented within various modes of capitalist control. In effect, the argument presented was that the capitalist and ownership classes could not rely solely on coercion and surveillance for the control of the working classes. He argued that the capitalists ruled as much through consensus as coercion (Gramsci, 1971). There was a need on the part of capital to incorporate the interests and demands of the working class through political discourses and the development of mechanisms of involvement, although these distorted working class interests and were represented by capitalist institutions in a manner biased towards the interests of the elite. Such social interests and demands were seen to be redefined around elite agendas through the articulation of working class interests in terms of ideologies, such as nationalism and populism (Laclau, 1977). So there is a tradition within Marxism of questioning the integrity and effectiveness of participation in a broader sense, but also of acknowledging that political and economic participation may reflect the changing balance of forces and relations between capital and labour. Marxists vary in their view of the effectiveness of these political structures according to what part of the Marxist tradition they belong.

This question as to whether institutions of regulation and participation were autonomous of capitalist processes and interests, and to what extent they could be, became a centre of discussion differentiating academic and political positions. In the 1960s and 1970s the French Marxist structuralist tradition, as represented by the work of Althusser (Althusser and Balibar, 1970) and Poulantzas (1973, 1975), began to introduce the notion of autonomy, especially relative autonomy, within an analysis of capital–labour–state relations. The argument was that an ensemble of institutions, such as the state, could be *relatively* autonomous of capitalist interests. The argument, very broadly, went as follows: capitalists were driven by short term and financially-oriented interests which in the long term could undermine the sustainability of capitalism by producing a lack of investment in the economic infrastructure and reproduction of labour (e.g., the lack of skill formation) and the political effects of greater worker exploitation (e.g., political instability and a crisis of legitimacy for capitalism). This leads to a pivotal role for the state which, having democratized to an extent during the twentieth century in the case of Europe, and to varying degrees in other contexts, must 'think' in the longer term on behalf of the capitalist system. This is influenced by the work of Engels (1972) who argued the state had the task of representing all capital's interests and not just that of any one segment. Through social strategies, such as the welfare state, investment in education, wage policies, and, of particular relevance to this chapter, the participation of workers, in terms of collective bargaining and forms of industrial democracy, the support and involvement of workers within capitalism could be, to varying degrees, guaranteed. This idea of regulation being essential to political and economic stability was picked up and developed by the French Regulation school (Aglietta, 1979). The British exponent of that school argued that the mode of regulation could be fairly autonomous of capitalist interests (Jessop, 1990). The problem for the state is that the interests of capital (and capitals) are not always clear. The state is seen as the institutional ensemble of forms of representation, intervention, and administration that require projects in their own right to create consistent forms of intervention and policy outputs (Jessop, 1990) some of which relate to the issue of participation: 'The operational autonomy of the state is a further massive complicating factor in this regard. Indeed, to the extent that it enables the state to pursue the interests of capital in general at the expense of particular capitals, it also enables it to damage the interests of capital in general. Accordingly, one must pay careful attention to the structurally inscribed strategic selectivity of the specific state forms and political regimes: and move away from the abstract, often essentialist theorization towards more detailed accounts of the interplay of social struggles and institutions' (Jessop, 2002: 41; see Martinez Lucio and MacKenzie, 2006, for a discussion).

None of the above denies the exploitative agendas of the state or capitalist systems of regulation, or their coercive dimensions in terms of surveillance and repression, but it does begin to establish a trajectory of study as to how the 'participative' processes within society may actually facilitate further capitalist development. Hence, when we refer to Marxism we see a very broad tradition and one which steadily engages with the regularity, longevity, and resilience of exploitative relations. One sees what Laclau and Mouffe (1985) consider to be a series of emergent projects where the political and ideological relations of society are related to capitalism in a more complex manner.

Academics and analysts of employment relations and participation have been influenced by such trajectories to varying degrees as the analysis below will demonstrate. They have dealt with issues of regulation and the role of participation through different views of capitalist interest (competing capitalist groups such as finance and industrial capitalism with the latter more likely to engage with labour agendas), political mediation (the effectiveness of trade unions, for example), state roles (the way the state can provide a social set of priorities for capitalist society), and regulatory systems (the way collective bargaining, for example, can alter the emphasis from economic to social priorities). Some see these as being relatively more autonomous of capitalist structures and ideology during particular moments than others. Some even see them as potential correctives for the nature of capitalism while others believe they are not, offering short term palliatives at very best. No discussion of Marxism or Marxist-inspired social analysis can proceed without an awareness of these debates and the differences they revealed within this tradition—however, the reality is that in many contemporary discussions of employment relation ill-informed caricatures of Marxism are increasingly common.

Hence, in terms of debates about participation, the issue of autonomy and position is central to the discussion of work and employment-related issues. In terms of industrial relations, the traditions discussed above inform various discussions. Hyman (1971) argued that Marxism was torn between optimistic and pessimistic approaches to questions of trade unionism and worker representation whether through representative organizations or vis-à-vis employers in the form of collective bargaining. For Allen (1966) collective bargaining almost became an end in itself for the trade union movement and its leadership. Clements (1977) and Clarke (1977) had similar reservations about unions being able to politicize and generalize the struggles around wages, although this pessimistic view of wage struggle and its potential for politicization is by no means shared (Kelly, 1988).

Given this, the focus of analysis in the 1970s and 1980s began to turn towards the workplace and to what is termed the labour process. These debates were concerned with Marx's notion of the transformation problem: that is to say, how bought labour could be transformed into performing labour. The initial debates in this area were influenced by the seminal work of Braverman (1974) who argued that in the context of industrial capitalism this transformation was enacted through various processes of managerial control. His focus was the Taylorization of work where direct forms of control derived from the separation of the conception of work from the execution of work. Increasingly management was concerned with the continuing division and fragmentation of labour. This would not just be pertinent to manufacturing but to white-collar work as well. In effect, we would see a major deskilling of labour. How is this relevant to our discussion? The first point is that within critical traditions the motives of management are not inspired necessarily by the 'softer', or more social aspects, of management strategy, such as participation. Second, the objective is to deskill the workforce and capture the knowledge of workers for the ends of capitalist development. This is what Thompson and Newsome (2004) consider the first and second wave of labour process theory (we will use and return to their metaphor of waves of labour process debate later on). However, these concerns and approaches shape many of the later waves. Other Labour Process theorists, such as Burawoy (1979, 1985), argued that such negative outcomes were not simply imposed from above by management but were the outcome of 'games' played and complex interactions between workers and managers. There is a political dimension in terms of production and there are coercive and consensus-based management approaches that can configure the quality of worker participation and limit its independent role. Friedman (1977) spoke of how managers were constantly shifting strategies between direct control and responsible autonomy: shaping and reshaping participation in relation to the balance of forces and the economic needs at any specific time. So participation varies in the extent to which it can be autonomous, and it is subject to control strategies and political forces at the (micro) workplace level.

Part of these early waves was a concern about autonomy and the extent to which workplace relations can have a greater autonomy from broader political, economic institutions and socio-economic relations. In effect, the issues of participation and control may be part of an ongoing re-establishing of boundaries and relations within a persistent antagonism between both sides of the employment relation which may not have a final resolution, either political or economic. Managers and workers will be tussling between modes of involvement (and forms of responsible autonomy) and modes of control (direct control in various guises) across time. Participation may be a game-like readjustment within the workplace.

The big question is to what extent this is the outcome of the socio-economic system, for instance, capitalism. According to Thompson (1990) the link between the labour process, class formation, and political transformation is not clear. It reflects the fact that struggles may be as much about resistance and defensive in orientation as they are about transformation and offensive in orientation (although the relation between these two is usually more symbiotic and complex than at first imagined so such a separation of levels maybe problematic). So the labour process needs to be understood as an arena in its own right which, while contextualized by capitalism and its employment relation, is not determined by it. The suggestion here is that all is not lost and the space for alternative configurations in the form of participation is broad. Hence, politically there may be forms of regulation which can correct the nature and extent of exploitation without transforming the nature of capitalist society. This autonomy of the labour process is important if we are to see how politics can create a basis for greater worker participation. It mirrors, theoretically, the argument by Edwards (1990) that the labour process is autonomous, even if it is fraught with tensions and antagonisms between workers and their managers.

The Levels and Politics of Participation: The Move from the Macro-Corporatism to Micro-Corporatism

One of the problems with the study of participation in the contemporary climate of Human Resource Management is the failure to locate participation within a broader framework and spectrum. The move to the micro, workplace level of participation has created among labour process theorists and specific streams of Marxist thought—not to say even 'mainstream' thinking—a tendency to downplay the role of other modes of participation and worker input into decision making. The withering of the political within HRM and the failure to discuss the state unless it is through the prism of the industrial relations, HRM interface (see Gregor Gall, Chapter 15) provides us with a particular template of analysis. Yet the Marxist variety of traditions has been concerned with three dimensions of worker participation vis-à-vis capital and the state.

The first tradition relates to the question of the state. In terms of participation the central aspect of the debate within political science has been the concern with corporatism and neo-corporatism. This discussion is by no means an exclusively Marxist construct (Lehmbruch, 1984; Schmitter, 1974). Such theorists argued that between the market and a state authoritarian approach there was an alternative mode of state intervention and representation in economic terms based on representing and involving socio-economic actors (normally labour and capital through their representative bodies). Schmitter (1974) spoke of state corporatism and societal corporatism. While corporatism tends to be associated with the dictatorial systems in Europe in 1930s Italy or in Spain from the 1940s to the 1970s (state corporatism), where the state determined who spoke on behalf of labour and capital within joint structures, it later became used as a term—'societal,' 'neo', or 'liberal' corporatism—to explain how governments consulted and involved trade unions and worker representatives within policy making and decision making. Trade unions would be consulted on employment relations issues, such as pay (where in some cases national organizations and governments would establish pay rates or increases at a national level as in countries such as Sweden) or on broader economic policy (as in Austria in the post-war period where trade unions and employer bodies were involved in consultations on economic policies) (Marin, 1990). Increasingly, the question of neo-corporatism is seen less in terms of strong structures of union participation at the level of the state, and more in terms of strategic initiatives which are flexible and tied around specific moments of restructuring and a concern with the supply side (see Jessop, 2002 for a critique). In recent years, this debate has mutated into a concern with the role of tripartite and union ventures into issues such as training and learning, with the model of labour involvement being focused on supply side agendas (Stuart, 2007).

The radical and Marxist position on such policies within Europe (especially Western European countries) during the 1970s and 1980s, focused on the motives and costs of such developments. Panitch (1981) argued that the main motive behind such macro-level strategies was the incorporation of labour into state and capitalist agendas at a time of crisis and wage-led inflation: and this is mirrored even at the time of writing this chapter with McIlroy's (2008) critique of union involvement in state policies of training in the UK. However, Panitch went on to argue that including trade unions within the state as a vehicle for controlling more radical or militant elements of the labour movement ran the risk of 'politicizing' the labour movement and industrial relations. Aspects of this argument were echoed by Hyman (1986) who pointed out that in the 1980s neo-corporatism became more a matter of dealing with the ongoing crisis within the modern and organized capitalist system. What emerges from such analyses is that the motives behind participation are often political and that participation may be used as a system of representation to emasculate the political potential and anti-capitalist sentiments of organized labour. However, such modes of participation can be unstable and can create a complex dialectical process as they empower labour in order to emasculate it—they create the basis and potential for instability.

Second, this state level of representation is paralleled by the development of regulation and participation through collective bargaining at the level of the industrial sector and the firm—especially the latter. The argument is that throughout the twentieth century in the United Kingdom, Western Europe, and the United States, the process of collective bargaining formed the most important basis for worker involvement through forms of bargaining on key working conditions between their agents (normally trade unions) and those of employers. The classical Marxist account of such forms of bargaining is that it was narrow in focus with a tendency to deal with particular aspects of the employment relation—thus it shifted attention away from broader political issues. Lenin spoke of workers developing a 'wage' or 'trade union' consciousness which was narrow and fragmented (Ehrenberg, 1983). According to Hyman (1971), this account is what underpins the pessimistic hypothesis and account of trade unions under capitalism. Positions within the Marxist traditions varied with some developing more instrumental approaches in terms of bargaining strategies and engaging with them, as with some of the Communist trade unions of Western Europe, and others from a more Anarcho-Syndicalist position seeing them as limiting the potential politics of industrial relations. Yet, there has always been a sanguine approach generally as to the ability of collective bargaining to act as a strong basis for worker participation within any form of capitalist system. Similar concerns were also developed with specific forms of industrial democracy and formal systems of co-opting workers into a role within corporate decision making as they were seen to incorporate labour within the agendas of capitalist corporations (Clarke, 1977).

However, during the 1980s the decline of labour representation and bargaining structures in the UK and US context led to a shift in the position of Marxists in relation to collective bargaining as a mode of representation. Concern with the impact of HRM-related modes of participation, such as quality circles, team working, and 'partnership' approaches (see Gregor Gall, Chapter 15), meant that traditional and independent collective bargaining could play a role for trade unions and workers in keeping the political and institutional boundary between labour and capital clear—collective bargaining became less of an issue of concern for Marxists in the light of an employer undermining of it in cases such as the United Kingdom and the United States. That collective bargaining became increasingly decentralized and reorganized around the local level (Katz, 1993), did not deter the argument that bargaining became an institution that could counter increasing change, fragmentation and individualization. Kelly (1996) began to see collective bargaining as a basis for militant as opposed to cooperative trade unionism which allowed the union to maintain an autonomous and independent agenda and set of structures. This is not an uncommon theme and concern—even among some classical pluralists and non-Marxists (Clegg, 1951). Yet in the context of what was perceived as a moment of industrial relations decline, bargaining as a mode of participation became a basis for maintaining effective influence by workers on the terms and conditions of their employment.

Hence third, this concern with defending bargaining as a way of regulating capital and maintaining worker representation in a more globalized and individualized system of capitalism comes in the wake of changes at the third level of worker participation; the workplace. These are dealt with in more detail later, but the main focus of Marxist concern is the way management develops systems of workplace representation that are seen to draw workers into the operational processes of the firm (Danford et al., 2005a,b; Garrahan and Stewart, 1992; Stewart and Wass, 1998). The argument is that workers are drawn into their own exploitation and into their control as groups and individuals through the mechanisms of new forms of workplace organization, such as team working. The focus of concern within radical circles is that the workplace is a terrain where many structures of representation, such as trade unions and collective bargaining, can be bypassed, exposing the individual to new forms of direct participation that are more concerned with economic/business issues than social issues in terms of employer interests. With the decline of state-level involvement for trade unions and bargaining roles in the UK and US the focus of analysis began to shift towards the study of workplace levels of participation and their potentially negative impact on workers. So when studying Marxist and Labour Process approaches we must appreciate that, while they can focus on various levels of the employment relation, the increasing reality is that the focus of the debate has moved onto the micro and workplace level.

Much of this critique has emerged due to the transmutation of social partnership and corporatist debate itself within pluralist and radical pluralist arenas within industrial relations: with the focus now being much more on the role of firm-level collaboration. For example, Haynes and Allen (2001) argued that social partnership represented one of the few alternative options for trade union survival and continuity in the context of a marketized system: a similar thesis was also forwarded by Ackers et al. (2005). Many have seen social partnership strategies as offering an important opportunity for a renewal of bargaining agendas and its content (Kochan and Osterman, 1994) and as an opportunity to rethink and revitalize forms of democratic participation in the firm (Ackers and Payne, 1998). This shift to the micro and the company level is therefore viewed in very different terms than the critical labour process perspective. It is seen in terms of political opportunity and choice, the realities of the context that exist for trade unions and the legacy of mutual gain and participation as a potential feature of industrial relations. On occasions in discussion between supporters and critics of social partnership it tends to oscillate into a binary and simple stand-off on the merits and demerits of it: whereby contextual issues are not taken into account (see Stuart and Martinez Lucio, 2005 for a review of these debates and their characteristics). Also much of this debate ignores the realities of non-union environments and the fact that dialogue can be structured in quite different ways in such contexts. Hence, much is debated in terms of a vision of industrial relations and work which has not been able to adapt to the changing nature of the employment relation and its complex individual and non-unionized collective characteristics. The legacy of the debates on corporatism whether Pluralist or Marxist continue to shape the way employment regulation are seen as when the debate focuses on micro level and fragmented features of the employment space.

PARTICIPATION AND LABOUR PROCESS DEBATES IN A CONTEXT OF CHANGE: THE FAILURE OF ALTERNATIVE MODELS

In terms of the critical discussions outlined above, the 1970s was not just focused on issues of worker control and resistance. Amnesia in personal terms is a common problem. It is also a problem in the academy. That discussion on forms of worker participation within industry and the workplace from critical, Marxist, and Labour Process perspectives is one that is a forgotten chapter, as far as much of the content of various leading conferences are concerned as we draw to the end of the 2000s. In the 1960s and 1970s two sets of discussions developed which involved a strong Marxist element. The first dealt with notions of worker participation in terms of co-operatives and worker-oriented organizations. Marx (1976: 449) was ambivalent about co-operatives. On the one hand, they showed workers could own and control their place of work; showing to all they could manage the workplace and provide an alternative approach to that of the 'master'. However, on the other hand, they were pockets of worker control within a context of capitalism and markets, which required greater political change and greater challenges to the social and political hierarchies that surrounded them to progress.

The extent to which workers owned or managed the organizations they worked in was a feature of discussion in the 1970s. There was also a range of debates on the way specific organizations had been subjected to worker intervention as an alternative to restructuring, as in the case of Cooley (1982). Workers and unions—alongside supportive experts—developed alternative views of production that permitted a more socially-oriented approach to the product and the way it was made. Yet a lack of supportive economic policies made such approaches vulnerable to the challenges of a capitalist and hostile context. The problem was that these were all islands of socialism in a sea of capitalism (Hyman, 1974).

In addition, there was the experience of Yugoslavia. While the memory of Communist Yugoslavia is currently linked to the tragic wars and ethnic tensions of the 1990s and beyond, this former country did consist of a model of workers' control which was highly elaborate and paid more attention to the voice of workers than most neighbouring Communist states (Warner, 1975). However, the problem of unclear lines between managers and unions, the lack of union autonomy, and the quite interventionist system of management structures were apparent (Warner, 1975). Hence, once more we see a relatively pessimistic and sanguine approach towards issues of control, participation, and worker representation within these alternative organizational configurations. Participation is constrained without genuine worker control, in terms of self-management committees, strategic worker ownership, and a greater say in questions of conception and not just execution, by developments at the macro, micro, and political levels.

These concerns played themselves out in terms of the great experiments of industrial democracy and worker participation in corporate decision making during the 1970s and early 1980s. Within Europe this was the age of industrial democracy—a range of proposals was developed that aimed to bring trade unions into the strategic decision-making processes of capitalism. In Sweden the attempt to develop Wage Earner Funds which would receive shares from the profits of firms and control them around regional funds, the development of worker directors on specific supervisory boards within larger German companies, and the proposals for worker directors through the Bullock Commission in the United Kingdom which led to an extensive experiment within the Post Office brought forth a wave of optimism regarding the influence workers would have through their representatives on the strategic decisions taken at the corporate level. In the case of Sweden, the Wage Earner Funds never developed as extensively as at first expected and in Britain employer opposition and the lack of preparedness of trade unions (Batstone et al., 1984) meant that the prospect of strong industrial democracy were soon dashed. Moreover, while in Germany trade unions did manage to locate themselves within various dimensions of strategic decision making, they were never in an imposing position. The European Union—the European Economic Community—would have to wait until the mid-1990s with the development of the European Works Council Directive to develop a semblance of trade union roles within transnational corporations and even then many question its systematic influence (Marginson and Hall, 2004; Wills 2004). The fate of industrial democracy as a higher social stage of capitalism has remained illusory. To this extent the failure of industrial relations regulation to deepen the political and institutional voice of workers within the firm paralleled the crisis, or lack of development and expansion, of the neo-corporatist model within Europe. The pessimists appear to have had their day within discussions on such topics although some would argue that a broader view of time frames and sensitivity to the links between different models of participation may allow for a slightly less pessimistic view (Martinez Lucio and Weston, 2007). Regardless of this, the emphasis was quickly turning to the micro level and the new deviancy of management within the workplace.

What one detects in this tradition is a concern with forms of involvement which are not fully supported and which are not located in an alternative political economy. However, the end of the 1970s and especially the 1980s gave rise to a new set of concerns in relation to the growing managerial emphasis on direct worker involvement at the micro level. The work of Harvie Ramsay (1977) was pivotal to the growing awareness of the politics of participation. His argument was that the relation between management and workers was antagonistic. He argued that one needed a longer term, historical view of worker participation within capitalism. At the heart of this was the tension between capital and labour, and the balance of forces between them. In moments of conflict and labour mobilization employers had no choice but to develop strategies of worker and trade union incorporation. The background of the 1960s and 1970s with their resurgent worker mobilizations and protests within Europe and the United States was a major factor in the attempts at industrial democracy and worker participation in the 1970s. Pateman (1970 quoted in Harley et al., 2005: 4) argued that the term participation was reclaimed by protest movements and the labour movement as a central demand in relation to the humanization of work. Participation was a terrain of engagement and in the 1970s it was labour who were articulating a broader project of emancipation through it.

Yet the project of emancipation through participation became more paradoxical (Harley et al., 2005: 12–13). Management began to respond to the need to address participation and began to reconstruct its image in a new and less collectivist manner. The 1980s and 1990s brought a new context of inward investment in the UK, a greater role for transnational corporations, and more managerial views of participation. The role of Japanese inward investors with their models of team working and quality circles (Stewart, 1996), the role of US investors with their non-union paternalistic models of individual participation, and the changing climate of industrial relations in the UK and US that saw a steady decline in the role of trade unions and collective bargaining systems (Katz, 1993), gave rise to a growing employer and management role in the balance of forces vis-à-vis labour.

CRITICAL VIEWS OF THE DIMENSIONS OF PARTICIPATION AS MODES OF CONFLICT

We can view these developments in another way and summarize the impact of such approaches on the way we view participation. What has emerged in the past twenty or so years is a view of participation in contemporary approaches to HRM that is concerned with the extent to which they undermine the autonomy of independent voice mechanisms. Participation is being remoulded managerially to undermine any autonomous and independent representative mechanisms and to tie them closer to the needs and agendas of capitalist organizations (Martinez Lucio and Simpson, 1992). The argument is that new modes of participation create spaces for involvement which are fragmented and disconnected from broader social and macro-oriented agendas. The foci of these new forms of involvement are now the corporate and production needs of the firm. This reflects a new micro-corporatism where the future of trade unions is tied to the future of the firm (Alonso, 1994). The end of participation is the economic and operational concerns of the firm as an economic and political unit.

This is reflected in the recent waves of Labour Process thinking: albeit without reference to the language of corporatism. Returning to the approach of Thompson and Newsome (2004), we have witnessed since the early 1990s a third and fourth wave of Labour Process theory drawing on the new dynamics of globalization and lean production: 'a wealth of qualitative research emerged illustrating the dark side of these lean production regimes. These accounts, heavily reliant on the control-resistance framework for their theoretical basis, reviewed these opportunities these new workplace regimes present to actively extend labour control … This evidence highlighted that, as a result, authority and real power move upward to management, whilst increased accountability and intensified work are forced downward to lower levels' (Thompson and Newsome, 2004: 147). This has led to a new fourth wave of research which has tried to reconnect concerns with the new labour process back into a broader picture of economic and industrial developments within global capital, and central to this is the context of greater performance measurement, increased emphasis on the outcomes of work and employment from an employer perspective, and the growing dominance of financial considerations (Thompson and Newsome, 2004).

The remoulding of participation is therefore central to these management-led endeavours. They occur in terms of various vectors. It is also essential for an understanding of the dynamics and dialectics of participation that we note the tensions in terms of vectors of analysis, such as the question of worker incorporation through indirect representation into capitalist interests, symbolic and cultural forms of participation, direct modes of participation that are workplace centred, and more individualized modes of participation. However, once these

---

Box 5.1 Dimensions and Vectors of Participation and Autonomy

Indirect Participation and Organizational Incorporation
Symbolic Participation and Cultural Incorporation
Direct Participation and Managerial and Operational Incorporation
The Individual and Participation and Social Exploitation
    However:
Agency and Participation as a New Space of Confrontation

Source: author

---

vectors are outlined we will endeavour to argue that the new language and processes of participation create new tensions and are not quite the new regimes of dominance they may at first appear to be.

The first vector is the renewed issue of trade union incorporation (Stuart and Martinez Lucio, 2005). The argument is at its most eloquent in what is denominated the University of West of England School which argues that in recent years we have seen a renewed interest in the language of partnership (Danford et al., 2005a, 2005b). This is not so much a social or macro-oriented partnership but one based on trade unions buying into the economic and business objectives of the firm in order to secure its role and a relative degree of influence within the firm. The argument is that new forms of social participation in terms of management–trade union relations in the form of partnership are imbalanced. They tie the trade union into a managerial agenda. Trade unions are allowed to play a role and represent the workforce so long as they can contribute to the value-added activities of the firm. In this respect, partnership is a legitimation device for securing managerial prerogative in a time of restructuring and change. Trade unions may have a role in this process and obtain some minimal social gains but ultimately it serves to close the debate within the workforce on alternative or distinct views of restructuring and change. Partnership agreements have been seen to be a feature of American and British industrial relations during the 1990s and 2000s. Critics, such as Beale (2005), Gall (2005), and Kelly (2004) have reinforced this concern with the way social partnership agreements commit trade unions to the restructuring of capital and compromise their autonomy and ability to respond more assertively to change. There is concern that such modes of involvement are built on confidentiality clauses with management, for example, which bind the trade union representatives in a firm or organization in terms of their ability to communicate or discuss sensitive issues with members. Moreover, they commit trade unions to working with management on issues thus creating the problem that they become, or are seen to become, a part of management. Kelly (1996) contrasts this with collective bargaining where unions are more independent of management by negotiating, but not implementing, decisions.

This responds to the historical concern of a school of thought within industrial relations that is both Marxist and non-Marxist, as in the case of Clegg (1951). Here unions are seen to be best serving members if they have a clear line of demarcation with management. Much may depend on the nature of regulation and the guarantees trade unions may have in terms of their role and independence (Martinez Lucio and Stuart, 2004): especially as in the United Kingdom partnership is normally an implicit or even explicit condition for an employer's recognition of a trade union within its workplaces which is not so much the case in most Western European countries. In fact, in the UK, new forms of involvement and communication are not always linked to trade unions in a strong and consistent manner in part due to the weak nature of regulation on the subject. A salient example of the disconnected nature of British strategies towards participation and consultation is the case of the new Information and Consultation agenda. The EU's Information and Consultation Directive of the late 1990s was actively opposed by the British New Labour Government due to the desire to revert to a softer form of regulation and to avoid stronger European variants (Taylor et al., 2007: 3). Hence, as the Directive was transposed it became watered down in the British context with management mediating its impact (Taylor et al, 2007: 4). In the course of their research Taylor et al. (2007) studied six cases in the UK—three of which were linked to the automobile industry. The study showed a poor record of participation on key restructuring issues—and a disconnection with traditional forms of trade union management relations:

This failure to consult raises wider questions about the wider political and legislative environment in the UK, where the law apparently allows companies peremptorily to make workers redundant ... Essentially, the Directive's transposition involved the 'de-Europeanization' of the idea of worker consultation. In continental Europe, the development of consultative structures (e.g. works councils) has represented the idea that labour rights, such as joining a union or being consulted and informed, are basic human rights and an extension of the principles of democracy. The UK's failure is ultimately a political failure as the government opposed in principle the ICE Directive and, under the impact of employers' influence, produced Regulations that significantly diluted what even in the original were hardly radical proposals.   (Taylor et al., 2007: 15)

This study mirrors many of the concerns in the UK about participation and consultation in industrial relations (Blyton and Turnbull, 2004; Marchington and Wilkinson, 2000). It also mirrors concerns with the role of similar modes of participation within transnational corporations in the form of European Works Councils (Ramsay, 1977; Wills, 2004). Overall the new collective modes of participation have been seen to be minimalist and unable to curb and limit management decision making—although the debate is quite varied (Fitzgerald, 2004).

   This use of new forms of indirect representation and more corporate-oriented participation in the form of partnership are seen to parallel—although not always link in with—new forms of symbolic participation. The question of participation is normally seen in institutional terms. That is to say it is seen as a series of processes which involve employees and workers directly or indirectly in decision making of one sort or another. However, participation is also symbolic in the sense that the interests and image of the worker are represented within the organization through a series of visual or abstract forms. This is nothing new but it is seen as an increasing feature of HRM. For example, companies in certain contexts conceive of the workforce and management forming part of a 'family' with shared interests and who associate with the ideals and symbols of a company (Oliver and Wilkinson, 1990). Whether this is merely rhetorical is a matter of much conjecture but there is an increasing interest in having the workforce represented in the communications and image of the firm, and vice-versa. However, any analysis of these phenomena requires an objective and less ethnic view of Japanese practices (Stewart, 1996). While not in a Marxist mould, but within a critical perspective, the work of Bacon and Storey (1996) argued that strategic HRM practices in some of the leading UK firms addressed and redefined the collective identity of the workforce through mechanisms, such as team working, management-led mass meetings, new forms of communication, and the development of mission statements and corporate values that place great store on the common interests of workers, managers, and owners. These new forms of corporate-oriented 'collective' modes of representation try to displace autonomous and independent collectivist forms (Martinez Lucio and Weston, 2002) and trade union engagement with them may actually serve to legitimate them and management's role within them (Stewart and Wass, 1998). They attempt to underpin new HRM modes of representation with an ideology and language which displaces antagonisms within the employment relation and reorganizes discussion in relation to competitor firms. Tension is thus a case of competition between firms and not conflict between classes (Alonso, 1994). Without this rhetoric and language it is difficult to mount the new forms of indirect participation, discussed earlier, in the form of partnership. The new forms are premised on a new vision of the employment relation as a mode of collaboration within the firm, not beyond it.

The third vector—and the most pivotal in terms of new forms of HRM—relates to direct forms of participation. Labour Process theory and studies in a variety of forms have focused on this aspect of contemporary participation which is viewed as a new mode of exploitation. The ironic twist in contemporary modes of management is that empowerment and involvement are deemed to be at the heart of new forms of exploitation. In *The Nissan Enigma*, Garrahan and Stewart (1992) described new management practices and focused on the way team working as inspired by Japanese models of management created a highly sophisticated system of control over workers. They argued that participation was underpinned by surveillance, peer pressure and competitive ideologies within the workplace. This set of arguments contrasted with those who argued that much depended on the type of teamwork and how it was regulated (Murakami, 1995) or developed within different economic, social, and cultural contexts (Mueller, 1994). Labour Process theory has engaged with such diversity but at the heart of critical debates is the fact that team working in recent times is less concerned with social interests and making work interesting and less fatiguing, despite the experiences in more 'progressive' firms such as Volvo (Hammarström and Lansbury, 1991) or the more regulated and union-led German context (Murakami, 1995). There was a new logic of transferring the burden of representation and control onto the shoulders of workers themselves within an environment of mutual worker vigilantism.

Hence, we begin to see the ironic inscription of the individual into their very own control. The final frontier for eroding autonomy within capitalism is to have the individual buy into their subjugation. This is the final sadistic turn in the age of Late Capitalism, the age of *self-harm* as the socio-economic system turns further inwards onto the body to extract ever more intense levels of worker activity and effort. Workers were seen to place themselves under pressure in certain circumstances— as in the case of Japan during the 1980s and 1990s—where they felt impelled to participate continuously in the providing of ideas and improvements through teams and suggestion schemes. The tying of performance-related pay and performance measurement to such processes can be seen to be propelling the workforce into 'doing' management's work and in effect becoming management albeit without the strategic and political role of senior managers (Danford, 2005a,b; Stewart, 2007). The workplace becomes a space where history, according to management, can be made and remade, where one's individual identity can be fulfilled and developed by participating, improving, and creating value (Stewart, 2006). Debates on stress in contemporary studies of work highlight the pressures that may emerge within regimes of TQM and new management practices. Social skills and communication skills are developed with the objective of enhancing participation as a means towards the end of greater productivity (Grugulis, 2007). In fact, the new regime of work is about creating for economic and not social purposes. A new functionalism prevails which reconfigures the dream of emancipation, and hence mutates it into a parody where the individual involves themselves in their own self-mutilation.

To say we are witnessing a 'dark side' of HRM is therefore a common feature of Labour Process theory (Thompson and Newsome, 2004). Yet it would be mislead-ing to see such developments as clear, linear, and inevitable. Labour Process theorists see such developments as a new arena of conflict and the basis for a new set of challenges. In part this is due to the outcomes we have described in terms of greater exploitation and control. There are new agendas of health and safety (Stewart, 1996, 2006). Questions of stress and physical integrity in the wake of greater control and performance have found themselves onto the agenda of industrial relations (Stewart, 2006). There is a curious opening in the way the materiality and physicality of work is now addressed and how trade unions may engage with such developments. Even within management circles the need to address the outcomes of new regimes of work are being addressed in a more open manner. However, there is also a new form of engagement and conflict within the process of participation and its new twists and turns. The way the use of quality management in the public sector provided a new terrain of engagement and difference within the workplace and organizational structures as stakeholders (unions, social groups, management, and others) battled it out to determine what it was the public wanted or what quality of service meant in reality (Kirkpatrick and Martinez Lucio, 1995; Martinez Lucio and MacKenzie, 1999). Struggles over quality of service have become linked with the quality of working life. In the workplace we have seen the meaning of flexibility and team working contested in many cases in terms of the way team rotation is decided, or how workers move between teams in order to deal with fatigue and monotony, and how participation is understood within teams (Martinez Lucio et al., 2000). In fact there is an argument that teamwork can create new common interests among employees that are critical and autonomous of management agendas given the supposed erosion of employee differences and hierarchies which have historically limited types of trade union solidarity (Blyton and Bacon, 1997).

This discussion informs us of *a new politics in participation*, and a new fragility within the new order of participation. In effect, agency is not eroded. That both Marxist and non-Marxist debates are identifying this means that we cannot reduce this solely to the political or theoretical dimensions of observers. However, what is seen to come of this may vary according to the perspectives of these observers with some seeing collective responses a more likely outcome (Stewart, 2006) while others see responses as more varied and fractured across different levels and actors (Clegg, 1994; Knights and Vurdubakis, 1994).

THE CONTRIBUTION OF MARXIST AND LABOUR PROCESS RESEARCH, AND THE CHALLENGE OF RENEWAL

Regardless of the depth and breadth of Marxist and Labour Process accounts, and regardless of different views regarding participation, there is a set of contributions that the Marxist and Labour Process accounts provide us with. They are empirical and analytical insights that go beyond just measuring participation and informing us as to its contingent aspect or that 'it does not always work'. They are insights that reveal the inbuilt tensions within the paradigm of participation and the development of participation in a capitalist context where ownership is not subject to any systematic social or political participation from workers. So how do these dimensions play themselves out in terms of the organization and management context?

The exposure of participation as *management rhetoric* is an important feature of these discussions. They point from within the critical perspective to a need for sanity in business schools and counterbalance to the more managerialist approaches to empowerment. They reveal the reality beneath the veil and the reality of organization. The critical and Marxist traditions reveal the nature of *management action* and how it is contextualized in terms of undermining collective mechanisms and independent voice. However, these traditions also reveal the *dialectics of participation* in terms of processes and outcomes. In terms of processes they draw attention to the degree of conflict and difference that exist in terms of the remit of participation and its interpretation, for example, the meaning of team working and the way workers have different understandings. They point to the way new forms of participation have been subjected to engagement in reality in terms of health and safety issues, the actual nature of influence, and the way they serve the customer or not. In fact, the terms in which participation and the outcomes of participation are studied by such observers is part of a 'menu' of new management practices that are more concerned with performance and productivity measures. They form a vital part of the new intensification of work and a new flexible internal and external labour market which is on capital's and not labour's terms.

The contribution of the Marxist debate has to be set alongside the challenges it is facing in dealing with the current context of change and the way in which the frame of analysis has been established. These provide us with the way the frame of analysis has shifted within Marxist and Labour Process debates. The current concern with participation has particular characteristics. The first is that the workplace is an obsessive focus within the Anglo-Saxon debate. The regulatory context and the political are engaged with less in such a context. Although many argue and remain insistent that 'better' systems of participation are usually tied together with a broader state and welfare perspective (Payne and Keep, 2005) this debate does not always connect with the workplace. This raises the issue that participation needs to reconsider a greater thematic link with the political in general and political science-based debates in particular. Another weakness is that the role of management as workers is not really discussed, and management is often seen as all empowered. The internal tensions around management and the exclusion of many tiers within decision making is not a central feature of the Labour Process debate. If anything, new modes of participation have an effect on locally-based and line-based management tiers. Klikauer (2007) is trying to open the debate regarding participation to a wider context by drawing on the Frankfurt School and the notion of the public domain within work. Using Habermas and related thinkers, he has begun a stream of discussion: he hopes that a dialogue about different notions of speech, discourse, and engagement may begin to emerge which sets the groundwork for an alternative engagement regarding 'public space' in the topic which is critical but which seeks viable alternatives. His argument is that labour must move away from instrumental communication and develop a new communicative rationality if it is to counter the greater colonization of the work sphere and its instrumentalization. This, presumably, requires a renewed discussion on not just the levels of participation and the relation between participants but on the principles and rights that underpin participation. This links back to our discussion of the way the alternatives discussed around industrial democracy and worker control in the 1970s marked a forgotten yet important moment in the discussion of participation (Hyman and Mason, 1995). If radical and critical debates do not do this we will remain encased in the agendas and practices that management set—critiquing in the absence of any alternative debate. In effect, we run the risk of our critiques mirroring the agendas of management in the way that 'alternative' debates on sexuality are shaped by the historic repression of sexuality they aim to remove (Foucault, 1979).

Autonomy is a pivotal issue and how it is constructed is important whether it is through separation and clear transactional relations, through bargaining and clear transactions, or through distinct ownership patterns. However, it is always felt that how the micro and macro relate to each other is a problem even in alternative modes of organization.

Issues of alternative combinations are less central to current discussions. Much of the debate is about the macro (regulatory or conflict-based) regulating the micro, or the eventual transformation of the nature of the relationship at the micro level. There is yet to be an agenda that ties together the different levels of regulation, participation and strategies that form the reality of the workplace through alternative views. In that respect, the managerialist HRM agenda has become uniquely hegemonic because it has set a debate in terms of the micro and operational dimensions at the expense of a broader social and political imagination.

REFERENCES

ACKERS, P. and PAYNE, J. (1998) 'British Trade Unions and Social Partnership: Rhetoric, Reality and Strategy', *International Journal of Human Resource Management*, 9(3): 529–50.
—— MARCHINGTON, M., WILKINSON, A., and DUNDON, T. (2005) 'Partnership and Voice, With or Without Unions', in M. Stuart and M. Martinez Lucio (eds), *Partnership and Modernisation in Employment Relations*, pp. 23–45. London: Routledge.
AGLIETTA, M. (1979) *A Theory of Capitalist Regulation*. London:Verso.
ALLEN, V. (1966) *Militant Unionism*. London: The Merlin Press Ltd.
ALONSO, L. E. (1994) 'Macro y microcorporatismo: las nuevas estrategias de la concertación social', *Revista Internacional de Sociología*, 8(9): 29–59.
ALTHUSSER, L. and BALIBAR, E. (1970) *Reading Capital*. London: NLB.
BACON, N. and STOREY, J. (1996) 'Individualism and Collectivism and the Changing Role of Trade Unions', in P. Ackers, C. Smith and P. Smith (eds), *The New Workplace and Trade Unionism*. London: Routledge.

BATSTONE, E., FERNER, A., and TERRY, M. (1984) *Consent and Efficiency*. Oxford: Blackwell.

BEALE, D. (2005) 'The Promotion and Prospects of Partnership at Inland Revenue: Employer and Union Hand in Hand?' in M. Stuart and M. Martinez Lucio (eds), *Partnership and Modernisation in Employment Relations*. London: Routledge.

BLYTON, P. and BACON, N. (1997) 'Recasting the Occupational Culture in Steel: Some Implications of Changing from Crews to Teams in the UK Steel Industry', *The Sociological Review*, 45(1): 79–101.

—— and TURNBULL, P. (2004) *The Dynamics of Employee Relations*. London: Macmillan.

BRAVERMAN, H. (1974) *Labour and Monopoly Capital*. New York: Monthly Review Press.

BURAWOY, M. (1979) *Manufacturing Consent: Changes in the Labour Process under Monopoly Capitalism*. Chicago: University of Chicago Press.

—— (1985) *The Politics of Production*. London: Verso.

CLARKE, T. (1977) 'Industrial Democracy: The Institutionalised Suppression of Industrial Conflict', in T. Clarke and L. Clements (eds), *Trade Unions under Capitalism*. Glasgow: Fontana.

CLEGG, H. A. (1951) *Industrial Democracy and Nationalization: A Study Prepared for the Fabian Society*. Oxford: Blackwell.

CLEGG, S. (1994) 'Power Relations and the Constitution of the Resistant Subject', in J. M. Jermier, D. Knights, and W. R. Nord (eds), *Resistance and Power*. London: Routledge.

CLEMENTS, L. (1977) 'Reference Groups and Trade Union Consciousness', in T. Clarke, and L. Clements (eds), *Trade Unions under Capitalism*. Glasgow: Fontana.

COLLINS, D. (1998) *Organizational Change: Sociological Perpsectives*. London: Routledge.

COOLEY, M. (1982) *Architect or Bee? The Human/Technology Relationship*. Boston: South End Press.

DANFORD, A. et al. (2005a) 'Employees' Experiences of Workplace Partnership in the Private and Public Sector', in M. Stuart and M. Martinez Lucio (eds), *Partnership and Modernisation in Employment Relations*. London: Routledge.

—— RICHARDSON, M., STEWART, P., TAILBY, S., and UPCHURCH, M. (2005b) *Partnership and the High Performance Workplace: Work and Employment Relations in the Aerospace Industry*. Basingstoke: Palgrave/Macmillan.

EDWARDS, P. K. (1990) 'Understanding Conflict in the Labour Process: The Logic and Autonomy of Struggle', in D. Knights and H. Wilmott (eds), *Labour Process Theory*. London: Macmillan.

EHRENBERG, J. (1983) 'Communists and Proletarians: Lenin on Consciousness and Spontaneity', *Studies in East European Thought*, 25(4): 285–306.

ENGELS, F. (1972 edition) *The Orgins of the Family, Private Property and the State*. New York: Pathfinder Press.

FITZGERALD, I. (2004) 'Introduction', in I. Fitzgerald and J. Stirling (eds), *European Works Councils: Pessimism of the Intellect, Optimism of the Will?* Routledge: London.

FOUCAULT, M. (1979) *The History of Sexuality*. London: Allen Unwin.

FRIEDMAN, A. (1977) *Industry and Labour*. Basingstoke: Macmillan.

GALL, G. (2005) 'Breaking With, and Breaking, "Partnership": The Case of the Postal Workers and Royal Mail in Britain', in M. Stuart and M. Martinez Lucio (eds), *Partnership and Modernisation in Employment Relations*. London: Routledge.

GARRAHAN, P. and STEWART, P. (1992) *The Nissan Enigma*. London: Mansell.

GRAMSCI, A. (1971) *Selections from the Prison Notebooks*. New York: International Publishers.

GRUGULIS, I. (2007) *Skills, Training and Human Resource Development*. London: Palgrave.

HAMMARSTRÖM, O. and LANSBURY, R. D. (1991) 'The Art of Building a Car: The Swedish Experience Re-examined', *New Technology, Work and Employment* 6(2): 85–90.

HARLEY, B., HYMAN, J., and THOMPSON, P. (2005) 'The Paradoxes of Participation', in B. Harley, J. Hyman, and P. Thompson (eds), *Participation and Democracy at Work: Essays in Honour of Harvie Ramsay*. London: Macmillan/Palgrave.

HAYNES, P. and ALLEN, M. (2001) 'Partnership as Union Strategy: A Preliminary Evaluation', *Employee Relations*, 23(2): 164–87.

HYMAN, J. and MASON, B. (1995) *Managing Employee Involvement and Participation*. London: Sage.

HYMAN, R. (1971) *Marxism and the Sociology of Trade Unionism*. London: Pluto.

——— (1974) 'Worhers Control and Revolutionary Theory', *Socialist Register*.

——— (1986) 'British Industrial Relations: The Limits of Corporatism', in O. Jacobi, B. Jessop, H. Kastendiek, and M. Regini (eds), *Economic Crisis, Trade Unions and the State*, pp. 79–104. London: Taylor and Frances.

JESSOP, B. (1990) *Theories of the Capitalist State*. Oxford: Polity.

——— (2002) *The Future of the Capitalist State*. Oxford: Polity.

KATZ, H. (1993) 'The Decentralization of Collective Bargaining', *Industrial and Labour Relations Review*, 47(1): 3–22.

KELLY, J. (1988) *Trade Unions and Socialist Politics*. London: Verso.

——— (1996) 'Union Militancy and Social Partnership', in P. Ackers, C. Smith, and P. Smith, (eds), *The New Workplace and Trade Unionism*. London: Routledge.

——— (2004) 'Social Partnership Agreements in Britain: Labor Cooperation and Compliance', *Industrial Relations*, 43(1): 267–92.

KIRKPATRICK, I. and MARTINEZ LUCIO, M. (1995) 'The Uses of "Quality" in the British Government's Reform of the Public Sector', in I. Kirkpatrick and M. M. Lucio (eds), *The Politics of Quality and the Management of Change in the Public Sector*. Routledge: London.

KLIKAUER, T. (2007) *Communication and Management at Work*. London: Palgrave.

KOCHAN, T. A. and OSTERMAN, T. A. (1994) *The Mutual Gains Enterprise: Forging a Winning Partnership among Labour, Management and Government*. Boston: Harvard University Press.

KNIGHTS, D. and VURDUBAKIS, R. (1994) 'Foucault, Power, Resistance and All That', in J. M. Jermier, D. Knights, and W. R. Nord (eds), *Resistance and Power*. London: Routledge.

LACLAU, E. (1977) *The Politics and Ideology in Marxist Theory*. London: Verso.

——— and MOUFFE, C. (1985) *Hegemony and Socialist Strategy*. London: Verso.

LEHMBRUCH, G. (1984) 'Corporatism in Decline?' in J. H. Goldthorpe (ed.), *Order and Conflict in Contemporary Capitalism*. Oxford: Clarendon.

——— (1917) *The State and Revolution* http://www.marxists.org/archive/lenin/works/1917/staterev/.

LENIN, V. I. (1961) 'On Strikes', in V. I. Lenin, *Collected Works*, vol. 4. London: Lawrence and Wishart.

MARCHINGTON, M. and WILKINSON, A. (2000) 'Direct Participation', in S. Bach and K. Sission (eds), *Personnel Management in Britain*. Oxford: Blackwell.

MARCUSE, H. (1964) *One-Dimensional Man: Studies in the Ideology of Advanced Industrial Society*. Boston: Beacon.

MARGINSON, P., HALL, M. J., Hoffman, A., and Muller, T. (2004) 'The Impact of European Works Councils on Management Decision-Making in UK- and US-based Multinationals: A Case Study Comparison', *British Journal of Industrial Relations*, 42: 209–33.

MARIN, B. (1990) *Generalized Political Exchange, Antagonistic Co-operation, and Integrated Policy Circuits.* Boulder, CO: Westview Press.

MARTINEZ LUCIO, M. and MACKENZIE, R. (1999) 'The Impact of Quality Management on Public Sector Industrial Relations', in S. Corby and G. White (eds), *Public Sector Employee Relations.* London: Routledge.

——— (2006) *Developments in Patterns of Regulation in Employment Relations: Re-appraising Views of the State in Industrial Relations Analysis.* Paper presented to the Conference Industrial Relations in the European Community 31 August to 2 September, Ljubljana Slovenia.

—— NOON, M. and JENKINS, S. (2000) 'The Flexible-Rigid Paradox of the Employment Relationship at Royal Mail', *British Journal of Industrial Relations*, June: 277–98.

—— and SIMPSON, D. (1992) 'Crisis and Discontinuity in Industrial Relations: The Rise of Human Resource Management and the Struggle over its Social Dimension', *International Journal of Human Resource Management*, September: 173–90.

—— and STUART, M. (2004) 'Swimming against the Tide: Social Partnership, Mutual Gains and the Revival of "Tired" HRM', *International Journal of Human Resource Management*, 15(2): 410–24.

—— and WESTON, S. (1992) 'The Politics and Complexity of Trade Union Responses to New Management Practices', *Human Resource Management Journal*, June: 77–91.

——— (2007) 'Preparing the Ground for a Social Europe? European Works Councils and European Regulatory Identity', in M. Whittall, H. Knudsen and F. Huijgen (eds), *Towards a European Labour Identity.* London: Taylor and Francis.

MARX, K. (1976) *Capital.* London: Penguin.

—— (2000) *Selected Writings*, (ed.) David McLellan. Oxford: OUP.

MCILROY, J. (2008) 'Ten Years of New Labour: Workplace Learning, Social Partnership and Union Revitalization in Britain', *British Journal of Industrial Relations*, 46(2): 283–313.

MUELLER, F. (1994) 'Teams between Hierarchy and Commitment: Change Strategies and the "Internal Environment"', *Journal of Management Studies*, 31(3): 383–404.

MÜLLER-JENTSCH, W. (2004) 'Theoretical Approaches to Industrial Relations', in B. E. KAUFMAN (ed.), *Theoretical Perspectives on Work and the Employment Relationship.* Illinois, IL: IIRA.

MURAKAMI, T. (1995) 'Introducing Teamworking—A Motor Case Study from Germany', *Industrial Relations Journal*, 26(4): 293–305.

OLIVER, N. and WILKINSON, B. (1990) *The Japanisation of British Industry.* Oxford: Blackwell.

PANITCH, L. (1981) 'Trade Unions and the Capitalist State', *New Left Review*, 125: 21–43.

PATEMAN, C. (1970) *Participation and Democratic Theory.* Cambridge: CUP.

PAYNE, J. and KEEP, E. (2005) 'Promoting Workplace Development', in B. Harley, J. Hyman, and P. Thompson (eds), *Participation and Democracy at Work: Essays in Honour of Harvie Ramsay.* London: Macmillan/Palgrave.

POULANTZAS, N. (1973) *Political Power and Social Classes.* London: NLB.

—— (1975) *Classes in Contemporary Capitalism.* London: NLB.

RAMSAY, H. (1977) 'Cycles of Control: Worker Participation in Sociological and Historical Perspective', *Industrial Relations Journal*, 28: 314–22.

SCHMITTER, P. (1974) 'Still the Century of Corporatism?' *Review of Politics*, 36(1): 85–131.

STEWART, P. (1996) 'Introduction', in P. Stewart (ed.), *Beyond Japanese Management: The End of Modern Times?* Aldershot: Frank Cass.

STEWART, P. (2006) 'Individualism and Collectivism in the Sociology of the Collective Worker', in L. E. Alonso and M. Martinez Lucio (eds), *Employment Relations in a Changing Society.* London: Palgrave.

—— and WASS, V. (1998) 'From "Embrace and Change" to "Engage and Change" Trade Union Renewal and New Management Strategies in the UK Automotive Industry?' *New Technology, Work and Employment,* 13(2): 77–93.

STUART, M. (2007) 'The Industrial Relations of Training and Learning', *European Journal of Industrial Relations,* 13(3): 269–80.

—— and MARTÍNEZ LUCIO, M. (2005) 'Partnership and the Modernisation of Employment Relations: An Introduction', in M. Stuart and M. Martinez Lucio (eds), *Partnership and the Modernisation of Employment Relations.* London: Routledge.

TAYLOR, P., BALDRY, C., DANFORD, A., and STEWART, R. (2007) ' "An umbrella full of holes?" Corporate Restructuring, Redundancy and the Effectiveness of ICE Regulations', International Industrial Relations Conference (Europe), September, Manchester, England.

THOMPSON, P. (1990) *The Nature of Work.* London: Macmillan.

—— and NEWSOME, K. (2004) 'Labour Process Theory, Work and the Employment Relation', in B. E. Kaufman (ed.), *Theoretical Perspectives on Work and the Employment Relationship* Illinois, IL: Cornell University Press.

TRAUB, R. (1978) 'Lenin and Taylor: The Fate of 'Scientific Management' in the (Early) Soviet Union', *Telos,* 37: 82–92.

WARNER, M. (1975) 'Whither Yugoslav Self-Management?', *Industrial Relations Journal,* 6(1): 65–72.

WILLS, J. (2004) 'Organising in the Global Economy: The Accor-IUF Trade Union Rights Agreement', in I. Fitzgerald and J. Stirling (eds), *European Works Councils: Pessimism of the Intellect, Optimism of the Will?* Routledge: London.

CHAPTER 6

AN ECONOMIC PERSPECTIVE ON EMPLOYEE PARTICIPATION

DAVID MARSDEN
ALMUDENA CAÑIBANO

INTRODUCTION

OVER the years, economists have looked at participation in organizations from a great many different angles, and to say that there is an 'economic approach' is a bold simplification. Nevertheless, there are certain strands running through the broad economics literature that distinguish it from the other disciplinary approaches. Following the editors' brief, we focus mainly on participation within organizations, and therefore leave out the extensive work on participation in the wider regulation of economic sectors and of the economy as a whole. We also take the employment relationship as the focus. In the path-breaking work of Coase (1937) and Simon (1951), the employment relationship is treated as a form of contractual framework in which workers agree to let managers direct their work within certain limits in exchange for their pay. Within this context, one can think of participation as an adaptation of the 'right to manage' form of the employment relationship according to which employees have varying degrees of input into decisions about work assignments and their coordination.

At a descriptive level, participatory forms are one of several possible ways of coordinating productive work within organizations. The debate among economists has tended to focus on the relative efficiency of different ways of organizing employment relationships. At one extreme, we have simple hierarchy, with management enjoying the full right to direct employees' work within a 'zone of acceptance', the range of tasks that employees agree falls within their respective jobs. At the other extreme, employees exert a very considerable degree of influence over their work priorities and enjoy a great deal of autonomy with regard to management over the timing and organization of their work.

Coase and Simon argue that firms have widely adopted the employment relationship in preference to other forms of contracting with those selling labour services because it is a more effective means of coordination under conditions of uncertainty about prices and about future labour needs. This highlights two of the key economic arguments concerning participation, namely information, because workers often understand better the details of their work than do their managers, and the necessary adaptation and renegotiation of job boundaries as organizational needs change, which are important because the right to manage is built upon a mutual and voluntary agreement when the employment relationship is entered into. The emphasis on coordination under conditions of uncertainty raises another set of issues that has received less attention within the economic approach, concerning the type of organizational architecture which provides the context for participation. Although Mintzberg may not spring to mind as a disciple of Coase and Simon, and probably not consider himself as such, his classification of organizational types presents a logical development of their work. Focusing on the contrast between simple hierarchy and full employee autonomy provides a rather limited two-dimensional view of participation which conceals many of its potential economic advantages. If the purpose of organizations is to coordinate human activity, then it follows that the constraints that this process has to obey will shape the design of employees' jobs. Mintzberg (1979) argues that organizations may coordinate the inputs or the outputs of work, and they may do so either *ex ante* by a process of standardization of routines and jobs, or *ex post* by an ongoing process 'mutual adjustment'. In a later section of this chapter, we argue that the spectrum between simple hierarchy and high autonomy assumes a different meaning depending on how organizations approach their coordination function.

At the centre of the argument in this chapter is the idea that the contribution of economic approaches to participation within organizations lies in their focus on the difficulties of coordination under conditions of uncertainty and limited information. Actors are subject to bounded rationality in the sense that their activities are mostly goal-oriented, an assumption shared by most economists as by Max Weber, but their calculative capacities are limited. In a world of perfect information and perfect markets, neither employment relationships nor employee participation are needed. Thus, the question arises as to how well different models of the employment relationship help to solve the resulting problems of coordination, and in so far as their solutions build on arrangements that endure over time, how these can be best adapted to changing needs.

In this chapter, we start with a brief historical overview of developments over the past forty years because it is useful to set theories in their wider historical context— why people posed the questions they did at a particular time. We then review a selection of the major theoretical approaches that illustrate the broad tent that encompasses the 'economic approach'. We then consider the diffusion and the ecology of participatory practices and how this has been interpreted. Next we present a partial survey of recent quantitative work on the performance effects of participatory practices updating that of Levine and Tyson (1990). Finally, we examine some of the conceptual problems posed by these studies before concluding.

BRIEF HISTORICAL OVERVIEW
OF THE DEBATE

In the 1960s and early 1970s, much of the work on participation focused less on its positive economic advantages than on the dysfunctional nature of what was commonly referred to as the bureaucratic model of blue- and white-collar work. 'Blue-collar blues' and 'white-collar woes' were two of the section headings of the US government task force report 'Work in America', published in 1973 (O'Toole, 1973). More educated workers with higher expectations were alienated by jobs that gave them little discretion and which were deprived of meaning because of the polarization between conception and execution. In France, the work of Georges Friedmann (1954), and his co-researchers, and in Scandinavia, the famous Swedish work organization experiments (Berggren, 1992), illustrate how widely the problem was perceived across the industrial world. From a narrowly economic point of view, worker alienation fed into reduced productivity because it was associated with high rates of absenteeism and labour turnover, worker discontent, and shop floor militancy. But it was also seen as harmful from the wider point of view of reduced worker and social well-being. The Work in America report highlighted also the cost of alienated work in terms of damage to physical and mental health, as well as its impact on women and minority workers.

Another element of the alienation and participation debate was to focus on the forms of spontaneous participation emerging from the shop floor, and threatening management control. In Britain, this was widely associated with the 'shop stewards' movement', but similar movements also took place in a number of continental European countries sparked by the Events of May 1968 in France and the Hot Autumn of 1969 in Italy (Spitaels, 1972). These 'bottom-up' movements revolved around what might be called the 'frontier of control', contesting the right to direct labour that management acquires through the employment contract, and offering a view of participation that revolves around joint decision making and negotiation.

By the late 1970s, a new theme was coming to the fore in terms of the positive benefits of employee voice for business performance. The argument was most prominently stated by Freeman and Medoff (1979, 1984) in the 'two faces of unionism', inspired by Hirschman's (1970) theory of 'exit, voice, and loyalty'. The two faces comprise one associated with zero-sum monopoly bargaining, long familiar to many economists, and one associated with a positive-sum interaction on account of the opportunities employee representatives provide for sharing information with management and which can lead to productivity improvements. Freeman and Medoff's paper stimulated a great deal of research on the effects of unions on various aspects of business performance, including productivity, labour turnover, absenteeism, and financial performance. By the time of Levine and Tyson's (1990) review, the evidence for positive productivity effects of employee participation was somewhat stronger than that for unions, although measurement problems and data limitations still leave much room for debate.

With the changing nature of modern economies, by the 1990s, two works stand out as signalling a new emphasis on participatory structures within organizations. Womack et al.'s (1990) account of lean production in the *Machine that changed the world* drew special attention to the innovations of Japanese lean production with its emphasis on devolving a number of decisions and responsibilities to shop floor workers and its use of team working. Participatory structures also attracted interest on account of the emerging knowledge economy, and the importance of 'know-ledge spillovers' as a source of growth for whole economies, and of competitive advantage for individual firms (Romer, 1994). Potential knowledge spillovers can play a key role both between and within organizations, and key questions concern the types of organizational arrangements that facilitate their use, and how far they are favoured by horizontal rather than vertical coordination mechanisms.

THEORIES LINKING PARTICIPATION TO PERFORMANCE

It has often been complained that the 'high-performance work system' models rely too heavily on empirical correlations and that there is little available theory to link participatory models to performance (Fleetwood and Hesketh, 2006). In fact, one can identify a large number or related theories, of which we give seven that are broadly-based on an economic approach.

Alienation

Although Blauner's 1960s classic study of alienation in modern American workplaces took its cue from Marx's early writings on wage labour, Adam Smith is also credited with a deep awareness of the limitations of his pin factory model of the division of labour. Excessive division of work tasks could harm workers' motivation and limit their ability to establish the social bonds in the workplace that can assist cooperation and productivity (Lamb, 1973). Setting his theory of moral sentiments alongside his wealth of nations has led many to question the status of the pin factory example: was it intended to stress the productivity of that kind of division of labour, or to illustrate a more general principle about the gains from specialization, skills, and productivity? Given the worker demotivation implicit in Blauner's (1964) account of alienation, where workers feel isolated, their gestures seem devoid of meaning to them, they have no influence over their work, and there is no scope for self-improvement, it is hard to envisage any other method of coordination succeeding than command and control. Following Smith's theory of moral sentiments, lack of scope for social interaction among workers in the pin factory would lead to a similar conclusion. The work process might function well until something goes wrong, but without the social bonds that support mutual adjustment, the solutions would depend on top-down interventions from management. Blauner's analysis in the US, like that of Touraine (1955, 1966) in France, supported an argument linking 'Taylorist' division of labour to certain economic dysfunctions by comparison with other models, notably craft organization, such as in contemporary printing, and in small batch manufacturing and semi-automated work places, such as in chemicals. While the human and social cost of alienation was reflected in dissatisfaction and illness, especially mental illness as observed by Work in America, the economic cost for the firm could be measured in absenteeism, turnover, and shop floor militancy, and their outcomes in terms of loss of productivity and product quality.

This led to a kind of negative case for increased employee participation: involving employees more in decisions relating to their work, and giving them enlarged and enriched jobs could help to mitigate the negative consequences of work in mass production. Perhaps because many economists lacked the necessary research skills, much of the running on the empirical side was made by work psychologists, a notable case represented by Hackman and Oldham's (1976) 'job characteristics model'. Their model reflects Blauner's analysis, arguing that skill variety, task identity, and task significance could enhance employees' experience of meaningfulness in their work, autonomy would counter the feeling of isolation and lack of influence, and feedback on the actual results of work activities would contribute to self-actualization through the knowledge of whether or not one has done a good job. In a wide-ranging review of 'before and after' studies applying this theory, Kelly (1992) found only modest support for the theory: job redesign increased job satisfaction, but it did not appear to raise motivation. Kelly's interpretation of this finding provides an interesting comment on the psychological approach. The omitted variable, so to speak, was the contractual nature of the employment relationship within which job redesign took place, or in terms of Marx's theory of alienation, the fact that labour services are bought and sold in a market relationship. Thus job enlargement and enrichment are always ambiguous, bringing scope for increased job satisfaction, but at the same time, enlarging the employee's productive obligations within the employment relationship. Thus, he showed that job performance improvements tended to occur either when the employer offered pay rises along with the job redesign, or when there were significant redundancies so that workers feared for their jobs.

Exit, Voice, and Productivity

Voice theories represent an alternative approach to examining the potentially positive effects of participation on productivity and other measures of organizational performance. Freeman and Medoff's (1979, 1984) landmark study adapted Hirschman's 'exit, voice, and loyalty' theory as a new starting point for looking at employee voice and productivity (Hirschman, 1970). Most organizations work well below their peak level of efficiency because of 'x-inefficiency' or 'organizational slack' (Liebenstein, 1966). Often, managers have difficulty obtaining the necessary information to improve efficiency levels because of information asymmetries between themselves and their subordinates. Workers often may not find it in their interest to share such information because managers may use it to retime their jobs, or even to make them redundant. In the long run, the resulting lower productivity will hold down the growth in wages, but if workers do not trust their employer to share productivity gains, there is little incentive for them to share information. Faced by depressed earnings with their current employers, workers may then quit, 'exit', to work for higher paying, higher-productivity firms, and in doing so, take the information with them. There might be other causes of efficiency loss, such as line manager incompetence or bullying behaviour whose resolution would benefit the organization if workers could inform other managers. Sharing ideas for improvements and expressing grievances to management facilitate the flow of information within organizations, and such 'voice' strategies can lead therefore to enhanced organizational performance.

'Voice' involves a prisoner's dilemma. Sharing information and sharing the productivity gains may be in everyone's interest, but the fear is that either side will take advantage of the other's weakness to pocket the lion's share of the gains. The risk is particularly great for workers because once the information is shared it cannot be withdrawn, and they have lost a vital resource in any power game. However, it could also run the other way if the employer makes initial concessions which are not reciprocated. Hence the argument for embedding information sharing within some kind of institutional framework which offers guarantees to both parties, such as formal participation schemes.

Freeman and Medoff introduce an additional argument for formalized employee voice in the workplace, namely, that individual voice may be inhibited by free-rider problems. This is particularly relevant for the kind of information that could cause the messenger to be perceived as a troublemaker, for example, if the line manager were incompetent or overbearing. In Freeman and Medoff's language, it is 'let Harry do it' while Tom and Dick keep their heads down. If Harry gets the grievance rectified, they all benefit, and if he gets marked as a troublemaker, Tom and Dick are still safe. Thus 'voice' could be stifled by a lack of protection for those exercising it. Hence, there is a second argument in favour of formal institutional arrangements to protect the exercise of voice. Although Freeman and Medoff's primary focus has been to explain the potential benefits of union representation, many of their voice arguments are of more general application, and have been widely used as a justification for participation.

Teams and Peer Group Monitoring

In their classic article on the theory of the firm, Alchian and Demsetz (1972) propose a theory of the firm based on the monitoring of effort by each party. Firms exist, they argue, because of the gains achieved by means of team production. However, in a world of selfish agents, these gains can only be realized if free-rider problems are overcome. In the example they give, loading a heavy object, it is the co-workers who can judge whether or not the others are lifting their share. What the firm provides is a contractual framework and an incentive structure to ensure that monitoring is carried out efficiently. They argue that a hierarchical structure will develop if specialist monitors, called managers, are more effective than team monitoring. The argument for the profit-oriented firm is that it is hard to monitor those entrusted with monitoring their co-workers, and so paying them the residual income after all costs have been deducted, that is profits, gives them an incentive to monitor effectively.

Whether or not hierarchical monitoring is more effective than peer monitoring depends heavily on the quality of the information on which it is to be based. Kolm (1969) illustrates the simplicity of the structure of information flows in a formal hierarchy compared with their multiplicity within a peer group in which each is monitoring the others. Thus if the relevant information can be simplified and codified, then a hierarchy will be more efficient in terms of costs and effectiveness than peer group monitoring. On the other hand, if the information is complex or strongly idiosyncratic, then peer monitoring may prove more advantageous. However, the effectiveness of peer monitoring may be constrained by group size. Williamson (1975) suggests that the motivation and the resources available are affected by group size. Bounded rationality means that above a certain group size, the monitoring of all by all becomes problematic, and if sanctioning free-riders is costly for the individuals doing it, the motivation to take them to task may also decline.

Peer group monitoring is a complex phenomenon. Although it may be in the interest of each individual to ensure there are no free-riders, the incentive to exert pressure must be sufficiently strong to overcome any reticence either to pressurize one's colleagues to work harder, or, more seriously, to 'snitch' on them to management. Williamson (1975) acknowledges the importance of atmosphere in work groups to their willingness to provide 'consummate' rather than 'perfunctory' performance. Although he does not set much store by 'trust' except as a mutual expectation about behaviour (Williamson, 1993), there is a fine line between enforcing cooperative behaviour within the group by informing management of a colleague's inadequate effort, and disloyal behaviour that would undermine teamwork. At what point do fellow team members interpret peer monitoring as opportunistic behaviour intended to curry favour with management at the expense of other group members? Some of the classic sociological studies of how work groups deal with 'rate busters' illustrate how the processes behind peer monitoring may cut both ways: to discourage 'shirking' but also to discourage actions that might undermine group performance norms (Burawoy, 1979; Dalton, 1948; Roy, 1955). This was echoed in a study of efficiency wages, Belman et al. (1992) found evidence of restriction of effort in workplaces with both cohesive work groups and unions. When the performance of individual workers depends on that of their peers, which is the whole point of Alchian and Demsetz's argument about the advantages of team production, then the group has powerful sanctions it can exert over members who deviate in either direction.

The question of peer group monitoring has returned to the fore in recent studies of incentive pay, notably, the use of team rewards and profit sharing. Using a data set that enabled them to measure peer monitoring, Freeman et al. (2008) argue that it may be one of the key factors behind the positive effect of group incentives on performance. They also found that peer monitoring but also peer group support were encouraged by group incentive pay.

'Frontiers of Control' and the Employment Relationship

Although not formalized into a testable theory, 'frontier of control' theories of participation have played a significant part in explaining persistent international differences in labour productivity. They lay behind two key drives for the reform of British employment legislation in the late 1960s and early 1970s. If Britain could develop legally binding collective agreements on the US model, then workflow management could be more predictable and less frequently interrupted by unofficial strikes, a view championed at that time in Britain by Professor Ben Roberts. There might be periodic set piece industrial conflicts, but in between contracts there would be none of the ongoing micro conflicts that were thought to have so damaged productivity in British plants. An alternative path was offered by the German experience of codetermination. It was argued that unlike the UK and US which had sought to combine the negotiation of change with pay bargaining in the form of productivity bargaining, the German model had in effect separated these two processes institutionally (Delamotte, 1971a). Unions and employer organizations could fight out the zero-sum battles over the distribution of the surplus in industry-level pay bargaining. However, the workplace was to be the locus for positive-sum negotiation between works' councillors and local management, from which the tactics of industrial warfare were banned for both parties: no strikes and no lockouts.

The term 'frontier of control' has a long radical history, as is shown by Hyman's (1975) Foreword to the reprinting of Goodrich's (1920) classic study of British workshop politics in the years up to 1920, and in similar studies such as that by Cole (1923). Nevertheless, it has its roots in the open-ended nature of the employment relationship and how the respective obligations of employee and employer are regulated. At its core lies management of the 'zone of acceptance', the range of tasks across which employees consent to management directing their labour, a concept that has played a key part for theorists ranging from Simon's (1951) formal theory of the employment relationship, to Rousseau's (1995) psychological contract theory. The recognition they all share is that the limits of the zone of acceptance will always include an important unwritten element. Even the most explicit employment contracts almost always contain a final catch-all clause to include any other duties as management may determine, the significance of which has been long recognized, as shown by Betters' (1931) historical study. Williamson (1975) shows that to specify these in a contract would involve multiple contingency clauses that would be far too costly to be workable for employment relationships. In other words, the zone of acceptance functions according to established practices of the workplace which emerge out of the day-to-day interaction between workers and their managers. Brown (1973) shows the central role of workplace custom which then spreads by means of equity arguments. Thus management errors of omission, for example, not enforcing a rule for one group of workers, become an argument for not applying it to others, on grounds of equity. Brown also shows how the politics of work group relationships, and the need to maintain a good bargaining relationship with management, determine which practices will become part of workplace custom and which will not. Thus, the scope of management's control over work assignments, and its application of workplace rules to regulate these, can be quite fluid. As new employees join the organization, these unwritten customs become for them the way their job is done in practice.

Writing about a period of very tight labour markets, and one in which the employment relationship was progressively displacing earlier forms of contracting for labour services, both Goodrich and especially Cole highlighted the phenomenon of 'creeping control' whereby the workforce eroded management's right to direct labour within this zone of acceptance. In doing so, they increased their own ability to regulate their work patterns and, in the process, obtain a more favourable wage–effort bargain. Goodrich's study sheds interesting light on the way the frontier of control is regulated, and the boundaries of jobs stabilized. Rather than seeking to codify the zone of acceptance, both parties sought agreement on the resources that they could bring to regulate the relationship and stabilize their bargaining power. Thus, the employers sought recognition in a number of landmark collective agreements in which unions recognized management's 'right to manage', separating the functions of managing employment contracts from coordination of the business. On the workers' side, Goodrich illustrates their moves to gain acceptance of regulatory principles that would enable them to keep to the spirit of the zone of acceptance they understood on joining the firm, in modern jargon, to reduce their exposure to post-contractual opportunism by the employer. Thus, insisting on the 'right to a trade' or occupation provides a guide to which tasks may be undertaken because of the processes and techniques learned during training. This is reinforced by control over a number of other key resources and activities that affect the bargaining power of both parties: hence, in his study, a focus on regulating discipline, dismissal, methods of payment, choice of supervisor, and so on. Apart from the first, none of these would determine directly the scope of a job, but each affects key resources in the implicit ongoing negotiation, and thus the ability of either party to enlarge or contract the range of tasks within the zone of acceptance, and to influence the procedures by which work is directed within this zone.

One factor helping to stabilize the zone of acceptance lies in the articulation between the institutions controlling these different resources, and limiting the degree to which they can be used in conjunction with each other. In an analysis of the systems of institutional participation in Britain, France, and Germany in the 1970s, one of the current authors showed that as a result of distributing the issues subject to employee influence across different bodies, each of which may have recourse to different types of sanctions, employees had acquired quite considerable degrees of voice over a range of issues whereas the process of incremental creeping control had been restricted. Thus, German works' councils gave German employees considerable voice over many aspects of their work organization, training, and jobs, but they were limited in how far these could be used in conjunction with wage bargaining and the rights to use the pressure tactics of industrial conflict which could be operated only outside the workplace at industry level (Marsden, 1978).

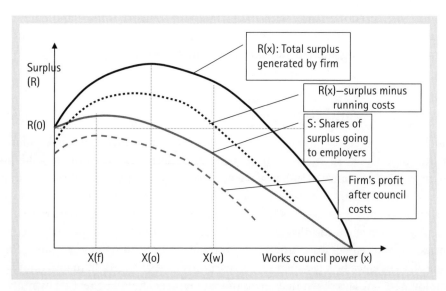

Figure 6.1 Freeman and Lazear's analysis of voice and power effects in participation

Similar arrangements applied in France, whereas in Britain the separation of powers was much less clear, and the frontier of control more fluid, a contributory factor to Britain's industrial productivity problems of that period.

One of the few attempts to formalize the division of functions between participation and bargaining activities was undertaken by Freeman and Lazear (1995) (see Figure 6.1). Their argument is based on the intuition that participation institutions require a certain amount of power before workers will share information with management without fearing that they are losing a vital resource in their power relations with management. However, as this power increases, so does the capacity to impede management's task of coordination. There is therefore a 'joint' or social optimum level of participation at X_o, which represents the maximum net gain from information sharing and efficient coordination for both parties as a whole. They also show how the employer's preferred level at X_f could be below this because as workers' power increases, so does their capacity to bargain for a larger share of the surplus (the workers' maximum absolute share is at X_w). If both parties were to negotiate their preferred levels of participation (between X_f and X_w), the resulting compromise could be below the socially optimum level, especially if the introduction of participation depends on the employer's initiative. Indeed, if they feared that employee powers would subsequently grow, they may well prefer to have no participation at all. Freeman and Lazear consider two possible solutions: legislation to compel both parties to move to the socially optimum level; and separation of the functions of productivity enhancing information sharing from bargaining over the division between wages and profits. They cite the German example in which works councils deal predominantly with the former and industry unions and employer organizations that negotiate over the latter. In this case, the two functions of information sharing and pay negotiation are institutionally separated.

Participation and Renegotiation

Much of the literature on participation focuses on teams and representative institutions which all involve an element of collective voice. This should not obscure the importance of individual employee voice in employment relationships once the relationship has been initiated. There is obviously scope for employee voice prior to hiring as the prospective employer and employee negotiate terms. Yet given the prevalence of long-term employment relationships in all major economies, there often comes a time when both parties need to revise the scope of the zone of acceptance because their respective needs have changed. In many countries, employment law lays down that terms of employment should be revised by mutual consent, but even under 'at will' regimes, where the employer may do this unilaterally, employers often choose to work by agreement in order to sustain employee motivation (Malcomson, 1997).

Economic contributions to our understanding of the process of renegotiating the zone of acceptance complement those from the psychological contract perspective (Conway and Briner, 2005). There has been considerable work at the aggregate level on the effects of different bargaining structures (Teulings and Hartog, 1998), but this also is beyond the scope of this chapter. There is, however, an important strand of thinking which can be traced back to the work of Walton and McKersie (1965) on different types of bargaining relationship, and notably, the contrast between 'distributive' bargaining where one party's gain is usually at the expense of the other, as in pay bargaining, and 'integrative' bargaining, where mutual gains may result, as in productivity bargaining.

Often the adaptation of the zone of acceptance conforms quite closely to the scope of integrative bargaining. A change in technology, organization methods, or just in job demands may take both parties beyond the understood zone of acceptance at the time of hiring. The employer could try to impose the change unilaterally, but with the risk that the discontented employee may leave, or stay on with reduced motivation. This may not be ideal for either party. On the other hand, the needed changes could be discussed. In an integrative negotiation, the aim is to find a mutually acceptable solution to a problem, which often requires give and take. Thus, to get the desired change, the employer may propose to alter the zone of acceptance in other areas that are favourable to the employee, or to provide organizational resources to make the employee's job easier. Often, employees fear that extending their job boundaries will lead to assignments which are beyond their competence, with the result that their performance would suffer incurring a loss of pay or worse.

For management to provide the necessary support, it needs to know the problem from the employee's perspective, so that information exchange is essential.

Team-level discussions with management provide one channel. Another potential channel which has been relatively under-explored from this perspective, is that of goal setting and performance appraisal, which have the potential to provide a forum for individual employee voice within long-term employment relationships. In their review of the work on goal setting and appraisal, Locke and Latham (2002) stress the importance of information exchange as one of the key benefits of participatory goal setting in which employees provide a significant input into the identification and choice of suitable performance objectives for their jobs. Marsden (2007) explores such ideas as a process of integrative negotiation using two illustrations based on the Centre for Economic Performance (CEP) research on performance-related pay. In the example of classroom teachers, altering the zone of acceptance meant shifting work priorities away from general educational goals towards an increased emphasis on pupil performance to help the school attract good applicants. The regular goal setting and appraisal process provided school managers with a forum in which these priorities could be discussed as well as measures of support that the school might give in order to assist their realization. The CEP research suggested that appraisal did not function in this way in all schools, but it appeared to do so in a significant and growing minority. In a second example, among non-medical hospital staff, the issue was to move the zone of acceptance in the direction of more flexible working time. In an example from another CEP project, a number of Royal Mail managers used return-to-work interviews as an opportunity to change hitherto tolerated absence patterns both by explaining the need for changed attendance patterns and where necessary by offering organizational support to assist the change (Marsden and Moriconi, 2009).

Although it has not been customary to think of goal setting and appraisal, and return-to-work interviews as forums for employee participation, their potential should not be underestimated. Integrative negotiation involves information exchange, and the search for solutions that take account of both parties' interests. With the steady decline of collective forms of employee voice in recent decades in many countries, the forums in which changing work obligations can be negotiated collectively have been reduced. Because work performance is strongly dependent on individual employees' perception of their bargain with the employer, such individual discussions can, but may not always, provide a framework within which it is possible to encourage individual employee voice in relation to mutual obligations framed by the zone of acceptance.

Organizational Structures and Participation

Some organizations coordinate activity by means of architectures which allow very little employee control, whereas others are designed to allow a great deal of autonomy. If we consider the way in which organizations fulfil their function of coordinating human activity, there are two basic principles (Lam, 2000; Mintzberg, 1979). When firms take over the role of coordinating activity from markets, they may do so either by specifying the inputs that employees are expected to provide, or they may specify their expected outputs. In the first case, managers are directly involved in designing the work processes and procedures employees should follow. To do this, they would require detailed information and knowledge about all aspects of the work involved. In the second, they focus on objectives, which, following Simon's perspective, economizes on the management knowledge required, but depends upon having appropriate incentives so that some key decisions about work organization are left to employees. The second principle relates to whether coordination is achieved by standardizing employee activities, whether inputs or outputs, or whether it is done by a process of mutual adjustment. Again, following Simon, standardization makes economic sense if demands are predictable to a large extent, whereas mutual adjustment of work roles and objectives is needed in more uncertain environments.

Combining these two principles, Lam and Mintzberg derive four organizational types: machine bureaucracy and professional bureaucracy, which respectively coordinate by standardizing inputs (work roles) or outputs (associated with different skills). Moving away from standardization, there are also two corresponding types of adhocracy, which use mutual adjustment: administrative adhocracy in which management determines the work roles, and operating adhocracy in which the focus is on coordinating outcomes or objectives. Following Lam's further development of the basic model, we can think of administrative adhocracy as illustrated by the 'J-form' (Japanese form) of organization, and operating adhocracy as the kind of very fluid work patterns found in research and development activities where the impossibility of predicting the sought for outcome with any precision means that work roles need to be highly adaptable.

In terms of the dimensions of employee participation, it is clear that these organizational models differ greatly with regard to job autonomy, job level decision making, as well as the scope of jobs and the capacity for employees to adjust them in the light of new information. Machine bureaucracy is perhaps closest to the model that preoccupied the writers on alienation in the 1960s being the one in which employees enjoy the lowest levels of job discretion. Operating adhocracy, on the other hand, would seem closest to the ideal against which machine bureaucracy was judged. One line of thinking on participation then is to seek ways of giving workers more control over work inputs, and lesser standardization of work roles, but while remaining within the same basic organizational model. Many of the classic studies and workplace experiments were set against the background of mass production systems in blue and white collar work (Berggren, 1992), as indeed are many of those reviewed below.

Broadening the issue by considering a wider range of organizational structures not only helps to put many of the participation initiatives and studies into perspective, but it also opens up another way of thinking about the economic arguments for its benefits, and about voice mechanisms and how they function. Mintzberg sought to link the choice of organizational types to the degree of uncertainty in the economic environment: standardization requires a stable environment so that economies of scale can be fully exploited. Research and development are highly uncertain environments both with regard to the product, which may fail technically, and its market demand which may not materialize. The implication is that the economic benefits of greater employee autonomy and decision making depend on informational factors and on environmental uncertainty. Hence firms may seek to adopt participation schemes within machine bureaucracies to mitigate their worst dysfunctions, but given the economic environment that led to the adoption of that model, there may be limited economic advantage for them to go further. In contrast, the structures based on mutual adjustment have many features of participation built into their architecture. Thus, administrative adhocracy, or J-form organizations, are built on the idea of fuzzy job boundaries, job rotation, and small group activities to solve problems as these are all activities that help to boost coordination by mutual adjustment—a process that requires a good deal of horizontal coordination.

Participation and the Knowledge Economy

Much of the early work on voice and participation was formulated in a static context. It is easy to imagine that gains from participation and knowledge sharing in 'mass production' were likely to show diminishing returns as production systems bedded down. Indeed, such factors could explain the short duration of quality circles that has been commonly observed in many Western organizations. However, in the knowledge economy, it has been argued that the returns to knowledge development are increasing, or at least continuous, rather than decreasing. This is one of the foundations of dynamic capabilities at the level of the firm (Dosi et al., 2001), and of 'endogenous growth' at that of an economy (Romer, 1994).

The role of participatory organization structures in knowledge development has been stressed for both blue collar and professional work. For the former, the argument has built on the idea that employees in all organizations have to deal from time to time with unusual and unanticipated operations. These give rise to opportunities for problem solving and learning. In traditional bureaucratic environments, such issues were often dealt with by technical experts, as was illustrated for French firms studied by Maurice, Sellier, and Silvestre (1986). In such cases, any learning that results remains in the possession of the managerial and technical hierarchy. In contrast, if such tasks are entrusted to intermediate level blue- and white-collar workers in participatory structures, then the learning occurs at this level and workers develop their diagnostic and intellectual skills, in addition to the practical ones directly related to their jobs (Koike, 2002; Koike and Inoki, 1990). On the basis of their case study comparison of plants with similar technologies in Japan and some other South-East Asian countries, Koike and Inoki argue that by engaging workers in these problem-solving activities and broadening their experience by job rotation, the Japanese plants were able to achieve higher levels of labour productivity.

Problem-solving activities and work group relations also played a critical part in Orr's (1996) study of Xerox photocopy engineers. Particularly important was the development of 'non-canonical' knowledge, the understanding of how the machines were used by clients as opposed to the 'canonical', codified knowledge of the repair manuals, and which the engineers shared among their teams by means of telling stories about different repair jobs they had undertaken (Brown and Duguid, 1991). According to the latter authors, the canonical knowledge was often organized in such a way that it directed attention away from the causes of malfunctions, and so impeded diagnosis and repair. Their account is consistent with Koike and Inoki's theory of skill and knowledge development out of unusual tasks, that is, the tasks that were not programmed by formal organizations. Likewise, in their study of New York traders, Beunza and Stark (2003) highlight the importance of lateral connections across organizational functions, in this case across different specialist trading desks, as a source of new knowledge and new opportunities for arbitrage.

In many respects, these examples underline the economic importance of Mintzberg's category of organizations based on 'adhocracy' and mutual adjustment rather than standardization, and of how important for certain types of economic activity it is to build participation into organization structures. Problem-solving activities appear to work best where information flows freely and work roles are fluid, and where unusual tasks can be turned into learning opportunities: in an adhocracy. However, which model a firm adopts may depend in part on how critical these are to provision of its key products and services.

DIFFUSION AND ORGANIZATIONAL ECOLOGY OF PARTICIPATORY PRACTICES

At the time of Levine and Tyson's (1990) survey, a major intellectual puzzle was how to reconcile the apparent economic benefits of participatory arrangements as shown by most of the studies they reviewed, and their limited diffusion in the United States, and a number of other advanced industrial economies. One argument that they advanced, as did other authors, such as Appelbaum and Batt (1994), was that participatory arrangements incur a high set-up cost for organizations with an uncertain economic return. To use the term of Bryson and Freeman (2008), they are high 'transaction cost' HR practices. There are several risks for lone innovators in an environment in which most firms use more traditional hierarchical methods. On seeing their investments in employee selection and training, competing firms may be tempted to poach their labour. Managers looking to other firms for their career advancement may wish to demonstrate their talents to potential future employers by pursuing more widely recognized criteria of success. Unions may be hostile, and employees with the experience of more traditional management methods may be suspicious of their current managers' motives when introducing participation. Such factors raise the cost of introducing participation, and so discourage innovator firms.

Nevertheless, after a slow start in the US and some other countries, work organization patterns that give more scope for employee participation have spread as shown by Osterman (2000), and in the EU, the European Working Conditions Survey (EWCS) shows a similar diffusion of team working and job-level participation practices. Nevertheless, the EU evidence also shows a great deal of diversity in the way these have been implemented. Lorenz and Valeyre (2005), using this survey, distinguish between job-level participatory structures that conform respectively to the 'lean' and the 'learning' models. In the former case, line management remains in close control, whereas in the latter, there is both more autonomy for team members and more scope is left in time management for employees to engage in problem solving and to learn on-the-job. Britain, Ireland, Spain, and to a lesser extent France, tended to follow the 'lean' model, and Germany and the Scandinavian countries, the 'learning' model. Linked to these country differences, Lorenz and Valeyre find differences in the strength of employment protection and vocational training both of which may provide platforms for capitalizing on learning opportunities, and national levels of R&D expenditures, their indicator of a knowledge-intensive economy.

EVIDENCE

In this section, we present an overview of recent empirical studies linking participation to performance which seeks to update that of Levine and Tyson (1990) (see Table 6.1). Our overview draws on a comprehensive sample of articles published in reputable refereed journals,[1] to render the task manageable and to assure quality. Other influential work published in books or any other kind of support was therefore excluded.

Following their example, we limit our coverage to quantitative studies. However, we introduce three main changes to their review. First, we decided to enlarge the range of performance measures considered, whereas their study focused on productivity effects. Indeed, most of the recent literature has analysed the effects of participation on a wide variety of performance measures, productivity being just one of many other indicators that ought to be taken into consideration. Hence, we added a column specifying the type of performance indicator based on two criteria: objectivity and type of outcome. With regard to the first, company performance can be objective, gauged from externally recorded and audited accounts, or subjective, based on the company respondent's perception. As for the type of outcome, we draw on Dyer and Reeves's (1995) differentiation between organizational and financial measures.

Second, we observed a tendency to homogenization of research strategies and methods, common to the general management literature (Scandura and Williams, 2000). This led us to omit the column named 'type of study', since most articles in our review would fit into the 'econometric' category.

Third, there has been a certain debate around the individual or complementary effects of new work practices, discussing whether they have a stronger impact when implemented as bundles (Green et al., 2006; Wood and DeMenezes, 2008). Therefore, we added a column that examines whether participation has been assessed in the study as an individual practice or as an element in a system of innovative work practices. More than 60 per cent of the articles applied the system's approach, supporting the complementarity or synergistic argument.

In consonance with Levine and Tyson (1990), articles were classified according to two key variables: type of participation (since representative participation was not studied in any of the articles, we only considered consultative, substantive and ownership participation) and effects of participation on performance. We encountered two main classification difficulties. On the one hand, the terminology on participation varies noticeably. We decided to include in the consultative category all practices labelled and described as *communication, information sharing, guidance, information meetings* or *grievance procedures.* Participation was considered substantive when portrayed as *empowerment, self-directed teams, employee autonomy, decentralized or participative decision making, work enrichment* or *job design.* Finally, ownership was associated with the terms *employee share options, employee ownership* and *employee stock ownership* and *financial participation.* When an article analyses the effects of several forms of participation, it is classified on the highest level of participation tested. However, following Levine and Tyson (1990) employee ownership is regarded individually no matter what other kinds of participation were included in the study.

On the other hand, with regard to the effect of participation on performance, in some articles the results obtained differed for different performance indicators, for instance, participation was positive for quality but negative or insignificant for profitability. In those cases, the article was categorized as 'inconclusive'. Huselid (1995) is an example of this problem. While being a seminal research piece and one of the most cited articles in the HRM literature, Huselid's results are different depending on the performance indicator considered. Whereas the practices labelled as 'employee motivation' (where participation is included) are positive and significantly related to productivity and Tobin's Q, they are negatively but non-significantly related to return on assets and turnover: therefore, Huselid (1995) is classified as 'inconclusive' in our table.

Several conclusions can be drawn from this table. To start, almost 80 per cent of the reviewed studies used subjective indicators of performance. For one thing, in the absence of independently sourced measures fitting the necessities of their research topic, researchers opt to use perceived indicators they can gather from respondents. Some highly-used databases, such as WERS, rely mainly on subjective measures. For another, there is evidence that objective and subjective measures are correlated and that their relationship to a wide range of independent variables is identical (Wall et al., 2004). In terms of level of outcomes, organizational measures are more commonly used than financial measures. This is consistent with the argument that participation and other HR practices have first an effect on indicators such as productivity, hence the space of time necessary to observe their relationship is shorter and less influenced by other parameters (Faems et al., 2005). Still, more than half of the articles we reviewed combine both methods in order to attain more powerful results. As far as the type of participation tested is concerned, we observe a prevalence of substantive participation. This goes in line with the above discussed theoretical issues, the higher the degree of worker involvement and influence, the greater the likelihood that those initiatives will have an influence on performance.

When compared to Levine and Tyson's (1990) table, the proportion of non-significant and inconclusive articles may be striking. This might be a consequence of the classification system explained above. Indeed, studies on the effects of participation are following the general trend in the management literature to use more than one outcome variable (Scandura and Williams, 2000). The increasing number of indicators utilized in the studies is therefore added to the usual measurement difficulties and the combination of both may be leading to inconclusive results. Although the search for more powerful results is commendable, the use of several performance indicators multiplies the number of causal relationships by which participation may influence performance. This question is familiar in the literature on union effects on performance: for example, unions may simultaneously raise performance through the beneficial effects of voice, but reduce profits by bargaining for a larger share of the surplus. Arguably, each of these relationships would need to be specified separately.

Another possible explanation to this lack of significance and conclusion relies on the movement towards institutional isomorphism, that is 'a constraining process that forces one unit in a population to resemble other units that face the same set of environmental conditions' (DiMaggio and Powell, 1983: 149). Management practices are institutionalized when organizations implement them insistently without clear indicators of their contribution to efficacy and efficiency (Tolbert and Zucker, 1983). It is conceivable that, initially, participation schemes were implemented because they reflected specific needs of the organization, and consequently had a real effect on its performance. However, once participation becomes a general practice that is required to attain social legitimacy, firms may introduce schemes without considering their true suitability to their needs, hence the increasingly common non-significant performance effect as it becomes more widespread.

Also noticeable is the increase of contingent and mediated models. Indeed, a growing number of papers are *opening the black box*, proposing the effects of participation on performance are moderated or mediated by other variables that had not been taken into consideration, such as technology (Larraza et al., 2006), organizational commitment (Paul and Anantharaman, 2003), or strategy (Guthrie et al., 2001).

Beyond the features captured in the table, this literature overview allowed us to identify certain interesting trends in the analysis of the effects of participation on performance. On the one hand, the studies have evolved in terms of their context and location. Whereas before 2000 most studies were undertaken in the US and the UK, lately the proportion of empirical work located in other geographical contexts has increased significantly. For instance, recent studies have been conducted in Europe, Asia, and Africa.[2] In general, the results of these studies indicate the importance of contextual factors, and so do not corroborate the idea that some human resource management practices may be universally applicable (Bjorkman and Xiucheng, 2002). Moreover, interest in sectors outside manufacturing has also increased in the last decade. Both services (Bartel, 2004; Paul and Anantharaman, 2003), and public services (Tessema and Soeters, 2006) have started to capture attention. However, an issue that does not seem to have evolved much is the continued focus on large firms. Indeed, small and medium enterprises remain somewhat neglected in this literature (Faems et al., 2005). The predominance of quantitative and cross-sectional studies over qualitative and longitudinal ones appears to be another structural characteristic of this literature. Even though the need for the latter two has been extensively claimed (Bjorkman and Xiucheng, 2002; Guest, 1997; Thompson, 2007) the difficulties of research access, particularly for longitudinal studies, seem to be delaying any progress.

On the other hand, few studies test explicit hypotheses directly derived from a theory. Indeed, following Fleetwood and Hesketh (2006) this field has to confront the problem of under-theorization and stop presuming that 'theory will emerge and develop via more, and/or better, empirical work'. Still, some conceptual frameworks are presented to explain the study's findings, as part of a general rationale. The resource-based view is certainly the most recurrent of those frameworks and states the firm is a bundle of distinctive resources that are key to developing competitive advantage, hence to increase performance (Barney, 1991; Wernerfelt, 1984). In this sense employees are considered as essential resources that need to be developed, protected, and maximally deployed. Nevertheless, the RBV, by its own description is a 'view' and not a theory, so it is difficult to derive precise, testable hypotheses. Although it has in recent years been associated more with a managerial than an economic perspective, yet it is related to economic approaches discussed in this chapter. Common themes include the individualization of the employment relationship, and the separation of human resource management performance enhancing practices from collective bargaining issues, which goes in line with Freeman and Lazear's study. Moreover, the RBV highlights the greater potential of intangible and knowledge-based resources in developing competitive advantage (Barney, 1991; Peteraf, 1993). A lot of these resources belong to employees and their tacit nature makes it difficult to exploit them without employee participation. As the 'exit, voice, and productivity' theory suggested, the organization can benefit greatly from the information obtained from employees. The RBV explains how firms that are able to acquire that information can gain a competitive advantage over their competitors, but it gives less attention to how to resolve some of the contractual difficulties inherent in the employment relationship, the conflicts of interest, and the problems of information sharing, and so on.

Over a decade ago, Guest (1997) stated theory should be reintroduced into the empirical debate in order to further develop the discipline. The theories linking participation and performance discussed in this chapter could certainly represent a contribution in that sense, providing future empirical studies with a more comprehensive framework of analysis. The increasing frequency of non-conclusive results as to the effect of participation on performance, suggests that improving empirical measures, for instance, additional performance measures, may not be the best route to more conclusive results. However, we find relevant the fact that the context in which the studies are undertaken is being taken into consideration. The introduction of variables, such as culture, institutional context, strategy, or sector may complicate the research design, but nevertheless move the field towards a better understanding of the relationship between participation and organizational performance.

Table 6.1 Recent studies of the performance effects of participation

Type of participation	Performance effects of participation											
	Positive			Non-significant or inconclusive			Contingent or mediated			Negative		
	Article	PI	Prac	Article	PI	Prac	Article	PI	Prac	Article	PI	Prac
Consultative	Apospori et al. (2008)	Sb / O,F	I	Bartel (2004)	Ob / F	I	Selvarajan et al. (2007)	Sb / F	S	Faems et al. (2005)	Ob / O,F	I
	Banker et al. (1996)	Ob / O	I	Chan et al. (2004)	Sb / O,F	S	Wright et al. (2003)	Ob / O,F	S			
	Björkman and Xiucheng (2002)	Sb / F	S	Gooderham et al. (2008)	Sb / F	I						
				Wood and DeMenezes (1998)	Ob,Sb /O,F	S						
	Michie and Sheehan (2005)	Ob/ O,F	I/S	Wood and DeMenezes (2008)	Ob, Sb / O	I/S						
Substantive	Ahmad and Schroeder (2003)	Sb / O	I	Bryson et al. (2005)	Sb / O,F	I	Datta et al. (2005)	Ob / O	S	McNabb and Whitfield (1997)	Sb / F	I
	Akhtar et al. (2008)	Sb / O,F	I	Cappelli and Neumark (2001)	Ob / O,F	I	Guerrero and Barraud (2004)	Ob,Sb /O,F	I/S			
	Arthur (1994)	Sb / O	S	Delaney and Huselid (1996)	Sb / O,F	I	Guthrie et al. (2002)	Sb / O	S			
	Bae and Lawler (2000)	Sb / O,F	S	Fey et al. (2000)	Sb / O,F	I	Hoque (1999)	Sb / O,F	S			
	Bae et al. (2003)	Sb / F	S	Fey and Björkman (2001)	Sb / O,F	I/S	Larraza et al. (2006)	Sb / O	S			
	Batt (2002)	Ob / O,F	I	Guest et al. (2003)	Ob,Sb /O,F	S	Ordiz and Fernández (2005)	Ob,Sb/ O,F	S			
	Horgan and Mühlau (2006)[3]	Sb / O	S	Harel and Tzafrir (1999)	Sb / O,F	I/S	Paul and Anantharaman (2003)	Sb / O,F	I			
	Ichniowski et al. (1997)	Ob/ O	S	Horgan and Mühlau (2006)	Sb / O	S	Vanderberg et al. (1999)	Ob / O,F	S			
	Katou and Budhwar (2006)	Sb / O	S	Huselid (1995)	Ob,Sb /O,F	S						
	Kaya (2006)	Sb / O,F	S	Huselid et al. (1997)	Ob / O,F	S						

Study	Indicators	Practices	Study	Indicators	Practices	Study	Indicators	Practices
MacDuffie (1995)	Ob, Sb/ O	I	Jayaram et al. (1999)	Sb / O	I	Faems et al. (2005)	Ob / O,F	I
Ordiz and Fernández (2005)	Ob,Sb/ O,F	S	Kalleberg and Moody (1994)	Sb / O,F	I			
Park et al. (2003)	Sb / O,F	S	Khatri (2000)	Sb / O,F	S			
Riordan et al. (2005)	Ob,Sb/ O,F	S	Orlitzky and Frenkel (2005)	Sb / O	S			
Vlachos (2008)	Sb / O,F	I	Ramsay et al. (2000)	Sb / O,F	S			
			Richard and Johnson (2001)	Ob,Sb /O,F	S			
			Tsai (2006)	Sb / O,F	I			
			Way (2002)	Ob / O	S			
			Wood et al. (2006)	Sb / O	I			
			Wright et al. (1999)	Ob / F	I			
			Zheng et al. (2006)	Sb / F	S	Guthrie et al. (2002)	Sb / O	S
Ownership Bae et al. (2003)	Sb / F	S	Wood and DeMenezes (1998)	Ob,Sb /O,F	S			
Gooderham et al. (2008)	Sb / F	I	Ramsay et al. (2000)	Sb / O,F	S			
Paul and Anantharaman (2003)	Sb / O,F	I						

Performance indicators: Ob: Objective; O: Organizational (absenteeism, turnover, quality, productivity, etc.); Sb: Subjective; F: Financial (sales, profits, share price, etc.).
Practices: I: Individual (the relationship between participation and performance has been directly analysed); S: Systems (participation is tested as a element of a system including other practices).

CONCLUSIONS

In this chapter, we consciously speak of economic approaches in the plural because it is misleading to force all the arguments covered in this short review into a single category. Concern about work organization and its effects has been a major issue within economics for a very long time. Lamb's (1973) study shows that Adam Smith himself was keenly aware of the two faces of the famous pin factory example. *Work in America* merely showed that 200 years later these tensions had still to be resolved. The approach of this chapter has been to look at participation against the canvas of the employment relationship, its organization, core processes, and their outcomes for organizational performance and social well-being.

Three key features differentiate these economic approaches from those of other disciplines: participation takes place within a market exchange relationship, in which there are simultaneously joint and diverging interests; the underlying contract is open-ended with regard to its content; and there are important information asymmetries inherent in that relationship. The open-ended nature of the employment relationship places the 'zone of acceptance' at its core, and participation can be understood as one of the processes by which the right to direct labour, the 'right to manage', is altered, and by which the zone itself may be adjusted from time to time. The more strongly the 'right to manage' is asserted, the more specialized managers become, and so the more acute are the problems of informational asymmetry. These can impede effective coordination, thus reducing organizational performance, and they may deprive management of sources of ideas for innovations. This said, these economic approaches need to be seen as complementary to other perspectives outlined in this volume.

There are many bridges to the other disciplines. Focusing on participation as a feature of the 'zone of acceptance' opens the way to considering how this is affected by other social processes, such as employment law, and employment relations. Legislation and collective agreements represent one type of channel which often implies a degree of compulsion. However, the institutional context may also affect the availability of alternative options for organizations. For example, if managers can dismiss employees easily, they may have less incentive to motivate them by means of interesting work—hence Lorenz and Valeyre's observation that the richer forms of participatory work organization were to be found in economies with stronger labour institutions. The behaviour of competitor firms may also affect the choices of individual firms, as Levine and Tyson, and Appelbaum and Batt observed, as poaching trained employees can undermine investments in employee participation programmes. The heritage of workplace relations can also affect the ability to develop participatory management. For reasons of low trust or adversarial relations, the zone of acceptance may have become very restricted in its scope, or rigid in relation to its boundaries. This could increase an organization's need for more participation, but it would also make it more difficult to operate. Similar factors could influence the degree to which peer group pressures operate to enhance or to restrict performance within work teams. The type of coordination system used by the organization can also be a significant factor, as suggested by Mintzberg's typology, although there are other typologies that could lead to the same conclusion. Much of the discussion of increased participation has taken place against a background of coordination strategies based on standardization and in which practices, such as team working, job rotation, and job discretion, are used in order to address problems of that approach. Yet in models that use mutual adjustment, these practices are often built into the organizational structure so that there is no need for special schemes.

One of the most striking findings of the survey of empirical studies included in this chapter is that it remains true that many more quantitative empirical studies show positive than negative effects of participation on organizational performance. Nevertheless, the picture is less clear-cut than it was at the time of Levine and Tyson's survey in 1990. This appears to be because of an increase in the studies counted as showing mixed or inconclusive results. There are several possible reasons for this. Some relate to measurement. Our survey includes a wider range of performance indicators than did Levine and Tyson, who focused on productivity. It is clear that the performance outcomes are sensitive to the type of measure chosen. Sometimes studies that show positive effects on productivity fail to show similar effects on financial performance measures. Another factor is that behind each process measure there can be big variations in design. For example, work on the British Workplace Employment Relations Survey shows that a measure, such as 'team working', may conceal great variations in team autonomy (Kersley et al., 2006: 90). Thus, changes in the mix of degrees of autonomy within the overall population of participation schemes could affect comparisons. Country coverage could also be a factor. Other factors which could account for less positive results this time concern the institutionalization of participation and its related practices as 'best practice', and in the types of organizations adopting them. All of these would caution against drawing strong conclusions from changes between the two surveys of studies. Nevertheless, the overall finding remains that quantitative empirical studies showing positive results continue to outnumber strongly those showing negative results.

Notes

The authors wish to thank the editors for their patience and encouragement throughout. The survey of recent studies on the effects of participation in The Evidence section is based on part of the doctoral thesis by Almudena Cañibano.

1. Journals included in the web of science. We covered major international journals known for their explicit HR focus (*Human Resource Management, International Journal of Human Resource Management, Personnel Psychology*), industrial relations journals (*Industrial Relations, British Journal of Industrial Relations*) and some general management journals in which relevant HR-related papers were likely to be found (*Academy of Management Journal, Academy of Management Review, Administrative Science Quarterly, Journal of Management, Journal of Management Studies, British Journal of Management*).

2. Greece (Apospori et al., 2008; Katou and Budhwar, 2006; Vlachos, 2008), Ireland and the Netherlands (Horgan and Muhlau, 2006), Spain (De Saa-Pérez and García-Falcón, 2002; Larraza et al., 2006), France (Guerrero and Barraud-Didier, 2004), Belgium (Faems et al., 2005), Eritrea (Ghebregiorgis and Karsten, 2007; Tessema and Soeters, 2006), The Philippines (Audea et al., 2005), India (Som, 2008), China (Ngo and Loi, 2008; Zheng et al., 2006), Pakistan (Khilji and Wang, 2006), etc.

3. Horgan and Mühlau (2006) test the same hypothesis for two different samples, one in Ireland and one in the Netherlands. The later showed a positive relationship between participation and performance, the former a non-significant one. Therefore, the article appears in both the positive and the non-significant table.

REFERENCES

AHMAD, S. and SCHROEDER, R. (2003) The impact of human resource management practices on operational performance: recognizing country and industry differences. *Journal of Operations Management*, 21: 19–43.

AKHTAR, S., DING, D., and GE, G. L. (2008) Strategic HRM practices and their impact on company performance in Chinese enterprises. *Human Resource Management*, 47(1): 15–32.

ALCHIAN, A. A. and DEMSETZ, H. (1972) Production, information costs, and economic organisation. *American Economic Review*, December: 777–95.

APOSPORI, E., NIKANDROU, I., BREWSTER, C., and PAPALEXANDRIS, N. (2008) HRM and organizational performance in Northern and Southern Europe. *The International Journal of Human Resource Management*, 19(7): 1187–207.

APPELBAUM, E. and BATT, R. (1994) *The new American workplace: transforming work systems in the United States*. Ithaca, NY: Cornell University Press.

ARTHUR, J. B. (1994) Effects of human resource systems on manufacturing performance and turnover. *Academy of Management Journal*, 37: 670–87.

AUDEA,T., TEO, S., and CRAWFORD, J. (2005) HRM professionals and their perceptions of HRM and firm performance in the Philippines. *International Journal of Human Resource Management*, 16(4): 532–52.

BAE, J., CHEN, S., DAVID T. W., LAWLER, J. J., and OCHIENG, F. (2003) Human resource strategy and firm performance in Pacific Rim countries. *The International Journal of Human Resource Management*, 14(8): 1308–32.

—— and LAWLER, J. J. (2000) Organizational and HRM strategies in Korea: impact on firm performance in an emerging economy. *Academy of Management Journal*, 43(3): 502–17.

BANKER, R. D., FIELD, J. M., SCHROEDER, R. G., and SINTIA, K. K. (1996) Impact of work teams on manufacturing performance: a longitudinal field study. *Academy of Management Journal*, 4(39): 867–91.

BARNEY, J. B. (1991) Firm resources and sustained competitive advantage. *Journal of Management*, 17(1): 99–120.

BARTEL, A. P. (2004) Human resource management and organizational performance: evidence from retail banking. *Industrial and Labor Relations Review*, 57(2): 198–203.

BATT, R. (2002) Managing customer services: human resource practices, quit rates and sales growth. *Academy of Management Journal*, 45(3): 587–97.

BELMAN, D., DRAGO, R., and WOODEN, M. (1992) Workgroups, efficiency wages and work effort. *Journal of Post-Keynesian Economics*, 14(4)summer: 497–521.

BERGGREN, C. (1992) *Alternatives to lean production: work organisation in the Swedish auto industry.* Ithaca, NY: ILR Press.

BETTERS, P. (1931) *The Personnel Classification Board: its history, activities and organisation.* Brookings Institution, Washington, DC.

BEUNZA, D. and STARK, D. (2003) The organization of responsiveness: innovation and recovery in the trading rooms of Lower Manhattan. *Socio-Economic Review*, 1(2): 135–64.

BJÖRKMAN, I. and XIUCHENG, F. (2002) Human resource management and the performance of Western firms in China. *The International Journal of Human Resource Management*, 13(6): 853–64.

BLAUNER, R. (1964) *Alienation and freedom: the factory worker and his industry.* Chicago: University of Chicago Press.

BOSELIE, P., PAAUWE, J., and JANSEN, P. (2001) Human resource management and performance: lessons from the Netherlands. *International Journal of Human Resource Management*, 12: 1107–25.

BROWN, J. S. and DUGUID, P. (1991) Organizational learning and communities-of-practice: toward a unified view of working, learning, and innovation. *Organization Science*, February, 2(1): 40–57.

BROWN, W. E. (1973) *Piecework bargaining.* London: Heinemann.

BRYSON, A., FORTH, J., and KIRBY, S. (2005) High-involvement management practices, trade union representation and workplace performance in Britain. *Scottish Journal of Political Economy*, 52(3): 451–94.

—— and FREEMAN, R. B. (2008) How does shared capitalism affect economic performance in the UK? CEP Discussion Paper 885, August. London: Centre for Economic Performance, London School of Economics.

BURAWOY, M. (1979) *Manufacturing consent: changes in the labor process under monopoly capitalism.* Chicago: University of Chicago Press.

CAPPELLI, P. and NEUMARK, P. (2001) Do 'high performance' work practices improve establishment-level outcomes? *Industrial and Labor Relations Review*, 54: 737–75.

CHAN, L., SHAFFER, M. A., and SNAPE, E. (2004) In search of sustained competitive advantage: the impact of organizational culture, competitive strategy and human resource management practices on firm performance. *The International Journal of Human Resource Management*, 15(1): 17–35.

COASE, R. H. (1937) The nature of the firm. *Economica*, November, 4(16): 386–405.

COLE, G. D. H. (1923) *Workshop organisation.* Oxford: Clarendon Press.

CONWAY, N. and BRINER, R. (2005) *Understanding psychological contracts at work: a critical evaluation of theory and research.* Oxford: Oxford University Press.

DALTON, M. (1948) The industrial 'rate buster': a characterisation. *Applied Anthropology*, Winter, pp. 5–18.

DATTA, D. P., GUTHRIE, J. P., and WRIGHT, P. M. (2005) Human resource management and labor productivity: does industry matter? *Academy of Management Journal*, 48(1): 135–45.

DELAMOTTE, Y. (1971a) British productivity agreements, German rationalisation agreements, and French employment security agreements. *Bulletin of the International Institute for Labour Studies*, pp. 30–44, ILO.

—— (1971b) *Les partenaires sociaux face aux problèmes de productivité et d'emploi.* Paris: OECD.

DELANEY, J. T. and HUSELID, M. A. (1996) The impact of human resource management practices on perceptions of organizational performance. *Academy of Management Journal*, 39(4): 949–69.

DE SAA-PEREZ, P. and GARCIA-FALCON, J. M. (2002) A resource-based view of human resource management and organizational capabilities development. *International Journal of Human Resource Management*, 13(1): 123–40.

DIMAGGIO, P. J. and POWELL, W. W. (1983) The iron cage revisited: institutional isomorphism and collective rationality in organizational fields. *American Sociological Review*, 48(2): 147–60.

Donovan (Chair) (1968) *Royal Commission on Trade Unions and Employers' Associations 1965–68.* Cmnd. 3623. London: HMSO.

DOSI, G., NELSON, R., and WINTER, S. (2001) *The nature and dynamics of organisation capabilities.* Oxford: Oxford University Press.

DYER, L. and REEVES, T. (1995). Human resource strategies and firm performance: what do we know and where do we need to go? *International Journal of Human Resource Management*, 6(3): 656–70.

FAEMS, D., SELS, L., DE WINNE, S., and MAES, J. (2005) The effect of individual HR domains on financial performance: evidence from Belgian small businesses. *The International Journal of Human Resource Management*, 16(5): 676–700.

FEY, C. F. and BJÖRKMAN, I. (2001) The effect of human resource management practices on MNC subsidiary performance in Russia. *Journal of International Business Studies*, 32(1): 59–76.

—— —— and PAVLOVSKAYA, A. (2000) The effect of human resource management practices on firm performance in Russia. *The International Journal of Human Resource Management*, 11(1): 1–18.

FLEETWOOD, S. and HESKETH, A. (2006) HRM-performance research: under-theorized and lacking explanatory power. *International Journal of Human Resource Management*, 17(12): 1977–993.

FORTH, J. and McNABB, R. (2008) Workplace performance: a comparison of subjective and objective measures in the 2004 Workplace Employment Relations Survey. *Industrial Relations Journal*, March, 39(2): 104–23.

FREEMAN, R., KRUSE, D., and BLASI, J. (2008) Worker responses to shirking under shared capitalism. *NBER Working Paper* no. 14227, August. Cambridge, MA: National Bureau of Economic Research.

—— and LAZEAR, E. (1995) An economic analysis of works councils, in J. Rogers and W. Streeck (eds), *Works Councils*, NBER, Chicago: University of Chicago Press.

—— and MEDOFF, J. (1979) The two faces of unionism. *Public Interest*, Fall(57): 69–93.

—— —— (1984) *What do unions do?* New York: Basic Books.

FRIEDMANN, G. (1954) *Problèmes humains du machinisme industriel.* Paris: Gallimard.

GHEBREGIORGIS, F. and KARSTEN, L. (2007) Human resource management and perform-ance in a developing country: the case of Eritrea. *International Journal of Human Resource Management*, 18(2): 312–32.

GOODERHAM, P., PARRY, E., and RINGDAL, K. (2008) The impact of bundles of strategic human resource management practices on the performance of European firms. *The International Journal of Human Resource Management*, 19(11): 2041–56.

GOODRICH, C. L. (1920) *The frontier of control: a study in British workshop politics.* London: Bell and Sons.

GREEN, K. W., WU, C., WHITTEN, D., and MEDLIN, B. (2006) The impact of strategic human resource management on firm performance and HR professionals' work attitude and work performance. *International Journal of Human Resource Management*, 17(4): 559–79.

GUERRERO, S. and BARRAUD-DIDIER, V. (2004) High-involvement practices and perform-ance of French firms. *The International Journal of Human Resource Management*, 15(8): 1408–23.

GUEST, D. E. (1997) Human resource management and performance: a review and research agenda. *The International Journal of Human Resource Management*, 8(3): 263–76.

—— MICHIE, J., CONWAY, N., and SHEEHAN, M. (2003) Human resource management and corporate performance in the UK. *British Journal of Industrial Relations*, June, 41(2): 291–314.

GUTHRIE, J. P., SPELL, C. S., and OCHOKI, R. (2002) Correlates and consequences of high involvement work practices: the role of competitive strategy. *The International Journal of Human Resource Management*, 13(1): 183–97.

HACKMAN, J. R. (1977) Work design, in J. R. Hackman and J. L. Suttle (eds), *Improving life at work.* (Reprinted in R. M, Steers and L. W. Porter (1991) pp. 418–43). Glenview, IL: Scott. Foresman.

—— and OLDHAM, G. (1976) Motivation through the design of work: test of a theory. *Organizational Behavior and Human Performance*, 16: 250–79.

HAREL, G. H. and TZAFRIR, S. S. (1999) The effect of human resource management practices on the perceptions of organizational and market performance of the firm. *Human Resource Management*, 38(3): 185–200.

HIRSCHMAN, A. O. (1970) *Exit, voice and loyalty: responses to decline in firms, organisations and states.* Cambridge, MA: Harvard University Press.

HOQUE, K. (1999) Human Resource Management and Performance in the UK Hotel Industry. *British Journal of Industrial Relations*, September, 37(3): 419–43.

HORGAN, J. and MHLAU, P. (2006) Human resource systems and employee performance in Ireland and the Netherlands: a test of the complementarity hypothesis. *The International Journal of Human Resource Management*, 17(3): 414–39.

HUSELID, M. (1995) The impact of human resource management practices on Turnover productivity, and corporate financial performance. *Academy of Management Journal*, 38: 673–703.

—— JACKSON, S. E., and SCHULER, R. S. (1997) Technical and strategic human resource management effectiveness as determinants of performance. *Academy of Management Journal*, 40: 171–88.

HYMAN, R. (1975) Foreword to the 1975 edition of CARTER L. GOODRICH (1920) *The frontier of control: a study in British workshop politics.* London: Bell and Sons; London: Pluto Press.

ICHNIOWSKI, C., SHAW, K., and PRENNSUCHI, G. (1997) The effects of human resource management practices on productivity: a study of steel finishing lines. *The American Economic Review*, 87(3): 291–313.

JAYARAM, J., DROGE, C., and VICKERY, S. K. (1999) The impact of human resource management practices on manufacturing performance. *Journal of Operations Management*, 18: 1–20.

KALLEBERG, A. L. and MOODY, J. W. (1994) Human resource management and organizational performance. *American Behavioral Scientist*, 37(7): 948–62.

KATOU, A. and BUDHWAR, P. S. (2006) Human resource management systems and organizational performance: a test of a mediating model in the Greek manufacturing context. *The International Journal of Human Resource Management*, 17(7): 1223–53.

KAYA, N. (2006) The impact of human resource management practices and corporate entrepreneurship on firm performance: evidence from Turkish firms. *The International Journal of Human Resource Management*, 17(12): 2074–90.

KELLY, J. (1992) Does job re-design theory explain job re-design outcomes? *Human Relations*, 45(8): 753–74.

KERSLEY, B., ALPIN, C., FORTH, J., BRYSON, A., BEWLEY, H., DIX, G., and OXENBRIDGE, S. (2006) *Inside the workplace: findings from the 2004 Workplace Employment Relations Survey*. London: Routledge.

KHATRI, N. (2000) Managing human resource for competitive advantage: a study of companies in Singapore. *The International Journal of Human Resource Management*, 11(2): 336–65.

KHILJI, S. and WANG, X. (2006) 'Intended' and 'implemented' HRM: the missing linchpin in strategic human resource management research. *International Journal of Human Resource Management*, 17(7): 1171–89.

KOIKE, K. (2002) Intellectual skills and competitive strength: is a radical change necessary? *Journal of Education and Work*, 15(4): 391–408.

—— and INOKI, T. (eds) (1990) *Skill formation in Japan and Southeast Asia*. Tokyo: University of Tokyo Press.

KOLM, S. C. (1969) Structuration informationnelle centralisée et hiérarchisée : une contribution à la théorie des organisations. *Revue Économique*, May, 20(3): 455–67.

LAM, A. (2000) Tacit knowledge, organizational learning and societal institutions: an integrated approach. *Organization Studies*, 21(3): 487–513.

LAMB, R. (1973) Adam Smith's concept of alienation. *Oxford Economic Papers*, July, 25(2): 275–85.

LARRAZA, M., URTASUN, A., and GARCÍA C. (2006) High-performance work systems and firms' operational performance: the moderating role of technology. *The International Journal of Human Resource Management*, 17(1): 70–85.

LEVINE D. I. and D'ANDREA TYSON, L. (1990) Participation, productivity, and the firm's environment, in A. S. Blinder (ed.), *Paying for productivity*, pp. 183–244. Washington, DC: Brookings Institution.

LIEBENSTEIN, H. (1966) Allocative efficiency vs. 'x-efficiency'. *American Economic Review*, June, 56(3): 392–415.

LOCKE, E. A. and LATHAM, G. P. (2002) Building a practically useful theory of goal setting and task motivation: a 35-year odyssey. *American Psychologist*, 57(9): 705–17.

LORENZ, E. and VALEYRE, A. (2005) Organisational innovation, human resource management and labour market structure: a comparaison of the EU-15. *Journal of Industrial Relations*, 47(4): 424–42.

LUPTON, T. (1963) *On the shop floor: two studies of workshop organisation and output*. Oxford: Pergamon Press.

MacDUFFIE, J. P. (1995) Human resource bundles and manufacturing performance: organizational logic and flexible production systems in the world auto industry. *Industrial and Labor Relations Review*, 48(2): 197–221.

MALCOMSON, J. M. (1997) Contracts, hold-up, and labor markets. *Journal of Economic Literature*, December, 35(4): 1916–57.

MARSDEN, D. W. (1978) *Industrial democracy and industrial control in West Germany, France and Great Britain*. Research Paper no. 4, London: Department of Employment (available online at *http://eprints.lse.ac.uk*).

—— (1999) *A theory of employment systems: micro-foundations of societal diversity*. Oxford: Oxford University Press.

—— (2007) Individual employee voice: renegotiation and performance management in public services. *International Journal of Human Resource Management*, July, 18(7): 1263–78.

—— and Moriconi, S. (2009) 'The Value of Rude Health: Employees' well-being, absence and workplace performance.' *Centre for Economic Performance, Discussion Paper #0919*, CEP, London School of Economics. *http://cep.lse.ac.uk/pubs/download/dp0919.pdf*

MAURICE, M., SELLIER, F., and SILVESTRE, J. J. (1986) *The social foundations of industrial power: a comparison of France and Germany*. Cambridge, MA: MIT Press.

McNABB, R. and WHITFIELD, K. (1997) Unions, flexibility, team working and financial performance. *Organization Studies*, 18(5): 821–938.

MICHIE, J. and SHEEHAN, M. (2005) Business strategy, human resources, labour market flexibility and competitive advantage. *The International Journal of Human Resource Management*, 16(3): 445–64.

MINTZBERG, H. (1979) *The structuring of organisations*. Englewood Cliffs, NJ: Prentice-Hall.

NGO, H. and LOI, R. (2008) Human resource flexibility, organizational culture and firm performance: an investigation of multinational firms in Hong Kong. *International Journal of Human Resource Management*, 19(9): 1654–66.

ORDIZ, M. and FERNÁNDEZ, E. (2005) Influence of the sector and the environment on human resource practices' effectiveness. *The International Journal of Human Resource Management*, 16(8): 1349–73.

ORLITZKY, M. and FRENKEL, S. J. (2005) Alternative pathways to high-performance workplaces. *The International Journal of Human Resource Management*, 16(8): 1325–48.

ORR, J. E. (1996) *Talking about machines: an ethnography of a modern job*. Ithaca, NY: ILR Press.

OSTERMAN, P. (2000) Work reorganization in an era of restructuring: trends in diffusion and effects on employee welfare. *Industrial and Labor Relations Review*, January, 53(2): 179–96.

O'TOOLE, J. (Chair: Special Task Force) (1973) *Work in America: report of a special task force to the Secretary of Health, Education and Welfare*. Cambridge, MA: MIT Press.

PARK, H. J., MITSUHASHI, H., FEY, C. F., and BJÖRKMAN, I. (2003) The effect of human resource management practices on Japanese MNC subsidiary performance: a partial mediating model. *The International Journal of Human Resource Management*, 14(8): 1391–406.

PAUL, A. K. and ANANTHARAMAN, R. N. (2003) Impact of people management practices on organizational performance: analysis of a causal model. *The International Journal of Human Resource Management,* 14(7): 1246–66.

PETERAF, M. A. (1993) The cornerstones of competitive advantage: a resourced-based view. *Strategic Management Journal,* 14(3): 179–91.

RAMSAY, H., SCHOLARIOS, D., and HARLEY, B. (2000) Employees and high-performance work systems: testing inside the black box. *British Journal of Industrial Relations,* 38(4): 501–31.

RICHARD, O. C. and JOHNSON, N. B. (2001) Strategic human resource management effectiveness and firm performance. *The International Journal of Human Resource Management,* 12(2): 299–310.

RIORDAN, C. M., VANDENBERG, R. J., and RICHARDSON, H. A. (2005) Employee involvement climate and organizational. *Human Resource Management,* 44(4): 471–88.

ROMER, P. (1994) The origins of endogenous growth. *Journal of Economic Perspectives,* winter, 8(1): 3–22.

ROUSSEAU, D. (1995) *Psychological contracts in organisations: understanding written and unwritten agreements.* Thousand Oaks, CA: Sage.

ROY, D. (1955) 'Efficiency' and 'the fix': informal intergroup relations in a piecework machine shop. *American Journal of Sociology,* 60: 255–66.

SCANDURA, T. A. and WILLIAMS, E. A. (2000) Research methodology in management: current practices, trends, and implications for future research. *Academy of Management Journal,* 43(6): 1248–64.

SELVARAJAN, T. T., RAMAMOORTHY, N., FLOOD, P. C., GUTHRIE, J. P., MACCURTAIN, S., and LIU, W. (2007) The role of human capital philosophy in promoting firm innovativeness and performance: test of a causal model. *The International Journal of Human Resource Management,* 18(8): 1456–70.

SIMON, H. A. (1951) A formal theory of the employment relationship. *Econometrica,* July, 19(3): 293–305.

SOM, A. (2008) Innovative human resource management and corporate performance in the context of economic liberalization in India. *International Journal of Human Resource Management,* 19(7): 1278–97.

SPITAELS, G. (ed.) (1972) *La crise des relations industrielles en Europe: diversité et unité, les réponses possibles.* Bruges: De Tempel.

TESSEMA, M. and SOETERS, J. (2006) Challenges and prospects of HRM in developing countries: testing the HRM-performance-link in Eritrean civil service. *International Journal of Human Resource Management,* 17(1): 1–20.

TEULINGS, C. and HARTOG, J. (1998) *Corporatism or competition? Labour contracts, institutions and wage structures in international comparison.* Cambridge: Cambridge University Press.

THOMPSON, M. (2007) Innovation in work practices: a practice perspective. *International Journal of Human Resource Management,* 18(7): 1298–1317.

TOLBERT, P. and ZUCKER, L. (1983) Institutional sources of change in the formal structure of organizations: the diffusion of civil service reform, 1880–1935. *Administrative Science Quarterly,* March, 28(1): 22–39.

TOURAINE, A. (1955) *L'évolution du travail ouvrier aux usines Renault.* Paris: Centre National de la Recherche Scientifique.

—— (1966) *La conscience ouvrière.* Paris: Seuil.

TSAI, C. (2006) High performance work systems and organizational performance: an empirical study of Taiwan's semiconductor design firms. *The International Journal of Human Resource Management*, 17(9): 1512–30.

VANDENBERG, R. J., RICHARDSON, H. A., and EASTMAN, L. J. (1999) The impact of High involvement work processes on organizational effectiveness: A second-order latent variable approach. *Group and Organization Management*, 24(3): 300–39.

VLACHOS, I. (2008) The effect of human resource practices on organizational performance: evidence from Greece. *The International Journal of Human Resource Management*, 19(1): 74–97.

WALL, T. D., MICHIE, J., PATTERSON, M., WOOD, S. J., CLEGG, C. W., and WEST, M. (2004) On the validity of subjective measures of company performance. *Personnel Psychology*, 57: 95–118.

WALTON, R. E. and MCKERSIE, R. B. (1965) *A behavioral theory of labour negotiations: an analysis of a social interaction system.* New York: McGraw-Hill.

WAY, S. A. (2002) High performance work systems and Intermediate indicators of firm performance within the US small business sector. *Journal of Management*, 28(6): 765–85.

WERNERFELT, B. (1984). A resource-based view of the firm. *Strategic Management Journal*, 5: 171–80.

WILLIAMSON, O. E. (1975) *Markets and hierarchies: analysis and antitrust implications.* New York: Free Press.

—— (1993) Calculativeness, trust, and economic organisation. *Journal of Law and Economics*, April, 36: 453–86.

WOMACK, J., JONES, D. T., and ROOS, D. (1990) *The machine that changed the world.* New York: Rawson Associates.

WOOD, S. and DE MENEZES, L. (2008) Comparing perspectives on high involvement management and organizational performance across the British economy. *The International Journal of Human Resource Management*, 19(4): 639–82.

—— —— (1998) High commitment management in the UK: evidence from the workplace industrial relations survey, and employers' manpower and skills practices survey. *Human Relations*, 51(4): 485–515.

—— HOLMAN, D., and STRIDE, C. (2006) Human resource management and performance in UK Call Centres. *British Journal of Industrial Relations*, 44(1): 99–124.

WRIGHT, P. M., GARDNER, T. M., and MOYNIHAN, L. M. (2003) Performance of business units. *Human Resource Management Journal*, 13(3): 21–36.

—— MCMAHAN, G. C., MCCORMICK, B., and SHERMAN, W. A. (1998) Strategy, Core Competence, and HR Involvement as determinants of HR Effectiveness and Refinery Performance. *The International Journal of Human Resource Management*, 37(1): 17–29.

ZHENG, C., MORRISON, M., and O'NEILL, G. (2006) An empirical study of high performance HRM practices in Chinese SMEs. *The International Journal of Human Resource Management*, 17(10): 1772–803.

PART III

FORMS OF PARTICIPATION IN PRACTICE

CHAPTER 7

DIRECT EMPLOYEE PARTICIPATION

ADRIAN WILKINSON
TONY DUNDON

INTRODUCTION

DIRECT employee participation has had a long history in management and industrial relations with various schemes and practices shaped by the different political, economic, and legal climates found in different countries. These climates also influence the demand (among employees and unions) for forms of participation in addition to the desire (by managers and employers) for the types of mechanisms used. In addition, the state has been a key player, both in its role as an employer and via its promotion of specific initiatives. Fad and fashions have been in evidence here as in other areas of management (Dietz et al., 2009; Dundon and Wilkinson, 2009).

However, we find that employers in different countries use the same terms for employee participation (engagement, voice, involvement, or empowerment) in different ways. Some forms of direct participation coexist and overlap with other techniques, such as suggestion schemes, quality circles, or consultative forums. In a European context, collective participation remains significant in certain countries, notably Germany and Sweden. A key issue is how direct and indirect participation coexist and the extent to which they complement or conflict with each other (Purcell and Georgiadis, 2006). The evolving regulatory frameworks add a new dimension to employee participation. Given the well documented decline in union voice, there is now greater interest in direct forms of participation (Marchington, 2006). Boxall et al. (2007: 215) report that:

Quality circles and other forms of small group problem solving have become commonplace in the Anglo-American world. These management driven forms of involvement are signed to serve employer goals of improved productivity and flexibility. However, our data suggests they increasingly meet the desire of workers to be involved in the things that relate most directly to them.

We organize our chapter in the following way. First, we define direct participation and consider the context in which participation has changed over time. Next, the issue of management choice over employee voice and participation is considered. We then review a framework against which to evaluate employee participation, and this is followed by an explanation of the types of schemes used in practice. Fourth is a consideration of the impacts on organizational performance and employee well-being that are often claimed to arise from employee participation. The chapter concludes by reviewing some of the current influences and policy choices in the area of direct employee participation.

Defining Direct Participation

Employee participation, involvement, and voice are somewhat elastic terms with considerable width in the range of definitions (see, for example, Dundon and Rollinson, 2004; Heller et al., 1998; Poole, 1986; Strauss, 2006; Wilkinson, 2002). The definitions may be as broad and all-inclusive as 'any form of delegation to or consultation with employees', or as narrow as a 'formal, ongoing structure of direct communications' such as through team briefing. Some authors refer to involvement as participation while others use empowerment, voice, or communications, often without extracting the conceptual meanings or differences that are used in practice (Parks, 1995). As Strauss (2006) points out, voice is a weaker term as it does not denote influence and may be no more than spitting in the wind. Equally, in one organization the term 'involvement' may be used to identify the same practice that another organization refers to as 'participatory'. Furthermore, in a single firm the labels used to describe a particular participation scheme may change over time and be rebranded as something new, while the structure and purpose of the mechanisms remains unchanged. As Gallie et al. (2001: 7) note, the literature on participation has rarely distinguished between the different forms that employee involvement in decision making could take. As a result, it is not easy to make precise comparisons about changes over time, and there are dangers that generalizations are made when in fact different practices are being compared (Marchington and Wilkinson, 2005).

We can try to make sense of the elasticity of the terms by seeing participation as an umbrella term covering all initiatives designed to engage employees. However, one can identify two rather different philosophies underlying participation (Wilkinson, 1998). First, the concept of industrial democracy (which draws from notions of industrial citizenship), sees participation as a fundamental democratic right for workers to extend a degree of control over managerial decision making in an organization. A prominent strand of the literature has its roots in notions of industrial citizenship and worker rights, and organizational democracy is a term widely used (Harrison and Freeman, 2004). This also brings in notions of free speech and human dignity (Budd, 2004). More recently this argument has been reframed in terms of stakeholders. Second, there is an argument around the economic efficiency model that suggests allowing employees an input into work and business decisions can help create better decisions and more understanding, and hence commitment (Boxall and Purcell, 2003).

Not surprisingly the picture is more complicated when we examine employee participation in international terms (Lansbury and Wailes, 2008). In European countries, for example, government policy and legislation provides for a statutory right to participation in certain areas, among both union and non-union establishments. In other countries, however, such as America or Australia, there is less emphasis on statutory provisions for employee involvement with a greater tendency to rely on the preferences of managers and unions, resulting in a mixed cocktail of direct and indirect participation in many organizations.

However, clearly much more important is what specific practices actually mean to the actors and whether such schemes can improve organizational effectiveness and employee well-being (Dundon et al., 2004). As this chapter is also concerned with clarifying what is meant by different participation schemes, we will evaluate the extent to which various practices allow workers to have a say in organizational decisions. At times the extent of such participation can be faddish and subject to managerial power; at other times it may be more extensive and embedded within an organization (Cox et al., 2006).

The Context for Direct Employee Participation

Employee participation has a long history in most Westernized economies (see Chapter 1). While we cannot assume that we have seen a simple development from command and control inspired by Taylor to the current emphasis on employee participation (Parks, 1995), a number of distinct phases can be traced in order to help place the role of participation in a contemporary context. The roots of modern participation can be seen in the Human Relations School in the 1940s and 1950s, although much of the emphasis was on groups and non-pecuniary rewards rather than specific schemes (Strauss, 2006: 780). The 1960s was often preoccupied with a search for job enrichment and enhanced worker motivation under a Quality of Working Life (QWL) banner. Managerial objectives tended to focus on employee skill acquisition and work enrichment. In the UK, examples at ICI and British Coal included semi-autonomous work groups to promote skill variety and job autonomy, inspired by the Tavistock Institute (Roeber, 1975; Trist et al., 1963). In practice, these schemes were more concerned with employee motivation as an outcome rather than as a mechanism that allowed workers to participate in organizational decisions. At the same time we saw an emphasis on power equalization and workers rights to participate (Strauss, 2006), which put more emphasis on representative bodies, such as codetermination in Germany and the abortive attempt to implement worker directors on the board of industry in the UK (Bullock, 1977).

From the 1980s and into the 1990s the context for participation changed significantly in Britain and the United States, with an approach driven from outside the formal institutions of industrial relations. The key agenda was business focused that stressed direct communications with individual employees which, in turn, marginalized trade union influence. This new wave of participation was neither interested in nor allowed employees to question managerial power (Marchington et al., 1992). In effect, this was a period of employee participation on management's terms in response to a concern with competition, especially Japanese production methods which spawned interest in TQM, Quality Circles, and Six Sigma (Wilkinson and Ackers, 1995).

The current business narrative is that organizations need to take the high road with high-value-added operations or be dragged down into competing for low-value-added jobs which are in danger of moving abroad (Handel and Levine, 2004). Organizations were encouraged to be flexible, innovative, and responsive, rather than seeking economies of scale through mass production (Piore and Sabel, 1983). The knowledge economy also provided impetus for involvement in decision making (Scarborough, 2003). These trends had implications for the management of employment and participation, in that compliance, hierarchy, and following rules were seen as less appropriate for modern employees. As Walton (1985: 76) put it, managers have 'begun to see that workers respond best—and most creatively—not when they are tightly controlled by management, placed in narrowly defined jobs, and treated like an unwelcome necessity, but instead when they are given broader responsibilities, encouraged to contribute, and helped to take satisfaction from their work'.

Many of the specific mechanisms to tap into such a labour resource became crystallized in models of high commitment management (Becker and Huselid, 2008; Huselid, 1995; Wright and Gardner, 2003), which emphasized the importance of employee participation to improve relations and increase organizational performance and profitability. As Strauss (2006: 778) observes it 'provides a win-win solution to a central organizational problem—how to satisfy workers' needs while simultaneously achieving organizational objectives'. However, in practice this is not always the case (Harley et al., 2005). There are also different perspectives in the literature, with one school of thought stressing the opportunities for involvement and worker discretion as a form of empowerment or as a human right, while others focus on tangible outcomes, such as skill acquisition or improved employee discretionary effort. The point is that discretion and participation may be of limited use if staff do not know how to use them (Wood and De Menezes, 2008).

MANAGEMENT CHOICE

The issue of employer choice has received surprisingly little attention in the existing employee involvement or voice literature (Purcell, 1995). One starting point is the concept of 'strategic choice'. Kochan et al. (1986) argues that the extent of organizational change has called into question traditional and institutionalized systems of management choice. In short, they suggest that managers are now the prime movers of organizational change despite the influence of other factors, such as labour and product markets.

There are three central tenants to the strategic choice model that apply to participation (see Figure 7.1). First, the ideologies of 'senior decision makers' either accord to a union or non-union system of employee voice. Second, these ideologies held by managers shape the type and nature of decisions made at a corporate (strategic), functional (line managers) and workplace (individual) level. The prevailing ideologies of managers can determine for instance whether employee participation will be direct and individual, or indirect and collective. Third, the choices management make then have implications (or 'outcomes') with regard to individual and organizational performance—such as lower levels of employee turnover or improved commitment and loyalty.

Much of the literature on strategy and choice tends to paint a top-down view of decision making, depicted in Table 7.1. A chief executive may design a new strategy on participation. The personnel director may decide what this strategy should look like (e.g., main components). Implementation may then be left to other managers

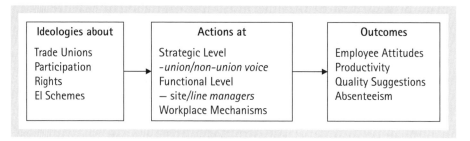

Figure 7.1 A strategic choice: a simplified specification

Source: Adapted from Godard (1997: 208).

and in turn the recipients of the policy will have some degree of choice as to how they operationalize and integrate different voice mechanisms.

However, this rational approach to choice, whereby the parties agree objectives, search for alternatives, evaluate, and then implement them tends to paint an over-simplified picture of the reality. Given that choice could encompass collective voice options, there is also likely to be tensions, as these incorporate additional layers of complexity that operate against the objectives of direct participation. Motivations for having collective voice (which can be union or non-union focused) may be different and indeed contradictory to those of direct employee participation channels. In practice, employer choice can be more 'political' which suggests that the top-down perspective often belies reality. Managers, supervisors and workers may themselves (in isolation of company policy) choose to institute and/or substitute voice through a personalized approach or due to historical legacies of custom and practice.

Overall, the idea of a simple model of managerial choice may not be so straightforward in reality. It is possible that regulatory rules and laws mean employers do things for the good of employees that they would otherwise neglect. Choice may also be constrained by management styles, worker or union actions, as well as the firms' cultural and historical legacies. But the roles of institutional, legal, and context-specific factors (e.g., labour and product markets and European directives) also seem important issues that tend to be neglected in the strategic, top-down view of employer choice. This leads to the possibility of *ad hoc* decisions or seemingly strategic choices that lack coherence.

Table 7.1 A top-down view of choice

1. Choice on Participation (Philosophy and Policy)	Board/MD/Union Negotiation
2. Choice on type of Participation mechanisms	Personnel/ Senior/Line Managers/Union Negotiation
3. Choice on method of implementation	Personnel/Senior/Line Managers
4. Choice on integrating Participation	Line Management/Employees/Union Reps

A Framework to Analyse Employee Participation

Given the issue with definitions and complexities that may surround employer choice for voice, we need a framework that can be used to analyse the extent to which various schemes genuinely allow employees to have a say in matters that affect them at work. What is important here is to be able to unpack the purpose, meaning, and subsequent impact of employee participation (Dundon et al., 2004). To this end a fourfold framework can be used: including the 'depth', 'level', 'scope', and 'form' of various participation schemes in actual practice (Dundon and Wilkinson, 2009; Marchington and Wilkinson, 2005).

First, the 'depth' to a direct participation scheme enables employees to have a say about organizational decisions (Marchington and Wilkinson, 2005). A greater depth may be evident when employees influence those decisions that are normally reserved for management (Dundon and Rollinson, 2004). The other end of the continuum may be a shallow depth, evident when employees are simply informed of the decisions management have made. Second is the 'level' at which participation takes place. This can be at a work group, department, plant, or corporate level. What is significant here is whether the schemes adopted by an organization actually take place at an appropriate managerial level. For example, involvement in a team meeting over future strategy would in most instances be inappropriate given that most team leaders would not have the authority to redesign organizational strategy. Third is the 'scope' of participation, that is, the topics on which employees can contribute. These range from relatively minor and insignificant matters, such as car parking spaces to more substantive issues, such as future investment strategies or plant relocation. Finally is the 'form' that participation takes. Direct employee participation, as noted earlier, has experienced a renewed focus since the 1980s and continued through the 1990s. Direct schemes typically include individual techniques, such as written and electronic communications, face-to-face meetings between managers and employees (e.g., quality circles or team briefing). Other forms of direct of participation are task-based (or problem solving) participation, where employees contribute directly to their job, either through focus groups, speak up programmes or suggestion schemes.

This framework allows for a more accurate description not only of the type of involvement and participation schemes in use, but the extent to which they may or may not engage employees (Marchington and Wilkinson, 2005). Figure 7.2 is more than a straightforward continuum from no involvement (information) to extensive worker participation (control). It illustrates the point that schemes can overlap and coexist. Central to this understanding of participation is power within the employment relationship, differentiated by the methods used (direct

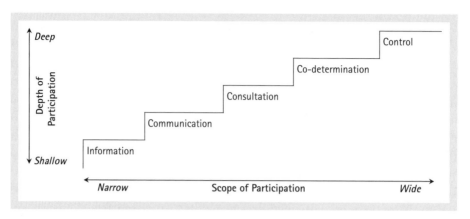

Figure 7.2 Escalator of employee participation

Source: Adapted from Marchington and Wilkinson, 2005.

or indirect classifications), the level at which participation takes place (individual to boardroom level), and the extent to which any particular technique is employee or management-centered.

Information Sharing

As noted earlier there has been a great deal of interest in recent years in management increasing downward communication to employees typically via newsletters, the management chain, or team briefing, which communicates organizational goals and the business position of the organization to 'win hearts and minds'. The logic here is that employees will be more understanding of the reasons for business decisions and as a result more committed to the organizations' action. Moreover, communication is direct to the workforce rather than being mediated by employee representation or trade unions. Thus, critics have argued that such schemes 'incorporate' workers and/or bypass trade unions (Ramsay, 1980). Clearly, communication in itself is a weak form of participation although communication practices vary in frequency and intensity. Some companies rely on their own internal newsletter to report a range of matters, from profits and new products to in-house welfare and employee development topics. More sophisticated techniques found by Marchington et al. (2001) included the use of electronic media, such as emails, company intranets, and senior management online discussion forums. However, concerns have been expressed with regard to how communication is used, in that the messages managers seek to communicate to workers may be used to reinforce managerial prerogatives. The way information is communicated can also be ineffective as many line managers responsible for disseminating corporate messages lack effective communication skills.

Upward Problem Solving

Upward problem-solving techniques seek to go further than communications by tapping into employee ideas for improvements. As with communication methods, problem-solving practices have increased, often inspired by Japanese work systems which encourage employees to offer ideas (Wilkinson et al., 1998). Upward problem-solving practices are designed to increase the stock of ideas available to management as well as encourage a more co-operative industrial relations climate. Specific techniques can range from employee suggestions schemes, focus groups, or quality circles to workforce attitude surveys (Wilkinson, 2002). The fundamental difference between these practices and communication methods is that they are upward (from employees to managers) rather than downward (managers disseminating information to workers).

At its simplest this may involve informing management of problems and letting them deal with it. A typical example in manufacturing would be workers having the ability to halt the line because of production problems. In the service industry, employees may be able to make customer-related decisions (often unanticipated) without seeking higher approval (e.g., replacing defective products), thereby indicating greater autonomy and responsibility at the point of production or service delivery. In relation to the framework for analysing employee participation shown earlier in Figure 7.2, it is clear that upward problem-solving techniques do offer a greater degree of depth than managerial communications. As Adler (1993a: 141) describes in his account of New United Motor Manufacturing Inc (NUMMI), 'the point is to get workers to participate in defining the standards and encourage them to constantly make suggestions to improve them'.

Voice Systems

Employee voice is the least precise of all participation mechanisms because in theory it can include all forms, both direct and indirect, in which employees have a say about matters that affect them at work (Boxall and Purcell, 2003). The best known explanation of the term voice goes back to Hirschman's (1970) classic work. However, Hirschman conceptualized 'voice' in a particular way and in a context of how organizations respond to decline and the term has been used in quite different contexts and applications elsewhere. His own definition was 'any attempt at all to change rather than to escape from an objectionable state of affairs' (Hirschman, 1970: 30). The point about voice is that its provision may secure general improvements. However, if exit is reduced this may force the discontented to take action within the organization, hence making voice more powerful.

Employees should have the opportunity to express their views and grievances openly and independently through a voice system rather than being able to raise only task-related problems. Of course 'voice' could be achieved through trade union organizations and collective bargaining, or through formally established grievance and disputes procedures, but non-union firms tend to favor direct participation through speak up schemes which offer employees protection if their complaints are not heard sympathetically as part of an alternative dispute resolution process (McCabe and Lewin, 1992). Dispute (grievance) procedures are sanctioned channels for employees to express discontent (Harlos, 2001: 326). They perform a number of functions to allow for employees to go above the immediate supervisor including counselling, investigation, conciliation, and feedback. Much of the available literature has looked at grievance systems and how these deal with collective agreement violation. Boroff and Lewin's (1997) analysis of survey responses from a non-union firm contradict the ideas of Hirschman and the findings of Freeman and Medoff. Examining those who indicated they had been subject to unfair work treatment, they reported that employee exercise of voice via grievance filing was positively-related to intent to leave, and loyalty was negatively-related to grievance filing. In short, loyal employees experiencing unfair treatment respond by suffering in silence. A study by Luchak (2003: 130) found that employees loyal to their organization are more likely to favour direct participation schemes, such as speak up programmes, than other employees who tend to be more calculative and use representative voice in the form of grievance filling.

Task Autonomy

Task autonomy is about allowing work groups a greater degree of control. It could be as simple as removing inspectors and getting workers to self-police or it could involve more significant restructuring of work units into cells (often around product flows) or the creation of semi-autonomous work groups, now commonly referred to as team working or self-managing teams. This differs from job rotation, enlargement, and enrichment in that the work group itself decides details of production and work group norms to a much larger extent than the former job restructuring schemes. Such teams can have autonomy, concerning task allocation and scheduling, monitoring of attendance, health and safety issues, the flow and pace of production, and can also be responsible for setting improvement targets (Wall and Martin, 1987). Teams can also have responsibility for the recruitment and training of temporary staff as well as controlling overtime levels. Developing a cell-base team structure is seen as helping communication, acceptance of change, and through peer pressure reduces the need for tight supervision and other forms of external control. Such groups can have what psychologists' term skill discretion (solving problems with the knowledge of the group) or means discretion (choice in organizing the means and tools of work)

(Cooper, 1973). These practices have a longer pedigree in seeking to counter the degradation of work and associated employee alienation (Proctor and Mueller, 2000), of which many schemes formed part of a series of work psychology experiments in the 1960s and 1970s (e.g., Tavistock Institute, QWL programs in the USA and Sweden). The criticisms levelled at task-participation are that outcomes often result in work intensification rather than job enrichment. Arguably, devolving more and more responsibilities to employees can increase stress levels. In other words, employees simply work harder rather than smarter (Delbridge et al., 1992).

Self-Management

This tends to be fairly rare in any real sense. Clearly self-managing work groups are a limited form of this approach, but are constrained by working within certain limits set by senior management (e.g., self-managing in relation to a set of work tasks). Ideally, self-management should involve divisions between managers and workers being eroded and decisions, rules, and executive authority no longer set by the few for the many (Semler, 1989). Bowen and Lawler (1992) refer to high involvement as a form of self-management participation, wherein business information is shared with workers and this affords employees the opportunity to have a say in wider business decisions.

Clearly the range and scope of direct participation mechanisms may overlap as many initiatives incorporate several similar features. For example, information is important to all forms of direct participation, not just as a separate mechanism in its own right. Some schemes are often unclear and ambiguous, ranging from the mechanistic descriptions of structures and procedures, to more organic techniques that shape attitudes and behaviours. Other mechanisms limit participation to formal institutions and procedures, such as memos, newsletters, or upward problem-solving methods, while day-to-day interactions between employee and management may engender more informal dimensions to participation, particularly within the smaller workplace devoid of many formalized HR systems (Wilkinson et al., 2007). At the same time, there are questions about whether or not informality can survive as a viable mechanism for independent employee participation in the absence of formal structures, especially if market conditions or senior management philosophies change (Wilkinson et al., 2004).

As we have noted, the use of various employee participatory initiatives intensified during the latter part of the 1980s and appears to have become more embedded and integrated with organizational practice during the 1990s. Marchington uses the term voice systems to suggest a certain overall coherence (Marchington, 2008), although we also need to know what different mechanisms mean in practice and what impact they have on organizational stakeholders, which is addressed next.

THE PRACTICE AND IMPACT OF DIRECT PARTICIPATION

There has been considerable criticism of the transformation thesis implying a shift from Fordism to Post-Fordism. It has been pointed out that the pursuit of flexibility has not led to widespread multi-skilling and indeed reflects sectoral change and opportunism rather than strategic choice. Lean production, as implemented, has strong elements of continuity with Taylorism. Nor has high trust relations appeared to be any more widespread than in previous times, with commitment largely calculative rather than employees working beyond contract or going the extra mile. Several studies seek to examine the impact of people management practices—which incorporate employee participation and voice—on organizational performance and employee well-being (Becker and Huselid, 1998; Dietz et al., 2009; Handel and Levine, 2004; Huselid, 1995; Locke and Schweiger, 1979; Miller and Monge, 1986; Wagner, 1994).

However, the extrapolation of survey evidence about the use of various involvement and participation schemes in many studies tells us very little about the impact or extensiveness of such techniques within a particular organization (Cox et al., 2006; Marchington, 2005). The ambiguity and lack of clarity about particular schemes is evident in relation to the impact such techniques are claimed to have on enhanced organizational performance (Dundon et al., 2004). First, it is difficult to isolate the cause and effect and demonstrate that participation can lead to better organizational performance given the whole range of other contextual influences. For example, labour turnover is likely to be influenced by the availability of other jobs, by relative pay levels, and by the presence, absence, or depth of particular participation schemes. Second is the unease associated with the reference to benchmarking: of assessing the date at which to start making 'before and after' comparisons. Should this be the date at which the new participative mechanisms (i.e., a quality circle or consultative committee) is actually introduced into the organization, or should it be some earlier or later date? For example, the claim that a quality circle saves money through a new work practice does not take into account that such ideas may have previously been channelled through a different route. This also leads on to a third concern, that of evaluating the so-called impact and on whose terms. Should assessments be made in relation to workers having some say (i.e., the process) or in terms of how things may be changed due to participation (i.e., the outcomes)? If it is the latter, then who gains? It remains the case that it is usually managers who decide what involvement and/or participation schemes to employ, at what level, depth, and over what issues (Wilkinson et al., 2004).

Clearly, effectiveness can be examined from a number of perspectives, and much depends on how one sees management motivation for the introduction of such initiatives. While there has been much discussion of direct participation from a humanist perspective there is no doubt that in the 1980s and 1990s management have regarded business considerations as the primary force behind these initiatives. Thus the participation wave of the last twenty-five years is much more business-oriented than the QWL movement of the 1970s. Furthermore, management has defined the redistribution of power in very narrow terms. The degree of participation offered is strictly within an agenda set by management and it tends not to extend to significant power sharing or participation in higher-level strategic decisions, such as product and investment plans. It is also true to say that radical forms of participation are not on the current agenda. In terms of whether it leads to greater worker influence over decisions the answer appears to be yes but within heavily constrained terms. Direct participation and voice may not always be liberating. Research suggests it can restrain autonomy or worker discretion and that opportunities 'to have voice do not in themselves confer perceptions of effectiveness' (Harlos, 2001: 335). Handel and Levine (2004: 38) report that it appears that involvement 'can improve organisational outcomes if the reforms are serious' but that the evidence on worker welfare is 'quite mixed'. According to Handel and Levine (2004: 39) the research suggests that when participation 'is not used as a form of speed-up, it gives workers more autonomy, recognizes the value of their contributions, improves job satisfaction and is often associated with lower quit rates'.

The research by Dundon et al. (2004) on employee voice also found that it could have a positive impact, in three general ways. The first is valuing employee contributions. This might lead to improved employee attitudes and behaviours, loyalty, commitment, and cooperative relations. The second impact relates to improved performance, including productivity and individual performance, lower absenteeism and (in a few cases) new business arising from employee ideas for improvement and efficiency. The final impact relates to improved managerial systems. This incorporates the managerial benefits from tapping into employee ideas; the informative and educational role of involvement along with improved employee relations.

Using the WERS data, Bryson (2004) finds that direct participation is associated with better employee perceptions of managerial responsiveness than either non-union representative voice or union participation. However, the combination of direct and non-union representative voice has the strongest effects. Union voice is not generally associated with perceptions of managerial responsiveness, but direct

voice mechanisms are associated with perceptions of greater managerial responsiveness. The negative union effects are strongest where the union representative is
part time, and Bryson (2004) suggests that union representation raises expectations
that may not be achieved due to time constraints. In short, direct voice tends to be
positively associated with perceptions of managerial responsiveness, and part-time
union representation shows a negative impact.

The prescriptive literature assumes that employees will welcome and indeed be
committed to the new approach. We do have evidence that workers welcome the
removal of irritants (e.g., close supervision) and welcome the opportunity to
address problems at the source as well as the ability to decide work allocation.
However, there is also evidence that employees are not sufficiently trained,
especially where participation is a result of downsizing. At other times, the
decision-making process is not clear or developed, so even when workers suggest
ideas management are unable to respond adequately and 'participation abandonment' is experienced (Adler, 1993a). Mechanisms are viewed either as bolted on and
lack coherence or integration to other human resource policies and practices, with
schemes left to dwindle as participation champions move on and new managers
have alternative agendas and objectives. These problems are partly the result of the
need to adapt to new production techniques and downsizing rather than enhancing participation *per se*. In other words, employee involvement is not without
costs, both in terms of establishing a new approach to management (involving
training costs, costs of new reward, and information systems) and in its operation
(involving issues of integration, consistency, and unintended consequences) (Lawler, 1996). Thus the new paradigm of work organization remains an ideal, with
elements adopted, but in an ad hoc piecemeal manner.

Recent analysis has looked at system design issues (Dietz et al., 2009) emphasizing that employees do not simply buy into rhetoric in an unconditional way and
their support is dependent upon trust in management and the systems used.
Employees interpret, evaluate, and (re)act to managerial initiatives that 'audit'
the viability of participation schemes and the benefits are likely to accrue to
workers. Thus, while employees may become immersed in a management discourse which makes it difficult for them to challenge any particular strategy, in
practice they may oppose the initiative implemented and indeed may subvert
management goals (Roberts and Wilkinson, 1991). Therefore it could be argued
that, although management try to limit the scope of participation, employees
themselves may question the extent to which they are treated and rewarded in
the organization as a whole, and the extent to which they participate in key
business decisions and hence construct their own independent agenda (Wilkinson,
2008).

So our argument is that we need to avoid a passive view of workers, as the
importance of such initiatives lies in the context of the translation of their supposed
formal properties within the real terrain of the organization and workplace.

This is also important in helping us understand whether direct participation erodes other forms of voice and involvement that may be indirect or collectivist in design. By restructuring work responsibilities and making the team central to the workplace, as well as encouraging employees to identify with managerial objectives, it can marginalize unions and in some cases is clearly intended to do so.

It is evident that direct participation impacts the role of middle managers and supervisors, from holders of expert power to facilitators or coaches responsible for tapping into employee ideas for improvement. Removal of expert power is perceived as a significant threat and participative management is seen as a burden to many middle managers and it is not surprising that they do not universally welcome it (Wilkinson, 2008). Their sense of anxiety is exacerbated by fears of job loss as levels in the hierarchy may be reduced as part of wider changes. Indeed some resist its introduction or alternatively go along with it but emphasize the 'hard', controlling aspects as a way of maintaining the existing power relationship. Moreover many see moves towards employee empowerment as 'soft' management removing their authority over subordinates. However, research suggests that opposition may owe more to the fact that they were not provided with the resources required, were not sufficiently trained, or were not evaluated on this in terms of performance appraisal and therefore did not see it as of much importance (Marchington and Wilkinson, 2005). In other cases, middle managers may feel that they gain influence over decisions taken elsewhere in the organization that affect their work. Some may also feel that it gives them a chance to show their initiative and so increases their career prospects despite losing a degree of functional expert power.

In practice, direct participation can be seen as depending contingently on other factors. For lower-level employees, involvement in organizations with more flexibly specialized processes, which rely on employee skill and discretion is associated with more influence over decisions than in organizations where there are routinized and standardized processes that are capable of being tightly controlled from above. Direct participation in terms of identifying and solving problems can be found at the New United Motor Manufacturing Inc. (NUMMI)–GM–Toyota joint venture in California, a Taylorized auto plant (Adler, 1993b).

CONCLUSIONS

In this chapter we have outlined, briefly, the context of employee participation over the last thirty years. We have also considered the changing contours of management choice, public policy and that the adoption of various participation schemes is often uneven and complicated. A utopian view of participation extending further and deeper as organizations become more democratic (Gratton, 2004) is not supported.

Moreover, we have sought to stress that the meanings and interpretations of such schemes are much more important than the type or number of techniques adopted. What is important is the depth to which participatory mechanisms are integrated with other organizational practices, the scope to which workers have a genuine say over matters that affect them, and the level at which participation occurs. Wood and De Menezes (2008: 676) conclude that management's overall orientation to the involvement and development of employees can be more significant than any specific practice. Equally, Bryson et al. (2006: 438) conclude that managerial responsiveness to the process of participation is as important for superior labour productivity as the existence of a formal voice regime.

At one level, the current practices of participation appear more embedded and less fragmented than they did in the early 1990s (Wilkinson et al., 2004). Attempts have been made to consolidate and integrate different involvement and participation mechanisms over time (Marchington et al., 2001). The dualism in the 1980s, of separated direct (individual) and indirect (union) involvement channels seems to be more intermingled with a range of schemes that overlap. Nevertheless, the employee participation practices remain no more than 'promising' (Leseure et al., 2004). Promising rather than best implies they may need customization before one could expect performance improvements.

Taken together, these developments suggest that the current policy environment holds better prospects for direct participation, because management has learned from the limitation of a weak form and a shallow depth to the participation initiatives of the 1980s and 1990s. It is too grand to talk of participative architecture but at least we are seeing some attempts to integrate participation. The challenges that lie ahead are determining how such a dynamic will be played out in practice, and how multiple schemes for participation can be embedded.

References

ADLER, P. (1993a) The learning bureaucracy: New United Motors Manufacturing, Inc., in B. Staw and L. Cummings (eds), *Research in Organizational Behaviour*, 15: 111–94. Greenwich, CT: JAI Press.

—— (1993b) Time-and-motion regained. *Harvard Business Review*, January–February: 97–108.

BECKER, B. and HUSELID, M. (1998) High performance work systems and firm performance synthesis of research and managerial implications, in G. Ferris (ed.), *Research in Personnel and Human Resources*, vol. 16, Stamford, CT: JAI Press.

—— —— (2008) Strategic Human Resources Management: Where Do We Go From Here? *Journal of Management*, 32(6): 898–925.

BOROFF, K. and LEWIN, D. (1997) Loyalty, voice and intent to exit a union firm: a conceptual and empirical analysis. *Industrial and Labour Relations Review*, 51(1): 50–63.

BOWEN, D. and LAWLER, E. (1992) The empowerment of service workers: what, why, how and when. *Sloan Management Review*, spring: 31–9.

BOXALL, P., HAYNES, P., and MACKY, K. (2007) Employee Voice and Voicelessness in New Zealand, in R. B. Freeman, P. Boxall, and P. Haynes (eds), *What Workers Say: Employee Voice in the Anglo-American Workplace*. Ithaca, NY: Cornell University Press.

—— and PURCELL, J. (2003) *Strategy and Human Resource Management*. London: Palgrave.

BRYSON, A. (2004) Managerial responsiveness to union and non-union worker voice in Britain. *Industrial Relations: A Journal of Economy and Society*, 43(1): 213–41.

—— CHARLWOOD, A., and FORTH, J. (2006) Worker voice, managerial response and labour productivity: an empirical investigation. *Industrial Relations Journal*, 37(5): 438–55.

BUDD, J. (2004) Employment with a human face: balancing efficiency, equity and voice. Ithaca, NY: ILR Press.

BULLOCK, A. (Lord) (1977) *Report of the Committee of Inquiry on Industrial Democracy*. London: HMSO (Cmnd. 6706).

COOPER, R. (1973) Task characteristics and intrinsic motivation. *Human Relations*, 26(August): 387–408.

COX, A., ZAGELMEYER, S., and MARCHINGTON, M. (2006) Embedding employee involvement and participation at work. *Human Resource Management Journal*, 16(3): 250–67.

DELBRIDGE, R., TURNBULL, P., and WILKINSON, B. (1992) Pushing back the frontiers: management control and work intensification under JIT/TQM factory regimes. *New Technology, Work and Employment*, 7(2): 97–106.

DIAMOND, W. and FREEMAN, R. (2001) What workers want from workplace organisations. *Report to the TUC's Promoting Unionism Task Group*. London: Trades Union Congress.

DIETZ G., WILKINSON, A., and REDMAN, T. (2009) Employee voice and participation, in *The Sage Handbook of Human Resource Management*. London: Sage.

DUNDON, T. (2009) Employee Participation, in T. Redman and A. Wilkinson (eds), *Contemporary Human Resource Management: Texts and Cases*, 3rd edition. Harlow: Pearson Education.

—— and ROLLINSON, D. (2004) *Employment Relations in Non-Union Firms*. London: Routledge.

—— and WILKINSON, A. (2009) Employee Participation, in T. Redman and A. Wilkinson (eds), *Contemporary Human Resource Management*. Pearson.

—— WILKINSON, A., MARCHINGTON, M., and ACKERS, P. (2004) The meanings and purpose of employee voice. *International Journal of Human Resource Management*, 15(6): 1150–71.

FREEMAN, R. and MEDOFF, J. (1984) *What do Unions do?* New York: Basic Books.

GALLIE, D., FELSTEAD, A., and GREEN, F. (2001) Employer Policies and Organizational Commitment in Britain 1992–97. *Journal of Management Studies*, 38: 1081–101.

GODARD, J. (1997) Whither strategic choice: do managerial IR ideologies matter? *Industrial Relations*, 36(2): 206–28.

GRATTON, L. (2004) *The Democratic Enterprise*. London: Prentice Hall.

HANDEL, M. and LEVINE, D. (2004) Editor's introduction: the effects of new work practices on workers. *Industrial Relations*, 43(1): 1–43.

HARLEY, B., HYMAN, J., and THOMPSON, P. (2005) *Participation and Democracy at Work: Essays in Honour of Harvie Ramsay*. London: Palgrave Macmillan.

HARLOS, K. (2001) When organizational voice systems fail: more on the deaf-ear syndrome and frustration effects. *Journal of Applied Behavioural Science*, 37(3): 324–42.

HARRISON, J. and FREEMAN, E. (2004) Is organizational democracy worth the effort? *Academy of Management Executives*, 18(3): 49–53.

HELLER, F., PUSIC, E., STRAUSS, G., and WILPERT, B. (1998) *Organisational Participation: Myth and Reality*. Oxford: Oxford University Press.

HIRSCHMAN, A. (1970) *Exit, voice and loyalty: responses to decline in firms, organizations and States*. Cambridge, MA: Harvard University Press.

HUSELID, M. (1995) The impact of human resource management practices on turnover, production and corporate financial performance. *Academy of Management Journal*, 38(3): 635–72.

KOCHAN, T., KATZ, H., and MCKERSIE, R. (1986) *The Transformation of American Industrial Relations*. New York: Basic Books.

LANSBURY, R. and WAILES, N. (2008) Employee involvement and direct participation, in P. Blyton, N. Bacon, J. Fiorito, and E. Heery (eds), *The Sage Handbook of Industrial Relations*, pp. 434–46. London: Sage Publications.

LAWLER, E. (1996) *From the Ground Up*. San Francisco: Jossey-Bass.

LESEURE, M. J., BAUER, J., BIRDI, K., NEELY, A., and DENYER, D. (2004) Adoption of Promising Practices: A Systematic Review of the Evidence. *International Journal of Management Reviews*, 5/6(3–4): 169–90.

LOCKE, E. and SCHWEIGER, D. (1979) Participation in decision-making: one more look, in B. Staw (ed.), *New Directions in Organizational Behavior*, 1: 265–339. Greenwich, CT: JAI Press.

LUCHAK, A. (2003) What kind of voice do loyal employees use? *British Journal of Industrial Relations*, 41(March): 115–34.

MARCHINGTON, M. (2005) Employee involvement: patterns and explanations, in B. Harley, J. Hyman, and P. Thompson (eds), *Participation and Democracy at Work: Essays in Honour of Harvie Ramsay*. London: Palgrave.

—— (2006) Employee voice systems, in P. Boxall, J. Purcell, and P. Wright (eds), *The Oxford Handbook of Human Resource Management*. Oxford: Oxford University Press.

—— Cooke, F., and Hebson, G. (2008) 'Human resource management across organizational boundaries', in Wilkinson, A., Redman, T., Snell, S., and Bacon, N. (eds). *Sage Handbook of Human Resource Management*. London: Sage.

—— GOODMAN, J., WILKINSON, A., and ACKERS, P. (1992) *New Developments in Employee Involvement*, Research Paper no. 2. London: Employment Department.

—— and WILKINSON, A. (2005) Direct participation, in S. Bach (ed.), *Personnel Management: A Comprehensive Guide to Theory and Practice* (4th edition). Oxford: Blackwell.

—— —— ACKERS, P., and DUNDON, T. (2001) *Management Choice and Employee Voice*. London: CIPD.

MCCABE, D. and LEWIN, D. (1992) Employee voice: a human resource management perspective. *California Management Review*, 34(3): 112–23.

MILLER, K. and MONGE, P. (1986) Participation, productivity and satisfaction: a meta-analytic review. *Academy of Management Journal*, 29(4): 727–53.

PARKS, S. (1995) Improving workplace performance, *Monthly Labor Review*, May: pp. 18–28.

PIORE, M. and SABEL, C. (1983) *The Second Industrial Divide*. New York: Basic Books.

POOLE, M. (1986) *Towards a New Industrial Democracy: Workers' Participation in Industry*. London: Routledge and Kegan Paul.

PROCTOR, S. and MUELLER, F. (eds) (2000) *Teamworking*. London: Macmillan.

PURCELL, J. (1995) Corporate strategy and its links with human resource strategy, in J. Storey (ed.), *Human Resource Management, A Critical Text*. London: Routledge.

PURCELL, J. and GEORGIADIS, K. (2006) Why should employees bother with worker voice? in R. Freeman, P. Boxall, and P. Haynes (eds), *What Workers Say: Employee Voice in the Anglo-Saxon World*. Ithaca, NY: Cornell University Press.

RAMSAY, H. (1980) Phantom participation: patterns of power and conflict. *Industrial Relations Journal*, 11(3): 46–59.

ROBERTS, I. and WILKINSON, A. (1991) Participation and purpose: boilermakers to bankers. *Critical Perspectives on Accounting*, 2: 385–413.

ROEBER, J. (1975) *Social Change at Work*. London: Heinemann.

SCARBOROUGH, H. (2003) Knowledge management, HRM and the innovation process. *International Journal of Manpower*, 124(5): 501–16.

SEMLER, R. (1989) Managing without managers. *Harvard Business Review*, September-October: 76–84.

STRAUSS, G. (2006) Worker participation—some under-considered issues. *Industrial Relations*, 45(4): 778–803.

TRIST, E., HIGGIN, G., MURRAY, H., and POLLOCK, A. (1963) *Organisational Choice: Capabilities of Groups at the Coalface Under Changing Technologies*. London: Tavistock Institute.

WAGNER, J. (1994) Participation's effect on performance and satisfaction: a reconsideration of research evidence. *Academy of Management Review*, 19: 312–30.

WALL, T. and MARTIN, R. (1987) Job and work design, in C. Cooper and I. Robertson (eds), *International Review of Industrial and Organisational Psychology*, pp. 61–91. Chichester: John Wiley.

WALTON, R. (1985) From control to commitment in the workplace. *Harvard Business Review*, 64(3): 77–84.

WILKINSON, A. (1998) Empowerment: a review and a critique. *Personnel Review*, 27(1): 40–56.

—— (2002) Empowerment, in M. Poole and M. Warner (eds), *International Encyclopaedia of Business and Management Handbook of Human Resource Management*. London: ITB Press.

—— (2008) Empowerment, in S. Clegg and J. Bailey (eds), *Encyclopaedia of Organizational Studies*. London: Sage.

—— and ACKERS, P. (1995) When two cultures meet: new industrial relations at Japanco, *International Journal of Human Resource Management*, 6(4): 849–71.

—— DUNDON, T., MARCHINGTON, M., and ACKERS, P. (2004) Changing patterns of employee voice. *Journal of Industrial Relations*, 46(3): 298–322.

—— —— and GRUGULIS, I. (2007) Information but not consultation: exploring employee involvement in SMEs. *International Journal of Human Resource Management*, 18(7): 1279–97.

—— REDMAN, T., SNAPE, E., and MARCHINGTON, M. (1998) *Managing With TQM: Theory and Practice*. London: Macmillan.

WRIGHT, P. and GARDNER, T. (2003) The human resource-firm performance relationship: methodological and theoretical challenges, in D. Holman, T. Wall, C. Clegg, P. Sparrow, and A. Howard (eds), *The New Workplace: A Guide to the Human Impact of Modern Working Practices*. Chichester: Wiley.

WOOD, S. and DE MENEZES, L. (2008) Coomparing perspectives on high involvement management and organizational performance across the British economy. *International Journal of Human Resource Management*, 19(4): 639–82.

......

CHAPTER 8

COLLECTIVE BARGAINING AS A FORM OF EMPLOYEE PARTICIPATION:

OBSERVATIONS ON THE UNITED STATES AND EUROPE

......

RICHARD N. BLOCK

PETER BERG

INTRODUCTION

......

INDUSTRIAL relations scholars have provided multiple rationales for the existence of collective bargaining. These include pluralism, industrial democracy, and industrial governance. The idea of industrial democracy or worker voice provides a basis for collective bargaining as a form of worker participation in economic decisions. As discussed in this book, worker participation can take different forms. Direct participation allows workers to participate in decisions related to their work. This form of participation is often part of an organizational process, such as high-performance work systems, in which workers engage in work process decisions and problem-solving activities around productivity and quality improvement (Appelbaum et al., 2000). Direct participation can also be obtained through legal mandates, which gives individual employees rights of ascent or refusal regarding issues relating to schedules or work demands (Berg et al., 2004: 344; Block, 2005).

In contrast, indirect participation is characterized by employee participation through independent representatives, (e.g., labour unions or works councils). These forms of representation are generally part of a legal structure that sets the parameters of participation. In some cases, the rights of labour unions, works councils, the bargaining process, and the formation of labour agreements are clearly defined and delineated. In other cases, these issues are left more open with the parties themselves determining the boundaries. Collective bargaining is a form of indirect employee participation in which worker representatives collectively negotiate wages and working conditions with employer representatives. The power of independent collective representatives varies across countries and depends in part on the rationale for the collective bargaining systems and bargaining structures that characterize the interaction between labour and management.

In this chapter, we compare and contrast the collective bargaining systems in the United States and Europe. In section two, we examine the rationale behind these collective bargaining systems by analysing labour legislation and key interpretive judicial decisions in the United States, and various treaties, legislation, and similar documents in Europe. These legal institutions clearly illustrate the greater status and scope of participation through collective bargaining in the Europe vis-à-vis the United States.

Section three focuses on bargaining structure and scope, union density, and union wage effects. We show that consistent with the legal support for collective bargaining participation in Europe, European countries have more centralized bargaining structures and broader bargaining scope than is found in the United States with union-negotiated terms and conditions being extended to the non-union sector in many countries. In the United States, the scope of bargaining is narrow, limited to 'mandatory subjects', specifically 'terms and conditions of employment', with those terms and conditions applying only within a legal bargaining unit. Morever, the definition of a 'mandatory subject' is in continuous litigation as employers attempt to narrow, and unions attempt to expand, the issues that must be bargained. As would be expected union density is also greater in Europe than the US. On the other hand, the union wage effect is greater in the

US than in Europe, as diffusion from the larger unionized sector in Europe raised the European non-union wage more than the diffusion from smaller US unionized sector raises the US non-union wage. Section four provides a summary and conclusion.

RATIONALE

United States

Because the collective bargaining system in the United States has its basis in laws and statutes rather than in the Constitution, legal doctrine essentially regulates collective bargaining. Thus, to understand the rationale or theory behind collective bargaining in the United States, one must examine the judicial decisions and legal debates as the system emerged.

The origin of law in the United State protecting collective bargaining was not based on principles of worker participation, or worker democracy, or any moral notions that workers should have rights to organize and bargain collectively.[1] Rather, when such legislation was passed, the rationale was to further broad economic goals. Providing workers collective bargaining rights was simply a means to reach those goals. Court decisions interpreting laws as they applied to collective bargaining generally reflected similar views.

The Common Law and Judicial Decisions through the Early 1920s

There was no legislation addressing collective bargaining for the first 120 years after the founding of the United States in 1776. Thus, the law applied to collective bargaining was the common law as interpreted by judges. In the earliest labour case, *Commonwealth v. Pullis*, in 1806, a jury found that a strike (then called a 'turnout') by journeymen shoemakers in Philadelphia to be a common law unlawful conspiracy to raise wages. In his charge to the jury, the recorder (judge) asked the jury to consider whether the combination of the journeyman was injurious to the public welfare because it interfered with the 'natural' determination of wages by supply and demand (Lieberman, 1960; Nelles, 1931). Thus, the recorder admonished the jury to focus more on the economic effects of the workers' actions than the interests of the workers in improving their standards of living.

Although the Massachusetts Supreme Court in *Commonwealth v. Hunt*, decided in 1842, ruled that the mere act of combining was not illegal and that legality would be determined by the actions of the workers (Oberer et al., 1986), a series of judicial decisions in the second half of the nineteenth century and into the first third of the twentieth century indicated that the law viewed the economic effects of worker organization as the most important consideration in determining the legal rights of labour. In *Walker v. Cronin*, decided in 1871, the Massachusetts Supreme Court ruled that an employer could seek damages from striking workers for losses during a strike (Oberer et al., 1986). In *Vegelahn v. Guntner*, decided in 1896, the Supreme Court of Massachusetts permitted picketing to be enjoined because of the prospective harm to the employer's business (Oberer et al., 1986). In *Loewe v. Lawlor*, decided in 1908, the US Supreme Court ruled that the antitrust laws applied to labour unions, because unions were a combination or conspiracy in restraint of trade (Lieberman, 1960; Oberer et al., 1986).[2]

Railroad Labour Relations

Legislation involving labour relations on the railroads illustrates from a different perspective the importance of economic factors in collective bargaining. In the second half of the nineteenth century, the railroads were among the more unionized industries in the United States. Carrier resistance to union recognition and wage demands often resulted in railroad strikes. Starting in the last quarter of the nineteenth century, when the railroads had become essential to the economic health of the country, concerns arose about the effects of railroad strikes on the public interest and the economy. This led to a string of late nineteenth- and early-twentieth-century legislation enacted between 1888 and 1920 that was designed to resolve disputes without strikes, generally through various forms of mediation and arbitration. All were unsuccessful because the results were not acceptable to both parties (Rehmus, 1976).

Importantly, the purpose of the legislation was not to guarantee the rights of railroad workers to organize. Rather, this legislation was designed to eliminate the economic loss and harm associated with collective bargaining, and, most importantly, labour conflict and strikes. Thus, the legislation was aimed at resolving disputes, and ameliorating the economic disruption caused by these disputes, rather than providing employees with the right to organize and bargain collectively (Dulles and Dubofsky, 1984; Rehmus, 1976; Wolf, 1927).

The Railway Labor Act (RLA), which currently governs labour relations in the railroads and airlines in the United States, was enacted in 1926 with the joint support of the carriers and unions, had no provision for determining representation. Like its predecessors, the RLA was designed to minimize the economic inconvenience caused by railroad strikes. Indeed, an administrative processs for representation was not added until the RLA was amended in 1934 (Eischen, 1976).

Collective Bargaining Generally

Union Recognition. There is no doubt that the National Labor Relations Act (NLRA), or Wagner Act, represented a watershed in labour relations in the United States. The law provided employees the right to self-organization and to bargain collectively. It is important to note, however, that the rationale for the Wagner Act was not based on any notions of human rights of workers to organize or bargain collectively, or some notion of the morality of collective bargaining or industrial democracy based on employee participation. Employee participation is not part of the 'Findings and Policies' that provided the rationale for passage of the Wagner (Cornell Law School, Undated). Thus, the NLRA was justified primarily on the reduction or elimination of industrial conflict (Cornell Law School, Undated).

The Wagner Act was passed after a predecessor law, Section 7(a) of the National Industrial Recovery Act (NIRA), proved ineffective in granting employees the right to unionize. The NIRA, passed in 1933, was enacted as a response to a perception that low prices contributed to the Depression. In essence, the NIRA permitted firms to fix prices as part of participation in a government programme. Among the requirements of programme participation was the obligation, under Section 7(a), to permit employees who so desired to organize and bargain collectively. (Bernstein, 1971)

Section 7(a) was unsuccessful in guaranteeing this right to employees, as it lacked effective enforcement mechanisms, and the entire NIRA was declared unconstitutional in 1935. Nevertheless, between the passage of the NIRA in 1933 and the Supreme Court decision declaring it unconstitutional, unions used the legislation to claim that the government supported unionization. The result was a wave of recognition strikes in 1934 that disrupted many industries. These strikes and the industrial conflict associated with union recognition were portrayed as obstructing interstate commerce, which then served as the constitutional rationale for the passage of the Wagner Act, given that the US Constitution limits national regulation of commerce to that commerce that is interstate (Bernstein, 1971).

Although the US Supreme Court in 1934 determined that the NIRA (and its labour provisions) were unconstitutional, the economic problems associated with strikes and industrial disruption still remained. These problems led to passage of the NLRA in 1935. The view underlying the NLRA was that the unwillingness of employers to recognize unions was the cause of industrial conflict and such conflict impaired and burdened interstate commerce (Bernstein, 1971).

The NLRA provided employees with the right to organize and bargain collectively, but the policy rationale for providing employees with this right was not based on human rights, or the moral notions of employee participation. Rather, the rationale was elimination of the disruption to the functioning of the economy caused by the failure of employers to recognize unions. Thus, at its core, the NLRA was passed to manage the industrial conflict that had accompanied the question of union recognition. Its purpose was to channel recognition disputes from the streets to the administrative offices of the National Labor Relations Board (NLRB). The law was successful in accomplishing that goal, as recognition strikes essentially disappeared after the constitutionality of the NLRA was upheld in 1937 (Bernstein, 1971). While industrial conflict continued to occur, it was generally over terms and conditions of employment.

In 1941, just four years after the NLRA was declared constitutional, the US Supreme Court granted employers the right to resist union organization through the exercise of the rights of free speech. Over the next forty years, this right was expanded as the NLRB and the courts permitted employers to require employees to attend meetings in which anti-union material was presented, decided to generally prevent the unions from entering the employer's premises or property to present arguments for unionization, and decided the content of what was said would not be regulated (Block and Wolkinson, 1986; Cingranelli, 2006; Midland National Life Insurance Company, 1982). It is not surprising that the rights of employers have expanded relative to unions in the United States, given that employee rights to organize collectively are not based on notions of fundamental human rights, that the general regulatory assumption in the US is that property rights are paramount, that markets are competitive and that impediments, such as unions, should be limited (Block et al., 2004).

Bargaining and Negotiations. Because the NLRA was not enacted with an underlying doctrine of worker democracy and participation, principles of adversarialism and collective bargaining limits were interpreted and built into the NLRA. NLRB decisions were the result of adversary proceedings before an administrative body and NLRB decisions could be appealed to the courts (Cornell Law School, Undated).

As a corollary to the resolution of the recognition matter, the NLRA required the employer to bargain with the union recognized by the administrative procedures of the NLRA. But because the NLRA provided no definition of the word 'bargain', when the NLRA was amended in 1947, a provision that defined the term 'bargain' was included. The provision stated:

[T]o bargain collectively is the performance of the mutual obligation of the employer and the representative of the employees to meet at reasonable times and confer in good faith with respect to wages, hours, and other terms and conditions of employment, or the negotiation of an agreement, or any question arising thereunder, and the execution of a written contract incorporating any agreement reached if requested by either party, but such obligation does not compel either party to agree to a proposal or require the making of a concession.

The Board and courts ruled that because the law required bargaining over 'wages, hours, and other terms and conditions of employment' (mandatory subjects) neither party had an obligation to bargain over matters that were not 'wages, hours, and other terms and conditions of employment' (permissive subjects). In practice, this meant the development of doctrine around issues about which the employer need not bargain. Fundamentally, the greater the number of issues that were determined to fall outside the definition of 'wages, hours, and other terms and conditions of employment', the greater the scope of management discretion in making decisions without negotiating with a union and the narrower the scope of employee participation in management decisions under collective bargaining.

The most important legal conflict on this matter involved management decisions that were fundamental to the business, such as decisions to close or relocate a facility, and at the same time, that affected employment. The Board and the courts were confronted with a choice: create an expansive definition of 'terms and conditions of employment', thereby enshrining into law a definition of bargaining that would encourage participation by unions in a range of management decisions; or create a narrow definition of 'terms and conditions of employment', limiting the scope of union participation in management decision making.

In 1964, in *Fibreboard v. NLRB*, the Supreme Court seemed to adopt the broad view. In *Fibreboard*, an employer decided to subcontract its maintenance function, essentially replacing its union-represented maintenance department with employees of a subcontractor. As a result, the employer terminated all of its maintenance department employees. The Supreme Court ruled that the employer had a legal obligation to negotiate with the union over the decision, stating:

The subject matter of the present dispute is well within the literal meaning of the phrase 'terms and conditions of employment' ... A stipulation with respect to the contracting out of work performed by members of the bargaining unit might appropriately be called a 'condition of employment'. The words even more plainly cover termination of employment which, as the facts of this case indicate, necessarily results from the contracting out of work performed by members of the established bargaining unit.   (*Fibreboard*, 1964)

While this statement from the court seemed to suggest the potential for a bargaining obligation a broad role for a union, and true participation, the concurring opinion stated otherwise:

The question posed is whether the particular decision sought to be made unilaterally by the employer in this case is a subject of mandatory collective bargaining within the statutory phrase 'terms and conditions of employment'. That is all the Court decides. The Court most assuredly does not decide that every managerial decision which necessarily terminates an individual's employment is subject to the duty to bargain. Nor does the Court decide that subcontracting decisions are as a general matter subject to that duty. The Court holds no more than that this employer's decision to subcontract this work, involving 'the replacement of employees in the existing bargaining unit with those of an independent contractor to do the same work under similar conditions of employment', is subject to the duty to bargain collectively.

I am fully aware that in this era of automation and onrushing technological change, no problems in the domestic economy are of greater concern than those involving job security and employment stability. Because of the potentially cruel impact upon the lives and fortunes of the working men and women of the Nation, these problems have understandably engaged the solicitous attention of government, of responsible private business, and particularly of organized labor. It is possible that in meeting these problems Congress may eventually decide to give organized labor or government a far heavier hand in controlling what until now have been considered the prerogatives of private business management. That path would mark a sharp departure from the traditional principles of a free enterprise economy. Whether we should follow it is, within constitutional limitations, for Congress to choose. But it is a path which Congress certainly did not choose when it enacted the Taft-Hartley Act. (379 U.S. 203, 218, 225–26)

Thus the concurring justices made it clear that they did not view the obligation to bargain under the National Labor Relations Act as a right to participate in major business decisions that would affect employment.

The question of whether the view of the majority or the concurrence would prevail was resolved seventeen years later, in 1981, in *First National Maintenance Corporation v. NLRB*. In this case, the employer, a provider of janitorial and maintenance services, terminated its contract with a client, Greenpark, a nursing home operator, in a dispute with Greenpark over the amount of the management fee Greenpark was obligated to pay to First National Maintenance. The employer also terminated its employees working at Greenpark. The Supreme Court found that First National Maintenance had no obligation to bargain with the union representing the Greenpark employees over the decision to terminate the Greenpark contract. In so ruling the Court observed that:

[I]n establishing what issues must be submitted to the process of bargaining, Congress had no expectation that the elected union representative would become an equal partner in the running of the business enterprise in which the union's members are employed. Despite the deliberate open-endedness of the statutory language, there is an undeniable limit to the subjects about which bargaining must take place.

The aim of labeling a matter a mandatory subject of bargaining, rather than simply permitting, but not requiring, bargaining, is to 'promote the fundamental purpose of the Act by bringing a problem of vital concern to labor and management within the framework established by Congress as most conducive to industrial peace' ... The concept of mandatory bargaining is premised on the belief that collective discussions backed by the parties' economic weapons will result in decisions that are better for both management and labor and for society as a whole ... This will be true, however, only if the subject proposed for discussion is amenable to resolution through the bargaining process. Management must be free from the constraints of the bargaining process to the extent essential for the running of a profitable business. It also must have some degree of certainty beforehand as to when it may proceed to reach decisions without fear of later evaluations labeling its conduct an unfair labor practice. Congress did not explicitly state what issues of mutual concern to union and management it intended to exclude from mandatory bargaining. Nonetheless, in view of an employer's need for unencumbered decisionmaking, bargaining over management decisions that have a substantial impact on the continued availability of employment should be required only if the benefit, for labor-management relations and the collective-bargaining process, outweighs the burden placed on the conduct of the business.   (452 U.S. 666, 675–77)

Thus, the court built a wall between labour and management, asserting that the system of labour relations in the United States did not remove from management the fundamental right to run the business free from union/employee involvement and participation. The language of the NLRA in 1935 and the Taft–Hartley Act of 1947 did not define what was meant by 'bargain collectively' and 'terms and conditions of employment'. Thus, the court, in *Fibreboard* and *First National Maintenance* could have interpreted those phrases broadly, consistent with principles of participation, or narrowly, thus limiting union participation. The court chose the latter option, consistent with the traditional US doctrine of private property rights and enhancing the functioning of the (presumed) competitive market. Bargaining is limited to mandatory subjects, essentially limiting the rights of unions to participate in many decisions that affect the firm and employees.

Europe

The European Union (EU), dominated by countries from continental Europe, is the polar opposite of the United States with respect to the employee participation through collective bargaining. Unlike in the US, where support for the institution of collective bargaining was seen as a vehicle for minimizing economic disruption, collective bargaining in continental Europe has long been seen as a component of human rights. Unions and collective bargaining are seen, in continental Europe, as part of industrial pluralism, the notion of generating a consensus among the different groups within the industrial relations system (Kerr et al., 1964). Notions of pluralism are consistent with developing overarching societal-level institutions that are seen as constraining what would otherwise be disproportionate employer power over employees (Block et al., 2004; Kelly, 2004). Developing consensus and offsetting employer power are accomplished through giving unions the right to participate, through appropriate structures, over matters that affect workers. This view stands in contrast to the United States where union participation through collective bargaining has been supported only when it is seen as enhancing economic efficiency, and has been impaired when it is viewed otherwise. In the EU, and especially in continental Europe, union participation and collective bargaining are part and parcel of social policy in the EU, which covers the multiple aspects of policy regarding employment (e.g., hours legislation, health and safety, etc.). In this chapter, we use European Community and, later, European Union treaties and policies to illustrate consensus views around collective bargaining and employee participation in Europe. As continental European countries dominate EC/EU policy making, we focus on countries in continental Europe.

Collective Bargaining Participation in the Early European Community and Member States

When the European Community was established by the Treaty of Rome in 1957, there was only minimal reference to social policy in general, let alone collective bargaining. Hepple (1993) argues that, when it was established, the EC was based on principles of economic neoliberalism through the establishment of a common market and the idea that a rising standard of living would result from the establishment of the EC. Springer (1994) notes that the main concern of the drafters of the Treaty of Rome with respect to social policy was the free movement of labour, as embodied in Articles 48–51 (Treaty Establishing the European Community, 1957).

It should be noted, however, that Articles 117 and 118 of the Treaty of Rome referenced the eventual harmonization of social systems and improved working conditions and standards of living and cooperation among the member countries in the social field, which was interpreted as giving the European Commission the authority to establish consultative mechanisms (Hepple, 1993). Separately, in 1961, the Council of Europe adopted the Social Charter which stated as fundamental principles the rights of workers to information and consultation and to participation in the improvement of working conditions and the working environment (Hantrais, 1995: 4).

At the same time, within the larger Member States, corporatist structures were developing that involved both labour and management at the national, sectoral, and regional levels. Germany developed a system of worker representation on boards of directors and works councils–employer negotiations at the workplace level, with unions and employer associations negotiating at the industry and regional levels (Daniel, 1978; Furstenburg 1998). In France, legislation provided unions with substantial influence out of proportion to their actual membership (Goetschy and Jobert, 1998). Italy has a history of national-level bargaining between the union confederations and the employer association that can be traced to the 1950s, with this national bargaining existing with industry and enterprise bargaining (Pelligrini, 1998). Among the relatively early members of the EC, Belgium, Denmark, and the Netherlands also had well-developed corporatist systems (Wallerstein et al., 1997). An industrial relations system characterized by a social partnership among employer organizations, unions, and government took root in Sweden in the early 1950s (Hammerstrom and Nilsson, 1998). Therefore, although the Treaty of Rome did not directly address social issues, employment, or collective bargaining, it is clear that worker representation and participation was established within the EC member states. Therefore, unlike in the US, worker representation, unions, and collective bargaining, often within corporatist-type structures, were seen as integral aspects of the economy in much of continental Europe.

Thus, it is not surprising that within a short period of time after establishment of the EC, these notions of structured worker representation and collective bargaining began to filter up to the community level. Between 1963 and 1971, joint labour–management sectoral committees were established at the community level in agriculture, road transport, inland waterway transport, sea fishing, and rail transport in order to make recommendations on terms and conditions of employment (Hepple, 1993). Although these committees did not negotiate collective bargaining agreements, largely due to employer resistance to such agreements, they did establish the principle of European level labour–management consultation. In addition, in 1970, the European Commission had discussed the importance of working with labour and management on economic policy (Hepple, 1993).

The Emergence of Social Policy and the Social Partners

With economic stagnation in the 1970s, the notion of improvements in the standard of living through economic liberalization began to recede in favour of the notion of the 'social market' (Hepple, 1993). The Treaty of Rome principle of harmonization of social systems was used as a basis for Community involvement in social matters. Although supporting the principle of subsidiarity, in 1974, the EC Council of Ministers adopted a resolution that supported, among other things, increasing involvement of management and labour in economic and social decisions and in the life of the undertaking (Hantrais, 1995: 5). This social action programme resolution resulted in actions on a range of social issues, including health and safety, and the rights of women (Hantrais, 1995: 5–6). It also resulted in the creation in 1975 of the European Foundation for the Improvement of Employment and Living Conditions (European Council, 1975; European Foundation, 2007). The establishment of the Foundation would serve to institutionalize research on employment and social issues within the EC and would be a component of an institutional structure that focused on employment and social policy.

EC legislation on social issues was, however, controversial, as it was viewed as compromising the principle of subsidiarity and could be inconsistent with laws in member states, primarily in the United Kingdom (Block et al., 2001; Hantrais, 1995). In addition, employer groups opposed Community-level legislation. Nevertheless, the Single European Act (SEA), passed in 1985, provided for qualified (less than unanimous) voting on less controversial social issues (health and safety, non-discrimination, worker consultation) and a social dialogue at the European level between representatives of labour and management (Hantrais, 1995).

The SEA led to the 1989 adoption of the Community Charter of the Fundamental Social Rights of Workers (Hantrais, 1995). Although the Charter did not establish binding legislation, it did announce that the EU had a continuing interest in social issues in the economy. The Charter addressed freedom of movement, improvement of living and working conditions, social protection, freedom of association and collective bargaining (the right of workers to organize and bargain collectively), vocational training, non-discrimination based on gender, health and safety, and protection of children, the elderly, and the disabled. It also included the following statement: '(t)he dialogue between the two sides of industry at European level which must be developed, may, if the parties deem it desirable, result in contractual relations, in particular at inter-occupational and sectoral level' (European Commission, Community Charter, 1989). Thus, the Charter was one additional step toward EU involvement in employment matters and recognition of the legitimacy and equality of labour and management as participants in determining employment and social policy.

Formal involvement of labour and management in EU policy making was incorporated in the Maastricht Treaty in 1992 (Treaty on European Union, 1992). The Maastricht Treaty supplemented the SEA-established principle of a qualified majority to adopt legislation on less controversial issues by permitting all Member States other than Britain to adopt social policies on controversial issues if those states agreed—it created a UK opt out (Block et al., 2001). It also required the European Commission to consult with representatives of management and labour prior to taking action in the social field (Treaty on European Union, 1992). Together, these provisions established a formal EU legislative involvement in the social field and institutionalized labour and management as actors at the community level in that legislative involvement.

The Maastricht Treaty was a formal recognition of labour as a recognized actor and participant in the EU decision-making system on matters of social policy and a social partner with management with some standing to represent workers throughout the community on community-level social legislation. It represented full integration of unions and collective bargaining into a European economy that was increasingly coming to be dominated by the EU. Moreover, the addition of a UK opt out removed the major barrier to the establishment of EU directives (legislation) in the social field that would create mandates in the Member States. According to the Maastricht Treaty, nothing could be proposed in the social field without labour and management input. Equally important, Maastricht made labour a formal advocacy group within the EU, permitting them to advocate for legislation above the national level (Block et al., 2001; Springer, 1994). Unions could also use their position to advocate research and to call attention to issues and problems.

Due to the UK opt out, Maastricht was the trigger for a series of directives in the more controversial areas of social policy. These included directives on employee consultation, sex discrimination, and part-time workers (Block et al., 2001). The 1997 Treaty of Amsterdam further incorporated labour and management in the EU legislative process related to social policy. Trade union and employer associations obtained the right to be consulted and comment on EU proposals for employment-related legislation. Article 138 of the Treaty of Amsterdam provides for a compulsory two-stage consultation procedure:

- before presenting proposals in the social policy field, the Commission is required to consult the social partners on the possible direction of Community action;
- if the Commission considers that Community action is desirable, it must consult the social partners on the actual content of the envisaged proposal.

The social partners are also consulted within advisory committees (e.g., the Advisory Committee on Safety and Health at Work), in the context of procedures aimed at garnering the views of interested parties, such as Green Papers, and systematically on the reports on transposal of Community legislation (Europa, 2007). This is not collective bargaining but part of a process of social dialogue incorporating union participation that is promoted by the EU as the way to negotiate change and implement social legislation. Furthermore, the peak associations of the parties involved in national collective bargaining are connected to the EU process of social dialogue and use it as a tool to move the EU agenda in ways that can promote EU directives for particular working conditions, such as parental leave, part-time equality, working time regulations, and minimum vacation leave. In addition, the process of social dialogue has helped win rights of consultation and information as well as European Works Council Legislation. Union participation in the EC legislative process is also enhanced by Article 118 that provides Member States the option of permitting labour and management to introduce measures to implement social directives, and formally gave labour and management the right to initiate the legislative process (Treaty of Amsterdam, 1997).

TRENDS AND EFFECTS OF DIFFERENT COLLECTIVE BARGAINING SYSTEMS

Given the different rationales behind the collective bargaining systems, one would expect different forms of representative participation in Europe and the United States. In fact, Europe and the United States have different bargaining structures with employers and worker representatives negotiating at different levels within the economy. Bargaining scope is also different across the two regions. The European Union has contributed to the expanded scope of bargaining in Europe. Union density is higher in Europe but union wage effects show a more mixed picture.

The United States

The legally-driven collective bargaining system in the United States results in bargaining being structured at a very decentralized level, as Section 9(b) of the

National Labor Relations Act limits a legal bargaining unit to 'the employer unit, craft unit, plant unit, or subdivision thereof' (National Labor Relations Board, Undated). This narrow definition of the bargaining unit promotes company and enterprise agreements, giving employers the ability to structure agreements to meet the needs of single or multi-enterprise bargaining units. The decentralized bargaining structure in the US gives employers great flexibility and in most cases, strengthens their bargaining power. Unions are also organized on craft or industry basis, but they do not negotiate industry-wide agreements unless employers agree to so negotiate, nor have they formed peak associations that engage in bargaining activity. Efforts by unions to establish pattern bargaining across company agreements has been reduced by declining union density, increasing global competition, and the mobility of capital in a digital technology world.

Union recognition procedures in the United States also contribute to decentralized bargaining structures. Before unions can negotiate on behalf of workers, they must show that at least 30 per cent of the employees in a defined bargaining unit would support union representation. If this can be shown, the NLRB approves the bargaining unit and administers a secret ballot election at the workplace in which the union must win 50% +1 of the votes for the right to bargain with the employer. This recognition process demands a high degree of union investment in organizing at a local level. In addition, the recognition process allows for extensive union avoidance tactics to influence employee votes. In 2001, labour unions won 54 per cent of all representation elections conducted, but only two-thirds of those victories actually achieved a collective bargaining agreement (Katz and Kochan, 2004: 155–7). Since employers are only obligated to bargain in good faith but not actually reach an agreement, resistance to union recognition is able to continue even after the representation election is won.

As discussed in section two, above, the scope of bargaining in the United States is limited by the legal designation of mandatory and permissive bargaining issues. This designation narrows the scope of bargaining in the US, increases employer prerogative, and restricts employee participation in issues through collective bargaining. Efforts to significantly expand the scope of bargaining are usually borne out of a crisis and are short-lived. For example, at various times union and management within the automobile and steel industries have negotiated union representatives serving on company boards (Lowell, 1985). These strategies have faded, however, as the economic crisis subsided or new management strategies emerge.

Thus, the macroeconomic rationale used to justify the role of labour unions in employment relations has resulted in a collective bargaining system with very decentralized bargaining structures and a narrow scope of bargaining. This has led to greater relative bargaining power for management and limited strategic choices of labour unions within the collective bargaining system.

Europe

In the pluralistic industrial relations systems in Europe, there exists multiple roles for collective representation, and the scope of collective represenation is broader than representing workers in a single bargaining unit. Collective bargaining among unions and employers or employer associations occurs at different levels across European countries. Collective representation also occurs in different forms at the workplace. In some cases, legislation or collective agreements determine specific roles for trade union representatives at the workplace as independent representatives or as part of a works council structure. In other cases, unions may not play an explicit bargaining role at the workplace but indirectly support local works councils through information and union training of works council leaders. Collective representation also plays an important role internationally at the EU level, where peak union and employer associations participate in EU policymaking through social dialogue. These multiple roles of collective representation have developed in a way consistent with the ideas of economic democracy that characterize Europe. We detail their structures below.

Collective Bargaining Structures

Although there is variation across European countries, bargaining structures in Europe are much more centralized than in the United States. Table 8.1 shows the levels of collective bargaining with regard to wages in various EU countries.

Although bargaining at the sectoral and enterprise level is most prevelant, a sizeble amount of bargaining is still inter-sectoral. In Ireland and Finland, inter-sectoral bargaining remains the dominant form of bargaining. In Germany, France, the Netherlands, Sweden, and Italy, sectoral bargaining supplemented by enterprise agreements is more common. The United Kingdom and the Czech Republic are good examples of countries in which enterprise-level bargaining is the dominant structure. Union membership density and coverage is higher in Europe than in the United States, and the centralized bargaining structures in Europe are consistent with this strength. The existence and continued viability of peak employer associations and legitimate union federations are key preconditions to inter-sectoral agreements. The coverage and recognized legitimacy of these social actors make national agreements on wage restraint, labour law reform, or training viable. These peak associations give collective actors power and authority to participate with employers and, in some cases, government, to negotiate change and set standards at a very centralized level, which is completely absent in the United States (EIRO, 2007: 22).

Although increased international competition and the pressure for more flexibility is contributing to a general trend toward the decentralization of bargaining in Europe (European Commission, 2006: 46–8), rather than dismantling centralized

Table 8.1 Levels of collective bargaining with regard to wages selected EU countries

	Inter-sectoral	Sector	Enterprise
Belgium	**	***	*
Czech Republic		*	***
Germany		***	**
France		**	**
Greece	**	***	*
Ireland	***	*	*
Italy	*	***	**
Hungary	*	**	***
The Netherlands	*	***	*
Finland	***	**	*
Sweden		***	*
United Kingdom		*	***

* existing level of collective bargaining
** important but not dominant level of collective bargaining
*** dominant level of collective bargaining
Inter-sectoral = Tripartite wage coordination or national bilateral agreements between peak federations
Source: European Commission, 2006: 47.

bargaining structures, the collective actors are using opening clauses in sectoral agreements to allow for local workplace negotiation on specific issues with trade union representatives or works councils. This approach to meeting local needs for flexibility has been described as 'coordinated decentralization' in which unions and/or employee representatives participate in negotiating flexibility with management. For example, the management of German enterprises has negotiated agreements with works councils that provide organization and working time flexibility within the limits of sectoral agreements (Bosch, 2004).

Workplace Representation

In most European countries, the main bodies for representing workers at the workplace are trade union representatives and works councils. Employee representation by a trade union is the norm in Cyprus, Ireland, and Sweden. The trade union has also been the single channel for representation in Poland. Trade union representation is also the norm in the United Kingdom, Estonia, and Latvia; however, these countries also allow the election of non-unionized employee representatives alongside union representatives. In the Czech Republic and Lithuania, works councils are the single channel of representation but are replaced by trade union representatives when they are elected to represent workers in the company. In Belgium, Denmark, Italy, Luxembourg, and Slovakia, a dual channel system of representation exists where trade unions dominate the works council. In contrast, the works council is more important than trade union representatives in Hungary and Slovenia. Works councils are viewed as complementary bodies to trade union representation in France, Greece, Portugal, and Spain. And in Germany, Austria, and the Netherlands, the works council is the only statutory body of workplace representation (European Commission, 2006: 65).

Although collective representation at the workplace takes many forms, it is conducted in a manner consisitent with EU directives on information and consultation rights. Within the EU, employers must provide employees with information on financial and business matters, employment levels, and structural changes to the business (e.g., closure, relocation, merger, takeover). Consultation on structural changes as well as the implementation of new technologies and working methods is also quite common across EU countries. Austria, Germany, the Netherlands, and Sweden go beyond simply information and consultation and provide workers with codetermination rights. France and Belgium also provide some codetermination rights on a limited set of issues (European Commission, 2006: 67).

In contrast, the United Kindom recently passed regulations on the information and consultation of employees. By 2008, those regulations will apply to organizations with fifty or more employees. Information and consultation procedures will only be established if a request is made by at least 10 per cent of the employees with at least fifteen employees participating. Once a valid request is made, employees can vote to recognize existing information and consultation arrangements as valid, or if no arrangements exist, employees can elect a team to negotiate such arrangements. After an agreement has been reached, it must be approved by 50 per cent of employees. If no negotiated agreement is reached within six months, the default statuatory scheme will apply, which is consistent with the basic information and consultation rights of the European Union (Statutory Instrument no. 3426, 2004). This procedure is cumbersome in comparison to Germany but for the first time gives employees in the United Kingdom the right to negotiate information and consultation arrangements over and above EU minimum criteria.

The effects of the differing rationales for collective bargaining in the United States and Europe are clear. In Europe, collective representatives are integrated across centralized bargaining structures, workplace participation bodies, and EU forms of social dialogue, providing unions leverage at each level to represent the interests of workers. In the United States, by contrast, union participation is limited to the legally designated bargaining unit and to terms and conditions of employment at that legally designated bargaining unit.

Union Density

Given the different rationales for participation through collective bargaining in the US, continental Europe, and the UK, it would be expected that the incidence of and

Table 8.2 Estimated union density, fourteen European union countries, Norway, Canada, United States, 2007

Country	Estimated percentage range
Finland	70–79
Sweden	70–79
Denmark	60–69
Belgium	50–59
Norway	50–59
Luxembourg	40–49
Austria	30–39
Ireland	30–39
Italy	30–39
Canada	20–29
Greece	20–29
United Kingdom	20–29
Germany	10–19
Netherlands	10–19
Portugal	10–19
Spain	10–19
United States	10–19
France	0–9

Sources: Organization for Economic Cooperation and Development.

trends in unionization in three areas would be substantially different. One would expect that unionization in the United States would be low, relative to the other two areas, and declining faster than unionization in the other two areas. Table 8.2, confirms that unionization in the United States is in the lowest grouping of all fifteen European Union countries. Figure 8.1 provides more detail on this comparison, presenting 2007 unionization data for the United States and ten European countries. As can be seen, of the ten European countries, the level of unionization in the United States exceeds only that of France. Despite their low level of union membership, French unions maintain power through a high coverage rate. The French state frequently exercises its right to extend collective agreements to non-affiliated employers and their employees. French Governments can also expand the jurisdiction of agreements by making them binding on employers in economically depressed regions where no bargaining partners are present (Van Ruysseveldt and Visser, 1996: 106). These practices by the state provide unions with power and protection beyond their membership numbers.

Turning from levels of unionization to trends in unionization, Figure 8.2 shows the twenty-eight-year trend in unionization in the United States and the ten European countries between 1980 and 2007. As can be seen, the general trend in unionization is downward in these countries. Figure 8.3, however, presents a different perspective by

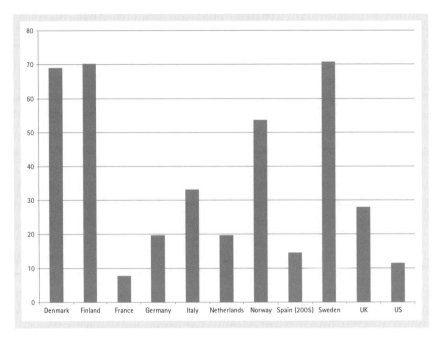

Figure 8.1 Percentage of employees who are union members, ten European countries and United States, 2007

Source: Organization for Economic Cooperation and Development.

comparing the precentage changes in the unionization rate between 1980 and 2007 for the United States and the ten European countries. As can be seen in Figure 8.3, the United States had a substantially greater decline than nine of the ten European countries. The percentage unionized in the US declined 48.2 per cent during this period. The average decline for the ten European countries was 17.4 per cent. For the nine continental European countries, the mean decline was 14.4 per cent, including France, which experienced a 57.2 per cent decline in the percentage unionized.

Union Wage Effects

Another useful way to examine the impact of participation through collective bargaining is to examine differences among countries in the union wage effect. Ideally, one would like to examine differences in a range of terms and conditions of employment. European–US comparisons of the impact of collective bargaining on terms and conditions of employment are complex, however, because labour stand-ards are much higher in Europe than the US (Block et al., 2003), and there are benefits, such as health insurance and paid annual leave, that are provided by European governments or that European governments mandate employers provide that must be negotiated through collective bargaining in the US. These government mandated benefits raise the 'floor' in Europe relative to the US, with result that

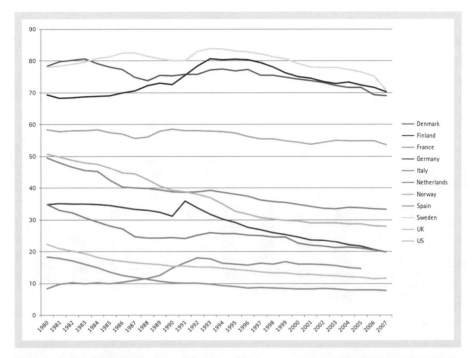

Figure 8.2 Percentage of employees who are union members, selected OECD Countries, 1980–2007

Source: Organization for Economic Cooperation and Development.

unions need not bargain for these provisions. The effect of this higher 'floor' on wage bargaining is ambiguous. It may result in lower negotiated wage increases for unionized vis-à-vis non-union workers in Europe than in the US because of a 'substitution effect;' unions may perceive they do not need wage increases as high as they might otherwise need because a relatively high level of benefits is provided, and employers may resist such wage increases because of the mandated floor. By the same token, unions in the US may perceive they need greater wage increases because of the low level of mandated benefits. A second reason a relativly low union wage premium may be observed in Europe is due to the adoption of the principle of extension in continental Europe—union negotiated wage increases are often extended to portions of the non-union sector, thus reducing the observed union–non-union differential (Blanchflower and Bryson, 2002).

On the other hand, the higher level of benefits could results in observing lower negotiated wage increases in the US relative to Europe. Unions in the US may be required to 'trade' wage increases for benefit increases. No such 'trade' may be required in Europe because the benefits are mandated.

Analysing union–non-union wage differentials for ten continental European countries for various sub-periods during the period 1994–1999, Blanchflower and Bryson

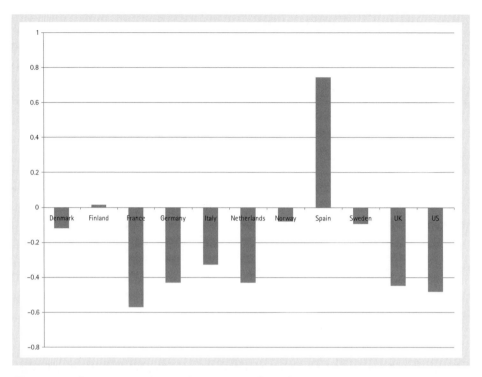

Figure 8.3 Percentage change in percent of employees who are union members, 1980–2007, selected OECD countries

Source: Organization for Economic Cooperation and Development.

(2002) found that the greatest differentials were in Austria, Denmark, and Portugal, with premia in the 15–18 per cent range, Norway and Spain were in the 5–10 per cent range, France and Germany in the 2–5 per cent; range, and Italy, the Netherlands, and Sweden exhibited a zero differential. Union wage premia in the UK have tended to be around 10 per cent. Estimates of annual waage premia for the period 1990–2001, ranged from about 4.4 per cent to about 17.7 per cent, depending on specification, controls, and data set examined. For the US, Blanchflower and Bryson estimate annual union–non-union wage differentials for the private sector in the period 1990–2001 to range from 14.3 per cent to 19.6 per cent. Blanchflower and Bryson note that their estimates are similar to five percentage points lower than other estimates.

Overall, it appears that the union wage premium in the US is high relative to the premium in the UK and in continental Europe. This relatively high and generally persistent union wage premium in the US most likely reflects strong anti-unionisn on the part of US employers and a large non-union sector. Non-union employers who so choose can successfully resist unionization using legal means without resorting to paying employees the 'union' wage (Block et al., 1996; Block et al., 2006). Given declining unionization in the US, the union wage premium is provided to a continually shrinking percentage of employees. It suggests that the unionized sector in the US has become increasingly isolated from the larger non-union sector. It also suggests, however, where unions are strong and can require employers to engage with them, essentially establishing participation, the wage benefits to unionized employees can be substantial vis-à-vis non-union employees.

SUMMARY AND CONCLUSIONS

The purpose of this chapter has been to examine the differing rationales for collective bargaining in the United States and Europe and how these rationales have affected the nature of participation through collective bargaining. The chapter has shown how the basis for collective bargaining in the United States has been the removal of impediments to economic efficiency caused by disputes over union recognition, while the basis for collective bargaining in Europe has generally been industrial pluralism and worker rights. In the United States, given the economic rationale for collective bargaining, in situations in which collective bargaining is perceived as impairing economic efficiency, the scope of participation through collective bargaining is narrowed. On the other hand, the pluralistic and worker rights rationale for collective bargaining in Europe has resulted in deep collective worker participation at all levels (community, country, region, sectoral, workplace) on a range of matters ranging from national policy to work scheduling.

Understood in this way, the variation in the scope of collective worker participation in the United States and Europe is placed in theoretical and historical context. The differences grow out of different assumptions about the very purpose of collective worker representation and the role of unions. In the United States, where unions and collective bargaining have traditionally been seen as disruptive of the economically efficient decisions made by unconstrained business, unionism is tolerated, resulting in a narrow scope of bargaining and minimalist formal participation. In Europe, where union and collective bargaining have traditionally been seen as Social Partners, one finds a broad scope of participation.

There are, of course, exceptions to these general rules. Bankruptcy law in the United States permits unions participation in bankruptcy proceedings, with what appears to be a substantial effect on bargaining outcomes of firms in bankruptcy (Hoffman, 2007; Terlep, 2007). In 2009, the UAW was actively involved in the decision of the US Government to provide financial aid to aid General Motors and Chrysler, and its health care trust now owns 17.5 per cent of General Motors (Shepardson and Aguilar, 2009) and 55 per cent of Chrysler (Kellogg and Maher, 2009). Nevertheless, the fundamental differences between the United States and Europe are well-established—participation through collective bargaining is narrow in the United States and generally broad in Europe.

As this chapter is being written in late 2009, legislation under consideration in the United States Congress and likely to be signed by a Democratic president if enacted, would ease the burdens on union organizing and recognition, increase the speed at which charges involving unlawful discriminatory discharge are processed, increase penalties on employers found to have unlawfully discriminatorily discharged employees, and provide for binding arbitration if an employer and a union are unable to agree on a first collective bargaining agreement (Library of Congress, Undated). Even if this legislation is enacted, it will not change the provisions of the labour law that define the scope of bargaining and limit agreements to a specific unit, and it is these that have resulted in a narrow scope for union participation through the the collective bargaining system in the United States.

NOTES

* The authors wish to thank Joo-Young Park for her invaluable research assistance. The volume editors and the participants in a workshop at the 2008 meeting of the Labor and Employment Relations Association provided helpful comments on an earlier draft of this paper.
1. The origins of labour law in the United States may be compared with the origins of law banning discrimination in employment.
2. See also *Duplex Printing Press Co. v. Deering*, US Supreme Court, 1921 (Lieberman, 1960; Oberer, Hanslowe, Andersen, and Heinsz, 1986).

REFERENCES

APPELBAUM, E., THOMAS, B., BERG, P., and KALLEBERG, A. L. (2000) *Manufacturing Advantage: Why High Performance Work Systems Pay Off*. Ithaca, NY: Cornell/ILR University Press.

BERG, P., APPELBAUM, E., BAILEY, T., and KALLEBERG, ARNE L. (2004) 'Contesting Time: International Comparisons of Employee Control of Working Time.' *Industrial and Labor Relations Review*, April, 57(3): 331–49.

BERNSTEIN, I. (1971) *Turbulent Years: A History of The American Worker 1933–1941*. Boston, MA: Houghton Mifflin.

BLANCHFLOWER, D. and BRYSON, A. (2002) Changes Over Time in Union Relative Wage Effects in the UK and the US Revisited, National Bureau of Economic Research, Working Paper 9395, December, at http://www.nber.org/papers/w9395, accessed 2 May 2007.

BLOCK, R. N. (2005) *Labour Standards in the Canadian Federal Jurisdiction: A Comparison with Canadian Provinces and Territories, States in the United States, and Selected European*

Nations, Report Prepared for the Federal Labour Standards Review Commission, Government of Canada, November.

—— (2006) Industrial Relations in the United States and Canada, in P. G. MICHAEL MORELY (ed.), *Global Industrial Relations,* pp. 25–51. London: Routledge.

—— BECK, J., and KRUGER, D. H. (1996) *Labor Law, Industrial Relations, and Employee Choice.* Kalamazoo, MI: W.E. Upjohn Institute for Employment Research.

—— BERG, P., and BELMAN, D. (2004) The Economic Dimension of the Employment Relationship, in J. Coyle-Shapiro, L. M. Shore, M. S. Taylor, and L. E. Tetrick (eds), *The Employment Relationship: Examining Psychological and Contextual Perspectives,* pp. 94–118. Oxford: Oxford University Press.

—— —— and Roberts, K. (2003) Comparing and Quantifying Labor Standards in the United States and the European Union. *International Journal of Comparative Labor Law and Industrial Relations,* 19(4): 441–67.

—— FRIEDMAN, S., KAMINISKI, M., and LEVIN, A. (2006) An Introduction to the Current State of Workers' Rights, in R. N. Block, *Justice on the Job: Perspectives on the Erosion of Collective Bargaining in the United States,* pp. 1–20. Kalamazoo, MI: W. E. Upjohn Institute for Employment Research.

—— ROBERTS, K., OZEKI, C., and ROOMKIN, M. (2001) Models of International Labor Standard. *Industrial Relations,* April: 258–92.

—— and WOLKINSON, B. W. (1986) Delay and the Union Election Campaign Revisited: A Theoretical and Empirical Analysis, in D. L. Lipsky (ed.), *Advances in Industrial and Labor Relations, vol. III,* pp. 43–82. Greenwich, CT: JAI Press.

BOSCH, G. (2004) 'The Changing Nature of Collective Bargaining in Germany: Coordinated Decentralization', in H. C. Katz, W. Lee, and J. Lee (eds), *The New Structure of Labor Relations. Tripartism and Decentralization,* pp. 84–118. Ithaca NY: ILR Press.

CINGRANELLI, D. L. (2006) International Election Standards and NLRB Representation Elections, in R. N. Block, *Justice on the Job: Perspectives on the Erosion of Collective Bargaining in the United States,* pp. 41–56. Kalamazoo, MI: W.E. Upjohn Institute for Employment Research.

Commonwealth v. Hunt, 45 Mass. (4 Metc. 111) 38 Am. Dec. 346 (Supreme Judicial Court of Massachusetts. Reprinted in Oberer, Hanslowe, Anderson and Heinsz (1986)).

Cornell Law School (Undated) *Legal Information Institute.* Retrieved 4 April 2007, from U.S. Code Collection, Title 29, Chapter 7, Subchapter II, Sec. 151: http://www.law.cornell.edu/uscode/html/uscode29/usc_sec_29_00000151----000-.html.

DANIEL, W. (1978) Industrial Democracy, in D. TORRINGTON (ed.), *Comparative Industrial Relations in Europe,* pp. 49–63. Westport, CT: Greenwood Press.

DAVIS, C. (2000) Loss of Board Representation at Wheeling-Pitt Fails to Stir Union Ire, *Pittsburgh Business Times,* 8 December, Retrieved 24 July 2008 from http://www.bizjournals.com/pittsburgh/stories/2000/12/11/story7.html.

DULLES, F. R. and DUBOFSKY, M. (1984) *Labor in America: A History,* 4th edition. Chicago, IL: Harlan Davidson Inc.

EIRO (2007) *Industrial Relations Developments in Europe 2006.* Luxembourg: Office of Publications of the European Commission.

EISCHEN, D. E. (1976) Representation Disputes and Their Resolution in the Railroad and Airline Industries, in C. M. Rehmus, *The Railway Labor Act at Fifty,* pp. 23–70. Washington, DC: National Mediation Board.

Europa (2007) *Social Dialogue and Employee Participation.* Section of EU web site. http://europa.eu/scadplus/leg/en/cha/c10716.htm.

European Commission (1989) *Community Charter of the Fundamental Social Rights of Workers.* Retrieved 20 June 2007, from Policy Studies Institute: http://www.psi.org.uk/publications/archivepdfs/Trade%20unions/TUAPP1.pdf.

——(2006) *Industrial Relations in Europe 2006.* Luxembourg: Office for Official Publications of the European Communities.

European Council (1975, 26 May) *Regulation (EEC) no. 1365/75 of the Council of 26 May 1975 on the creation of a European Foundation for the Improvement of Living and Working Conditions.* Retrieved 21 June 2007, from Eur-Lex: http://eur-lex.europa.eu/smartapi/cgi/sga_doc?smartapi!celexapi!prod!CELEXnumdoc&lg=EN&numdoc=31975R1365&model=guichett.

European Foundation for the Improvement of Employment and Living Conditions (2007, 16 April) *About the Foundation: FAQ.* Retrieved 21 June 2007, from http://www.eurofound.europa.eu/about/faq/index.htm.

FURSTENBERG, F. (1998) Employment Relations in Germany, in G. Bamber and R. Lansbury (eds), *International and Comparative Employment Relations,* pp. 201–23. London: Thousand Oaks New Delhi: Sage.

GOETSCHY, J. and JOBERT, A. (1998) Employment Relations in France, in G. Bamber and R. Lansbury (eds), *International and Comparative Employment Relations,* pp. 169–200. London: Thousand Oaks New Delhi: Sage.

HAMMERSTROM, O. and NILSSON, T. (1998) Employment Relations in Sweden, in G. Bamber and R. Lansbury (eds), *International and Comparative Employment Relations,* pp. 224–48. London: Thousand Oaks New Delhi: Sage.

HANTRAIS, L. (1995) *Social Policy in the European Union.* New York: St. Martin's Press.

HEPPLE, B. (1993) *European Social Dialogue—Alibi or Opportunity?* London and Worthing: College Hill Press.

HOFFMAN, B. G. (2007) UAW to Run Dana Retiree Benefits. *Detroit News,* 7 July.

KATZ, H. and KOCHAN, T. (2004) *An Introduction to Collective Bargaining and Industrial Relations,* 3rd edition. New York: McGraw Hill/Irwin.

KELLY, J. (2004) Industrial Relations Approaches to the Employment Relationship, in J. Coyle-Shapiro, L. M. Shore, M. S. Taylor, and L. E. Tetrick, *The Employment Relationship: Examining Psychological and Contextual Perspectives,* pp. 48–64. Oxford: Oxford University Press.

KERR, C., DUNLOP, J. T., HARBISON, F., and MYERS, A. C. (1964) *Industrialism and Industrial Man.* New York: Oxford University Press.

Library of Congress (Undated) Thomas: The Employee Free Choice Act. Retrieved 27 August 2008 at http://thomas.loc.gov/cgi-bin/query/D?c110:1:./temp/~c110cpq9ex::.

LIEBERMAN, E. (1960) *Unions Before the Bar.* New York: Oxford Book Company.

LOWELL, J. (1985) Chrysler Pact Spawns Dissension in the Ranks. *Ward's Auto World* December. Retrieved on 24 July 2004 from http://findarticles.com/p/articles/mi_m3165/is_v21/ai_4044975.

MAYNARD, M. and BUNKLEY, N. (2007) Auto Union Leader Finds Comfort Level. *The New York Times,* 16 May.

Midland National Life Insurance Company (1982) 263 NLRB 127, 1982.

National Labor Relations Board (Undated) National Labor Relations Act. Retrieved 27 August 2008, at http://www.nlrb.gov/about_us/overview/national_labor_relations_act.aspx.

NELLES, W. (1931) 'The First American Labor Case', *Yale Law Journal*, pp. 165–93, excerpted in W. Oberer, T. J. Heinsz, and D. Nolan (2002) *Labor Law: Collective Bargaining in a Free Society*, pp. 3–11, 5th edition, St. Paul, Minnesota: West Group.

New York Times (1994) Company News: Union Representative is Approved for Board. 29 January.

PELLEGRINI, C. (1998) Employment Relation in Italy, in G. Bamber and R. Lansbury, *International and Comparative Employment Relations*, pp. 144–68. London: Thousand Oaks, and New Delhi: Sage.

OBERER, W., HEINSZ, T. J., and NOLAN, D. (2002) *Labor Law: Collective Bargaining in a Free Society*, pp. 3–11, 5th edition, St. Paul, Minnesota: West Group.

OBERER, W. E., HANSLOWE, K. L., ANDERSON, J. R., and HEINSZ, T. (1986) *Labor Law: Collective Bargaining in a Free Society*, 3rd edition, St. Paul: West Group.

Organization for Economic Cooperation and Development (undated) Stat Abstracts, http://stats.oecd.org/WBOS/Index.aspx?DatasetCode=CSP6, accessed 26 April 2007.

RAUWALD, C., CHON, G., and STOLL, J. D. (2007) Cerberus to Buy 80.1% Stake in Chrysler in $7.4 Billion Deal, *The Wall Street Journal*, 14 May.

REHMUS, C. H. (1976) Evolution of Legislation Affecting Collective Bargaining in the Railroad and Airline Industries, in C. M. Rehmus, *The Railway Labor Act At Fifty*, pp. 1–22. Washington, DC: National Mediation Board.

SEIFERT, H. and MASSA-WIRTH, H. (2005) Pacts for Employment and Competitiveness in Germany. *Industrial Relations Journal*, 36(3), 217–40.

SPRINGER, B. (1994) *The European Union and Its Citizens: The Social Agenda*. Wesport, CT: Greenwood Publishing Group.

Statutory Instrument no. 3426. (2004) *The Information and Constulation of Employees Regulations*. Internet version of Statutory Instruments. Queen's Printer of Acts of Parliament. http://www.opsi.gov.uk/si/si2004/20043426.htm.

TERLEP, S. (2007) UAW to Push Delphi Deal. *Detroit News*, 25 June.

Treaty of Amsterdam Amending the Treaty on European Union (1997, 10 November). *The Treaties Establishing the European Communities, and Related Acts*. Retrieved 20 June 2007, from Europa: http://europa.eu.int/eur-lex/en/treaties/dat/amsterdam.html.

Treaty on European Union (1992, 29 July) Retrieved 20 June 2007, from Europa: http://eur-lex.europa.eu/en/treaties/dat/11992M/htm/11992M.html#0090000015.

Treaty of Rome (1957, 25 March) Retrieved 14 June 2007, from Hellenic Resources Network: http://www.hri.org/docs/Rome57/index.html.

VAN RUYSSEVELDT, J. and VISSER, J. (1996) *Industrial Relations in Europe*. London: Sage Publications.

WALLERSTEIN, M. M., GOLDEN, M., and LANGE, P. (1997, April) Unions, Employer Associations, and Wage Setting Institutions in Northern and Central Europe, 1950–1992. *Industrial and Labor Relations Review*, 50(3): 379–401.

WOLF, H. D. (1927) *The Railroad Labor Board*. Chicago, IL: University of Chicago Press.

CHAPTER 9

EMPLOYER STRATEGIES TOWARDS NON-UNION COLLECTIVE VOICE

PAUL J. GOLLAN

UNTIL the last few years it was apparent that little was known about the effectiveness of non-union collective voice[1] (NCV) and employee representation in non-unionized firms[2] are composed, their independence from managerial influence, and their 'representativeness'. With few exceptions, there is limited documentation about management strategies and union responses towards NCV, and the impact of such structures on influencing managerial decisions (Dundon and Gollan, 2007; Gollan, 2000, 2001, 2007, 2009; Lloyd, 2001; Taras and Kaufman, 2006; Terry, 1999; Watling and Snook, 2003).

NCV has tended to play a minimal role in many Anglo industrial relations systems, with few formal processes or legal requirements[3]. However, the lack of representative structures covering increasing numbers of non-union employees due to declining levels of trade union density and legislative changes banning closed shop or compulsory union arrangements have prompted the current interest in NCV arrangements.

This chapter explores management strategies towards, and the development of, NCV arrangements and union responses to such arrangements in predominately English speaking countries.[4] It also tracks the development of dual channel NCV and union voice arrangements and examines the interplay between channels of NCV and trade unions.

Overall this chapter reviews the current theory and raises debates around management strategies and issues involved in the process of transition from NCV to unionism. Finally, the chapter concludes by developing a framework underpinning management strategies towards NCV arrangements and union responses to such arrangements.

Due to the complexity of, and the variations in, NCV arrangements precise definitions are problematical. However, four common elements can be identified. First, only employees in the organization can be members of the representative body. Second, there is no or only limited formal linkage to outside trade unions or external employee representative bodies. Third, a degree of resources is supplied by the organization in which the employee representative body is based. Fourth, there is a representation of employees' interests or agency function, as opposed to more direct forms of individual participation and involvement.[5] However, the range of issues considered by NCV varies considerably, and often reflects on the body's level and structure in the organization (i.e., ranging from workplace/work zone safety committees to company-wide joint employee–management bodies) (also see Gollan, 2000: 410–11).

NCV arrangements may take the form of peer review panels, safety committees, works councils, consultative councils/committees (CCs), or joint consultative committees (JCCs). In addition, the official terminology varies (i.e., CCs and JCCs) between jurisdictions and even among research surveys. In reality the variations in terminology do not equate to differences of form or function. According to Taras and Copping (1998), in general, NCV arrangements are routinized forums in which non-union employees meet with management to discuss issues at either the plant or enterprise level.

NCV in Perspective

Some commentators would suggest that structures representing the interests of employees through collective bargaining—legally enforced or not—may give more legitimacy and efficacy to the decision-making process (Hyman, 1997) ensuring greater organizational commitment, and be a complement for existing union structures. Hyman (1997) also suggests that non-union employee representation forms have the capacity to assist unionism in workplaces where they are given many responsibilities and especially when enforced through statutory rights. Others have suggested that the question is not whether NCV structures will weaken unions, but rather whether unions will be prevented from developing a strong presence where there is an existing NCV arrangement (Terry, 2003). In essence, this argument is based on the premise that 'confident, assertive unionism can still make effective use of collective action to obtain management concessions' (Terry, 2003: 491). Based on UK evidence, Fishman (1995: 7) has stated, 'There is surely no inherent reason why a works council should inhibit union growth.' These views are often linked to the notion of workplace 'partnership', which stresses the need to transform the traditional adversarial and conflictual forms of behaviour to a consensus-based approach (Terry, 2003).

In contrast, other commentators have suggested that NCV arrangements along the lines of works councils have 'consolidated a more recent shift to non-unionism' (Kelly, 1996: 56). This rationale is premised on the belief that employer-initiated structures are based on employers' terms and cannot be effective in providing a true voice for employees' issues and concerns because they institutionalize worker cooperation, thus limiting scope for trade union action (Kelly, 1996; Lloyd, 2001). Some argue that NCV arrangements, such as works councils, are used by management as 'cosmetic' devices (Terry, 1999) or are little more than 'symbolic' forms of representation (Wills, 2000) as a means to avoid trade unions. These commentators also state that such structures are often packed with 'hand-picked management cronies' or in the cases where employees can elect representatives (including union members), will not be fully independent of the company and will not have the backing of national union organizers to enforce action or outcomes.

In North America, Taras and Kaufman's (1999: 13) evidence indicates that where union representation is strong (or at least where there is a valid union threat) NCV arrangements are likely to be more effective for employees than they would be in the absence of unions. In their example of Imperial Oil employees in Canada, such structures are described as 'the toothless dog got molars'. They also predict that managerial attention to NCV arrangements would diminish when co-existing with a weak union movement (Taras and Kaufman, 1999).

Taras and Kaufman (1999: 16) also suggest that when NCV arrangements are examined through the lens of industrial relations laws and institutions, with an assumption that the interests of workers and employers are different then the flaws of NCV are starkly exposed. The way these industrial relations laws are structured is premised on the belief that there will be a conflict of interests between the employee and employer, and conflict is natural in that relationship. Since there is an inequity of power in the employment relationship then institutions, such as unions and tribunals, are established as a means to redress this perceived inequity and to channel this conflict of interests. They suggest that this pluralistic view of the workplace raises issues of power, influence, bargaining, confrontation, independence, and the articulation of separate agendas (Taras and Kaufman, 1999: 16).

Taras and Copping's (1998) research into NCV arrangements at Imperial Oil in Canada suggests a cautionary note. An important finding of their investigation was that the company allowed perceptions of 'worker power and influence to develop', and representatives 'over-estimated their capacity to halt corporate-level initiatives' (Taras and Copping, 1998: 39). Thus this experience contributed to 'widened expectations–achievements gaps' creating frustration, lost of trust, and the impetus for union organizing certification. Interestingly Taras and Copping (1998: 40) also highlight that the principal inhibiting condition of unionization 'was the desire by employees to give management a chance to "correct its errors"'. They state that employees worked with management until 'all vestiges of trust were dissipated. Had the company been more responsive to worker discontent . . . there is little doubt that the union would have failed', and employees were reluctant to form a union even though they were frustrated with voice arrangements.

An interesting insight into employee views of NCV was presented in the Freeman and Rogers (1998) survey of American private sector workers. Given a choice between joint committees, unions, or laws protecting individual rights, some 63 per cent chose joint committees, 20 per cent opted for unions, and 15 per cent favoured individual rights. When presented with the choice of a voice structure run jointly by employees and management or one run by employees only, 85 per cent of respondents to the study choose the first option (Freeman and Rogers, 1998).

In the US, Kaufman's (2003: 25) research at Delta Air Lines would seem to confirm that if the motive and purpose of non-union voice arrangements is to foster cooperative and positive employee relations, then employees feel satisfied with their jobs and will often express commitment to the company. As Kaufman therefore suggests, an indirect by-product of such voice arrangements is that many of the conditions that lead employees to seek outside representation are not present. However, Kaufman also argues that if firms establish NCV arrangements for the explicit purpose of avoiding or keeping out unions, this may lead to negative outcomes as employees' perceptions and expectations are not met and they quickly grow disillusioned (Kaufman, 2003: 25).

Research would suggest that NCV arrangements are driven by three principal factors—viable union threat, a means to increase the flow of information and communication, and to provide a more harmonious and consensual workplace culture.[6] For example, Taras and Kaufman (1999: iii) argue that in North America 'non-union systems operate best when they exist in the shadow of viable union threat'. Lipset and Meltz (2000) and Verma (2000) have also indicated that the higher the union membership in an industry, the more likely the presence of NCV arrangements in that industry.

Case study research in the UK by Bonner and Gollan (2005), Gollan (2000, 2001, 2003, 2005, 2007), Lloyd (2001), Terry (1999), and Watling and Snook (2003) have indicated that for a large majority of non-union firms the main aim of NCV is to increase the flow information and communication, rather than negotiation. Most of these organizations see non-union representation and consultation as providing a more effective channel of communication than unions, stressing more 'harmonious' and less conflictual relations with the workforce, thus building and encouraging an atmosphere of mutual cooperation.

Research by Frenkel et al. (1995) in Australia also suggests that the increasing trend towards 'knowledge, work, and people centeredness' along with rising skill and education levels and more sophisticated employer strategies have given rise to a more consensual workplace culture. As a result, it is suggested that traditional bases of collectivism through trade unions, stemming from an atmosphere of alienating work relations through command and control management-style, are eroded (Colling, 2003).

From these studies it would appear that NCV arrangements have been viewed as a means of increasing company productivity and efficiency, and promoting an understanding of company policy rather than as an effective forum of collective representation for the interests of employees.

As Taras and Kaufman (1999) highlight from a US perspective, a natural instinct for industrial relations research is to compare NCV arrangements to unions, with little acknowledgement of, or research into, comparing NCV to a situation of no representation (also see Freeman et al., 2007; Haynes, 2005). This, they say, raises the question of whether NCV arrangements provide advantages to employees over no representation. Taras and Kaufman conclude that NCV arrangements do indeed 'provide workers with benefits that exceed what they could accomplish on their own. The positive benefits include improved communication, both bottom-up and top-down, greater access to managerial decision makers, the venue and means to express voice opportunities for leadership and positions' (Taras and Kaufman, 1999: 20). Similarly, Haynes' (2005) research into the lightly unionized New Zealand hotel industry over a ten-year period would suggest that while NCV arrangements may be less effective than union representation, in a non-union setting they may provide a measure of influence that would otherwise be denied to such workers.

MANAGEMENT STRATEGIES TOWARDS NCV

It is suggested that NCV arrangements are an integral element in providing the diffusion of information provision and employee involvement through consultation as a means to enhance organizational performance. According to Taras and

Kaufman (1999), the discussion of NCV by its advocates is embedded in the rhetoric of HRM. Opponents view NCV arrangements as simply company-initiated 'subterfuge to pacify and deceive workers, who might otherwise seek union representation' (Taras and Kaufman, 1999: 16). As such, they describe NCV arrangements as 'brittle' and unions as 'durable and independent'.

Alternatively, proponents view NCV arrangements as a means to foster 'genuine labour-management harmony, thus NCV arrangements are cooperative compared to unions which are considered adversarial' (Taras and Kaufman, 1999: 16) and encourage a 'singularity of purpose' between workers and managers for the good of the common enterprise', or a 'mutuality of interests' based on a 'win–win' outcome as part of the strategic HRM agenda.

For some firms, NCV arrangements are part of a progressive vision of employee relations (Taras and Kaufman, 1999: 9) embraced both by early welfare capitalist philosophies (Jacoby, 1997) and by a modern high-performance workplace focus. Taras and Kaufman 1999: 9) suggest that firms become committed to NCV 'because of its value to the development of harmonious relations with workers, and the belief that it has the capacity to deliver tangible benefits to the firm and its workforce (although these benefits appear difficult to quantify)'. Moreover, in unorganized workplaces little is known about why employees represented by other non-union arrangements reject or show little interest in trade union representation. Examples in North America have included Imperial Oil (Taras, 2000), which was coined 'fortress Imperial' due to employees' reluctance to embrace trade unions, and Delta Air Lines (Kaufman, 2003). Jacoby (1997) highlights this within the context of 'welfare capitalism' where comprehensive employee involvement and people-centred programmes were able to reduce the effect of union organizing campaigns.

Thus NCV voice arrangements can also be perceived as organs aligning common interests of employees and employers, while unions can be perceived as more independent entities. As such, unions can be seen as operating in separate domains, in pursuit of agendas that sometimes conflict with those of employers. This line of argument would suggest that NCV arrangements are complementary to unions although through coexistence may develop interdependences with union arrangements.

Willman, Bryson, and Gomez (2003) see the rationale for employer demand for voice in terms of the product market model based on the beneficial effects on firm performance.[7] In particular, they explore the positive effects attached to representation in the workplace based on economic utility and psychological benefits (also see Freeman and Rogers, 1999). They see voice (including NCV) in the context of institutional economics with the emergence of different voice arrangements based on a contracting problem—'make or buy decision on the part of the employer' (Willman et al., 2003: 3).

As part of their analysis they suggest, 'the probability of union voice within an establishment may be defined in terms of the values of and relationships between' three variables: employee propensity to join a union; union propensity to organize at a workplace, and employer propensity to deal with a union (Willman et al., 2003: 3). Union voice may have a number of complex or varied combinations. For example, employees become active around a grievance or set of grievances and seek to join a union. A union may focus its organizing activity within a particular workplace or industry and force the employer to recognize a union. Or an employer may pre-emptively recognize a union by choosing a particular union. Significantly, they suggest that, 'employer preference for a particular voice regime is likely to be a prime factor in its emergence'. They also add that while employer preferences may change due to a number of factors (legislation, union campaigns, employee dissatisfaction, industrial action, etc.) there is 'stickiness' to regime choice based on the high cost of switching (Willman et al., 2003: 4).

Applying transaction costs economics to employment, the decision to make (own voice) or buy (contract voice) is based on a number of factors. These include the specificity of the asset (the type of employee), frequency of the interaction (voice exchange through consultation and bargaining), its uncertainty (permanent or temporary employee and the need for a voice arrangement), and its governance structures (voice effectiveness and value). According to transaction cost economics the more idiosyncratic or unpredictable, and the greater frequency of interaction and duration of exchange, the greater the likelihood of the employer 'making' their own voice arrangement. Such a choice will be governed by bounded rationality and trust between parties (i.e., expectation of opportunism by the other party). The limitation of the model is explaining why there is continued existence of different governance mechanisms (or voice arrangements) for similar transactions (e.g., consultation and bargaining).

Making voice would require an employer to create a non-union voice arrangement which would be perceived as legitimate by employees. Buying voice would mean subcontracting out to a trade union all aspects of voice provision. Hybrid or hedge (or dual channel) forms of voice arrangements with a mixture of union and non-union voice structures could be established based on the nature of the transaction process (asset specificity, frequency, and uncertainty) or the behaviour of the other party (boundedness of rationality, expectation or perception of opportunism, and risk preference) (Willman et al., 2003: 8).

From an employer perspective the choice of which option to apply will be dependent on a number of factors and influences. For example, where both risks are equally high (e.g., a lack of HR expertise or experience, or a union is militant or too weak to deliver voice) employers may hedge and opt for the compromise or hybrid option and adopt a dual channel of union and non-union voice. This may also include an 'experiential' or trial period for existing arrangements to accurately assess the outcomes of the voice arrangements. In addition, the 'pure' administrative cost of voice is highest in the make case and lowest in the buy

Table 9.1 Voice regime—effectiveness, risk, direct cost, and switching cost

Channel	Buy (union)	Hedge (dual)	Make (NCV)
Direct cost	low	high	high
Switching cost	high	high	low
Risk/opportunism	high	med	low
Effectiveness in meeting firm's objectives	med	med	high

Source: Adapted from Willman et al., 2003: 28.

case and hedging is the highest cost option overall although the one with the lowest risk (see Table 9.1).

Another important factor is the union threat effect. The union threat effect could be perceived as a source of employee power by employers, and may become a compelling reason for employers to launch non-union voice arrangements, such as NCV arrangements (Taras and Kaufman, 1999). Lipset and Meltz's (2000) and Verma's (2000) research also suggest that the higher the union membership in an industry, the more likely the penetration of NCV arrangements in that industry (also see Taras and Kaufman, 1999).

All these pressures are likely to encourage conformity to existing practice (DiMaggio and Powell, 1983; Willman et al., 2003), reinforce the benefits of an institutional framework and highlight the difficulties and limitations for firms of acting in isolation (Appelbaum and Batt, 1994; Levine and Tyson, 1990).

While there are a number of disadvantages for the 'first mover' to adopt NCV arrangements, other institutional considerations may overcome such first mover disadvantages and encourage adoption of certain voice arrangements. In particular, there appear to be two key factors: first, trade union and employer association action through the adoption of voice arrangements in collective agreements and initiatives contained in new standards and codes; second, union action to separate issues for integrative bargaining and consultation and those for distributive bargaining (Freeman and Lazear, 1995).

Freeman and Medoff (1984) highlight these integrative and distributive functions of unions both as bargaining agents over the distribution of the surplus of labour–management cooperation and as a collective voice to raise productivity. In other words, they impact on both the distribution and the size of the surplus. It is argued that these two activities can interfere with each other, in that the information shared in raising productivity can be used strategically to increase the share of the surplus. As such it is suggested that cooperation can be fragile and tenuous.

Finally, legislative frameworks may encourage the adoption of certain types of collective voice arrangements. Appelbaum and Batt's (1994) analysis of the impediments to the diffusion of high-performance work systems[8] (including voice arrangements) suggests, 'an important role for public policy in developing an institutional framework that would support, rather than undermine, the transformation to high-performance work systems'.

They go on to argue, 'A more hospitable institutional setting might enable recent or newly emerging high-performance systems to survive the challenges posed by low-wage, low-skill competitors and by poor macroeconomic performance' (Appelbaum and Batt, 1994: 159–60). In addition, Appelbaum and Batt (1994) have applied institutional theory as a means to explain labour-market adaptations prompted by trigger events generating the diffusion of new 'solutions' to employment/ labour management problems. Importantly, the incentive for 'first moving' is likely to be asset specificity.

It is also argued that switching costs are high with employers tending to 'stick' to existing arrangements; where switching does occur it tends to be to a dual channel voice arrangement (Willman et al., 2003). This is premised on the belief that employers make rational decisions/choices within certain constraints or pressures. A rational choice model sets out free choices for firms to maximize utility (benefits over costs). Under bounded rationality it is assumed that such choices are constrained by limited access to relevant information or employers are limited in their capacity to deal with all the necessary information, thus creating conditions for opportunistic behaviour by other parties.

Applying agency and incentive theory to employee participation may address the principal agent problem and assist employers to make more informed decisions, since managers cannot easily monitor performance of their subordinates (creating incentives for employees to 'shirk').[9] In addition, participation may create scope for peer group pressures encouraging cooperative solutions. It could also be assumed that cooperation in the workplace gives rise to a prisoner's dilemma problem (all would be better off if no one 'shirked', but each one privately has an incentive to free-ride if they think it will go undetected). As such, colleagues may be better at detecting who is 'shirking' than supervisors and managers, thus voice may engender positive motivation via increased levels of employee participation leading to increased levels of commitment. Such peer group pressures can be reinforced by other procedures (appraisals and performance-related pay) which make pay dependent on team or firm performance.

In addition, voice may provide more factual information about the practical difficulties of measuring all aspects of work performance. Voice arrangements may also provide information about employee orientations to their work, and the appropriateness of different kinds of incentives. This is in addition to providing a channel for renegotiating terms of employment, such as implementing new pay systems.

A critical appraisal of management strategies can be found in Forrant's (2000) review of metalworking plants in the US. He argued that corporations have been intent on gaining hegemony on the shop floor, with efforts by managers to create interest in various participation and continuous improvement schemes in the 'context of the implicit and explicit threats to employment security that global production flexibility provides to corporations' (Forrant, 2000: 751). He goes on to suggest that even where unions are present, these global market pressures have allowed managers to shift production arbitrarily to gain even the slightest competitive advantage. Workers and their unions are thus squeezed between a rock and a hard place. They are accused of being backward thinkers should they refuse to consider management-proposed work changes that might give their plant a chance to prosper, yet they are equally damned when they accede, only to have managers 'pick their brains' and transfer the work to places in less expensive parts of the world (Forrant, 2000: 752).

However, as Marchington et al. (2001) have suggested, the idea of a simple model of employer choice towards collective voice may not be so clear. A number of factors may impinge on employer options towards choice of voice arrangements. Certain regulatory rules and laws may encourage or force certain behaviours that otherwise would not have taken place (such as a legal requirement for health and safety committees or the establishment of information and consultation arrangements). Other forces and influences may also be at work such as a particular management culture or attitudes of management that may constrain or inhibit certain strategies, such as excluding trade union involvement in collective bargaining. Union or employee behaviour and actions may also influence the choice of consultation or representation model. Finally, the organization's cultural and historical attitude towards employee consultation and representation may also be a significant factor (Marchington et al., 2001).

It could be argued that the term employee 'voice' may obscure the traditional distinction between employee involvement and consultation mechanisms that are soft on power, and bargaining which is hard on power. Managers and employers may regard the involvement and consultation aspects of employee voice as desirable as a means to improve firm performance, for example, direct communications to inform employees of what managers expect, and employees providing suggestions to improve productivity. However, employers are less keen on the bargaining side of 'employee voice', for example, fighting redundancy plans or demanding higher wages in return for increased productivity.

Taras and Kaufman (1999: 15–16) have expressed this more succinctly, 'very few employers are genuinely interested in fostering collective worker identity. [It's] ... like inviting a pet bear into the house, there is an omnipresent fear that the creature cannot be controlled although it can be pacified, temporarily, by feeding it a rich diet.'

The concept of 'welfare capitalism' has been explored in the US by Jacoby (1997) who suggests that NCV arrangements are a sophisticated management strategy to reduce employee turnover and provide welfare support to employees through consensual employment relations. He argues that as a result the need for interest representation through traditional unions is reduced and replaced by more paternalistic approaches and management-style. This can be achieved through higher pay, wide provision of employee benefits, and most importantly greater employee voice through participation arrangements including non-union employee representation voice mechanisms.

Thus employers gain greater organizational commitment from employees in exchange for their willingness to voluntarily forgo collective representation through an independent voice mechanism such as trade unions (Colling, 2003). In his study of Delta Air Lines, Kaufman (2003) describes its management approach as 'enlightened paternalism', where employees frequently spoke of the company as 'mother Delta' or the 'family' management model which required great expense and effort devoted to securing and maintaining employee loyalty and *esprit de corps*. However, Taras and Kaufman's (1999) review of NCV arrangements in the United States and Canada suggest that while it could be assumed that the creation of NCV arrangements by some firms may be part of a welfare capitalism strategy in light of greater employment insecurities, it can also be seen in many workplaces as part of a 'high performance' human resource management and more participative strategy rather than a paternalistic model.

Fairris' (1995: 494) historical study of US company unions[10] during the 1920s suggests that such voice mechanisms cannot be understood entirely in terms of employers' efforts to block independent unionization or to foster greater worker loyalty through the paternalistic provisions of welfare capitalism. Fairris argues that these NCV arrangements were 'mechanisms by which workers voiced their concerns about shop floor conditions to employers instead of exiting the firm'. According to Fairris, they were an effective method for addressing workers' shop floor discontent, and as a result led to both increased productivity and enhanced safety and thus were 'mutually beneficial for labor and management'. However, Fairris (1995: 495) states that during this period the transition from institutions based on avoiding employee exit from the firm to arrangements promoting employee voice was rife with conflict 'as each party strove to shape the new regime to its own advantage' both in terms of workplace power and shop floor rewards.

Fairris (1995: 496) further argues that the 'emergence of these voice demands, was in part the unintended consequence of employers' efforts to reduce labour turnover through welfare benefits. Such efforts increased the cost of the exit option for workers and thus encouraged demands for an alternative mechanism for expressing shop floor discontent.' While the value of Fairris' research may have less relevance in today's environment, it nevertheless highlights the benefit of company unions from a worker and management perspective, which served to prevent the distributional losses they would have encountered with independent trade unions.

MANAGEMENT STRATEGIES TOWARDS NCV AND UNION RESPONSES—A FRAMEWORK

Wheeler and McClendon (1991) suggest that an individual's decision to unionize is based on the 'gap' in employees' expectations (aims and goals) and achievements (outcomes). This can prompt movement (choice) along three paths.

- Path one—Perceived reduction in employee rights or privileges. Employees move along a 'threat' path, acting aggressively against employer (industrial action, strikes, stoppages).
- Path two—Other factors act as a trigger (legislation, market conditions, etc.) with employees following a 'frustration' path and hoping to resolve this by peaceful means (consultation and negotiation). Only if peaceful pursuit is blocked by the employer will employees move to aggressive activity. Brett (1980: 48) found that management's refusal to change unsatisfactory conditions in response to worker complaints incites such frustration, because it ignores the condition that led to the complaints and also denies the legitimacy of employee influence.
- Path three—Dissatisfied employees can follow a 'calculation' path in which they vote for a union (e.g., under new UK legislation on union recognition). Neither frustration nor threat need be present in this case.

Despite these three paths, union organizing efforts are moderated, mediated, and influenced by inhibiting or facilitating conditions (Kaufman, 1997). As Taras and Copping (1998) argue, the 'emotional intensity' of frustration with the expectation–achievement gap (either derived from expectancy or equity theory) motivates and acts as a catalyst for action. In the words of Taras and Copping (1998: 26), 'Thus, frustration incites a search for a solution, but also heightens emotional intensity, so that the rational elements of the succeeding behaviour may be mixed with a tendency to read provocation into incidents that would ordinarily be taken for granted.'

Figure 9.1 below sets out a framework highlighting the major themes and influences on the interplay between NCV and union voice arrangements. In particular, the model shows that a number of processes are involved in the mobilization of union representation and its interaction with employer strategies and interplay with NCV arrangements. It starts from the premise that certain internal and external contextual variables create an expectation and achievement–satisfaction gap, which management attempts to fill by creating a voice arrangement. This may be achieved through a single representation channel buying in a union or by establishing a non-union voice mechanism.

However, management may decide to 'hedge' by recognizing a union and establishing an additional voice arrangement creating two voice channels as a

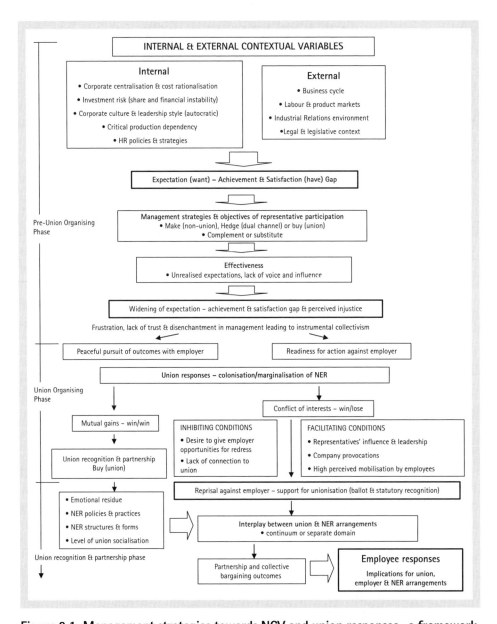

Figure 9.1 Management strategies towards NCV and union responses—a framework

Source: Adapted from Wheeler and McClendon, 1991:60.

means to address lack of employee voice and mediate union demands. Such strategies determine whether NCV arrangements are established as a complement to or a substitute for union representation. It is suggested that when such NCV arrangements, are established they create certain employee expectations about outcomes from such arrangements. If these expectations are not realized, a widening of the gap between expectation and achievement results in greater frustration, lack of trust and disenchantment in management leading to instrumental collectivism due to a lack of perceived effectiveness. This could manifest itself either as the peaceful pursuit of desired outcomes through mutual gains by union recognition by the employer and/or employer-employee partnership.

These arrangements lead to certain partnership and collective bargaining outcomes, which in turn influence employee responses and perceptions. Alternatively, union responses may be expressed through a readiness for action against an employer based on a conflict of interests as an expression of a 'win' and 'lose' strategy. This will be meditated by union responses, in particular union strategies to colonize or to marginalize NCV arrangements.

Under the union recognition/partnership path a number of factors may influence the type and level of interplay between union and NCV arrangements including NCV policies and practices, NCV structures and forms, and the level of union socialization. Under the 'win/lose' conflict path, the reprisal against the employer through support of unionization may be influenced by a number of conditions. One inhibiting condition may be the desire by certain sections of the workforce to give the employer opportunities for redress, the lack of desire to be members of a trade union, or the lack of connection to the union movement among employees. This may be due to more individualist, cultural, and societal values towards or lack of historical connection to unions. More facilitating conditions include the strength of the union representatives' influence and leadership, company views and opinions towards unions, and high perceived mobilization by employees. As a result, these conditions and influences will affect the interplay between union and NCV arrangements, and in so doing will have implications for unions, the employer and NCV.

Discussion

Management Strategies Towards and Objectives of NCV Arrangements

Central to management strategies in the implementation of NCV is the rationale for establishing such structures, given that managers initiate, and are the architects for, such arrangements. The case studies provide a number of reasons for the establishment of NCV arrangements. In summary, there are five principal reasons why managers established such schemes. First, they were a means to improve information flows and communication between employees and managers in organizations. Second, such arrangements may act as a 'safety valve' especially in the absence of an active union presence. Some companies with a long history of formal consultation structures see this as a primary reason for low levels of industrial conflict. Third, an NCV arrangement may help to facilitate the process of organizational and workplace change by enabling management and employees to highlight issues of concern at an early stage thus reducing potential conflict at the implementation stage. Fourth, NCV could potentially increase organizational performance through increased productivity and quality by providing a forum for new ideas and employee input thus increasing employees' understanding of business behaviour and producing greater levels of satisfaction and commitment. Finally, NCV arrangements may be used as an alternative for negotiations in situations where there is little active union or collective bargaining or as an attempt to undermine the union's position.

It could be argued that these results reinforce Willman, Bryson, and Gomez's (2003) thesis, which provides a rationale for an employer's demand for non-voice in terms of transaction costs economic benefits on firm performance. In this approach the decision to make (own voice by establishing NCV) or buy (contract voice by recognizing a union) is based on the type of employee, the amount of consultation and bargaining, the level of permanency of the need for voice, and its value and effectiveness in providing organizational outcomes.

The research would suggest a primary reason for establishing NCV arrangements was to create a single channel of representation without 'third party' intervention and a desire for a more direct relationship with employees.

This seems to reflect transaction cost economics theory which states that firms having higher levels of product market or service delivery risk are likely to act in a risk-averse manner, based on 'potential' rather than actual cost. Notably for employers, the legislative environment and union strategies towards voice arrangements will influence risk-averse activity by firms.

Other important reasons for introducing NCV arrangements in these organizations were to establish a representation structure to fill the void or 'representation gap' in the absence of unions and to assist in management initiatives, such as encouraging organizational change initiatives, establishing a forum for new ideas, and improving commitment to the company.

Overall, the research examined in this chapter point to an increasing adoption of NCV structures as part of sophisticated HRM and High Involvement Management (HIM) approaches, which emphasize communication and consultation. This would lend support to Flood and Toner's (1997) research, which suggested that non-union status may reduce an adversarial climate associated with unions and enable management to gain greater cooperation from employees in making unpopular changes and economies without the threat of industrial action, demarcation, or other forms of retribution.

Taras and Copping (1998) argue that in the absence of a serious union threat, management's preoccupation with NCV diminishes. However, when confronted by a union threat management awakens to pay greater attention to workplace issues that address the needs of employees. However, Bacon and Storey (2000: 423) have argued in their review of employer strategies towards union and employer partnership, 'those organisations acting as if they would prefer unions to "wither on the vine" discovered that the insecurity felt by employees was a potential future problem'.

Union Responses and Approaches towards NCV Arrangements

An important theme explored in this chapter has been union responses and approaches towards NCV arrangements. This has provided an opportunity to review union strategies and approaches towards NCV and, in particular, whether they employed tactics of 'colonization' in terms of union members and representatives being activity involved in such arrangements, or a 'marginalization' approach where union members and representatives actively avoided any involvement in NCV arrangements. The research would suggest that these strategies are particularly important in organizations, that have established NCV arrangements for the purposes of union avoidance. Equally important are employees' attitudes towards unions and their potential impact in providing the conditions for unionization.

Taras and Copping's (1998: 36) study of Imperial Oil in Canada suggests that in developing a unionization process model for application in non-union workplaces it is clear that an element of dissatisfaction is a necessary precondition to the unionization process. The findings from the cases presented in this thesis would seem to reinforce this view. Importantly, dissatisfaction over certain issues considered by employees as important and the notion of 'trust' (or lack of) between management and employees were even more critical to the unionization process.

Kim's (2004) research in Korea suggests that promoting NCV may not prevent union organizing and mobilization completely, since union and NCV channels may satisfy different needs and outcomes. Given that many employers have previously pursued NCV to avoid unionization, these differences may have significant policy implications.[11] In addition, Kim's research suggests that a lack of enthusiasm among employees for NCV arrangements may reflect perceptions of employees that representatives in NCV arrangements are *de facto* subordinates of employers and thus lack the capacity to represent employee interests effectively, providing fertile ground for union mobilization.

Importantly, the process of unionization at Eurotunnel (Gollan, 2007) was not driven by a rational, utility-maximizing calculation with the desire to use the union as a threat to restore lost bargaining power within a non-union context. Employees had little prior knowledge of unions due to the company's recruitment policies which were focused on people who had not been union members. As with Taras and Copping's (1998: 37) Imperial Oil case, the subsequent organizing drive and campaign phase was not union focused but management centred.

Applying the frustration and disenchantment path from Figure 9.1, the peaceful pursuit of outcomes through consultation with the employer is first used to resolve issues and differences. This period is associated with discussion over possible unionization and time to resolve issues and assess management responses.

However, level and influence of unionization may be dependent on the success of union strategies towards organizing potential members. Terry (2003: 498) has argued, 'The clear lesson . . . is that trade unions to retain credibility and legitimacy at all levels, may from time to time need to demonstrate their continued capacity for the exercise of economic sanctions against employers, in particular with regard to the classic, distributional issues of pay and conditions.' He goes on to suggest, 'paradoxically perhaps, the continued availability of such sanctions is one demonstration of the continuing strength of the partnership approach. (Controlled) conflict at the sectional level, usually over pay and conditions; cooperation at the workplace is the consistent formula; the one reinforcing and complementing the other.'

To reinforce this point, in many ways the partnership agreement at Eurotunnel (Gollan, 2007) protected the vagaries of management-style rather than extracted increased wages and conditions with the subsequent unrealized expectations resulting in dissatisfaction, disenchantment, and frustration. Employees' perceptions that they were unable to influence management decision making and the subsequent feelings of powerlessness, lack of trust in management, and ineffective voice through the company CC in the face of cost cutting, changes to working hours practices, shift patterns, pay and benefits, staffing issues (including recruitment and redundancies), and level of centralization of decision making were facilitating variables of great importance in the unionization process. Another important element in the unionization process was that over the years perceptions of worker power and influence were developed with elected delegates on the CC overestimating their capacity to halt company-level initiatives resulting in unrealized expectations on the part of employees.

The Eurotunnel (Gollan, 2007) study would also suggest that many employees felt they were as individuals best able to deal with certain traditional trade union issues. The risk for the union was Eurotunnel employees' perception of a lack of effective union voice could potentially impact negatively on the influence that unions have on management decisions and undermine its legitimacy at the workplace. Deakin et al's. (2002: 349) research suggests that effective union voice through employer–union partnership arrangements is dependent on its perceived strength and sophistication. However, they also caution that the sustainability of partnership arrangements will be dependent on how employers and unions manage the 'exogenous shocks' in the form of economic downturns and changes in systems of employment regulations (Deakin et al., 2002: 351).

In addition, union approaches in terms of a union's drive to curb management prerogatives may be due to the union's unwillingness to accommodate changes in periods of rapidly changing markets and technologies. It could be argued that when firms are in financial difficulty, unions' inability to adapt to the external environment hurts the 'image' of unions not only to employers but also current to potential members, further widening trade union legitimacy and authority at the workplace.

These issues could also be seen as the challenge for not only employer and union partnership at Eurotunnel, but could more generally have implications for employer and union partnership in the future. As Brown (2000) has stated, workplace partnership can be said to be a reflection of union weakness and to an extent reflects a decline in influence and power. Terry (2003: 498) highlights a degree of caution for trade unions under partnerships. In particular, thought should be given to the handling of distributive issues within partnership agreements in light of the rhetoric of cooperation and shared objectives, which can undermine the degree of union independence and restrict the level of force that can be brought to bear on management.

Concluding Comments

The framework in Figure 9.1 outlines a number of processes that are involved in the mobilization of union representation and its interaction with employer strategies, and the interplay with NCV arrangements. It starts from the premise that certain internal and external contextual variables create an expectation and achievement–satisfaction gap, which management tries to fill by creating a voice arrangement, either through a single representation channel by buying in a union or by making a non-union voice mechanism.

However, management may decide to 'hedge' by recognizing a union and establishing an additional voice arrangement creating two voice channels as a means to address employee expectations and mediate union demands. It is suggested that when employer-initiated voice arrangement are established they create certain employee expectations about outcomes. If these expectations are not realized, a widening of the gap between expectation and achievement leads to greater frustration, lack of trust, and disenchantment in management leading to instrumental collectivism. This could manifest itself in either the peaceful pursuit of desired outcomes through mutual gains in the form of union recognition by the employer and/or employer–employee partnership, or through union readiness for action against an employer based on a conflict of interests and a 'win' and 'lose' strategy. This will be mediated by union responses, in particular union strategies to colonize or to marginalize NCV arrangements.

The findings in this chapter could potentially have far-reaching implications for employers, unions, and government policy regarding the structures needed for providing effective consultation and representation. Given the devolution of decision making in many organizations and the greater focus on employee commitment and effective organizational change, these findings are of particular interest. They suggest that if employers wish to encourage an alignment of interests between employee behaviour and organizational goals, they need to place greater emphasis on giving employees a greater say in the decision-making process and having influence over workplace issues, address the expectations of employees, and at times an acknowledgement of differing interests may be essential conditions for a more effective decision-making process.

Under the union recognition/partnership path, a number of factors may influence the type and level of interplay between union and NCV arrangements, such as emotional residue, NCV policies and practices, NCV structures and forms, and the level of union socialization. Under the 'win/lose' conflict path, the reprisal against the employer through support of unionization may be influenced by a number of conditions. One inhibiting condition may be the desire among certain sections of the workforce to give the employer opportunities for redress, and the lack of desire to be members of a trade union or a lack of connection to the union movement among employees. This may be due to more individualist cultural and societal values towards, or lack of historical connection to, unions. More facilitating conditions include the strength of union representative influence and leadership, company views and opinions towards unions, and high perceived mobilization by employees. As a result of these conditions and influences, the interplay between union and NCV arrangements lead to particular partnership and collective bargaining outcomes influencing employee responses and perceptions, and in so doing have implications for unions, the employer, and NCV arrangements.

The findings highlight that unions not only have to fear employer hostility but also employee apathy and questions concerning union efficacy at workplace level. While management may support and sponsor the union arrangements to bolster partnership, if employee support is not forthcoming and ebbs away, substitution by NCV arrangements could be seen as a legitimate alternative strategy.

However, as Gollan's (2007) Eurotunnel case demonstrates, while management may go to considerable lengths to keep independent union voice out of the workplace, the case also raises important issues of the risk for employers in such a strategy and the potential negative impact and unproductive consequences that may result. Likewise for trade unions in partnership arrangements similar to those at

Eurotunnel, the language and rhetoric of partnership emphasize consensual business-driven outcomes, but whether such arrangements are compatible with the longer-term dynamic of collective bargaining and pay determination is questionable.

While such partnership arrangements are often based on complex pay formulae linked to productivity and inflation indices, in the absence of traditional conflictual behaviour within a largely unitarist arrangement, the success of such arrangements is yet to be seen. It could be argued that a necessary condition of effective partnership is the overt expression of disagreement, 'reinforcing the legitimacy and credibility of unions as independent bearers of employee interest. Supine trade unions serve neither the interest of their members nor ironically, of employers' (Terry, 2003: 500). As Martin et al. (2003: 610) have suggested 'there is a danger for unions following and promoting partnership strategies ... [they] risk endangering their independence and alienating sections of the membership who have joined them to provide representation and opposition rather than because they were a business partner'.

Importantly the research suggests that the old dichotomy of a union versus non-union channels of voice is likely to prove inadequate in shaping future representation arrangements. Instead the focus could be more fruitfully directed towards the quality of employee representation and resultant climate of employment relations, manifested in a mosaic of substance and process.[12] Embracing this alternative orientation has important consequences for management strategies and union responses to NCV arrangements in establishing effective workplace research arrangements.

In summary, the evidence demonstrates that only by establishing mechanisms that enable employees to have legitimate voice and allow differences to emerge will managers be able to channel such differences into more productive outcomes. Pivotal to this is the effectiveness and power of NCV and union arrangements. Processes that underpin the representation of employees' interests and rights are at the core of effectiveness of such bodies. The findings in this chapter would suggest that incorporating a degree of collective bargaining as a complement to or as part of an NCV process could provide more productive outcomes for employers and more just outcomes for employees.

The findings would indicate that the existence of a mechanism—union or non-union—for communication or consultation between management and employees at the workplace may not be a sufficient condition for representation of employee interests. This study highlights the importance of the interplay between NCV and union voice arrangements for effective employee voice over workplace issues. This understanding of the interplay between non-union and union representative voice arrangements may be essential for achieving and maintaining employee satisfaction. Finally, while trade unions may provide greater voice than non-union arrangements (thus the reluctance of management to provide such voice arrangements), the strength of voice is dependent on the legitimacy and effectiveness of trade unions in representing employees' interests at the workplace. And that in turn depends on the union being perceived by the workforce as both representative and able to act effectively.

Notes

1. NCV structures can also be referred to as non-union employee representation, union-independent forms of employee representation or alternative forms of employee representation. However, it is recognized that while such representative structures may be formally independent of trade unionism these structures may also involve union members. Moreover, these structures may operate with, against, or in the absence of union organization. In this chapter, voice is defined as the means not only to communicate or consult but to potentially influence the decision-making process. However, it may be argued that influence provides the foundation for power and the expression of that power through industrial 'muscle', and consequently acknowledges that voice and influence are linked but nonetheless different constructs with different purposes (Greenfield and Pleasure, 1993: 193–4).
2. Non-union firms in this context are firms which do not recognize a registered independent trade union for the purposes of collective bargaining. It does not preclude that such firms may have union members.
3. However, there are formal requirements that health and safety committees be established in some union and non-union workplaces.
4. As Freeman et al. (2007: 1) suggest, despite being located in three different geographic areas, these highly-developed English speaking countries have a common legal tradition, close political and economic ties, and 'are linked by flows of people, goods, and capital'.
5. Other forms of direct participation may include TQM teams, self-managed work teams, and quality circles. Importantly, these forms of direct participation are not representational in nature as they include every worker in the work group. Recent research from the European Works Council Study Group has suggested that direct employee involvement is lower in organizations with formal representative structures. This may imply that direct and indirect employee involvement are to some extent acting as substitutes for each other (Fenton-O'Creevy et al., 1998: 24). Unions may be present in NCV bodies if they are representing certain workplace constituencies but not in an official union capacity. In other words, NCV representatives from an Anglo perspective can be unionized in membership but not in deed.
6. See below for further details on management strategies towards NCV.
7. Recent research findings by Batt et al. (2002) applying Freeman and Medoff's (1984) exit voice model suggest that union institutions and management policies that facilitate voice can significantly reduce exit, despite significant declines in union density and controlling for team-based voice mechanisms, pay and other human resources practices that are affected by collective bargaining. Importantly, they suggest that union representation and direct participation (e.g., problem-solving groups and self-directed teams) may be viewed as complementary vehicles for employee voice at work.

8. The High Performance Work Systems approach includes practices that invest in the skills of the workforce and provide the opportunity and incentives for employees to use those skills effectively (also see Appelbaum et al., 2000).

9. Agency theory recognizes that the interests of principals (owners) and agents (managers) are not the same and that the principal and agent must align their differing interests. NCV and employee participation arrangements may play an important role in motivating employees and managers through information sharing. Agency theory can also be influenced by a number of psychological and social processes, for example, procedural justice and notions of fairness in which NCV can have a pivotal role.

10. From a European perspective these can be considered NCV arrangements.

11. Alternatively, NCV may substitute for unionism if NCV arrangements are given a negotiating function similar to unions to enhance employment conditions.

12. I would like to thank Professor David Marsden for this point.

References

APPELBAUM, E. and BATT, R. (1994) *The New American Workplace: Transforming Work Systems in the United States*. Ithaca, NY: ILR Press (imprint of Cornell University Press).

—— BAILEY, T., BERG, P., and KALLEBERG, A. (2000) *Manufacturing Advantage: Why High Performance Work Systems Pay Off*. Ithaca, NY: ILR Press (imprint of Cornell University Press).

BACON, N. and STOREY, J. (2000) 'New Employee Relations Strategies in Britain: Towards Individualism or Partnership?' *British Journal of Industrial Relations*, 38(3): 407–27.

BATT, R., COLVIN, A., and KEEFE, J. (2002) 'Employee Voice, Human Resource Practices and Quit Rates: Evidence from the Telecommunications Industry', *Industrial and Labor Relations Review*, 55(4): 573–94.

BONNER, C. and GOLLAN, P. J. (2005) 'A Bridge Over Troubled Water—A Decade of Representation at South West Water', *Employee Relations*, 27(3): 238–58.

BRETT, J. M. (1980) 'Why Employees Want Unions', *Organisational Dynamics*, 8(4): 47–59.

BROWN, W. (2000) 'Annual Review Article: Putting Partnership into Practice', *British Journal of Industrial Relations*, 38(2): 299–316.

COLLING, T. (2003) 'Managing without Unions: The Sources and Limitations of Individualism', in P. EDWARDS (ed.), *Industrial Relations: Theory and Practice* (2nd edition), pp. 368–91. Oxford: Wiley-Blackwell.

DEAKIN, S., HOBBS, R., KONZELMAWN, S., and WILKINSON, F. (2002) 'Partnership, Ownership and Control: The Impact of Corporate Governance on Employment Relations', *Employee Relations*, 24(2): 335–52.

DIMAGGIO, P. J. and POWELL, W. W. (1983) 'The Iron Cage Revisited: Institutional Isomorphism and Collective Rationality in Organisational Fields', *American Sociological Review*, 48(2): 147–60.

DUNDON, T. and GOLLAN, P. J. (2007) 'Re-conceptualizing Voice in the Non-union Workplace', *The International Journal of Human Resource Management*, 18(7): 1182–98.

FAIRRIS, P. (1995) 'From Exit to Voice in Shopfloor Government: The Case of Company Unions', *Business History Review*, 69(4): 493–529.

FENTON-O'CREEVEY, M., WOOD, S., and CALLEROT, E. (1998) *Employee Involvement within European Multinationals*, European Works Council Study Group, Stage 1 Unpublished Research Report, July.

FISHMAN, N. (1995) *TUC Consultative Document: Collective Representation at Work—Practical Political Considerations*, Unpublished, London.

FLOOD, F. C. and TONER, B. (1997) 'Large Non-Union Companies: How Do They Avoid a Catch 22?' *British Journal of Industrial Relations*, 35(2): 257–77.

FORRANT, R. (2000) 'Between a rock and a hard place: US industrial unions, shop-floor participation and the lean, mean global economy', *Cambridge Journal of Economics*, 24: 751–69.

FREEMAN, R. B., BOXALL, P., and HAYNES, P. (2007) *What Workers Say*. Ithaca, NY and London: ILR Press.

—— and LAZEAR, E. P. (1995) 'An Economic Analysis of Works Councils', in J. Rogers and W. Streeck (eds), *Works Councils: Consultation, Representation and Cooperation in Industrial Relations*. Chicago and London: The University of Chicago Press.

—— and MEDOFF. J. L. (1984) *What Do Unions Do?* New York: Basic Books.

—— and ROGERS, J. (1998) 'What Do Workers Want? Voice, Representation and Power in the American Workplace' in S. Estreider (ed.), *Employee Representation in the Emerging Workplace: Alternatives Supplements to Collective Bargaining*, Proceedings of New York University 50th Annual Conference on Labor. Boston, MA: Kluwer Law International.

—— —— (1999) *What Workers Want*. Ithaca, NY: ILR Press.

FRENKEL, S., KORCZYNSKI, M., DONAGHUE, L., and SHIRE, K. (1995) 'Re-constituting Work: Trends Towards Knowledge Work and Info-normative Control, *Work, Employment and Society*, 9(4): 773–96.

GREENFIELD, P. A. and PLEASURE, R. J. (1993) 'Representatives of their own choosing: finding workers' voice in the legitimacy and power of their unions', in B. E. Kaufman and M. M. Kleiner (eds), *Employee Representation: Alternatives and Future Directions*, pp. 169–95. Madison, WI: Industrial Relations Research Association.

GOLLAN, P. J. (2000) 'Non-union Forms of Employee Representation in the United Kingdom and Australia', in B. E. Kaufman and D. G. Taras (eds), *Non-union Employee Representation: History, Contemporary Practice, and Policy*, pp. 410–49, Armonk, NY: M.E. Sharpe.

—— (2001) 'Tunnel Vision: Non-union Employee Representation at Eurotunnel', *Employee Relations*, 23(4): 376–400.

—— (2003) 'Faces of Non-union Representation in the UK—Management Strategies, Processes and Practice', *International Employment Relations Review*, 9(2): 1–28.

—— (2005) 'Representative Voice—The Interplay between Non-union and Union Representation Arrangements at Eurotunnel', *Advances in Industrial and Labor Relations*, p. 14. Greenwich, CT: JAI Press.

—— (2007) *Employee Representation in Non-Union Firms*. London: Sage Publications.

—— (2009) 'Non-Union Employee Representation: A Review of Existing Evidence from the Advanced English Speaking Countries', *International Journal of Management Reviews* (forthcoming).

HAYNES, P. (2005) 'Filling the Vacumm? Non-union Employee Voice in the Auckland Hotel Industry', *Employee Relations*, 27(3): 259–71.

HYMAN, R. (1997) 'The Future of Employee Representation', *British Journal of Industrial Relations*, 35(3): 309–36.

JACOBY, S. M. (1997) *Modern Manors: Welfare Capitalism Since the New Deal*, Princeton, NJ: Princeton University Press.

KAUFMAN, B. E. (1997) 'The Future of the Labor Movement: A Look at the Fundamentals', Paper Presented at the Spring Meetings of the Industrial Relations Research Association.

—— (2003) 'High-Level Employee Involvement at Delta Air Lines', *Human Resource Management*, 42(2): 175–90.

KELLY, J. (1996) 'Works Councils: Union Advance or Marginalisation?' in A. McColgan (ed.), *The Future of Labour Law*. London: Mansell.

KIM, D. (2004) 'Employees' Perspective on Non-union Representation: A Comparison with Unions', Discussion Paper, School of Business, Korea University.

LEVINE, D. I. and TYSON, L. D. A. (1990) 'Participation, Productivity and the Firm's Environment', in A. S. Binder (ed.), *Paying for Productivity: A Look at the Evidence*. Washington, DC: Brookings Institution.

LIPSET, S. M. and MELTZ, N. M. (2000) 'Estimates of Nonunion Employee Representation in the United States and Canada: How Different Are the Two Countries?' in B. E. Kaufman and D. G. Taras (eds), *Nonunion Employee Representation*, pp. 223–30. Armonk, NY: M.E. Sharpe.

LLOYD, C. (2001) 'What do Employee Councils Do? The Impact of Non-union Forms of Representation on Trade Union Organisation', *Industrial Relations Journal*, 32(4): 313–27.

MARCHINGTON, M., WILKINSON, A., ACKERS, P., and DUNDON, T. (2001) *Management Choice and Employee Voice, Research Report*. London: CIPD.

———— (2005) *Human Resource Management at Work: People Management and Development*, 3rd edition. London: CIPD.

MARTIN, G., PATE, J., BEAUMONT, P., and MURDOCH, A. (2003) 'The Uncertain Road to Partnership: An Acting Research Perspective on "New Industrial Relations"', in the UK Offshore Oil Industry', *Employee Relations*, 25(6): 594–612.

TARAS, D. G. (2000) 'Contemporary Experience with the Rockefeller Plan: Imperial Oil's Joint Industrial Council', in B. E. Kaufman and D. G. Taras (eds), *Non-union Employee Representation: History, Contemporary Practice, and Policy*, pp. 231–58. Armonk, NJ: M.E. Sharpe.

—— and COPPING, J. (1998) 'The Transition from Formal Nonunion Representation to Unionization: A Contemporary Case', *Industrial and Labor Relations Review*, 52(1): 22–44.

—— and KAUFMAN, B. E. (1999) *What do Nonunions Do? What Should We Do About Them?* MIT Task Force Working Paper #WP 14, Prepared for the 25–26 May, conference 'Symposium on Changing Employment Relations and new Institutions of Representation', 1 September, Washington, DC. (Accessed on web 13-11-04 at http://mitsloan.mit.edu/iwer/taskforce.html).

Taras, D. G. and Kaufman, B. E. (2006) 'Nonunion Employee Representation in North America: Diversity, Controversy, and Uncertain Future', *Industrial Relations Journal*, 37(5): 513–42.

Terry, M. (1999) 'Systems of Collective Representation in Non-union Firms in the UK', *Industrial Relations Journal*, 30(1): 16–30.

—— (2003) 'Partnership and Trade Unions in the UK', *Economic and Industrial Democracy*. 24(4): 485–507.

Verma, A. (2000) 'Employee Involvement and Representation in Nonunion firms: What Canadian Employers Do and Why?' in B. E. Kaufman and D. G. Taras (eds), *Nonunion Employee Representation*, pp. 307–27. Armonk, NY: ME Sharpe.

Watling, D. and Snook, J. (2003) 'Works Council and Trade Unions: Complementary or Competitive? The Case of SAGCo', *Industrial Relations Journal*, 34(3): 260–70.

Wheeler, H. N. and McClendon, J. A. (1991) 'The Individual Decision to Unionize', in G. Strauss, D. G. Gallagher, and J. Fiorito (eds), *The State of the Unions*, pp. 47–83. Madison, WI: Industrial Relations Research Association.

Willman, P., Bryson, A., and Gomez, R. (2003) 'Why Do Voice Regimes Differ?' Centre for Economic Performance, Working Paper no. CEPDP0591, November, London School of Economics.

Wills, J. (2000) 'Great Expectations: Three Years in the Life of a European Works Council', *European Journal of Industrial Relations*, 6(1): 85–107.

CHAPTER 10

WORKER DIRECTORS AND WORKER OWNERSHIP/ COOPERATIVES

RAYMOND MARKEY

NICOLA BALNAVE

GREG PATMORE

INTRODUCTION

EMPLOYEE participation in organizational decision making at the strategic management level is manifested in two main ways: one, employee representatives sitting alongside shareholder representatives on the boards of public companies and state-owned enterprises; and two, producer cooperatives in which the workers own the organization. Producer cooperatives are also likely to have extensive employee representation on their boards. However, the two forms of participation fundamentally differ. Employee representation on the boards of public companies and state-owned enterprises constitutes employee *participation as employees*, in common with the other forms of participation examined in this book. Producer cooperatives owned by the employees constitutes *participation as owners*. This means that the motivational bases for each approach differ, even when some structures are similar.

There are also overlapping or hybrid cases of participation. Profit sharing, covered elsewhere in this book, is one instance. It appeals to similar motivational factors as cooperatives, although it falls short of full employee ownership. In addition, there are cases in Eastern Europe and Africa of unions buying a proportion of shares in order to gain board representation as shareholders (Kollonay-Lehoczky, 1997: 176–7, 184–5; Musa et al., 1997: 309–10). Both instances involve employee *participation as owners*, but the workers remain employees and these approaches may coexist with other forms of employee *participation as employees*.

This chapter separately examines the two approaches to employee participation in organizational decision making at the strategic management level. It analyses the incidence and effectiveness of each form of participation. The chapter concludes with general observations about the comparative viability and basis for each form.

EMPLOYEE REPRESENTATION ON BOARDS OF MANAGEMENT (ERB)

Incidence of ERB

ERB varies greatly in terms of incidence, proportion of the board, and method of selection. In some countries their role is defined by legislation, and in others by agreement with unions. Employee board members might be elected by employees, or appointed by works councils, unions, or management. They may constitute one or two members of a board, or even be equal in number to other board members. Eligibility for ERB is confined to employees in many cases, but may include union officials or others. In most instances ERB requires instigation by employee representatives even where there is legislation.

ERB is particularly widespread throughout Europe. European approaches to corporate governance tend towards a stakeholder model, whereby employees and the community are recognized alongside shareholders as stakeholders in companies. This contrasts with the Anglo-Saxon model that solely recognizes shareholders as stakeholders. In Western Europe a statutory basis for employee representatives on company boards exists in Denmark, Sweden, Norway, Finland, Austria, Germany,

France, the Netherlands, and Luxembourg. Ireland, Greece, and Portugal have similar provisions applying to state-owned enterprises only, and Spanish savings banks as well as state-owned companies are covered by legislation for employee representation on boards (Kluge, 2005: 169–70; Kluge and Stollt, 2007; Simons and Kluge, 2004). Belgium and Italy have ERB in some major state sector organizations only. Efforts to introduce general provisions for ERB failed in Britain in the late 1970s (Clegg, 1979: 439–43; Knudsen, 1995: 53–4; Taylor, 1980: 164–71).

Considerable variety in approach exists in Western Europe as shown by Table 10.1, although in most cases ERBs enjoy the same rights and obligations as other directors. One major variation occurs because of a dual board structure in some countries, notably the Rhineland countries of Germany, Austria, and the Netherlands, which have management and supervisory boards. The latter's role is to oversee the everyday management decisions of the company, appoint members of the management board, and develop broad policy and philosophies of the company. It is on the supervisory board that principal rights for employee representation exist in Austria, the Netherlands, and Germany. Representatives of employees sit on the management boards of Sweden, Norway, and Luxembourg. In Denmark representatives sit on both boards, and in France on one or the other.

Germany has the oldest commitment to ERB dating back to 1922. West German codetermination legislation of 1951 and 1952 included ERB, which was extended in 1976 and in 1995 extended to the public sector. Legislation for ERB spread generally in Europe in the 1970s, notably in Scandinavia. However, the proportion of all German employees represented by ERB provisions fell from 31 to 25 per cent from 1986 to 1996 as a result of the growth of small- and medium-sized enterprises (SMEs) and different company structures (Knudsen, 1995: 32–4, 44–5; Report of the Commission on Codetermination, 1998).

In many formerly Communist Eastern European countries ERB also exists. These countries moved towards enterprise co-management at multi-levels in the 1970s and 1980s to improve efficiency. In the former Yugoslavia an extensive system of workers' self-management existed from the 1950s, whereby the workers' assembly of all employees chose managers and ratified company policy. During the 1990s transition to market economies in these countries new labour regulations and bases for employee participation were developed as part of a process of extensive privatization, but in many cases the new systems of representation have been influenced by their history (Kavcic, 1997; Kollonay-Lehoczky, 1997). Table 10.2 shows considerable variety in approach among and within these countries, complicated by different approaches for state and privatized companies.

The extent of ERB in Europe has encouraged efforts to generalize ERB at the European Union (EU) level. An attempt to introduce obligatory EU level regulations for ERB based on the German model in the European Commission's draft Fifth Directive on European Company Law of 1972 ultimately failed to overcome sustained opposition from employers and the British Government, and it was

Table 10.1 West European employee representation on company boards

Country	Criteria	Number of reps.	Nomination	Selection	Eligibility	Board structure
Denmark	Ltd liability, >35 employees	2 on SB (1973); 1/3 or min. 2/5 MB (1980)	Not specified	Employee vote	Employees only	dual
Sweden	Ltd liability, >25 employees	Min. 2 on MB (1973)	Local union		Employees but no formal obligation	single
Norway	Ltd liability, >50 employees (1973); >30 employees (1989)	Up to 1/3 MB	Employees	Employee vote, unless unions agree to choose	Employees only	single
Finland	Ltd liability, >150 employees (1991);	Max. 4 or 1/4 SB or MB	By personnel groups (e.g. blue & white collar)	Employee vote in 2 groups	Employees only	choice
Austria		1/3 SB	Works council		Works councillors	dual
Germany	Private sector a) iron, steel, coal >1,000 employees; b) private sector 500–2,000 employees; c) private sector >2,000 employees; d) public sector (1995)	a) 1/2 SB (5), neutral chair, 1 on MB (1951); b) 1/3 SB (1952); c) 1/2 SB (1976);	a) 2 works council, 3 union; b) works council & employees; c) union 2/3, & employees;	a) general meeting shareholders; b) employee vote; c) employee vote, or delegates' assembly if >8,000 employees;	a) employees, & union nominations; b) employees only; c) employees & union nominations	dual
Netherlands	large cos: €16 m capital, >100 employees, works council exists	1/3 SB	works council	general meeting shareholders	no employees	dual

Country		Appointed by	Voting	Eligibility	Choice
France	a) state enterprises (>50%); b) privatised cos.; c) non-mandatory private cos.; d) cos. with works councils	a) up to 1/3 SB or MB; b) 2–3 on SB or MB; c) max. 1/3 SB or MB; d) 2 works council observers	a) employees; b) employees; c) employees; d) works councillors	a) employee vote; b) employee vote; c) employee vote; d) works councils appoint observers	employees only	
Luxembourg	ltd liability, >1,000 employees	1/3 MB	works council	works council	employees only except iron/steel	single
Ireland	20 state enterprises/agencies	mainly 1/3	unions	employee vote	employees only	single
Greece	state enterprises	2–3	employees but unions de facto	employee vote	employees only	single
Portugal	state enterprises	1 (rarely implemented)	works council & employees;	employee vote	employees only	single
Spain	state enterprises & savings banks	2	most representative unions		no restrictions	single
Malta	10 state enterprises	1 on MB	works council	Employee vote	no restrictions	single

SB: Supervisory board. MB: management board.

Sources: Hagen, 2008; Kluge and Stollt, 2006, 2007; Simons and Kluge, 2004; Stollt and Kluge, 2005.

Table 10.2 East European employee representation on company boards

Country	Criteria	Number of reps.	Nomination	Selection	Eligibility	Board structure
Czech Republic	a) joint stock cos > 50 employees; b) state-owned cos.	1/3 SB	a) private sector: union or works council & employees; b) state-owned: process agreed with union	employee vote	a) private sector: employees & union officials; b) state-owned: employees only	dual
Hungary	joint stock & limited liability cos. >200 employees	1/3 SB; where MB only by agreement with works council	works council in consultation with unions		employees only	choice
Poland	privatised cos: a) state holds >50% shares b) state holds <50% shares c) >500 employees; state-owned cos. remain covered by 1981 workers' self management Act	a) 2/5 SB; b) 2–4 on SB; c) additionally 1 on MB works council participates in appointing managing director	employees &/or union	employee vote	no restrictions	dual
Slovakia	a) joint stock cos. >50 employees; b) State-owned cos.	a) 1/3 SB; b) 1/2 SB	a) employees in private sector; b) union in state-owned cos.	a) employee vote in private sector; b) in state-owned cos. employee vote + 1 union appointed	employees only	dual
Slovenia	a) joint stock cos. with SB (most) b) joint stock cos. with MB only fulfilling 2 of 3 criteria: >50 employees, >€7.3 m. turnover, assets >€3.65 m.	a) 1/3–1/2 SB + 1 on MB where >500 employees; b) 1/5–1/3 MB	a) SB members appointed by works council; MB 1 works council nominated, appointed shareholders; b) MB members appointed by works council		no restrictions	choice
Romania	all cos. with union	min. 1 on MB advisory only	union		no restrictions	single

SB: Supervisory board. MB: management board.

Sources: Kluge and Stollt, 2006, 2007; Stollt and Kluge, 2005.

finally dropped in 1983. Trade unions in countries with developed systems of ERB, notably Germany, also feared that the EU-wide proposals would dilute existing national systems (Cressey, 1997: 30–31; Goetschy, 2003; Taylor, 2006: 40–42; Veersma and Swinkels, 2005: 190–95). However, the 2001 European Company (SE) Statute, effective in October 2004, revisited the issue more flexibly with adoption of an associated Directive on ERB. Companies which operate across a number of Member States of the EU may register as an SE in order to operate within one set of corporate regulations. For registration, companies are required to initiate negotiation with a special negotiating body of employee representatives (union and/or works council) from each country in which they operate, to determine the nature of employee involvement in the decision-making processes of the new SE. This involvement may include ERB, works councils, and trade union representation. The outcome of the negotiations, however, depends on the existing legal requirements for employee involvement in decision making in the Member States in which the company operates. A key objective of the SE statute is to prevent the undermining of existing national provisions for ERB in member states through formation of an SE. The corollary of this is that ERB is only mandatory for an SE where it is already a feature of national legislation (Taylor, 2006: 42–4; Veersma and Swinkel, 2005). In this way, the SE Statute attempts to overcome employer opposition as well as trade union fears.

Outside continental Europe systematic legislated approaches to ERB are rarer. Where ERB occurs it is commonly the result of public sector initiatives in statutory authorities or public enterprises. In the United Kingdom, for example, the TGWU traditionally had a seat on the Mersey Docks and Harbour Board, and in the 1960s and 1970s this became a growing phenomenon. In 1967 when the steel industry was nationalized, the British Steel Corporation instituted fourteen worker directors, nominated by the TUC (Trades' Union Congress) Steel Committee. These directors represented a minority of a unitary board of management. While some claimed that they succeeded in humanizing company policy, others were more critical of their lack of impact on decision making (Taylor, 1980). From 1978–1979 the British Post Office experimented with union and management parity on a board which also included a small third group of independent consumer representatives, but the new Conservative Government refused to renew the arrangement, particularly in the light of management hostility to the scheme (Batstone et al., 1983).

Australian Governments have instigated ERBs for statutory authorities and corporations from the 1950s, particularly at the state government level. In 1952 a trade union representative was included on the board of the newly established New South Wales (NSW) Electricity Commission. Other state electricity authorities followed suit over the next few years, as did the NSW State Dockyard, the railways and the State Superannuation Board (Baird, 1978). From the 1970s this became more common. The incidence of ERB grew from 15 to 29 per cent of public sector workplaces in Australia from 1990 to 1995. At the federal level ERB appeared on statutory authorities, such as the Australian Broadcasting Commission (ABC), Qantas, Australia Post, Telstra (the telecommunications authority), and the Reserve Bank, particularly under the federal Labor Party Government from 1983–1996. In some of these instances, however, this was the result of appointment of a union official to a board vacancy, rather then the creation of a board position specifically for an employee representative. Currently ERB occurs in Area Health Services and universities, which are statutory authorities governed by boards or councils, but also in many libraries, museums, schools, and technical colleges which also have boards or councils but do not enjoy the full autonomy of a statutory authority. In New Zealand a union representative was appointed to the Air New Zealand board in 1985, but few other examples have occurred. In the British and Australian cases union appointments were also the norm, with the ABC and Australian universities being more exceptional in providing for election of representatives by all employees, although usually these positions have been taken by unionists (Markey, 2003: 130–32).

Public sector ERB in Britain and Australia, however, has declined since the 1980s and 1990s respectively, for two main reasons. First, policy under Conservative Governments did not favour ERB and it was discontinued, although in Australia at a state as opposed to national government level it has not declined so much because of the persistence of Labor Governments at that level. Second, widespread privatization of public sector enterprises in developed economies, such as Britain and Australia, has led to the abandonment of ERB in those enterprises affected, such as Qantas and Telstra. This process has also occurred in other countries as a result of privatization.

Elsewhere, in much of Africa, ERB on state authorities and enterprises was practiced extensively in the post-colonial era, when many African nations developed a large public sector. Egypt and Algeria were prominent examples from the 1950s and 1960s respectively. ERB was part of broader socialist approaches to industrial organization, with Algeria adopting its own form of workers' self-management, *autogestion*. Similarly, ERB was instigated in state enterprises in Tanzania after the Arusha declaration of 1967 ushered in a policy of self-management and common ownership of industry. Ghana was another prominent example of ERB in a large state sector. Most of these examples of ERB involved union-nominated employee representatives who constituted 30–40 per cent of the board. However, these approaches have enjoyed very limited success. Unions have been reluctant to play a positive role in ERB, and in the socialist African nations, such as Egypt, Algeria, and Tanzania, the process became corrupted as management boards and unions became dominated by ruling party representatives. The incidence of employee board representation has declined in developing African economies in recent years, as a consequence of World Bank and IMF policies insisting on privatization as a prerequisite for economic aid. As elsewhere, privatized firms generally have not persisted with ERB arrangements (Kester, 2007: 32–5, 288; Musa, 2001: 233–7; Musa et al., 1997: 313–15).

Outside Europe, where employee representatives on company boards occur in the private sector without statutory requirement, it has often been a result of agreements between unions and management. For example, in the USA from the 1980s a small number of firms in the steel and airline industries included union-nominated directors on their boards. This was part of the industrial relations response to the crisis undergone by these industries at that time, often alongside 'concession bargaining' by the unions to keep the companies afloat (Katz, 1993: 93–4; McKersie, 2001; Strauss, 2001). In Australia ERB grew from 4 to 11 per cent of private sector workplaces with twenty or more employees from 1990 to 1995. The industry sector where it was most common was Property and Business Services, 16 per cent (Markey, 2003).

Finally, Japan warrants mention as a special case. Kuwahara characterizes Japanese firms as 'quasi-employee managed' even though there are no members of company boards who are nominated or elected by employees or their unions. Nevertheless, most board members are former long-term employees, nominated by the president of the firm to the shareholders' meeting. While these commonly come from senior managers' ranks, they have usually risen through the company, and frequently have been enterprise union members and officials (Kuwahara, 2004; Suzuki, 2005).

Effectiveness of ERB

Effectiveness of ERB may be evaluated by different criteria. For example, it has commonly been alleged that ERB is disruptive of corporate governance, particularly in hindering companies' ability to innovate because it tends to produce an emphasis on defending the status quo (Kluge, 2005: 164, 173). More importantly for our purposes, a number of practical limitations frequently have been identified with ERB as a form of employee participation (Strauss, 1998: 139–40). First, the scope of ERB is confined to larger limited liability or joint stock companies, since SMEs are commonly unincorporated and lack boards of directors, but SMEs represent a major proportion of employment. Second, employee board representatives have limited powers because they do not constitute a majority on the board, key decisions frequently are not made at board level, and management exercises a significant degree of power through controlling the agenda and flow of relevant information. A recent survey of employee representatives in the EU found that overall they did not consider their influence on board decisions to be great, but that it varied according to the issue. The greatest influence perceived by these employee representatives concerned health and safety and industrial relations, and the least over appointment/dismissal of management and strategic issues, such as accounts and budgets, general economic position and strategic planning (Carley, 2005: 239–40). This confirms earlier observations that ERB's specialization in administration of social policies and personnel administration has contributed significantly to 'developing modern, employee-friendly personnel management styles' (Knudsen, 1995: 44–5). Third, effective participation in governance processes may require technical skills that employee representatives lack for evaluating accounting, legal, marketing, and strategic data. However, few board directors with a business background would enjoy expertise in all these areas and the problem may be dealt with by adequate induction and training processes for board members, and by maintaining a balance of different expertise on the board. Fourth, communications between board representatives and the employees sometimes has been a concern of unions fearing that worker directors become isolated from workers 'at the top of a pyramid of corporate power' (Taylor, 2006: 44–5). Communication also may be hindered because board members are expected to respect confidentiality concerning board deliberations, partly since sensitive information could reach competitors (O'Kelly, 2005: 229). Fifth, a related issue concerns role conflict: are ERBs primarily representing employees' interests, which might be short term, or are they co-managers, primarily representing the welfare of the organization as a whole. However, this perceived role conflict assumes that employees' interests are separate from, or even 'outside' those of the firm, and that managers' perceptions of what is best for the firm are necessarily free of self-interest and short-term objectives. Both assumptions are contestable, and represent a denial of the stakeholder model of corporate governance.

Retrenchment and union-management issues are most likely to generate role conflict (O'Kelly, 2005: 229). One strategy adopted in Sweden (Levinson, 2001; Nilsson, 2004) and in some cases in the US, has been for ERBs to absent themselves from deliberations directly relating to industrial relations matters. However, this does not address the related common criticism by employee organizations that their representatives are prone to becoming incorporated by the boards, and a 'transmission belt' for management thinking to the workforce. It is noteworthy in this regard that a 2004 survey of EU ERBs found that while they were evenly divided over whether they primarily saw themselves as general board members, or representatives of specific employee interests, far greater proportions of employees, works councils, unions, other board members, and management saw them as primarily representatives of specific employee interests (Carley, 2005: 240–43).

It seems that these issues are best dealt with in those countries operating with the stakeholder model of corporate governance. In Germany and other European countries ERBs are only one manifestation of representative employee participation, with others including employee works councils and strong unions. The overwhelming theme of recent research which examines multiple forms of participation, including direct participative processes of teamwork and autonomous work groups is that they are mutually supportive and work best as part of a broader system: participation begets participation (Gollan and Markey, 2001: 324). In cases such as those in the USA, where ERB has been introduced piecemeal and as a result of economic crisis, many of the disappointments associated with the practice of board representation seem more likely to become substantial obstacles.

The German codetermination system was credited with contributing signifi- cantly to German industry's competitiveness by the 1998 Commission on Codetermination (Report of the Commission on Codetermination, 1998; Taylor, 2006: 45–6). It is impossible to isolate the precise economic impact of codetemina- tion, but the implementation of the 1976 Codetermination Act preceded a period of unprecedented economic prosperity in Germany, and has not impacted negatively upon foreign investment which is more affected by infrastructure, market dynam- ics, and workforce qualifications. In December 2006, the Biedenkopf Commission recommended greater flexibility in negotiated collective agreements regarding proportion and election of employee representatives and the role of the supervisory board, inclusion of employee representatives from foreign subsidiaries, and choice between dual and monist board structures. However, union representatives could not agree on employers' proposal for a reduction in parity employee representation on supervisory boards, and negotiated optional codetermination. The government has not legislated for change because it sought a mutually agreed position from employers and unions (Müller, 2007).

In Sweden and Denmark support for ERB has been strong from employers and unions, although the unions originally proposed legislation. The Swedish system evolved during a period of considerable modernization, restructuring, and techno- logical innovation. Recent surveys have indicated a high degree of satisfaction with the system on the part of management, labour directors, and unions (Edlund and Viklund, 1993: 47–8; Levinson, 2001; Taylor, 2005: 161). A 1998 Swedish survey of chief executives found that 60 per cent believed ERB had contributed to cooperation, improved worker understanding of board decisions, and facilitated employee support for difficult decisions. In Denmark the measures for ERB initially encountered employer resistance. However, 60 per cent of Danish employ- ees are now employed in enterprises with ERB, and over two-thirds of companies employing more than 200 have instigated ERB, although employees in most smaller companies have failed to initiate ERB. Studies indicate strong employee support, though many felt that power effectively remained concentrated on com- pany boards and that employee representatives were hindered by their confidenti- ality obligation. Nonetheless, there is wide acknowledgement that the system has generated greater employee understanding of management goals and contributed to a competitive edge for these countries (Knudsen, 1995: 91; Taylor, 2006: 46–7). For Sweden, Edlund and Viklund (1993: 48) note that 'the right of representation on company boards has mainly come to be regarded as a means of keeping the union informed, rather than a means of directly influencing corporate decision-making'. European unions generally appear to have overcome their fears about the isolation of worker directors (Taylor, 2006: 45).

Recent reports in all of the European countries with legislated ERB tend to confirm a moderately positive outlook. It is also confirmed by the high proportion of new European Companies (SEs) which have maintained ERB, where it might have been avoided or diluted, including a large proportion of German-based companies which have adopted single board structures for SE registration. There is no evidence allowing a conclusion that company performance is impacted upon negatively by ERB. Countries with extensive forms of ERB generally enjoy a strong position in global markets and a positive rating for microeconomic attractiveness as business locations (Kluge, 2005: 173–5).

A recent survey of 500 representatives in 10 EU countries indicated different types of relationship with management and unions. The majority receive full-time paid release from employers to fulfil their duties, and most of the remainder receive part-time release, but trade unions are the main provider of training, support, and advice in a small majority of cases. Works councils and employees generally are seen as the most important relationship for these representatives. However, demographically they were not very representative of the wider workforce. They were 'clearly a group of mainly middle-aged men with shopfloor or clerical jobs, with relatively long service on the boards of the companies for which they work and strong links to trade unions' (Carley, 2005: 233–8).

PRODUCER COOPERATIVES

Producer cooperatives, otherwise known as industrial or workers' cooperatives, may be considered an advanced form of worker participation. While the recent literature on employee participation in Western economies has largely neglected producer cooperatives, they previously attracted considerable attention focusing on particular examples such as Mondragon in the Basque Region of Spain (Bradley and Gelb, 1981, 1982, 1987; Johnson and Whyte, 1977; Thomas and Logan, 1982; Whyte and Whyte, 1988) and the Plywood Cooperatives in the Pacific North West of the USA (Craig and Pencavel, 1992). There was also considerable interest in the labour-managed firms in Yugoslavia before its disintegration. However, as this form of organization was mandated for all enterprises above a certain size, they are of limited relevance to the experience of producer cooperatives in mixed Western economies (Leete-Guy, 1991: 65). The major issues within the producer cooperative literature examined here are defining producer cooperatives, tracking their life cycle, and their impact on productivity, employment, and wages.

Producer cooperatives form part of a broader cooperative movement that includes consumer cooperatives, agricultural cooperatives, and cooperative banks. There is no generally accepted definition of producer cooperatives. However, as Jones (1978: 150) presents, there are a number of characteristics on which most commentators would agree:

(i) The enterprise is autonomous; (ii) workers are able to become members of the enterprise, usually by nominal holdings of share capital; (iii) formal provisions exist for direct and indirect participation in control and management at all levels in the enterprise by worker-members; (iv) workers share in income remaining after payment of material costs and do so by virtue of their functional role as workers; and (v) the cooperative principles of 'one-member-one-vote' and 'limited return on capital' apply.

These characteristics, particularly those related to worker participation (combining participation in profits, ownership, and decision making), largely distinguish producer cooperatives from capitalist firms (Estrin and Shlomowitz, 1988: 61; Jones, 1978: 150). The principle of one vote for each member irrespective of the number of shares also applies to consumer cooperatives and cooperative banks, in which workers can also be members through their role as consumers and may have some influence on the employment practices of these cooperatives if allowed to participate in general meetings and on the boards of directors (Balnave and Patmore, 2006: 61). The management of producer cooperatives run the firm in the interests of workers and the members receive a share of the profits. While workers in non-cooperative private sector firms may share in profits and participate in management through forms of profit sharing, employee representation, and employee shareholding, the enterprise is run for the profit of private shareholders rather than workers. (Derrick, 1981: 106; Estrin et al., 1987: 45).

There is a difference in the literature as to what constitutes workers' ownership of a producer cooperative. A purist definition restricts membership to workers only. This principle underlies the Mondragon producer cooperatives where all and only current workers are members (Jones, 1978: 151). In the case of French workers' production cooperatives (WCO), each cooperator is simultaneously 'co-owner' and 'cooperator' (Bataille-Chedotel and Hutzinger, 2004: 91). However, membership of traditional French producer cooperatives is not confined to current workers (Jones, 1978: 151). In other cases, such as the Plywood cooperatives of the Pacific Northwest in the USA (Craig and Pencavel, 1992: 1084), not all workers are members. The link between ownership and employment can break down if the cooperatives hire non-member staff to meet increases in demand for its products (Leete-Guy, 1991: 64). Lindkvist and Westenholz (1991: 324) take a more liberal view of worker ownership, arguing that for a producer cooperative, more than half the employees have share capital and at least one-third of the employees must be owners.

Producer cooperatives also differ in the degree to which members directly participate in management and decision making. Leete-Guy (1991: 64) argues that in 'labour-managed firms', participation in the management of the cooperative is part of the job. In the context of British producer cooperatives, Jones (1978: 151) notes that while the principle of 'one-member-one-vote' has meant that in some cooperatives worker–members have formed the majority of the committee of management, in the vast majority of cases direct worker participation has been provided through some form of works committee. In contrast, French producer cooperatives have been subject to a legal requirement that at least two-thirds of the policy-making board be current workers (Jones, 1978: 151). Kandathil and Varman (2007) note that worker ownership does not automatically lead to 'psychological ownership', particularly when involving the takeover of existing firms as a last resort in order to save jobs. In such cases, there are incidences where no formal mechanisms for institutionalizing worker participation are established, while in other situations, such mechanisms may not lead to enhanced worker participation. Management may not provide the level of information expected by workers and/or workers may not be able to comprehend or indeed trust the information provided, particularly if the organization has had a history of distrust between management and employees.

There are several ways by which producer cooperatives are formed. They can be new start-up firms. Alternatively, as noted above, they can involve workers taking over existing firms. Some producer cooperatives were established to deal with some kind of crisis such as job losses and firm closure. While some buyout may involve workers purchasing firms that are closing due to issues of commercial viability, in other cases owners of viable firms may find them difficult to sell due to short-term losses resulting from mismanagement or because they are not considered sufficiently viable by potential buyers (Paton, 1991: 30–32).

The confidence of workers to proceed with the buyout depends upon the attitudes of external parties. Trade unions have generally been suspicious of producer cooperatives or hostile to them. According to Bradley and Gelb (1981: 212), organized labour perceives attempts at worker control as legitimating, and thus strengthening, the real control held by capital, and further, that labour opposition to increased capitalist power is fragmented and thus weakened by co-operativism. Nevertheless, periods of unemployment make trade unions more sympathetic to the establishment of producer cooperatives as a means of saving jobs. Governments can also be sympathetic to establishing producer cooperatives during periods of unemployment to preserve jobs and sustain regional economies. Overall, however, the larger the producer cooperative sector in a particular economy, the greater the credibility of the idea, and more support there is for the establishment of producer cooperatives (Paton, 1991: 30–32).

One question raised is why many producer cooperatives do not survive. Arising from the Webbs (1914), there is the idea that producer cooperatives degenerate into non-participatory organizations. The Webbs (1914: 21), who were concerned about the lack of success of producer cooperatives compared to consumer cooperatives prior to the First World War, doubted the abilities of workers to exercise self-discipline in regard to production output and quality. They also believed the workers in producer cooperatives did not have a requisite knowledge of the market and could not change existing work practices to meet shifting market needs. Producer cooperatives can also be weakened by a 'collective selfishness' if they are successful and the original members retire. Members, to avoid diluting their equity, will take in new workers as hired labour rather than members. By the time the members retire the value of the shares has become so high that they can be only purchased by the remaining members or outside investors. Very few workers end up owning or controlling the enterprise (Whyte: 1991: 83–4). Members with entrepreneurial ability or financial resources may seek finally to convert the producer cooperative into a capitalist enterprise (Leete-Guy, 1991: 66, 69). The Mondragon cooperatives have overcome the tendency to degenerate by allowing members to own the company but not hold individual shares that can be bought or sold. Non-member employees are also limited to 10 per cent (Whyte: 1991: 97).

One important constraint for the establishment and growth of producer cooperatives is a shortage of capital. As Craig et al. (1995: 126) note, producer cooperatives can be 'inherently risky institutions'. Workers may put all their own wealth into the producer cooperative rather than diversifying it and even provide personal loans to the producer cooperative beyond their shareholdings. Members prefer immediate rewards to retaining profits for protection against a downturn in economic activity and investment in new technology, marketing methods or plant. Even where producer cooperatives begin with state of the art technology, they do not generally develop the capacity for applied research in order to remain competitive (Whyte, 1991: 84). This 'underinvestment effect' was put forward by Vanek (1975: 446–50), a leading microeconomic theorist of producer cooperatives, as a major explanation for the comparative failure of producer cooperative compared to the capitalist firm.

Despite the calls by Vanek (1975: 454–5) for external financing of producer cooperatives to counter underinvestment, there are limitations. Traditional finan-cial institutions have been reluctant to lend capital to producer cooperatives. Where members have decided to form a producer cooperative in crisis situations, financial institutions can be concerned with lending to enterprises that have been abandoned by their capitalist owners. If the enterprise is profitable the capital costs can be higher because lending institutions are unfamiliar with or unsympathetic towards producer cooperatives. (Lindkvist and Westenholz, 1991: 327). While Jefferis and Thomas (1986: 96) agreed with Vanek that there was a problem of undercapitalization with producer cooperatives, in their study of printing and clothing cooperatives in the UK, the problem arose from an 'inability of coop members to raise sufficient external finance (for a variety of reasons) rather than a conscious decision not to do so.' Thomas (1990: 181–2) also argues that small capitalist firms and producer cooperatives report similar problems in obtaining external finance. They both use external loans from friendly sources, such as family, friends, and sympathizers, and commercial sources, such as banks. Small business owners may feel similar concerns about making risky decisions in regard to retained surpluses and do not rely on external equity any more than most co-operatives. While cooperative banks, such as those in Spain and the United Kingdom, are sympathetic to producer cooperatives, they also have to protect their own equity and the interests of existing cooperatives by ensuring that they finance new cooperatives which do not compete with established cooperatives (Jefferis and Mason, 1990: 221; Whyte and Whyte, 1988: 86).

What impact do producer cooperatives have on productivity, employment, and wages? The advocates of cooperatives (Logue and Yates, 2006: 687) argue that producer cooperatives perform better than their private sector counterparts with higher levels of morale, loyalty, output, and productivity. Workers have a financial stake and participate in the firm. As there is no separation of interests between workers and owners, there are no bargaining costs and workers may contribute to firm productivity as they are more willing to reveal information concerning production problems and opportunities than in a private firm. Supervisory costs will also be reduced as workers are motivated to monitor each others' efforts. Profit sharing by the producer cooperative will also give them a premium over capitalist firms by attracting workers with high levels of ability or work effort (Ben-Ner, 1988: 292–6; Craig et al., 1995: 124–6).

However, the findings from studies of productivity in producer cooperatives vary. Estrin, Jones, and Svejnar (1987) in a study of five Western economies found that the overall effect of producer cooperatives on productivity was positive. The most positive impact on productivity arose from profit sharing, with individual share ownership and participation in decision making by workers having a slightly lesser impact. Grunberg (1991: 119) in a study of the plywood cooperatives challenged the link between commitment to the firm, work satisfaction and productivity. He speculated that while the 'loose supervisory climate' increased work satisfaction, it contributed to lower levels of work effort. Generally studies of producer cooperatives have shown that the sharing of profits does have an impact on productivity, but there are variations between countries. When comparative data is available for both producer cooperatives and comparable capitalist firms, empirical evidence is inconclusive concerning the superior productivity of producer cooperatives (Bonin et al., 1993: 1302–304; Craig et al., 1995: 158).

Producer cooperatives have been found to provide more stable employment in the face of variations in output price than other types of enterprises (Bonin et al., 1993: 1315; Craig and Pencavel, 1992: 1096; Thomas and Logan, 1982: 155). As Bonin et al. (1993: 1315) suggest, this also means that the return to labour must be more flexible and reflective of product market conditions than in the capitalist firm.

Pencavel, Pistaferri, and Schivardi (2006) reached such conclusions in their study of Italian producer cooperatives—these enterprises having more volatile wages and less volatile employment than their capitalist counterparts. While they found this 'consistent with the notion that enterprises where workers command a greater voice will protect workers from employment reductions' (2006: 42), they also found that producer cooperatives had 14 per cent lower wages than capitalist enterprises. Jeffris and Thomas (1986: 91) in a study of UK clothing and printing cooperatives found that most cooperatives were paying below the average wage. They argued that this reflected their precarious position within a capitalist economy and the rate of wages was not a matter of choice but all that the cooperatives could afford. By contrast, studies of the Mondragon producer cooperatives found that their members had greater wealth and earnings than employees in capitalist enterprises (Thomas and Logan, 1982: 155). However, this should be qualified by the constraints to income differentials with the ratio of the lowest to highest payment being one to three. As a result, the lowest paid members of Mondragon receive slightly more than their counterparts in the non-cooperative sector, while it has been estimated that managers receive less than half (Bonin et al., 1993: 1294; Bradley and Gelb, 1987: 79–80).

Conclusions

Employee representatives on the boards of companies and producer cooperatives are both major, if often neglected, forms of employee participation in strategic decision making. Internationally, ERBs are the norm for large companies in Europe as a result of long traditions of a stakeholder approach to corporate governance, in contrast with the Anglo-Saxon shareholder model. In Europe, where it has the strongest foothold, generalized legislation is the main basis for ERB. Producer cooperatives, on the other hand, do not enjoy the support of legislation in this way. They consequently are more dispersed throughout the world as a minority approach, usually for smaller organizations as a result of frequent difficulties in developing large-scale capital. Both manifestations of employee participation are clearly viable, however. European practice suggests that ERBs may play effective roles in corporate governance, to the benefit of management, employees, and organizations as a whole, in the private as well as public sectors. The European experience also suggests that ERB works best in association with other extensive forms of employee participation, such as works councils and union representation. Producer cooperatives also appear to be at least as effective as other firms in terms of productivity and effectiveness, as well as offering advantages to employees of a share in profits and a voice in running the organization. Both forms of employee participation have been long-lived and enjoy strong prospects for continuance, although neither appears likely to become internationally dominant forms in the immediate future.

REFERENCES

BAIRD, J. (1978) 'Trade Unions and Industrial Democracy', in *Proceedings of the International Conference on Industrial Democracy*, p. 259. Adelaide: CCH, 259.

BALNAVE, N. and PATMORE, G. (2006) 'Localism and Rochdale Co-operation: The Junee District Co-operative Society', *Labour History*, 91: 47–68.

BATAILLE-CHEDOTEL, F. and HUTZINGER, F. (2004) 'Faces of Governance of Production Co-operatives: An Exploratory Study of Ten French Co-operatives', *Annals of Public and Co-operative Economy*, 75(1): 89–111.

BATSTONE, E., FERNER, A., and TERRY, M. (1983) *Unions on the Board: An Experiment in Industrial Democracy*. Oxford: Blackwell.

BEN-NER, A. (1988) 'The Life Cycle of Worker-Owned Firms in Market Economies', *Journal of Economic Behaviour and Organization*, 10: 287–313.

BONIN, J. P., JONES, D. C., and PUTTERMAN, L. (1993) 'Theoretical and Empirical Studies of Producer Co-operatives: Will Ever the Twain Meet?' *Journal of Economic Literature*, 21: 1290–320.

BRADLEY, K. and GELB, A. (1981) 'Motivation and Control in the Mondragon Experiment', *British Journal of Industrial Relations*, 19(2): 211–31.

—— —— (1982) 'The Replication and Sustainability of the Mondragon Experiment', *British Journal of Industrial Relations*, 20(1): 20–33.

—— —— (1987) 'Cooperative Labour Relations: Mondragon's Response to Recession', *British Journal of Industrial Relations*, 25(1): 77–99.

CARLEY, M. (2005) 'Board-Level Employee Representatives in Nine Countries: A Snapshot', *Transfer*, 11(2): 231–44.

CLEGG, H. (1979) *The Changing System of Industrial Relations in Great Britain*. Oxford: Blackwell.

CRAIG, B., PENCAVEL, J. (1992) 'The Behaviour of Worker Co-operatives: The Plywood Companies of the Pacific Northwest', *The American Economic Review*, 82(5): 1083–4.

—— —— FARBER, M., and KRUEGER, A. (1995) 'Participation and Productivity: A Comparison of Worker Cooperatives and Conventional Firms in the Plywood Industry', *Brookings Papers: Microeconomics*, pp. 121–74.

CRESSEY, P. (1997) 'Transnational works councils and macro European, developments', in R. Markey and J. Monat (eds), *Innovation and Employee Participation Through Works Councils. International Case Studies*, pp. 29–48. Aldershot, Avebury.

DERRICK, P. (1981) 'Prospects for Industrial Co-operatives—An Alternative to Industrial Democracy', *Long Range Planning*, 14(4): 106–14.

EDLUND, S. and VIKLUND, B. (1993) 'Perspectives in the Area of Participative Management: the Swedish Case', *Bulletin of Comparative Labour Relations*, 27: 43–66.

ESTRIN, S., JONES, D. C., and SVEJNAR, J. (1987) 'The Productivity Effects of Worker Participation: Producer Co-operatives in Western Economies', *Journal of Comparative Economics*, 11: 40–61.

—— and SHLOMOWITZ, R. (1988) 'Income Sharing, Employee Ownership and Worker Democracy: Theory and Evidence', *Annals of Public and Co-operative Economy*, 59(1): 43–66.

GOETSCHY, J. (2003) 'EU Social Policy and Developments in Worker Involvement', in M. Gold (ed.), *New Frontiers of Democratic Participation at Work*. Aldershot: Ashgate.

GOLLAN, P. J. and MARKEY, R. (2001) 'Conclusions: Models of Diversity and Interaction', in R. Markey, P. Gollan, A. Hodgkinson, A. Chouraqui, and U. Veersma (eds), *Models of Employee Participation in a Changing Global Environment: Diversity and Interaction*, pp. 322–43. Aldershot: Ashgate.

GRUNBERG, L. (1991) 'The Plywood Co-operatives: Some Disturbing Findings', in R. Russell and V. Rus (eds), *International Handbook of Participation in Organizations*, vol. 2, pp. 103–22. Oxford: Oxford University Press.

HAGEN, I. (2008) 'The Current System of Employee Board-Level Representation in Norway', Worker-Participation.Eu, European Trade Union Institute, http://www.worker-participation.eu/, accessed 15 August 2008.

JEFFERIS, K. and MASON, N. (1990) 'Financing Worker Co-operatives in EC Countries', *Annals of Public and Co-operative Economy*, 61(2/3): 213–44.

—— and THOMAS, A. (1986) 'Conditions for Financial Viability in Workers' Co-operatives. The Case of UK Clothing and Printing Co-ops', *Annals of Public and Co-operative Economy*, 57(1): 79–102.

JOHNSON, A. G. and WHYTE, W. F. (1977) 'The Mondragon System of Worker Production Cooperatives', *Industrial and Labor Relations Review*, 31(1): 18–30.

JONES, D. C. (1978) 'Producer Cooperatives in Industrialized Western Economies: An Overview', *Annals of Public and Co-operative Economy*, 49(2): 149–61.

KANDATHIL, G. M. and VARMAN, R. (2007) 'Contradictions of Employee Involvement, Information Sharing and Expectations: A Case Study of an Indian Worker Cooperative', *Economic and Industrial Democracy*, 28(1): 140–74.

KATZ, H. (1993) 'The Restructuring of Labour Relations in the United States', *Bulletin of Comparative Labour Relations*, 27: 89–100.

KAVCIC, B. (1997) 'Slovenia: From Self-management to Co-determination', in R. Markey and J. Monat (eds), *Innovation and Employee Participation Through Works Councils. International Case Studies*, pp. 210–20. Aldershot: Avebury.

KESTER, G. (2007) *Trade Unions and Workplace Democracy in Africa*. Aldershot: Ashgate.

KLUGE, N. (2005) 'Corporate Governance with Co-determination—A Key Element of the European Social Model', *Transfer*, 11(2): 163–78.

—— and STOLLT, M. (2006) 'Workers' Representation at Board Level in the New EU Member States', in N. Kluge and M. Stollt (eds), *The European Co : Prospects for Worker Board Level Participation in the Enlarged EU*, pp. 70–74. Brussels: European Trade Union Institute.

—————— (2007) 'Worker Board-level Participation in the EU-27', at SEEurope: www.seeurope-network.org, accessed 24 April 2007.

KNUDSEN, H. (1995) *Employee Participation in Europe*. London: Sage.

KOLLONAY-LEHOCZKY, C. (1997) 'The Emergence of New Forms of Workers' Participation in Central and Eastern Europe', in R. Markey and J. Monat (eds), *Innovation and*

Employee Participation Through Works Councils. International Case Studies, pp. 169–89. Aldershot: Avebury.

KUWAHARA, Y. (2004) 'Employment Relations in Japan', in J. Greg, R. Bamber, D. Lansbury and N. Wailes (eds), *International and Comparative Employment Relations. Globalisation and the Developed Market Economies* (4th edition) pp. 277–305. Sydney: Allen and Unwin.

LEETE-GUY, F. (1991) 'Federal Structure and the Viability of Labour Managed Firms in Mixed Economies', in R. Russell and V. Rus (eds), *International Handbook of Participation in Organizations*, vol. 2, pp. 64–79. Oxford: Oxford University Press.

LEVINSON, K. (2001) 'Employee Representatives on Company Boards in Sweden', *Industrial Relations Journal*, 32(3): 264–74.

LINDKVIST, L. and WESTENHOLZ, A. (1991) 'Employee-Owned Companies in the Nordic Countries', in R. Russell and V. Rus (eds), *International Handbook of Participation in Organizations*, vol. 2, pp. 323–43. Oxford: Oxford University Press.

LOGUE, J. and YATES, J. S. (2006) 'Co-operatives, Worker Owned Enterprises, Productivity and the International Labour Organisation', *Economic and Industrial Democracy*, 27(4): 686–90.

McKERSIE, R. (2001) 'Labor's Voice at the Strategic Level of the Firm', *Transfer*, 7(3): 480–93.

MARKEY, R. (2003) 'A Stakeholder Approach to Corporate Governance: Employee Representatives on Boards of Management', in P. Gollan and G. Patmore (eds), *Partnership at Work. The Challenge of Industrial Democracy. Labor Essays 2003*, pp. 122–33. Sydney: Pluto Press.

MÜLLER, T. (2007) 'The "Biedenkopf Commission" Sees no Need for Fundamental Reform of German Co-determination', *Transfer*, 1/2007: 156–59.

MUSA, E. (2001) 'Workers' Participation in Ghana: A Case Study of a State-Owned Enterprise in Transition to Privatisation', in R. Markey, P. Gollan, A. Hodgkinson, A. Chouraqui, and U. Veersma (eds), *Models of Employee Participation in a Changing Global Environment*, pp. 232–46. Aldershot: Ashgate.

——SHABIDI, J., MSOLA, H., and KIDWANGA, J. (1997) 'Workers' Participation under Structural Adjustment: For Whose Interests? The Case Study of a Tanzanian Private Enterprise', in R. Markey and J. Monat (eds), *Innovation and Employee Participation Through Works Councils. International Case Studies*, pp. 307–31. Aldershot: Avebury.

NILSSON, R. (2004) 'Sweden', in Simons, R., and Kluge, N. (eds). Workers' participation at board level in the EU-15 countries. Reports on the national system and practices, pp. 111–25. Brussels: Hans Böckler Foundation and European Trade Union Institute.

O'KELLY, K. (2005) 'A European Project for Employee Board-level Representatives: Issues, Roles and Responsibilities', *Transfer*, 11(2): 221–30.

PATON, R. (1991) 'Worker Takeovers of Failing and Bankrupt Enterprises in Europe', in R. Russell and V. Rus (eds), *International Handbook of Participation in Organizations*, vol. 2, pp. 28–42. Oxford: Oxford University Press.

PENCAVEL, J., PISTAFERRI, L., and SCHIVARDI, F. (2006) 'Wages, Employment, and Capital in Capitalist and Worker-owned Firms', *Industrial and Labour Relations Review*, 60(1): 23–44.

Report of the Commission on Codetermination (Germany) (1998) cited at eiroline (1998/06; website of the European Foundation for the Improvement of Living and Working Conditions), 'Report assesses co-determination and recommends modernisation': http://www.eiro.eurofound.ie/1998/06, accessed 1 June 2000.

SIMONS, R. and KLUGE, N. (eds) (2004) *Workers' Participation at Board level in the EU-15 Countries. Reports on the National Systems and Practices.* Brussels: Hans Böckler Foundation and European Trade Union Institute.

STOLLT, M. and KLUGE, N. (eds) (2005) *Worker Board-Level Representation in the New EU Member States: Country Reports on the National Systems and Practices*. Brussels: Social Development Agency and European Trade Union Institute.

STRAUSS, G. (1998) 'Collective Bargaining, Unions and Participation', in F. Heller, E. Pusic, G. Strauuss, and B. Wilpert, *Organizational Participation. Myth and Reality*, pp. 97–143. New York: Oxford University Press.

—— (2001) 'American Experience with Union-Nominated Boards of Directors', in R. Markey, P. Gollan, A. Hodgkinson, A. Chouraqui, and U. Veersma (eds), *Models of Employee Participation in a Changing Global Environment*, pp. 97–118. Aldershot: Ashgate.

SUZUKI, F. (2005) 'Corporate Governance Reform and Industrial Democracy in Japan', *Japan Labour Review*, 2(1): 81–104.

TAYLOR, R. (1980) *The Fifth Estate. Britain's Unions in the Modern World*. London: Pan.

—— (2005) 'Industrial Democracy and the European Traditions', *Transfer*, 11(2): 155–62.

—— (2006) ' "Taking Responsibility in an SE"—A New Challenge for Workers from Different Cultural and Political Backgrounds', in N. Kluge and M. Stollt (eds), *The European Co. : Prospects for Worker Board Level Participation in the Enlarged EU*. Brussels: European Trade Union Institute, pp. 40–49.

THOMAS, A. (1990) 'Financing Worker Co-operatives in EC Countries', *Annals of Public and Co-operative Economy*, 61(2/3): 175–211.

THOMAS, H. and LOGAN, C. (1982) *Mondragon. An Economic Analysis*. London: George Allen and Unwin.

VANEK, J. (1975) 'The Basic Theory of Financing of Participatory Firms', in J. Vanek (ed.), *Self-Management: Economic Liberation of Man*, pp. 445–55. Penguin: Harmondsworth.

VEERSMA, U. and SWINKELS, S. (2005) 'Participation in European Companies: Views from Social Partners in Three Member States', *Transfer*, 11(2): 189–206.

WEBB, S. and WEBB, B. (1914) 'Co-operative Production and Profit Sharing', *New Statesman Special Supplement*. London.

WHYTE, W. F. (1991) 'Learning from Mondragon', in R. RUSSELL and V. Rus (eds), *International Handbook of Participation in Organizations*, vol. 2, pp. 83–102. Oxford: Oxford University Press.

—— and WHYTE, K. K. (1988) *Making Mondragon. The Growth and the Dynamics of the Worker Cooperative Complex*. Cornell: ILR Press.

CHAPTER 11

EMPLOYEE PARTICIPATION THROUGH NON-UNION FORMS OF EMPLOYEE REPRESENTATION

BRUCE E. KAUFMAN

DAPHNE G. TARAS

As earlier chapters of this book have described, employee participation in business organizations can be structured and delivered in many different ways. The distinctive approach considered here is indirect participation through forms of non-union employee representation (NER). As detailed below, NER comes in many varieties and serves many functions; it is also often the subject of considerable controversy and divergent opinion. Adding to the subject's interest, NER's importance also appears to be on the upswing—a product of both decline in the traditional form of indirect employee voice (trade unions) and the concomitant rise of more elaborate and formal plans of employee involvement (EI) in industry.

Our chapter is organized into five main parts. Section 1 defines NER and provides a thumbnail sketch of its historical evolution; Section 2 describes the various forms of NER and its alternative functions; Section 3 synthesizes these diverse forms and functions into four distinct models/strategies of NER (called the 'four faces' of NER); Section 4 provides a brief overview of theorizing on NER; and Section 5 surveys the recent empirical literature on NER, with emphasis on evidence regarding NER's performance and strengths and weaknesses. The chapter ends with a brief recapitulation of the main theme—that is, NER exhibits great diversity in form, purpose, and outcome and sweeping generalizations are therefore hazardous.

NER: Definition and History

Non-union employee representation may be generically defined as one or more employees who act in an agency function for other employees in dealings with management over issues of mutual concern, including the terms and conditions under which people work (Kaufman and Taras, 2000: 7). Selected workers' representatives meet with managers, usually in committee-type structures in which communication and exchange of thoughts is fostered. Representatives usually are internal to the company and serve leadership roles for limited terms. NER is based on a *quid pro quo* between managers and workers. In setting up such plans, management expects that the plans will encourage cooperative, advisory, and consultative modes of interaction so that problems can be creatively resolved and frictions amicably reduced. In taking on a representational function, workers expect that NER will provide a meaningful forum for employee voice, a capacity to influence managerial decision making, and recognition by managers that workers have a right to fair and respectful treatment.

Informal examples of NER no doubt go back to the beginning of organized human civilization, as in the building of the pyramids when the Israelite workers asked Moses to present their grievances to the Pharaoh. As a formal practice in modern business organizations, NER dates to the late nineteenth century. Around the 1870s the large-scale industrial enterprise and corporate form of business began to appear, such as railroads, steel mills, and electrical utilities. These companies grew to include tens of thousands of employees and sometimes five thousand or more worked together in a single plant or mill. Managing such a large agglomeration of people was a significant challenge, as was maintaining harmonious employer–employee relations. With these challenges in mind, we see in the late nineteenth century the emergence of many employer initiatives in what today would be considered the province of human resource management (HRM). Examples include incentive pay schemes, insurance and pension benefits, training programmes, and even company housing (Kaufman, 2008). Another such initiative was a permanently-organized employee committee or council formed to meet with management to talk over problems, deal with grievances and promote improved communication and esprit d'corps (Basset, 1919; National Industrial Conference Board, 1919). Such bodies appeared more or less simultaneously in Britain, Germany, and the United States and a decade later in Japan (Gospel, 1992; Kaufman, 2008; Rogers and Streeck, 1995; Totten, 1967). They went under many different names, but common English language versions were 'shop committee', 'works council', and 'cooperation plan'.

In the aftermath of the First World War the NER movement went in different directions. The government of Weimar Germany in 1920 enacted legislation that mandated works councils and spelled out their form and function, while in Britain NER was largely absorbed into what became known as Whitley Councils—joint industry-wide councils with unions as the representatives of employees. Only in North America, and to some degree in Japan, did NER survive in the form that we focus on in this chapter—an organization voluntarily established, structured, and operated by the employer. The most common name given to the North American variety of NER was 'employee representation' (Kaufman and Taras, 2000).

The early heyday of NER was in the United States during the Welfare Capitalism movement of the 1920s (Bernstein, 1960). A number of major American corporations, some with branch plants in Canada and Japan (e.g., General Electric, International Harvester), created formal plans of employee representation in their factories (Jacoby, 1991; Taras, 2000a). Each plant was divided into election districts, the workers in each district elected a representative, and the representatives met as a council with management representatives on a periodic basis to discuss issues of joint interest. Often the plant councils formed subsidiary representation bodies, such as joint safety committees and social welfare committees.

These NER plans were intended to give employees an avenue for voice, participation and due process and, in this spirit, were sometimes called 'plans of industrial democracy' (Leitch, 1919). Critics charged, however, they were a counterfeit or sham form of industrial democracy since the plans were created, financed, and operated by management to promote the interests of the company, presumptively at the expense of workers (Brody, 1994; Dunn, 1926; Gitelman, 1988). The critics pejoratively called the ER bodies 'company unions' and claimed their main purpose was to deceive and co-opt workers so they did not organize into independent trade unions. The proponents of NER responded that some unions were themselves often discriminatory, authoritarian, and corrupt, while the NER plans had a demonstrable record of promoting improved terms and conditions of employment and the resolution of grievances (Kaufman, 2000; Leiserson, 1928). The early battle lines formed from these divergent views and have shaped the contours of the ongoing debate.

NER in North America came to another fork in the road in the 1930s. The collapse of Welfare Capitalism and the ensuing cascade of wage cuts, speed ups, and large-scale layoffs set off by the Great Depression soured workers and the public against Big Business. To raise wages and restore humanity to the workplace, the American Government did an about face and enacted the National Labour Relations Act (NLRA) in 1935 with the purpose of promoting greater unionization. Towards that end, the NLRA also banned almost all forms of NER. This ban remains in effect to this day, although the boundary line between what is a legal and illegal type of NER moves modestly back and forth over time (Kaufman, 1999; LeRoy, 2000; National Labour Relations Board, 2001). Canada, by way of contrast, followed a different route. It passed NLRA-type legislation a decade later but it did not at the same time ban NER (Taras, 1997a, 2006). Thus, for the next half century NER has followed along two divergent routes in North America—legal in Canada and illegal in the US.

Regardless of whether NER was legal or illegal, until the 1980s it remained a largely forgotten topic in North America, examined only occasionally and most often critically by labour historians (e.g., Gitelman, 1988; Ozanne, 1967). A major part of the reason was that in both Canada and the United States unions succeeded in organizing most large industrial companies and thus NER looked like a moot issue (MacDowell, 2000). Two things happened, however, to reawaken interest in NER.

The first is the rise of academic and managerial interest in new forms of work organization and people management, often called 'high performance' or 'high involvement' work systems (Applebaum et al., 2000; Kochan et al., 1986; Lawler, 1992). In the 1980s, this movement also was inspired by the Japanese economic miracle and the more participative model that was associated with the Japanese-style of management. The high-performance system utilizes a number of complementary components, including self-managed work teams, gain sharing pay systems, extensive training, and egalitarian corporate cultures, but by wide agreement the linchpin practice is extensive and formalized employee involvement (Cappelli and Neumark, 2001; Lawler et al., 1992; MacMahan et al., 1998). In small work groups and for certain tightly focused production problems, EI can be conducted through one-on-one discussion or direct forms of group participation, such as when a quality circle meets with a manager (Wilkinson et al., 2007). In larger workplaces, and for many plant- or company-wide operational, financial, and human resource issues, direct participation is neither feasible nor cost-effective and thus EI needs to be implemented through some type of indirect representational body, such as a plant-level employee committee or joint industrial council. In the US, however, these bodies remain illegal under the NLRA if they in some substantive way engage in bilateral dealing between managers and workers over employment-related issues. (Representational committees in transportation industries covered under the Railway Labour Act are permissible, however.) From this disjunction ensued into the 1990s a growing body of commentary and debate about the pros and cons of NER as a way to promote more EI and competitive industry (Commission on the Future of Worker–Management Relations, 1994; Hiatt and Gold, 2000; LeRoy, 1997; Maryott, 1997; Taras, 2003).

The second stimulus to renewed interest in NER came from the cumulatively large decline in union coverage of the workforce by the century's end and, particularly in the American workplace, the consequent opening up of an (allegedly) large 'participation/representation gap'. When trade unions represented the majority of workers in the industrial core of the economy, NER had little apparent role to serve. By the 1990s, however, private sector union density had moderately declined in Canada and sharply declined in the United States—to such an extent in the USA that by 2000 only one in ten private sector workers was covered by collective bargaining. Concern thus developed about finding alternative organizational means to provide workers with voice, representation, and due process in business firms—a concern heightened by the empirical findings of Freeman and Rogers (1999) that in the USA the decline in unions had opened up a huge gap between the amount of voice and representation workers want and how much firms provide. Hence, North American industrial relations (IR) academics, despite widespread scepticism/hostility towards NER (e.g., Adams, 1993; Kochan, 1995), started to join legal scholars and reconsider whether employee representation could indeed serve as a useful alternative voice mechanism in the workplace (e. g., Kaufman and Kleiner, 1993; Lewin and Mitchell, 1992; Strauss, 1995; Taras, 1998).

For reasons just described, explicit focus on NER (distinguished from broader research on EI) was through most of the 1990s a largely North American topic. In the last decade, however, interest in NER has rapidly taken on international dimensions, albeit more slowly in countries outside the Anglo-American orbit (Gumbrell-McCormick and Hyman, 2006). The twofold explanation discussed above applies as well. In countries, such as Australia, Britain, Germany, Ireland, and Japan, union density has been noticeably trending downward, while interest in EI and high-performance work systems has been rapidly growing (Ackers, et al., 2006). Evidence of a substantial-sized participation/representation gap also has been found for many of these countries (Freeman et al., 2007; Towers, 1997). As in North America, academic attitudes towards NER in Europe and Australasia were initially rather frosty and sceptical (e.g., Guest and Hoque, 1994; Hyman, 1997), only to then did it gradually warm up and take on a cautiously positive perspective. Indeed, the academic literature on NER from outside North America has been expanding at a rapid rate and now comprises the bulk of the research output on this topic (see Gollan, 2007, for an extensive bibliography).

The booming literature on NER in Europe (particularly Ireland and the United Kingdom) has origins in two other factors. The first is the establishment of numerous 'greenfield' plants by multinational corporations from Japan and the

United States. In most cases, these companies are committed to a non-union strategy and used various forms of NER as part of their programme (Watling and Snook, 2003; Dundon et al., 2006). Second, in 1998 the European Commission proposed a directive on 'information and consultation of employees' that would, if adopted, mandate companies in member countries to establish consultative employee representational committees in all workplaces with more than fifty employees. Particularly for the UK, the directive promised a rather substantial increase in such committees relative to the existing situation. After much debate and negotiation, a less binding version was adopted in 2002 and implemented in 2005 as the European Directive on Information and Consultation (Hall, 2006).

NER: Forms and Functions

NER is an umbrella term for an unusually diverse set of forms and practices. Further, the nomenclature varies from country to country. In Canada, for example, NER may be called a Joint Industrial Council (JIC) or Employee–Management Advisory Committees (EMACs), while in the UK a popular term is Joint Consultative Committee (JCC). In the USA, NER flies somewhat 'under the radar' as productivity committees, employee involvement groups, plant advisory councils, and other such permutations.

We have endeavored to capture most of the different forms and functions of NER in Table 11.1 (based on Taras and Kaufman, 2006; also see Dundon et al., 2006). (Recall NER is limited to voluntarily-created representational bodies, so European-style works councils are excluded.) We have organized Table 11.1 into six dimensions. We treat each consecutively.

Form. A glance down the first column of Table 11.1 shows that there are many ways of providing NER at the workplace. The column starts from the small-scale forms of representation (e.g., an ombud) and works down to the larger and more complex types. Some forms are *ad hoc* or informal, while others are long-standing and highly developed. Most committees or advisory groups operate at the shop floor or department level, such as a joint safety committee. However, other forms of NER, such as a plant consultative committee or joint industrial council, cover all departments in a plant or company and often provide access to high-level executives or even the board of directors (for examples, see Dundon et al., 2006; Gollan, 2007; Kaufman, 2003a; Taras, 2000b; Terry, 1999). In public sector organizations, a common form of NER is some type of staff association (Marsden, 2003). Also distinctive, while employers most often create NER bodies, in some cases workers take the initiative and create and run these plans. Examples include identity-based groups for women, minorities, and gay/lesbian workers and employee professional associations (Helfgott, 2000; Verma, 2000).

The highest level and most formally structured type of NER, such as a modern-day JIC/JCC or 1920s-style employee representation plan, are the most intensively studied. These plans frequently involve elected worker representatives operating under a constitution that sets out the NER systems' forms, functions, and procedures. Part of both academic and legal interest in these high-level NER forms is because they come closest in form and function to traditional-type labour unions.

Functions. Just as NER comes in many different shapes and sizes, so too does it seek to serve a variety of different functions, listed in column 2 of Table 11.1. One of the most common reasons that firms operate NER systems is to improve the communication flow between workers and managers, and provide workers with various forms of voice (Dundon et al., 2004). Particularly in large companies, NER can help bridge the often large divide that separates top executives from shop floor workers, ensuring that communication is both more rapid and less filtered and distorted (Kaufman, 2003a). A downside of such 'skip-level' reporting, however, is that it often causes discomfort for foremen and supervisors who feel left out or exposed to scrutiny. As a result, they often tacitly oppose or actively sabotage NER. Finally, NER also facilitates more personal contact between managers and workers, counteracting the deadening effect of bureaucracy. For these reasons NER is more often adopted in larger-size firms.

Another function of NER is to provide greater workplace justice and more effective dispute resolution. The NER plans of the 1920s, for example, often acted as a grievance system, sometimes culminating in arbitration by a top-level executive. Modern NER plans continue this tradition of in-house dispute resolution, rarely utilizing third-party arbitrators (Estreicher, 2004; Ewing, 1990; McCabe and Lewin, 1992).

A more complex function, especially in the more highly developed and formal NER systems, is negotiation and adjustment of wages and other terms, and conditions of employment. Few employers create NER plans for bargaining or negotiation purposes and many plans explicitly state that their purpose is limited to communication, consultation, and other such 'integrative' functions. The reality is necessarily more complex. The broader the mandate and scope of the NER plan, the more likely it is that part of the communication employees want to have with managers is about their wages, benefits, and conditions. Employers can rule this part of the conversation out of bounds, but then they also undercut the willingness of employees to participate (the 'what's in it for me' issue). Hence, companies with larger NER plans inevitably engage in a certain amount of 'collective dealing' with employees about their economic concerns, albeit in the form of dialogue and employee lobbying rather than overt 'across the table' negotiation and bargaining (Chiesa and Rhyason, 2000; MacDougall, 2000; Taras, 2000b; Terry, 1999).

Table 11.1 Examples of diversity of NER plans

1. Forms	2. Functions	3. Topics	4. Representation modes	5. Extent of power	6. Degree of permanence
Ombud	Communication and Information Flow	Benefits, including Pensions and Health Insurance	Internal to the Firm (e.g., elected representative from among workers in the group)	Completely Co-opted by Management	Short-term, Ad Hoc Committee
Joint Safety Committee	Production and Organizational Coordination	Safety/Health	External to the Firm (e.g., players' agents in sports)	Scope of Power (e.g., single topic or broad authority)	Time-limited, until a Problem is Solved
Dispute Resolution Panel	Employee Morale and Esprit de Corps	Working Conditions	Representatives Appointed by Management	Informal Consultation	Disbandable Structure upon Notice by One or the other Party
Scanlon Plan and Gain Sharing Committee	Education and Training of Employees	Grievances/Dispute Resolution	Representatives Elected by Workers (secret ballot)	Advisory Groups	Permanent Structure
Departmental Production and Coordination Committee	Employee Relations and Disposition of Irritants	Management Problems	Degree of Independence Given to Representatives	Decisions made by Consensus only	
Quality Improvement Committee	Employee Involvement	Employee Relations Climate	Ability to Seek Professional Expertise Outside Firm	'Dealing With' Management through Preparation of Formal Positions	
Gender/Ethnic/Sex Identity Groups	Corporate Culture	Production Issues		Chairing or Co-Chairing meetings	
Employee-Management Advisory Committees	Cooperation and Common Purpose	Equipment/Capital Issues		Developing the Agenda	

(cont.)

Table 11.1 (*Continued*)

1. Forms	2. Functions	3. Topics	4. Representation modes	5. Extent of power	6. Degree of permanence
Cross-Divisional Council for Employment Issues	Management and Employee Development	Customer Service		Negotiating	
Plant Council	'Trojan Horse' for Union Organizing	Quality of Products and Production		Distribution of minutes and positions	
Employee Committee on Board of Directors	Union Substitution	Business Strategy		Ability to Take Action to Promote Positions	
Company-Wide Representation Systems (JIC, JCC)	Union Avoidance	Wages and other Terms and Conditions of Employment		Vote-Taking in NER; majority wins	
Staff Associations	Lobbying Government	Status of the Occupation		Worker Veto Power over Change	
Professional Advocacy Groups					

As indicated in Table 11.1, NER also plays a number of other functions besides dealing with traditional terms and conditions of employment, such as improved production efficiency, morale building, and union avoidance. These functions are discussed in more detail later in the chapter, so we move on.

Topics/Subjects. The third dimension of NER is the substantive content of decision making. What are the sets of issues over which NER forums exercise influence? In addition to wages and conditions of work, a wide variety of other subjects are handled by forms of NER, listed in column 3 of Table 11.1. These subjects vary according to the type of NER. The decentralized, small-scale forms of NER typically target only one subject, while larger-scale NER may handle a variety. NER forums often discuss the social aspects of work, orientation of new employees, the interpretation of handbooks and manuals, and the rectification of various irritants at the workplace. Dental and extended health care plans are reviewed, pension plans are examined, and suggestions are made for improvements. At the Dofasco company in Canada, an employee group for many years was charged with joint oversight of the massive pension plans (Harshaw, 2000). Joint health and safety committees are another common form of NER at the workplace.

Representation Modes. Worker representatives come to their jobs in a variety of ways, and the type of representation often is related to the formality and complexity of the NER plan. Table 11.1, column 4, identifies a variety of distinctions that can be used to describe the modes of representation. Typically representatives are elected by their constituency group to serve a set term in office (often two years). At the shop floor level, the election may involve an informal show of hands; in large-size NER plans a secret ballot may be used. In other cases, elections are thought to unduly introduce a divisive political aspect and representatives are instead selected through an intensive interview process before a joint manager–employee committee. In other cases representatives are appointed by management, or chosen by management from nominations provided by employees. In this respect, the degree and form of democratic practice varies widely—as it does among unions. Also paralleling the union case, not all workers are anxious to participate, to vote, or to become representatives. Apathy often is a factor.

As most NER is enterprise-based, the representatives come from within the firm's workforce. Representatives usually are employees engaged in similar work to the workers they represent. There also are circumstances in which representatives are external to the firm. For example, professional associations may provide agents or experts to help advance their members' interests in interactions with employers (e.g., in disciplinary hearings or in contract negotiations). External worker advocacy groups, often staffed by lawyers, may provide representational services to non-union workers (Taras, 2007).

Extent of Power. The issue of power is one of the most controversial parts of NER. NER forms are designed to function largely in a consultative and advisory capacity. One of the employer's goals is to promote greater harmony and cooperation in the workplace. From this perspective, all forms of collective bargaining are anathema since they introduce an adversarial 'we versus them' mentality into employee relations and emphasize 'splitting the pie' instead of 'growing the pie'. For this reason, most forms of NER eschew formal bargaining, forbid selection of worker representatives from outside the enterprise, provide no independent financial resources or outside professional counsel, and lack the right to strike.

Not unexpectedly, for these reasons critics view NER plans as fatally flawed because they allow workers to exercise *voice* but not the *muscle* needed to make employers listen and compromise (Brody, 1994; Butler, 2005; Freeman and Medoff, 1984; Haynes and Fryer, 2001). Critics also allege that NER plans are used to co-opt, manipulate, and create 'false consciousness' among the workers (Barenberg, 1993). A common charge, for example, is that NER either 'wins' for the employees what the company had already decided to give, or is used to 'sell' or 'sugar-coat' give backs to the company. Another line of thought is that companies would never create a NER plan in the first place if it did not in the end promote their interests, presumably at the expense of employees' interests. Given these (alleged) defects, critics of NER often refer to it as a 'sham', 'toothless dog', or 'collective begging'.

But another and more positive side to the story also exists. Although NER plans have less open and obvious forms of power than trade unions, they nonetheless provide subtle and 'under the surface' channels of influence for workers (Cone, 2000; Kaufman, 2003a; Taras, 2000b). To their proponents, the relevant comparison is not between NER and trade unions, since the two are intended to serve different purposes, but NER and the non-union firm with no form of collective consultation (the 'no voice' option). They claim that NER inevitably gains 'wins' for employees, perhaps modest at any one time but cumulatively significant over time. This happens for several reasons.

When a company creates a NER plan, for example, it raises the expectations of employees that they will be consulted and have influence. This expectation creates a form of leverage for workers, since if the company reneges then morale plummets and the risk of unionization rises. Relatedly, forming a NER body is an invitation to employees to offer their opinions and requests. Having asked for employee voice, the company then has to consider that repeatedly saying 'No' carries its own cost in terms of undercutting the viability of the employee forum and scuttling employee goodwill. Another consideration is that NER is created to foster cooperation and mutual gain and thus employees must see some 'wins' on their side if the system is to have longevity and effectiveness. NER also exerts indirect bargaining power on employers in the sense that they deliberately pay high wages and benefits in order to take distributive issues 'off the table' so the NER can focus on win–win issues. And, finally, attention again should be highlighted on the power NER plans acquire from employers' desire to avoid unionization; the union threat effect boosts the efficacy of NER in delivering gains to workers.

Having said all of this, the fact remains that most forms of NER exist at the discretion of employers and have influence only to the extent employers see that NER serves their long-term interests. Absent a strike threat, independent financial resources, and outside counsel, NER is relatively powerless to change an employer's 'No' to a 'Yes'. Also a problem, NER—like non-union ADR systems—may not yield fair outcomes for employees if companies give them one-sided rules of operation. In the end, the extent to which the non-union system delivers either distributive fairness (in outcomes) or procedural fairness (in processes) depends on managerial choice and consent.

Degree of Permanence. Finally, in the last column of Table 11.1, are the temporal attributes of NER, ranging from the most temporary to most permanent. At the top of the chart are short-term and *ad hoc*-type plans usually created to deal with a specific non-recurring problem or topic. At an intermediate point on the temporal spectrum are various joint committees and councils that are established and operate for several years or more. They may end because the problem they are addressing disappears or a new management team decides to try a different EI strategy. Permanent NER structures exist within companies for a long period of time. Often the permanent NER plans are a well-integrated part of a larger human resource management philosophy of progressive 'high road' employer–employee relations. In North America, some NER plans exist for decades, such as at Imperial Oil in Canada (Taras, 2000b) and Polaroid in the USA (Kaufman, 1999). (The NLRB forced Polaroid to disband the NER plan in the early 1990s.) In Europe, NER plans have gained much longer lifespans because larger-sized companies are now mandated by EU directives to have consultative plans. Outside individual companies, relatively long-lived NER groups can also be found in the form of professional associations and a few employee lobbying groups.

Although some NER plans have considerable longevity, more often they have a relatively short 'half-life'. NER, apparently, is a difficult system to maintain in an equilibrium (Dundon et al., 2006; Terry, 1999). Firms often create them during a crisis, to solve a specific problem, or as a reaction to the latest management 'fad of the month'. For a short while the plans command both management attention and worker interest. Come back in a few years, however, and frequently the committees have lost energy or been completely disbanded; in other cases they have turned into an independent union. Keeping NER plans energized and productive over the longer term is a major management challenge.

Some scholars (e.g., Weiler, 1990) argue that on both efficiency and industrial democracy grounds non-union employers in North America should be required by law to establish some kind of joint forum for consultation and employee voice, perhaps along European lines. Doing so, they contend, would help stabilize NER and provide permanency and power. At a practical and political level, such a proposal in the current environment can safely be described as 'dead on arrival'; not only will most companies strongly oppose it but so too will organized labour (fearing a competitive and weaker form of representation for employees). Some scholars (e.g., Kaufman and Levine, 2000) also oppose it on grounds that such a 'one size fits all' approach will impose higher costs on all firms but yield significant productivity gains in only a subset. Others argue that true employee power is best delivered when it is initiated by employees themselves rather than through policies or laws and that the acts of mobilization and articulation of interests yields more effective voice (Sims, 2008).

The Four Faces of NER

Non-union employee representation is one of the most controversial topics in the labour policy arena. Part of the reason is that NER is a tangled web consisting of many different threads of values and perspectives. Along this line, Freeman and Medoff (1984) famously noted that trade unions have two different 'faces' and the conclusions one reaches about unions hinge critically on which face is examined. In an earlier article (Taras and Kaufman, 2006), we advanced the same proposition about NER, but posited that NER has four faces. The purpose of our 'four faces' is to systematize and distinguish some of the diverse perspectives previously noted, particularly regarding the purpose and effects of NER.

These four faces of NER are summarized in Table 11.2. They represent different dimensions or 'realities' of NER. Although these four faces are presented here as separate entities, in real life they frequently commingle. Since these four faces are presented in our earlier article and are also well described in Table 11.2, we limit our discussion here.

Evolutionary Voice Face. One perspective on NER is that it provides a 'way station' in the development of employee voice and industrial democracy. In this view, the industrial relations landscape is conceptualized as a continuum (Bernstein, 1960; Derber, 1970). At the starting point is a regime of individual bargaining, employer unilateralism, and absence of any mechanism for employee voice and representation. This is the traditional workplace that characterized early twentieth-century capitalism and, to a significant if less hard edged degree, many workplaces today. As societies evolve, employees and the public demand a more humanized and democratic form of workforce governance. Since the dominant political and business elites strenuously oppose unions, a first step is an employer-created form of NER. Although perhaps marginally effective, NER does not, in this view, alter the basic imbalance in power and control exercised by capital over labour (Brody, 1994; Ozanne, 1967); it does, however, give workers and their leaders initial experience in collective action (Timur, 2004). Hence, workers grow dissatisfied with NER, come to see it as a largely

Table 11.2 Four faces of NER

	Evolutionary	Unity of interest	Union avoidance	Complementary
Purpose	Gradual improvement of labour's economic position and democratizing of the workplace	Create a harmonious workplace in which workers are aligned with drivers of firm success	To suppress demand for unions through union suppression and union substitution tactics	Beneficial interaction of the unique competencies of unions and non-union systems
Paradigm	History, Institutional (Evolutionary) Economics, pluralist Industrial Relations	Unitarist Human Resource Management, Organizational Development	Traditional IR for Union Suppression, paternalist/unitarist HRM for union substitution	Combination of IR and HRM
Utility to Firm	Economies of scale in dealing with workers in groups; achieving better systems of voice among workers; superior worker–manager communication vehicle	Alignment of workers to firm's goals, reduce adversarialism, improve communication	Early warning system to detect employee discontent and union organizing, reduces employees' desire for union representation, vehicle for weeding out union activists and buying time to defeat the union drive	Captures advantages of unions (e.g., standardized wages and benefits, taking wages out of competition) and advantages of non-union representation in internal workforce governance (e.g., non-adversarial form of collective voice)
Utility to Workers	Gradual expansion of wages and benefits, greater voice and due process, substitutes independence for paternalism and autocracy	Greater voice and influence in firm, direct access to management, higher morale, improved pay and benefits.	Company may raise wages and benefits and improve conditions to keep out union, workers may be so alienated by hard ball tactics that it builds more support for the union	Workers may get the best of both systems; workers get benefits of unionization without paying dues, while turning attention to other workplace issues
Utility to Unions	Worker demand for unions gradually increases, union density rises over time	If non-union system not managed well, may lead dissatisfied workers to unionize	The firm may over do firings and repression, leading to 'backfire' effect in which employees have a greater demand for union representation	Positive: unions retain their contribution as negotiators of terms and conditions of employment, making union organizing attractive; Negative: free-riding by workers makes unionization difficult
Examples of Worksite Practices	Evolution of dispute resolution from 'open door' to formal grievance system, replacement of informal and subjective HRM practices for written and formal procedures	Joint committee on gain sharing, peer review dispute resolution panel, employee representatives on board of directors	Union substitution uses many high-performance HRM practices; union suppression relies on heavy use of external consultants and attorneys, frequent terminations	Collective bargaining of economic package, use of joint worker-management committees on working conditions, quality of worklife

empty promise, and decide to replace it with a genuine type of industrial democracy in the form of an independent trade union.

Unity of Interest. It is employers who most often create NER and from their perspective it has a second face. Employers look at NER as a component of their human resource management system and utilize it to the extent it, like other HRM practices, adds to profit and competitive advantage. NER adds to profit through a variety of channels, such as improved information and communication, better coordination of production, and increased employee morale. According to many managers who practice NER, the ultimate objective is to promote improved organizational performance by fostering greater cooperation and unity of interest in the workplace, such as in the modern high-performance work system (Kaufman, 2003b). An additional but largely indirect benefit is that workers lose interest in union representation. The NER plans at Delta Air Lines and Imperial Oil are prime examples of this type of cooperative/union substitution strategy in action (Chiesa and Rhyason, 2000; Cone, 2000; Kaufman, 2003a; Taras, 2000b).

Union Avoidance. This face posits that the primary purpose of NER plans is union avoidance (Bernstein, 1960; Lawler, 1990; Lloyd, 2001; Terry, 1999). From this perspective, employers—particularly where less constrained by laws and social norms—have a considerable aversion toward unions, reflecting in part philosophical disagreements (e.g., individualism versus collectivism, protection of employers' prerogatives and property rights) but equally or more so the threat that unions pose toward employers' profits and managerial control of the workforce. As part of their union avoidance strategy, companies often adopt NER. Critics of NER argue that the workers gain little from NER; that is, the benefits are at best temporary and at worst manipulative and delusional, as when companies use NER to 'educate' and 'persuade' employees of the need for give backs (Barenberg, 1993; Basken, 2000; Hiatt and Gold, 2000; Upchurch et al., 2006). But the case against NER is much stronger, they argue, because often it is used to fend off unionism as part of companies' overt or covert 'stick' strategy of union suppression. Union suppression keeps out unions by negative methods that rely on fear, coercion, and punishment, such as harassment and discharge of union activists, infiltrating the workforce with spies, and spreading rumors and disinformation about unions and their supporters (Friedman et al., 1994). Once the union is defeated, employer interest in NER rapidly fades and it is back to 'business as usual'.

Complementary Voice. The fourth face looks at NER as a complement to trade unionism, not a substitute as in the second and third face. In this view, NER and trade unionism occupy separate domains and serve different goals and functions. This being the case, it is not a matter of 'one or the other' but how best to 'mix and match' the two into a composite system of 'dual channel' voice. For example, in Britain dual channel voice arrangements have proliferated over the last decade as employers move to supplement 'union only voice' with a combination of union and NER voice. The latter, they find, is often better at addressing integrative issues and avoiding adversarialism (Gollan, 2007). In the Canadian context, Taras (1997) has described how the mix of unions and NER complement each other— the unions use their power to stabilize and advance the wage structure and companies use NER to fine-tune their internal employment policies and practices. Similarly, Chaykowski's (2000) study of the National Joint Council system in Canada found that it continued to serve a useful communication and consultation role even after the introduction of public sector collective bargaining in the 1960s.

NER Theory

The information in Tables 11.1 and 11.2 helps provide a framework and taxonomy for understanding NER. Several studies have endeavored to go further and develop theoretical models for understanding why employers do (or do not) adopt NER, difference in NER adoption rates across countries, and NER's effects on outcomes, such as productivity and profits. We briefly describe two of the most important (also see Dundon et al., 2006; Gollan, 2007; Willman et al., 2006).

The first model is by Freeman and Lazear (1995). They used the model to analyse European works councils, but it applies equally well to various types of NER. The question they seek to answer is the factors that determine an employer's choice of the breadth and depth of voice provided to employees in the workplace. In their model, the employer's objective is maximum profit. More workplace voice for employees has two offsetting effects on profit. More voice adds to profit to the extent it increases labour productivity, such as through improved communication, coordination, and morale. But more voice also subtracts from profit to the extent it increases the collective capacity of workers to bargain for higher wages and other cost-increasing terms and conditions of employment. (The fact that NER creates extra profit but also raises labour cost is called the 'Catch 22' of employee representation by Flood and Toner (1997).) Given this, Freeman and Lazear show that the employer will increase voice options as long as the marginal profit gain in higher productivity exceeds the marginal profit loss from higher labour compensation; when the two become equal the optimal level of voice (from the employer perspective) has been reached. An interesting insight of their model is that while this voice level may be optimal for the employer, it is likely to be suboptimal from a social point of view. The reason is that society gains from the extra productivity of employee voice but firms stop short of the maximum possible productivity gain because they seek to limit redistribution of profit to labour.

A second model is developed by Kaufman and Levine (2000). Their approach is to consider NER as a factor input, along with capital and labour, that firms can use to produce output. Just as with the labour input, a firm can calculate the marginal revenue product of NER (the extra revenue gained by using an additional unit of NER in production) which, in turn, can be used to generate a downward sloped NER factor input demand curve. Given a cost (price) of producing NER (assumed for simplicity to be a constant per unit), it is possible to use the demand curve to determine the firm's optimal level of NER. This model yields three implications: first, firms adopt NER when the profit gain from higher productivity exceeds the cost of producing the NER; second, firms that get a higher productivity gain from NER, or have a lower cost of producing NER, will adopt more of it in terms of both breadth and depth; and, third, factors such as extensive internal labour markets and a full employment macroeconomy increase the productivity pay-off of NER and thus promote more adoption of it. Kaufman and Levine also conclude, like Freeman and Lazear, that firms are likely to underinvest in NER, although they tie the reasons to various market failures rather than concerns over rent redistribution; they also argue that the choice of NER versus trade unions as the optimal form of voice rests in part on the degree to which labour markets are competitive—the more non-competitive they are, the more favoured are unions as a way to balance employers' power advantage in wage determination.

Empirical Research on NER

The empirical research on the forms, functions, and effects of NER is growing at a rapid rate, albeit from a quite small base circa: the early to mid-1990s. Illustrative of the topic's resurgence, symposiums on NER have recently appeared in *Journal of Labour Research* (Winter, 1999), *Socio-Economic Review* (May, 2006), and *Industrial Relations Journal* (September, 2006).

In North America, early research on NER was limited largely to historical studies of company unions in the pre-Wagner Act era and law review articles debating the efficacy and interpretation of the NLRA's ban on workplace representational committees. Otherwise it was largely ignored by HRM and IR scholars (but see Lewin and Mitchell, 1992; Kaufman and Kleiner, 1993)—in the former case because they concentrated on direct and small-scale forms of employee participation and in the latter because NER was widely regarded as a socially retrograde employee relations practice (e.g., 'union busting'). The real beginning of modern NER research in the United States and Canada is a 1997 conference on the subject in Banff, Canada and the book that grew out of it, *Nonunion Employee Representation*

(Kaufman and Taras, 2000). The conference and book helped highlight and legitimize the topic in HRM/IR circles, while the law review literature continues apace.

In Britain, NER did not have the same controversial history so the historical literature on the topic is much smaller. But, conversely, research by HRM and IR scholars started earlier and has blossomed more fully. The first wave of research bearing on NER—carried out as part of a larger project on EI—came from a group of employment scholars at the Manchester Business School, summarized in the book *New Developments in Employee Involvement* (Marchington et al., 1992). This group, with the addition of Dundon and partially relocated to Loughborough University, did a second wave of research on EI and NER in the late 1990s, summarized in *Management Choice and Employee Voice* (Marchington et al., 2001). Their research continues to this day (see Ackers et al., 2006), although the team has further dispersed to include Griffith University and NUI Galway. Joining them post-2000 have been many other authors, a number of whom are cited below. Particularly active has been Paul Gollan, who has contributed more than a half-dozen in-depth case studies of NER among UK companies, summarized in the recent book *Employee Representation in Non-Union Firms* (Gollan, 2007).

Empirical research on NER is also appearing in other countries, such as Australia (Benson, 2000; Gollan, 2000; Pyman et al., 2006), Germany (Addison et al., 2000; Gospel and Willman, 2005), Japan (Morishima and Tsuru, 2000), and South Korea (Kim and Kim, 2004). The majority of studies are case studies of NER at individual companies; however, an expanding number of quantitative analyses are also appearing. Here is a brief summary of salient points in this literature.

History, Growth, and Extent. The case studies reveal that some companies have operated NER for several decades or more, although due to the dominance of unionism (both quantitatively and in terms of scholarly interest) these non-union representation plans largely remained in the shadows (see Butler, 2005; Gollan, 2007; LeRoy, 2000; Taras, 2000b). Starting in the early 1990s, NER plans began to noticeably proliferate; evidence from Britain, however, suggests a level-ling off or even modest dip in larger-scale JCC-type bodies (Gollan, 2007). NER in one form or another now seems to be fairly widespread, although still significantly less than all forms of EI considered as a whole. A national survey of the United States and Canada by Lipset and Meltz (2000), for example, found that roughly 50 per cent of employees in non-union companies participated in some type of collaborative work group but only about 20 per cent were covered by some type of NER. Similar results appear in Britain. According to data from the 2004 Workplace Employment Relations Survey (WERS), 93 per cent of firms reported some kind of direct participation but only 49 per cent had some kind of representative voice (union or non-union) and only 21 per cent had a solely non-union form (Bryson et al., 2006).

Form/Structure/Purpose/Power. Diversity is the hallmark of modern NER in terms of form, structure, purpose, and power. This fact makes large-scale generalizations about NER difficult-to-treacherous. Comparative case studies of companies find they adopt an incredibly diverse set of NER bodies; indeed, no two companies do it alike (Gollan, 2007; Kaufman, 1999; Terry, 1999; Wilkinson et al., 2004).

Part of this diversity is explicable in terms of the different reasons companies adopt NER and the functions they intend it to serve. Empirical research finds that companies adopt NER for what may be characterized as both 'offensive' and 'defensive' reasons. The offensive reasons are tied to higher business performance and competitive advantage, generally as part of an effort to create or enhance a unitarist-type work system. Here NER has a more 'HRM flavour' and is often an integral part of a larger EI system. The defensive reasons are related to managerial attempts to minimize 'bads' or 'costs', such as keeping out trade unions and satisfying new legal mandates. Here NER has a more 'IR/Legal flavour', operates in a more overtly pluralist employment relation, and tends to more closely mimic the form and function of trade unions.

Peeling back the layers of NER further, case studies find that companies adopt NER with one or a combination of nine different goals in mind. The first is to promote improved communication between management and employees; the second is to improve employee morale and organizational commitment; the third is to improve the coordination and efficiency of the production process; the fourth is to obtain employees' ideas, knowledge, and participation in problem solving; a fifth is to provide a forum for the airing and reconciliation of different interests and points of view; a sixth is to achieve greater procedural and distributive justice in employer–employee dispute/grievance resolution; a seventh is to achieve a positive image with stakeholders as a progressive employer; an eighth is to minimize trade union organization and control and, correlatively, maintain or strengthen management control; and a ninth is to satisfy legal regulations (Gollan, 2007; Kaufman, 2003a; Terry, 1999).

In keeping with the management science maxim 'structure follows strategy', the diversity in NER forms and structures (noted above) is at least partly explicable in terms of the relative importance individual companies give to these nine goals. Among the six companies with some form of NER studied by Kaufman (1999), for example, one was oriented towards improved production and felt little union threat, while another was more oriented towards improved communication and felt a large union threat. The former adopted an EI system that mostly relied on direct participation (e.g., self-managed work teams, special project groups) but then added-on several small-scale NER forms, such as a plant review board and peer review dispute resolution panel. The other company also adopted a mix of direct and indirect participation, but gave more emphasis to large scale and more centralized indirect forms. Thus, it created small continuous improvement teams but then also created division-wide employee councils (with employee-selected representatives and written by-laws) and put employee representatives on the corporation's board of directors.

Outcomes and Effectiveness. Diversity is again the theme when it comes to the effectiveness and outcomes of NER. A number of writers have reached relatively positive conclusions about the performance of NER, while a number of others have tended toward the negative side. If there is a common denominator, it is probably that the pluses and minuses tend to be modest sized in absolute value and relative to other drivers of business performance and employee well-being, indicating that NER's effects—whether for good or bad—are in the grand scheme of things most often on the margin.

The attractiveness of NER is that it promises a win–win outcome for both employers and employees. That is, successful NER serves management's interests by increasing organizational performance and harmony; it also serves employees' interests by improving the terms and conditions of work and satisfaction with the job and company in a relatively non-adversarial manner. In this respect, large-scale surveys of workers in several countries reveal that a large majority of employees say they prefer some kind of joint cooperative form of representation at work rather than a more traditional adversarial trade union (Freeman and Rogers, 1999; Freeman et al., 2007).

But does NER really deliver the goods? Evidence on the effectiveness of NER and its effect on employment outcomes is available from two different sources. The first is personal testimony from managers and workers; the second is quantitative evidence, generally from large-scale surveys. Both yield a mixed picture.

To start, the effect of NER seems to depend on the extent to which it is used for integrative (unitarist) versus bargaining (pluralist) purposes or, alternatively, what we earlier framed as offensive versus defensive purposes. Most studies (Terry, 1999) conclude that NER is relatively ineffective as a forum for distributive bargaining and employee interest representation. The reason is that NER bodies lack the power, resources, and autonomy necessary to exert real leverage on the company—a fact not surprising since they are created by employers whose goal is to use them to *increase* profit, not to subtract from profit by creating an in-house bargaining agent. NER particularly fails to deliver positive, long-lasting outcomes for employees, and often employers, in four situations: the first is when it is primarily used as an overt union avoidance device; the second is when the firm's environment forces significant cost cutting; the third is when management gives the NER little scope or power for influence and, at the same time, continues to make unilateral decisions on important HRM issues; and the fourth is when management takes action (or fails to take such) that represents in the eyes of employees a serious breach in trust, a breaking of past commitments, or egregious opportunism (Gollan, 2006; Moriguchi, 2005; Taras and Copping, 1998; Upchurch et al., 2006; Watling and Snook, 2003). In these cases the firm's employees frequently decide to seek union representation.

NER enjoys its greatest success when used as part of a long run high-involvement employment strategy emphasizing competitive advantage through people. As much as possible, these companies endeavour to pay high wages and provide good benefits and working conditions as a way to take divisive distributive ('bargaining') issues off the table, thus allowing NER to focus on integrative 'win–win' issues (Kaufman, 2003a; Taras, 2000b). In these types of high-performing organizations, it can be difficult to quantitatively isolate the positive effect of NER since it is only one part of a larger, synergistic HRM system (Bryson et al., 2006). Nonetheless, several statistical studies have found positive NER effects on productivity, wages and/or quits (Addison et al., 2000; Batt et al., 2002; Fairris, 1997; Pencavel, 2006). Another study found that employees had a more favourable perception of managerial responsiveness in companies with NER plans than with trade unions (Bryson, 2004). The success of some NER plans is also revealed by the fact that a core group of corporate adopters maintain it over a long period of time and devote considerable management time and resources into it. Asked to identify the major contribution NER makes to organizational performance, the managers most often identify factors such as 'improved climate' or 'greater cooperation' rather than some more tangible and specific outcome. Paradoxically for NER, at least one study finds that the more satisfied and committed are employees (a 'good climate') the more likely they are to shift from representational voice to direct voice with managers (Luchak, 2003).

Case studies reveal successful large-scale NER is a challenge to successfully manage and requires considerable employer commitment and attention; it also requires significant upfront investment and can quickly atrophy (Taras and Copping, 1998; Upchurch et al., 2006). A key part of the challenge is to manage employee expectations, for reasons earlier explained. Also, NER is a management challenge because its success is conditional on a number of complex and not always easy to control factors ('mediating variables'). One is trust between the company and workers; a second is managerial responsiveness to employee concerns and opinions; a third is emphasis on integrative problem solving (rather than distributive bargaining); a fourth is a supportive economic environment in which the company is profitable and workers enjoy some measure of job security (rather than a situation of ongoing cost-cutting and significant layoffs); and a fifth is a 'human asset' HRM strategy that makes workers partners in a longer-term business relationship (rather than 'hired hands' in a short 'in and out' relationship).

CONCLUSION

Non-union forms of employee representation are one method for implementing employee participation in organizations. In this respect, they are both a complement and substitute for other methods, such as direct forms of participation (e.g., self-managed work teams, quality circles) and other forms of indirect participation (e.g., trade unions).

NER has been practiced in industry for more than a century, with considerable diversity and variation both across countries and over time. Few topics related to employee participation, or industrial relations and labour policy in general, have been as controversial. The last twenty years have seen an upswing in interest in NER, fuelled partly by the popularity of high-performance work systems and the leading role of employee involvement therein and also the decline of union-provided voice in many countries. In this context, NER has attracted attention as a potentially useful middle way (or third way) between 'no voice' and 'union voice'.

In practice, smaller-scale and 'single issue' forms of NER (e.g., safety, gain sharing, production, dispute resolution committees) have proliferated the most; the incidence of NER then decreases as one moves up the ladder in terms of breadth and depth of scale, issues covered, and decision-making ability. NER plans that cover employees in entire plants or companies and have purview over all joint issues of concern, such as some JIC's and JCC's, are scattered throughout industry (except in the USA where they are largely illegal), but remain a distinctly minority phenomenon. So far, however, it is these larger NER plans that have attracted the most research interest.

Just as the form and function of NER plans vary greatly, so do their outcomes and effectiveness. Many NER plans have a short half-life, while others operate effectively for decades. Similarly, some NER plans make a noticeable difference in company performance and employee job satisfaction, while many others have only a marginal effect or none at all. The same divided evidence also applies to whether NER plans on balance inhibit or promote union organization. In this regard, we are simply repeating the conclusion reached by noted industrial relations scholar, William Leiserson (1928) eight decades ago in his in-depth review of NER plans of the 1920s. He observed, 'Almost anything that may be said of employee representation will be true.' The same statement remains valid today.

REFERENCES

ACKERS, P., MARCHINGTON, M., WILKINSON, A., and DUNDON, T. (2006) 'Employee Participation in Britain: From Collective Bargaining and Industrial Democracy to Employee Involvement and Social Partnership—Two Decades of Manchester/Loughborough Research', *Decision*, 33(1): 75–87.

ADAMS, R. (1993) 'The North American Model of Employee Representational Participation: "A Hollow Mockery" ', *Comparative Labour Law Journal*, 15(1) 201–11.

ADDISON, J. T., SCHNABEL, C., and WAGNER, J. (2000) 'Nonunion Employee Representation in Germany', in B. Kaufman and D. Taras (eds), *Nonunion Employee Representation: History, Contemporary Practice, and Policy*, pp. 365–85. Armonk, NY: ME Sharpe.

APPELBAUM, E., BAILEY, T., BERG, P., and KALLEBERG, A. (2000) *Manufacturing Advantage: Why High-Performance Work Systems Pay Off*. Ithaca, NY: Cornell University/ILR Press.

BARENBERG, M. (1993) 'The Political Economy of the Wagner Act: Power, Symbol, and Workplace Cooperation', *Harvard Law Review*, 106, May: 1379–496.

BASKEN, R. (2000) 'My Experience with Unionization of Nonunion Employee Representation Plans in Canada', in B. Kaufmanand D. Taras (eds), *Nonunion Employee Representation: History, Contemporary Practice, and Policy*, pp. 487–97. Armonk, NY: M.E. Sharpe.

BASSET, W. (1919) *When the Workmen Help You Manage*. New York: Century.

BATT, R., COLVIN, A., and KEEFE, J. (2002) 'Employee Voice, Human Resource Practices and Quit Rates: Evidence from the Telecommunications Industry', *Industrial and Labour Relations Review*, 55(4): 573–94.

BENSON, J. (2000) 'Employee Voice in Union and Non-union Australian Workplaces', *British Journal of Industrial Relations*, 38(3): 453–59.

BERNSTEIN, I. (1960) *The Lean Years: A History of the American Worker 1920–1933*. Boston, MA: Houghton Mifflin.

BRODY, D. (1994) 'Section 8(a)(2) and the Origins of the Wagner Act', in S. Friedman et al. (eds), *Restoring the Promise of American Labour Law*. Ithaca, NY: ILR Press.

BRYSON, A. (2004) 'Managerial Responsiveness to Union and Non-union Voice', *Industrial Relations*, 43(1): 213–41.

—— CHARLWOOD, A., and FORTH, J. (2006) 'Worker Voice, Managerial Responsiveness and Labour Productivity: An Empirical Investigation', *Industrial Relations Journal*, 37(5): 438–56.

BUTLER, P. (2005) 'Non-union Employee Representation: Exploring the Efficacy of the Voice Process', *Employee Relations*, 27(3): 272–88.

CAPPELLI, P. and NEUMARK, D. (2001) 'Do "High-Performance" Work Practices Improve Establishment-Level Outcomes?' *Industrial and Labour Relations Review*, 54, July: 737–75.

CHARLWOOD, A. (2006) 'What Determined Employer Voice Choice in Britain in the Twentieth Century? A Critique of the "Sound of Silence" Model', *Socio-Economic Review*, 4(2): 301–10.

CHAYKOWSKI, R. (2000) 'Advancing Labour-Management Relations Through Consultation: The Role of the National Joint Council of the Public Service of Canada', in B. Kaufman and D. Taras (eds), *Nonunion Employee Representation: History, Contemporary Practice, and Policy*, pp. 328–47. Armonk, NY: M.E. Sharpe.

CHIESA, R. and RHYASON, K. (2000) 'Production District Industrial Council at Imperial Oil Ltd. The Perspective from the Employee Side', in B. Kaufman and D. Taras (eds), *Nonunion Employee Representation: History, Contemporary Practice, and Policy*, pp. 474–76. Armonk, NY: M.E. Sharpe.

Commission on the Future of Worker–Management Relations (1994) *Report and Recommendations*. Washington: US Dept. of Labour and Dept. of Commerce.

CONE, C. (2000) 'Delta Personnel Board Council', in B. Kaufman and D. Taras (eds), *Nonunion Employee Representation: History, Contemporary Practice, and Policy*, pp. 469–73. Armonk, NY: M.E. Sharpe.

DERBER, M. (1970) *The American Ideal of Industrial Democracy.* Urbana, IL: University of Illinois Press.

DUNDON, T., CURRAN, D., RYAN, P., and MALONEY, M. (2006) 'Conceptualizing the Dynamics of Employee Information and Consultation: Evidence from the Republic of Ireland', *Industrial Relations Journal,* 37(5): 492–512.

——WILKINSON, A., MARCHINGTON, M., and P. ACKERS. (2004) 'The Meaning and Purpose of Employee Voice', *International Journal of Human Resource Management,* 15(6): 1149–70.

DUNN, R. (1926) *American Company Unions.* Chicago: Trade Union Educational League.

ESTREICHER, S. (2004) 'Alternative Dispute Resolution in the Employment Arena', *Proceedings of the New York University Annual Conference on Labour.* New York: International Law Publications.

EWING, D. (1990) *Justice on the Job: Resolving Grievances in the Nonunion Workplace.* Boston, MA: Harvard Business School Press.

FAIRRIS, D. (1997) *Shopfloor Matters: Labour–Management Relations in Twentieth-Century Manufacturing.* London: Routledge.

FLOOD, F. and TONER, B. (1997) 'Large Non-Union Companies: How Do They Avoid a Catch 22?' *British Journal of Industrial Relations,* 35(2): 257–77.

FREEMAN, R., BOXALL, P., and HAYNES, P. (2007) *What Workers Say: Employee Voice in the Anglo-American Workplace.* Ithaca, NY: Cornell University Press.

—— and LAZEAR, E. (1995) 'An Economic Analysis of Works Councils', in J. Rogers and W. Streeck (eds), *Works Councils: Consultation, Representation, and Cooperation in Industrial Relations,* pp. 27–52. Chicago: University of Chicago Press.

——and MEDOFF, J. (1984) *What Do Unions Do?* New York: Basic Books.

——and ROGERS, J. (1999) *What Workers Want.* Ithaca, NY: Cornell University Press.

FRIEDMAN, S., HURD, R., OSWALD, R., and SEEBER, R. (eds) (1994) *Restoring the Promise of American Labour Law.* Ithaca, NY: Cornell University Press.

GITELMAN, H. (1988) *Legacy of the Ludlow Massacre.* Philadelphia, PA: University of Pennsylvania Press.

GOLLAN, P. (2000) 'Nonunion Forms of Employee Representation in the United Kingdom and Australia', in B. Kaufman and D. Taras (eds), *Nonunion Employee Representation: History, Contemporary Practice, and Policy,* pp. 410–52. Armonk, NY: M.E. Sharpe.

—— (2006) 'Twin Tracks—Employee Representation at Eurotunnel Revisited', *Industrial Relations,* 45(4): 606–49.

—— (2007) *Employee Representation in Non-Union Firms.* London: Sage.

GOSPEL, H. (1992) *Markets, Firms, and the Management of Labour in Modern Britain.* Cambridge: Cambridge University Press.

——and WILLMAN, P. (2005) 'Statutory Information Disclosure for Consultation and Bargaining in Germany, France, and the UK', in J. Storey (ed.), *Adding Value Through Information and Consultation.* Basingstoke: Palgrave Macmillan.

GUEST, D. and HOQUE, P. (1994) 'The Good, the Bad, and the Ugly: Employment Relations in Non-Union Workplaces', *Human Resource Management Journal,* 5(1): 1–14.

GUMBRELL-MCCORMICK, R. and HYMAN, R. (2006) 'Embedded Collectivism? Workplace Representation in France and Germany', *Industrial Relations Journal,* 37(5): 473–91.

HALL, M. (2006) 'A Cool Response to the ICE Regulations? Employer and Trade Union Approaches to the New Legal Framework for Information and Consultation', *Industrial Relations Journal,* 37(5): 456–72.

HARSHAW, M. (2000) 'Nonunion Employee Representation at Dofasco', in B. Kaufman and D. Taras (eds), *Nonunion Employee Representation: History, Contemporary Practice, and Policy*, pp. 463–8. Armonk, NY: M.E. Sharpe.

HAYNES, P. and FRYER, G. (2001) 'More Form Than Substance? Collective Bargaining and Employee Voice in the Auckland Luxury Hotel Industry', *International Journal of Employment Studies*, 9(2): 109–30.

HELFGOTT, R. (2000) 'The Effectiveness of Diversity Networks in Providing Collective Voice for Employees', in B. Kaufman and D. Taras (eds), *Nonunion Employee Representation: History, Contemporary Practice, and Policy*, pp. 348–64. Armonk, NY: M.E. Sharpe.

HIATT, J. and GOLD, L. (2000) 'Employer-Employee Committees: A Union Perspective', in B. Kaufman and D. Taras (eds), *Nonunion Employee Representation: History, Contemporary Practice, and Policy*, pp. 498–511. Armonk, NY: M.E. Sharpe.

HYMAN, R. (1997) 'The Future of Employee Representation', *British Journal of Industrial Relations*, 35(3): 309–36.

JACOBY, S. (1991) 'Pacific Ties: Industrial Relations and Employment Systems in Japan and the United States', in H. Harris and N. Lichtenstein (eds), *Industrial Democracy in America: The Ambiguous Promise*. Cambridge: Cambridge University Press, pp. 206–48.

KAUFMAN, B. (1999) 'Does the NLRA Constrain Employee Involvement and Participation Programs in Nonunion Companies?: A Reassessment', *Yale Law and Policy Review*, 17(2): 729–811.

—— (2000) 'The Case for the Company Union', *Labour History*, 41(3): 321–50.

—— (2003a) 'High-Level Employee Involvement at Delta Air Lines', *Human Resource Management*, 42(2): 175–190.

—— (2003b) 'The Quest for Cooperation and Unity of Interest in Industry', in B. Kaufman, R. Beaumont, and R. Helfgott (eds), *Industrial Relations to Human Resources and Beyond: The Evolving Process of Employee Relations Management*, pp. 115–46. Armonk, NY: M.E. Sharpe.

—— (2008) *Managing the Human Factor: The Early Years of Human Resource Management in American Industry*. Ithaca, NY: Cornell University Press.

—— and KLEINER, M. (eds) (1993) *Employee Representation: Alternatives and Future Directions*. Madison: Industrial Relations Research Association.

—— and LEVINE, D. (2000) 'An Economic Analysis of Employee Representation', in B. Kaufman and D. Taras (eds), *Nonunion Employee Representation: History, Contemporary Practice, and Policy*, pp. 149–75. Armonk, NY: M.E. Sharpe.

—— and TARAS, D. (2000) *Non-union Employee Representation: History, Contemporary Practice, and Policy*. Armonk, NY: M.E. Sharpe.

KIM, D. and KIM, H. (2004) 'A Comparison of the Effectiveness of Unions and Non-Union Works Councils in Korea: Can Non-Union Employee Representation Substitute for Trade Unionism?' *International Journal of Human Resource Management*, 15(6): 1069–93.

KOCHAN, T. (1995) 'Using the Dunlop Report to Achieve Mutual Gains', *Industrial Relations*, 34(3): 350–67.

—— KATZ, H. and MCKERSIE, R. (1986) *The Transformation of American Industrial Relations*. New York: Basic.

LAWLER, E. (1992) *Ultimate Advantage: Creating the High-Involvement Organization*. San Francisco: Jossey-Bass.

—— ALBERS, S. and LEDFORD Jr., G. (1992) *Employee Involvement and Total Quality Management: Practices and Results in Fortune 1000 Companies*. San Francisco: Jossey-Bass.

LAWLER, J. (1990) *Unionization and Deunionization: Strategy, Tactics, and Outcomes.* Columbia: University of South Carolina Press.

LEISERSON, W. (1928) 'The Accomplishments and Significance of Employee Representation'. *Personnel*, 4, February, pp. 119–35.

LEITCH, J. (1919) *Man-to-Man: The Story of Industrial Democracy.* New York: Forbes.

LEROY, M. (1997) ' "Dealing With" Employee Involvement in Nonunion Workplaces: Empirical Research Implications for the TEAM Act', *Notre Dame Law Review*, 72(1): 31–82.

—— (2000) 'Do Employee Participation Groups Violate Section 8(a)(2) of the National Labour Relations Act? An Empirical Analysis', in B. Kaufman and D. Taras (eds), *Nonunion Employee Representation: History, Contemporary Practice, and Policy*, pp. 287–306. Armonk, NY: M.E. Sharpe.

LEWIN, D. and MITCHELL, D. (1992) 'Systems of Employee Voice: Theoretical and Empirical Perspectives', *California Management Review*, 35, spring, pp. 95–111.

LIPSET, S. and MELTZ, N. (2000) 'Estimates of Nonunion Employee Representation in the United States and Canada: How Different Are the Two Countries?' in B. Kaufman and D. Taras (eds), *Nonunion Employee Representation: History, Contemporary Practice, and Policy*, pp. 223–30. Armonk, NY: M.E. Sharpe.

LLOYD, C. (2001) 'What do Employee Councils Do? The Impact of Non-union Forms of Representation on Trade Union Organization', *Industrial Relations Journal*, 32(4): 313–27.

LUCHAK, A. (2003) 'What Kind of Voice Do Loyal Employees Use?', *British Journal of Industrial Relations*, 41(1): 115–34.

McCABE, D. and LEWIN, D. (1992) 'Employee Voice: A Human Resource Management Perspective', *California Management Review*, 35, spring: 112–23.

MACDOUGALL, K. (2000) 'Nonunion Employee Representation at the Royal Canadian Mounted Police', in B. Kaufman and D. Taras (eds), *Nonunion Employee Representation: History, Contemporary Practice, and Policy*, pp. 477–82. Armonk, NY: M.E. Sharpe.

MACDOWELL, L. (2000) 'Company Unionism in Canada', in B. Kaufman and D. Taras (eds), *Nonunion Employee Representation: History, Contemporary Practice, and Policy*, pp. 96–120. Armonk, NY: M.E. Sharpe.

MACMAHAN, G., BELL, M., and VIRICK, M. (1998) 'Strategic Human Resource Management: Employee Involvement, Diversity, and International Issues', *Human Resource Management Review*, 8, Fall: 193–214.

MARCHINGTON, M., GOODMAN, J., WILKINSON, A., and ACKERS, P. (1992) *New Developments in Employee Involvement.* Employment Department Research Series no. 2. London: HMSO.

—— WILKINSON, A., ACKERS, P., and DUNDON, T. (2001) *Management Choice and Employee Voice.* London: Chartered Institute of Personnel Professionals.

MARSDEN, D. (2003) 'Individual Employee Voice: Renegotiation and Performance Management in Public Services', *International Journal of Human Resource Management*, 18(7): 1263–78.

MARYOTT, M. (1997) 'Participate at Your Peril: The Need for Resolution of the Conflict Surrounding Employee Participation Programs by the TEAM Act of 1997', *Pepperdine Law Review*, 24: 1291–326.

MORIGUCHI, C. (2005) 'Did American Welfare Capitalists Breach Their Implicit Contracts During the Great Depression? Preliminary Findings from Company-Level Data', *Industrial and Labour Relations Review*, 59(1): 51–81.

MORISHIMA, M. and TSURU, T. (2000) 'Nonunion Employee Representation in Japan', in B. Kaufman and D. Taras (eds), *Nonunion Employee Representation: History, Contemporary Practice, and Policy*, pp. 386–409. Armonk, NY: M.E. Sharpe.

National Industrial Conference Board (1919) *Works Councils in the United States.* Research Report no. 21. New York: National Industrial Conference Board.

National Labour Relations Board. (2001) *Crown Cork & Seal Company, Inc.*, Case 16-CA-18316; 20 July. Washington, DC: National Labour Relations Board.

OZANNE, R. (1967) *A Century of Labour-Management Relations at McCormick and International Harvester.* Madison: University of Wisconsin Press.

PENCAVEL, J. (2003) 'Company Unions, Wages, and Hours', in D. Lewin and B. Kaufman (eds), *Advances in Industrial and Labour Relations*, vol. 12, pp. 7–38. New York: Elsevier.

——(2006) 'Company Unions, Wages, and Work Hours', in D. Lewin and B. Kaufman (eds), *Advances in Industrial and Labor Relations*, vol. 12, pp. 7–38. New York: Elsevier.

PYMAN, A., COOPER, B., TEICHER, J. and HOLLAND, P. (2006) 'A Comparison of the Effectiveness of Employee Voice Arrangements in Australia', *Industrial Relations Journal*, 37(6): 543–59.

ROGERS, J. and STREECK, W. (1995) *Works Councils: Consultation, Representation, and Cooperation in Industrial Relations.* Chicago: University of Chicago Press.

SIMS, A. (2008) 'Fireside Chat', Speech given to the Canadian Industrial Relations Association, Calgary Chapter meeting, May.

STRAUSS, G. (1995) 'Is the New Deal System Collapsing? With What Might It be Replaced?' *Industrial Relations*, 34(3): 329–49.

TARAS, D. (1997a) 'Why Non-Union Representation is Legal in Canada', *Relations Industrielles*, 52(4): 761–80.

——(1997b) 'Managerial Intentions and Wage Determination in the Canadian Petroleum Industry', *Industrial Relations*, 36(2): 178–205.

——(1998) 'Nonunion Representation: Complement or Threat to Unions?' *Proceedings of the Fiftieth Annual Meeting.* Madison: Industrial Relations Research Association, pp. 281–90.

——(2000a) 'Portrait of Nonunion Employee Representation in Canada: History, Law and Contemporary Plans', in B. Kaufman and D. Taras (eds), *Nonunion Employee Representation: History, Contemporary Practice, and Policy*, pp. 121–48. Armonk, NY: M.E. Sharpe.

——(2000b) 'Contemporary Experience with the Rockefeller Plan: Imperial Oil's Joint Industrial Council', in B. Kaufman and D. Taras (eds), *Nonunion Employee Representation: History, Contemporary Practice, and Policy*, pp. 231–58. Armonk, NY: M.E. Sharpe.

——(2003) 'Employee Voice: Evolution from Employee Representation to Employee Involvement', in B. Kaufman, R. Beaumont, and R. Helfgott (eds), *Industrial Relations to Human Resources and Beyond: The Evolution of Employee Relations Management*, pp. 293–329. Armonk, NY: M.E. Sharpe.

——(2006) 'Determining Employer Intent: When is a Voice Forum found to be Unlawful under Canadian Law?' *Socio-Economic Review*, 4(2): 321–36.

——(2007) 'Reconciling Differences Differently: Employee Voice in Public Policymaking and Workplace Governance', *Comparative Labor Law and Policy Journal*, 28: 167–91.

——and COPPING, J. (1998) 'The Transition from Formal Nonunion Representation to Unionization: A Contemporary Case', *Industrial and Labour Relations Review*, 52(1): 22–44.

TARAS, D. and KAUFMAN, B. (2006) 'Non-Union Employee Representation in North America: Diversity, Controversy, and Uncertain Future', *Industrial Relations Journal*, 37 (5): 513–42.

TERRY, M. (1999) 'Systems of Collective Employee Representation in Non-union Firms in the UK', *Industrial Relations Journal*, 30(1): 16–30.

TIMUR, A. T. (2004) *Transition to Unionism: Differences Between Nonunion Representation Forums and Greenfield Sites*. Ph.D. Dissertation, Haskayne School of Business, University of Calgary.

TOTTEN, G. (1967) 'Collective Bargaining and Works Councils as Innovations in Industrial Relations in Japan During the 1920s', in R. Dore (ed.), *Aspects of Social Change in Modern Japan*, pp. 203–44. Princeton: Princeton University Press.

TOWERS, B. (1997) *The Representation Gap: Change and Reform in the British and American Workplace*. New York: Oxford University Press.

UPCHURCH, M., RICHARDSON, M., and STEWART, P. (2006) 'Employee Representation and Partnership in the Non-Union Sector: A Paradox of Intentions', *Human Resource Management Journal*, 16(4): 393–410.

VERMA, A. (2000) 'Employee Involvement and Representation in Nonunion Firms: What Canadian Employers Do and Why?', in B. E. Kaufman and D. G. Taras, *Nonunion Employee Representation: History, Contemporary Practice, and Policy*, pp. 303–27. Armonk, NY: M. E. Sharpe.

WATLING, D. and SNOOK, J. (2003) 'Works Council and Trade Unions: Complementary or Competitive: The Case of SAGCo', *Industrial Relations Journal*, 34(3): 260–70.

WEILER, P. (1990) *Governing the Workplace*. Cambridge: Harvard University Press.

—— DUNDON, T., MARCHINGTON, M., and ACKERS, P. (2004) 'Changing Patterns of Employee Voice', *Journal of Industrial Relations*, 46(3): 298–322.

—— —— and GRUGULIS, I. (2007) 'Information But Not Consultation: Exploring Employee Involvement in SME's', *International Journal of Human Resource Management*, 18(7): 1279–97.

WILLMAN, P., BRYSON, A., and GOMEZ, R. (2006) 'The Sound of Silence: Which Employers Choose No Employee Voice and Why?', *Socio-Economic Review*, 4(2): 283–300.

CHAPTER 12

WORKS COUNCILS:

THE EUROPEAN MODEL
OF INDUSTRIAL
DEMOCRACY?

REBECCA GUMBRELL-McCORMICK

RICHARD HYMAN

In this chapter we focus on works councils, adopting the definition of Rogers and Streeck (1995: 6): 'institutionalized bodies for representative communication between a single employer ('management') and the employees ('workforce') of a single plant or enterprise ('workplace')'. We are concerned with countries with *generalized* systems of representation—hence where participation structures exist largely independently of management wishes—and not with those where representative bodies may be established voluntarily through localized management (or union) initiatives. We also limit attention to bodies with the capacity to discuss a broad agenda of employment- and work-related issues; this means, for example, that we ignore statutory health and safety committees, which exist in many countries without works councils. On this definition, works councils are almost exclusively a phenomenon of continental Western Europe, and we discuss below why this is the case. Our focus is also specifically on *national* institutions; we do not examine the one instance of mandatory supranational structures, European

Works Councils. Nor do we consider board-level employee representation, though in some countries—notably Germany—this can reinforce the influence of works councils.

Works councils differ substantially between countries in their status (established by law or by comprehensive collective agreement), their powers and functions (from information to consultation and—rather infrequently— codetermination), and hence their capacity to exert significant influence over management decision making, their composition (employee-only, or joint management–worker), and their relationship with trade unions external to the company. In this chapter we give principal attention to six European countries with very different works council systems: Germany, the Netherlands, Belgium, France, Italy, and Sweden.

Varieties of Works Councils

The term 'works council' is a literal translation of the German *Betriebsrat* or Dutch *ondernemingsraad*, but not of the French *comité d'entreprise*, and even less so of the Italian *rappresentanza*. And even where an apparently identical term is used in different languages, this does not necessarily mean that the institutions are identical (Biagi, 2001: 483). In one of the earliest comparative analyses of European experience, Sorge (1976: 278) referred to the 'bewildering variety of industrial democracy institutions', adding that while 'there are noticeable clusters of institutional features across national borders', there also exist 'national institutions which cannot be conveniently fitted into an international system of types'. This is one cogent reason to commence analysis with a survey of national institutional arrangements.

As we have noted, works councils as defined above are widespread in continental Europe but extremely rare elsewhere. In the USA, where the Commission on the Future of Worker–Management Relations (the Dunlop Commission) was established in 1993 to propose solutions to the widening 'representation gap', its report did not even consider the possibility of legislation on works councils. In other non-European countries, if council-like structures have been established it has typically been in emulation of European models, often to little effect. For example, in South Africa a 'workplace forum' system was established after the end of apartheid, to a large extent informed by German codetermination. But to establish a forum requires trade union initiative, and very few exist because most unions have viewed the new structures with suspicion (Wood and Mahabir, 2001: 230). In Taiwan, joint committees with elected employee representatives are in theory mandatory, but there are no sanctions if management disregards the legal requirements, and coverage rates are very low (Han and Chiu, 2000). However in Korea, where labour management councils have been obligatory in larger firms since 1980, they do appear to function relatively effectively (Kato et al., 2005; Kleiner and Lee, 1997).

Within Europe there are also negative examples. British employers overwhelmingly regard mandatory councils as a challenge to their own managerial prerogatives, and most unions have also considered them a threat to their 'single channel' of representation. In Central and Eastern Europe, the principle of joint employee–management structures was typically rejected after 1989 because unfettered managerial prerogative was regarded as an essential element in the invention of a market economy—notably in Poland, where the leaders of *Solidarność* in government rejected the ideas of industrial democracy with which they had flirted in opposition (Federowicz and Levitas, 1995). One exception is Hungary, where mandatory works councils were introduced in 1992 under the influence of German experience; but their functions are purely informational and consultative, and most observers consider their significance limited (Frege, 2002; Tóth, 1997). In some other countries (for example, the Czech Republic) the law permits the formation of councils on a voluntary basis. Almost certainly the closest to a Western European 'strong' works council system is in Slovenia, in part perhaps because of popular attachment to the former Yugoslav tradition of self-management (Stanojević, 2003).

How should we understand the European specificity of works councils? It is common to see independent representation of employee interests within the company as one expression of the 'European social model'—a concept notoriously difficult to define (Ebbinghaus, 1999; Jepsen and Serrano Pascual, 2006). An important principle (on which there is a broad consensus between the social-democratic and Christian-democratic traditions which are predominant in much of Western Europe) is that firms are social institutions with a variety of stakeholders, not simply economic institutions accountable only to their shareholders; and that employees are thus in an important sense 'citizens' of the company in which they work. This principle is incompatible with the common law models of company law which prevail in the Anglophone countries. Jackson (2005), in a study of mandatory board-level employee representation, concludes that civil law systems are a necessary but not sufficient condition for such provisions. This also seems to apply to those countries with strong works council systems. What other conditions apply?

In discussing peak-level institutions of cross-class cooperation, Therborn (1992: 36) distinguishes between what he terms 'an institutionalization of partnership and consensus' and 'an institutionalization, one might perhaps even say ritualization, of conflict'. Which dynamic underlies the creation of national works council systems? According to Sorge (1976: 284), works councils tend to be legally mandated where state repression long ago provoked the rise of a radical, indeed revolutionary labour movement, and governments then had to create order by imposing institutions of workplace employee representation designed to bypass more militant class-wide mobilization. Hence as Knudsen (1995: 18) suggests, 'the common ground for participation has emerged historically through social compromises which have crystallized from social struggles'; and as Ramsay (1977) argues, there appear to occur 'cycles of control' through which new institutions are created in response to phases of oppositional worker mobilization. This is evident from both the French and the German cases, outlined below. We may also note that governments have more recently encouraged participative mechanisms in order to achieve employee support, or at least acquiescence, in productivity-enhancing changes in work organization. Hence there is an inherent ambiguity or contradiction underlying works council systems: they may be designed in part to promote workers' rights by facilitating collective 'voice' over key aspects of the employment relationship, but often to a greater extent are intended to foster industrial peace and productive efficiency when these goals are considered problematic.

Such ambiguities are certainly the case with the Information and Consultation Directive (2002/14/EC) adopted by the European Union (EU) in 2002. The European Commission wished to make mechanisms for employee representation obligatory in member states as part of a project of modernizing production systems, and this was supported by most trade unions as a means of strengthening employee voice in the face of increasing restructuring of production and decentralization of industrial relations. But not only did the sheer diversity of national systems across the EU make any standard mechanism impossible to define, the lack of any immediate background of 'social struggles' made it easy for reluctant governments and employers' organizations to resist. The eventual Directive gives workers in larger companies (with over fifty employees) a right to be informed about the undertaking's economic situation, and informed and consulted about employment prospects and about decisions likely to lead to substantial changes in work organization or contractual relations, including redundancies and transfers (Carley et al., 2005: 11, 32; European Commission, 2006: Chapter 3). It does not, however, prescribe works councils as defined above: there is a complex triggering procedure before a mechanism becomes mandatory, and while an 'information and consultation committee' is the default mechanism, other far less institutionalized procedures are possible in companies.

In the remainder of this section we summarize the institutional arrangements in each of our six countries, explaining their historical evolution and outlining their actual functioning. In the process we will highlight key ambiguities and controversies in contemporary discussion. These accounts will be used for comparative thematic analysis in the final part of the chapter.

Germany

We start with Germany, where works councils (*Betriebsräte*) were invented, and where the rights assigned to employee representatives are usually considered the strongest of any national system; for that reason will go into more detail in this section than in those following.

Workplace representation structures first developed in the late nineteenth century in response to the growth of socialist trade unionism. Some employers established voluntary factory committees, and these were made obligatory in all industries deemed essential for the 1914–1918 war effort (Müller-Jentsch, 1995: 53). The wartime rise of revolutionary workers' councils prompted a law on works councils (*Betriebsrätegesetz*) in 1920 (Fürstenberg, 1978).

To some extent, history was repeated after 1945, when radical works councils emerged and a newly unified trade union movement pressed for a substantial programme of industrial and economic democracy. The 1952 *Betriebsverfassungsgesetz* (Works Constitution Act), creating a representative structure separate from the unions and without the right to negotiate or strike, was perceived as a defeat for the labour movement. The significance of works councils has, however, altered over time, partly through legislative amendments but primarily through an evolution in the triangular relationship between councils, unions, and managements.

Codetermination operates at two levels. In all but the smallest companies (fewer than five employees) there is a requirement to establish a works council, elected by the workforce every four years; and in all firms with over 2,000 employees the latter are represented on the supervisory board, in practice through a combination of works councillors and outside trade union officials. In this chapter we do not discuss board-level representation, though it should be noted that participation in the supervisory board reinforces the status and informational resources of works council members.

Works councils are employee-only bodies which in larger firms are in constant contact with management. Their size varies in line with the number of employees, and in larger establishments (over 200 employees), one or more works councillors have full-time release from their normal work. Councils are elected every four years. Since 1972 it has been possible to establish a central works council in multi-plant companies.

There are rights to information over a range of business and financial questions, consultation over a broader set of employment matters, and codetermination (giving at least a provisional veto) on hiring and firing, payment and grading systems, and the regulation of working time. While councils are mandatory, there is no obligation on the employer to take the initiative; this must be triggered by a group of employees or a trade union with membership in the workplace. In practice, councils are absent in many firms, particularly the smallest.

The separation of functions between unions and councils was initially regarded as a recipe for divide and rule, but things turned out differently: 'the two levels in the dual system are mutually reinforcing' (Thelen, 1991: 16). According to most calculations, over 75 per cent of councillors (and an even higher proportion of council presidents) are unionists, elected on a union 'slate'. Unions need the councils to provide a channel of information and communication, to monitor the application of collective agreements, and often to help with recruitment; councils need the unions for training, information, and advice, and as a source of legitimacy in defending broad collective principles against the particularistic interests of their constituents (Hege and Dufour, 1995; Jacobi et al., 1998: 212; Müller-Jentsch, 1995: 75; Streeck, 1992).

One should not assume, however, that a strong works council functioning as the extended arm of the union is the norm. In the first substantial empirical account of works council status and practice, Kotthoff (1981) found that roughly two-thirds were management-dominated. However, when Kotthoff (1994) returned to the same workplaces he discovered a significant transformation: some two-thirds of councils were by his criteria now effective representatives of employee interests, cooperating on equal terms with the external union. Even smaller employers, often as a result of a generational change in management, saw the value of a strong council which could provide a stable counterpart on the employee side. Similar results were reported by Schmidt and Trinczek (1991) and by Bosch (1997), who found a reciprocal process involving a professionalization of personnel management and a self-confident, relatively autonomous works council leadership. The two sides were engaged in close day-to-day relationships, each recognizing that a strong counterpart could paradoxically enhance its own status in dealing with other managers, on the one hand, and the workforce, on the other.

In recent years this delicate balance has faced three interconnected challenges: German unification, intensified international competition, and a decentralization of bargaining. First, after unification in 1990, west German labour law was applied to the east. Most commentators were sceptical whether works councils could operate effectively without the normative underpinnings which had evolved over several decades in the west. Frege (1999) disputed this view, but much research indicated that councils in the east disregarded union policy in defence of workplace interests in a context of intense industrial restructuring.

Second, 'company egoism' (or *Betriebsegoismus*) became common in both parts of Germany with the end of the 'economic miracle'. Many firms facing economic difficulties (especially smaller establishments) withdrew from their employers' associations or disregarded sectoral agreements. This required the acquiescence of works councils, while unions often turned a blind eye if the only alternative seemed to be job losses (Streeck and Hassel, 2003: 113). To maintain some coordination of the growing trend to 'wildcat cooperation' (Streeck 1984), sectoral agreements increasingly included 'hardship clauses' permitting firms in economic difficulties to negotiate exemptions from the prescribed wages and conditions. In addition, 'employment pacts' were agreed in many major firms, allowing deviations from sectoral agreements in exchange for job security guarantees (Kommission Mitbestimmung, 1998).

Third, many employers, particularly in private services, have begun to resist the formation of councils, or at least to ensure the election of management-friendly councillors (Bormann, 2007; Dribbusch, 2003). There is a growing 'exclusion zone' of firms covered neither by a collective agreement nor by a works council, encompassing a high proportion of workplaces, but (since the traditional institutions are still firmly established in larger firms) a far smaller proportion of employees. Only 4 per cent of establishments with between five and twenty employees have a works council, as against over 90 per cent of those with more than 500. There is also significant disparity between east and west Germany, and an even more substantial difference between manufacturing and services (Gumbrell-McCormick and Hyman, 2006). However, as Frege argues (2002: 233), 'most available empirical evidence suggests that works councils currently remain a stable institution'; and Kotthoff (1998) insists that while substantively they have been weakened in their relations with the employer, procedurally they remain strong: they are if anything more necessary as 'co-managers' of painful restructuring.

The Netherlands

Dutch works councils were legally constituted by the 1950 *Wet op de Onderne-mingsraden* (WOR), revised in 1971, 1979, and 1998, forming part of a complex set of institutions to regulate labour relations in the spirit of the post-war 'social-democratic compromise'. The Foundation of Labour (*Stichting van de Arbeid*), a joint body representing employers and employees, was founded in 1945, reflecting the Dutch tradition of a pragmatic, cooperative, and consultative approach to industrial relations. Another 1950 law created the tripartite Social and Economic Council (*Sociaal-Economische Raad*). As part of the same 'historic compromise', the two sides of industry accepted 'management's right to manage' and 'free collective bargaining' (Visser, 1995: 89–90).

Works councils became mandatory in establishments with over twenty-five employees, for the specific purpose of contributing 'to the best functioning of the enterprise' (Visser, 1995: 89). They were not designed as organs of representation or voice for the workforce, but as a channel of communication. The councils were to be made up of employees, with the employer as chair. There were no sanctions to ensure compliance; and indeed, few councils were set up until the 1960s, neither employers nor trade unions showing much enthusiasm. Unions were suspicious of the councils as 'paternalistic' institutions and concentrated instead on collective bargaining, primarily at industry or sector level, and on the new bipartite industry boards. Employers, for their part, were more likely to set up councils in larger firms, and in those with a modern personnel department (Visser, 1995: 90).

The 1971 reform raised the threshold for mandatory councils to firms with 100 or more employees, and extended their purpose to consultation and representation (Visser, 1995: 91), but left most of the remaining aspects of the system in place. The most important and controversial provision of the 1979 reform removed the requirement for the employer to act as chair; but to retain the consensual, 'problem-solving' approach, it prescribed obligatory consultation and mediation. In the 1998 reform, the threshold was lowered again, this time to fifty or more employees (van het Kaar, 2003), and councils' powers were extended.

Although they were slow to build up, there was a fivefold expansion in numbers from the late 1970s to the late 1980s—though much of the growth was in the education sector, covered by special legislation in 1982 (Looise, 1989: 271). Today, the Netherlands has one of the highest rates of coverage of works councils: in 2002, 71 per cent of establishments with fifty employees or more had councils, rising to 94 per cent in firms with 200 or more (van het Kaar, 2003). In addition, one-third of establishments with fewer than fifty employees have a personnel delegation (*perso-neelsvertegenwoordiging*), according to a provision created in 1998. Around 68 per cent of the workforce have either a works council or a personnel delegate at their workplace (van het Kaar, 2003).

Works councils, especially since the 1998 reform, have considerable powers. Their right to information and consultation is very broad, encompassing 'each and every decision that touches upon the continuity of the organization, such as mergers, acquisitions, closures, dislocations, substantial expansions, or reductions' (Engelen, 2004: 499). They monitor the firm's implementation of legislation on equal opportunities, health and safety, and other work-related areas. They enjoy consultation rights on economic and financial matters, and must be informed and consulted in a timely manner. Further, they have codetermination rights over pension insurance, the arrangement of working hours and holidays, health and safety and rules concerning hiring, firing, promotion, training, and grievance handling. In disagreements over plans for restructuring or redundancies, the employer must postpone their implementation while an amicable solution is sought. This 'capacity to create negative dilemmas for management' is often used by councils as a bargaining chip in order to influence 'strategic policy issues', without actually having to invoke the formal power of appeal (Teulings, 1989: 81).

Trade unions, though at first relatively uninterested in the councils, now place more emphasis on them. They have long organized union slates for elections, and provide training and technical assistance. However, the unions, especially the largest confederation (the *Federatie van Nederlandse Vakvereningen*, FNV), have been keen to protect their own primacy over the councils, and to maintain the formal separation between the two, but have come 'to accept the works council as the main body for worker representation' at company level (Looise and Drucker,

2003: 384). Employers also came to recognize the advantages of councils, particularly in situations of restructuring and redundancies (Visser, 1995: 92). In contrast to many other countries, their coverage and influence seem to have increased in the past decade (Looise and Drucker, 2003).

Recently, however, there has been concern that their effectiveness is under threat from changes in the nature of employing organizations. On the one hand, internationalization of ownership means that strategic decisions are increasingly taken outside the Netherlands; on the other, decentralization of decision making *within* companies, including mechanisms for direct employee participation, may undermine councils' relevance from below. These concerns—which are certainly mirrored in other European countries—led the Ministry of Labour (*Ministerie van Sociale Zaken en Werkgelegenheid*) to commission a detailed study of Dutch codetermination, which set out 'four scenarios' for the future, including the opposing possibilities of closer integration with trade unions, and closer integration with management detached from trade union input (van het Kaar and Smit, 2006). At the time of writing, there has been no outcome at the level of public policy.

Belgium

In Belgium the main institutions of workplace employee representation were established by law in September 1948. Works councils, known in the two national languages as *ondernemingsraden* and *conseils d'entreprise*, are strongly integrated into the system of industrial relations and are accepted by both sides of industry, although there are disagreements over their powers and the rules regulating them (Delbar, 2003).

Works councils were one of the institutions of employee participation envisaged by the 'social pact' of 1944 between the leading employer and trade union organizations, through which 'workers were given some social benefits if the unions were willing to leave the capitalist enterprise structure and its economic decision-making alone' (Hancké and Wijgaerts, 1989: 194). Most of these institutions were established in the immediate post-war period, resulting in 'one of the most formalized participation structures in Europe' (Vilrokx and Van Leemput, 1992: 362). The 1948 law created representation and consultation bodies at all levels of the economy. At the peak was the Central Economic Council (*Centrale Raad voor het Bedrijfsleven*, CRB or *Conseil centrale de l'économie*, CCE), an advisory body comprising equal numbers of employer and union representatives along with independent experts (Vilrokx and Van Leemput, 1992: 372). This was complemented by a National Labour Council (*Nationale Arbeidsraad*, NAR; *Conseil national du travail*, CNT) created in 1952 and devoted to social affairs. Works councils were assigned primarily information and consultation functions, with no powers of negotiation and limited rights of codetermination. They have equal numbers of elected employee representatives and nominated employers' representatives, with the employer acting as chair and a workers' representative as secretary. In 1952, another representative body was established on similar lines, responsible for workplace health, safety, and the working environment; since 1996 this has been known as the committee for safety and protection at work (*comité voor preventie en bescherming op het werk*, CPBW or *comité pour la prévention et protection au travail*, CPPT). Finally, there were workplace union delegations (*syndicale delegatie* or *délégation syndicale*), chosen (informally or formally) by trade union members and/or officials (Devolder et al., 2005) and recognized by the employer for collective negotiation and individual representation of the workforce (Vilrokx and Van Leemput, 1992: 377).

Works councils were initially mandatory in all enterprises with over 200 employees; reduced to 150 by a national agreement in 1958 (Devolder et al., 2005) and to 100 in 1979. Recent proposals to lower it still further to fifty have foundered because of employer resistance (Delbar, 2003), but will need to be revisited following a European Court ruling in 2007 that Belgium is in breach of the requirements of the Information and Consultation Directive. Employee representatives (and also those on health and safety committees) are chosen through 'social elections' every four years; only the recognized trade union confederations may present slates: the socialist ABVV/FGTB, the largely Catholic ACV/CSC, and the liberal ACLVB/CGSLB. If there are more than fifteen managers, their representatives are elected from slates named by the NCK/CNC, although non-union 'house lists' are also allowed for this category of worker. There is a requirement for 'proportionality' of women and men for each group of employees (blue-collar, white-collar, young workers, and managers).

Works council powers include the right to receive information on economic and financial matters; consultation on work organization, working conditions, new technology, training, restructuring, collective redundancies, early retirement, and closure; codetermination on criteria for dismissal and reemployment, work rules, annual holidays and paid study leave; and monitoring of the application of social legislation, redeployment of disabled workers, vocational skills criteria and the employment of young workers. Following the closure of Renault's Vilvoorde plant without proper consultation, the 'Renault' law of 1998 tightened the mandatory consultation procedure and strengthened the sanctions against any breach (Delbar, 2003). Since 1996, companies have been required to discuss detailed annual company reports or 'social balance sheets' with their councils; and a distinctive feature of the Belgian system is the provision for an independent auditor to advise the council on these reports and on other information provided by management (De Beelde and Leydens, 2002; Delbar, 2003).

Initially, works councils achieved limited implantation, and were described by Gevers (1973) as a 'marginal phenomenon'. In particular the ABVV/FGTB adopted a radical goal of workers' control in the early 1970s, incompatible with the collab-orative mission of the councils (Dambre, 1985: 203). Council coverage is limited by the size threshold: of the Belgian workforce of approximately 4 million, roughly one-third are in enterprises with over 100 employees (and half in firms with fifty or more); in the elections for works councils in 2000, the electorate was only about 1.2 million in just over 3,000 companies (Oste and Vilrokx, 2000). Just under 19,000 employee representatives were elected, of whom 30 per cent were women (Delbar, 2003)—a proportion which increased to 34 per cent in 2008 (Perin, 2008). Accord-ing to the ACV/CSC, both major confederations are finding it increasingly difficult to obtain sufficient candidates (interview, December 2007).

Today, works councils are highly institutionalized, well demarcated from trade union delegations as consultative rather than negotiating bodies, but often working closely with them. On some issues, councils can wield considerable influence. Their operation is rarely confrontational, and they concentrate on financial and economic information, consultation on work rules, hiring, and dismissal procedures.

In Spain, the institutions of workplace representation resemble those described below in the case of France: personnel delegates (delegados de personal), works committees (comités de empresa) and trade union delegates (delegados sindicales), with relatively significant formal rights assigned by legislation in 1980 and 1986. while there is in principle a 'dual system', in practice the former two institutions are closely integrated with the two main unions, and indeed provide a forum within which they can reconcile their different priorities (Escobar, 1995: 183; Martínez Lucio, 1992: 501). In Portugal the Constitution gives employees the right 'to create workers' commissions for the defence of their interests and democratic involvement in the workplace' (interven-ção democrática na vida da empresa). However, employers and unions (which, as in other Mediterranean countries, are able to have their own representatives—delegados sindicais—at workplace level) have few incentives to make this right effective. The coverage of comissões de trabalhadores is patchy, and most of those that exist on paper are inactive (Barreto and Nauman, 1998: 415). In Greece, with many background similarities to the other Mediterranean countries, the law provides for voluntary works councils; neither employers nor unions have shown any enthusiasm for the institution, and scarcely any have been established (Broughton, 2005: 214–5).

France

The Mediterranean countries are marked by a history of adversarial industrial relations and intense social and political cleavages. In France, Italy, Portugal, and Spain, Communist parties were for decades the strongest in Western Europe, and the trade unions linked to these parties were for some time the largest within ideologically divided labour movements. Some form of works council system is legally mandated in all four countries; not surprisingly, the context often makes their functioning problematic.

In France, the first legally instituted mechanism of worker participation and representation—the *délégués du personnel* (personnel delegates, DP)—was established by the 'popular front' government in 1936. They cover all establishments with more than ten employees, with an obligation on the employer to organize elections. The delegates represent employees (individually or collectively) with grievances regarding the application of legal or contractual rules (Tchobanian, 1995: 117). They have no bargaining powers and no formal links to trade unions, though practice is often very different.

The end of the Second World War and a new upsurge of labour militancy brought the creation of *comités d'entreprise* (works committees, CE), established by government decree in 1945 and ratified by legislation in 1946 (Eyraud and Tchobanian, 1985: 257). They are mandatory in firms with more than fifty employees, and intended as a forum for information and consultation on social and economic matters between the employer, who chairs the *comité*, and elected employee representatives. They lack formal bargaining powers and have no code-termination rights. The nationally recognized 'representative' unions have a privileged role: they alone can nominate candidates in the first round of elections, and only if these fail to attract half the available votes is there a second round open to all. The term of office, initially two years, was extended to four in 2005. *Comités* have a budget of at least 0.2 per cent of the company's revenues, to be spent on social and welfare activities (Dufour and Mouriaux, 1986; Tchobanian, 1995). Multi-plant firms sometimes have a two-tier structure, with the workplace body called a *comité d'établissement*. Following the mass social protests and general strike of May 1968, further legislation enabled unions to appoint workplace delegates (*délégués syndicaux*, DS) and branches (*sections syndicales*).

The system of employee representation was overhauled in 1982 with the four *lois Auroux*. The first and most innovative provided for 'expression groups' (*groupes d'expression directe*) in enterprises with over 200 employees, as a forum through which employees could express their views on the content, conditions, and organization of their work. The second required all firms with more than 200 employees to negotiate each year over pay and working time, and mandated sectoral negotiations (annually on minimum pay rates and every five years on job classifications). The third made workplace health and safety committees (*comités d'hygiène, de sécurité et des conditions de travail*) obligatory in firms with over fifty employees, while the fourth gave CEs powers of scrutiny over a wider range of issues, including hiring and firing, and expanded rights to receive company information. (A fifth law, in 1983, extended representation rights in firms with majority public ownership.)

How effective are these institutions? Some recent commentators describe an 'implosion' of French industrial relations (Rosanvallon, 1998: 240): a de facto individualization of employment regulation within an elaborate framework of collective representation. Andolfatto and Labbé (2000: 49–50, 111) report that workplace representatives are ageing; fewer activists combine more tasks, reinforcing the long-established practice of *cumul de mandats* and resulting in a 'professionalisation of representation', with declining contact with the workforce. On this reading, the whole structure of collective representation has become a façade while workplace reality involves a new managerialism (Goyer and Hancké, 2004: 176, 189–93).

The European Foundation (2006) reports a sharp deterioration in working conditions in France in the past decade; while Coutrot (1998: 253–61) refers to 'a regime of silent violence': control through a combination of external economic pressures, internal management authority, and 'material and symbolic incentives'. Employer 'violence' is manifested in a wide range of anti-union practices; for example, Andolfatto and Labbé (2000: 108) report that 15,000 'protected' representatives are dismissed each year despite the legal provisions. Further, France is the continental European country with the most developed American-style HRM, and has witnessed a 'spread of individualization' (Jenkins, 2000: Chapter 4).

Yet the discourse of democratic participation and expression has become rooted in the trade unions, especially the CFDT. Parsons (2005: 144) argues that 'direct expression' has had a creative, empowering effect where unions are well represented and employers have a modern, constructive approach. It is also apparent that trade unions, after a long period of declining influence, are now 'reunionizing' many *comités* (Dufour and Hege with Dubas, 2005). Moreover, because the organizational shell of autonomous collective representation remains, it is easier to give it new content than to fill an organizational vacuum. An official survey in 1998 showed that a DP, CE, and/or DS existed in 75 per cent of establishments with twenty or more employees, and 97 percent of those with 100 or more; only 12 per cent of all employees in firms with twenty or more workers had no independent representation. The coverage rate, particularly in smaller firms, was thus higher than in Germany. Even in small workplaces, formal trade union representation is the norm (Dufour et al., 2004: 15).

Do these conflicting assessments reflect increasingly different realities? Today, while the pattern in small firms and in the private service sector remains mixed, representative institutions are virtually omnipresent in large manufacturing firms and the public sector, commonly with a significant cadre of union activists who control the CE, systematic links to external union(s), and a continued ability to mobilize collective action.

Italy

In Italy, in contrast to the other Mediterranean countries, there exist functional equivalents of works councils that wield considerable codetermination capacity. Workplace representative institutions date back to the start of the twentieth century. Ad hoc committees created in individual companies became formalized as *commissioni interne* (internal commissions) elected by union members. The system became generalized by collective agreements during and after the First World War, partly (as in Germany) to bypass more radical rank-and-file organizations, but the commissions were abolished under fascism (Regalia, 1995: 217–8). After the fall of Mussolini they were re-established through a national agreement.

The powers of the *commissioni* were limited, and their effectiveness was further reduced by the ideological fragmentation of Italian unionism between the *Confederazione generale italiana del lavoro* (CGIL), the *Confederazione italiana dei sindacati lavoratori* (CISL) and the *Unione italiana del lavoro* (UIL). Often they served as little more than vehicles for a popularity contest between the rival unions, with employers regularly interfering to ensure the election of candidates they considered compliant. Representatives—in stark contrast to German works councillors—lacked protection against victimization: often the fate of activists in the Communist-oriented CGIL.

The position was transformed by the escalation of spontaneous industrial militancy in the 'hot autumn' of 1969. Though the official union confederations did not initiate the strike wave they were its main beneficiary, with rapid gains in membership. The rank-and-file committees that often led the struggles were institutionalized as union-based factory councils, displacing the *commissioni*. These organizational gains were reinforced by the novel representational rights conveyed by the 1970 Workers' Statute (*Statuto dei diritti dei lavoratori*): the new law introduced the notion of a workplace trade union representative structure (*rappresentanza sindacale aziendale*, RSA) in firms with over fifteen employees, with an array of legal prerogatives and protections, but without defining the nature or composition of the new mechanisms.

There is a duality inherent in the Italian model, which is at one and the same time a workplace trade union body (as the adjective *sindacale* signifies) and a council elected by and from all employees (Regalia, 1995: 221; Terry, 1993: 141). The legal protections enjoyed by workplace union representatives (*delegati*) facilitated the growth of an active bargaining culture at shop floor level (Sciarra, 1977) and were an important resource when the decade of mobilization in the 1970s gave way to economic uncertainty and the rationalization of production in the 1980s. Major employers were obliged to negotiate change with employee representatives; as Wedderburn put it (1990: 172), 'the *Statuto* did not impose any general duty to bargain, but ensured that the *rappresentanza* clung like a limpet to the walls of every enterprise'. There developed a pragmatic process of 'microcorporatism' (Regini, 1991) involving the 'formalized proceduralization' of company industrial relations (Negrelli, 1991). This contrasts with British experience at the time, when shop stewards, lacking analogous statutory rights, were largely unable to resist unilateral imposition of restructuring by management (Terry, 1993: 143).

Particularly in hard times, factory councils required external union support: a study in the early 1980s (Regalia, 1984) described workplace delegates as 'elected and abandoned'. This is one reason why the main confederations were anxious to formalize the constitutional arrangements; and following a tripartite national agreement in 1993—a characteristically Italian process whereby collective bargaining gave detailed shape to legal prescription—the status of the workplace structures has been more clearly prescribed, under the revised title *rappresentanza sindacale unitaria* (RSU). However the duality of status and function remains evident: two-thirds of the members are directly elected by the workforce, but the other third is nominated, in effect, by the main confederations (who today act largely in concert). Hence elements of single- and dual-channel systems are combined. In the public sector, however, all delegates are directly elected.

RSUs are elected triennially. There is a lack of official statistics on their extent, but there is a broad consensus that a large majority of employees in all but the smallest firms are covered (Muratore, 2003). In general, the main unions seem able to dominate the election process. Even more than in other countries, a 'dual-channel' system is effectively union-controlled; and the particularly strong rights enjoyed by union delegates under the 1970 legislation result in an unusually powerful representative mechanism.

Sweden

In Scandinavia—where rates of union membership are the highest in the world—employees' workplace interests are typically represented by the unions' local organizations. In recent decades there has been a trend to the creation of parallel and overlapping 'cooperation committees', as with the committees or councils established in Norway by a central agreement in 1966 (Dølvik and Stokke, 1998; Lismoen, 2003); these are effectively union-based equivalents of (joint) works councils. In Denmark, similar committees were first established through a central agreement in 1947, subsequently revised a number of times. This procedure reflected commitment to the 'voluntary' principle of industrial relations, in response to government proposals to legislate on the issue (Knudsen, 1995: 82–3). In principle, non-unionists can be elected, but shop stewards (*tillidsrepræsentanten*) are *ex officio* members and typically play a leading role. These committees 'are characterized by a high degree of involvement and codetermination in the day-to-day business of companies' (Jørgensen, 2003). There are similar provisions in Finland, in this case based on legislation first enacted in 1978, primarily designed to strengthen the bargaining role of shop stewards (Lilja, 1998: 175; Parviainen, 2003).

In Sweden, a central agreement between the main union and employers' confederations in 1946 established joint works councils (*företagsnämnderna*), with employee representatives elected exclusively by trade union members (Brulin, 1995: 193). However, they possessed only limited powers, and despite revisions to the agreement in 1966 the councils were seen by many unionists as ineffectual.

Particularly against the background of rapid technological change and work restructuring, the employers' insistence on unrestricted managerial prerogative came under increasing challenge.

The outcome was a partial shift in the 1970s from 'voluntarism' to legal regulation. In 1974 the *Förtroendemannalagen* (FML) gave workplace union representatives (the literal equivalent of German *Vertrauensleute*, but with a far stronger role) the right to time off with pay, office facilities, and protection against victimization. This was followed by the highly contentious 1976 law on codetermination (*Medbestämmandelagen*, MBL) which obliged employers to give union representatives detailed information on business matters and negotiate before making significant changes to work arrangements or employment conditions. Workplace representatives also obtained an interim right to veto changes which seriously affected employment security. Firms in breach of these obligations became liable to financial penalties (Berg, 2003). In this context, the works council agreement was terminated.

The MBL required employers to negotiate over change, but they were not obliged to reach agreement (Brulin, 1995: 198–9; Kjellberg, 1998: 106); despite the title of the law, this did not mandate codetermination. This is of course the essence of information and consultation arrangements in most other countries. However, after six years of negotiation the unions and employers at central level supplemented the legislation by a 'development agreement' (*Utvecklingsavtal*, UVA) which encouraged joint regulation of changes in work organization and the work environment, along similar lines to the 'cooperation committees' in other Nordic countries. The UVA prescribed local negotiations on the exercise of codetermination at workplace level, and opened the possibility of creating 'bipartite participation and information bodies'. Few agreements along these lines were negotiated, but 'the local parties often act as though they have a local agreement' (Brulin, 1995: 199–200). Hence though assessments of the impact of the UVA differ, it does appear to have stimulated more intensive union involvement in managerial decision making, initially only after the strategic decisions were already taken but increasingly at an earlier stage (Kjellberg, 1998: 107–108).

Single-channel representation is the essence of the Swedish system: the unions' workplace stewards (*förtroendevalda*) and 'clubs' (*klubbar*) are the sole institutional intermediary between management and the workforce. Can one therefore speak of works councils in Sweden? If one accepts the definition of Frege (2002: 223) that councils 'are workplace-based institutions ... that have status and functions distinct from, though not necessarily in competition with, those of unions', the answer is no. But on the definition cited from Rogers and Streeck at the outset of this chapter—'institutionalized bodies for representative communication'—it seems appropriate to refer to Swedish works councils, or at least to functionally equivalent mechanisms.

THEMES AND ISSUES: COMPARING
AND CONTRASTING

Works councils in our six European countries share largely similar origins, in the sense that most came about in response to conflict between labour and capital, either around the beginning of the twentieth century, just after the First World War or after the Second. Their aims were shaped by their origins: to restore or preserve industrial and social peace, by giving workers a stake in society and a voice at the workplace. But they differ greatly in terms of their composition, modes of selection, powers, and responsibilities, and links to other industrial relations institutions. In this section we compare and contrast the six national models described above, beginning with their formal requirements and regulations; then looking at key issues in their practical operation: their representativeness, the balance between different sections of workforce interests; and their relationship with trade unions. We conclude by considering the extent to which councils (still) allow workers an effective voice at work.

Formal Requirements, Rules and Regulations

One simple distinction is between national systems established by law and those that are the outcome of peak-level collective agreement (which may in turn possess legally binding status); but reality is rather more complex. Certainly we can say that the Dutch, French, and German systems are legislatively based (even if the law to some extent gave force to the wishes of the 'social partners'). But in Sweden and Italy the two processes have interacted. In the former, as we have seen, the central agreement of 1946 created rather ineffectual councils; they were given stronger powers by the MBL of 1976; but this in turn was given practical effect by the UVA six years later. In the latter, collective agreements after each world war institutionalized the system of *commissioni*; but it was the law of 1970 which created mechanisms with real teeth—though the 1993 national agreement first gave a clear definition to the *rappresentanza*. In Belgium, councils were established by law in 1948; but this resulted from a peak-level agreement, as did many subsequent amendments.

According to the definition we have adopted, works councils are *mandatory* bodies. However, there are at least four qualifications to be made. First, there is normally a size threshold for the requirement to take effect. As we have seen, in Germany it is only five, although councils take on additional functions and powers as the workforce grows; in Italy it is fifteen; in France and the Netherlands it is fifty; while in Belgium it is currently a hundred. Only in Sweden is there no size limit.

Second, establishing a council often requires some form of 'trigger'. As already indicated, the Belgian and French systems put the onus on the employer to hold 'social elections', whereas there is no automatic obligation in Germany and the Netherlands. Rather, the workforce (in Germany this requires only three employees to act) or a trade union must take the initiative. The same is the case in Italy and Sweden. In smaller firms in particular, the 'default option' of no works council tends to prevail. There is a lack of reliable data for most countries, and it appears that patterns are highly uneven. The lower the size threshold, the higher the proportion of firms (though less so of employees) without works councils even though covered by the law. Germany is a striking example: councils exist in only 11 per cent of eligible firms and establishments (Carley et al., 2005: 24), though they cover roughly half the eligible workforce.

Third, works councils require the employer's cooperation in order to function effectively. It takes two to engage in meaningful information and consultation. Most legal prescriptions require that information on the specified issues be provided accurately and in good time, and that the employer consult in good faith before taking final decisions. But it typically takes a qualitative judgment to assess whether an employer has genuinely complied. Even more fundamentally, protection is needed for employees who initiate the creation of a works council, stand for election, and exercise their functions if elected. The strongest rules are in Germany and Belgium, but all countries under consideration have some legal protection.

This leads to the fourth qualification: that requirements have to be observed voluntarily or else enforced. What *sanctions* are available to persuade recalcitrant employers to establish a works council, subject to the necessary 'triggers'; to provide the specified information and engage properly in consultation; and more fundamentally, to refrain from victimization of employee representatives or those who seek to exercise their legal rights? More specifically, who is responsible for complaining if an employer breaches the law (or legally binding agreement); in what type of court; what is the delay before a case is heard; what penalties may be imposed if the employer is found guilty; and what happens if the employer then fails to comply with the judgment? In general, European countries possess labour inspectorates who can initiate prosecutions, but normally on individual rather than collective issues; hence typically it is up to aggrieved employees, or their union, to bring complaints. Most countries (though not, for example, the Netherlands) have specialized labour courts or tribunals which can often provide speedier decisions than normal courts. In theory, penalties can be significant: for example, in France, Germany, and Italy an employer in serious breach of the law is liable not only to a substantial fine but even to a year's imprisonment. Some local magistrates in Italy may be prepared to utilize draconian powers, but in general it seems that the penalties for non-compliance are in practice relatively trivial, at least for a large and wealthy company. Hence the more powerful sanction may well be the opprobrium an employer may incur if found to be flouting national labour law—a factor which seems to have contributed to the decision by McDonalds in France to rescind its dismissal of candidates for the post of *délégué* (Braud, 2002).

The *composition* of the councils and the *number* of councillors are important variables. In Germany, Italy, and Sweden, all councillors, including the chair, are representatives of the employees. Belgium and France have joint councils, and the employer acts as chair; this was also the case in the Netherlands until the law of 1979 brought the Dutch system more into line with the German. The number of councillors at a firm or establishment varies between countries: the minimum is one (Germany) but France, Italy and the Netherlands require at least three. France has a maximum of fifteen elected employee councillors; Belgium and the Netherlands twenty-five. In Italy and Germany, there is no absolute maximum. There are generally requirements for some councillors to come from particular categories of workers—for example, manual and white collar—and in some countries for a gender balance, as we discuss below.

Election by the workforce is the most common form of selection, although some employee representatives (for example, representatives of trade union confederations in Italy) are appointed, as are most management representatives. Elections in our six countries are usually open to all employees, but this is often qualified by length of service (usually six months to one year), age (over sixteen or eighteen), and sometimes by contractual status (full-time, or with permanent contracts).

Representatives, Representativeness, and Representation

The relationship between representatives and those they represent is 'ambivalent and evanescent' (Regalia, 1988: 351). Are workers' representatives to be *delegates*, mandated to follow a particular position (note the French term *délégués du personnel* and the Italian *delegati*) or are they free to reach their own conclusions on the basis of the information they receive? The 'parliamentary' model prevails: works councillors have the autonomy to take their own decisions until required to stand for re-election—though some national systems do provide, exceptionally, for initiatives to recall councillors who have lost employees' confidence, and others permit councillors to convene workforce assemblies in order to report back on contentious issues.

Yet in many countries, the question is often posed: are representatives truly representative? The *representation* of the workforce of a company or establishment is an explicit aim of works councils in some systems, but not all. (It was not one of the original aims under Dutch law, but was added in the 1971 reforms.) Here a definitional ambiguity is evident. 'In one common meaning of the word, to be representative is to share the main characteristics of a broader population; but trade union and other employee representatives are never representative in this sense (if only because they normally require a distinctive set of motivational qualities); and it is unlikely that a 'representative sample' of a workforce would be well suited to the functions of interest representation' (Hyman, 1997: 310).

Hege and Dufour (1995: 93) argue that 'a differentiation from the rank and file is necessary for the process of representation itself'. First, a coherent employee 'voice' has to be constructed from a multiplicity of interests, aspirations and grievances within the workforce; effective representatives must be sufficiently detached to be able to filter and prioritize these, in many cases seeking to align what are at first sight contradictory demands. Second, they need a strategic, long-term perspective in order to assess the costs and benefits, risks and opportunities of any course of action.

Yet detachment opens the possibility that representatives may become unresponsive to the workforce and perhaps too close to management. Particularly in large companies or establishments where senior councillors are freed from regular duties, either by law (as in Germany) or by custom and practice, the role of representative may become viewed as an attractive career option. Müller-Jentsch (1995: 57) writes of 'the increasing professionalization of a works councillor's role' in Germany; Teulings (1989: 76) noted that in the Netherlands 'the distance between the leaders and followers has increased sharply in the past five years'. Bureaucratization and professionalization are reinforced by the increasingly diversified activities of works councils. Larger German councils contain a network of subcommittees to deal with specific issues, such as wage setting, accident prevention, white-collar employees, female workers, young workers and apprentices, social welfare, and physically handicapped persons. In Belgium, the works council may be divided into subcommittees, acting as preparatory work groups on such functional specialisms as employment, social services, or work rules.

The close day-to-day interaction and 'collaboration in good faith' between councillors and management can on occasion degenerate into corruption. The Volkswagen scandal—it was revealed in 2005 that leaders of its works council had been bribed with luxury 'sex tours' to agree to restructuring plans—was doubtless exceptional but tarnished the image of codetermination in Germany. An important challenge in all countries is therefore to bridge the two meanings of representativeness: to sustain both relative autonomy and representational legitimacy.

Proportionality and Diversity of Interests

A less sensational but far more common problem than corruption is that the line of least resistance in representation may be to express the interests of those sections of the workforce that possess collective strength and assertiveness, neglecting those who are less vocal but for that reason more in need of representation. In general, electoral systems provide for proportional representation (Biagi, 2001: 501), which can in principle allow under-represented groups to organize round their own candidates. In some German workplaces in the 1970s, Turkish workers who were not represented on official union lists were able to vote a few of their own members into office; and this in turn forced the unions to construct more inclusive electoral slates. But such instances are rare.

Most studies reveal a tendency for men, older age groups, and more highly-skilled workers to be over-represented on works councils, though available data are limited. Engelen (2004: 500–505) cites a large-scale survey of Dutch works councils in 1998 in arguing that there is a 'growing discrepancy between the composition of the works council and the composition of the workforce'. Women made up only 25 per cent of councillors but 40 per cent of the workforce in the enterprises studied. Younger workers, ethnic minorities, those working part-time and on non-standard or temporary contracts were also under-represented. An official analysis of French social elections in 2000–2001 found a rather narrower gender gap: 32 per cent of those elected were women, as against 40 per cent of the electorate (Amossé and Lemoigne, 2004).

This effect may be attenuated in systems which have quotas for gender representation. This has been the case since 1978 in Belgium, but a study in 1997 (Ramioul, 1997) found that women were still seriously under-represented. Since 2001, German law has required at least proportionality for women if they are in a minority at the workplace—but not if they constitute the majority of employees. Some 80 per cent of larger firms (over 100 employees) comply with the law (Dribbusch, 2007). France also introduced a law on gender equality in 2001 (the *loi Génisson*) applying to a wide range of workplace issues, including representation on the *comités*; but there were no clear sanctions; an official study in 2004 found its implementation 'mediocre'.

The gender imbalance is typically far greater among leadership positions than in works council membership more generally. However, Dribbusch (2007) reports findings from smaller German enterprises (under 200 employees), where bureau-cracies are presumably less entrenched, showing that often younger women are increasingly elected as chair or vice-chair of the *Betriebsrat*. A comprehensive study by Hege et al. (2001) found that women were slightly *over*-represented in the post of secretary (the employer always chairs the *comité*), and tended to be younger than male secretaries. They were more likely to have been elected on non-union lists and in councils that had only recently been established. It would be unwise to draw firm conclusions, and to assume that correlation is the same as causality, but the results are intriguing. They may suggest, positively, that the involvement of women is increasing in line with generational change, or negatively, that established councils in larger, more unionized undertakings are still obstructive. This would fit with the suggestion in other studies that works councils, especially long-established ones, may develop an elite of councillors who become, or are perceived as being, increasingly distant from the majority of employees.

Councils and Unions

It is common to distinguish between single-channel systems (where trade unions possess a monopoly right of representation) and dual-channel systems where unions and councils have distinct bases of representation. As our national accounts show, there is no such clear-cut dichotomy in practice. Sweden is our one case where councils (or their functional equivalent) are simply the plant-level unit of the union; everywhere else there is an institutional separation, but this is qualified in different ways.

In part this is true even at the formal level, in particular as concerns electoral arrangements. In Belgium, nominations are restricted to union-sponsored lists; in France, the same is true unless the union nominees fail to obtain the votes of a majority of the electorate in the first round of elections (as often happens). In both Germany and the Netherlands, candidates may be nominated either by groups of employees or by unions with members in the workplace. The Italian system is a hybrid, since (in the private sector) the unions can directly appoint a third of the representatives as well as submitting lists of candidates for the other seats. The law may also prescribe working relationships between councils and unions: for example, in Germany an outside union official can participate in the activities of the *Betriebsrat* if a quarter of its members so request.

Dufour and Hege have argued (2002: 171) that 'effective representation normally depends on resources extending well beyond formal rights'; and in terms of informal operation, the union–council link is typically intimate. In most countries, generational changes have led to an ageing population of representatives and to increasing difficulty in attracting new candidates; union officials may need to work hard to 'cultivate' new talent and may at times appear to be 'parachuting' in individuals, whether or not these have the support of the workforce. In the day-to-day work of representation there is a more general need for mutual support, as noted above. This is one reason why, in France, many of those elected to *comités* as non-unionists subsequently affiliate with one or other union. As a corollary, the fear often expressed that works councils may supplant employees' attachment to trade unionism is probably misplaced. As Brewster et al. argue (2007: 69), 'it is clear that a central concern for unions should not be whether the one form of representation erodes the other. Rather, it is what is *done* on these respective bodies that should be their main preoccupation.'

CONCLUSION: ARE WORKS COUNCILS (STILL) EFFECTIVE VOICE MECHANISMS?

Works councils are engaged in a complex and problematic balancing act. First, their primary relationship is with the employees whom they represent: articulating their wishes and interests, and in the process redefining these. The very notion of representativeness, as we have seen, can be deeply ambiguous. Second, they are interlocutors of management; but this relationship can be precarious and contradictory. Third, those workplace representatives who are subject to external union authority nevertheless exercise some autonomy, while those who are in theory independent typically depend on external union organization for support and legitimation.

Negotiating this complex three-way relationship is difficult at the best of times. For most analysts, however, it has become increasingly precarious in recent years, as a result of interlocking changes in work organization, the structure of employment, corporate ownership, and the global economy.

The reorganization of production in pursuit of enhanced productivity, often in the context of a decentralization of collective bargaining, has confronted works councils with new challenges (Terry, 1994: 227). These demand new and sophisticated technical expertise, increasing the need for specialist advice and training but at the same time creating new risks of detachment between representatives and rank and file, as leading councillors themselves become de facto co-managers.

Changes in the structure of employment involve both sectoral shifts—from manufacturing to services—and the growth of part-time, temporary, and sub-contracted work. In part these trends are linked to the growing feminization of employment. This means that in most countries the weight of employment is shifting to sectors and groups where trade unions have traditionally been weakly implanted, and with little tradition of collective identity. This certainly helps explain the growth of a 'works council-free' area in Germany; if in practice triggering works councils requires union initiative, while the existence of councils can itself provide a springboard for unionization, then collective representation may be subject to a double-bind. And within enterprises which do possess collective representation, the growing diversity of occupational interests accentuates the difficulties of constructing a coherent synthesis.

In terms of company ownership, the acceleration of mergers and takeovers and the growing trend to internationalization create two obvious problems for works councils. First, the constituencies to be represented are shifting, and the carefully established understandings between representatives and managements are frequently disrupted by corporate restructuring. More radically, as the 2006 Dutch study emphasized, national company management may no longer possess the capacity to reach meaningful agreement with employee representatives.

The impact of economic globalization is pervasive: above all, in the overriding compulsion of competitiveness. Consensus in one workplace—the original official rationale of works council systems—is all too easily transformed into concession bargaining, as managements force local representatives into a competitive process of acquiescence in a drive for reduced labour costs. The implication is that the only employee interest which can be effectively defended is to avoid plant closure and minimize job losses.

In the last decades of the twentieth century, there were ambitious projects in many of our countries for works councils to articulate new, 'qualitative' demands and to engage proactively in reshaping the work environment and working life more generally. It would be a sad paradox if the trend in the twenty-first century is towards more sophisticated mechanisms of employee voice but diminished influence over management decisions.

References

AMOSSÉ, T. and LEMOIGNE, C. (2004) *Les femmes dans les comités d'entreprise et délégations uniques du personnel: une parité encore lointaine*. Paris: DARES.

ANDOLFATTO, D. and LABBÉ, D. (2000) *Sociologie des syndicats*. Paris: La Découverte.

BARRETO, J. and NAUMANN, R. (1998) 'Portugal: Industrial Relations under Democracy', in A. Ferner and R. Hyman (eds), *Changing Industrial Relations in Europe*, pp. 395–425. Oxford, Blackwell.

BERG, A. (2003) *Works Councils and Other Workplace Employee Representation and Participation Structures: Sweden*. http://www.eurofound.europa.eu/eiro/2003/09/tfeature/se0309103t.htm.

BIAGI, M. (2001) 'Forms of Employee Representational Participation', in R. Blanpain, C. Engels, and G. Bamber (eds), *Comparative Labour Law and Industrial Relations in Industrialized Market Economies*, 7th edition, pp. 483–524. The Hague: Kluwer.

BORMANN, S. (2007) *Angriff auf die Mitbestimmung. Unternehmensstrategien gegen Betriebsräte: Der Fall Schlecker*. Berlin: edition sigma.

BOSCH, A. (1997) *Vom Interessenkonflikt zur Kultur der Rationalität: Neue Handlungsbeziehungen zwischen Management und Betriebsrat*. Munich and Mering: Rainer Hampp.

BRAUD, M. (2002) 'Industrial Action Hits Mcdonald's Restaurants and Franchises' http://www.eurofound.europa.eu/eiro/2002/02/feature/fr0202104f.htm.

BREWSTER, C., WOOD, G., CROUCHER, R., and BROOKES, M. (2007) 'Are Works Councils and Joint Consultative Committees a Threat to Trade Unions? A Comparative Analysis', *Economic and Industrial Democracy*, 28(1): 49–77.

BRIEFS, U. (1989) 'Codetermination in the Federal Republic of Germany: An Appraisal of a Secular Experience', in G. Széll, P. Blyton, and C. Cornforth (eds), *The State, Trade Unions and Self-Management*, pp. 63–74. Berlin: de Gruyter.

BROUGHTON, A. (2005) 'European Comparative Practice in Information and Consultation', in J. Storey (ed.), *Adding Value through Information and Consultation*, pp. 200–18. Basingstoke: Palgrave Macmillan.

BRULIN, D. (1995) 'Sweden: Joint Councils under Strong Unionism', in J. Rogers and W. Streeck (eds), *Works Councils: Consultation, Representation and Cooperation in Industrial Relations*, pp. 189–216. Chicago: University of Chicago Press.

CARLEY, M., BARADEL, A., and WELZ, C. (2005) *Works Councils: Workplace Representation and Participation Structures*. Dublin: European Foundation.

COUTROT, T. (1998) *L'entreprise néo-libérale, nouvel utopie capitaliste?* Paris: La Découverte.

DAMBRE, W. (1985) *Geschiedenis van de ondernemingsraden in België*. The Hague: Kluwer.

DE BEELDE, I. and LEYDENS, H. (2002) 'Audit Expectations in Works Councils', *Economic and Industrial Democracy*, 23(2): 229–69.

DELBAR, C. (2003) *Works Councils and Other Workplace Employee Representation and Participation Structures: Belgium*. http://www.eurofound.europa.eu/eiro/2003/09/tfeature/be0309304t.htm.

DEVOLDER, C., CAUSARANO, P., HYMAN, R., KOHL, H., and BERGGREN, L. (2005) 'Syndicalismes à l'entreprise: Des avancées à l'ambiguïté' in P. Pasture, M. Pigenet and J.-L. Robert (eds), *L'apogée des syndicalismes en Europe occidentale 1960–1985*. Paris: Publications de la Sorbonne, pp. 109–37.

DØLVIK, J. E. and STOKKE, T. A. (1998) 'Norway: The Revival of Centralised Concertation', in A. Ferner and R. Hyman (eds), *Changing Industrial Relations in Europe*. Oxford: Blackwell, pp. 118–45.

DRIBBUSCH, H. (2003) *Gewerkschaftliche Mitgliedergewinnung im Dienstleistungssektor: Ein Drei-Länder-Vergleich im Einzelhandel*. Berlin: edition sigma.

—— (2007) *Women Still Underrepresented on Works Councils*. http://www.eurofound. europa.eu/eiro/2007/04/articles/de0704029i.htm.

DUFOUR, C. and HEGE, A. (2002) *L'Europe syndicale: La représentation des salariés en France, Allemagne, Grande-Bretagne et Italie*. Brussels: P.I.E.-Peter Lang.

—— —— with DUBAS, A. (2005) *Resyndicalisation ou changement de paradigme?* Noisy-le-Grand: IRES.

—— —— MALAN, A., and ZOUARY, P. (2004) *Post-enquête Réponse*. Noisy-le-Grand: IRES.

—— and MOURIAUX, M.-F. (1986) *Comités d'entreprise: Quarante ans après*. Noisy-le-Grand: IRES.

EBBINGHAUS, B. (1999) 'Does a European Social Model Exist and Can It Survive?' in G. Huemer, M. Mesch, and F. Traxler (eds), *The Role of Employer Associations and Labour Unions in the EMU*, pp.1–26. Aldershot: Ashgate.

ENGELEN, E. (2004) 'Problems of Descriptive Representation in Dutch Works Councils', *Political Studies*, 52(3): 491–507.

ESCOBAR, M. (1995) 'Spain: Works Councils or Unions', in J. Rogers and W. Streeck (eds), *Works Councils: Consultation, Representation and Cooperation in Industrial Relations*, pp. 153–88. Chicago: University of Chicago Press.

European Commission (2006) *Industrial Relations in Europe 2006*. http://ec.europa.eu/employment_social/social_dialogue/docs/ir_report2006_en.pdf.

European Foundation (2006) *A Review of Working Conditions in France*. http://www.eurofound.eu.int/ewco/surveys/FR0603SR01/FR0603SR01.htm.

EYRAUD, F. and TCHOBANIAN, R. (1985) 'The Auroux Reforms and Company Level Industrial Relations in France', *British Journal of Industrial Relations*, 23(2): 241–59.

FEDEROWICZ, M. and LEVITAS, A. (1995) 'Poland: Councils under Communism and Neoliberalism', in J. Rogers and W. Streeck (eds), *Works Councils: Consultation, Representation and Cooperation in Industrial Relations*, pp. 283–312. Chicago: University of Chicago Press.

FREGE, C. M. (1999) 'Understanding Union Effectiveness in Central Eastern Europe: Hungary and Slovenia', *European Journal of Industrial Relations*, 8(1): 53–76.

—— (2002) 'A Critical Assessment of the Theoretical and Empirical Research on German Works Councils', *British Journal of Industrial Relations*, 40(2): 241–59.

FÜRSTENBERG, F. (1978) *Workers' Participation in Management in the Federal Republic of Germany.* Geneva: IILS.

GEVERS, P. (1973) 'Ondernemingsraden, Randverschijnsel in de Belgische Industriële Democratiseringsbeweging?' Ph.D. thesis, Katholieke Universiteit Leuven.

GOYER, M. and HANCKÉ, B. (2004) 'Labour in French Corporate Governance: The Missing Link', in H. Gospel and A. Pendleton (eds), *Corporate Governance and Labour Management*, pp. 173–96. Oxford: OUP.

GUMBRELL-McCORMICK, R. and HYMAN, R. (2006) 'Embedded Collectivism? Workplace Representation in France and Germany', *Industrial Relations Journal*, 37(5): 473–91.

HAN, T.-S. and CHIU, S.-F. (2000) 'Industrial Democracy and Institutional Environments: A Comparison of Germany and Taiwan', *Economic and Industrial Democracy*, 21(2): 147–82.

HANCKÉ, B. and WIJGAERTS, D. (1989) 'Belgian Unionism and Self-Management', in G. Széll, P. Blyton, and C. Cornforth (eds), *The State, Trade Unions and Self-Management.* Berlin: de Gruyter, pp. 187–210.

HEGE, A. and DUFOUR, C. (1995) 'Decentralization and Legitimacy in Employee Representation: A Franco-German Comparison', *European Journal of Industrial Relations*, 1(1): 83–99.

—— —— and NUNES, C. (2001) *Les femmes secrétaires de comité d'entreprise: une parité trompeuse?* Paris: DARES.

HYMAN, R. (1997) 'The Future of Employee Representation', *British Journal of Industrial Relations*, 35(3): 309–36.

JACKSON, G. (2005) 'Employee Representation in the Board Compared: A Fuzzy Sets Analysis of Corporate Governance, Unionism and Political Institutions', *Industrielle Beziehungen*, 12(3): 1–28.

JACOBI, O., KELLER, B., and MÜLLER-JENTSCH, W. (1998) 'Germany: Facing New Challenges', in A. Ferner and R. Hyman (eds), *Changing Industrial Relations in Europe*, pp. 190–238. Oxford: Blackwell.

JENKINS, A. (2000) *Employment Relations in France: Evolution and Innovation.* New York: Kluwer.

JEPSEN, M. and SERRANO PASCUAL, A. (eds) (2006) *Unwrapping the European Social Model.* Bristol: Policy Press.

JØRGENSEN, C. (2003) *Works Councils and Other Workplace Employee Representation and Participation Structures: Denmark.* http://www.eurofound.europa.eu/eiro/2003/09/tfeature/dk0309102t.htm.

KATO, T., LEE, J., LEE, K.-S., and RYU, J.-S. (2005) 'Employee Participation and Involvement in Korea: Evidence from a New Survey and Field Research', *International Economic Journal*, 19(2): 251–81.

KJELLBERG, A. (1998) 'Sweden: Restoring the Model?' in A. Ferner and R. Hyman (eds), *Changing Industrial Relations in Europe*, pp. 74–117. Oxford: Blackwell.

KLEINER, M. M. and LEE, Y.-M. (1997) 'Works Councils and Unionization: Lessons from South Korea', *Industrial Relations*, 36(1): 1–16.

KNUDSEN, H. (1995) *Employee Participation in Europe.* London: Sage.

KOMMISSION MITBESTIMMUNG (1998) *Mitbestimmung und neue Unternehmenskulturen: Bilanz und Perspektiven.* Gütersloh: Bertelsmann Stiftung.

KOOPMANN, K. (1981) *Vertrauensleute: Arbeitervertretung im Betrieb.* Hamburg: VSA.

KOTTHOFF, H. (1981) *Betriebsräte und betriebliche Herrschaft: Eine Typologie von Partizipationsmustern im Industriebetrieb.* Frankfurt: Campus.

—— (1994) *Betriebsräte und Bürgerstatus: Wandel und Kontinuität betrieblicher Mitbestimmung.* Munich and Mering: Rainer Hampp.

—— (1998) 'Mitbestimmung in Zeiten interessenpolitischer Rückscritte: Betriebsräte zwischen Beteiligungsofferten und "gnadenlosem Kostensenkungsdiktat"', *Industrielle Beziehungen,* 5(1): 76–100.

LILJA, K. (1998) 'Finland: Continuity and Modest Moves towards Company-Level Corporatism', in A. Ferner and R. Hyman (eds), *Changing Industrial Relations in Europe,* pp. 171–89. Oxford: Blackwell.

LISMOEN, H. (2003) *Works Councils and Other Workplace Employee Representation and Participation Structures: Norway.* http://www.eurofound.europa.eu/eiro/2003/09/tfeature/no0309102t.htm.

LOOISE, J. C. (1989) 'The Recent Growth in Employees' Representation in The Netherlands: Defying the Times?' in C.J. Lammers and G. Széll (eds), *International Handbook of Participation in Organizations Volume I,* pp. 268–84. Oxford: OUP.

LOOISE, J. K. and DRUCKER, M. (2003) 'Dutch Works Councils in Times of Transition: The Effects of Changes in Society, Organizations and Work on the Position of Works Councils', *Economic and Industrial Democracy,* 24(3): 379–409.

MARTÍNEZ LUCIO, M. (1992) 'Spain: Constructing Institutions and Actors in a Context of Change', in A. Ferner and R. Hyman (eds), *Industrial Relations in the New Europe,* pp. 482–523. Oxford: Blackwell.

MÜLLER-JENTSCH, W. (1995) 'Germany: From Collective Voice to Co-management', in J. Rogers and W. Streeck (eds), *Works Councils: Consultation, Representation and Cooperation in Industrial Relations,* pp. 53–78. Chicago: University of Chicago Press.

MURATORE, L. (2003) *Works Councils and Other Workplace Employee Representation and Participation Structures: Italy.* http://www.eurofound.europa.eu/eiro/2003/09/tfeature/ito309304t.htm.

NEGRELLI, S. (1991) *La società dentro l'empresa.* Milan: FrancoAngeli.

OSTE, J. and VILROKX, J. (2000) *Social Elections Bring Little Change.* http://www.eurofound.europa.eu/eiro/2000/06/feature/be0006316f.htm.

PARSONS, N. (2005) *French Industrial Relations in the New World Economy.* London: Routledge.

PARVIAINEN, S. (2003) *Works Councils and Other Workplace Employee Representation and Participation Structures: Finland.* http://www.eurofound.europa.eu/eiro/2003/09/tfeature/fi0309203t.htm.

PERIN, E. (2008) *Women Win Seats in Workplace Elections but Remain Underrepresented.* http://www.eurofound.europa.eu/eiro/2008/07/articles/be0807029i.htm.

PINAUD, H. (1996) 'Participation in France', in G. Kester and H. Pinaud (eds), *Trade Unions and Democratic Participation: A Scenario for the Twenty-First Century,* pp. 4–134. Aldershot: Avebury.

RAMIOUL, M. (1997) *Women in the Belgian Labour Market: Discrimination Persists.* http://www.eurofound.europa.eu/eiro/1997/09/feature/be9709216f.htm.

RAMSAY, H. (1977) 'Cycles of Control: Worker Participation in Sociological and Historical Perspective', *Sociology*, 1(3): 481–506.

REGALIA, I. (1984) *Eletti e abandonnati: Modelli e stili di rappresantanza in fabbrica.* Bologna: il Mulino.

—— (1988) 'Democracy and Unions: Towards a Critical Appraisal', *Economic and Industrial Democracy*, 9(3): 345–71.

—— (1995) 'Italy: The Costs and Benefits of Informality', in J. Rogers and W. Streeck (eds), *Works Councils: Consultation, Representation and Cooperation in Industrial Relations*, pp. 217–41. Chicago: University of Chicago Press.

REGINI, M. (1991) *Confini mobili.* Bologna: il Mulino.

ROGERS, J. and STREECK, W. (1995) 'The Study of Works Councils: Concepts and Problems', in J. Rogers and W. Streeck (eds), *Works Councils: Consultation, Representation and Cooperation in Industrial Relations*, pp. 3–26. Chicago: University of Chicago Press.

ROSANVALLON, P. (1998) *La question syndicale.* Paris: Hachette.

SCHMIDT, R. and TRINCZEK, R. (1991) 'Duales System: Tarifliche und betriebliche Interessenvertretung', in W. Müller-Jentsch (ed.), *Konfliktpartnerschaft: Akteure und Institutionen der industriellen Beziehungen*, pp. 167–99. Munich and Mering: Rainer Hampp.

SCIARRA, S. (1977) 'The Rise of the Italian Shop Steward', *Industrial Law Journal*, 6(1): 35–44.

SORGE, A. (1976) 'The Evolution of Industrial Democracy in the Countries of the European Community', *British Journal of Industrial Relations*, 14(3): 274–94.

STANOJEVIĆ, M. (2003) 'Workers' Power in Transition Economies: The Cases of Serbia and Slovenia', *European Journal of Industrial Relations*, 9(3): 283–301.

STREECK, W. (1984) 'Neo-Corporatist Industrial Relations and the Economic Crisis in West Germany', in J. H. Goldthorpe (ed.), *Order and Conflict in Contemporary Capitalism*, pp. 291–314. Oxford: Clarendon.

—— (1992) 'Codetermination: After Four Decades', in W. Streeck (ed.), *Social Institutions and Economic Performance*, pp. 137–68. London: Sage.

—— (1995) 'Works Councils in Western Europe: From Consultation to Participation', in J. Rogers and W. Streeck (eds), *Works Councils: Consultation, Representation and Cooperation in Industrial Relations*, pp. 313–48. Chicago: University of Chicago Press.

—— and HASSEL, A. (2003) 'The Crumbling Pillars of Social Partnership', *West European Politics*, 26(4): 101–24.

TCHOBANIAN, R. (1995) 'France: From Conflict to Social Dialogue?' in J. Rogers and W. Streeck (eds), *Works Councils: Consultation, Representation and Cooperation in Industrial Relations*, pp. 115–52. Chicago: University of Chicago Press.

TERRY, M. (1993) 'Workplace Unions and Workplace Industrial Relations: The Italian Experience', *Industrial Relations Journal*, 24(2): 138–50.

—— (1994) 'Workplace Unionism: Redefining Structures and Objectives', in R. Hyman and A. Ferner (eds), *New Frontiers in European Industrial Relations*, pp. 223–49. Oxford: Blackwell.

TEULINGS, A. W. M. (1989) 'A Political Bargaining Theory of Codetermination', in G. Széll, P. Blyton, and C. Cornforth (eds.), *The State, Trade Unions and Self-Management*, pp. 75–101. Berlin: de Gruyter.

THELEN, K. A. (1991) *Union of Parts: Labor Politics in Postwar Germany.* Ithaca, NY: Cornell UP.

THERBORN, G. (1992) 'Lessons from "Corporatist" Theorizations', in J. Pekkarinen, M. Pohjola, and B. Rowthorn (eds), *Social Corporatism: A Superior Economic System?*, pp. 24–43. Oxford: Clarendon Press.

TÓTH, A. (1997) 'The Invention of Works Councils in Hungary', *European Journal of Industrial Relations*, 3(2): 161–81.

VAN HET KAAR, R. (2003) *Works Councils and Other Workplace Employee Representation and Participation Structures: The Netherlands.* http://www.eurofound.europa.eu/eiro/2003/09/tfeature/nl0309102t.htm.

—— and SMIT, E. (eds) (2006) *Vier scenario's voor de toekomst van de medezeggenschap: Een onderzoek in opdracht van het Ministerie van SZW.* http://docs.szw.nl/pdf/129/2006/129_2006_3_9664.pdf.

VILROKX, J. and VAN LEEMPUT, J. (1992) 'Belgium: A New Stability in Industrial Relations?' in A. FERNER and R. HYMAN (eds), *Industrial Relations in the New Europe*, pp. 357–92. Oxford: Blackwell.

VISSER, J. (1995) 'The Netherlands: From Paternalism to Representation', in J. Rogers and W. Streeck (eds), *Works Councils: Consultation, Representation and Cooperation in Industrial Relations*, pp. 79–114. Chicago: University of Chicago Press.

WEDDERBURN, K. W. (Lord) (1990) 'The Italian Workers' Statute: Some British Reflections', *Industrial Law Journal*, 19(3): 154–91.

WOOD, G. and MAHABIR, P. (2001) 'South Africa's Workplace Forum System: A Failed. Experiment in the Democratization of Work?', *Industrial Relations Journal*, 32(3): 230–43.

CHAPTER 13

EMPLOYEE SHARE OWNERSHIP

ERIC KAARSEMAKER

ANDREW PENDLETON

ERIK POUTSMA

INTRODUCTION

EMPLOYEE share ownership involves employees acquiring shares in their employer so that they become shareholders. In recent years governments in North America, Europe, Australasia, and Asia have promoted various forms of employee share ownership, though the incidence of schemes and the level of employee participation varies considerably between countries (Pendleton et al., 2001; Poutsma, 2001; Vaughan-Whitehead, 1995). In principle, employee ownership gives employees additional rights to those normally expected by employees: a right to share in the company's profits, access to information on company finances and operations, and rights to participate in the management of the company (Rousseau and Shperling, 2003). These may bring about fundamental changes in employee attitudes and behaviour, which may in turn be reflected in a range of company-level outcomes such as productivity and financial performance.

Employee share ownership takes a variety of forms, some of which may have greater significance and effects than others. Employees may acquire large proportions of company shares, possibly the entire share capital, or just a small minority stake. Shares may be held individually or collectively. Participation in the share ownership plan may be limited to just a few individuals, typically senior managers, or open to the entire workforce. The extent to which employees possess profit sharing, information, and participation rights also varies considerably (Ben-Ner and Jones, 1995). This variety means that generalizations about employee share ownership have to be made with caution, as will become evident in the chapter.

Perspectives on the significance of employee share ownership vary widely. Policy makers in some countries argue that aligning workers' interests with those of the firm and its shareholders will provide incentives for employees to work 'harder and smarter'. Some go further and see it as heralding a significant change in the nature of employment in advanced industrial societies because it blurs traditional boundaries between workers and owners (Gates, 1998; Rousseau and Shperling, 2003). Widespread employee share ownership may create a form of 'economic democracy', whereby employees acquire a greater share of national wealth (Blair et al., 2000). However, some doubt that it will become a widespread form of corporate organization, because coordinating diverse worker interests is costly (Hansmann, 1996) and employee ownership will dilute managerial and owner incentives (Jensen and Meckling, 1979). Others have viewed it as a sham: owning small proportions of company shares (as is the case in most share ownership plans), exposes employees to the risks of ownership but not its potential gains (D'Art, 1992). Some have argued that employee share ownership is a tool to undermine trade unions and head off employee dissent when labour is strong (Ramsay, 1977; see Pendleton, 2005).

The modern academic literature on employee share ownership dates back to the late 1970s, with the emergence of the Employee Stock Ownership Plan (ESOP) in the USA. These origins of the recent literature have coloured the theoretical perspectives and approach of much contemporary analysis of this topic. Much of the literature in the 1970s and 1980s examined majority employee ownership. The major issues were the impact on employee attitudes and behaviour (Long, 1978; Rhodes and Steer 1981), the role of participation in decisions (Hammer et al., 1982; Long, 1981), the implications for trade unions (Hammer and Stern 1986; Stern et al 1983), and the impact on performance (Conte and Svejnar, 1990; Long, 1980). In the more recent literature (late 1980s onwards), the focus has tended to be on more modest levels of employee ownership. However, the concerns, assumptions, and questions from the earlier literature have largely carried over into this newer literature. Yet it is questionable whether these are entirely appropriate or relevant for the analysis of 'mainstream' employee share plans in otherwise conventionally-owned companies. It also means that some issues that are pertinent to 'mainstream' employee share ownership plans, such as factors influencing voluntary employee participation and the wealth effects of employee share ownership, have been barely considered.

In the chapter we deal with the following. We first provide more details of the various types of employee share ownership plans, before providing information on the incidence of employee share ownership. Then, we examine the factors associated with the use of employee share ownership plans by companies ('determinants'). Following this, we discuss the factors associated with employee participation in share plans where such participation is voluntary. We then review the extensive literature on the effects of employee share ownership on attitudes, behaviour, and performance.

Types of Employee Share Ownership

Employee share ownership plans can take several different forms. At the outset it is important to distinguish between share ownership where employees own a substantial proportion of company shares and that where employees own a small minority, typically 5 per cent or less. In modern industrialized economies, the latter is more common and, because this type of share ownership is concentrated in larger firms, employee coverage is far higher. Although both forms of employee share ownership have features in common—they typically use the same mechanisms to transfer shares to employees—they usually have a very different character. In majority employee-owned firms, employees may have a strong sense of ownership, and may expect to be deeply involved in the governance and management of the firm. Employee ownership may have come about via an employee buyout or by an exiting owner wanting to pass on the business to the employees. By contrast, in 'mainstream' employee share ownership, the plans will typically be one of several components of the company's reward package, and employees may have little expectation or interest in participating in governance and management. Instead their orientation to the plan may be primarily financial (French, 1987).

In the USA and UK, majority employee share ownership has often been achieved via an ESOP—Employee Stock Ownership Plan. This is a mechanism by which shares can be acquired by a trust on behalf of employees (Pendleton, 2001). Share acquisition might be financed by a loan to the trust, possibly provided by the company. Alternatively, shares might be gifted to the trust by the company. In most cases the shares will be distributed over time to individual employees (tax arrangements may necessitate this) but in some cases shares are held in trust in perpetuity so that there is collective ownership (the John Lewis Partnership is the most well-known UK example). Where shares are distributed, the typical process is for a share of annual profits to be passed to the trust so that it can pay off the loan. As the loan is repaid, shares are released from the trust to employees.

The advantage of this arrangement is that employees acquire ownership at little or no direct personal cost or risk. The disadvantage can be that ownership comes cheaply to employees, with the result that they may not take on the full responsibilities of ownership.

Another route to employee ownership is direct purchase by employees but this obviously carries a great deal more risk for employees and the potential for this route to ownership is restricted by employees' liquidity constraints. Some firms combine direct purchases by employees and acquisition of shares by a trust. Some combine individual and collective ownership.

In 'mainstream' employee share ownership plans, employees typically acquire shares in three main ways. The first is donation of shares by the company to employees or the purchase of shares on employees' behalf by the company, often using similar mechanisms to those described above. The Share Incentive Plan (SIP) in the UK enables companies to distribute shares to employees (though potentially with differential allocations linked to performance criteria). The second route is purchase of shares by employees, typically on favourable terms. For instance, the Share Incentive Plan allows employees to subscribe up to £1,500 each year to 'Partnership Shares'. Contributions are encouraged by very favourable tax concessions and the potential for companies to match employee contributions with additional shares ('Matching Shares'). Contributory schemes are also common in some other countries, such as the United States (so-called Section 423 plans) and France (where employee contributions to the Plan Epargne d'Entreprise—company savings plan—can be channelled into company shares). A variant is the 401(k) pension plan in the United States in which employees can allocate funds to employer shares (and receive them as matches for pension contributions) in some firms. The final means of acquiring shares is share options. Here, employees take out options to purchase shares at some point in the future (typically three to ten years time). When the options can be exercised, employees may choose not to exercise, to acquire and immediately sell ('cashless exercise'), or purchase and retain the shares. In the UK's SAYE (or 'Sharesave') scheme, employees enter a savings plan to save the money to purchase the shares.[1]

The arrangements by which employees become shareholders has important implications for the character and effects of employee share ownership. Clearly, some schemes—most notably free share distributions—facilitate involvement by all or nearly all employees whereas in others participation is dependent on employee willingness to contribute financially. Where participation is voluntary, participation rates may be low, with the result that the hypothesized effects of share ownership on employee behaviour and company performance may not be realized. Voluntary participation also means that some groups of employees (possibly those with higher disposable income) may be more likely to participate in the plan than others, thereby limiting the redistributive potential of employee share ownership.

Overall, the character of share ownership can vary considerably between companies. In some, employees own a substantial proportion of the company with all employees participating in ownership equally. In others, a minority of employees may own a small proportion of the company's shares. These considerations should be borne in mind when assessing the character and effects of employee share ownership plans.

Incidence of Employee Share Ownership

The incidence of employee share ownership plans varies considerably by country, as does the number of employee participants. The United States is seen as the paragon of employee share ownership, with schemes promoting employee share ownership emerging in the 1920s (Blair et al., 2000). The recent phase of employee ownership dates from ESOP legislation in the mid-1970s. Currently, nearly 10,000 companies use an ESOP, a stock bonus plan, or a stock-based profit sharing plan, and about eleven million employees are thought to participate in these (National Center for Employee Ownership, 2008). Companies totalling 750 have a 401 (k) pension plan with substantial holdings in company stock (around 1.5 million employees), 3,000 offer broad-based stock options, and around 4,000 have a stock purchase plan. This combination of contributory and non-contributory share ownership plans is estimated to involve about 20 per cent of the US private sector workforce in share ownership (Blasi et al., 2003). Most publicly-traded companies offer minority employee ownership, with the combined employee share of the company under 10 per cent in most cases. By contrast, employee ownership in privately-owned companies is often far more substantial.

Employee share ownership in the United Kingdom also dates from the 1970s and 1980s. There are two main all-employee plans with favourable tax status: the Save As You Earn share option scheme (introduced in 1980) and the Share Incentive Plan (introduced in 2000 to replace Approved Profit Sharing (1978)). In addition, there are two other tax approved plans which, though usually selective, can be used for all employees: the Company Share Options Plan (introduced in 1984 as Discretionary Share Options, and revised in 1996) and Enterprise Management Incentives (introduced in 2000). In 2005–2006 1,400 companies operated one or both of the all-employee plans (HMRC, 2008).

In mainland Europe there is a wide divergence between companies in the promotion of and incidence of share ownership plans (Pendleton et al., 2001). France appears to have the highest incidence with a well-developed employee savings system allowing employees to channel bonuses and savings into employer stock. Germany has not traditionally promoted employee share ownership but has recently announced measures to promote it (April 2008). In Western Europe, the countries with the lowest use of employee share ownership have tended to be the Mediterranean countries (Greece, Italy, Portugal, and Spain), though Spain is notable for the Mondragon cooperatives in the Basque region. For a while some Eastern European countries had high levels of employee ownership as a result of the transition from soviet-style economies but this has faded in most cases (Mygind et al., 2006).

It is noticeable that, for the most part, share ownership plans are most prevalent in the Anglo-American economies or what Hall and Soskice call the 'liberal market economies' (2001). In part, this is because governments in these economies have passed legislation and offered tax concessions to promote these plans. Comparative studies have shown that regulation and fiscal concessions are key influences on the national incidence of financial participation schemes (Poutsma, 2001; Poutsma et al., 2003; Uvalic, 1991; Vaughan-Whitehead, 1995). But the deeper question concerns why governments have pursued these policies? Part of the answer lies in well-developed stock markets. The liberal market economies (USA, Canada, UK, etc.) are notable for having relatively large numbers of stock market listed firms, and for having active secondary equity markets with dispersed ownership (see Gospel and Pendleton, Chapter 21). The level of protection for small shareholders is also said to be higher in the liberal market economies (La Porta et al., 1997). Much of the potential attractiveness of company shares lies in their liquidity: where shares are easily convertible into cash they will be more attractive to the employee.

The greater dispersion, transparency, and liquidity of ownership in the liberal market economies comes at a price. Ownership is often said to take a 'low commitment' form, leaving firms at the mercy of exiting shareholders. This low commitment relationship is said to extend also to the company–employee relationship (Black et al., 2007; Blair, 1995). The appeal of employee share ownership to policy makers and corporate managers is that it is a means of promoting employee commitment that is consistent with the norms of governance and business organization in the liberal market economies. It also provides an alternative to statutory forms of employee involvement in decisions (e.g., works councils) that are found in many European countries.

DETERMINANTS OF EMPLOYEE SHARE OWNERSHIP

As well as national differences in the promotion and incidence of share ownership plans, there are also clear differences *within* countries. Certain kinds of firms are far more likely to use employee share ownership plans than others.

In general, 'mainstream' employee share ownership plans, where a small minority of equity is acquired by employees, are mainly found in larger, stock market listed firms (Pendleton et al., 2001). They also tend to be especially prevalent in the financial services sector. It is much less easy to generalize about firms with majority employee ownership as there are far fewer of them, and the reasons for conversion to employee ownership tend to be idiosyncratic. The discussion that follows therefore focuses on firms with minority employee ownership plans. We consider the factors and characteristics associated with the use of ESO schemes.

The literature on this topic is substantial and long-standing (Bryson and Freeman, 2007; Cheadle, 1989; Festing et al., 1999; Jones and Kato, 1993; Kato and Morishima, 2002; Kruse, 1996; Pendleton, 1997; Poole, 1989; Poutsma and Huijgen, 1999). It tends to use a principal–agent framework, in which the employer or management is considered to be the principal and employees the agents. The issue is how the principal gets the agents to do what the principal wants (Jensen and Meckling, 1976). Opportunities for moral hazard and adverse selection are greater in some workplaces than others, and the costs of countering these will be correspondingly greater. The general presumption has been that employee share ownership will be used as a substitute for other forms of monitoring when the latter are costly, such as when teamwork makes individual performance pay difficult to use (Pliskin and Jones, 1997). Studies of determinants therefore concern themselves with the costs of monitoring. Since these are difficult to measure directly, proxies based on characteristics of the company, workplace, and employees are used. In the course of this agency-inspired literature a number of factors have been important, and these are considered in turn.

Size

Information asymmetries and monitoring are said to become more costly as firm size, and managerial hierarchies, increase. For this reason, size is widely predicted to be associated with the adoption and use of share plans, and indeed many studies find this to be the case (Festing et al., 1999; Kruse, 1996; Kruse et al., 2007; Landau et al., 2007; Pendleton, 1997; Pendleton et al., 2001). It seems likely that the high fixed costs of introducing share ownership plans are also important in explaining the size distribution of share schemes (Lenne et al., 2006; Pendleton, 1997). However, a major theoretical problem arising from the use of share plans by large firms is that incentive effects are likely to be inversely related to size because of the free-rider effect. Hence, the rationale for using share ownership plans is not so obvious (Prendergast, 1999). The literature deals with this by emphasizing the need for complementary forms of employee participation to engender cooperation and peer pressure, and thereby overcome any tendencies towards free-riding.

An alternative possibility is that employee share ownership is not used to provide 'high-powered' incentives (see below).

Characteristics of Work Settings and Workforces

Information asymmetries and monitoring problems could be more intense in work situations where individual performance and output is hard to measure because of tacit elements of the work, task interdependence, and product immateriality and complexity (Alchian and Demsetz, 1972; Ben-Ner et al., 2000; Kruse, 1996; Sesil et al., 2002). There are a range of measures which may be used to proxy these processes: the proportions of various categories of staff, the proportion of highly-educated staff, the complexity/interdependence of work tasks, the use of auto-mated technology, capital intensity, investments in R&D, and growth opportunities (ratio of market to book value) (Core and Guay, 2001; Frye, 2004). To varying levels, these all may indicate degrees of indeterminacy in the nature of tasks and products. For instance, higher-ranked staff are assumed to undertake more com-plex tasks (more costly to monitor) and to have more discretion (greater oppor-tunities to make 'wrong' decisions).

The findings to date have been ambiguous and contradictory. There is some evidence that share plans are more likely to be found in sectors with high propor-tions of professionals, such as the professional services and computer services industry (Kruse et al., 2006), and that stock options are more likely to be used when production is human capital intensive and employee performance hard to monitor (Jones et al., 2006). However, other studies have found no connection between share plans and workforce composition (Pendleton et al., 2001), while others have found unexpected relationships. Pliskin and Jones (1997), for instance, found a positive relationship between stock purchase plans and machine-paced work, contrary to expectations.

Risk

Agency theory predicts that optimal contracts will be a trade-off between incentives and risk. There is substantial evidence elsewhere in the pay literature that firms facing high risk are less likely to use incentives-based pay schemes, probably due to employee risk aversion (Bloom and Milkovitch, 1998). It has been suggested that the need to pay premia to employees to compensate them for bearing sig-nificant risk can make contingent rewards costly for firms. However, Prendergast (2002) posits a positive relation between risk and incentives, since in more uncer-tain settings the principal is often better off delegating responsibility to the agent (s), and the delegation necessitates the use of incentives. Oyer (2004) argues that when uncertainty is high, fixed wage contracts require frequent revision and the transaction costs of doing this can be prohibitively costly. To retain the best employees, it is better to tie compensation to a measure that correlates with the business cycle, such as share price. Most studies do not measure the role of risk in the firm's operating environment (Sesil et al., 2002 being an exception) but it is common for measures of product competition to be used. The results, however, tend to be inconclusive.

Liquidity Constraints

According to Yermack (1995), firms with severe cash constraints and high capital needs may substitute shares for cash pay. For instance, IT companies that have not yet secured positive income streams and are investing heavily relative to their assets may use equity-based pay (especially options) for this reason. Core and Guay (2001) found that firms use non-executive option grants as a substitute for cash compensation to a greater extent when they face cash flow constraints and when the costs of external capital are greater. However, Jones et al. (2006) found no support for this in a Finnish panel study.

Assessment

The clearest conclusion from the determinants literature is that 'mainstream' stock plans are most likely to be found in large, stock market listed companies. Yet share ownership is a 'noisy' reward in these firms because many of the influences on share price are outside company, let alone employee, control. Coupled with the free-rider factor in larger firms, a line-of-sight issue (it is difficult for employees to see how their behaviour influences share price), and inconsistent empirical results for monitoring costs, this casts doubt on the agency perspective. It seems questionable that firms use share ownership plans as simple, direct, or 'high-powered' incentives. Given that firms and workplaces using share plans also use other, more high-powered incentives, it may be that share plans are used for alternative objectives (Pendleton, 2006). A perspective gaining ground in the literature is that share plans signal to employees that investments in human capital will be protected or insured (Blair, 1995; Robinson and Zhang, 2005). They guarantee that employees will share in the fruits of human capital development and in so doing encourage employees to invest in firm-specific human capital despite the insecurity and risk of so doing. This perspective might help to explain the preponderance of share ownership in listed firms. In liberal market economies, it is said to be difficult for listed firms to commit to their workforces because of the 'uncommitted' nature and structure of shareholding by institutional investors (Gospel and Pendleton, Chapter 21).

In turn, employees may be reluctant to commit to the firm. Employee share ownership is a means of developing commitment, using instruments that are well developed in this kind of economy.

Employee Participation in Share Ownership

One issue that has received little attention in the literature is employee participation in employee share ownership. Why do some employees participate, and others do not? What factors influence levels of participation in share ownership plans? The reason for this gap in the literature seems to be its origins in the ESOP and majority employee ownership literature in the 1970s: here this issue is of little interest because typically all employees receive shares. However, many 'mainstream' share plans are voluntary, and thus this issue is far more relevant. A literature is starting to emerge (Degeorge et al., 2004; Pendleton, 2009), drawing on insights that have emerged in the US literature on 401(k) pension plans. This literature tends to focus on individual-level influences on participation: as yet there has been little empirical work on company-level influences, such as communications, about share plans. It finds that employee orientations to plans are predominantly financial and that employees' capacity (income, etc.) to participate is a key influence on participation (Brown et al., 2008; Dewe et al., 1988; Pendleton, 2009).

Job position and income are the most important influences on participation and contributions to voluntary share ownership plans. A recent European Foundation study using the 2005 European Working Conditions Survey finds that employees in managerial positions are more than four times as likely to participate in these schemes as skilled, semi-skilled, or unskilled 'blue-collar' workers (Welz and Fernández-Macías, 2007). This applies after controlling for sector, establishment size, and education. Kruse et al. (2007) find a similar picture in the USA, while in the UK Pendleton (2009) finds that income is the most important factor influencing both the decision to participate and the level of contributions.

Financial participation is also distributed unevenly between the sexes and between types of contract: the European Foundation study found that men are more likely to participate than women, and workers on permanent contracts are more likely to participate than those on temporary contracts, suggesting that financial participation is subject to similar forms of differentiation as general pay structures. The type of employee most likely to have shares in their company is a male manager in the financial sector with a tertiary level of education.

These findings are important because they cast doubt on the claim that employee share ownership *per se* will lead to a more equal distribution of wealth. Although some kinds of share plan may have redistributive tendencies (e.g., free share distributions to all employees), others (e.g., voluntary subscriptions-based plans) clearly do not.

A further issue that is starting to emerge is the degree of concentration of employee savings in company shares (Blasi and Kruse, 2006). Any employee share ownership plan, especially one with tax benefits, may encourage employees to hold 'all their eggs in one basket'. There is now extensive evidence that many employees with 401(k) pensions plans tend to invest disproportionately in employer shares where there is the potential to do so. This has been criticized because in most cases concentration will deliver lower returns than a diversified portfolio (Meulbroek, 2005), and because employee share ownership aligns financial and human capital risk (i.e., employment tends to be most at risk when share values are most under threat). Recent evidence indicates that share plan participants behave similarly to 401(k) plan participants: Pendleton (2008) has found that nearly 20 per cent of share plan participants have 50 per cent or more of their savings tied up in employer shares. Those on higher incomes are more likely to tie up their savings in this way. This evidence indicates that the criticism of employee share ownership that it induces employees to take risky decisions is well founded. There is a growing belief among advocates of share ownership that greater financial education is necessary to counter this tendency.

IMPACT OF EMPLOYEE SHARE OWNERSHIP PLANS ON EMPLOYEE ATTITUDES

A primary rationale among policy makers for employee share ownership has been its apparent capacity to influence employee attitudes and behaviour, such as turnover, turnover intention, commitment, motivation, and satisfaction, and thus to affect company performance. Since the 1970s there has been a rich vein of research into the relationship between employee ownership and employee attitudes and behaviour, mainly conducted in the US and UK. Over fifty quantitative academic studies have been conducted and more than two-thirds have found a favourable relationship between employee ownership and employee attitudes and behaviour. The results of most of the remainder have been inconclusive.

Employee ownership has been widely predicted to have favourable effects on employee attitudes and behaviour. In a landmark study, Klein (1987) identified three ways in which employee ownership affects attitudes: one, intrinsic satisfaction—ownership per se is sufficient to bring about attitudinal and behavioural change; two, extrinsic satisfaction—ownership leads to attitudinal and behavioural change because it is financially rewarding; and three, instrumental satisfaction—ownership brings about attitudinal and behavioural change by facilitating other outcomes that are desired by employees such as participation in decision making.

Pierce and colleagues (1991, 2001, 2003) developed theory further by proposing that employee ownership leads to a change in an employee's mindset, which they coined *psychological ownership*. It is this changed mindset that in turn leads to attitudinal and behavioural change. Pierce et al. (2001, 2003) further claimed that psychological ownership emerges because it satisfies certain human motives such as *self-efficacy* (being able to exert control over one's direct environment), *self-identity* (ownership as an expression of the self), and *having a place* (the need to have a place of one's own). These motives can be satisfied in organizations—empirical evidence shows people expressing feelings of ownership towards their work, their job, the product of their work, and their organization (Pierce et al., 2001: 300–301; 2003: 88–91). Several empirical studies have shown the important role played by 'psychological ownership' in employee share ownership plans (Kaarsemaker, 2006; Pendleton, 2001; Pendleton et al., 1998; Wagner et al., 2003).

In Pierce et al.'s view, a sense of ownership develops in at least three ways: one, through enhanced *control* over particular organizational factors, such as the job, department, procedures, or product lines; two, through increased information about, and more *intimate knowledge* of particular organizational factors; and three, through *self-investment* (of one's time, skills, ideas, energy) into the potential target of ownership (Pierce et al., 2001: 301–302; 2003: 92–3).

Although there is clear evidence that employee ownership is associated with psychological ownership and commitment, there are some issues that require further investigation. First, no studies have compared the attitudinal effects of different types of employee ownership (ESOPs, share options, direct ownership, etc.). Also, most have used simplistic measures of employee ownership, such as whether employees are shareholders or not. Only about 15 per cent have used more sophisticated measures of employee ownership such as the size of the individual employees' stakes. Second, it is not fully clear under what conditions employee share ownership has favourable effects on psychological ownership and work attitudes/behaviour. It has been apparent for some time that employee ownership needs to fit with other organizational practices, such as employee involvement in decisions, but for the most part the relative importance of these other practices has not been determined. Even though participation in decision making is found to influence employee attitudes (as in Pendleton et al., 1998), few studies have analysed the interactions between employee ownership and participation (exceptions include Freeman et al., 2004 and Kaarsemaker, 2006).

It is apparent from the literature that the fit with other HR practices (besides participation in decision making) with employee ownership should be considered (Bernstein, 1976; Kaarsemaker and Poutsma, 2006; Rosen et al., 2005). Ownership of an asset comes with a few rights—the right to use the asset, the right to its returns, and the right to sell it. These rights need to be translated into HRM practices. Besides participation in decision making, these practices include: information sharing, profit sharing, training for business literacy (so that employees can understand information and participate in a meaningful way), and means for resolving disputes. Together with employee ownership, these practices theoretically form a 'high-performance work system' that can signal to employees the importance of employee ownership to the firm and its leadership (Kaarsemaker and Poutsma, 2006). Together, these practices may underwrite an 'ownership culture', and it is within organizations that possess such a culture that the strongest impacts of employee ownership on employee attitudes and behaviour have been found (Beyster and Economy, 2007; Blasi et al., 2003; De Jong *and Van Witteloostuijn, 2004*; Gittell, 2003; Kaarsemaker, 2006; Maaløe, 1998; Rosen et al., 2005). However, the relative importance of these HR practices, and the means through which they affect attitudes, needs to be further tested.

In sum, as predicted by theory, empirical research on the impact of employee ownership on employee attitudes and behaviour has found strong evidence that employee ownership has positive effects. However, the research to date has a number of significant shortcomings. It has not clearly distinguished the various types of employee ownership, and measures of employee ownership have often been simplistic. Most studies have neglected the mechanisms underlying the relationships between employee ownership and employee attitudes and behaviour, as well as the conditions under which employee ownership yields effects.

The Impact of Employee Share Ownership on Workplace and Company Performance

The most important rationale for employee share ownership among policy makers has been its apparent potential to enhance company performance (CEC, 2002; HM Treasury, 1998). The 'hard' version of this rationale suggests that linking employee rewards to corporate outcomes, such as share price, will provide a direct incentive for employees to work in ways that are conducive to good collective performance. The 'softer' version suggests that making employees owners will support favourable attitudes and behaviour, as outlined in the previous section. Other possibilities include a 'sorting' effect: employee share plans will attract high-quality employees and those who are favourably inclined to share-based rewards to employment in the company (Lazear, 2000). Further explanations emphasize the capacity of share plans to retain valuable employees either by signalling the firm's commitment to these employees (Blair, 1995; Robinson and Zhang, 2005), by 'locking-in' employees through the deferred character of share plans (Sengupta et al., 2007), or by aligning employee rewards with the business cycle (share price tends to be higher when alternative employment opportunities are greater) (Oyer, 2004).

There is a great deal of evidence on the relationship between share ownership plans and performance, with more than seventy studies since the 1970s. The research on the impacts of employee ownership on firm performance has investigated relationships with financial performance measures (such as profit margins and return on assets) and with productivity measures (such as value added per employee and sales per employee). In some studies, the performance measures have been taken from company accounts (see OXERA, 2007, for instance), while in others (such as those based on the UK Workplace Employment Relations Surveys) subjective evaluations of relative workplace performance have been used.

There are several surveys of the literature that provide a useful guide to research findings so far (Conte and Svejnar, 1990; Doucouliagos, 1995; Kruse and Blasi, 1997; Pérotin and Robinson, 2003). The consensus from this literature can be stated as follows. Employee share ownership has positive effects on performance (especially productivity) but these outcomes are often small and/or statistically insignificant. Positive effects tend to be larger and stronger among firms with majority employee ownership than among firms with 'mainstream' employee share plans (Doucouliagos, 1995), though there is some evidence to the contrary (Conte and Svejnar, 1988). Finally, the effects of employee ownership are greater, or are only achieved (as in General Accounting Office, 1987), when there is also participation in decision making.

Although these findings are widespread, there are several problems with research on this topic. The first is the theoretical basis of the performance prediction. Given the free-rider effect mentioned earlier, it is perhaps unlikely that share ownership alone will bring about performance enhancements. This is the reason why the literature emphasizes the importance of participation in decisions and complementary HRM practices to accompany share ownership. By generating cooperation, peer pressure, and an ownership culture these practices will mitigate any tendencies for employees to free-ride in the share ownership plan. The theory and evidence on this is not, however, clear cut. While complementary practices may support more favourable employee attitudes and behaviour, as outlined in the previous section, it is not axiomatic that these will feed through to corporate level performance because the latter will be affected by a variety of other factors.

Empirically, results are diverse. Though some studies provide clear evidence of the combined effects of share ownership and participation on performance (Kato and Morishima 2002), others find that participation does not add to the effects of share ownership (Kalmi et al., 2006; Ohkusa and Ohtake, 1997; Robinson and Wilson, 2006). Some studies find differences between types of participation: for instance, Addison and Belfield (2001) find that share plans have positive effects on financial performance in workplaces with downward communication (e.g., team briefing) but not those with 'upward' participation, such as quality circles. Finally, some studies find that participation can detract from positive effects of share ownership in certain circumstances, such as when all or most employees are involved in the share plan (Pendleton and Robinson, 2008).

Further problems with research into the effects of share ownership on performance include the tendency to conflate majority and minority share ownership, and the tendency not to distinguish clearly between types of share ownership plan (i.e., voluntary purchase plans versus free share distributions) even though they might function in very different ways. There is also a range of important methodological problems affecting most studies to varying extents. These include selection bias and reverse causality, omitted variable bias, and the cross-sectional nature of many studies. As a result it is difficult to conclude beyond doubt that share ownership improves company performance.

PARTICIPATION

The relationship between employee share ownership and other forms of employee involvement and participation has pervaded the literature. It has been widely argued that participation in decision making is necessary for employee share plans to secure attitudinal change and to achieve improvements in company productivity. There is also widespread evidence that share plans are more likely to be found in participative firms and workplaces. However, it is not always clear what forms of employee participation are likely to have the most synergistic effects. There is some evidence from WERS that 'downward communication' (team briefings, etc.) are more likely to have a complementary relationship with share ownership than 'upwards participation' (participation in decisions) (Addison and Belfield, 2001) but at this stage diverse measures of participation across the literature mean that no firm conclusions can be drawn.

One issue that has contributed to a lack of clarity in predictions about complementarities between share plans and other forms of participation is the tendency to conflate 'mainstream' share plans (minority ownership in conventionally-owned large firms) with majority or fully worker-owned companies. Participation may function in different ways between the two types of organization. In conventional firms, participation appears to be necessary to counter the free-rider and line-of-sight problems found in larger, listed firms. But there is the possibility that too much participation might impede the authority and status relationships that pervade many of these organizations. By contrast, in employee-owned firms extensive participation appears vital for employees to realize a full sense of ownership, given that the right to determine how an asset is used is a fundamental component of ownership. Even so, finding a balance between employee participation in decisions and managers' ability to manage can be challenging.

Evidence on linkages between employee share ownership and indirect or representative participation is more complex. There are substantial differences between countries in the structure and nature of representative participation (see chapters in this book). Some countries have decentralized systems of indirect participation, others have centralized arrangements, and others still have combinations of the two. Some countries, such as the UK, have mainly single channel representation (all or most representation occurs through union and bargaining channels) while others, such as Germany, have dual systems (union representation in collective bargaining and separate representation through works councils). This means that generalizations about linkages with share ownership are difficult to make. That said, there is consistent evidence over many years that share ownership plans tend to be found in unionized establishments in the UK (Gregg and Machin, 1988; Pendleton, 1997), and there is also some evidence that the conjunction has favourable impacts on workplace performance (Sengupta, 2008). Elsewhere in Europe, the evidence is less supportive (Festing et al., 1999; Poutsma et al., 2006). However, even where union representation and employee share ownership coexist, the two function largely independently of each other (Pendleton, 2005), with little union involvement in the design, implementation, and operation of employee share plans in most cases. The major exception is majority employee-owned firms where unions were involved in mounting the buyout.

Much of the separation between union representation and employee share ownership plans can be attributed to union suspicion. Unions have traditionally been wary of share ownership plans because of fears that it may either bypass and undermine union representation or draw unions into representing shareholder interests. There have been fears that employers may use share ownership to weaken union representation. Although many unions are now more favourably inclined towards share ownership plans (share plans have not had dire effects on union representation in most cases), there is residual suspicion of employer motives among some unions in some countries (Pendleton et al., 2003). This is often well founded as some employer groups have highlighted the apparent potential of share plans to decentralize bargaining and secure greater pay flexibility. However, share ownership plans function independently of pay bargaining to a large extent because they are governed by separate regulation (securities laws, etc.). As a result their capacity to bring about major changes in bargaining structure is probably very limited.

Conclusions

At the start of this chapter we highlighted several perspectives on employee share ownership. These either argued that share ownership will bring about fundamental changes to the employment relationship or else they will change very little. The logic of the evidence presented in this chapter is that the truth is generally somewhere in-between. Most share ownership plans do not appear to fundamentally transform the employment relationship. This is because in most cases the amount of equity passing to employees is proportionally small, and there is little expectation on the part of those involved that share ownership will transform the way the company is run. But there are exceptions, especially where there is substantial employee ownership. However, even focusing on minority ownership there is substantial evidence of attitudinal and behavioural impacts in certain circumstances. There is also enough evidence to suggest that share ownership has favourable effects on company and workplace performance. Despite this consensus, it is also apparent that there is a lack of clarity in the approach to research. The literature has not distinguished clearly between levels or types of ownership, nor indeed between types of complementary participation. Nor has it fully addressed some issues, such as the factors influencing employee participation in voluntary share ownership plans. There is therefore a rich agenda for future research in this area.

Note

1. 'Phantom shares' are a variant of share ownership. These are instruments linked to shares but which do not have the legal rights associated with actual share ownership.

References

Addison, J. and Belfield, C. (2001) 'Updating the determinants of firm performance: estimation using the 1998 UK Workplace Employee Relations Survey'. *British Journal of Industrial Relations*, 39(3): 341–66.

ALCHIAN, A. A. and DEMSETZ, H. (1972) 'Production, information costs, and economic organization'. *American Economic Review,* 62(5): 777–95.

BEN-NER, A., BURNS, W. A., DOW, G., and PUTTERMAN (2000) 'Employee ownership: an empirical exploration' in M. M. Blair and T. A. Kochan, The New Relationship: Human Capital in the American Corporation, pp. 194–233. Washington DC: Brookings Institution.

—— and JONES, D. C. (1995) 'Employee participation, ownership and productivity: a theoretical framework'. *Industrial Relations,* 34(4): 532–54.

BERNSTEIN, P. (1976) *Workplace Democratization: Its Internal Dynamics.* Kent, OH: Kent State University Press.

BEYSTER, J. and Economy, P. (2007) *The SAIC Solution: How we Built an $8 Billion Employee-Owned Technology Company.* Hoboken, NJ: Wiley.

BLACK, B., GOSPEL, H., and PENDLETON, A. (2007) 'Finance, corporate governance, and the employment relationship'. *Industrial Relations,* 46(3): 643–50.

BLAIR, M. (1995) *Ownership and Control: Rethinking Corporate Governance for the Twenty-First Century,* pp. 241–98. Washington, DC: Brookings Institution.

—— KRUSE, D., and BLASI, J. (2000) 'Employee ownership: an unstable form or a stabilizing force?' in M. Blair and T. Kochan (eds), *The New Relationship. Human Capital in the American Corporation.* Washington, DC: Brookings Institution.

BLASI, J. and KRUSE, D. (2006) 'Are diversification and employee ownership incompatible?' *Journal of Employee Ownership Law and Finance,* 18(4): 19–38.

—— —— and Bernstein, A. (2003) *In the Company of Owners: The Truth about Stock Options (and Why Every Employee should Have Them).* New York: Basic Books.

BLOOM, M. and MILKOVICH, G. (1998) 'Relationships among risk, incentive pay, and organizational performance'. *Academy of Management Journal,* 41(3): 283–97.

BROWN, M., LANDAU, I., MITCHELL, R., O'CONNELL, A., and Ramsay, I. (2008) 'Why do employees participate in employee share plans? A conceptual framework'. *Labour and Industry,* 18(3): 45–72.

BRYSON, A. and FREEMAN, R. (2007) 'Doing the right thing? Does fair share capitalism improve workplace performance?' London: Department of Trade and Industry, Employment Relations Research Series no. 81.

CHEADLE, A. (1989) 'Explaining patterns of profit sharing activity'. *Industrial Relations,* 28(3): 398–400.

Commission of the European Communities (2002) *Communication from the Commission to the Council, the European Parliament, the Economic and Social Committee and the Committee of the Regions: on a Framework for the Promotion of Employee Financial Participation.* Brussels: Commission of the European Communities, COM (2002) 364 final.

CONTE, M. and SVENJAR, J. (1990) 'The performance effects of employee ownership plans', in A. Blinder (ed.), *Paying for Productivity: A Look at the Evidence,* pp. 143–72. Washington, DC: Brookings Institution.

CONTE, M. A. and SVEJNAR, J. (1988) 'Productivity effects of worker participation in management, profit-sharing, worker ownership of assets and unionization in U.S. firms.' *International Journal of Industrial Organization,* 6(1): 139–51.

CORE, J. and GUY, W. R. (2001) Stock option plans for non-exectutive employees. *Journal of Financial Economics,* 61(2): 253–87.

—— and WAYNE, G. (2001) 'Stock option plans for non-executive employees'. *Journal of Financial Economics,* 61(2): 253–87.

D'Art, D. (1992) *Economic Democracy and Financial Participation: A Comparative Study.* London: Routledge.

DEGEORGE, F., JENTER, D., MOEL, A., and TUFANO, P. (2004) 'Selling company shares to reluctant employees: France Telecom's experience'. *Journal of Financial Economics*, 71(1): 169–202.

DE JONG, G. and VAN WITTELOOSTUIJN (2004) Successful corporate democracy: sustainable cooperation of capital and labour in the Dutch Breman Group. *Academy of Management Executive*, 18(3): 54–66.

DEWE, P., DUNN, S., and RICHARDSON, R. (1988) 'Employee share option schemes, why workers are attracted to them'. *British Journal of Industrial Relations*, 26(1): 1–20.

DOUCOULIAGOS, C. (1995) 'Worker participation and productivity in labor-managed and participatory capitalist firms: a meta-analysis'. *Industrial and Labor Relations Review*, 49(1): 58–77.

FESTING, M., GROENING, Y., KABST, R., and WEBER, W. (1999) 'Financial participation in Europe—determinants and outcomes'. *Economic and Industrial Democracy*, 20(2): 295–329.

FREEMAN, R., KRUSE, D., and BLASI, J. (2004) 'Monitoring colleagues at work and free rider problem: profit sharing, employee ownership, broad-based stock options and workplace performance in the United States'.

FRENCH, J. L. (1987) 'Employee perspectives on stock ownership: financial investment or mechanism of control?' *Academy of Management Review*, 12(3): 427–35.

FRYE, M. (2004) 'Equity-based compensation for employees: firm performance and determinants'. *Journal of Financial Research*, 27(1): 31–54.

GATES, J. (1998) *The Ownership Solution*. London: Penguin.

GITTELL, J. H. (2003) *The Southwest Airlines Way: Using the Power of Relationships to Achieve High Performance*. New York: McGraw-Hill.

GREGG, P. and MACHIN, S. (1988) 'Unions and the incidence of performance-linked pay schemes in Britain'. *International Journal of Industrial Organisation*, (6): 91–107.

HALL, P. and SOSKICE, D. (eds) (2001) *Varieties of Capitalism: The Institutional Foundations of Comparative Advantage*. Oxford: Oxford University Press.

HAMMER, T. and STERN, R. (1986) 'A yo-yo model of cooperation: union participation at the Rath Packing Company'. *Industrial and Labor Relations Review*, 39(3): 337–49.

—— —— and Gurdon, M. (1982) 'Workers' ownership and attitudes towards participation', in F. Lindenfeld and J. Rothschild-Whitt (eds), *Workplace Democracy and Social Change*. Boston, MA: Porter Sargent.

HANSMANN, H. (1996) *The Ownership of Enterprise*. Cambridge, MA: Belknap.

HMRC (2008) www.hmrc.gov.uk/stats/emp_share_schemes/companies/.pdf.

HM Treasury (1998) *Consultation on Employee Share Ownership*. London: HM Treasury.

JENSEN, M. and MECKLING, W. (1976) 'Theory of the firm: managerial behavior, agency costs and ownership structure'. *Journal of Financial Economics*, 3(4): 305–60.

—— —— (1979) 'Rights and production functions: an application to labor-managed firms and codetermination'. *Journal of Business*, 52(4): 469–506.

JONES, D., KALMI, P., and MKINENÄKINEN, M. (2006) 'The determinants of stock option compensation: evidence from Finland'. *Industrial Relations*, 45(3): 437–68.

—— and KATO, T. (1993) 'Employee stock ownership plans and productivity in Japanese manufacturing firms'. *British Journal of Industrial Relations*, 31(3): 331–46.

KAARSEMAKER, E. (2006) *Employee Ownership and Human Resource Management: A Theoretical and Empirical Treatise with a Digression on the Dutch Context*. Doctoral Dissertation. Radboud University: Nijmegen.

KAARSEMAKER, E. and POUTSMA, E. (2006) 'The fit of employee ownership with other human resource management practices: theoretical and empirical suggestions regarding the existence of an ownership high-performance work system, or theory O'. *Economic and Industrial Democracy*, 27(2): 669–85.

KALMI, P., PENDLETON, A., and POUTSMA, E. (2006) 'The relationship between financial participation and other forms of employee participation: new survey evidence from Europe'. *Economic and Industrial Democracy*, 27(4): 637–67.

KATO, T. and MORISHIMA, M. (2002) 'The productivity effects of participatory employment practices: evidence from new Japanese panel data'. *Industrial Relations*, 41(4): 487–520.

KLEIN, K. (1987) 'Employee stock ownership and employee attitudes: a test of three models'. *Journal of Applied Psychology*, 72(2): 319–32.

KRUSE, D. (1996) 'Why do firms adopt profit sharing and employee ownership plans'. *British Journal of Industrial Relations*, 34(4): 515–38.

—— (2002) 'Research evidence on the prevalence and effects of employee ownership'. *Journal of Employee Ownership Law and Finance*, 14(4): 65–90.

—— and BLASI, J. (1997) 'Employee ownership, employee attitudes, and firm performance: a review of the evidence', in D. Lewin, D. Mitchell, and M. Zaira, (eds), *The Human Resource Management Handbook*. London: JAI Press.

—— —— and PARK, R. (2007) 'Shared capitalism in the U.S. economy: prevalence, characteristics, and employee views of financial participation in enterprises'. Paper presented for the Russell Sage/NBER Conference in New York City, October 2006.

—— FREEMAN, R., BLASI, J., BUCHELE, R., SCHARF, A., RODGERS, L., and MACKIN, C. (2004) 'Motivating employee-owners in ESOP firms: human resource policies and company performance', in V. Pérotin, and A. Robinson, (eds), *Employee Participation, Firm Performance and Survival*. Amsterdam: JAI Press.

KRUSE, D. L., BLASI, J. R., and PARK, R. (2008) 'Shared capitalism in the U.S. economy?' *Prevalence, Characteristics, and Employee Views of Financial Participation in Enterprises*. Cambridge, MA: NBER.

La PORTA, R., LOPEZ-DE-SILANES, F., SCHLEIFER, A., and VISHNY, R. (1997) 'Legal determinants of external finance'. *Journal of Finance*, 52, 1131–50.

LANDAU, I., MITCHELL, R., O'CONNELL, A., and RAMSAY, I. (2007) 'An overview of existing data on employee share ownership in Australia'. Research Report, University of Melbourne Law School.

LAZEAR, E. (2000) 'Performance pay and productivity'. *American Economic Review*, 90: 1346–61.

LENNE, J., MITCHELL, R., and RAMSAY, I. (2006) 'Employee share ownership schemes in Australia: a survey of key issues and themes'. *International Journal of Employment Studies*, 14: 1–34.

LOGUE, J. and YATES, J. (2001) *The Real World of Employee Ownership*. Ithaca, NY: Cornell University Press.

LONG, R. (1978) 'The relative effects of share ownership vs. control on job attitudes in an employee-owned company.' *Human Relations*, 31(9), 753–63.

—— (1980) 'Job attitudes and organizational performance under employee ownership'. *Academy of Management Journal*, 23(4), 726–37.

—— (1981) 'The effects of formal employee participation in ownership and decision-making on perceived and desired patterns of organizational influence: a longitudinal study'. *Human Relations*, 34(10): 847–76.

MAALØE, E. (1998) *The Employee Owner: Organizational and Individual Change within Manufacturing Companies as Participation and Sharing Grow and Expand.* Copenhagen: Academic Press.

MCNABB, R. and WHITFIELD, K. (1998) 'The impact of financial participation and employee involvement on financial performance'. *Scottish Journal of Political Economy,* 45(2): 171–89.

MEULBROEK, L. (2005) 'Company stock in pension plans: how costly is it?' *Journal of Law and Economics,* 48(2): 443–74.

MYGIND, N., DEMINA, N., GREGORIC, A., and KAPELYUSHNIKOV, R. (2006) 'Corporate Governance Cycles During Transition: A Comparison of Russia and Slovenia'. *Corporate Ownership & Control,* 3: 52–64.

National Center for Employee Ownership (2008).

OHKUSA, Y. and OHTAKE, F. (1997) 'The productivity effects of information sharing, profit sharing, and ESOPs'. *Journal of the Japanese and International Economies,* 11(3): 385–402.

OXERA (2007) *Tax-advantaged Employee Share Schemes: Analysis of Productivity Effects.* London: HM Revenue and Customs.

OYER, P. (2004) 'Why do firms use incentives that have no incentive effects?' *Journal of Finance,* 59: 1619–49.

PENDLETON, A. (1997) 'Characteristics of workplaces with financial participation: evidence from the WIRS'. *Industrial Relations Journal,* 28: 103–19.

—— (2001) *Employee Ownership, Participation and Governance: A Study of ESOPs in the UK.* London and New York: Routledge.

—— (2005) 'Employee share ownership, employment relationships, and corporate governance', in B. Harley, J. Hyman, and P. Thompson, (eds), *Participation and Democracy at Work: Essays in Honour of Harvie Ramsay.* London: Palgrave.

—— (2006) 'Incentives, monitoring, and employee stock ownership plans: new evidence and interpretations'. *Industrial Relations,* 45(4): 753–77.

—— (2008) 'Do participants in employee share ownership plans acquire too many shares?' Unpublished *mimeo.*

—— (2009) 'Employee participation in employee share ownership: an evaluation of the factors associated with participation and contributions in Save As You Earn plans'. *British Journal of Management,* forthcoming.

—— Poutsma, E., Brewster, C., and Van Ommeren, J. (2001) *Employee Share Ownership and Profit Sharing in the European Union.* Dublin: European Foundation for the Improvement of Living and Working Conditions.

—— —— Van Ommeren, J., and Brewster, C. (2003) 'The incidence and determinants of employee share ownership and profit sharing in Europe', in T. Kato and J. Pliskin (eds), *The Determinants of the Incidence and the Effects of Participatory Organizations.* Amsterdam: JAI Press.

—— and Robinson, A. (2008) 'Employee share ownership and productivity: an interaction-based approach'. Unpublished paper.

—— Wilson, N. and Wright, M. (1998) 'The perception and effects of share ownership: empirical evidence from employee buy-outs'. *British Journal of Industrial Relations,* 36(1): 99–123.

PÉROTIN, V. and Robinson, A. (2003) 'Employee participation in profit and ownership: a review of the issues and evidence.' Luxembourg: European Parliament.

PIERCE, J., KOSTOVA, T., and DIRKS, K. (2001) 'Towards a theory of psychological ownership in organizations.' *Academy of Management Review,* 26(2): 298–310.

PIERCE, J., KOSTOVA, T., and DIRKS, K. (2003) 'The state of psychological ownership: integrating and extending a century of research'. *Review of General Psychology,* 7(1): 84–107.

—— —— RUBENFELD, S., and Morgan, S. (1991) 'Employee ownership: a conceptual model of process and effects'. *Academy of Management Review,* 16(1): 121–44.

PLISKIN, J. and JONES, D. (1997) 'Determinants of the incidence of group incentives: evidence from Canada'. *The Canadian Journal of Economics,* (30)4: 1027.

POOLE, M. (1989) *The Origins of Economic Democracy: Profit-Sharing and Employee-Shareholding Schemes.* London: Routledge.

POUTSMA, E. (2001) 'Recent trends in employee financial participation in the European Union'. Luxembourg: Office for Official Publications of the European Communities.

—— Hendrickx, J., and Huijgen, F. (2003) 'Employee participation in Europe: in search of the participative workplace'. *Economic and Industrial Democracy,* 24: 45–76.

—— and Huijgen, F. (1999) 'European diversity in the use of participation schemes'. *Economic and Industrial Democracy,* 20: 197–223.

—— KALMI, P., and PENDLETON, A. (2006) 'The relationship between financial participation and other forms of employee participation: new survey evidence from Europe.' *Economic and Industrial Democracy,* 27(2): 637–68.

POUTSMA, E., LIGTHART, P., and SCHOUTEN, R. (2005) 'Employee share ownership in Europe. The influence of US Multinationals'. *Management Revue,* 16(1): 99–122.

PRENDERGAST, C. (1999) 'The provision of incentives in firms'. *Journal of Economic Literature,* 37: 7–63.

—— (2002) 'The tenuous trade-off between risk and incentives'. *The Journal of Political Economy,* 110(5): 1071.

RAMSAY, H. (1977) 'Cycles of control: worker participation in sociological and historical perspective'. *Sociology,* 11: 481–506.

RHODES, S. and STEERS, R. (1981) 'Conventional vs. worker-owned organizations'. *Human Relations,* 34(12): 1013–35.

ROBINSON, A. and WILSON, N. (2006) 'Employee financial participation and productivity: an empirical reappraisal'. *British Journal of Industrial Relations,* 44(1): 31–50.

—— and Zhang, H. (2005) 'Employee share ownership: safeguarding investments in human capital'. *British Journal of Industrial Relations,* 43(3): 469–88.

ROSEN, C., CASE, J., and STAUBUS, M. (2005) *Equity: Why Employee Ownership is Good for Business.* Boston, MA: Harvard Business School Press.

—— KLEIN, K., and YOUNG, K. (1986) *Employee Ownership in America: The Equity Solution.* Lexington, MA: Lexington Books.

ROUSSEAU, D. and Shperling, Z. (2003) 'Pieces of the action: ownership and the changing employment relationship'. *Academy of Management Review,* 28: 553–70.

Russell, R., Hochner, A., and Perry, S. (1979) 'Participation, influence, and worker-ownership'. *Industrial Relations,* 18(3): 330–41.

SENGUPTA, S. (2008) 'The impact of employee-share-ownership schemes on performance in unionized and non-unionized workplaces'. *Industrial Relations Journal,* 39(3): 170–90.

—— Whitfield, K., and McNabb, R. (2007) 'Employee share ownership and performance: golden path or golden handcuffs?' *International Journal of Human Resource Management,* 18(8): 1507–38.

SESIL, J., KROUMOVA, M., BLASI, J., and KRUSE, D. (2002), 'Broad-based employee stock options in US 'new economy' firms,' *British Journal of Industrial Relations,* 40: 273–94.

STERN, R., WHYTE, W., HAMMER, T., and MEEK, G. (1983) 'The union and the transition to employee ownership', in W. Whyte, T. Hammer, C. Meek, and R. Stern (eds), *Worker Participation and Ownership*. Ithaca, NY: ILR Press.

US General Accounting Office. (1987) *Employee stock ownership plans: little evidence of effects on corporate performance* (Office Report to the Chairman, Committee on Finance, U.S. Senate no. GAO/PEMD-88-1). Washington, DC: General Accounting Office.

UVALIC, M. (ed.) (1991) *The Promotion of Employee Participation in Profits and Enterprise Results*. Social Europe, Supplement 3/91, Commission of the European Communities, Office for Official Publications of the European Communities, Luxembourg.

VAUGHAN-WHITEHEAD, D. (1995) *Workers' Financial Participation: East-West Experiences*. Geneva: International Labour Office.

WAGNER, S., PARKER, C., and CHRISTIANSEN, N. (2003) 'Employees that think and act like owners: effects of ownership beliefs and behaviors on organizational effectiveness'. *Personnel Psychology*, 56(4): 847–71.

WELZ, C. and FERNÁNDEZ-MACÍAS, E. (2008) 'Financial participation of employees in the European Union: much ado about nothing?' *European Journal of Industrial Relations, 14* (4), 479–97.

YERMACK, D. (1995) 'Do corporations award CED stock options effectively?' *Journal of Financial Economics*, 39(2–3): 237–69.

CHAPTER 14

FINANCIAL PARTICIPATION

IAN KESSLER

FINANCIAL participation is a mechanism by which employees are provided with a stake in the performance or ownership of an organization. This stake is reflected in remunerative arrangements, typically in the form of a payment linked to a corporate outcome measure or to an allocation of shares in the company (Vaughan-Whitehead, 1995: 1). It is a mechanism which has attracted considerable interest from policymakers, practitioners, and academics. This interest derives from the hybrid nature of financial participation: it is as likely to be considered in the context of developing a reward system as it is in debates on forms of employee participation and involvement. However, its potential potency as a form of employee participation cannot be doubted, not only directly involving workers in corporate financial performance with a payout of some kind, but also providing the basis for broader staff engagement with the kind of organizational decision making likely to affect that performance.

The extensive interest can also be linked to the diverse and significant implications associated with financial participation as it addresses some of the key tenets underpinning capitalist economies. Financial participation challenges the traditional distribution of corporate outcomes, whether as profits or other gains, and even more fundamentally confronts established property and ownership rights where based upon the allocation of company shares to employees. Founded upon such radical principles, it is not surprising that this form of participation has attracted contributions from various academic disciplines. The debates stimulated are highlighted by the spectrum of political views voiced about financial participation. Some have seen it as a form of 'popular capitalism', which by extending ownership and profit distribution more widely to employees strengthens the prevailing economic system (Rosen and Young, 1991: 4). Others have regarded it as a means of subverting this system, especially if manifest in full employee ownership of companies or control of profits. Psychologists have interrogated the assumptions surrounding this political hyperbole, considering whether such participation really does affect employee attitudes and behaviours. In contrast, financial commentators have been preoccupied by the possible influence of such participation on the nature of corporate governance. While the economic consequences of such participation in terms of earnings, employment, and productivity at societal and organizational levels have stimulated interest among researchers and policymakers.

This chapter presents a structured and systematic overview of the character, use and consequences of financial participation, with a view to exploring the contributions made by these different research communities to ongoing debate and understanding. In doing so, it also provides a map to facilitate movement through the considerable volume of material on the topic. It is divided into the following parts: the first, considers approaches to financial participation; the second, the adoption of schemes; and finally, outcomes of various kinds.

Approaches to Financial Participation

Approaches to financial participation comprise two elements: design and objectives. It is a testament to the importance of this form of participation to various stakeholders that these elements have been sensitive to the interests of both organizations and governments. While organizations have had considerable discretion in designing schemes which reflect their own needs and circumstances, states in many developed countries have also had their own independent agendas encouraging support for particular types of scheme in pursuit of discrete political, economic and social aims.

Design

Financial participation is a generic label for a number of schemes, varying along dimensions that most crucially relate to the nature of participation, the level of participation and eligibility for participation. The forms taken by financial participation along these dimensions helps account for the diverse views that such an approach has attracted; whether or not financial participation has radical organizational or societal consequences might well depend on the character of the scheme in question.

The *nature* of financial participation revolves around whether employees directly participate in the distribution of organizational outcomes, typically in the form of a cash-based payout, or in the ownership of the company where they acquire shares in it. There are hybrid schemes which combine cash and shares: for example, cash linked to an organizational outcome may be used to buy shares on behalf of the employees. The Wage Earner Funds introduced in Sweden from the mid-1980s provide an example of this hybrid approach. These funds were financed by a tax on 'excess' profits and used to buy shares in Swedish companies (Whyman, 2006). Clearly, it is also the case that the value of shares to employees may well be realized only when they are sold to generate a cash sum. However, it is a significant distinction with implications for the way in which schemes are structured and operated. Pendleton et al. (2001:9) highlight the ways in which cash and share-based schemes might vary according to:

- the liquidity of payment (cash versus shares);
- the timescale of the reward (current versus future benefits);
- the immediacy of the link (direct versus indirect); and
- the perspective (cash-based schemes looking backwards on past corporate performance and share-based forward to potential performance).

Profit sharing is the most commonly cited form of cash-based scheme, with the employee payout triggered when profits reach a certain level or improve by a certain proportion over a given period. This payout is usually in the form of a lump sum provided to the employee in addition to base pay and comprising a non-consolidated, variable element of earnings. Profit is not the only organizational outcome used to generate such a cash payment, although other financial outcomes are most often adopted in the context of gain sharing schemes. Two such schemes, in currency for over fifty years and using outcomes perceived as more sensitive to employee behaviour than profit, have received particular prominence: the Rucker and Scanlon Plans. The Scanlon Plan is founded on a baseline ratio of labour costs to the sales value of production; while the Rucker Plan is rooted in the ratio of labour costs to production value (actual net sales plus or minus inventory changes, minus outside purchased material and services, www.qualitydigest.com/jul/gainshre.html, accessed 27.9.07). An improvement or gain in this ratio stimulates a payment which, as the term implies, is shared between employer and employee on an agreed basis. More recently, gain sharing schemes have moved towards less complex formulae, being based upon the sharing of productivity gains or quality improvements. (Harrington, 2000: 326).

Shares can also be distributed in different ways. A given proportion may be allocated to employees free of charge or on preferential terms at issue. Alternatively, employees may be given an option to buy a number of shares on a deferred basis, over an extended period at a particular price. In Britain, the Save-As-You-Earn Employee Share Owning Scheme is an example of the latter approach. This is a scheme approved by the government which allows employees to save on a regular basis to buy shares at a given price and make gains if the price appreciates over that period with a reduced tax liability. On a slightly grander scale, Employee Share Ownership Plans (ESOP) involve a loan to an employee benefit trust, which then purchases company stock and distributes it through periodic payments to each employee's ESOP account (Vaughan-Whitehead, 1995: 2).

The *level* of participation is an issue of scale, the degree of employee involvement in a scheme. Schemes vary in terms of the proportion of total profits and shares allocated to employees: the higher the proportion the higher the level of participation. However, such schemes provide the basis for another, less direct form of involvement. This is a participative infrastructure, for instance, in the form of suggestion schemes or joint management and employee or union committees which allow for some influence over organizational performance. The rationale for this infrastructure is a 'line of sight' which claims that the effect of financial participation is likely to depend on whether workers can influence corporate outcomes. This feature is particularly explicit in gain sharing. As Wilson and Bowey (1982: 348) note:

Management-worker co-operation in the Scanlon Plan is effected through productivity committees consisting of representatives of both management and unions ... This is, perhaps, the key feature of the Scanlon plan that has led to so much of its success, since the productivity committees enable the workforce to genuinely participate in the management of their jobs.

This supportive infrastructure is not, however, an intrinsic feature of financial participation, its presence being a key differentiator between schemes in practice.

Finally, financial participation schemes vary along the eligibility dimension, being open to the whole workforce or restricted to particular sections. The tax benefits provided by state sponsored schemes have typically been founded on the condition that they are open to all workers. This is the case with the British SAYE scheme and the more recent Share Incentive Plan which allows companies to give all employees up to £3,000 worth of shares a year. It is also a feature of statutory schemes in France which cover profit sharing and share ownership schemes (Vaughan-Whitehead, 1995). However companies developing their own schemes have scope to be more exclusive, limiting coverage to particular groups, say executives, or varying payouts according to individual performance.

Objectives

Financial participation has been underpinned by a varied range of objectives. It follows that the intention of a scheme needs to be empirically established. Poutsma (2001: 21) provides a fairly exhaustive list of the aims 'at company level' for financial participation—a bundle of 'positive' reasons:

- generating productivity increases
- enhancing flexibility of remuneration
- gaining tax advantages
- providing employee benefits

and a further cluster of 'negative' reasons:

- discouraging union
- defending against a takeover
- financing a troubled company.

Many of these reasons can be extended from the company to the societal level, informing government attempts to encourage financial participation. Productivity gains and wage flexibility, in particular, are macroeconomic objectives with implications for national growth, employment, and earnings levels. In addition, however, national government support for such schemes has been driven by ideological and normative considerations. In Britain, the privatization of utilities instigated by Margaret Thatcher's Conservative Government in the 1980s was often accompanied by the issue of shares to employees as way of harnessing their support. For example, the privatization of British Telecommunications in 1984 was accompanied by the issuing of fifty-four shares free to every employee. Less instrumental aims can also be indentified, with states viewing financial participation as part of a social justice or rights agenda, linking schemes to notions of industrial citizenship and economic democracy. As Gordon Brown, then British Chancellor, noted in introducing statutory support for employee share ownership in 2000: 'So that millions of hard working people have a stake in the business whose wealth they create, we will remove the old barriers to a new share owning democracy' (quoted in Michie and Oughton, 2005). It is noteworthy that the European Union, in encouraging financial participation over recent years, has viewed it as a way of 'achieving a wider distribution of wealth generated by the enterprise which the employed persons have helped to produce' (Poutsma, 2001: 21).

The company-level objectives distinguished by Poutsma (2001) are essentially predicated on the assumption that financial participation might contribute to corporate 'success'. Some focus on how financial participation secures such success by encouraging positive employee attitudes and behaviours; others place greater emphasis on its potential to reduce labour cost. Giving employees a stake in the company might encourage a greater organizational commitment, which translates into higher productivity. This might be an affective commitment, with such participation encouraging an emotional attachment to the company, or an instrumental commitment deriving from the additional reward promised by it. Alternatively, the payout to the employee might more directly feed through to 'desired' behaviours without the mediating effect of attitudinal change. The treatment of financial participation by the human resource management literature reflects this distinction. Viewed as part of a 'high commitment' bundle of management practices, profit sharing and employee share ownership are assumed to create an emotional attachment to the organization which encourages positive behaviours (Richardson and Thompson, 1999). Seen as a 'high-performance' technique, they are seen to acquire an incentive effect which impacts more directly on productivity (Wood, 1999).

At the same time, it might be argued that financial participation has negative organizational affects; demotivating employees, fostering negative behaviours and generating higher costs. Such participation often requires employees to take a heightened share of the risks associated with fluctuating company performance; with employees typically risk adverse, this might require a premium to compensate for the heightened uncertainty. The increased likelihood of 'free-riding', the ability of employees to 'hide' and yet still benefit where pay is linked to the aggregate measure of company performance, might also dampen employee enthusiasm.

The use of financial participation to discourage trade unions might also be seen to fall within attempts to deploy such schemes to change employee attitudes and behaviours. Where employee rewards rely on the performance of the company rather than the efforts of trade union negotiators, workers might shift their allegiance from the latter to the former. As Scanlon (1948: 60) highlights in a case study of gain sharing in a US company, 'Beginning with 1938 for six consecutive years the (gainsharing) bonus was paid. The employees were well aware of the fact that they were receiving this bonus for staying out of the union.'

Trade unions have typically been suspicious of financial participation. In providing advice to its members on profit sharing, one British trade union noted, 'The real danger of profit related pay is that it is often an attempt to take part of the paybill out of the collective bargaining arena, where employees through their unions have a voice, into the domain of management discretion' (IPCS, 1988). However, trade union views on such schemes have not been unambiguously hostile. Unions have found it difficult to resist the enhanced benefits of schemes, especially where they have complemented rather than substituted for regular pay increases. Indeed, in Brazil (Zylberstajn, 2002) the union position has been safeguarded by a constitutional obligation on employers to implement profit and share ownership schemes through the medium of collective bargaining. More generally, such schemes have also been viewed as providing an opportunity for unions to leverage their influence: if members' pay is likely to depend on strategic, board level decisions, related to such issues as product development and capital investment which determine profit, then there is a case for unions being involved in such decision making.

The use of financial participation to gain tax advantages and develop greater wage flexibility suggests a relationship with corporate performance-driven less by changes in employee attitudes and behaviour and more by certain cost benefits or efficiencies. The tax advantages which derive from government approved schemes certainly have value to employees as the direct beneficiaries with a reduced financial burden on incomes or capital gains. However, the employer has much to gain as well, with tax advantages providing an opportunity to generate better value for money from the paybill. More significantly, profit sharing has been presented as a means of building into the pay determination process a strong affordability element. This view (Weitzman, 1984), significantly influencing public policy developments in the UK and the US in the 1980s and 1990s, suggests that by linking pay to profits, organizations create a mechanism which provides high pay-outs when the company is best placed to afford them, while deflating increases in 'troubled times'. The workers also stand to benefit from such a system, as the automatic reduction of paybill costs in the context of weak corporate performance negates the need for job losses.

The empirical evidence on the kinds of managerial objectives underpinning the introduction of financial participation places considerable weight upon employee attitudes. A survey of around 500 companies from across the European Unions (Van Den Blucke, 1999) found the most popular reasons were 'to encourage employees to take a greater interest in the success of the company' and 'to create a feeling amongst employees of belonging to one company and sharing common goals'; those goals which were related to productivity and cost-efficient remuner-ation were much less commonly cited. Kruse (1996) in a longitudinal study of a similar number of US companies finds a more mixed picture. Exploring the importance of goals close to those identified by Poutsma (2001) he finds some support for productivity-related motives, with higher research and development expenditure among those firms who had previously introduced profit sharing, and flexibility-related motives, with higher variance in profits prior to the adoption of a scheme.

The design and range of objectives underpinning the use of financial participa-tions raise a number of questions. The first relates to actual practice: what types of scheme are being adopted? The second touches upon patterns of take-up: are there patterns in the implementation of profit sharing and employee share ownership schemes? The third is associated with outcomes: to what extent does evidence support the achievement of the aims outlined. These questions are addressed in the succeeding sections.

Implementation and Patterns of Practice

The adoption of financial participation has been sensitive to a variety of influences across time and space. These have been reflected in a number of analytical approaches:

Time:

- A political economy approach suggesting a link to changes in industrial development.
- A management-style approach proposing a link to shifts in managerial values and beliefs.

Space:

- A national employment systems approach relating patterns to institutional differences between countries in the regulation of the employment relationship.
- A contingency approach positing an association with features of an organization, its workforce or industry.

Financial participation has a long history. Peach and Wren (1992: 13) point to the profit sharing arrangements 'recognised as early as 1775 by French economist, A. R. J. Turgot and practised by the Parisian house painting firm *Maison Leclaire*'; while Schloss (1907) writing about developments at the end of the nineteenth century can point to forty-nine employers with profit sharing schemes from a variety of industries. From these early days the difficulties associated with these schemes were fully recognized. Marriot (1971: 179) reports on an American survey undertaken in 1896 which showed that of fifty plans noted at the time, thirty-three had been abandoned permanently.

Despite these acknowledged problems the popularity of such schemes has continued to 'wax and wane'. Mathews (1989), tracing the start-up of profit sharing schemes in Britain between 1880 and 1940, shows a pattern of 'decline and fall' with a peak every ten years. Ramsay (1977) suggests such cycles reflect the balance of power between labour and capital: in times of worker strength management seeks to extend employee participation so attempting to 'defuse' potential resistance. Mathew's (1989: 445) analysis provides some support for this model, noting an increase in the introduction of profit sharing at times of industrial unrest and a decline during more peaceful periods. However, it is a view which does not fit easily with the continued and increasing popularity of financial participation in countries where union strength has been on the wane. In Britain, for example, there has been a significant growth in the number and coverage of profit sharing schemes at a time of relative union weakness; thus, the number of approved profit-related pay schemes rose from 1,175 covering 232,000 employees in 1990 to 12,740 schemes embracing 3,596,000 workers in 1996 (IDS Report, 1996).

While the implementation of financial participation varies over time in any given country as a response to shifting social, political, and economic conditions, differences in the national take-up of schemes endure. This suggests deep-seated values and institutions which influence national choices on the adoption of financial participation. Poole (1989: 27) provides one of the most comprehensive analytical frameworks for exploring such differences, pointing to the influence of statutory frameworks, as well as labour and management ideologies, on patterns of financial participation between countries.

Certainly data from various sources highlight these national differences. The Employee Participation in Organizational Change survey undertaken by the European Foundation for the Improvement of Living and Working Conditions in 1996 found that in organizations with fifty employees or more, countries coalesced into three groups in adopting profit sharing: the UK and France where a significant proportion of organizations had introduced a scheme, 40 per cent and 57 per cent respectively; Sweden, the Netherlands, and Germany where a noteworthy but smaller proportion of organizations had done so, between 10 per cent and 20 per cent; and Portugal and Italy where very few organizations had taken-up a scheme, around 5 per cent. There was much less evidence of variation by country in the case of share ownership schemes with the UK standing alone as a country where a noteworthy proportion of organizations, around a quarter, had a scheme; in all other countries the figure was well below 10 per cent.

The data collected by the CRANET study, covering organizations with 200 or more employees, confirm these findings. There are, however, some differences: in the Netherlands, along with the UK and France, larger organizations were likely to have profit sharing schemes; while France and the Netherlands also joined the UK in having a significant proportion of organizations, around a quarter, with share ownership schemes. (Pendleton and Poutsma, 2004: 16). These surveys are not, however, particularly sensitive to the coverage of schemes or more particularly to how open they are to different occupational groups. A more recent survey of over 150 companies across the EU suggests that countries, such as Denmark and the UK, were much more likely to have schemes restricted to management only, while others, for instance, France, the Netherlands, and Finland, extended their schemes to all employees (Poutsma, 2006: 16).

These findings lend support to the influence of the state on the take-up of financial participation schemes between countries. It has been noted that, 'the incidence of profit-sharing, as revealed by the 1999 CRANET survey correlates with the presence of legislation encouraging the use of profit sharing in some form'

(Pendleton and Poutsma, 2004: 17). Indeed, there are signs that path dependent cultural values might also account for the patterns. The relatively extensive use of profit sharing in France, for instance, reflects the long standing use of financial participation as management practice and mechanism for regulating relations between labour and capital (Pendleton and Poutsma, 2004: 21–2). It has also been suggested that patterns of corporate governance help explain these differences. In seeking to explain higher levels of financial participation in Britain than in Germany and France, Kabst et al. (2006: 575) note, 'As the degree of sophistication of the UK capital markets as well as acceptance of capital investments within the British population is more widespread in comparison to Germany and France, employee share ownership is more likely to be seen in British organizations.'

The final approach suggests that there may be features of industries, organizations, work, and employment which cut across national differences to influence the take-up of financial participation. Agency theory, the predominant model for the study of financial participation, has implicitly been based on a notion of contingency. Financial participation is seen as a means of aligning the interests of principal and agent where the costs of direct monitoring and individual incentives are prohibitively high, a situation particularly likely in the case of certain employee groups, such as management or those working with technologies, allowing considerable worker discretion. However, reviewing the research on these relationships Pendleton (2006: 758) concludes that 'Empirical findings relating to the nature of job tasks and work technology provide mainly unsupportive evidence for the view that share ownership plans are used to ameliorate monitoring costs in complex work settings.' Drawing upon data from the British Workplace Employment relations survey, 1998, he finds that rather than substituting for monitoring and individual incentives, share ownership may well complement, compensating for the weak motivation effects of such mechanisms.

The adoption of financial participation has also been related to features of organizational structure. For instance, across the European Union smaller organizations and family-owned businesses are much less likely to have any form of financial participation, perhaps reflecting concerns about diluting ownership rights. Financial participation has also been found to vary by industry, being particularly prominent in financial and banking services. One contingent factor, which has been consistently explored, has been union presence. Again the evidence is far from conclusive, perhaps reflecting union ambiguity on schemes. There are studies from Canada (Long, 1989), the US (Cooke, 1994), Germany (Heywood et al., 1998) and Britain (Poole, 1989) which suggest that unionization is negatively related to the presence of profit sharing, but other studies from the same countries show no association between union presence and such schemes (Gregg and Machin, 1988; Kruse, 1993).

IMPACT

Process

Much of the research on financial participation has concentrated on its impact, but before considering this work, it is worth dwelling on the issue of process as it relates to profit sharing and employee share ownership: *how* schemes are adopted and run in practice. This is often overlooked by researchers, perhaps reflecting an assumption that in operational terms such schemes are relatively unproblematic, mechanistically conforming to fixed rules associated with eligibility and distribution. The neglect of process, however, risks obscuring the contested nature of financial participation. It also obscures the possibility that the way a scheme is designed, implemented, and operated may well affect its impact.

Hyman and Mason's (1995) distinction between involvement and participation helps draw attention to the different ways in which profit sharing and employee share ownership schemes might be used within an organizational context comprising competing worker and management interests. As a mechanism for employee *involvement* such schemes are seen as driven by management in pursuit of sectional goals linked to corporate outcomes with joint decision making limited to narrow task-related activities; as a basis for employee *participation* such schemes are viewed more as a response to the collective interest of the workforce, allowing employee influence over power-related issues. Ben-Ner and Jones (1995) build upon this distinction in noting that financial participation can generate two types of employee rights: rights of control which entail determination of the objectives of the organization, the positions that individuals occupy, and the functions they perform; and rights of return which include the 'financial and physical pay-off generated from the operation of the organisation'. While cash-based schemes appear more likely to generate rights of return and shares ownership rights of control, it remains an empirical question as to just what rights are generated by particular schemes in a given context. More to the point, such a distinction encourages a focus on how the configuration of rights under a scheme affects the balance of power between labour and capital.

There have been relatively few attempts to explore the influence of rights and power on the introduction or operation of financial participation. An exception is Collins's (1995) work on the 'death' of a gain sharing scheme in a US manufacturing firm during the late 1980s. He identified a range of 'political games' played by those with a stake in the scheme. The most common of these were 'calculation games', which involved managerial manipulation of the bonus calculation to minimize payouts. Other games included those relating to the operation of the joint board reviewing the scheme, with attempts to tamper with the agenda as a means of pursuing respective management–non-management interests; and 'suggestion scheme games', where, for instance, management underfunded the implementation of suggestions so reducing the likely cost benefits and, in turn, payouts under the gain sharing scheme.

Recognition that financial participation schemes are underpinned by a political process connects to a long-standing acknowledgement in the industrial relations literature that the *way* in which a reward system is developed can be as important to its 'success' as its design (Bowey et al., 1982). Support for this proposition in the context of financial participation is found in the work of Kim (1999) who high-lighted that the survival of gain sharing plans in American and Canadian firms was related to union involvement in their administration. It is also reflected in the experimental work of Cooper et al. (1992) which revealed that the social dilemmas around 'free-riding' were ameliorated if organizations used fair distribution rules in gain sharing schemes developed on a participative basis.

There has also been some research on the obstacles to the further development of financial participation. A survey of companies in six EU countries found that the legal framework, often too complicated and restrictive, was the main barrier, although over half of the companies also suggested that the administrative costs associated with schemes were prohibitively high. While acknowledging general difficulties, this survey, in addition, highlighted some differences in barriers between countries. For example, while in most countries trade unions were not seen as a major obstacle, in Spain they were viewed as a significant barrier; moreover Finland stood out as a country where the employees were simply not interested in the long-term benefits associated with schemes (Poutsma, 2006).

Consequences

The absence of work on process issues associated with financial participation is partly related to the relative dearth of case study work on schemes, a method-ology well suited to exploring the complexities associated with their ongoing operation. Those researching financial participation have mainly adopted quan-titative approaches, particularly in studying the consequences of profit sharing and employee share ownership. This methodological bias has implications for developing an understanding of outcomes. Given the range of objectives under-pinning the use of financial participation, the aims of a scheme can never be assumed. Surveys often look at outcomes without any consideration of intention. It is noteworthy that researchers routinely assume that financial participation is part of a 'high commitment' bundle of management practices, while it could equally be used as part of cost minimization strategies. This is not to deny the possible effects of schemes regardless of intent, but such an approach is still founded on an under-theorized view on the relationship between schemes and consequences which ignores intention and meaning.

A considerable proportion of the studies are also cross-sectional leaving open questions about the direction of causation. It is also the case that in practice, few surveys have sought to explore the relationship between attitudinal, behavioural, and corporate outcomes. Certainly hypothesized models have been put forward theorizing these relationships (Pierce et al., 1991) but few have been fully tested.

Research on the consequences of financial participation has largely revolved around the achievement of corporate and broader societal objectives for such schemes. There has been work on macroeconomic effects, especially on whether the use of profit sharing affects employment, with findings calling into question this link (Blanchflower and Oswald, 1988). There have also been studies on the impact of schemes on the role of the unions, again the findings suggesting that this appears to be limited (Pendleton et al., 1995) As Pendleton et al. (2001: 23) note in a EU-wide study: 'There is no evidence that any form of financial participation weakens the representative role of trade unions or works councils within an enterprise.'

Much of the research has been pitched at the corporate level and focused on employee organizational performance, employee attitudes, behaviour, and organizational outcomes. These outcomes are considered in turn.

Attempts to explore the relationship between financial participation and corporate performance have used various outcomes measures, including financial performance measures, such as return on capital employed, sales per employee, or simply sales turnover (for summary of measures adopted by studies see OXERA, 2007). The findings from this research point in the same direction, providing support for a positive relationship between financial participation and these outcomes. This was the main finding of a review undertaken by Kruse and Blasi (1995) of twenty-seven mainly US studies. This relationship has continued to hold in studies in other countries as well. For example, a recent study in the UK on the productivity effects of tax advantaged employee share schemes (OXERA, 2007), found long run productivity increases among those firms using such schemes. There has, however, been a growing interest in exploring this relationship further with a recognition that it may be contingent. As Long (2000: 477) has stressed:

Although there is substantial evidence that, on average, employee profit sharing improves company performance, little is known about the conditions under which it does so or the mechanisms through which it operates.

The investigation of these conditions and mechanisms has been along two lines. The first has considered whether the use of financial participation in combination with other, complementary practices is conducive to a positive relationship between financial participation and corporate performance. Such an approach is part of a broader perspective which views 'bundles' of human resource management practices as more likely to impact positively on organizational performance than disconnected or isolated initiatives. In fact this is a stream of thought that connects to traditional debates on financial participation, particularly related to gain sharing schemes, which prescribed the value of supportive employee involvement systems. Recent evidence provides some support for this relationship. Long's Canadian study found that where firms used profit sharing in combination with a 'high-involvement' management philosophy and extensive communication about schemes they had better organizational outcomes. Pendleton (1997) using British Workplace Employment Relations data similarly found that there was a strong link between schemes and outcomes in workplaces that used information sharing mechanisms and had white-collar union recognition agreements.

The second line of investigation has looked at the form of financial participation in considering impact on organizational outcomes. Robinson and Wilson (2006) suggest that cash-based arrangements are likely to create a more direct link between employee efforts and profits which leads to a strong but short-term productivity impact, while share-based schemes create a more deep-seated shift in employee attitudes and behaviour which affects productivity in a more sustained way. This view finds support from a British study on tax advantaged financial participation schemes indicating that while firms using Save as You Earn employee share ownership schemes have a 4.1 per cent long run improvement in productivity, those using the Approved Profit Sharing schemes show no significant improvement (OXERA, 2007).

There have been few attempts to explore the different routes by which cash and share-based schemes might affect organizational outcomes, in other words considering whether the changes in employee attitudes feed through to influence corporate performance. There have, however, been a number of studies which have explored whether financial participation schemes do in fact shift employee attitudes in predicted ways, and especially whether they lead to higher levels of employee commitment. The theoretical models underpinning this relationship have tended to become more refined over the years. Early research produced mixed results on whether financial participation was associated with positive or negative employee attitudes. A longitudinal study by Dunne et al. (1991) covering employees in a UK manufacturing firm found no difference in attitudes between those who were involved and not involved in the share ownership scheme, although those who were not involved but considered joining developed negative views over time. The development of negative attitudes was also highlighted in a US study by Kruse (1984), a finding related to the weakening of employee involvement over the years. In contrast Poole and Jenkins in a survey covering some 2,000 UK employees concluded 'that the argument that employee financial participation is linked with a positive set of attitudes on a wide range of aspects of company policy clearly received considerable support from this inquiry' (1990: 327).

More recent studies have sought to build upon this work by exploring mechanisms by which employee attitudes might change under such schemes. Pendleton et al. (1998), for example, propose a two-stage model that suggests that any commitment generated by employee buyout schemes is dependent on employees developing a genuine sense of ownership, which is seen to derive from relatively high levels of share ownership. Coyle Shapiro et al. (2002) in a longitudinal study of around 140 UK employees in an aerospace company found that positive employee attitudes were crucially related to employees viewing profit sharing as an act of reciprocity on the part of management: if employees felt profit sharing was provided by the organization in exchange for their contribution, they were more likely to trust management and be commitment to the organization.

A final stream of research on the consequence of financial participation has concentrated on behavioural outcomes. Such outcomes are a crucial link between attitudinal change and improved organizational performance. As noted earlier, 'desired' behaviours might well be generated directly by financial participation without the need for an attitudinal shift but hypothesized models have tended to view the organizational commitment generated by financial participation as encouraging behavioural shifts. Pendleton et al. (1998) found that a feeling of psychological ownership generated by schemes fed through to commitment and then to behaviours such as a willingness to 'work harder' for the company. Similarly Chiu and Wei-Chi (2007) found that organizational commitment mediated the relationship between the combined use of cash and stock-based schemes and organizational citizenship behaviour in their survey of employees in a Taiwanese electronic company.

The behavioural consequences of financial participation have not always been clearly set out in analytical models seeking to explore the impact of schemes. Pierce et al. (1991), for example, simply note 'behavioural responses' to financial partici- pation, without unpacking the form these might take; while Florowski (1987) conflates a range of organizational and employee outcomes. However, research on behavioural outcomes has typically focused on employee productivity, turn- over, and absenteeism. The theorized link between such behaviour and organiza- tional performance has rested in large part on agency theory; however, human capital theory has also informed some of these models. Thus, in providing greater wage and labour cost flexibility in response to shifting economic conditions, profit sharing helps ensure greater employment stability and a return of the investment by employers in the training of their staff. Robinson and Zhang's (2005) work on employee share ownership schemes provides some conformation of the link between financial participation and the acquisition, and retention of skills along the lines predicted by human capital theory. They find that employee participation rates in employee share ownership schemes are likely to increase in workplaces where skill acquisition takes time and the majority of workers require and receive extensive training.

There is also some support for a relationship between financial participation and lower rates of turnover and absenteeism. Wilson and Peel (1991) found that quit rates and absenteeism were lower in over fifty UK engineering firms where profit sharing and other forms of participation were in place. In a survey of men in non-union jobs between 1988 and 1994, Azfar and Danninger (2001) revealed that those covered by profit sharing were less likely to quit their jobs. They also noted that these men were likely to receive more frequent training. Arthur and Jelf's (1999) longitudinal study highlighted that the introduction of gain sharing schemes was followed by a gradual and permanent decline in absenteeism; while similar findings were revealed by Brown et al. (1999) in the case of employee share owning schemes introduced across 127 French firms.

Other, less mainstream behavioural measures have been used to explore the impact of financial participation. Arthur and Aiman-Smith (2001), for example, draw upon the notion of double-loop learning to consider what impact gain sharing has upon the volume and nature of suggestions in organizations. In a survey of employees in a US manufacturing plant, they revealed that there was limited scope for gain sharing to generate 'first order' incremental suggestions on change to established routines and that these quickly tended to peter out. They were replaced, however, by more radical and innovative 'second order' suggestions, which increased over time. In one of the few attempts to measure the before and after behavioural affects on the shift to financial participation, Hatcher and Ross (1991) found that the shift from piecework to gain sharing in a US manufacturing organization was associated with a decrease in employee grievances and improvement in product with lower defect rates.

Summary and Conclusion

Financial participation has been an enduring feature of the social, political, and economic landscape since the emergence of industrial organizations at the end of the eighteenth century. There are few signs to suggest that interest is waning as commentators, policymakers, and practitioners continue to debate and develop initiatives related to it. This chapter has suggested that in large part financial participation has attracted this attention because it covers a range of practices capable of acting as a vehicle for a variety of organizational and societal objectives. The typical distinction was drawn between cash and share-based schemes and consideration given to how these schemes had been used to pursue corporate objectives linked to employee attitudes and costs as well as political objectives related to social justice, macroeconomic well-being or partisan ideologies. The pursuit of these goals and, in particular, the take-up of different schemes was seen as highly sensitive to circumstances across time and space. The 'waxing and waning' of practice and interest in financial participation over the years was variously attributed by researchers to worker power and business conditions, while patterns in the take-up of schemes were related to national institutions and statutory frameworks as well as to features of organizations, industries, and occupations.

Despite the focus on design, objectives, and adoption, it was clear that most of the research on financial participation had focused on the consequences of schemes. This work was seen as concentrating on whether and how financial participation impacted on employee attitudes and behaviours and on organizational performance. Research suggested a positive relationship between financial participation and various organizational outcomes; however this work was increasingly seeking to explore the conditions under which this relationship held. This had promoted interest in financial participation as part of a bundle of management practices and in the need to unpack the effects of different types of financial participation scheme. Research on employee attitudes suggested a less conclusive relationship with financial participation, but similarly it was moving down the path of exploring the mechanisms by which schemes might prompt greater employee commitment. Finally, some of the limitations of this research were highlighted. A more detailed exploration of process was seen as essential to a fuller appreciation of the issue of power and control which might underpin the use of financial participation, while a greater sensitivity to the normative and political rationale might also be built into models exploring the take-up and consequences of schemes.

REFERENCES

ARTHUR, J. and AIMAN-SMITH, L. (2001) 'Gainsharing and Organizational Learning: An Analysis of Employee suggestions Over Time', *Academy of Management Journal*, 44(4): 737–54.

—— and JELF, G. (1999) 'The Effects of Gainsharing on Grievance Rates and Absenteeism', *Journal of Labor Relations*, 20(1): 133–46.

AZFAR, O. and DANNINGER, J. (2001) 'Profit Sharing, Employment Stability and Wage Growth', *Industrial and Labor Relations Review*, 54(3): 619–30.

BEN-NER, A. and JONES, D. (1995) 'Incentives, Monitoring and Employee Stock Ownership Plans: New Evidence and Interpretations', *Industrial Relations*, 45(4): 753–75.

BLANCHFLOWER, D. and OSWALD, A. (1988) 'Profit Related Pay: Prose Discovered', *The Economic Journal*, 98: 720–30.

BOWEY, A., THORPE, R., and MITCHELL, F. (1982) *Effects of Incentive Payment Systems*. London: Department of Employment.

BROWN, S., FAKHFAKH, SESSIONS, J. (1999) 'Absenteeism and Employee Sharing: An Empirical Analysis based on French Panel Data 1981–91', *Industrial and Labor Relations Review*, 52(2): 234–52.

CHIU, S. and WEI-CHI, T. (2007) 'The Linkage between Profit Sharing and Organizational Citizenship Behaviour', *International Journal of Human Resource Management*, 18(6): 1098–115.

COLLINS, D. (1995) 'A Socio-Political Theory of Workplace Democracy: Class Conflict, Constituent Reactions and Organisation Outcomes at a Gainsharing Facility', *Organization Science*, 6(6): 628–44.

COOKE, W. (1994) 'Employee Participation Programs, Group-Based Incentives and Company Performance: A Union-Non-Union Comparison', *Industrial and Labor Review*, 47: 594–609.

COOPER, C., DYCK, B., and FROHLICH, J. (1992) 'Improving Effectiveness of Gainsharing: The Role of Fairness and Participation', *Administrative Science Quarterly*, 37: 471–90.

COYLE SHAPIRO, J., MORROW, P., RICHARDSON, R., and DUNNE, S. (2002) 'Using Profit Sharing to Enhance Employee Attitudes: A Longitudinal Examination of the Effects on Trust and Commitment', *Human Resource Management*, 41(4): 423–37.

DUNNE, S., RICHARDSON, R., and DEWE, P. (1991) 'The Impact of Employee Share Ownership on Worker Attitudes: A Longitudinal Case Study', *Human Resource Management Journal*, 1(3): 1–18.

FLORKOWSKI, G. (1987) 'The Organizational Impact of Profit Sharing', *Academy of Management Review*, 12(4): 622–36.

GREGG, P. and MACHIN, S. (1988) 'Unions and the Incidence of Performance Linked Pay Schemes in Britain', *International Journal of Organizations*, 6: 91–107.

HARRINGTON, J. (2000) 'Team Based Pay', in R. Thorpe and G. Homan (eds), *Strategic Reward Systems*. London: Prentice Hall.

HATCHER, L. and ROSS, T. (1991) 'From Individual Incentives to an Organization Wide Gainsharing Plan', *Journal of Organizational Behavior*, 21: 169–83.

HEYWOOD, J., HUBLER, O., and JIRJAHN, U. (1998) 'Variable Payment Schemes and Industrial Relations: Evidence from German', *KYKLOS*, 51: 237–57.

HYMAN, J. and MASON, B. (1995) *Managing Employee Involvement and Participation*. London: Sage.

IDS Report (1996) 'Huge Growth in Profit Related Pay', October, 723: 2–3.

IPCS (1988) *Fair Share? A Negotiators Guide to Profit Sharing*. London: IPCS.

KABST, R., MATLASKE, W., and SCHMELTER, A. (2006) 'Financial Participation in British, French and German Organisations: A Neo-Institutional Perspective', *Economic and Industrial Democracy*, 27(4): 565–85.

KIM, D. (1999) 'Determinants of the Survival of Gainsharing Programs', *Industrial and Labor Relations Review*, 53(1): 21–41.

KRUSE, D. (1984) *Employee Ownership and Employee Attitudes: Two Case Studies*. Pennsylvania: Norwood Editions.

—— (1993) *Profit Sharing: Does it Make a Difference?* Kalamazoo: Upjohn Institute.

—— (1996) 'Why do Firms Adopt Profit Sharing and Employee Share Ownership Plans?' *British Journal of Industrial Relations*, 34: 515–38.

—— and BLASI, J. (1995) *Employee Ownership, Employee Attitudes and Firm Performance: A Review of the Evidence*, NBER Working Paper Series 5277. Cambridge, MA: National Bureau of Economic Research.

LONG, R. (1989) 'Patterns of Workplace Innovation in Canada', *Relations Industrielles*, 44: 805–26.

—— (2000) 'Employee Profit Sharing', *Relations Industrielles*, 55(3): 477–504.

MATHEWS, D. (1989) 'The British Experience of Profit Sharing', *The Economic History Review*, 42(4): 439–64.

MARRIOT, R. (1971) *Incentive Payment Systems*. London: Staples Press.

MEULLER, F. (1996) 'Human Resources as Strategic Assets', *Journal of Management Studies,* 33(6): 757–85.

MICHIE, J. and OUGHTON, C. (2005) 'Employee Ownership Trusts and Corporate Governance', *Corporate Governance,* 13: 4–8.

OXERA (2007) *Tax Advantaged Employee Share Scheme: Analysis of Productivity Effects.* London: HM Revenue and Customs.

PEACH, E. and WREN, S. (1992) 'Pay for Performance from Antiquity to the 1950s', in B. Hopkins, and T. Mawhinney (eds), *Pay for Performance form Antiquity to the 1950s, in Pay for Performance.* New York: Haworth Press.

PENDLETON, A. (1997) 'Characteristics of Workplaces with Financial Participation: Evidence from the Workplace Industrial Relations Survey', *Industrial Relations Journal,* 28: 103–19.

—— (2006) 'Incentives, Monitoring and Employee Stock Ownership Plans: New Evidence and Interpretations', *Industrial Relations,* 45(4): 753–75.

—— and POUTSMA, E. (2004) *Financial Participation: The Role of Governments and Social Partners.* Dublin: European Foundation.

—— —— BREWSTER, C., and VAN OMMEREN, J. (2001) *Employee Share Ownership and Profit Sharing in the EU.* Dublin: European Foundation for the Improvement of Living and Working Conditions.

—— ROBINSON, A. and WILSON, N. (1995) 'Does Employee Ownership Weaken Trade Unions? Recent Evidence from the UK Bus Industry', *Economics and Democracy,* 16(4): 577–605.

—— WILSON, N., WRIGHT, M. et al. (1998) 'The Perceptions and Effects of Share Ownership: Empirical Evidence from Employee Buy Outs', *British Journal of Industrial Relations,* 36(1): 99–123.

PIERCE, J., RUBENFELD, A., and MORGAN, S. (1991) 'Employee Ownership: A Conceptual Model of Process and Effects', *Academy of Management Review.* 16(1): 121–41.

POOLE, M. (1989) *The Origins of Economic Democracy.* London: Routledge.

—— and JENKINS, G. (1990) 'Human Resource Management and Profit Sharing: Employee Attitudes and a National Survey', *International Journal of Human Resource Management,* 3 (3): 322–36.

POUTSMA, E. (2001) *Recent Trends in Employee Financial Participation in the European Union.* Dublin: European Foundation.

—— (ed.) (2006) *Changing Patterns of Employee Financial Participation.* Nijmegen: Nijmegen School of Management.

RAMSEY, H. (1977) 'Cycles of Control: Worker Participation in Sociological and Historical Perspectives', *Sociology,* 11(3): 481–506.

RICHARDSON, R. and THOMPSON, M. (1999) *The Impact of People Management on Business Performance.* London: IPD.

ROBINSON, A. and WILSON, N. (2006) 'Employee Financial Participation and Productivity: An Empirical Reappraisal', *British Journal of Industrial Relations,* 44(1): 31–50.

—— and ZHANG, H. (2005) 'Employee Share Ownership Safeguarding Investments in Human Capital', *British Journal of Industrial Relations,* 43(3): 469–88.

ROSEN, C. and YOUNG, K. (1991) *Understanding Employee Ownership.* Cornell: ILR Press.

SCANLON, J. (1948) 'Profit Sharing under Collective Bargaining: Three Case Studies', *Industrial and Labor Relations Review,* 2(1): 58–75.

SCHLOSS, D. (1907) *Methods of Industrial Remuneration.* London: Willmans and Norgate.

VAN DEN BLUCKE, F. (1999) *A Company Perspective of Financial Participation in the European Union: Objectives and Obstacles.* Brussels: Research Centre for Financial Participation.

VAUGHAN-WHITEHEAD, D. (1995) *Workers' Financial Participation*. Geneva: ILO.

WEITZMAN, M. (1984) *The Share Economy*. Cambridge, MA: Harvard University Press.

WHYMAN, P. (2006) 'Post Keynesianism, Socialisation of Investment and Swedish Wage Earner Funds', *Cambridge Journal of Economics*, 30(1): 49–68.

WILSON, F. and BOWEY, A. (1982) 'Profit and Performance Based Systems', in A. Bowey (ed.), *Managing Salary and Wage Systems*. Aldershot: Gower.

WILSON, N. and PEEL, M. (1991) 'The Impact on Absenteeism and Quits of Profit Sharing and Other Forms of Employee Participation', *Industrial and Labor Review*, 44(3): 454–71.

WOOD, S. (1999) 'Human Resource Management and Performance', *International Journal of Management Review*, 1: 397–413.

ZYLBERSTAJN, H. (2002) 'The Brazilian Case: Performance Pay and Workers' Rights', in M. Brown and J. Heywood (eds), *Pay for Performance*. London: M.E. Sharpe.

PART IV

PROCESSES AND OUTCOMES

CHAPTER 15

LABOUR UNION RESPONSES TO PARTICIPATION IN EMPLOYING ORGANIZATIONS

GREGOR GALL

INTRODUCTION

LABOUR unions[1] have historically sought 'participation' in employing organizations as they have attempted to gain the organizational and institutional means by which to protect and advance their members' interests beyond the (limited) scope conventionally allowed by capitalists and capitalism. To achieve participation would for unions seem to represent some considerable movement towards achieving either workers' control or the codetermination of the employment relationship and the workplace. For labour unionism, participation concerns not simply the means to regulate the employment relationship from within the employing organization but also from without through both external intervention into the workplace and extra workplace regulation, giving testimony to unions acting as both economic and political agencies. However, the majority of systems of participation have originated from employers with almost all the remainder derived from initiatives of governments or states. The broad purposes of participation, for employers, concern generating workers' consent for and cooperation with managerial aims and objectives. For government and states, the former are just as salient as facilitating industrial harmony and social stability so that appropriate conditions for economic growth under capitalism are provided. Thus, little participation is created either at the behest of workers-cum-unions or directly by them.[2] Alongside this, the widespread absence of systems of participation (Freeman and Rogers 1999, 2006; Kersley et al., 2006) is a conscious and deliberate employer policy (Blyton and Turnbull, 2004: 253). So, wanting forms of worker control but always being the weaker party in the employment relationship, the historical dilemma for labour unionism is whether entering participation will strengthen or weaken its ability to prosecute its members' interests, and whether avenues of participation augment or undermine its preferred primary *modus operandi*, namely, collective bargaining.

This chapter will firstly provide a multilayered theorization of labour unionism's relationship to participation—essentially one of the political economy of participation—in order to provide the basis for examining unions' experience of, and response to, participation. This requires an exposition of the broad parameters of the relationship between labour unionism and participation before examining the conceptual implications of these parameters. In doing so, participation is defined broadly as the reality, rhetoric, and aspiration of worker involvement in task determination as well as contributing to higher-level, decision-making processes concerning the employment relationship, enterprise and markets, whether coming from workers, employers, or states (Marchington et al., 1992). This then concerns, with varying degrees of depth and breadth, direct and indirect participation at different levels of employing organizations and over an array of subjects.[3] In essence, the focus will then be on bilateral arenas of engagement between workers and employer representatives which are not formally and conceptually predicated on the involvement of any third parties.

THE PARTICIPATION PROBLEMATIC

Unions are predicated on their members (and workers at large and potential members) having separate and different interests from those of employers (and their managers). Labour unionism's *raison d'etre* is the organizational representation of these interests, pursued through mobilization (of whatever form and extent) but primarily operationalized in the workplace through collective bargaining and primarily focused on immediate economic and micro-political issues in the workplace. Simply put at this level, labour unionism's role is to represent the interests of the exploited against the exploiters (employers or capital) and those (governments, states) which support the exploiters' aims and activities. But having separate and different interests does not necessarily presuppose those interests are antithetical to those of employers, either some or all of the time. Rather, there may be instances when workers and employers have similar or overlapping (rather the same) interests, just as there may be instances when workers and employers have opposing and contradictory interests (Cressey and MacInnes, 1980; Edwards, 1986). Indeed, both similar and contradictory interests are possible at one and the same time over different issues, giving testimony to the multidimensional, dialectical nature of the relationship between capital and labour (Hyman, 2001). And, while calculations of when, where, and how interests coincide are indeterminant, the constant dialectic of interests, of antagonism and intersection of interests, is an unceasing one under capitalism. Alongside this, recognition is needed of the dynamic but contingent process of contention between those interests, where interdependency exists and the complexion of this interdependency varies according to the balance of power between the two parties as a result of, *inter alia*, labour and product market changes. In this framework, the notion of a dialectical relationship between objective and subjective recognition, indeed construction, of workers' interests (Kelly, 1998) is critical. The same can be said of the interplay between oppositional ideas and workers' power where 'marginal' ideas can then seem more credible if workers are more willing to engage with them because they become more commonsensical.

Following from this, workers' immediate, short-term interests concern the substantive material conditions regarding the outcomes of the wage–effort bargain as well as the procedural means by which the wage–effort bargain is itself determined, where the factors involved comprise power, authority, and control in the trifurcated relationship between employer, union, and workers. Where worker–employer interests coincide, to some degree, there is the possibility of coalitions or alliances of varying lengths of time. Where interests do not coincide, conflict, whether open or hidden, will ensue for varying lengths of time. The absence of open conflict should not be presumed to indicate the presence of harmony and cooperation. Concomitant, whether labour unionism deems its members' interests are more or less compatible with those of employers is primarily a matter of ideology and consciousness. Unions predisposed to an oppositional ideology are more likely to believe members' interests will not be best served by participation while those unions predisposed to a cooperative ideology are more likely to argue the contrary. Consequently, labour unionism's approach towards participation is neither predicated on conflict nor cooperation per se. Rather, its approach is one that will be contingent upon the interplay of material interests, power resources, and members' consciousness, which is, in turn, infused and influenced by ideology, leading across time and space to a number of possible outcomes vis-à-vis participation. In this configuration, the significance of union leverage is noteworthy for unions with oppositional ideologies but without power to operationalize these will act differently from unions that have these and the wherewithal to operationalize. In other words, the power play of pragmatism and accommodation is evident in the overall union problematic (Kelly, 1996b; Martinez Lucio and Stuart, 2005).

Labour unions operate through mechanisms of collective bargaining and regulation of intra-firm labour markets (by job control and demarcation). The substance of both mechanisms concerns the immediate, direct issues of the wage–effort bargain like contractual (and custom and practice) terms and conditions. These are, largely, economistic. But participation, in its widest sense, is of a more political nature and offers tantalizing possibilities of extending extant workplace control to the higher institutions of the enterprise and market because there are certain aspects of participation which would suggest that all of employers' affairs which have bearing on workers should be subject to participation. Thus, the implication, at least, is that decision making on investment, products, ownership, and strategy should be party to codetermination. But, as will be discussed later, the obstacles to realizing that aspiration are sizeable, as are the dangers for unions, in attempting to do so.

Where participation comes from employers and governments/states, unions will approach these with a critical eye to working out their response and do so in regard of the array of factors outlined above. This will often be subject to processes of debate and dialogue within their own different formal structures and processes of democracy and participation.[4] However, those originating with employers or heavily influenced by employers will be the subject of more scepticism than those emanating from government/state because the latter's political complexion can be relatively more or less favourable to labour unionism depending on the complexion of the political parties in office, and state initiatives may reflect the political power of organized labour. In any case, the relationship between employers and the government/state is significant because each can influence the other in regard of their own activity on the presence or absence of systems of participation and their complexion and form. Where initiatives for participation come from labour unionism, a more embedded process of internal debate leading to policy positions being adopted has taken place. Broadly speaking, in periods of growing leverage for organized labour, minorities within labour movements will seek means of participation to reify, extend, and legitimize this leverage while other minorities will seek similar means of participation to control and manage the extension of leverage, indicating the tensions within labour unions over power, interests, and politics. The majority will continue with the *modus operandi* of collective bargaining. In periods of shrinking leverage, some minorities will envisage that systems of labour-initiated participation can act as a bulwark against further erosion of influence. The paradox is that in the former periods, unions are more likely to be able to achieve such goals compared to the latter periods precisely because of the changing balance of power between themselves, employers, and state.

For employers, participation is also potentially thorny. The dominant employer tendency is to manage in an intrinsically unilateralist manner. So in common with their approach to labour unionism per se, their concerns are whether participation reinforces or erodes their control—their managerial prerogative—over work and workers, and to what extent (albeit where control is not an end in itself but a means to productivity and production of profit). For example, employers' control may be reinforced and extended by participation through acquisition of worker tacit knowledge or further legitimacy (Parker and Slaughter, 1985). The concrete issue is whether this will happen in a particular situation or era, and whether there are internal (workforce) or external (government) compulsions to adopt participation. Thereafter, the issues arise of what forms and processes of participation more or less support employer interests should they feel inclined or compelled to do so. Consequently, we can view participation as indicative of capital's simultaneous strength and weakness vis-à-vis being able to command but also need participation as a means of socializing and reifying expropriation of surplus labour.

For some employers, the more fearful or paranoid, an issue will be whether participation prefigures—in capacity and consciousness building senses—forms of workers' control. Here, the fear is that participation can raise workers' horizons and aspirations, making employer power and authority open to question and challenge. Moreover, some employers recognize that they cannot foresee, much less guarantee, whether their intentions for participation will be realized in the form of desired outcomes because the environment and processes in which participation operates are indeterminant. Conversely, other employers will make an observation that what is on their side in present circumstances is that new forms of participation are inserted into the totality of both existing systems of private property rights and ownership, and existing hierarchies of authority and control so that scope for fundamental challenge is so severely limited as to be almost non-existent.

So are there any revolutionary or subversive implications to participation? Although participation is inserted into existing capitalist structures, it is not merely this which suggests that the answer to the question is almost totally in the negative. Participation has often been placed on a continuum and sometimes an escalator (Blyton and Turnbull, 2004; Marchington, 1992). One inference from these is that each level or component is not self-limiting or inhibiting—in other words, the ability to reach the next higher stage is possible from attaining the 'previous' one. This is unproven, for employer or government design of participation does not lend itself to expansion and upgrading. Only in periods of revolutionary upheavals, as per Argentina, Bolivia, and Venezuela in the late 1990s/ to early 2000s, does the questioning of ownership concretely arise and only in these situations may such creeping control be possible. Yet here, both new (worker) and old (employer or state) forms of participation were deployed. And, regardless of which position one adopts on the Ramsay (1977, 1991) versus Manchester camp (Ackers et al., 1992; Marchington et al. 1993) exchange on 'cycles' and 'waves', there is wide consensus that power relations, material interests, and ideology are crucial to understanding the dynamics and intentions of contemporary participation (including 'involvement' and 'empowerment'). Even the Manchester camp would no doubt agree that both employer and government/state initiatives can be challenging for labour unionism and that there is porosity to both employer and government/state initiatives for the kinds of reason discussed previously without suggesting that there is much scope for workers challenging management for more fundamental control through employers' participation schemes.

Having touched upon a discussion of the possible revolutionary implications of participation, two further questions are in order. First, whether participating in participation becomes self-limiting where the independent organs of worker representation—unions—are regarded as being harbingers, or potentially prefigurative, of workers' power or socialism. For some radicals and Marxists, this is not an issue, for they hold that labour unionism is inherently reformist, and thus has no emancipatory or revolutionary potential, for it seeks to better the terms of, not abolish, wage labour. Rather, workers' power will be arrived at through new forms of organization like soviets or workers' councils. But for other radicals and Marxists, a widely divergent conclusion has been reached: while labour unionism is in intention and current practice reformist, it may also be transformed through the development of contradictions and struggles into an emancipatory agency. Thus, participating in participation takes on another and arguably more serious connotation because this emancipatory or revolutionary potential may be crushed or diverted. Consequently, participating should be spurned or approached in a very specific and conscious manner. Second, whether labour unionism is inherently conservative with regard to participation because while it contests the wage–effort bargain, it does so in economic rather than political terms. If this is the case, labour unionism is not well predisposed to approaching the higher level participation issues of what is produced and how it is produced. Therefore, the issue becomes that, for workers, approaching participation through labour unions may then be counterproductive.

Before deploying this political economy of participation in a more applied manner, it is worth noting that both workers and unions do not necessarily have matching approaches towards participation. Workers face direct participation in a different way from labour unionism, it being both institution and 'secondary organization' (Offe and Wisenthal, 1985). Indeed, direct participation conceives no role for a third (and representational) party. Through direct participation, workers can theoretically exercise influence on both wage–effort bargain and labour process without recourse to labour unionism. This is true of union and non-union workers alike though its persuasiveness is arguably greater for the latter which consciously reject labour unionism. So, generally speaking, one could anticipate a less critical and more positively engaged response to participation from those that are non-union members compared to those that are not. This arises because unions act as tribunes for workers *per se* and/or sectionalist vanguards for specific groups of workers. Either way, a more developed oppositional consciousness is required of these workers. Labour unionism also faces indirect participation in a different way from workers for, as a representational and bargaining agent, it has interests that are different but not necessarily separate from those of workers and its members. Here its concern is that as both bureaucracy and organization, indirect participation may reinforce or erode its indirect representative role. For example, unions may see their interests bound up with protecting the robustness of union–management bilateral institutions from erosion by other forums of exchange and not as innovative means to influence the direct and immediate experience of work and employment. Furthermore, workers may prefer what seem like more immediate and direct ways of influencing their experience of work and employment. For unions, there is an issue of possible substitution, with workers wanting participation and where they believe they can do without, and do better without, a union, particularly under the HRM derived discourse of empowerment (Freeman and Rogers, 1999, 2006; TUC, 2008). Under indirect participation, employers may be willing to provide resources to solidify these nominally 'independent' non-union forums.

Participation 'before' Participation

From the 1960s to as late as the mid-1980s, participation under the rubric of workers' economic and industrial democratic aspirations and derived from state initiatives, reflecting a less unequal balance of power between capital and labour, existed in a relatively widespread manner in many Western economies (Lane, 1986; Mueller et al., 2000). What light can labour unionism's experience here of participation from a different era shed on contemporary, employer-initiated participation? There are numerous workplace studies to draw upon (Beynon, 1973; Nichols and Armstrong, 1974; Nichols and Beynon, 1977) where the context of the balance of class forces and the terms were different—for 'enrichment' then, read 'empowerment' now—but where the pressures and dynamics of capitalism and work and employment under capitalism show a historical similarity. One instance is of participation back 'then' transmogrifying into what is now known as involvement, and thus coming to constitute employer attempts at work intensification and management by stress (Danford, 1999; Parker and Slaughter, 1985, 1988, 1994). But three key differences between then and now come to mind. Employers are attempting to lay the responsibility on individual workers for their individual and collective work predicaments through an ideological assault of incorporation where employers' responsibilities also become those of workers; the notion of extending 'free collective bargaining' to encroach upon management (Coates and Topham, 1970) is a degraded one because of the shrunken breadth and depth of collective bargaining as well as its narrow economism; and the horizons of labour unionism are considerably narrowed so that demands like 'opening the books' are seldom now made.

That said, previous research identified that for shop stewards, the contending challenges and opportunities emanating from participation concerned role conflict, incorporation and loss of contact with members as well as access to information, management, and decision making (Marchington and Armstrong, 1981, 1984). Here, some of the variability in steward perceptions and responses was attributed to political worldviews, where left-wing views were more critical of management (Marchington and Armstrong, 1984). Moreover, a number of salient points emerge for labour unionism per se. One is that unions should be concerned with analysing the power resources and attendant ideologies that underpin, give rise to, and shape schemes of participation. Power gives the option of exercising initiative while lack of power tends to compel reaction and accommodation. And despite a variety of union reactions to participation, each was limited by its superficiality, which ill prepared them for later employer-initiated participation. Consequently, unions would benefit by creating the intellectual and mobilizing capacities to respond to, and develop, participation schemes. For example, developing the critical theory of employer-inspired union incorporation would be useful for some consideration. In the former period in Britain, bodies such as the Institute for Workers' Control did this, and it is evident that worker incorporation remains a key employer objective and practice today. Furthermore, the practice of consultation, as a potential harbinger of employee involvement, concerned marginal issues within a predetermined management framework (MacInnes, 1985), so this perspective is still valid.

CONTESTED TERRAIN *AND* TERRAIN FOR STRUGGLE?

In contemporary Western economies, it is common to talk of a 'representation gap', whereby labour unionism is now a shrunken force, non-union institutions have not fully, in qualitative and quantitative terms, taken up the vacated space and workers still desire representation (Blyton and Turnbull, 2004: 275; Freeman and Rogers, 1999; Kelly, 1998: 46; Kersley et al., 2006). Consequently, labour unions still wish participation for workers and their members but they find what is on offer, primarily from employers, is far from appetising or satisfactory. Yet, simultaneously, they are confronted with the forced choice of participating in participation as they cannot compel their own preferred forms of participation from without.

Employer power is derived from ownership and control of the means of production, distribution, and exchange and, following from this, the paraphernalia of a monopoly of the means of organized violence and a hegemonic ideology and legal framework that support the rights of private property. From these flows, *inter alia*, the ability and right to hire and fire. Meanwhile, union power is derived from labour scarcity, disruptive capacity, and political influence (Batstone, 1988). Nonetheless—and because of this—the dichotomous relationship between capital and organized labour is acted out on the terrain of participation and through participation itself. The sense of both 'nonetheless' and 'because' is that participation is a superstructure built on top of the base of the quintessential nature of the relationship between employer and worker under capitalism, whereby the latter necessarily pervades any superstructure. And, therefore, antagonism and intersection of interests as well as processes of conflict and cooperation are played out in the arenas and institutions of participation. The current swing of the pendulum of power towards employers, making this underlying dynamic more often than not subterranean, should not obscure recognition of this.

So an enduring problematic for unions is whether they should be inside or outside 'the tent'—the tent being the institutions and arenas of participation through which employer power is often exercised. Put in a heuristic manner, being on the 'inside' presumes that: one, employer power can be contested within the tent, leading to the exercise of a countervailing force; two, being outside is to self-induce marginalization and isolation from contesting employer power; and three, allowing employers untrammelled and uncontested access to workers merely reinforces their dominance. Being on the 'outside' presumes: one, contamination of workers from employer ideology; two, incorporation of labour unionism into employer values and interest; and three, the creation of an independent, outside power base can influence what goes on inside through infringement and osmosis. Notwithstanding variation in the sub-forms and sub-purposes of participation, the double-edged nature of this dilemma for labour unionism is acute. However, in those arenas established at the behest of governments/states, the challenge can be less acute because of the possibility of different, non-employer forces shaping and influencing the purpose and form of the participation (on the outcomes concerning European Works Councils see, for example, Hall and Marginson (2005)). Nonetheless, many workplace unionisms are so impotent that they feel, sooner or later, compelled to become involved in participation for the fear of being 'outside' is worse than the consequences of being on the 'inside'.

Yet, the challenge for labour unionism is even more complex than this because most of the immediately preceding discussion pertained to indirect forms of participation where unions are more able to have a role because both they and the form of participation here are representative institutions and processes (even if this involves no elections or worker choice). In other words, there is a space in which unions can operate, whether seen as legitimate or not by employers, because they are intermediaries. Where direct participation is concerned, the axis of the primary relationship, stemming from employer intention, is an unmediated one between worker and supervisor/manager and where the agenda is a productivity one. The limited ideological and organizational resources of individual workers suggest such an agenda is far more difficult to resist in periods of labour quiescence. Indeed, where participation is part of employer-led HRM agendas, then the attempt is to also advance into workers' minds and colonize them with their ideology. This gives a new twist to the 'frontier of control' (Goodrich, 1975) and indicates employers are not 'sharing' control to regain it, as per Flanders' dictum, but 'sharing' control to extend it. Producing profit under market economies and the fragility of many production systems (like 'just-in-time') demands employers seek high levels of worker consent and cooperation—mere compliance is no longer deemed sufficient. In this, empowerment can be read as enslavement because superordinates cannot and will not empower subordinates. Where there is a collective aspect to the worker–manager relationship in direct participation, there are greater opportunities for resistance to management, and where labour unionism is defined as being an oppositional force, labour unionism may then find an entry point. All other things being equal, such possibilities depend on the type and form of direct participation. So, in cases of team working and problem-solving groups, there is arguably less opportunity because the focus is the immediacy of work, while in team briefings and meetings, for example, which are one step removed from the conducting of work itself, a more contestable bilateral manager–managed relationship exists.

THE MEANS OF PARTICIPATION

In the last thirty years, with the ascendancy of employer power, increasing penetration of unitarist ideology (through HRM) into employer circles and the state stepping back from a regulatory role in collective employment relations, it has been common for participation studies in Western economies to concentrate on where and what employers have done proactively—rather than focusing on what they have not done vis-à-vis participation so that 'presence', not 'absence', has been the order of the day. This has tended to give the student of employment relations a partial representation of the array of the means of participation, whereby recognition and understanding of new and existing means of state-derived participation are downplayed. So aside from the direct and indirect, collectively and individually-orientated initiatives from employers (e.g., quality circles, team working, staff councils, partnership agreements, profit-related pay, employee share ownership schemes, 360 degree appraisals), there is a panoply of other means of statutory-based participation, largely of an indirect and representative nature, such as health and safety representatives, joint consultative councils, works councils, workplace committees, worker directors, and redundancies committees. However, some of these are not mandatory unless certain worker support thresholds are attained and not all stipulate a role for unions. Setting aside their derivation for the moment, the form, scope, depth, and site of participation all afford greater or lesser opportunities and threats to labour unionism. Those that concern direct and immediate participation and work on an individual basis are less amenable to union influence than those that are indirect and work on a longer term basis. The former concern 'soft power' and the latter 'hard power'.

Labour Unionism Praxis

By and large, labour unionism has not engaged in what could be described as praxis over employer-initiated participation, that is, theoretically-informed practice (Ramsay, 1991), this being also true of its consideration of, and reflection on, HRM and new management techniques (NMT) (Martinez Lucio and Weston, 1992). Quite apart from the economism's hegemony within labour unionism, the rise of accommodation to capital through 'new realism', and the decline of oppositional union intellectuals, one of the main reasons for this outcome is that consideration of participation has been subsumed within a wider consideration of HRM/NMT (in the case of Britain, see GMB, 1993, n.d.; Heaton and Linn, 1989; MSF, 1994; NUCPS, n.d.; TUC, 1994). These analyses stressed the drive for productivity, fragmentation of collectives, and promotion of individualism as well as pushing for workers' 'hearts and minds' through attitudinal restructuring. While this submerging is eminently sensible, in so doing unions have missed a trick. The sense in which HRM/NMT threaten labour unionism through marginalization by deploying exclusion strategies can accommodate an understanding of the employers' intention for participation. Here, schemes of participation are used to supersede or erode existing bilateral (union–employer) channels of exchange and negotiation. But this then also ignores the specificity of participation, whereby while

HRM/NMT proclaim mutuality of interests of capital and labour, participation offers a means by which this can be operationalized in the workplace and in so doing creates the possibility of a reified ideological barrier between workers and labour unionisms. And it also attempts to reconfigure and reconstruct workplace and worker collectivism. Thus, the 'new' collectivism is one that is created by employers to serve their interests. In this sense, participation is more dangerous and pernicious than HRM/NMT because it offers the possibility of putting 'meat on the bones' of employers' mutuality agenda. So, participation then warrants its own detailed and extended consideration. Of course, that does not mean that overall union positions cannot be identified, for their responses reflect the contending pressures on workers of antagonism and cooperation. But it does mean that they are skewed towards being fundamentally non-strategic, *ad hoc* and immediately reactive. Consequently, the range of responses is both more narrowed and more superficial.

From union responses, in Britain and the United States particularly, the following attitudes and behaviours are identifiable: one, to look for the positives and potentials from a position of subscribing to the idea of mutuality of interests between capital and labour (which leads unions to seek partnership with employers); two, readiness to agitate around expected discrepancies of theory and practice and criticize when promises or expectations are not delivered upon; three, the belief that participation represents the reassertion of right to manage as union displacement; four, take the opportunity of, and through, participation to posit alternative conceptions of participation because employer-initiated versions concern 'soft' power; and five, seek to bargain over participation and deal with issues that arise from it within existing bilateral channels. Such responses (both of intention and practice) can then usefully be grouped within those types of broad categories identified by writers when evaluating union responses to management initiatives like HRM, team working, and employee involvement in Britain (Bacon and Blyton, 2004; Carr, 1994; Hyman and Mason, 1995; Marchington, 1995; Martinez Lucio and Weston, 1992; cf. Blyton and Turnbull, 2004: 260; Marchington and Wilkinson, 2005). These comprise: a) embracement and constructive engagement via partnership and cooperative approaches towards employers; b) pragmatic bargaining, where the introduction, processes, and outcomes of participation are subject to existing bargaining procedures, whereby negotiation takes place not over what is introduced and when but how and in what form; and c) reluctant critical engagement which seeks damage limitation and subversion with importance attached to preventing marginalization and maintaining independence.

However, the dynamics of responses require recognizing that many unions started with outright opposition, or agnosticism and indifference, or scepticism and cynicism (George and Levie, 1984; Marchington, 1995; Marchington and Wilkinson, 2005; Ramsay, 1991) but then amended these to one of the above three categories after unnecessarily ceding control to management through abstentionism, creating distance from their memberships and inability to sustain opposition when members were 'participating' (Beaumont, 1991; Fisher, 1995) in the cases of then major British left-wing unions, ASTMS and TGWU. Likewise, heterogeneity of intra-union response requires acknowledgement for one cannot speak of a union response in the singular. Thus, Hyman and Mason (1995: 151–5) suggested that workplace unionisms tend to have more critical responses than national unionisms because they faced participation in more immediate and forceful manners. However, equally observable has been that gaps have emerged between (national) policy and (local) practice because workplace unions have been unable or unwilling to implement national policy positions for lack of support from members or a less critical view of participation. In North America, resistance to employer participation has been greater in Canada than in the United States, because of higher mobilizing and ideological capacities (Beaumont, 1991). Nonetheless, even within the US, labour unionism has become bifurcated vis-à-vis participation, with acceptance for reasons of impotence and economic necessity competing with rejection for reasons of work intensification and threats to union presence (Beaumont, 1991).

Marginalization and Avoidance

Writers such as Marchington and Wilkinson (Marchington, 1992, 1995; Marchington and Wilkinson, 2005; Wilkinson, 1998) noted that whether by design or default, there is a possibility of union marginalization resultant upon employers introducing participation systems and schemes. This inference's thrust can be extended to pertain to non-union workplaces in terms of union avoidance. In both scenarios of marginalization and avoidance, processes of suppression and substitution are intended to deny and obstruct workers' access to resources of collective power and ideology of an oppositional nature. Sometimes, these resources are independent, that is, they are union-based from either inside or outside workplaces, while in others the resources are derived primarily from state action like statutory works councils. But if participation is the 'velvet glove' in the employers' armory, then we should not in our focus upon participation forget that victimization, and threats thereof, are the 'iron fist' which the same employers also deploy. The specific context for the prospects of marginalization and avoidance is that schemes of participation—like the presence of HRM techniques—are more commonly found in unionized workplaces than in non-union workplaces (on Britain, see Cully et al., 1999; Kersley et al., 2006), and there is a greater preponderance of schemes of participation in workplaces where the employer believes there to be potential or actual union organizing.

Labour unionism faces the various dilemmas outlined earlier. Regarding works councils, Kelly (1996a) argued that they have a corrosive intent and capacity while Hyman (1996) argued that they can be colonized by unions and redeployed for their own purposes. Heery et al., (2004) concluded the balance of evidence favoured Hyman. Yet a more robust assessment can be gained by positing that in spite of the 'intention' of works councils, the other key part of the equation to understanding their impact is to recognize the differing environments into which they are inserted, comprising, *inter alia*, strong existing, weak existing, or emergent labour unionisms. Consequently, a number of possibilities emerge—*inter alia* strong labour unionism crushes and/or captures work councils, weak labour unionism is further corroded by or captures work councils, and emergent labour unionism is corroded by or captures work councils. Such outcomes are based on considerations of union and worker power and ideology. Thus, the complexity and indeterminacy of employment relations compels that the issue is not a choice between either Kelly or Hyman, nor to say just that both are possible. Rather, it is to identify the possible and probable outcomes, and the dynamics leading to these, depending on a number of contextual and contingent factors. With this in place, analysis is then able to posit whether and at what point works councils, in this instance, become self-limiting or self-enabling.

PARTICIPATING IN PARTICIPATION

There are contingent dangers for unions in participating and not participating in participation—indirectly through direct participation and directly through indirect participation. Employers will often approach existing workplace unionism for cooperation on introducing, and acting supportively within and without, participation schemes. Here, employers seek union endorsement to provide legitimacy for participation in order to generate worker cooperation. Where opposition is the preferred response, union deliberation on feasible and effective external opposition will consider whether participation can be stopped or watered down, and what the employer's commitment to participation was and to what form. Deliberation on feasible and effective internal opposition will consider whether labour unionism's relationship with members and workers would be strengthened or weakened. So, where union power has been eroded, with the consequence that worker attachment to labour unionism itself has been reduced, labour unionism faces the dilemma of whether it can attempt to enter the participation arena in order to win back that attachment in order to rebuild itself. A particular aspect of the challenge is that because participation may be seen by some workers as the 'next best thing' or 'only show in town', they become even less receptive to the overture from weakened labour unionism. Here, there is a 'Catch 22' situation—workers will not attach themselves to unions until they are stronger and unions will not become stronger until workers attach themselves to unions. The danger of cementing union weakness is present, for part of the purpose of participation is the attitudinal restructuring of workers yet there is a still paucity of recent research to show whether the rather unspectacular gains for employers of early participation schemes (Kelly and Kelly, 1991; Guest and Dewe, 1991; Wright and Edwards, 1998) have continued or not.

Earlier, the issue of historic self-limitation arising from worker participation in participation was raised. Empirically, this is a hard proposition to test for a successful workers' revolution has not existed in the current epoch and instances of mere revolutionary upheaval have been very few. Nonetheless, where revolutionary upheaval has taken place in recent times—Argentina, Bolivia, and Venezuela—existing, new and old forms of governance and participation have been deployed by workers. In these instances, when management and employers are removed or flee, then existing employer-constructed institutions of participation no longer play the same role and they are transformed into different organs with different roles and powers. Indeed, an oxymoron exists here for in these situations, the existing institutions cease to be the existing institutions. What is less clear are what roles labour unionism play here for there are important differences within and between labour unionism in these countries with regard to relations in the past and present to the state and governing parties.

PARTICIPATION AND PARTNERSHIP

Influenced by 'third way' type politics, which eschew both social democracy and unregulated capitalism, some labour unionisms have viewed partnership as a modern means of maintaining and extending their workplace, firm, and societal influence in difficult times. So, despite its lack of boundary definition, many unions not only welcomed partnership from employers and government, but they have also fought for it from them and in so doing put forward their own preferred definitions of partnership.[5] As a distinct form of indirect participation, its opportunities and threats for unions are as they were outlined previously. According to different studies, the experience of unions testifies to the anticipated fault lines. In the financial services sector in Britain, where partnership is more extensive and embedded than elsewhere, partnership was found to have eroded bargaining and promoted consultation within the framework of an employer-led agenda (Gall, 2008). This evidence of incorporation and atrophy as well as relative strategic influence 'beyond' confines of conventional collective bargaining were found elsewhere (Guest and Peccei, 2001; Kelly, 1996b; 2004; Martinez Lucio and Stuart, 2005; Stuart and Martinez Lucio, 2002; Terry 2003).

TEAM WORKING

Team working is now widespread in contemporary workplaces (for Britain, see Kersley et al., 2006) and like other employer participation initiatives has standard aims emanating from the unitarist and capitalist value systems. Most critically informed studies of team working have examined its implications for work organization and workers. Where extant studies have touched upon labour unionism, they have indicated the impact of team working on union attachment and influence has been multifaceted—positive, negative, neutral, and ambiguous—for reasons concerning operation of labour markets, employer product market positions, and union responses (Bacon and Blyton, 2006; Martinez Lucio et al., 2000; McCabe and Black, 1997; Pollert, 1996). More specifically, what type of team working, means of introduction, environment of operation, and so on were also found to be additional, important variables. Little evidence of genuine 'empowerment' of workers was found. Rather, controlled autonomy, manufactured discretion, and extra responsibility without power were evident. In this sense, extant workplace labour unionism has not been pushed aside by the creation of independent sources of workers' power.

One particularly salient issue is whether team working has brought about attitudinal restructuring, that is, reduced 'them-and-us' factory class-conscious perceptions among workers and positive subscription to a management world view, for such attitudes have an important bearing on labour unionism. Some studies (Appelbaum et al., 2000) suggest team working can lay the basis for creating enterprise attachment and partnership where employers have successfully seduced workers while others (Barker, 1993) indicate that management control increases through worker self-induced suppression of oppositionalism. Consequently, these types of studies purport to show that team working reduces 'them-and-us' attitudes, albeit for different reasons. Whether this would be deemed 'good' or 'bad' in the case of the former type of studies would hinge on the orientation of the union, namely, whether it looked favourably upon partnership or not. However, it seems more studies have indicated team working can reinforce 'them-and-us' attitudes as well as fragment them without this being an aid to management (Bacon and

Blyton, 2005; Coupland et al., 2005). Moreover, teams can offer collective resistance to employers where employers infringe upon their 'autonomy' in both union and non-union environments under a number of circumstances (Gall 2003; McKinlay and Taylor, 1996). One aspect of this is where workforces have defended 'traditional' team working against the 'modern' employer versions. Another is that workers appropriate the notion of the 'team' to use against management. Such outcomes, as intimated above, are not necessarily supports for labour unionism, for workers' attachment to, and participation in, unions is more complex and contingent than this.[6]

TRANSNATIONAL DIFFERENCE

Nation state-based configurations of the 'triangle' (Hyman, 2001) of market, class, and society in English-speaking countries, as well as how their labour unionisms relates to each of these poles of attraction, clearly differ. That said, the contrast between the generic configuration found here and that found in northern and southern Europe is marked. But these distinctions indicate that the nature, dynamics and environments vis-à-vis participation are variations underneath of a central theme of capitalism—'varieties of capitalism' in other words. Consequently, the preceding discussion of participation must be viewed with one eye to cross-national applicability and another eye to country-specific applicability. Thus, one can say that the same underlying interests and processes are evident but the outcomes differ because of the national environments in which these operate.

CONCLUSION

Contemporary times have witnessed a huge increase in pseudo- and partial-participation in the form of employee involvement and HRM practices. Although often labelled a fad, in generic terms, participation has had many mutations and a longer shelf life than other NMT. The obvious question here is whether participation has contributed to hollowing out and atrophy of workplace unionism, subsequently weakening national unions and labour unionism per se. Critical analysis would probably answer in the positive, but make clear the relationship between participation as a cause and symptom here is complex, stress the contributory impact of other wider factors, and processes, and underline the limitations enforced on participation by workers and unions. Yet, it also apparent that the paucity of union debate on participation since the mid-1990s indicates that some of the hopes for improving the quality of working life via it have evaporated while labour unionism has generally been overcome by the ascendancy of employer power where participation has played a role. Unions have begrudgingly accepted that reality of participation and NMT/HRM despite localized and sporadic resistance. 'Running to stand still' has been the order of the day for unions, either through trying to combat the erosion of terms and conditions of employment or through 'union organizing' to rebuild presence and strength. So, to paraphrase and adapt Marx, unions have made their own history (as conscious agencies) but not always in circumstances of their own choosing. And, it is this point which means that the analysis contained herein is one which must be viewed as a contingent one given the contextual nature of the epoch in which labour unionism is presently operating. Therein lies the hope and prospect that the malaise of labour unionism here may not be a permanent phenomenon.

Notes

My thanks are to John Kelly, Miguel Martinez Lucio, and Adrian Wilkinson for comments on an earlier draft.

1. The term 'labour' unions is used because most major unions are no longer 'trade' but general unions where many 'trades' and none are submerged within or where trades no longer have significance in qualitative or quantitative terms. Using this term focuses upon the more fundamental aspect of unions as collective bodies of workers whose organizational *raison d'etre* is regulating the wage–effort bargain.

2. One example, albeit not exclusively, is that of worker cooperatives although many are established when conventional employers decide that generating profit value is no longer possible in a particular enterprise.

3. Although collective bargaining can rightly be located within the ambit of wider participation as an indirect form, owing to its fulsome consideration elsewhere, it will not be considered here. This is also the case with 'union organizing' as a means by which to create bargaining leverage.

4. On partnership, see Martinez Lucio and Stuart (2005) on the internal process and debate within British unions.

5. Something similar can be said about a number of unions' attempts to use the Information and Consultation Regulations in Britain from 2005 to gain further institutional rights within employing organizations in order to act as credible bargaining partners within a mutual gains paradigm.

6. Essentially, the same sequence of points vis-à-vis team working are true for financial participation (profit sharing, worker share ownership and worker buyouts (see summaries and research in Pendleton, 2001, 2005)).

REFERENCES

ACKERS, P., MARCHINGTON, M., WILKINSON, A., and GOODMAN, J. (1992) 'The use of cycles? Explaining employee involvement in the 1990s' *Industrial Relations Journal*, 23(4): 268–83.

APPELBAUM, E., BAILEY, T., BERG, P., and KALLEBERG, A. (2000) *Manufacturing Advantage: Why High Performance Work Systems Pay Off*. Ithaca, NY: Cornell University Press.

BACON, N. and BLYTON, P. (2004) 'Trade union responses to workplace restructuring' *Work, Employment and Society*, 18(4): 749–73.

————— (2005) 'Worker responses to teamworking: exploring employee attributions of managerial motives', *International Journal of Human Resource Management*, 16(2): 238–55.

————— (2006) 'Union cooperation in a context of job insecurity: negotiated outcomes from teamworking', *British Journal of Industrial Relations*, 44(2): 215–38.

BARKER, J. (1993) 'Tightening the iron cage: concertive control in self-managing teams', *Administrative Science Quarterly*, 38(3): 408–37.

BATSTONE, E. (1988) 'The frontier of control', in D. Gallie (ed.), *Employment in Britain*, pp. 218–47. Oxford: Blackwell.

BEAUMONT, P. (1991) 'Trade unions and HRM', *Industrial Relations Journal*, 22(4): 300–308.

BEYNON, H. (1973) *Working for Ford*. London: Penguin.

BLYTON, P. and TURNBULL, P. (2004) *The Dynamics of Employee Relations*, 3rd edition. Basingstoke: Palgrave Macmillan.

CARR, F. (1994) 'Introducing team working—a motor industry case study' *Industrial Relations Journal* 25(3): 199–209.

COATES, K. and TOPHAM, T. (eds) (1970) *Workers' Control*. London: Panther.

COUPLAND, C., BLYTON, P., and BACON, N. (2005) 'A longitudinal study of the influence of shopfloor work teams on expressions of "us" and "them".' *Human Relations*, 58(8): 1055–81.

CRESSEY, P. and MACINNES, J. (1980) 'Voting for Ford', *Capital and Class*, 11: 5–33.

CULLY, M., WOODLAND, S., O'REILLY, A., and DIX, G. (1999) *Britain at Work—As Depicted by the 1998 Workplace Employee Relations Survey*. London: Routledge.

DANFORD, A. (1999) *Japanese Management Techniques and British Workers*. London: Mansell.

EDWARDS, P. (1986) *Conflict at Work: A Materialist Analysis of Workplace Relations*. Oxford: Basil Blackwell.

FISHER, J. (1995) 'The trade union response to HRM in the UK: the case of the TGWU' *Human Resource Management Journal*, 5(3): 7–23.

FREEMAN, R. and ROGERS, J. (1999, 2006) *What Workers Want*. Ithaca NY: ILR Press.

GALL, G. (2003) *The Meaning of Militancy? Postal Workers and Industrial Relations*. Aldershot: Ashgate.

———— (2008) *Labour Unionism in the Financial Services Sector—Struggling for Rights and Representation*. Aldershot: Ashgate.

GEORGE, M. and LEVIE, H. (1984) *Japanese Competition and the British Workplace*, Centre for Alternative Industrial and Technological Systems, London.

GMB (1993) *HRM/TQM*, GMB—Britain's general union, London.

———— (n.d.) *Human Resource Management—A Trade Union Response*, GMB—Britain's general union, Glasgow.

GOODRICH, C. (1975) *The Frontier of Control: A Study in British Workshop Politics*. London: Pluto.

GUEST, D. and DEWE, P. (1991) 'Company or trade union: which wins workers' allegiance? A study of commitment in the UK electronics industry', *British Journal of Industrial Relations*, 29(1): 75–96.

—— and PECCEI, R. (2001) 'Partnership at work: mutuality and the balance of advantage' *British Journal of Industrial Relations*, 39(2): 207–36.

HALL, M. and MARGINSON, P. (2005) 'Trojan horse or paper tigers? Assessing the significance of European works councils', in B. Harley, J. Hyman, and P. Thompson (eds), *Participation and Democracy at Work*, pp. 204–221. Basingstoke: Palgrave Macmillan.

HEATON, N. and LINN, I. (1989) *Fighting Back: A Report on Shop Steward Response to New Management Techniques in TGWU Region 10*. Barnsley: TGWU Region 10/Northern College.

HEERY, E., HEALY, G., and TAYLOR, P. (2004) 'Representation at work: themes and issues', in G. Healy, E. Heery, P. Taylor, and W. Brown (eds), *The Future of Worker Representation*, pp. 1–36. Basingstoke: Palgrave Macmillan.

HYMAN, J. and MASON, B. (1995) *Managing Employee Involvement and Participation*. London: Sage.

HYMAN, R. (1996) 'Is there a case for statutory works councils in Britain?' in A. McColgan (ed.), *The Future of Labour Law*, pp. 64–84. London: Mansell.

—— (2001) *Understanding European Trade Unionism: Between Market, Class and Society*. London: Sage.

KELLY, J. (1996a) 'Works councils: union advance or marginalization?' in A. McColgan (ed.), *The Future of Labour Law*, pp. 46–63. London: Mansell.

—— (1996b) 'Union militancy and social partnership', in P. Ackers, C. Smith, and P. Smith, (eds), *The New Workplace and Trade Unionism*, pp. 77–109. London: Routledge.

—— (1998) *Rethinking Industrial Relations: Mobilization, Collectivism and Long Waves*. London: Routledge.

—— (2004) 'Social partnership agreements in Britain: labor co-operation and compliance', *Industrial Relations*, 43(1): 267–92.

—— and KELLY, C. (1991) 'Them and us: social psychology and the new industrial relations', *British Journal of Industrial Relations*, 29(1): 25–48.

KERSLEY, B., ALPIN, C., FORTH, J., BRYSON, A., BEWLEY, H., DIX, G., and OXENBRIDGE, S. (2006) *Inside the Workplace: Findings from the 2004 Workplace Employment Relations Survey*, Abingdon: Routledge.

LANE, T. (1986) 'Economic democracy: are the trade unions equipped?' *Industrial Relations Journal* 17(4): 321–8.

MACINNES, J. (1985) 'Conjuring up consultation', *British Journal of Industrial Relations* 23(1): 93–113.

MARCHINGTON, M. (1992) *Managing the Team: A Guide to Successful Employee Involvement*. Oxford: Blackwell.

—— (1995) 'Involvement and participation', in J. Storey (ed.), *Human Resource Management— A Critical Text*, pp. 280–308. London: Routledge.

—— (2005) 'Employee involvement: patterns and explanations', in B. Harley, J. Hyman, and P. Thompson (eds), *Participation and Democracy at Work*, pp. 20–37. Basingstoke: Palgrave Macmillan.

—— and ARMSTRONG, R. (1981) 'Employee participation: problems for the shop steward', *Industrial Relations Journal* 12(1): 46–61.

—— —— (1984) 'Employee participation: some problems for some shop stewards', *Industrial Relations Journal*, 15(1): 68–81.

Marchington, M. Goodman, J., Wilkinson, A., and Ackers, P. (1992) *New Developments in Employee Involvement.* Sheffield: Employment Department.

—— Wilkinson, A. (2005) 'Direct participation and involvement', in S. Bach (eds), *Managing Human Resources: Personnel Management in Transition*, pp. 398–423. Oxford: Blackwell.

—— —— Ackers, P., and Goodman, J. (1993) 'The influence of managerial relations on waves of employee involvement' *British Journal of Industrial Relations*, 31 (4): 553–76.

Martinez Lucio, M., Jenkins, S., and Noon, M. (2000) 'Management strategy, union identity and oppositionalism: team work in the Royal Mail', in S. Proctor and F. Mueller (eds), *Teamworking*, pp. 262–79. Basingstoke: Macmillan.

—— and Stuart, M. (2005) 'Suspicious minds? Partnership, trade union strategy and the politics of contemporary employment relations', in P. Stewart (ed.), *Employment, Trade Union Renewal and the Future of Work: The Experience of Work and Organizational Change*, pp. 212–230. Basingstoke: Palgrave Macmillan.

—— and Weston, S. (1992) 'The politics and complexity of trade union responses to new management techniques' *Human Resource Management Journal* 2(4): 77–91.

McCabe, D. and Black, J. (1997) '"Something's gotta give": trade unions and the road to teamworking' *Employee Relations*, 19(2): 110–27.

McKinlay, A. and Taylor, P. (1996) 'Power, surveillance and resistance: inside the "factory of the future"', in P. Ackers, C. Smith, and P. Smith (eds), *The New Workplace and Trade Unionism*, pp. 279–300. London: Routledge.

MSF (1994) *New Management: An MSF Guide*, Manufacturing, Science and Finance Union, London.

Mueller, F., Procter, S., and Buchanan, D. (2000) 'Teamworking in its context(s): antecedents, nature and dimension', *Human Relations*, 53(11): 1387–424.

Nichols, T. and Armstrong, P. (1974) *Workers Divided: A Study of Shopfloor Politics*, London: Fontana.

—— and Beynon, H. (1977) *Living with Capitalism: Class Relations and the Modern Factory*, London: Routledge.

NUCPS (n.d.) *Human Resource Management*, Environment and Transport Group, National Union of Civil and Public Servants, London.

Offe, C. and Wisenthal, H. (1985) 'Two logics of collective action', in C. Offe (ed.), *Disorganised Capitalism: Contemporary Transformation of Work and Politics*, pp. 170–220. Cambridge: Polity.

Parker, M. and Slaughter, J. (1985) *Inside the Circle: A Union Guide to QWL.* Boston: South End Press.

—— —— (1988) *Choosing Sides: Unions and the Team Concept*, Boston: South End Press.

—— —— (1994) *Working Smart: A Union Guide to Participation Programs and Reengineering.* Detroit, MI: Labor Notes.

Pendleton, A. (2001) *Employee Ownership, Participation and Governance.* London: Routledge.

—— (2005) 'Employee share ownership, employment relationships and corporate governances', in B. Harley, J. Hyman, and P. Thompson (eds), *Participation and Democracy at Work*, pp. 75–93. Basingstoke: Palgrave.

Pollert, A. (1996) '"Team work" on the assembly line: contradiction and the dynamics of union resilience', in P. Ackers, C. Smith, and P. Smith (eds), *The New Workplace and Trade Unionism*, pp. 178–209. London: Routledge.

RAMSAY, H. (1977) 'Cycles of control: worker participation in sociological and historical perspective', *Sociology*, 11(3): 481–506.

—— (1991) 'Reinventing the wheel? A review of the development and performance of employee involvement', *Human Resource Management Journal*, 1(4): 1–22.

STUART, M. and MARTINEZ LUCIO, M. (2002) 'Social partnership and the mutual gains organisation: remaking involvement and trust at the British workplace', *Economic and Industrial Democracy*, 23(2): 177–200.

TERRY, M. (2003) 'Can "Partnership" reverse the decline of British trade unions?' *Work, Employment and Society*, 17(3): 459–72.

TUC (1994) *Human Resource Management—A Trade Union Response*, Trades Union Congress, London.

—— (2008) *Why Do Workers Want? An Agenda for the Workplace from the Workplace*, Trades Union Congress, London.

WILKINSON, A. (1998) 'Empowerment: theory and practice', *Personnel Review* 27(1): 40–56.

WRIGHT, M. and EDWARDS, P. (1998) 'Does teamworking work, and if so, why? A case study in the aluminium industry', *Economic and Industrial Democracy*, 19(1): 59–90.

CHAPTER 16

VOICE IN THE WILDERNESS? THE SHIFT FROM UNION TO NON-UNION VOICE IN BRITAIN

RAFAEL GOMEZ

ALEX BRYSON

PAUL WILLMAN

INTRODUCTION

DURING the past quarter century, the proportion of workers in Britain with access to union representation—either as dues paying members or covered by workplace collective agreements—declined from over half of the employed population to just under a third. Britain, of course, was not alone in this regard. The United States lost a similar proportion of its unionized workforce during the same period (see Figure 16.1 below).

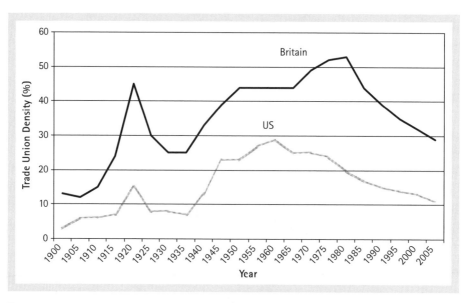

Figure 16.1 Trade union density in Britain and the United States (%)

Sources: Authors calculations. US source data from Troy and Sheflin (1985). US data from Bain and Price (1980) Tables 3.1 and 4.1. Supplemented for the US with Bureau of Labor Statistics (BLS) data. British data from Booth (1995: Table 2.1) and supplemented with BSAS (various waves using authors calculations).

In contrast to the other major episodes of large-scale union decline, as occurred in the first interwar period, Britain was not experiencing a widespread recession or substantial price deflation (two factors often cited as causes of union decline). In the latter half of the period, Britain and America experienced historically low unemployment rates yet the fall continued. A chronic decline of this magnitude stands out as a sharp departure from prior experience and represents a marked shift in the provision of workplace voice in the British economy. The significance of this shift is further compounded by the fact that collective representation is often viewed—even by trade union critics—as the principal source of employee voice.[1] The decline in union voice witnessed in Britain over this period appears to suggest that collective voice has either been replaced with something else (a supply side effect), shunted aside by employees (a demand side effect), or perhaps some combination of both.

From the perspective of social science inquiry, this departure presents a potential learning opportunity not to be missed. Employment Relations (ER) research is not often viewed as a laboratory science, and under normal circumstances controlled experiments testing the effects of organizational and labour market changes are not possible. However, by focusing on this period in British history it is possible to draw lessons and reach conclusions that under more normal circumstances are hard to tease out from outcomes of smaller magnitude and shorter duration.

This chapter offers seven observations on the nature of workplace voice and its determinants in Britain since the early 1980s; in each case focusing on implications for well-known debates about worker participation, labour relations, human resource management and organizational behaviour. Drawing thematic observations and forming conclusions on the basis of previous work is not the same as testing causal hypotheses. Nor does the empirical work we do sample from here (much of it our own) constitute an experiment in any scientific sense. Nonetheless, the major outlines of what has happened to workplace voice in Britain over the past twenty-five years does speak fairly directly to themes that have figured prominently in questions of union membership demise (Gospel and Wood, 2003), human resource management ascendancy (Machin and Wood, 2005) and new forms of employment relations (Dundon et al., 2004; Marsden, 2004), at both the theoretical and practical level.[2]

More importantly for the purposes of this book, understanding the conditions under which employee voice mechanisms emerge inside the workplace helps to uncover where, given structural shifts in the economy, voice provision may be heading in the future. Identifying which forms of voice are best suited to differing socio-economic and industrial environments can provide answers to questions of just how varied, new, and unorthodox workplace voice can be. These answers will also help determine whether, in the context of union representation declines, employees will still have access to meaningful forms of two-way communication in the future, and just how and where in the employment relations landscape these forms might be found.

Seven Key Observations about Employee Voice

Below we outline seven important themes or observations that have arisen from recent studies on workplace voice in Britain, and which any framework (or set of models) purporting to understand participation at the workplace needs to address. The section then ends with a set of general conclusions.

Observation 1. There are a wide variety of formal voice regimes that extend beyond the traditional confines of collective voice provided by unions.

Formal systems of voice provision in Britain, what have been termed 'voice regimes' in the literature (Bryson et al., 2004), are found in more varied forms than previously imagined and typically documented. Even within the traditional union voice sector, there can be direct and representative forms of voice that coexist side-by-side, the latter representing the form of voice found in a majority of unionized environments in Britain (Bryson and Gomez, 2003).[3]

The lack of attention paid to this broader nature of voice provision is due in large part to the fact that most of the writing in this area has focused almost exclusively on the American case where, for legal reasons, it is often more difficult to combine union with non-union forms of voice (LeRoy, 2006). In Britain there exists a voluntarist framework that has granted the parties to industrial relations a considerable degree of freedom to choose their preferred or agreed institutional arrangements (Clegg, 1979). Employers have therefore had a substantial amount of choice as to the voice regime(s) they adopt.

In Britain, detailed data on unions and voice at the workplace span the period 1980–2004. These two decades broadly coincide with two well-defined political eras. First, there was the Thatcher era, during which a significant expansion of employer choice was generated by a series of deregulatory measures that reduced legal support for trade union activity (Willman and Bryson, 2007). The second era was dominated by New Labour which, much to the chagrin of its trade union supporters, did little to reverse many of the earlier Tory reforms. Employers in the UK were therefore virtually unconstrained in the period up to 2004 in their ability to offer voice and to mix union and non-union alternatives at the establishment level.[4]

This period of relative managerial freedom allowed unionized employers to supplement union representation with non-union voice without having to incur the costs of terminating relationships with unions. It also allowed newly born firms to bypass unions altogether and to establish their own 'brand' of non-union voice (Willman and Bryson, 2007). This situation contrasts starkly with the US, where the legal system clearly identifies certain non-union voice and HRM practices as illegal, in order to preserve unions' 'sole agent' status (LeRoy, 2006).[5] While the virtues of such a system for trade union strength can be debated—with many allies of the union movement insisting that this aspect of the Wagner Act model is the worst of all possible worlds for unions and employees (Adams, 1998)—it is true that it has not allowed any viable non-union voice system to grow alongside the union representative channel.

The absence of statutorily enforceable voice in Britain means that most firms are 'born' voice free and as a consequence have had to choose whether to remain in this default position, or to adopt a formal voice regime sometime after their set-up date. Employers have been equally unconstrained in their adoption decision, as there are several voice regimes in Britain to choose from. Voice regimes may combine union and non-union voice. They may also combine direct and representative voice mechanisms. One can identify the choice set facing firms based on a series of questions asked of workplaces in the Workplace Employment Relations Survey series (WERS). These questions can capture employer options in voice regime provision. The choice set basically boils down to four mutually exclusive options depicted in Figure 16.2 (Panel A) and set out in detail below:

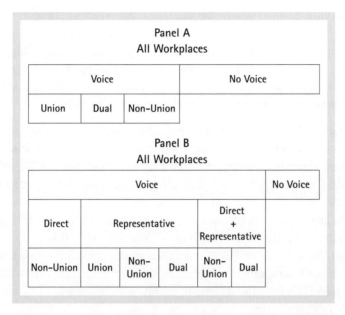

Figure 16.2 Voice regime choice in Britain for all workplaces

- To Buy (i.e., Union Voice). This is closest to the Freeman and Medoff (1984) view of voice where the employer subcontracts to one or more unions the exclusive responsibility for the generation of voice. This involves, in Williamson's (1983) terms, a long-term relational contract in which the employer's direct costs in the production of voice are low but the risks of supplier (i.e., union) opportunism are high. In our survey data these are workplaces with one or more unions recognized for pay bargaining or union representatives on-site.

- To Make (i.e., Non-Union Voice). This is akin to the 'sophisticated HRM' approach, but in the voice context involves employers choosing directly to provide a set of formal employee voice mechanisms excluding third party (i.e., union) intervention. The administrative costs of providing this type of voice are correspondingly higher and while there is a risk that the approach may not generate the voice required, there are no counterparty risks. In the context of British WERS surveys, this includes: the presence of joint consultative committee meeting at least once a month; non-union representative on-site; problem-solving groups; regular meetings between management and employees which allow for two-way communication; and finally, team briefings that occur at least once a month and devote time to employees' questions/views.

- To Hedge (i.e., Dual Channel Voice). Following the logic in Williamson (1991) this is a mixed option in which union and non-union voice mechanisms coexist. This may be seen as a form of employer hedging, attempting to control both cost and risk. For simplicity, we have treated this as a single option, acknowledging that a range of hybrids are possible across firms.

- To Maintain the No Voice Default (i.e., No Voice). These are workplaces defined by the absence of any voice measures highlighted above. These workplaces may have one-way communication practices, such as suggestion box schemes, that could substitute for formal two-way voice, but even here previous work has demonstrated that the uptake of these methods inside no voice workplaces has been rather minimal (Bryson et al., 2007).

Going further and distinguishing between *direct* and *representative* voice dimensions of the choice set, a sixfold typology emerges. Direct voice is a non-union phenomenon, though combinations with union voice (which by definition is representative) are also possible. These added dimensions are depicted in Panel B of Figure 2.[6]

To see which of the voice regimes conceptualized above is most prevalent in the British economy, or alternatively stated, to see how well this conceptualization coheres with the 'facts' as revealed by various waves of WERS surveys, we need to cast our gaze at Observation 2 below.

Observation 2. Despite the decline in union voice, the overall incidence of voice has actually remained constant over time.

There is a persistent group of workplaces, roughly one in five, that do not adopt any formal voice regime in each wave of the WERS stretching back to 1984.[7] These are the No Voice Default workplaces identified in the last bullet point of Observation 1 above (there is more to say about these workplaces in our final observation). Thus four out of five workplaces have consistently provided some voice to their employees. This is demonstrated in the first two rows (Panel A) of Table 16.1.

Table 16.1 Voice regimes in Britain for all workplaces, 1984–2004

Type of voice arrangement	1984	1990	1998	2004
Panel A: All Workplaces				
1 No voice	16	19	18	14
2. Voice (all types)	84	81	82	86
Panel B: Voice Workplaces Only				
3.1 Union only	24	14	9	6
3.2 Dual (union and non-union)	43	39	32	33
3.3 Non-union only	17	28	41	47
All Observations	1,973	2,045	1,911	1,579

Notes: All cells in percentages. Base is workplaces with twenty-five or more employees. Union voice is defined as one or more recognized trade unions or a joint consultative committee meeting at least once a month with representatives chosen through union channels. Non-union voice is defined as a joint consultative committee meeting at least once a month with representatives not chosen through union channels, regular meetings between senior management and the workforce or briefing groups.

Source: Authors' calculations from various waves of WERS surveys.

This constancy in the overall incidence of voice in Britain masks an internal shift within the voice sector itself. Table 16.1 Panel B, which isolates changes in the voice sector only from 1984 onwards, demonstrates that the dominant form of voice provision in British workplaces, as far back as 1990, was the non-union variety; either as a standalone (i.e., Make) regime or as part of some dual combination (Hedge) with union voice. Union only voice, on the other hand, has witnessed a steady decline, as has dual voice, both of which have been substituted by the exclusive use of non-union voice. This is represented in Figure 16.3, as shifts in union forms of voice have clearly been substituted by non-union regimes.

Why, then, has the overall incidence of voice remained constant, despite the large falls in the previously dominant union voice form? To answer this question we need to invoke the idea of voice as a *generic need* among workers (and hence a derived need for employers). Voice is *generic* in the sense that it is demanded (implicitly or explicitly) by workers irrespective of time and place and, as such, is an inherent requirement for most employers to provide.[8] Demand for voice is expected to remain roughly constant.

Voice can (and is) supplied by an assortment of institutional actors: the state (in the form of statutory provision and legal regulation); the firm (in the form of non-union voice); and by unions (in the form of collective representation). Union voice, being one of many methods for providing voice to workers, is one form of delivery that resides within a *solution market*: this is where a specific buyer (in this case a workplace) seeks a specific solution to a problem (the problem of supplying voice

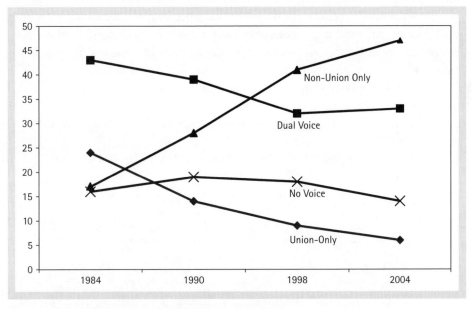

Figure 16.3 Voice regimes in Britain, 1984–2004 (%)

Source: Authors' calculations from various waves of WERS surveys.

to its employees) based on all possible solutions (the fourfold options presented in Observation 1). Specific forms of voice compete with each other for dominance in this solution market. What should shift, therefore, are the specific ways (solutions) in which voice is delivered and not the overall provision of voice.[9] We would expect voice regime choices to be determined by their relative costs, regulatory regimes, the absence of employee demand in some sectors and a whole host of other internal and external factors to the firm and workplace (Bryson et al., 2007; Dundon et al., 2005).

Union representation, in this context, can be viewed as a victim of shifting cost-benefit decisions on the part of new firms (Bryson et al., 2007) and to some extent new workers as well (Bryson et al., 2005b; Machin, 2003).

Observation 3. The prevailing voice regime in Britain for much of the post-war era (i.e., union only voice) lost the bulk of its market share to non-union rivals primarily because of ecological factors.

The ecological phenomenon alluded to above refers to a voluntarist employment relations environment, where statute does not dictate voice choices, and where new workplaces are born with 'no voice' as their default. New employers choose to either: one, wait before investing in voice; two, live indefinitely with no voice; and/or three, immediately adopt their own non-union voice regime. In Table 16.2 we see how workplace set-up date is linked closely to the incidence of voice regime, with newer workplaces set up after 1960 having a significantly greater incidence of non-union voice.

Why is it that employers started to move away from union voice and towards non-union voice? One principal reason for this is that non-union voice typically involves fewer lock-in effects, in the sense that once in place, removing a union is much more costly (and in extremis may involve costly plant closure) than the costs incurred from jettisoning an internally produced form of non-union voice.[10]

Another reason for the shift is that non-union voice alternatives have grown in visibility/reliability over time, with firms increasingly able to hire expert HRM managers with administrative experience in non-union voice provision. There is also some evidence that employers became disenchanted with union voice.[11]

Table 16.2 Incidence of voice regimes in Britain in 1984 for all workplaces by set-up date

Voice regime	By set up date			
	<1960 [1]	1960–1974 [2]	1975–1984 [3]	Diff [1]–[3]
1. Union Voice	28	23	16	−12
2. Dual Channel	43	42	42	−1
3. Non-Union Voice	13	22	22	+9
4. No Voice	17	13	20	+3

Note: All cells in percentages. Columns may not up add to 100 due to rounding.

Source: Authors' Calculations based on WERS 1984.

Older firms that had originally adopted union voice did not, it should be emphasized, abandon union voice completely. Rather, they supplemented union voice with non-union voice (Bryson et al., 2007). This suggests that greater lock-in and path dependence are associated with union voice regimes. Very few firms switch from the union to no voice option, suggesting as well that there is experiential learning associated with voice provision generally. Over time workplaces are likely to become cognizant of the hard to observe benefits associated with employee voice provision and wish not to lose those in an effort to weaken union voice. This drift from union only to non-union voice mixing can been characterized as a 'long goodbye' for traditional union only voice (Willman et al., 2007), rather than a sudden shift from one voice equilibrium to another. These conclusions are further elaborated in our next observation.

Observation 4. When viewed over a long enough time period, spanning most of the past century, the rise and fall of union membership in Britain is akin to a Product Life Cycle (PLC).

Unlike the generic form of voice, whose demand is constant, union voice is a specific solution (one of many) to the problem of satiating employee voice.[12] This means that like most methods for solving a given problem, it has a fairly pre-determined life cycle as any product meeting an inherent need would. This is the well-known product life cycle (PLC) concept, which is a useful tool for understanding a product's success or failure over time. It is usually represented in a diagram that relates time on the horizontal axis to some measure of product success (such as sales) on the vertical axis. Because a PLC is dynamic and involves two variables (time and sales) it is best shown graphically. If one compares Panel A in Figure 16.4, where a typical PLC is depicted, with our original Figure 16.1, we see a striking similarity between PLC and union density and membership. This, we argue, is not a coincidence, as there are several features of the product life cycle (PLC) model that are applicable in the case of union voice demise in Britain.

Focusing on Figure 16.4, Panel A, the diagram shows the five stages in a typical product's PLC.[13] As product markets grow, mature, and then decline over time, a firm's marketing strategy must evolve to the changes in buyer behaviour and the changing competitive environment. The state is also often called upon to adjust industrial regulations and consumer protections as a consequence of technological changes that occur through the course of a PLC.

The five stages of the typical PLC depicted above and their relevance to union voice are as follows:

1. *Introduction.* The uptake of a new product is often slow. There are several reasons for this. Technology is new and uncertain. Distributors still have contracts with older products and producers. Buyers are still unaware of the new product or are uncertain of its benefits. If the product is truly new, in the sense of offering a technological improvement and not merely a different brand, competition from

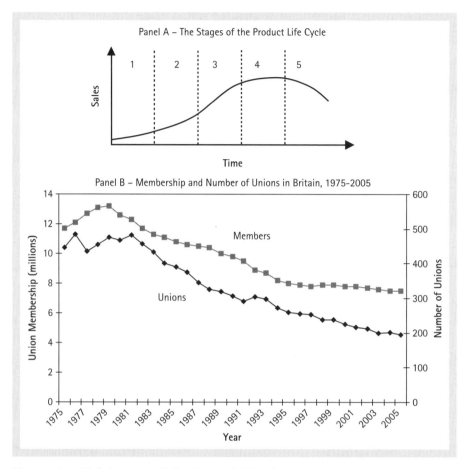

Figure 16.4 PLC theory and the rise and fall of union membership

Source: Authors calculations from The Annual Reports of the Certification Officer.

other brands and products would be low at this stage. For example, in the initial stages of the home personal computer, companies like Olivetti were major players while giants like IBM were more concerned with large mainframe and institutional computers. Unions for a time were just such a 'unique technology' for delivering voice. They were the only kids on the block for much of the past century.

2. *Growth phase.* Growth of sales occurs at an accelerating rate. The causes of growth can be varied but one can surmise that if first users are satisfied, they then pass on favourable word-of-mouth to other consumers for the product. Wider distribution and more visibility also increase sales. More competitors enter, but this actually expands the market. For example, the growth of car technology in the United States in 1910 had over 200 domestic car companies where as today it has only three domestic automakers. Unions experienced

a similar explosion in growth in the early part of the twentieth century, peaking in Britain in the 1970s (see Figure 16.4, Panel B) and declining ever since.

3. *Shake out phase.* Demand is still increasing but at a slower rate. The weakest competitors are leaving the market. Concentration and merger activity begins. Airlines in the passenger air travel industry witnessed numerous mergers and failures after the terrorist attacks on 11 September 2001, a time which for a period dramatically lowered passenger travel. In Figure 16.4, Panel B, we see a second line trailing underneath the membership line showing the number of trade unions peaking, as noted in Willman and Bryson (2006), just as membership begins to plunge. Soon after this inflection point, both follow the same trend, with each declining and reinforcing the inevitable demise.

4. *Maturity.* Market penetration is now very high. Most consumers have bought the product. Technology has stabilized and only minor modifications are possible within the existing product range. There is not much room for growth but neither is there much decline. The period of relative union growth and stability in Britain is the mid-to-late 1970s.

5. *Decline.* New, more technologically advanced, products make their appearance and substitute for the existing product. Changes in the consumer's needs or external changes (perhaps in complementary technology) could make products obsolete. For example, if the price of petrol increases, this may make obsolete the internal combustion engine and cause permanent declines in cars with these engines. In most cases, the PLC's fifth stage is shown with sales declining to zero. But what happens after a product begins to decline is not predestined. Indeed, as we shall see in a moment, firms (like union organizations perhaps) can do much to relaunch or forestall a product's decline in this last stage.

The major PLC-unionization similarities seen above are linked to the fact that union voice, like any formal solution to a problem, is susceptible to competition from other newer solutions (i.e., technologies) for solving the same problem in a better (i.e., more reliable, less costly) fashion. We have seen evidence of this already in Observations 2 and 3, in that dual channel voice replaced union only solutions for older workplaces and stand-alone non-union voice became the norm for newer workplaces. Second, there is in the PLC model, both buyer and 'supplier/distributor' reticence at the early stages of any technological or product introduction. This makes initial uptake for a new product hard to initiate, even if there is latent demand from a significant segment of buyers. This is akin to the reticence that both employers and governments displayed to unions at the turn of the last century.[14] In some geographic regions of the US, for example, unions never managed to take hold primarily because of employer hostility, and still today those regions remain largely union free (Lipset et al., 2004). Similarly, at the other tail of the PLC, lies buyer fatigue, which makes the demise of an outmoded technology often hard to forestall.

In between these two stages is a substantial period of buyer and supplier acceptance, which if extensive enough and accompanied by strong learning or experiential benefits, can imply durable lock-in and/or brand loyalty. That is, once customers sample an experiential product, they tend to stick with it, as do close relatives and associates of these consumers. Similar patterns have been found in the union sector (Blanden and Machin, 2002; Gomez and Gunderson, 2004). These effects make an existing cohort of users loyal and attached to a particular solution, but often leave successive generations of new customers more likely to wait, or to pick newer and/or better forms of voice, leaving older users stuck with an inferior (though relatively more net beneficial) choice.

Union membership, therefore, exhibits many of the properties of a particular solution to a problem (i.e., an experiential product) that over time exhibits rising, constant, and ultimately falling buyer take-up. In this sense, firms can be seen as both the suppliers of particular voice regimes for their workers and also buyers or adopters of voice: only that their demand for voice is a derived one, much like computer manufactures who buy computer chips. Silicon chips are bought only to the extent that there is a pull factor associated with consumer preferences and demands for computers. Union voice, therefore, like an Intel chip, is one type of voice (silicon chip) that firms may be forced (through worker pressure) to adopt over other forms (in-house brands).

Over time, if employee pressure for union voice abets, or if firms are determined to forestall collective representation at the workplace, union voice is likely to decline where substitutes are available. Unions themselves may have also helped to foster some of this decline, by paradoxically being successful in retaining union members at unionized workplaces. Because of the high lock-in effects associated with experiential products, such as unionism, once a member signs on or a workplace is organized, the chance of losing membership is lowered (other than that due to job loss or plant closure).[15] In the case of a firm, it becomes rather hard to remove a union once in place. This makes trade union officials' need for new workplace organization and new member recruitment seem less profitable than member retention.

Observation 5. Workers have stopped joining unions, even where they are present at the workplace and representing workers.

There is some symmetry in the workplace effects we have documented above and the observations drawn from employee—as opposed to employer—voice choices. The key here is that new workers are increasingly less likely to be exposed to unions through social networks at an early enough stage in their lives and careers. Early exposure proves crucial because most of the benefits that unions provide today are not found in the visible wage premium.[16] The benefits instead reside with more hard to observe non-wage benefits. Most of what unions do is only revealed *after* a worker becomes a member or joins a unionized workplace; this is akin to what, in consumer theory, is known as a classic 'experience good' (Bryson et al., 2005a; Gomez and Gunderson, 2004). Because union voice is much like an experience good, this presents problems for unions in attracting new members, as they need to expose the benefits of their trade union voice prior to purchase, whereas workers are well aware of all the costs as reflected in membership dues and possible penalties related to threats made by recalcitrant employers that threaten or punish workers for joining a union and trying to organize (Logan, 2002).

In this context, it is important to point out a relevant feature of the British system; namely it does not compel workers to join a union or pay union dues even if employees are represented by the union.[17] This creates an incentive for workers to free-ride. This has become a large problem for unions in Britain: the free-rider rate rose dramatically in the 1980s and 1990s (Bryson and Freeman, 2007). New behavioural economic work explaining how procrastination fosters decision delay, in scenarios where decision making involves future benefits coupled with immediate costs—which describes union membership almost perfectly for most workers—is instructive. In the absence of compulsory due payments—so-called agency or 'closed shop' laws—workers desiring unionization can nevertheless rationalize their free representation by insisting that 'I may want to join the union, but since I do not have to pay dues and I am not compelled to do so, I will wait another day, and the next day the same rationalization is undertaken, and so on.' This worker bypass effect helps to explain the rise in 'never membership' in Britain over the last few decades as seen in Figure 16.5.

An important underlying question is how well this worker-level analysis fits in with the general thrust of the chapter and book, which is predicated on employer-level analyses? The answer lies primarily in understanding worker demands for voice, which may engender employer or government/statutory supply. Specifically, to the extent that new workers increasingly fail to translate their latent desire for some form of collective representation into effective demand for union voice (Freeman and Rogers, 1999)—because they have never had any exposure to it through family or first jobs (Gomez and Gunderson, 2004)—the provision of union voice becomes harder to 'sell' in the voice market. Substitutes gradually emerge and workers have no real comparison upon which to make judgements.

This is evidenced by Figure 16.5 below, which demonstrates that the majority of union membership decline (the falling line) in Britain was accounted for by rising 'never membership' or non-adoption (the rising line), as opposed to worker ex-membership (the constant line on the bottom). People were not increasingly leaving unions: they simply stopped joining to the same extent as they had done before (Bryson et al., 2005b).[18]

Observation 6. Voice regimes are found to be differentially associated with the presence and intensity of progressive HRM polices at the workplace level.

In the recent past, it has often been taken as given that voice and modern forms of Human Resource Management (HRM) were substitutes (Guest, 1989; Kochan, 1980). The rise of one (HRM) was clearly correlated with demise of union voice, hence rationales for the channel by which HRM displaced union voice were proffered (Belfield and Heywood, 2004).[19]

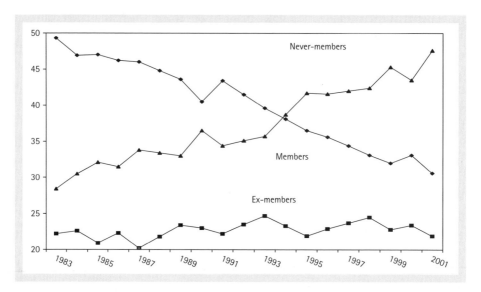

Figure 16.5 Trends in union membership split by never, current, and ex-members, 1983–2001 (%)

Note: Mid-point rates have been interpolated for years in which the survey was not conducted (1988 and 1992) and years in which the question on ex-membership was not asked (1994 and 1997).

Source: Estimates from data in Bryson et al. (2005b).

The reality proves to be a little more complicated than earlier work may have imagined. If one examines the four typologies of voice regime choice established at the outset, one finds workplaces with no formal voice and union only voice have the lowest adoption of HRM practices. Otherwise, however, there are significant positive correlations between non-union and dual voice and HRM innovative practices. The functioning of HRM appears to require formal voice structures. The evolutionary and transaction cost literatures point the way in explaining the creative capabilities aspect associated with innovation creation and adoption.

Even more nuance emerges when one focuses only on the voice sector. That is, by looking at workplaces that provide voice, there appears to be a hierarchy of voice provision that emerges with respect to HRM intensity. Union only voice is last and non-union and dual channel voice become virtually indistinguishable in their leading position. This is confirmed and reinforced by the findings of regression analyses, where factors that give rise to both union voice and HRM (such as firm size) are controlled for. Table 16.3 provides a picture of these raw and adjusted associations, showing how the relation between HRM and dual and non-union voice remain strong even when controls are added.

As can been seen from earlier discussion and in Table 16.3, the greater part of the union voice sector in the UK is dual channel and hence also to a material degree

Table 16.3 Voice regimes and mean HRM scores in Britain for all
         workplaces, 1998

Voice Regime	Raw HRM score	Adjusted HRM score
1. No Voice	5.71	6.97
2. Union Only	6.41	6.83
3. Non-Union Only	6.86	7.56
4. Dual Voice	7.51	7.64

Note: HRM Score is a count of 13 progressive HRM practices. Each practice is weighted equally such that if a workplace had one practice it would be allocated a score of 1 and so on. The maximum value is therefore 13. The Raw score is merely the mean of the score by voice regime. The Adjusted score is based on coefficients taken from the regression of HRM scores with extensive controls for workplace characteristics such as workplace size accounted for.

Source: Based on estimates found in Tables 2 (row 14) and 7 (row 9) in Bryson et al. (2007).

non-union. This perhaps explains much of the compatibility between union presence and HRM. Union only voice regimes, however, are more similar to no voice regimes in their relationship to HRM. In this sense, the UK case may not be a good basis for generalization to other labour markets. Where employers face a straight choice between union or non-union voice (as in the US), the implications for HRM adoption and use may be very different.

Observation 7. In the absence of a closed shop or statutory voice provisions, some employers will always choose the no voice option.

Around one-fifth of British workplaces have no formal voice mechanisms. Some firms are simply small enough to rely on informal face-to-face communication (Willman et al., 2006) while others seem to have a preference for 'no voice'. For example, even after controlling for size, sector, industry and other employer characteristics, firms owned and operated by single family owners are less likely to employ a formal voice regime. They also tend to have fewer HRM practices (Bryson et al., 2007).

The likely reason for this finding centres on the broader costs/benefits and perceptions of the returns to voice for such employers. The expectation of accruing all the benefits of workplace voice or HRM, without investing in a system of voice provision and thus bypassing costs of implementing these innovations formally, is perhaps too high a temptation for those owner–managers who can also appropriate all the rents/profits should this riskier strategy pay off. Managers who cannot appropriate the rents directly, as is the case in the public sector, are more likely to implement a voice regime or allow one to form (i.e., unions), knowing that the net benefits (on a risk adjusted basis) are higher this way and perhaps also make their jobs as managers easier. This is one explanation for the high rates of public sector unionism in many labour markets around the world.

CONCLUSIONS

This chapter deals with the emergence, presence, and gradual transformation of workplace voice in Britain. Britain is an interesting case because it has sustained one of the longest and most prolonged falls in union representation in the Western world. Some have interpreted this as a move away from institutionalized voice by both workers and employers in the face of global product market competition and attendant needs for greater labour flexibility. This chapter has shown that union collective representation has been *supplanted* by non-union voice in new workplaces and, where union voice persists in older workplaces, it has been *supplemented* by non-union voice. The incidence of 'no voice' workplaces has remained roughly constant. The absence of formal voice in a significant minority of workplaces can be linked to certain observable firm characteristics, such as size, network externalities, ownership and age of enterprise (Bryson et al., 2007).

This chapter has defined workplace voice by partially drawing on insights from consumer theory, industrial organization, and transaction cost economics. The central notion is that voice represents an inherent or generic need for workers (and to some extent for employers as well given that their demand is largely a derived demand from employees). Irrespective of time and place, demand for workplace voice in an industrialized society does not generally go away. Much like the basic need to communicate or to travel, voice is something whose demand is fairly constant. In its absence, the workplace suffers from the consequences of 'no voice' through higher absenteeism, turnover, and other negative side effects (Budd, 2004). Attempts to root out the need for voice through automation, Fordist assembly line manufacturing, and scientific management have historically experienced limited success (Kaufman, 2003).

The inherent need for voice at work, in turn, gives rise to derived or secondary needs, which represent the manner in which workers and employers have solved the problem of supplying voice at the workplace. For workers, the demand for voice and its various forms can be linked to the number and types of needs or problems workers face at the workplace. The greater the number of needs expressed, the more likely it is that workers will desire voice, and more specifically union as opposed to non-union voice, whether they are in the UK or the US (Bryson and Freeman, 2006, 2007).

Traditionally, union collective agreements were the preferred regime/technology for supplying voice to workers. But like any technique for solving a problem, it can be superseded or displaced by rival forms. It has often been asserted that HRM is one such substitute. The evidence for Britain suggests that HRM is more of a complement than a direct substitute for voice. What has undermined union voice is the use of non-union direct forms of voice—such as problem-solving groups, meetings between management and the workforce, and team briefings—which usually entail sharing information and consultation, as opposed to negotiation, and have an individual rather than a collective flavour.

In seeking to explain this transformation of voice in British workplaces, evidence from consumer behaviour theory is useful. We suggest that conceiving of voice as an experience good is appropriate. Since most workplaces are born without an off the shelf voice system(s) in place, management has to create and implement a specific set of practices which allow voice to emerge. They must also learn how these systems of workplace voice function in order to receive a stream of benefits, whereas the costs for workers and firms (in terms of time and money) are better known and experienced upfront.

In very small organizations this learning may not require too much formalization and voice can therefore remain informal and not very complex. However, in organizations with non-trivial numbers of employees, the structures used to facilitate voice provision are not self-evident.

Historically, the demand on the part of workers for union representation offered a solution to the voice provision problem for large employers. The nature of union representation made it a 'collective form of voice' suitable in an era of large manufacturing industries, standardized jobs and the demands of mass consumer markets. Unions flattened wage structures and many workers were employed in unionized workplaces, thus creating a self-reinforcing loop in which workers identified with the 'common dreams' and aspirations afforded by collective voice.[20] The high water mark for this type of voice provision in Britain, and most Anglo-Saxon countries, was the early 1970s. Until that time, firms new and old were still buying into 'union representation' as the appropriate solution for voice provision.

Union voice still remains quite durable in the sense that very few firms and/or employees seek to derecognize a union once it is formed. Workers themselves display much higher tenure and lower turnover when there is union voice at the firm (Fernie and Metcalf, 1995), affirming some of the positive net benefits provided by union voice. The reasons for this behaviour have much to do, we believe, with the experiential nature of voice regimes; union voice being the prototypical form for older workplaces. Because the benefits of a given way of delivering voice are unknown to managers prior to adoption, there are elements of risk and uncertainty involved in adopting any new technology or process innovation. Workplace voice is one such innovation and so employers and employees often have to use external cues to base their adoption decisions upon. The prevailing technology offers one such cue, and if industry leaders are increasingly employing non-union voice, it may be wise for others to do likewise. Once chosen, a given voice regime has informational advantages that newer, perhaps 'technically' better voice regimes do not.

Evidence linking employer networks—both internal via multi-establishment firms and external networks through affiliation in industry associations—to greater voice provision is another feature of the voice story. This is an added facet of the 'experience-good' model in that experience goods have larger network externalities and path dependent effects associated with them. To the extent that a prevailing technology takes hold, sometimes for historically accidental reasons, learning by doing, lock-in and network effects all combine to create positive feedbacks that make a given system of voice provision dominant; leaving another, perhaps 'better', form languishing.

Another part of the experience-good story is switching in and out of voice regimes, which can be characterized in a number of ways (e.g., experimentation, optimization as the external environment changes or even as 'flailing'). There is evidence that new workplaces often delay adopting a formal voice regime—a large number of workplaces with 'no voice' are younger establishments (e.g., more likely to be set up in the earliest 'birth cohort' as seen in Table 16.2). This too is a feature of experience goods since they tend to generate greater switching costs and lock-in effects than technologies whose qualities are well known prior to adoption. Firms that know lock-in will spend more time searching before implementing a voice regime that will be difficult to undo. Thus the gross benefits of voice regimes as stand-alone solutions are not enough to encourage adoption; hence the puzzle that many labour relations scholars have noted (i.e., Why don't better ways of managing employees and doing things diffuse more rapidly and ubiquitously?) can be accounted for by characterizing voice in this way.

Finally, the rise of Human Resource Management, we argue, is not the cause of union voice decline. HRM and most forms of voice—dual channel and non-union voice—act as complements rather than substitutes at the workplace level in Britain. The reasons for complementarity can be located in the functions served by HRM and those served by voice. It would appear that voice is required to make HRM and other progressive workplace practices work more effectively. The transaction cost and evolutionary schools predict that governance costs fall if workers have greater organizational capabilities that aid in the sharing of tacit knowledge among workers and between employees and management. This may explain why certain forms of voice—such as non-union and dual systems that combine union and non-union voice— are systematically related to more, rather than fewer, progressive HRM workplace practices.

In the final analysis, it may be that the flexible way in which voice provision can occur in Britain has afforded unions, despite the large falls in overall membership, a lifeline that has otherwise been absent in the US. Voice has not disappeared into the wilderness in Britain, despite the ebbing of its traditional collective provision, though workers may still be better served by forms of voice that carry third party (i.e., union or statutory) representation.

Notes

1. The definition of formal employee voice in this chapter is a variant of the definition developed by Hirschman (1970) in his seminal monograph and later elaborated and appropriated to unions in the labour market by Freeman and Medoff (1984). We refer to *formal voice* as any institutionalized form of two-way communication between management and employees. As we show later, this definition extends beyond union voice and non-union forms of representation and includes direct forms of two-way communication such as problem-solving groups. Also included are the statutory systems of works council voice developed as part of the European Union (EU) directive on workplace consultation. For more, see Bryson et al. (2004); Dundon et al. (2005). Broader definitions of voice are also invoked for the labour market as a whole and for society more generally. In this context see the work by Adrian Wilkinson and his colleagues (Wilkinson et al., 2004) and John Budd's *Employment with a Human Face* (2004).

2. As early as the 1980s, writers (mostly in the US as this is where the union decline was already well underway) were noting the growth of the non-union sector and delving into its systems of employee management and voice (see Verma and Kochan, 1985). For a very early overview, see Foulkes, Fred K. (1980), *Personnel Policies in Large Non-union Companies*. New York: Prentice Hall.

3. Though the exact proportions have shifted slightly since the earliest waves of the WERS surveys, roughly seven out of ten unionized workplaces offer a combination of direct and collective forms of voice, as opposed to collective voice forms only (see Table 1, p. 19 in Bryson et al., 2007).

4. The implementation of the EU directive on worker consultation and the recognition legislation, both signed into law in early 2000, have changed this landscape slightly. However, its impact in the period 1998–2004 has been minimal. The vast majority of union bargaining agreements are still entered into voluntarily (Gall, 2004). For more, see Gospel and Willman (2003); Moore (2004); Wood et al. (2003).

5. Canada is an intriguing mix of the two systems. Its union recognition procedures are akin to the US Wagner Act but Canadian law neither prohibits non-union voice nor does it have statutory provisions (apart from over health and safety) for works councils (Taras, 2006). Nevertheless, it appears that the non-union voice sector in Canada is one-fifth the size of the voice sector in Britain (Lipset et al., 2004).

6. A concrete illustration of a dual channel voice regime is provided in a recent bulletin circulated to staff at the London School of Economics, which already had a collective bargaining agreement in place, and which describes the creation of a new Staff Consultative Committee: 'SCC terms of Reference: 1. To consider and identify and be consulted on issues, trends and developments relating to LSE strategy, policy and governance likely to have an impact on the working environment at LSE with the exception of matters concerning individuals; 2. To communicate its views on these matters to the relevant individuals or bodies within LSE and to request further information relevant to its deliberations. 3. The SCC shall have no decision making powers (which committees retain) or negotiating powers in respect of staff matter (which remains the purview of the trades unions) and is not a part of the governance structure and is self-standing body.'

7. The proportion of no voice workplaces has actually declined a little since 1998. In the latest wave of WERS data, one in seven workplaces are identified as no voice workplaces.

8. There is evidence that employee voice is associated with worker engagement, motivation and satisfaction, health and well-being. However, formal institutionalized voice may not be needed in the smallest workplaces where one-to-one communication is feasible. Furthermore employers may have little derived need for voice where they rely little on worker inputs for their competitive advantage.

9. This follows from a well-known Industrial Relations notion, articulated by Jack Barbash in the following aphorism 'Like Nature, Industrial Relations abhors a Vacuum'. The notion is that actors in the system compete to fill a space already carved out by the inherent need for voice. In its absence, Barbash, Meltz, and Hebden all separately identify the (negative) consequences that follow from the pursuit of a union free strategy and consequent lack of voice. For more, see Barbash (1987), Hebden and Stern (1998); Meltz (1989) .

10. An interesting question is perhaps why the fear of lock-in may have risen over time? It could be due to the increased rate of technological change and product market competition more generally, which means that firms are increasingly concerned about the penalty of lock-in to any existing technology or managerial innovation.

11. Shift share analyses show that under one-third of the fall in union recognition between 1984 and 1998 was accounted for by compositional change among employers, which is consistent with a decline in employer tastes for union voice (Bryson et al., 2004). Blanchflower and Bryson (2008) show that compositional effects account for one-third of the union decline in the private sector between 1984 and 2004.

12. Unions offer other solutions for workers and firms as well. For workers, they provide direct wage and non-wage benefits. For firms, according to Gospel (1992) unions often help firms maintain collusive arrangements and protection from external competition.

13. This life cycle can equally apply to a specific technology or industry.

14. The struggle for ever increasing worker rights and the fundamental right to organize began much earlier than this. The repeal of the Combination Laws in 1824 in Britain— which meant that trade unions were no longer illegal—began the slow but eventual process of trade union recognition at the workplace level. See Chapter 2 of Booth (1995) for a fuller account.

15. There is an important caveat of note here. We know that workplace-level union density has declined markedly among unionized workplaces. This is due to new employees choosing non-membership, which shows up as rising never membership even in union workplaces (Bryson et al., 2005b). Once this begins then the experiential component at workplace level begins to unravel.

16. There is still a substantial premium in the US and smaller but significant premium in Britain (Blanchflower and Bryson, 2008; Bryson, 2007).

17. The closed shop was made legally unenforceable in 1991.

18. By 2005 52 per cent of employees in Britain were never members (Bryson, 2007).

19. The most recent evidence for Britain has pointed in the direction of no relation at all (Machin and Wood, 2005).

20. See Todd Gitlin's well-known book of the same name, *The Twilight of Common Dreams*. New York: Owl Books, 1996.

References

ADAMS, R. J. (1998) 'Trade Unions', in M. Poole and M. Warner (eds), *The Handbook of Human Resource Management*, pp. 817–25. London: International Thomson Business Press.

BAIN, R. SAYERS, G., and PRICE, R. J. (1980) *Profiles of Union Growth: A Comparative Statistical Portrait of Eight Countries*. Basil Blackwell: London.

BARBASH, J. (1987) 'Like Nature, Industrial Relations Abhors a Vacuum: The Case of the Union Free Strategy', *Industrial Relations/Relations Industrielles*, 42(1): 168–79.

BELFIELD, C. R. and HEYWOOD, J. S. (2004) 'Do HRM Practices Influence the Desire for Unionization? Evidence across Workers, Workplaces, and Co-Workers for Great Britain', *Journal of Labor Research*, 25(2): 279–300.

BLANCHFLOWER, D. G. and BRYSON, A. (2008) *Union Decline in Britain*, CEP Discussion Paper no. 0864.

BLANDEN, J. and MACHIN, S. (2002) 'Cross-Generation Correlations of Union Status For Young People in Britain', CEP Discussion Papers 0553, Centre for Economic Performance, LSE.

BOOTH, A. (1995) *The Economics of the Trade Union*. Cambridge: Cambridge University Press.

BRYSON, A. (2007) 'New Labour, New unions?' in A. Park, J. Curtice, K. Thomson, M. Phillips, and M. Johnson (eds), *British Social Attitudes: The 23rd Report—Perspectives on a Changing Society*, pp. 183–211. London: Sage.

——FORTH, J., and KIRBY, S. (2005a). 'High-Performance Practices, Trade Union Representation and Workplace Performance in Britain', *Scottish Journal of Political Economy*, 53(3): 451–91.

——and FREEMAN, R. (2006) 'Worker Needs and Voice in the US and the UK', *NBER Working Paper no. 12310* National Bureau of Economic Research. Cambridge, MA:

————(2007) 'What Voice Do British Workers Want?' in R. Freeman, P. Boxall, and P. Haynes (eds), *What Workers Say: Employee Voice in the Anglo-American Workplace*, pp. 72–96. Ithaca and London: Cornell University Press.

——and GOMEZ, R. (2003) 'Buying into Union Membership', in H. Gospel and S. Wood (eds), *Representing Workers: Union recognition and membership in Britain*, pp. 51–71. London: Routledge.

————(2005) 'Why Have Workers Stopped Joining Unions?: Accounting for the Rise in Never—Membership in Britian.' *British Journal of Industrial Relations*, 43(1): 67–92.

——— GUNDERSON, M., and MELTZ, N. (2005b) 'Youth Adult Differences in Demand for Unionization: Are American, British and Canadian Workers All That Different?" *Journal of Labor Research*, 26(1): 155–67.

BRYSON, A., GOMEZ, R., KRETSCHMER, T., and WILLMAN, P. (2007) 'The Diffusion of Workplace Voice and High-commitment Human Resource Management Practices in Britain, 1984–1998'. *Industrial and Corporate Change*, 16(3): 395–426.

—— WILLMAN, P., and GOMEZ, R. (2004) 'The End of the Affair? The Decline in Employers' Propensity to Unionize' in J. Kelly and P. Willman (eds) *Union Organization and Activity*, pp. 129–149. London: Routledge.

BUDD, J. (2004) *Employment with Human Face: Balancing Efficiency, Equity, and Voice*. Ithaca and London: ILR Press/Cornell University Press.

CLEGG, H. A. (1979) *The System of Industrial Relations in Great Britain*. Oxford: Blackwell.

DUNDON, T., WILKINSON, A. J., MARCHINGTON, M., and ACKERS, P. (2004) 'The Meanings and Purpose of Employee Voice', *The International Journal of Human Resource Management*, 156(1): 1149–70.

—— —— —— (2005) 'The Management of Voice in Non-Union Organisations: Managers' Perspectives', *Employee Relations*, 27(3): 307–19.

FERNIE, S. and METCALF, D. (1995) 'Participation, Contingent Pay, Representation and Workplace Performance: Evidence from Great Britain.' *British Journal of Industrial Relations*, 33(3): 379–415.

FREEMAN, R. and MEDOFF, J. (1984) *What Do Unions Do?* New York: Basic Books.

—— and ROGERS, J. (1999) *What Workers Want*. Ithaca, NY: Cornell University Press and the Russell Sage Foundation.

GALL, G. (2004) 'Trade Union Recognition in Britain, 1995–2002: Turning a Corner?' *Industrial Relations Journal*, 35(3): 249–70.

GOMEZ, R. and GUNDERSON, M. (2004) 'The Experience-Good Model of Union Membership', in P. V. Wunnava (ed.), *The Changing Role of Unions: New Forms of Representation*. New York: M.E. Sharpe.

GOSPEL, H. (1992) *Markets, Firms and the Management of Labour in Modern Britain*. Cambridge: Cambridge University Press.

—— and WILLMAN, P. (2003) 'Dilemmas in Worker Representation—Information, Consultation, and Negotiation', in H. Gospel and S. Wood (eds), *Representing Workers: Trade Union Recognition and Membership in Britain*, pp. 144–165. London: Routledge.

—— and WOOD, S. J. (2003) *Representing Workers: Trade Union Recognition and Membership in Britain*. Routledge: London.

GUEST, D. E. (1989) 'Human Resource Management: Its Implications for Industrial Relations and Trade Unions', in J. Storey (ed.), *New Perspectives on Human Resource Management*, pp. 41–55. London: Routledge.

—— and CONWAY, N. (1999) 'Peering into the Black Hole: The Downside of the New Employment Relations in the UK', *British Journal of Industrial Relations*, 37(3): 367–90.

HEBDON, R. and STERN, H. (1998) 'Tradeoffs Among Expressions of Industrial Conflict: Public Sector Strike Bans and Grievance Arbitrations', *Industrial and Labor Relations Review*, 51(2): 204–21.

HIRSCHMAN, A. (1970) *Exit, Voice and Loyalty*. Cambridge: Harvard University Press.

KAUFMAN, B. E. (2003) 'Sumner Slichter on Personnel Management and Employee Representation in the Pre-New Deal Era', in B. E. Kaufman and D. Lewin (eds), *Advances in Industrial and Labor Relations*, 12: 223–69

KOCHAN, T. A. (1980) *Collective Bargaining and Industrial Relations.* Homewood, III: RICHARD D. IRWIN.

LEROY, M. H. (2006) 'The Power to Create or Obstruct Employee Voice: Does US Public Policy Skew Employer Preference for "No Voice" Workplaces?' *Socio-Economic Review,* 4(3): 311–19.

LIPSET, S. M., MELTZ, N. M., GOMEZ, R., and KATCHANOVSKI, I. (2004) *The Paradox of American Unionism: Why Americans Like Unions More than Canadians Do But Join Much Less.* Ithaca, NY: Cornell University Press.

LOGAN, J. (2002) 'Consultants, Lawyers and the Union-Free Movement in the United States since the 1970s', *Industrial Relations Journal,* 33(3): 197–214.

MACHIN, S. (2003) 'Trade Union Decline, New Workplaces and New Workers', in H. Gospel and S. Wood (eds), *Representing Workers: Union Recognition and Membership in Britain,* pp. 15–28. London: Routledge.

—— and WOOD, S. (2005) 'Human Resource Management as a Substitute For Trade Unions in British Workplaces', *Industrial and Labor Relations Review,* 58(2): 201–18.

MARCHINGTON, M., WILKINSON, A. J., ACKERS, P., and GOODMAN, J. (1993) 'The Influence of Managerial Relations on Waves of Employee Involvement', *British Journal of Industrial Relations,* 31(4): 553–77.

MARSDEN, D. (2004) 'The 'Network Economy' and Models of the Employment Contract: Psychological, Economic, and Legal', *British Journal of Industrial Relations,* 42(4): 659–84.

MELTZ, N. (1989) 'Industrial Relations: Balancing Efficiency and Equity', in J. Barbash and K. Barbash, (eds), *Theories and Concepts in Comparative Industrial Relations,* pp. 109–113. Columbia: Universality of South Carolina Press.

MOORE, S., (2004) 'Union Mobilization and Counter-Mobilization in the Statutory Recognition Process', in John Kelly and Paul Willman (eds), *Union Organization and Activity,* pp. 7–31. London: Routledge.

TARAS, D. G. (2006) 'Nonunion Representation and Employer Intent: How Canadian Courts and Labour Boards Determine the Legal Status of Nonunion Plans'. *Socio-Economic Review,* 4(2): 321–36.

TROY, L. and SHEFLIN, N. (1985) *The U.S. Union Sourcebook.* West Orange, NJ: Industrial Relations Data and Information (IRDI)Services.

WILLIAMSON, O. E. (1983) *Markets and Hierarchies: Analysis and Antitrust Implications.* New York: Free Press.

—— (1991) 'Comparative Economic Organization: The Analysis of Discrete Structural Alternatives', *Administrative Science Quarterly,* 36(2): 269–98.

WILLMAN, P. and BRYSON, A. (2006) 'Accounting for Collective Action: Resource Acquisition and Mobilisation in British Unions', *Centre for Economic Performance,* Discussion Paper no. 768.

WILLMAN, P. and BRYSON, A. (2007) 'Union Organization in Great Britain', *Journal of Labor Research,* 28(1): 93–115.

—— —— and GOMEZ, R. (2006) 'The Sound of Silence: Which Employers Choose 'No Voice' and Why?' *Socio-Economic Review,* 4(3): 283–99.

—— —— —— (2007) 'The Long Goodbye: New Establishments and the Fall of Union Voice in Britain', *The International Journal of Human Resource Management,* 18(7): 1318–34.

WILKINSON, A., DUNDON, T., MARCHINGTON, M., and ACKERS, P. (2004) 'Changing Patterns of Employee Voice', *Journal of Industrial Relations*, 46(3): 298–322.

WOOD, S., MOORE, S., and EWING, K. (2003) 'The Impact of the Trade Union Recognition Procedure under the Employment Relations Act 2000–2', in S. Wood and H. Gospel (eds), *Representing Workers: Union Recognition and Membership in Britain*, pp. 119–144. London: Routledge.

VERMA, A. and KOCHAN, T. A. (1985) 'The Growth and Nature of the Nonunion Sector within a Firm', in T. A. Kochan (ed.), *Challenges and Choices Facing American Labor*, pp. 89–127. Cambridge, MA: MIT Press.

CHAPTER 17

HIGH INVOLVEMENT MANAGEMENT AND PERFORMANCE

STEPHEN WOOD

WORKER participation is an end in itself—it provides an opportunity for workers to influence events. It is assumed, though, that it will provide not only greater procedural justice but fairer substantive outcomes. Its impact on individual and organizational performance may be positive as it may increase workers' job satisfaction and commitment to their work and organization. But studies of the association between job satisfaction and individual performance suggest it may not be that strong, and may depend on the type of job (Judge et al., 2001). Nor is the link between participation and performance, individual or organizational, necessarily positive.

Indeed, worker participation has commonly been seen as having detrimental effects on organizational performance, at least in managerial circles. This was particularly the case in the 1960s and 1970s in liberal market economies, such as the UK and USA. The most prominent formal means of participation, trade union representation, was perceived to be associated with lowering productivity and raising wages, and consequently in private sector firms with lower levels of profits, a perception that was borne out by much research (Metcalf, 2003; Wall et al., 2004). Trade unionism was also implicated in macro-economic failings, and particularly the high inflation and low productivity growth that characterized the UK and to a lesser extent the USA. Discussions of alternatives or complementary methods, such as Works Councils or Workers on the Board, were shrouded in accusations that they too would be unfavourable for the performance of organizations and, by implication, economies. If nothing else, they would at least slow up decision making (Marchington and Loveridge, 1979: 175–9).

Currently, the possible negative link between participation and performance is one of the justifications for the stakeholder model of organizations, as it is argued that given the diverse range of interests of stakeholders, managers should make trade-offs between shareholders' and others' objectives. Fulfilling the interests of workers in having a say in decisions that affect their jobs and livelihoods may be one such trade-off, as it may help the legitimacy and harmony of the organization, but not without added costs for the organization.

However, in the 1970s there emerged a new emphasis on a form of participation that might have positive effects on performance. This is what Lawler (1986) called the 'high involvement model' or Walton (1985) the 'high commitment model'. It was portrayed as providing enhanced participation that would have a virtuous effect on organizational performance, while boosting workers' job satisfaction. It has become a crucial part of management thought with an appeal that is different from other forms of participation. It, along with work enrichment, has consequently sometimes been used by managers to ward off new forms of formal participation, such as worker–directors, as they argued it was more relevant to both workers and managements. Moreover, its positive links to performance began to be treated as so secure that it became widely known as the 'high performance work system', a term probably first popularized by the US Government in the early 1990s (US Department of Labor, 1993). This increased focus on high involvement management in the past twenty years as a source of performance gains for organizations is consistent with the conclusion of Levine and Tyson's (1990: 203–204) review of pre-1990s participation studies: that long lasting productivity gains are more likely to be associated with what they term 'substantive participation', which involves the decentralization of decisions to the shop floor and participative work groups, than the formal consultative arrangements and other voice mechanisms that have been at the centre of industrial relations.

A stream of research followed that examined if the high involvement human resource system was indeed associated with higher performance. Overviews of the initial studies of these tended to conclude that they were demonstrating that it was (Becker and Gerhart, 1996; Guest, 1997). Nonetheless, as the number of studies grew, the results were uneven across studies and performance measures within the individual studies (Wall and Wood, 2005). Moreover, the measures of human resource systems that were correlated with performance also varied considerably in the studies. While most of the researchers make reference to high involvement management, in some of the studies its key aspects were neglected. This difference in the emphasis given to high involvement management in the studies means that we can compare the results of those that unequivocally measure it with those where it is less central to see if high involvement management has distinctive performance effects.

In this chapter I will first introduce the concept of high involvement management as a form of participation, then the key studies that have directly measured high involvement management to show how they have explored high involvement management and its links to performance. I will then compare the results of these studies with others within the human resource management (HRM)-performance research stream to see if they reveal stronger performance relationships than do these others.

High Involvement Management

Lawler's concept of high involvement management and Walton's high commitment approach, which can be treated as synonymous, grew out of their earlier concern with work enrichment. The central feature of this is the development of distinctive job design principles that reverse the narrow job specifications and rigid divisions of labour associated with Taylor's Scientific Management, or what Walton calls the 'control' model. Redesigning Taylorist jobs so they 'combine planning and implementation' (Walton, 1985: 79) would increase worker satisfaction, so it is claimed, through greater autonomy and more challenging work.

High involvement management, in contrast to a narrow redesigning of jobs, meant workers participating not only in changing their roles, but also in what Benson and Lawler (2003: 156) call 'opportunities to . . . participate in the business as a whole'. This organizational participation or involvement extends beyond the role involvement associated with work enrichment (Wall et al., 2004). To adapt a phrase from a manager in the UK car industry in the late 1980s, it involves workers having two jobs: one to make the product, and one to think of better ways of doing their job and making the product. We thus use the term high involvement management to refer to practices offering workers opportunities for organizational involvement, either directly or indirectly through the use of information dissemination and training specifically to aid involvement. This is consistent with Lawler's (1986, 1991) identification of the enhancement of the power, skills, and knowledge of workers as the core elements of high involvement management.

High involvement management thus involves first, work organization practices, such as team working, flexible job descriptions, and idea capturing schemes, which are means of encouraging greater flexibility, proactivity, and collaboration; and, second, practices that give workers the opportunities for the acquisition of skills and knowledge that are needed to ensure that they have the capacities to work in an involved way. These include intensive training geared towards team working, functional flexibility and idea generation, and team briefing and information sharing, particularly about the economics and market of the business.

A useful way of thinking about high involvement management is to contrast it with individualized piecework systems where the payment system is the fulcrum of an organization's approach to personnel management as well as their production management. The issue about piecework systems is not so much about whether they work or if individuals will respond to the monetary incentives they provide, though there has been a long-standing debate about the effectiveness of monetary incentives; it is rather about the effect of their working, as they often work so well that workers will literally concentrate only on the 'piece'. Klein (1976: 7) showed how it narrows operators' perceptions of their job to such an extent that this simply means 'the immediate job cycle' (i.e. the time it takes for them to fulfil a task, which in many Taylorist regimes was a matter of seconds). The culture surrounding piecework means that performing the narrow tasks workers do is all that mattered, 'not making a good product or being in any way concerned with the wider objectives of the firm' (Klein, 1976).

The thrust of the high involvement management model is the development of broader horizons among all workers—the opposite of the tunnel vision associated with piecework—so that they will think of better ways of doing their jobs, connect what they do with what others do, and take initiative in the face of novel problems. In the language of much modern management theory they will participate in a continuous improvement culture. This came to the fore in the wake of the effective adoption of quality circles and other idea capturing schemes in Japanese firms, which were seen as highly successful innovators, particularly in manufacturing (Cappelli and Neumark, 2001; Jürgens, 1989; Wood, 1991, 1993).

The adoption of high involvement management is aimed at eliciting a high level of commitment to one's work and organization so that such proactive behaviour is largely self-regulating rather than controlled by sanctions and pressures external to the individual. The use of the prefix 'high' is important, first because a minimum level of cooperation and commitment is required for any work system, including piecework, to function; and second, because the aim is to induce more than proficient performance, the adaptation and proactivity that Griffin, Neal, and Parker (2007) increasingly see as characterizing modern work requirements.

A number of motivational or supporting practices are also associated with high involvement management (Appelbaum et al., 2000; Forth and Millward, 2004: 100; de Menezes and Wood, 2006). Lawler includes these reward systems, along with power, skills, and knowledge, as a dimension of high involvement management, as he reasoned 'basing rewards on organizational performance is one way to ensure that employees are involved in and care about the perform-ance of their company' (Lawler et al., 1995: 18). This implies they are general incentives to perform and not specifically for individuals to make use of oppor-tunities for participation or to gain the skills required in a high involvement regime. Such motivational practices might include, along with incentive pay-ment systems, minimal status differentials, internal recruitment, and job security guarantees.

Some of these practices were commonplace before high involvement manage-ment, particularly internal recruitment and incentive schemes. Indeed, part of the modernization agenda for human resource management has focused on the need to change the form of the internal recruitment system, as it was thought that promotion had been dominated by the seniority principle when it needed to be more strongly linked to performance. Incentive pay systems—perhaps linked more to group- and organizational-level performance—were also thought to be desirable as part of a more performance-oriented organization.

But there is no reason why following such prescriptions should be accompan-ied with high involvement practices, and indeed Arthur (1994) includes perform-ance-related pay in his characterization of its opposite, the control model. Some writers like Becker and Huselid (1998) who include it in their model of the high performance work system appear to treat it as pivotal to what might be seen as a more literal high performance system centred on performance management techniques rather than employee involvement (Wood, 1999: 394). Incentive schemes have in fact long been a source of controversy within human resource management and beyond (Beer et al., 1984); for example, advocates of total quality management such as Deming (1986) associate them with the control strategy and were deeply critical of performance-related pay. Because of such controversies and the long-standing use of internal promotion and incentive schemes, we would not expect these and the other motivational supports that are often associated conceptually with high involvement management to be in practice uniquely associated with it.

There is also no reason to expect that high involvement management is always accompanied by work enrichment. Indeed, the hallmark of the Japanese manage-ment system is to introduce high involvement management into systems that remain Taylorist in key respects, and particularly in the lack of job autonomy or task variety (Wood, 1989). Its use is often associated with production systems where the basic task system and technology are not changed, as in assembly line car manufacturing.

CORE HIGH INVOLVEMENT MANAGEMENT–PERFORMANCE STUDIES

The research studies that developed in the wake of the claims that high involvement management represented a novel high performance management system typically measures a set of human resource practices and correlates these with one or more organizational performance measure. The variety of practices included in the stream of studies is large, as recent reviews of them have documented (Wall and Wood, 2005; Wood and Wall, 2007). Moreover, their underlying concepts are not the same, and, while most authors of the studies included in such reviews make some reference to high involvement management in their background theoretical discussion, many include practices not specific to high involvement management as conceived above or at least do not isolate the effect of motivational supports from the core high involvement practices. As such, collectively they are best treated, as many do, as the human resource management–performance studies.

An important emphasis in this literature is on the merits of practices being used together as a coherent package, which is typically taken to be a set of practices that 'mutually reinforce each other' (Hoque, 1999: 422). In order to capture the package, the majority of studies have used composite measures of practices, for example, an index that measures the total use of the practices or classifications based on cluster analysis that distinguish sets of organizations based on their similar combined use of practices. If a coherent set simply refers to a complement of practices that are best in each of the domains of high involvement management then such methods may be appropriate for assessing the extent of their use on performance, though it masks the precise impact of particular practices. This concealment becomes particularly significant if the motivational practices are not unique to high involvement systems as it may be that it is these, not the high involvement practices, that account for any performance effects identified. Moreover, neither method adequately tests mutual reinforcement which implies that the presence of a practice adds to the effect of another, and vice versa. Such synergistic relationships should be tested by assessing the impact of the interaction of two or more practices on performances.

Indexes can be contrasted with scales (DeVellis, 1991), which measure an underlying construct and the items constituting it are assumed to reflect or be caused by it, and the association between them is explained by the construct.[1] Applied to high involvement management, scales measure an underlying orientation that explains the use of the practices, as have been used in some of the human resource management–performance studies (Wood and de Menezes, 1998; 2008).

In these terms, studies that either concentrate on individual high involvement practices or measure a high involvement orientation through a scale based on some form of latent variable analysis (Bartholomew and Knott, 1999; Wood, 1999) most directly measure high involvement management. Studies that include indexes of practices that are solely high involvement practices may be treated likewise, but the vast majority of such studies include other practices (the exception is MacDuffie, 1995), and it is not possible in these to isolate the contribution of high involvement management, particularly relative to motivational practices as many of these indexes are concentrated on motivational practices. Finally, there are some human resource management–performance studies that either include few or no high involvement practices. I now present the key studies in which the unique impact of high involvement management can be isolated. For ease of presentation this set of studies will be called the high involvement management studies.

Wood and de Menezes's Direct Measure of High Involvement Management

Wood and de Menezes (2008) included in their study a set of high involvement practices, motivational supports, and work enrichment practices, as well as total quality management practices. They used data from the UK's Workplace Employee Relations Survey of 1998, which included a survey based on managerial respondents of 2,191 workplaces across the whole economy, private and public.

Wood and de Menezes compare three different performance models: high involvement management as a set of complementary best practices, as a set of practices that have synergistic effects on each other, and as an underlying high involvement orientation or philosophy. Consequently, they first established whether an orientation underlaid the use of practices associated with high involvement management, such as teamwork, quality circles, functional flexibility, suggestion schemes, information dissemination, and training geared to aiding these (reported in full by de Menezes and Wood, 2006), since they do not take for granted that these practices are uniquely reflective of the orientation. They found strong correlations among all the practices and then showed that these correlations were explained by a common factor and thus they tended to be used as a single coherent system, that reflected an underlying high involvement orientation. They were thus able to measure the high involvement orientation by a scale.

Though the use of some of the motivational support practices was correlated with the high involvement orientation, they were not a part of it nor did they form a unified set. The work enrichment measures were also discrete from high involvement management or the individual motivational supports. This confirms that the use of high involvement management is not limited to contexts where jobs have high levels of autonomy and that the use of the motivational supports may be quite common without high involvement management.[2]

Wood and de Menezes (2008) found that the high involvement orientation was linked to both the level and rate of change in labour productivity. But it was not, however, a main factor, since its relationship with productivity was moderated by total quality management and its association with the rate of change in productivity was moderated by a motivational support, variable pay. Total quality management was a main effect in both the level and rate of change of productivity equations. The high involvement orientation was not related to labour turnover, and its association with absenteeism is the opposite of that predicted: the greater the level of the orientation, the higher the absence.

Though these results were mixed they compared favourably with the tests of the association between individual practices and organizational performance conducted by Wood and de Menezes. These revealed no relationships between practices, or any of the two-way interactions between them, and any of the performance measures, the rate of change in productivity, labour turnover, and absenteeism. Thus there was no support for the complementary or synergistic perspective.

The support offered by the study for the orientations perspective implies that it is the high involvement orientation underlying the use of practices not the practices per se that is associated with the two productivity measures. However, in both cases the relationship is moderated. Moreover, Wood and de Menezes also found that the practices that were most strongly related to productivity were job variety and method control, both dimensions of enriched jobs. And in the case of productivity change the variable pay was a main effect as well as moderator of its relationship with high involvement management. Wood and de Menezes' study shows the advantage of testing competing hypotheses and differentiating different aspects of human resource management as the links to performance vary across them and between performance measures.

MacDuffie

MacDuffie (1995), in a similar vein to Wood and de Menezes (2008), distinguished key high involvement practices from supporting human resource practices. The former constitute what he called a flexible work system, and was concerned with 'how work is organized, in terms of both formal work structures and the allocation of work responsibilities and the participation of employees in production-related problem-solving activity' (p. 207). It was measured by an index of six items, made up of the percentage of the workforce involved in: one, teams; and two, employee involvement groups; the number of production-related suggestions received from employees; the percentage of suggestions implemented; the extent of job rotation; and the degree of production worker involvement in quality tasks.

A second system is the human resource system, which included motivational supports but also general skill acquisition practices, in contrast to the specific high involvement skill acquisition practices included in the Wood and de Menezes (2008) measure. The human resource system was measured by an index based on the following practices: staff selection was based on an openness to learning, rather than on previous relevant experience; minimal status barriers between managers and workers (i.e., harmonization across grades); training provided for: one, new recruits; and two, experienced production and other staff; and pay levels that are dependent on plant performance.

Using data from a study of sixty-two car assembly plants, the majority of which were in the USA, Europe, and Japan, MacDuffie found that both indices were related to labour productivity, defined as the labour hours to build a vehicle; but the work system factor was not significant when the human resource factor was controlled for. The two-way interaction between the two indices was not significant.

MacDuffie (1995) also measured a third system, the lean production or buffer-less system (Womack et al., 1990) (i.e., a just in time, minimal inventory system is used). This was measured by an index of low stocks, work in progress, and space dedicated to final repair, and was also found to be related to productivity. More-over, the three-way interaction between lean production and the work and human resource system was significantly related to productivity; moreover in the equation including this, none of the three factors was independently related to productivity.

Examining the effects on the quality of production, MacDuffie found that when two-way interaction terms were included in the quality model, lean production was positively related to quality, and the work system–lean interaction was significantly related to it—in other words, the work system had an effect on it when used with lean production. Contrary to what was expected, the human resource system was negatively related to quality when the interactions were included in quality equations.

This study is consistent with Wood and de Menezes in that it shows that the association between work systems and the level of productivity is moderated by a third factor: lean production, which is similar to Wood and de Menezes' total quality management. However, the motivational supports also moderate this association in MacDuffie's study.

Wright, McCormick, Sherman, and McMahon's Distinction between Participation and Skills and Motivational Supports

Wright, McCormick, Sherman, and McMahan (1999) distinguished employee participation from human resource practices. Employee participation was defined as direct organizational involvement, and specifically as giving individuals at a lower level in the organization 'a greater voice in one or more areas of organizational performance' (p. 552). It was measured by a ten-item measure of participation in such activities as: resolving customer-generated problems; problem-solving teams; departmental or functional area goal setting and planning; statistically tracking and recording process variation and performance. The authors (p. 566) explicitly treated this as a measure of Lawler's high involvement management.

Human resource practices were 'the organizational activities directed at managing the pool of human capital and ensuring that capital is employed towards the fulfilment of organizational goals' (p. 552); it was thus 'the means through which firms can increase the skills of the workforce and provide incentives for workforce members to contribute'. Four types of human resource practice were measured, all by multiple-item indexes: selection; training; equitable compensation; and appraisal. The skills dimension of human resource practices covered all skill acquisition and not just that specific to participation in a high involvement regime.

Using data from a sample of thirty-six petro-chemical refineries in the USA, performance was measured by a financial performance index created from the refinery's profit margin in the year of the study (1993), average annual profit growth in the five years 1988–1993, and average annual sales growth in the five years 1988–1993. Neither participation nor any of the human resource practices was positively related to financial performance. Training was, however, negatively related to it.

However, the interaction between participation and three of the four human resource practices—selection, compensation, and appraisal—was significantly related to performance, showing they form a synergistic relationship. The effect of these human resource practices on performance depends on the level of participation. This finding is consistent with Wood and de Menezes' and MacDuffie's as it shows that the impact of high involvement management on performance is moderated by a third factor; in this case it is the motivational supports. Wright et al. did not, however, examine operational management methods.

Cappelli and Neumark: Longitudinal Analysis

Cappelli and Neumark's (2001) study assessed the impact of high involvement practices individually. They saw employee involvement at the core of the high performance system and particularly highlighted teamwork as 'the typical mechanism through which employee involvement operates'. Although Cappelli and Neumark also argued that other practices, such as suggestion schemes and job rotation, can create a sense of involvement too. High involvement practices included in the study were team meetings (including quality circles), self-managed teams, job rotation, cross-training, and teamwork training, while the other measures included were pay for skill, profit sharing, and total quality management, which was treated as a form of employee involvement.

Using the National Employers' Survey of the USA in establishments with twenty or more employees in the private manufacturing and service sectors, Cappelli and

Neumark examined the impact of the practices on performance in two panel data sets, one over seventeen years, the other over twenty. They found that no practice was positively associated with productivity, measured by sales per worker. The one significant result was a negative association between job rotation and productivity. Nor was there any strong evidence of synergies between key practices, as measured by two-way interactions between practices; but the interaction between profitsharing and self-managed teams was significant in some specifications. Overall, this study found no strong relationship, using a longitudinal design rather than the cross-sectional one used in the three studies discussed so far. The study did not, however, examine the integrated use of the practices.

Birdi, Clegg, Patterson, Robinson, Stride, Wall, and Wood: Extending High Involvement Management to Lean Production with Longitudinal Analysis

Birdi, Clegg, Patterson, Robinson, Stride, Wall, and Wood (2008), in a study of UK manufacturing companies, measured high involvement management by two single-item measures: empowerment and teamwork. Respondents, chief executives or directors, were given a description of the practice by the interviewer. In the case of empowerment it was defined as 'passing considerable responsibility for operational management to individuals or teams (rather than keeping all decision-making at the managerial level)', and team-based working was defined as 'placing operators into teams with their own responsibilities and giving them freedom to allocate work between team members'. A third human resource practice, extensive training, concerned all development as opposed to training for narrow specific job needs or simply that involved in equipping people for high involvement management. Birdi et al. also included three operational management techniques associated with lean production—just in time, total quality management, and supply-chain partnering—as well as advanced manufacturing technology. Total quality management was, though, defined such that it entailed employee involvement, namely: 'seeking continuous change to improve quality and making all staff responsible for the quality of their work. Such practices include Kaizon and Continuous Improvement.'

Birdi et al.'s study was longitudinal, as it involved analysing the performance of 308 UK companies over 22 years, and the extent to which the introduction of a practice had some effect on this. Productivity was measured by value-added, as derived from the company's profit and loss account.

Of the seven practices examined, only empowerment and extensive training had an impact on value-added following their introduction, though the size of the effect of extensive training varied across firms. However, Birdi et al. also showed that the performance of all practices—human resource or operational—was strengthened by teamwork. Empowerment and extensive training also enhanced the effect of total quality management, while empowerment had a similar effect on the impact of supply-chain partnering, and extensive training on just in time.

Birdi et al.'s key measures of high involvement management thus had the decisive effects: empowerment had a crucial independent effect on productivity and had a synergistic relationship with total quality management and supply-chain partnering. Additionally, teamwork had a synergistic effect on all other practices. Thus, although using a longitudinal design like Cappelli and Neumark (2001), Birdi et al. found a stronger link between the individual high involvement practices and productivity than did their study. Nonetheless, the discovery of a synergistic relationship between empowerment and total quality management chimes with Wood and de Menezes, and MacDuffie's results. However, their empowerment measure did not separate high involvement management from work enrichment.

Overview of High Involvement Management Studies

The results of these studies are uneven, both across studies and performance measures within studies. Such differences are not readily explicable. For example, there are differences between studies with relatively similar designs. The starkest variation is between the two most similar studies, the longitudinal studies by Cappelli and Neumark (2001) and Birdi et al. (2008) that both concentrate on assessing individual practice effects on productivity. The former finds no practices linked to it, and the latter gets quite strong relationships, particularly involving empowerment. The practices in the studies are, however, different, and the data are taken from different countries, the USA and the UK respectively.

However, with the exception of this conflict, there is some commonality in findings on productivity between the other studies. The relationship between high involvement management or practices and performance is moderated by a third factor in the majority of studies. In Wood and de Menezes' (2008) study, high involvement management's relationship is moderated by total quality management; in MacDuffie's (1995) lean production (related to total quality management) is similarly a moderator but so also is the human resource system (training and motivational supports); the latter is similar to Wright et al.'s (1999) results where the moderator is human resource management (training, selection, and motivational supports). While in Birdi et al.'s (2008) study the empowerment that incorporates an element of high involvement management is the main predictor of productivity, its effect is enhanced by team working, another element of high involvement management.

COMPARING THE STUDIES OF THE HIGH INVOLVEMENT MANAGEMENT STUDIES WITH OTHER HRM-PERFORMANCE STUDIES

We will now contrast the results of the high involvement management studies with those in which the unique contribution of high involvement management or practices can be isolated with those HRM-performance studies where it cannot or where no high involvement practice is measured. That these studies do not necessarily prioritize high involvement practices over others is not grounds for criticism, as they may be targeting a different or broader notion of modern human resource management of which high involvement management is a part. Some are simply including motivational supports as part of high involvement management, as do Guthrie (2001) and Batt (2002); but, as Wood and de Menezes's results suggest, these are not likely to be uniquely associated with it.

Guthrie's study is a good example of one in which the results are positive for all performance measures investigated. It uses an index of high involvement management that included work organization practices (employee participatory programmes, teams and cross-training or cross-utilization) but was dominated by general skill and knowledge acquisition practices and motivational supports, such as training focused on future needs, total hours of training, internal promotion, performance-based promotions, and attitude surveys. Guthrie found in his study of 164 New Zealand private sector companies that this index of practice use was positively associated with firm productivity, measured by sales per employee, and negatively associated with the average annual rate of employee turnover.

Batt's study also yields similar positive results. Her core index, measuring work design, was based on two measures of job discretion and two measures of team participation. It thus combines the organizational involvement that characterizes high involvement management with the role involvement entailed in work enrichment. The measure was related to both performance measures investigated, positively to sales growth, and negatively to the quit rate. Another index, of human resource incentives, was related to sales growth but not the quit rate.

An example of a study that used cluster analysis rather than an index was Arthur's research in thirty US steel mills in which he discriminated, on the basis of their similarity in the use of certain practices, between those plants adopting what he called high commitment management and those using the high control approach. The high involvement practices in the study were high levels of employee involvement in managerial decisions and formal participation programmes, and training in group problem solving, while other practices included general training, zero or low levels of incentive pay, formal grievance procedures, and social gatherings. The measure also included the percentage of craft workers and supervisor/worker ratio.

The high commitment plants were found to be associated with all the performance measures included in the studies: higher labour efficiency, lower scrap rates and lower labour turnover.

The oft-cited Huselid (1995) study is one in which the results are less clear-cut. He measured two dimensions of high performance systems that nominally reflect my distinction between high involvement management and motivational supports. He identified these on the basis of principle component analysis, labelling the first 'employee skills and organizational structures', and the second 'employee motivation'. Of the three high involvement management practices included in the study, two—participation in quality circles or labour management teams and information sharing—were included in the skills and organizational factor, while the third, appraisal is in the motivational. The remaining ten practices were mainly, in our terms, motivational, but do not all load on the motivation factor. In particular company-level or gain sharing incentive schemes are included in the skills and organization factor. Job analysis, which is not necessarily a high involvement practice, is also included in that measure. The intelligibility of the factors in terms of either the high involvement management concept or Huselid's own terms is not then totally clear, particularly as one would expect incentive payment schemes to be under employee motivation.

Using data from a sample of 968 organizations with over 100 employees from all major industries in the US private sector, the employee motivation factor, but not employee skills and organizational structures, was significantly positively associated with productivity and to Tobin q's measure of market value. In contrast, the employee skills and organizational structures index was related to the gross rate of return on assets but only weakly associated with Tobin's q and not at all with productivity. There were thus differences between the performance measures that were associated with the two factors—a variation that Huselid leaves unexplained. Neither factor was related to labour turnover.

The above studies produce results that show associations between measures of human resource management systems and performance. Other studies reporting, as Guthrie and Arthur do, associations between their human resource system measure and all the performance measures assessed include, Bae and Lawler (2000), Datta, Guthrie, and Wright (2005), Hoque (1999), Ichniowski, Shaw, and Prennushi (1997). However, there are also a few such studies in which mixed results were found (Wright et al., 2003) or no association between human resource management and performance was found, most notably those by Guest and Hoque (1994), Guest, Michie, Conway, and Sheehan (2003), and Way (2002).

Collectively the results of these studies are no better or worse than those of the high involvement management studies.[3] Both sets of studies include diverse combinations of practices; what distinguishes the high involvement management studies is not their exclusion of motivational practices but their ability to assess the association between these and performance indicators separately from those of high involvement practices. The majority of both types of studies do reveal an association between a human resource management measure and at least one performance indicator, and there is no discernable difference in the extent of significant results between them. More generally, there is no obvious pattern to the results that suggests the diversity is systematically related to the characteristics of the studies—for example, that more promising results are found in studies that are cross-sectional, use questionnaires rather than interviews, or use audited performance data (for more detail on the methodologies of studies, see Wall and Wood, 2005).

Moreover, of the three studies in Wall and Wood's (2005) analysis of HRM-performance studies that did not include a high involvement practice, two of them found a positive association between their measure of human resource management and the performance measures investigated: Koch and McGrath's (1996), and Youndt, Snell, Dean, and Lepak (1996), both found the indexes they used to measure a human capital-based approach were significantly associated with labour productivity. The third study, by Fey, Bjürkman, and Pavlovskaya (2000) assessed the independent impact of nine practices, the majority of which were motivational practices, and found that only two practices were associated with their measure of overall firm performance—job security and the salary level for employees—in their sample of 101 foreign firms operating in Russia.

On the basis of this comparison between the high involvement management studies and the other studies, we cannot conclude that high involvement management has a distinctive effect on performance that is relative to other human resource approaches. Equally, though, there is sufficient evidence in the studies to suggest it does have some impact, or at least that the research points to potential links between high involvement management and performance outcomes.

Conclusion

The study of high involvement management has been part of the wider human resource management–performance research stream. The studies in the stream differ in their foci, measures of practices and performance measures, as well as samples and methods of data collection. The results vary across studies, including across performance measures in the individual studies.

Only a minority of these studies isolate the distinctive impact of high involvement management, as many treat it as part of a broader modern or sophisticated human resource management. On the one hand, from the former studies we get a picture that high involvement management does have an effect, particularly on productivity, but this effect may well be moderated by, or dependent on, other factors, especially operational management practices. On the other hand, a comparison of these studies with those that do not allow one to isolate the impact of high involvement management, or neglect it totally, shows that they do not yield stronger (or weaker) results than the others. It is because of this that we need to have more studies that do allow one to differentiate precisely the effects of types of practices and orientations.

The comparisons of high involvement management with other practices or approaches available in some studies suggest that it may not be uniquely related to performance. In particular Wood and de Menezes's (2008) study that directly compares high involvement management with work enrichment implies that it may not be as decisive as—or at least any more important than—that. It is certainly premature to conclude that high involvement management—or any form of human resource management—merits the high performance management tag.

The way forward is to design studies of high involvement management that include data on: one, a comprehensive range of the high involvement practices; two, job design; three, other human resource practices; and four, practices from other areas of management (e.g. operational management). It is important to include operational management practices to assess the extent to which they depend on high involvement management being successful or enable high involvement methods to work. There is a clear need to assess the relationship between all practices prior to any attempt to develop composite measures. This will determine the nature of any integrated use of practice or managerial orientations. Then we need to test competing hypotheses, and in particularly assess the relationships between individual practices and performance, individually and jointly through interaction terms, and compare these with the relationships involving orientations.

Overcoming some of the common weaknesses of the studies (Wall and Wood, 2005, summarize these well), including their over-reliance on single sources for data on both practices and performance data, should also be encouraged. The heterogeneity in the nature of the studies as we have seen limits the conclusions one can make from the research stream; and studies that replicate the measures of others should be welcomed (Sitkin, 2007).

The focus of the studies to date has been on establishing the link between high involvement management or human resource management and performance, rather than exploring the mechanisms that may explain any relationship. This focus is perhaps understandable given the novelty of the research area and the innovative nature of high involvement management. Why invest resources in theorizing or exploring a link that may not exist? But given the promising results of the studies reviewed here, future research could more readily include measures of the potential mediators, such as employee satisfaction and well-being, better structuring and organization of work systems, initiative and proactive behaviour of workers, and individual and organizational learning.

Notes

1. Indexes are sometimes known as formative scales, as they are created on the basis of items that precede or cause the construct they purport to measure, or indeed may not even represent a single concept. In this terminology, what are referred to in this chapter as scales would be reflective scales (Dinamantopoulos and Siguaw, 2006).

2. This is consistent with Barnard and Rodgers' (2000) research in Singapore which found that neither internal recruitment nor job stability was associated with a measure of high performance work systems based on high involvement management practices.

3. A table summarizing the studies in the terms of this chapter is available from the author; s.j.wood@sheffield.ac.uk; for other tables summarizing the studies, see Becker and Gerhart, 1996; Wall and Wood, 2005; Wood and de Menezes, 2008; Wood and Wall, 2007 .

References

Appelbaum, E., Bailey, T., Berg, P., and Kalleberg, A. L. (2000) *Manufacturing Advantage: Why High Performance Work Systems Pay Off*. Ithiaca, NY: Cornell University Press.

Arthur, J. B. (1994) 'Effects of human resource systems on manufacturing performance and turnover', *Academy of Management Journal*, 7: 670–87.

Bae, J. and Lawler, J. J. (2000) 'Organizational and HRM strategies in Korea: Impact on firm performance in an emerging economy', *Academy of Management Journal*, 43(3): 502–17.

Barnard, M. and Rodgers, R. A. (2000) 'How are internally oriented HRM policies related to high-performance practices? Evidence from Singapore', *International Journal of Human Resource Management*, 11(6): 1017–46.

Bartholomew, D. J. and Knott, M. K. (1999) *Latent Variable Models and Factor Analysis*, 2nd edition. London: Arnold.

Batt, R. (2002) 'Managing customer services: Human resource practices, quit rates, and sales growth', *Academy of Management Journal*, 45(3): 587–97.

Becker, B. E. and Gerhart, B. (1996) 'The impact of human resource management on organizational performance: Progress and prospects', *Academy of Management Journal*, 39(4): 779–801.

—— and Huselid, M. A. (1998) 'High performance work systems and firm performance: A synthesis of research and managerial implications', in G. R. Ferris (ed.), *Research in Personnel and Human Resources*, 16: 53–101. Stamford, CT: JAI Press.

Beer, M., Spector, B., Lawrence, P., Mills, D., and Walton, R. (1984) *Managing Human Assets*. New York: The Free Press.

Benson, G. S. and Lawler III, E. E. (2003) 'Employee involvement: Utilization, impacts and future prospects', in D. Holman, T. Wall, C. Clegg, P. Sparrow, and A. Howard (eds), *The Essentials of the New Workplace*, pp. 155–73. London: Wiley.

Birdi, K., Clegg, C., Patterson, M., Robinson, A., Stride, C., Wall, T., and Wood, S. (2008) 'Contemporary manufacturing practices and company performance: A longitudinal study', *Personnel Psychology*, 61(3): 467–501.

Cappelli, P. and Neumark, D. (2001) 'Do "high performance" work practices improve establishment-level outcomes?' *Industrial and Labor Relations Review*, 54(4): 737–75.

DATTA, D. K., GUTHRIE, J. P., and WRIGHT, P. M. (2005) 'Human resource management and labor productivity; Does industry matter?', *Academy of Management Journal*, 48(1): 135–45.

DEMING, W. E. (1986) *Out of the Crisis: Quality, Productivity and Competitive Position*. Cambridge: Cambridge University Press.

DEVELLIS, R. F. (1991) *Scale Development: Theory and Applications*. Newbury Park, California: Sage.

DINAMANTOPOULOS, A. and SIGUAW, J. (2006) 'Formative versus reflective indictors in organizational measure development: A comparison and empirical illustration', *British Journal of Management*, 17(4): 263–82.

FEY, C. F., BJÖRKMAN, I., and PAVLOVSKAYA, A. (2000) 'The effect of human resource management practices on firm performance in Russia', *International Journal of Human Resource Management*, 11(1): 1–18.

FORTH, J. and MILLWARD, N. (2004) 'High-involvement management and pay in Britain', *Industrial Relations*, 43(1): 98–119.

GRIFFIN, M. A., NEAL, A., and PARKER, S. K. (2007) 'A new model of work role performance: Positive behavior in uncertain and interdependent contexts', *Academy of Management Journal*, 50(2): 327–47.

GUEST, D. (1997) 'Human resource management and performance: A review and research agenda', *International Human Resource Management*, 8(3): 263–76.

—— and HOQUE, K. (1994) 'The good, the bad and the ugly: Employee relations in new non-union workplaces', *Human Resource Management Journal*, 5(1): 1–14.

—— MICHIE, J., CONWAY, N., and SHEHAN, M. (2003) 'Human resource management and corporate performance in the UK', *British Journal of Industrial Relations*, 41(2): 291–314.

GUTHRIE, J. P. (2001) 'High involvement work practices, turnover and productivity: Evidence from New Zealand', *Academy of Management Journal*, 44(1): 180–90.

HOQUE, K. (1999) 'Human resource management and performance in the UK hotel industry', *British Journal of Industrial Relations*, 37(3): 419–43.

HUSELID, M. A. (1995) 'The impact of human resource management practices on turnover, productivity, and corporate financial performance', *Academy of Management Journal*, 38 (3): 635–72.

ICHNIOWSKI, C., SHAW, K., and PRENNUSHI, G. (1997) 'The effects of human resource management practices on productivity: A study of steel finishing lines', *American Economic Review*, 87(3): 291–313.

JUDGE, T. A., THORESEN, C. J., BONO, J. E., and PATTON, G. K. (2001) 'The job satisfaction-job performance relationship: A qualitative-quantitative review,' *Psychological Bulletin*, 127(3): 376–407.

JÜRGENS, U. (1989) 'The transfer of Japanese management concepts in the international automobile industry', in S. Wood (ed.), *The Transformation of Work?* pp. 204–18. London: Unwin Hyman.

KLEIN, L. (1976) *New Forms of Work Organisation*. Cambridge: Cambridge University Press.

KOCH, M. J. and MCGRATH, R. G. (1996) 'Improving labor productivity: Human resource management policies do matter', *Strategic Management Journal*, 17: 335–54.

LAWLER, E. E. (1986) *High Involvement Management*. San Francisco, CA: Jossey-Bass.

—— (1991) 'Participative Management Strategies', in J. W. Jones, B. W. Steffy, and D. W. Bray (eds), *Applying Psychology in Business. The Handbook for Managers and Human Resource Professionals*, pp. 578–86. Lexington, MA: Lexington Books.

Lawler, E. E., Mohrman, S. A., and Ledford Jr., G. E., (1995) *Creating High Performance Organizations*. San Francisco, CA: Jossey-Bass.

Levine, D. I. and Tyson, L. D'Andrea (1990) 'Participation, productivity and the firm's environment', in A. S. Blinder (ed.), *Paying for Productivity*, pp. 183–243. Washington, DC: The Brookings Institute.

MacDuffie, J. P. (1995) 'Human resource bundles and manufacturing performance: Organizational logic and flexible production systems in the world auto industry', *Industrial and Labor Relations Review*, 48(2): 197–221.

Marchington, M. and Loveridge, R. (1979) 'Non-participation: the management view? *Journal of Management Studies*, 16(2): 170–84.

de Menezes, L. M. and Wood, S. (2006) 'The reality of flexible work systems in Britain', *International Journal of Human Resource Management*, 17(1): 1–33.

Metcalf, D. (2003) Unions and productivity, financial performance and investment: International evidence, in J. T. Addison and C. Schnabel (eds), *International Handbook of Trade Unions*, pp. 118–71. Cheltenham: Edward Elgar.

Sitkin, S. (2007) 'Promoting a more generative and sustainable organizational science', *Journal of Organizational Behavior*, 28(7): 841–48.

US Department of Labor (1993) *High Performance Work Practices*. Washington, DC: US Department of Labor.

Wall, T. D. and Wood, S. J. (2005) 'The romance of human resource management and performance, and the case for big science', *Human Relations*, 58(4): 429–62.

———— and Leach, D. J. (2004) 'Empowerment and performance', in C. L. Cooper and I. T. Robertson (eds), *International Review of Industrial and Organizational Psychology*, 19: 1–46. London: Wiley.

Walton, R. E. (1985) 'From "control" to "commitment" in the workplace', *Harvard Business Review*, 63(2): 77–84.

Way, S. A. (2002) 'High performance work systems and intermediate indicators of firm performance within the US small business sector', *Journal of Management*, 28(6): 765–85.

Womack, J., Jones, D. T., and Roos, D. (1990) *The Machine that Changed the World*. New York: Rawson.

Wood, S. (1989) 'Japanization and/or Toyotaism?' *Work, Employment and Society*, 5(4): 567–600.

—— (1991) 'Japanization and/or Toyotaism?' *Work, Employment and Society*, 5(4): 567–600.

—— (1993) 'The Japanization of Fordism?' *Economic and Industrial Democracy*, Vol. 14, No. 4, November, 538–55.

—— (1999) 'Getting the measure of the transformed high-performance organization', *British Journal of Industrial Relations*, 37(3): 391–417.

—— and de Menezes, L. M. (1998) 'High Commitment Management in the UK: Evidence from the Workplace Industrial Relations Survey and Employers' Manpower and Skills Practices Survey', *Human Relations*, Vol. 51, No, 4, 485–517.

———— (2008) 'Comparing perspectives on high involvement management and organizational performance across the British economy', *International Journal of Human Resource Management*, 19(4): 639–83.

Wood, S. J. and Wall, T. D. (2007) 'Human resource management and employee voice', *International Journal of Human Resource Management*, 18(7): 1335–1372.

WRIGHT, P. M., GARDNER, T. M., and MOYNIHAN, L. M. (2003) 'The impact of HR practices on the performance of business units', *Human Resource Management Journal*, 13(3): 21–36.

WRIGHT, P. M., McCORMICK, B., SHERMAN, W. S., and McMAHON, G. C. (1999) 'The role of human resource practices in petro-chemical refinery performance', *International Journal of Human Resource Management*, 10(4): 551–71.

YOUNDT, M. A., SNELL, S. A., DEAN, J. E., and LEPAK, D. P. (1996) 'Human resource management, manufacturing strategy, and firm performance', *Academy of Management Journal*, 39(4): 36–65.

CHAPTER 18

EMPLOYEE VOICE AND MUTUAL GAINS

DAVID LEWIN

INTRODUCTION

THE idea that employee exercise of voice may result in mutual gains to employer and employee is well known, however, this idea has largely been developed and 'tested' in unionized employment relationships that feature formal collective bargaining by employer and employee representatives which leads in most instances to a written agreement (contract). On the one hand, this is not surprising because from a theoretical perspective mutual gains-type bargaining has as its antecedents prior concepts of integrative (or cooperative or variable sum or win–win) negotiations, and because from an applied perspective union–management negotiations over a first contract or successor contracts constitute proactive behaviour that culminates in the establishment of terms, conditions, and related 'rules' of the employment relationship.

On the other hand, this is quite surprising in light of the well documented decline in (private sector) union membership and collective bargaining, and the equally well documented growth in non-union enterprises of dispute resolution systems and practices which, by definition, are not jointly determined by employer and employees. Outside of the US these systems and practices are often labelled non-union employee representation (NER) whereas in the US they are typically labelled alternative dispute resolution (ADR), meaning an alternative not only to unionized employee representation but especially to use of the external legal/judicial system for resolving employment disputes. Under each of these employment dispute resolution systems and practices non-union employees can be said to directly exercise voice and to do so much in the same way as unionized employees. However, non-union employment dispute systems and practices vary considerably in the extent to which employees can be represented by others, such as peers or outside counsel, and in this respect depart considerably from the representation of unionized employees by shop stewards, committee men and women, and progressively higher-ranking union officials. In any case, whether and to what extent mutual gains to employer and employee result from the presence and use of NER and ADR systems and practices is largely unknown. Hence, this chapter focuses on employee voice in non-union enterprises and addresses the question, 'Do mutual gains to employer and employee result from non-union employees' exercise of voice?'

To answer this question, the first section provides a brief review of the literature on employee voice and mutual gains which focuses on how they are linked. The second section summarizes the evidence, including a new source of evidence, about the incidence of ADR systems and practices in (US-based) non-union enterprises. The third section draws on a sample of such enterprises to estimate the extent to which employees actually exercise voice under these ADR systems and practices. In the fourth section, survey, interview, and archival data drawn from four of these non-union enterprises are analysed to document and assess the extent to which employee exercise of voice under these enterprises' ADR systems and practices result in mutual gains to employer and employee. The fifth section summarizes the main conclusions of this study and derives certain implications for a broadened theoretical perspective on employee voice and mutual gains.

EMPLOYEE VOICE AND MUTUAL GAINS

The concept of employee voice is largely derived from the work of Hirschman (1970), who addressed the question of why dissatisfied customers of companies and dissatisfied citizens of nation states might not simply leave and become customers of other companies or citizens of other nation states, respectively. Such leaving or, as Hirschman labelled it, 'exit', would clearly be consistent with, indeed predicted by, neoclassical economic theory which assumes (among other things) perfectly functioning product and labour markets, complete information, and the full mobility of capital and labour. But as Hirschman observed, some dissatisfied customers (and citizens) do not exit, rather they stay and fight—or as he put it, exercise 'voice'—in attempting to have their dissatisfaction redressed. These customers (and citizens), said Hirschman, are clearly more loyal than those who exit, therefore customer (and citizen) loyalty should be positively correlated with voice and negatively correlated with exit.

This key insight has been drawn upon by many labour economists and industrial relations specialists to model and analyse the exit–voice trade-off in the employment relationship (Freeman and Medoff, 1984; Lewin, 2007). Predictions in this regard are the same as those pertaining to customers and citizens, that is, some dissatisfied employees will choose to exercise voice rather than exit/quit their jobs and seek employment elsewhere, and those who exercise such voice are more loyal than those who exit/quit. Some scholars, notably those who focus strongly on this exit– voice trade-off, have found empirical support for the trade-off (Freeman, 1980). These findings have emanated largely from studies of unionized employees who exercise voice by filing grievances using the grievance procedures contained in union–management collective bargaining agreements. Among such employees, the main empirical finding is that grievance filing (i.e., voice) is significantly negatively correlated with quitting (i.e., exit). Other scholars, however, have included the third component of Hirschman's analytical framework, that is, loyalty, in their studies, and find that contrary to prediction employee loyalty is inversely correlated with voice (Boroff and Lewin, 1997; Lewin and Boroff, 1996). These studies, which include both unionized and non-union employees and firms, also find that (consistent with a priori prediction) employee loyalty is inversely correlated with exit. It therefore appears that the dominant behaviour among (unionized and non-union) employees who are dissatisfied with their employment relationship is to suffer in silence rather than exercise voice or exit their employment relationships (Rusbelt et al., 1988).

The concept of mutual gains has it antecedents in behavioural theory and research on collective bargaining. For example, Walton and McKersie (1965), distinguished distributive bargaining from integrative bargaining between union-ized employees and management. Distributive bargaining is characterized as a fixed-sum game in which what one party loses the other party gains, negotiation agenda items are posed as issues about which the parties are in conflict, each side uses power tactics in attempting to influence the other side's reservation price and resistance point, and negotiations are largely adversarial in nature. Integrative bargaining is characterized as a variable-sum game in which both sides may win or lose, negotiation agenda items are posed as problems to be solved, both sides openly exchange information in attempting to serve their mutual interests, and negotiations are largely cooperative in nature. More popularly, distributive bar-gaining is typically labelled win–lose-type negotiations and integrative bargaining is typically labelled win–win-type negotiations (Fisher and Ury, 1981).

More recently, the concept of integrative bargaining has evolved into interest-based negotiations (IBN) in which the negotiating parties jointly: 1) identify key mutual interests; 2) gather and share information required to analyse these inter-ests; 3) generate decision-making options, and 4) choose options 'that offer the highest mutual gains for the parties' (McKersie et al., 2008: 68). Whether and to what extent IBN is conceptually or empirically different from integrative bargaining is disputable. Nevertheless, several notable case examples of IBN and integrative bargaining in the context of union–management relations have been documented.[1] What this research has not addressed, however, is whether and to what extent mutual gains to management and employees can result from ADR and other types of non-union employee voice—which is the issue taken up in this chapter.

Non-union ADR Systems: Incidence and Causality

Several studies conducted during the last two decades or so have estimated the extent to which ADR systems have been adopted by non-union enterprises.[2] Collectively these estimates range between approximately one-sixth and one-half of non-union enterprises, with the variation in this regard being influenced by level of enterprise (e.g., entire company versus local establishment/facility), industry coverage, sampling frame, type of respondent, time period, and other factors. In an attempt to obtain a more precise, contemporary estimate of the incidence of ADR systems in non-union enterprises, a new survey was designed and administered in mid-2007 to a sample of 1,150 business units of US-based publicly traded companies. This random sample was drawn from the 2006 COMPUSTAT business unit financial reporting file and represented 20 per cent of all business units and 28 per cent of all non-union businesses included in that file. In order to maximize the response rate the survey was administered in several ways, including electronically (i.e., online), by telephone, by mailed hard copy, and in a few instances by direct interview. These multiple methods yielded an overall response rate of 65.8 per cent (i.e., 757/1150). A summary of the main findings from this survey is presented in Table 18.1.

As of 2006, some 63 per cent of the business units included in this sample had one or another type of ADR system in place. The dominant type of ADR system in these non-union businesses is a multi-step appeal/complaint procedure similar in some respects to the grievance procedure that prevails in unionized businesses; 71 per cent of the non-union businesses with ADR systems have such a multi-step procedure. The most common single ADR practice (method) in these non-union businesses is arbitration, which is present in almost 80 per cent of the non-union businesses that have multi-step ADR systems and in almost 70 per cent of the non-union businesses that have any type of ADR system. No other single ADR practice is present in a majority of the non-union businesses with ADR systems. Following arbitration, the next most common ADR practices in these businesses are an

Table 18.1 ADR system presence and type in non-union business units

ADR system present		
Response	Frequency	Per cent
Yes	478	63.1
No	273	36.1
Don't know	6	0.8
Total	757	100
Multi-step procedure		
Response	Frequency	Per cent
Yes	340	71.1
No	137	28.7
Don't know	1	0.2
Total	478	100
Specific ADR practice		
Category	Frequency	Per cent*
Arbitration	354	74.1
Mediation	87	18.2
Upper management review	149	31.2
Peer review	104	21.8
Employee hot line	216	45.2

*Does not total 100 per cent due to multiple ADR practices within business units.

Source: ADR system survey of 1,150 non-union business units, 2007.

employee hot line (45 per cent), upper management review (31 per cent), peer review (22 per cent), and mediation (18 per cent).

Industrial relations scholars have offered a variety of explanations for the rise and diffusion of ADR systems in non-union businesses, notably, threat explanations, on the one hand, and strategic HR/IR explanations, on the other hand. According to the data presented in Table 18.2, the primary reason, expressed by 79 per cent of the respondents, why the non-union businesses included in this study have adopted ADR systems is to avoid employment litigation (i.e., the litigation threat). The secondary reason for such adoption, expressed by 54 per cent of the respondents, is to avoid unionization (i.e., the unionization threat). By contrast, only 22 per cent of the respondents in these non-union businesses indicated that the identification of workplace issues/problems (i.e., a strategic rationale) was a reason for their businesses' adoption of an ADR system, and only 19 per cent indicated that an ADR system was adopted as a component of a larger high-involvement work system (i.e., another strategic rationale). Further according to the data in Table 18.2, this pattern of findings is even more pronounced when it comes to non-union businesses' adoption of arbitration as a specific ADR practice.

Table 18.2 Reasons for ADR system adoption by non-union businesses

Reason for adoption		
Category	Frequency	Per cent[*]
Employment litigation avoidance	599	79.1
Unionization avoidance	410	54.2
Identification of workplace issues/problems	168	22.2
Part of high-involvement work system	143	18.9
Competitor has an ADR system	45	5.9
Top management's ethical beliefs	9	1.2
Don't know	17	2.2
Reason for adopting arbitration		
Category	Frequency	Per cent[*]
Employment litigation avoidance	617	81.5
Unionization avoidance	431	56.9
Identification of workplace issues/problems	147	19.4
Part of high-involvement work system	125	16.5
Competitor has an ADR system	56	7.4
Top management's ethical beliefs	12	1.6
Don't know	5	0.7

[*]Does not total 100 per cent due to multiple reasons for ADR system and arbitration adoption.

Source: ADR systems survey of non-union business units, 2007.

Non-union ADR Systems and Employee Exercise of Voice

It is one thing for non-union businesses to have ADR systems in place, quite another thing for employees to use these systems. Hence the question naturally arises, 'To what extent do non-union employees use their employers' ADR systems?' Prior research on this question suggests that annually, on average, about 5 of every 100 non-union employees of businesses with ADR systems actually use these systems, meaning that they file a written complaint or 'grievance'. According to the data collected for the present study, however, and as shown in Table 18.3, the annual complaint/grievance filing rate in this sample of non-union businesses during the five year period from 2002 to 2006 was 13.5 per cent. This is a 'hard' complaint/grievance filing rate, meaning that it includes only written complaints/grievances filed by employees at the first step of the formal employment dispute resolution systems that covered them and in which they were eligible to engage in such filing. Stated differently, this overall complaint/grievance filing rate does not include informal discussion of potential complaints/grievances by non-union employees with their peers, supervisors, or managers. Prior research (e.g., Lewin and Peterson, 1988) as well as certain other data obtained during the

Table 18.3 Annual average ADR system usage
           rates in non-union business units,
           2002–2006

Usage rates	
Year	Per cent*
2002	12.6
2003	13.3
2004	13.8
2005	14.1
2006	13.7
2002–2006	13.5

*Based on number of complaints/grievances filed annually per
100 employees.

Source: ADR system survey of non-union business units, 2007.
N = 424 out of 757 non-union business units with ADR systems
(i.e., 56 per cent).

course of this study, indicate that informal grievance rates among unionized and non-union employees are between five and ten times higher than formal grievance filing rates. In any case, not only is the aforementioned 13.5 per cent grievance filing rate among non-union employees considerably higher than has previously been reported, it is also higher than the typical grievance filing rate in unionized businesses. What factors might explain this relatively high complaint/grievance filing?

First, and as suggested by the non-union ADR system incidence data discussed above, it is no longer unusual or novel for a non-union business to have such a system in place; indeed, it is in fact the norm. Analogously, this means that employees of such businesses are not doing something unusual (or highly improbable) if they file complaints/grievances under such systems. Second, non-union employers typically describe in considerable detail their particular ADR systems, communicate these descriptions widely to employees, and often encourage employees to make use of these systems (i.e., exercise voice). Here there may well be an analogy to the speak-up systems that many of these non-union businesses maintain for their customers whereby such customers are encouraged to bring their concerns about product/service availability, quality, price, and repair to the attention of management (i.e., exercise voice). In both instances, that is, regarding ADR systems for employees and speak-up systems for customers, these non-union businesses apparently prefer voice over exit or, in other words, retention over turnover. From this analytical perspective, an ADR system for employees is viewed as a mechanism for retaining and perhaps enhancing a non-union business's human capital, and a speak-up system for customers is viewed as a mechanism for retaining and thereby increasing the lifetime revenue obtained from customers.

Third, developments in information technology, in particular the widespread use of personal computers and intranets by non-union businesses, makes it much easier and simpler than previously for employees of these businesses to file written complaints/grievances and to obtain responses from management to those complaints/grievances. Indeed, this 'causal' factor was cited by a substantial majority of the respondents of the non-union businesses that were surveyed for this study, and also by a substantial majority of the employees of the four non-union businesses that served as the 'mutual gains' research sites for this study. Fourth, some ADR system usage in the non-union businesses included in this study consists of complaints/grievances that employees initially pursued through litigation but which were subsequently referred—moved—by the courts to these ADR systems for resolution. Such action almost always occurred in cases in which non-union employees alleged one or another type of employment discrimination, and apparently occurred only in those instances in which the non-union businesses in question had ADR systems featuring arbitration. This is, of course, consistent with and reflective of the 'deferral to arbitration' doctrine that the US Supreme Court has articulated during the last decade or so in employment discrimination cases involving non-union businesses.

Regarding the issues about which employees of non-union businesses exercise voice using these businesses' ADR systems, those involving performance appraisal, promotion, compensation, work location, and work environment are the most common, as shown in Table 18.4. Next in terms of the frequency with which they are pursued through these ADR systems are issues involving leave time and arrangements (such as paid versus non-paid), job title and discipline, including termination from employment. Relatively low frequency of ADR system usage apparently occurs with regard to the issue of employment discrimination, however,

Table 18.4 Issues about which employees exercise voice in non-union ADR systems

Issue	Frequency	Per cent[*]
Performance appraisal	236	55.6
Promotion (denial)	201	47.4
Compensation (e.g., bonus eligibility)	189	44.6
Work location	175	41.3
Work environment (e.g., cleanliness)	164	38.7
Leave time/arrangements (e.g., medical)	95	22.4
Job title	79	18.6
Discipline (e.g., termination, suspension)	74	17.5
Employment discrimination	29	6.8

[*]Does not total 100 per cent due to multiple issues about which employees exercise voice.
Source: ADR system survey of non-union business units, 2007.
N = 424 out of 757 non-union business units with ADR systems (i.e., 56 per cent).

the complexity attending non-union employees' initial filing of employment discrimination cases with the courts and subsequent referral of such cases by the courts to these non-union businesses' ADR systems implies that the usage rate for this issue is somewhat higher than the survey-based usage rate shown in Table 18.4. Nevertheless, on the whole these data suggest a conclusion that is contrary to received wisdom about non-union ADR, namely, that the scope of issues over which non-union employees exercise voice is larger than the scope of issues over which unionized employees exercise voice through collectively bargained grievance procedures.

Further, just as unionized employees are known to influence management practices through grievance filing, so too can non-union employees exercise such influence. In particular, survey respondents in about three-quarters of the non-union businesses included in this study indicated that they had revised their supervisor training practices in response to employee grievance filing; well over half of these non-union businesses modified employee compensation, work shifts, and working conditions in response to employee grievance filing; about one-third of these non-union businesses changed their workplace safety and training practices in response to employee grievance filing; and approximately one-quarter of these non-union businesses altered their promotion and per-formance evaluation practices in response to employee grievance filing. To the extent that such changes in management practices are beneficial to the non-union businesses and employees included in this study, they attest not only to the influence that non-union employees can exercise through the use of ADR (and, by inference, other types of non-union employment dispute resolution systems and practices) but to the mutual gains that can result from non-union employee exercise of voice.

Under a non-union business's ADR system, all of the employees covered by that system presumably have an equal likelihood of using that system. The ADR system usage data presented in Table 18.5 do not support this presumption. Instead, they indicate that men are more likely than women, middle-aged employees are more likely than younger and older employees, home country located employees are more likely that other country located employees, and non-supervisory and non-managerial employees are more likely than supervisors and managers to use their non-union businesses' ADR systems. With regard to gender, age, and position (i.e., supervisor/manager versus employee), these findings comport with those previously reported in studies of non-union ADR.[3] Nevertheless, from a broader perspective, non-union businesses' ADR systems cover a much wider range of employees than the grievance systems of unionized businesses. In the latter, only members of a bargain-ing unit are eligible to use the grievance procedure specified in the collective bargaining agreement, whereas in the former all employees up to and sometimes including middle management are eligible to use the ADR system. Hence, even though supervisors and managers of non-union businesses are significantly less

Table 18.5 Employee use of non-union ADR systems by demographic characteristics

Employee characteristic	Frequency*	Per cent
Gender		
Male	276	65.1
Female	148	34.9
Total	424	100
Age		
Younger (i.e., 18–34 years of age)	116	27.4
Middle (i.e., 34–54 years of age)	233	54.9
Older (i.e., 55 and above years of age)	75	17.7
Total	424	100
Location		
Home country (of company)	314	74.1
Outside home country (of company)	110	25.9
Total	424	100
Position		
Non-supervisory, non-managerial employee	346	81.6
Supervisory and managerial employee	78	18.4
Total	424	100

*Based on forced choice within each employee characteristic category.

Source: ADR system survey of non-union business units, 2007.

N = 424 out of 757 non-union business units with ADR systems (i.e., 56 per cent).

likely than non-supervisory and non-managerial employees of those businesses to actually use these businesses' ADR systems, the fact that some supervisors and managers of these non-union businesses do use these systems indicates that 'employee' exercise of voice is more pervasive, occupationally or job title wise, in non-union than in unionized businesses.

Non-union ADR Systems, Employee Exercise of Voice and Mutual Gains

Having established the widespread existence of ADR systems in non-union enterprises and having shown that these systems are in fact used by non-union employees more frequently than has previously been thought, attention now turns to the key question posed at the outset of this chapter, namely, 'Do mutual gains to employer and employee result from non-union employees' exercise of voice?' For this purpose, four of the non-union businesses that responded to the aforementioned survey and that have ADR systems in place were selected for participation in the second phase of this study.[4] Research wise, this phase featured archival analysis of company ADR (and related) records over a five-year period; 2) in-depth interviews with executives in each company; and 3) selection of samples of employees in each company and administration of a survey to those employees. Table 18.6 presents descriptive data for each of the four companies, the interviewees, and the employee samples.

Among these four non-union companies, two have had ADR systems in place for about a decade and a half, one for about a decade, and one for about half a decade. In two of these companies, arbitration is the final step of the ADR system; in one of these companies, a senior management committee is the final step of the ADR system; and in one of these companies, the Chief Executive Officer (CEO) is the final step of the ADR system. Two of the four companies' ADR systems include peer review as a formal step and one includes mediation as a formal step. Further, in two of these companies employees who use the ADR system can be represented by outside counsel, in another of these companies employees who use the ADR system can be represented by a colleague, and in still another of these companies employees who use the ADR system are not permitted to be represented.

Archival analysis of ADR system data and documents in these four companies showed the following. First, during the five-year period from 2002 to 2006, twelve complaints/grievances per 100 employees were filed annually on average, ranging between nine and sixteen on a per company basis and between ten and fourteen on a per year basis. Second, all but two of these complaints/grievances were settled/ decided within three months of their filing, another was settled/decide within four months of its filing, and another was settled/decided within six months of its filing. Third, in each company either quarterly or bi-annual meetings of senior executives and line managers were held to discuss ADR system activity, issues, settlements, and follow-up actions. Fourth, each of the four companies amended or revised its ADR system specifications on at least one occasion during the 2002–2006 period. Fifth, in two of these companies lawsuits filed by certain of their employees alleging employment discrimination were referred by the courts to the companies for settlement under the companies' ADR systems.

In order to identify and analyse the mutual gains resulting from employee exercise of voice in non-union enterprises, an interview protocol was designed and administered to the top five executives in each of the four participating companies. In particular, this purposive sample included the General Manager (GM), Chief Operating Officer (COO), Chief Human Resources Officer (CHRO), Chief Financial Officer (CFO), and Chief Marketing Officer (CMO) in each company.[5] The specific questions included in the protocol focused on the benefits and costs (i.e., gains and losses) that the interviewees perceived to be associated with or result from ADR system usage in their respective companies. All of the executives were interviewed twice, with the interviews averaging about two hours each.

Table 18.6 Selected characteristics of four non-union business units, ADR systems, executive interview, and employee survey samples

Characteristic	Business unit			
	A	B	C	D
Industry	Aerospace	Medical supplies	Information technology	Entertainment
Years ADR system in place	15	10	5	15
ADR practices	Arbitration peer review	CEO final step mediation	Peer Review	Arbitration
Employee representative	Outside counsel	None	Peer	Outside counsel
Average annual employment, 2002–2006	46,400	21,600	28,400	18,700
ADR system usage rate, 2002–2006	16.2	11.4	9.2	13.8
Average time to settlement of ADR issues	2.6 months	1.8 months	1.4 months	2.3 months
Executives interviewed by job title	CEO	CEO	CEO	CEO
	COO	President	President	COO
	SVP-HR	SVP-HR	VP-HR	CHRO
	CFO	SVP-marketing	Treasurer	SVP-marketing
	General counsel	General counsel	General counsel	General counsel
Surveyed, Employees, Sample size,	380	285	325	255
Respondents and response rate	226	174	206	184
	59.50%	61.10%	63.40%	72.6

Source: Archival analysis, top executive interview data, and employee survey data.

The interviews were audio taped, after which the tapes were transcribed and the qualitative responses to interview questions were coded and thereby transformed into data for subsequent analysis.

The second interviews of these executives were conducted approximately four months after the first interviews, and were designed to probe certain of the areas of ADR benefits and costs that emerged from a survey of samples of employees in each company that had used—filed one or more complaints/grievances under— each company's ADR system during the 2002–2006 period.[6] The selection of these employee samples was based on the preceding archival analysis and was then stratified by type of issue over which complaints/grievances were filed, employee job title/occupational category, level of complaint/grievance decision, and decision result. This selection procedure yielded a total sample of 1,245 employees to whom the survey was administered by mailed hard copy followed by two mailed postcard requests and one telephone request for survey completion and return. The overall response rate to this survey was 63.5 per cent (790/ 1,245), with the postcard and telephone follow-up requests generating about 13 per cent of this total. These employee survey data together with the aforementioned executive interview data permit the analysis of mutual gains under these four non-union ADR systems.

To begin this analysis, consider the views of top executives about the benefits and costs of the ADR systems in their respective companies. As shown in Table 18.7,

Table 18.7 Summary of top executive ratings of ADR system benefits and costs

Item	Rank
ADR System Benefit	
Providing a source of information about employee relations issues/problems	1
Identifying ineffective supervision/management	2
Clarifying company HR policies/practices	3
Reducing employee dissatisfaction	4
Reducing employment litigation	5
Increasing employee retention	6
Avoiding employee unionization	7
Enabling employees to communicate with top management	8
Serving as a form of employee participation in the organization	9
Strengthening employee discipline	10
ADR System Cost	
Resources required to maintain/operate an ADR system	1
Loss of productive time	2
Reduced supervisor morale	3
Loss of decision-making control	4
Retention of low performing employees	5

Source: Interviews of five top executives in each of four non-union business units with ADR systems (N = 20).

these executives perceive the main benefits of their ADR systems to be (in order of importance): 1) providing a source of information about employment relations issues/problems; 2) identifying ineffective supervision/management; 3) clarifying company HR policies/practices; 4) reducing employee dissatisfaction; 5) reducing employment litigation; 6) increasing employee retention; 7) avoiding employee unionization; 8) enabling employees to communicate with top management; 9) serving as a form of employee participation in the organization; and 10) strengthening employee discipline. When asked if their companies would be 'better off with or without an ADR system', nineteen of the twenty interviewed executives responded 'better off with an ADR system'.[7]

This ranking of ADR systems benefits varies by the particular positions that these executives hold in their respective organizations. To illustrate, the GMs and COOs of these companies are significantly more likely than the CHROs and CMOs to rate 'providing a source of information about employment relations issues/problems', 'identifying ineffective supervision/management', and 'enabling employees to communicate with top management' as the main benefits of their companies' ADR systems. CHROs and CMOs are significantly more likely than GMs, COOs, and CFOs to rate 'clarifying company HR policies/practices', 'reducing employee satisfaction', and 'increasing employee retention' as the main benefits of their companies' ADR systems. CFOs are significantly more likely than all other top executives to rate 'reducing employment litigation' and 'avoiding employee unionization' as the main benefits of their companies' ADR systems.[8]

Turning to the perceived costs of their respective ADR systems, the executives interviewed for this study identified the following (in order of importance): 1) resources required to maintain/operate an ADR system; 2) loss of 'productive' time; 3) reduced supervisor morale; 4) loss of decision-making control; and 5) retention of low performing employees. The CFOs in these companies were significantly more likely than the CHROs and CMOs to rate 'resources required to maintain/operate an ADR system' and 'loss of productive time' as the main costs of their companies' ADR systems; COOs were significantly more likely than all other executives to rate 'loss of decision-making control' as the main cost of their companies' ADR systems; and CHROs and CMOs were significantly more likely than CEOs, COOs and CFOs to rate 'reduced supervisor morale' and 'retention of low performing employees' as the main costs of their companies' ADR systems.

When asked specifically, 'Do the benefits of your company's ADR system exceed its costs?' seventeen of the twenty interviewed executives responded 'yes', two responded 'no', and one responded 'they are equal'. As a validity check on the responses to this question, a subsequent question asked, 'Do the costs of your company's ADR system exceed its benefits?' Responding to this question, sixteen of the interviewed executives responded 'no', two responded 'yes', one responded 'they are equal', and one responded 'I don't know'. With only two inconsistent answers to this pair of questions, it appears that the top executives in the four companies that participated in this (phase of the) study clearly judge their companies' ADR systems to be providing net benefits, in fact, substantially so. But does this necessarily mean that these systems and employee exercise of voice through them produces mutual gains?

The data presented in Table 18.8 are helpful for answering this question. They show that employees in the four participating companies who actually filed complaints/grievances under their companies ADR systems rate the benefits of these systems as follows (in order of importance): 1) redressing ineffective supervision/management; 2) clarifying company HR policies/practices; 3) improved working conditions, 4) increased training; 5) fairer promotion decisions; 6) communicating with top management; 7) increased employee satisfaction; 8) increased employee retention; 9) improved family–work life balance; and 10) reduced employment discrimination.[9] While some of these benefits of ADR systems differ from those indentified by company executives others are similar or even identical to them, including such top-rated benefits as 'redressing ineffective supervision/management' and 'clarifying company HR policies/practices', and such mid-rated benefits as 'communicating with top management' and 'increased employee satisfaction'. In light of prior theorizing about non-union enterprises' rationale for adopting ADR systems and the specific benefits of such systems identified by the top executives of these companies during their first interviews, the employees who were surveyed for this study were asked their views about the effects of the ADR

Table 18.8 Summary of non–union employee ratings of ADR system benefits and costs

Item	Rank
ADR system benefit	
Redressing ineffective supervision/management	1
Clarifying company HR policies/practices	2
Improved working conditions	3
Increased training	4
Fairer promotion decisions	5
Communicating with top management	6
Increased employee satisfaction	7
Increased employee retention	8
Improved family–work life balance	9
Reduced employment discrimination	10
Loss of productive time	1
ADR system cost	
Time required to reach decisions about complaints/grievances	2
Failure of management to learn from prior complaints/grievances	3
Reduced supervisor morale	4
Retention of low performing employees	5

Source: Survey of employees of non-union business units with ADR systems who used those systems at least once during 2002–2006 (response rate = 63.5 per cent, i.e., 790/1,245).

systems in their companies on employee 'demand' for unionization and for employment litigation. For this purpose, the relevant survey questions and their associated rating scales were structured such that answers could range from large positive demand, scaled at $+3$, to large negative demand, scaled at -3, with the choice 'no effect on demand' scaled at 0. On the whole, these employees judged such effects to be small to negligible; specifically, their mean rating of the effects of ADR systems on potential employee unionization was -0.4 and their mean rating of the effects of ADR systems on potential employment litigation was $+0.6$. Hence, in these two important respects, the employees of the four companies included in this study—employees who have had personal experience with these companies' ADR systems—differ from the top executives of these companies. Nevertheless, when it comes to certain other benefits of ADR systems, these same employees share quite similar views with the top executives of their companies.

Much the same can be said about employee views of the costs of the ADR systems that prevail in their companies. When asked about such costs,[10] these employees rated the following (in order of importance): 1) loss of productive time; 2) time required to reach decisions about complaints/grievances; 3) failure of management to learn from prior complaints/grievances; 4) reduced supervisor morale; and 5) retention of low performing employees. Notably, three of these costs are the same as those identified by top executives of these companies whereas 'time required to reach decisions about complaints/grievances' and 'failure of management to learn from prior complaints/grievances' are different costs from those identified by top executives. Because prior research has identified fear of retaliation as having a significant negative effect on non-union (and unionized) employees' filing of complaints/grievances,[11] the employees surveyed for this study were asked to indicate whether and to what extent they considered such fear of retaliation to be a 'cost' of their own companies' ADR systems. Surprisingly, perhaps, these employees judged this cost to be small indeed; the mean rating of their responses to a question about fear of retaliation for filing a complaint/ grievance under their respective companies' ADR systems was 1.4 on a 1 = very small, 7 = very large rating scale. This finding is not so surprising, however, when one considers the relatively high rates of ADR system usage in these companies, the involvement of peers and external third parties in these ADR systems, and the relatively swift grievance settlements that occurred in these companies, at least during 2002–2006.

As with the top executives of these four companies, the sample of employees in these companies who had filed complaints/grievances under their companies' ADR systems were specifically asked, 'Do the benefits of your company's ADR system exceed its costs?' Of the 790 employees who answered this question, 84.1 per cent (664/790) responded 'yes', 8.2 per cent (65/790) responded 'no', and 7.7 per cent (61/ 790) responded 'about equal'. Also as with the top executives, a validity check on the responses to this question was conducted by including the subsequent question in the survey: 'Do the costs of your company's ADR system exceed its benefits?' In answering this question, 82.1 per cent (649/790) of the employees responded 'no', 7.5 per cent (59/790) responded 'yes', and 10.4 per cent (82/790) responded 'about equal'. Given the quite consistent answers to this pair of questions, it appears that employees that participated in this study judge their companies' ADR systems to be providing net benefits—in fact and as with the dominant view expressed by the top executives of these companies, substantially so. In sum, this combination of interview and survey evidence obtained from top executives and employees, respectively, in the four non-union companies that participated in this study leads to the conclusion that mutual gains result from/can be attributed to the ADR systems in these companies.

Further supporting this conclusion are certain qualitative examples of ADR system benefits in these four companies that were identified and elaborated by the executives and employees that participated in the study. Four pairs of examples, one offered by an executive and the other by an employee in each of the participating companies, are summarized below.[12]

Company A, Aerospace; Executive (COO). Our ADR system has been around since the early 1990s and was adopted because quite a few of our professional employees were telling us that they had no systematic way of bringing work problems to our attention or, when they did, there was little or no subsequent action or feedback. This probably says something about the main type of employee we have in our business, who are engineers and who prefer order, systems, and procedures in all aspects of the business. We did some benchmarking in this area and decided to go the whole hog by adopting a dispute resolution procedure that culminates in third-party arbitration. In my experience—I've been the COO for the last seven years and am an engineer by training—our system has worked pretty well. We don't get a lot of complaints, but when we do we try to act on them quickly by investigating them carefully, reaching decisions, and then providing detailed feedback to the employees [who filed the complaints]. As I see it, this has helped us to clarify our HR policies, improve our supervision, and in some instances retain valuable employees. There are costs to this system, of course, but you can't get value from a system like ours without investing in it.

Company A, Aerospace; Employee (Mechanical Engineer). I've been with this company for eighteen years and I think we've come a long way in the way we handle employee relations. When I started with the company, if you had a complaint you basically could only bring it to your supervisor and hope that some sort of action would be taken. This was a hit and miss process and you never really new what decisions management had reached about your complaints. After the company adopted its ADR system, this began to change and I think that for the last several years everyone pretty much knows how management had handled employee complaints and what actions they've taken to deal with those complaints ... You asked if I'd ever used our ADR system, and the answer is "yes, twice". Once I used this system to complain about a performance review that I thought was unwarranted because I was rated 'poor' in certain areas. My complaint was reviewed pretty quickly, as I recall, and changes were made to that review so that 'average' became my lowest rating in any area. My supervisor wasn't too happy about this but he told me that he'd discussed the matter with upper management and understood why the change was made. The next time I used the ADR system was to complain about a promotion that I thought I'd been denied. That complaint took longer to get an answer to, several weeks I think, and I was told that the promotion wouldn't be granted at that time but might be granted the next year if my performance improved. I guess it did because I was promoted the next year.

Company B, Medical Supplies; Executive (CMO). This has always been a strongly customer-oriented company and we've been doing customer satisfaction surveys for, oh, about fifteen years. We also have a speak-up system for customers in which they can contact us to get specific information about or complain about a product or a service or a salesperson, or just about anything else. Those of us in marketing think that these two things have helped us retain our customers, especially the best ones. I think it was about ten years ago that my predecessor [as CMO] together with our CHRO at the time 'sold' the rest of senior management on adopting a speak-up-type system for our employees, which is now popularly referred to as an ADR system. His main reasoning seemed to be that our employees are our customers, too—internal customers I guess you'd say—so we should have some type of system that allows them to get their complaints addressed when they need to. I've been surprised at how well this system has been received, especially by management. Of course this may be because our CEO really believes in this system. As a matter of fact and as you may know, the CEO is the last step in our ADR system and he usually winds up deciding two or three of the employee complaints yearly. I know of at least three instances in which he's reversed the decisions of lower management, but he's always careful to explain why he's reached these decisions. I think this has helped us spot and correct certain employee relations problems and keep some of these problems out of the court system. It's also helped to retain some key employees.

Company B, Medical Supplies; Employee (Salesperson). I've worked for three different companies during the last eleven years and know how salespeople can be treated. In my first company it was simply a matter of how much revenue you could generate for the company. Sales meant a hell of a lot but service didn't. I raised this issue several times with my manager but got nowhere, so after a couple of years I moved to another company. That company was better than the first when it came to serving customers, but as an employee if you had an issue or problem you were expected either to work it out yourself or get your supervisor to deal with it. Well, that might be OK in general but not when your supervisor was the problem! I left that company two years ago and have been with my present company for six years and expect that I'll be here quite a while longer. Here we have a [ADR] system for employees that allows you to raise issues and get them addressed; you don't have to be quiet about these problems or just bring them to the attention of your supervisor. Two years ago I felt that I had to spend quite a lot of money to improve the quality of service to the customers in my geography [i.e., geographical area] and that was going to cut the margins on sales to those customers. My supervisor disagreed with me and disallowed the cost increase. So, it took this issue through the ADR system and it wound up being decided by the CEO himself. I didn't quite expect that and was nervous when I found out about it, but it turned out that he not only approved the cost increase but changed the company's policy in this area to give more weight to the quality of customer service and somewhat less weight to sales margin.

Company C, Information Technology; Executive (CHRO). This is a progressive company that really does believe that employees are a key asset. You probably don't think this is unusual because, after all, these days we sell solutions as much or more than products to our customers. But having worked for two other competitor companies I can tell you that most of the time when companies say they have progressive HR or employee relations policies they usually emphasize things like teamwork, decentralization and a strong company culture. We have these things in my company, but we don't pretend that everyone shares the same goals or that we don't have conflicts at work. This is a demanding business and sometimes our employees see these demands as inappropriate or unfair. This is where our ADR system comes in to play. We've had this system for about five years—I've been CHRO for three years and was Associate CHRO for three years before that—and it's really helped us to clarify our work practices, reduce employee dissatisfaction, and even make fairer promotion decisions. Our system doesn't involve third parties, such as an arbitrator, but we do have peer review and a top management committee as formal ADR steps. In the last two years, work–family life balance and promotion issues have been the subject of employee complaints, and I think that the way we addressed these complaints using the ADR system has worked to the company's benefit and our employees' benefit. These are 'win–wins', though we spend quite a lot of time and money in maintaining and sometimes modifying our ADR system.

Company C, Information Technology; Employee (Production Specialist). This is a pretty exciting business and its gotten more exciting as we've shifted from what you might call an almost exclusive emphasis on products to a balance of products and services—business solutions, its called. I've worked here for seven years and during that time more and more demands have been made on us who actually produce 'things'. Decisions that used to be made by my supervisor are now made by my team and sometimes by me alone. I'm getting paid more than I used to and the money is pretty good, but sometimes the job demands get out of hand. That's where our ADR system becomes important. I've used that system twice, once when I felt that my team was too small to get the job done and the second time when the company wanted me to relocate. I didn't originally think I'd use the ADR system for either of these issues, but I found that I couldn't get any resolution of them from my supervisor. So, I filed complaints using the ADR system. The first issue got settled pretty quickly at the peer review step, and the result was that our team was increased from four to five members. That was a really good decision and we were really able to accomplish our work on time and with a higher level of quality. Our supervisor wound up benefitting from this and turned out to be a 'happy camper'. The second issue took a lot longer to get settled, probably because it went to the top management committee. That committee decided that I didn't have to relocate, but they also wound up allocating more resources to my department so that jobs in other locations could be filled. In the end, my supervisor was pretty happy with that decision, too.

Company D, Entertainment; Executive (GM). This is a fast-paced business with a lot of creative people working here. Of course that's pretty much true of any business in our industry, but I think our business does better than most in recognizing that conflicts among creative types are very common—normal, you might say—and therefore it pays to have an organized, systematic way of dealing with those conflicts. In a nutshell, this is why we have an ADR system and have had for quite a while. One of the key aspects of this system, in my opinion, is that arbitration is the final step. I think that when employees see that the company is willing to turn over to a neutral third party decision-making responsibility on an issue of, say, suspension or termination, they believe that the company is trying to deal with them fairly. You can't have every employment dispute go to arbitration, of course, and we have only a few cases a year that go that far. Sometimes the decisions reached in the ADR system, including cases decided short of arbitration, wind up overturning the decisions of lower management, but our managers recognize this risk and the truth is that their decisions are much more likely to be supported than overturned. This is one benefit of this system; another is that it clarifies some of our HR practices; another is that is reduces employee dissatisfaction. I even think that this system has helped us to attract and retain some key talent, though others might disagree with that. We also regularly use our ADR system data to identify workplace issues and to improve supervisory training.

Company D, Entertainment; Employee (Facility Manager). I've held the position of Facility Manager for three years and before that I worked directly for the previous Facility Manager. About four years ago I filed a complaint under our ADR system. I was reluctant to do so because my complaint was one of sexual harassment and it involved two of my co-workers. [This employee is a male as were his co-workers at the time.] I discussed this matter on a confidential basis with my boss, the Facility Manager, and she told me that she had had other problems with these same two employees, and that if I was willing to pursue my complaint through the ADR system she would back me to the hilt. While I didn't want to put myself in the middle of a bigger dispute, I felt that my choices were either to file the complaint or to quit. Obviously, I did file the complaint and what surprised me was that the review of my complaint was speeded up—expedited, I believe they called it—so that it went to arbitration about three weeks after I filed it. About two weeks after that I received notice of the arbitrator's decision and also the company's decision, which was to fire the two co-workers. In fact, the company made a big deal about this decision and publicized it throughout the company. One year later my boss was promoted to another position and I was promoted to Facility Manager. I was surprised to learn that even though I am now a manager in this company, I am still eligible to use the ADR system. I don't expect that I will do so, but I think this shows that the company is really interested in dealing with work conflicts no matter who they involve.

These four paired examples do not, of course, establish the basis for broad generalizations about employee voice and mutual gains in non-union enterprises. Nevertheless, they can help scholars to think more deeply about the concept of mutual gains, the study of mutual gains as between the unionized and non-union sectors, and the possibility that mutual gains to employers and employees may result from the widespread availability and quite considerable use of non-union ADR systems.[13]

CONCLUSIONS AND IMPLICATIONS FOR MUTUAL GAINS THEORY

Heretofore, theory and research on mutual gains has focused largely on employee exercise of voice in unionized settings featuring collective bargaining between representatives of management and labour which typically leads to formal written agreements (i.e., contracts) that contain grievance procedures. It is through both bargaining, per se, and grievance procedures that unionized employees exercise voice in the employment relationship and which on occasion lead to mutual gains. By contrast, this chapter focuses on employee voice in non-union enterprises and addresses the question, 'Do mutual gains to employer and employee result from non-union employees' exercise of voice?'

The short answer to this question is 'yes' based on the findings from the study reported herein. These main findings are: one, a substantial majority (almost two-thirds) of a large sample of US-based non-union businesses that were surveyed in mid-2007 reported having one or another type of ADR system in place; two, these ADR systems are not only available but are actually used by employees, as indicated by the estimated 13.5 per cent annual complaint/grievance filing rate among the employees of these businesses during 2002–2006; three, top executives of four non-union businesses with ADR systems that participated in this study indicated through lengthy interviews that they strongly believe that their businesses are 'better off' for having these ADR systems and that the benefits derived from these systems substantially exceed their costs; four, a large sample of employees of these four non-union businesses indicated through survey responses that they believe that the benefits derived from these businesses' ADR systems substantially exceed their costs; and five, specific examples of the benefits derived from/attributed to these ADR systems were provided by a top executive–employee pair in each of these four non-union businesses.

What do these findings imply for theorizing about mutual gains or, more pointedly, employee voice and mutual gains? Surely one implication is that such theorizing should not be circumscribed by reliance upon a purely collective context. While the presence of an employee union, the expression of collective voice by union representatives in negotiations with management representatives, the existence of a collective bargaining agreement, and the existence and use of grievance procedures by unionized employees facilitates the analysis of employee voice and mutual gains, these conditions or attributes also restrict such analysis. Indeed, these restrictions have grown larger and more untenable as unionism and collective bargaining coverage have declined and as the incidence of non-union ADR systems has substantially increased. Stated differently, employee voice can be—and is—exercised outside of a collective context, therefore, the analysis of mutual gains resulting from employee exercise of voice should also occur outside of (or in addition to) the collective context.

Another implication of the findings from this study is that judgements about mutual gains resulting from employee exercise of voice in non-union settings must rely heavily on the individual rather than the group or organization as the primary unit of analysis. As is evident from the present study, individual executives and employees provided the basic data by which mutual gains associated with employee exercise of voice were assessed. This is admittedly an additive or cumulative-type of analysis, meaning that the views expressed by individual executives and individual employees were merged and compared, respectively, in order to draw conclusions about employee voice and mutual gains. Nevertheless, there is a certain 'real' quality to this type of analysis, especially when compared to studies of mutual gains that rely on examples of 'innovative' provisions of collective bargaining agreements,[14] and this reality should be more fully and explicitly considered in theorizing about employee voice and mutual gains.

Finally, this study's findings serve as a reminder that 'employee voice' may be exercised not only by non-management employees but by management employees as well. In other words, managers (and even executives) are employees, too. This observation is underscored by recognizing that in unionized enterprises only employees who are members of the bargaining unit are eligible to use the grievance procedures contained in collective bargaining agreements, whereas in non-union enterprises most employees, including supervisors and managers (up to the mid-management level), are eligible to use these enterprises' ADR systems. It is easy to overlook this reality when mutual gains theory focuses primarily on employee voice exercised in a collective context.

Notes

1. See, as examples, Adler (1993); Bacon and Blyton (2006); Cutcher-Gershenfeld; et al. (2006); Deakin et al. (2002); Eaton et al. (2004); Mckersie et al. (2008); Rubenstein (2003); Rubenstein and Kochan (2001).
2. See, as examples, Colvin (2003); Delaney et al. (1989); Feuille and Chachere (1995); Feuille and Delaney (1992); Ichniowski; et al. (1989); Lewin (2005, 2008a, 2008b); Lipsky, et al. (1997, 2003); McCabe (1988); Westin and Felieu (1988).
3. The findings regarding gender and age differences also comport with those previously reported in studies of unionized grievance procedures (see, for example, Lewin and Peterson, 1988). By contrast, the data concerning home country located versus non-home country located employee usage of non-union ADR systems appear to be the first reported in the literature on this topic.
4. These four businesses constitute a 'purposive' sample based on: 1) 458 of the 757 that responded to the survey by indicating that they had a formal ADR system in place; 2) 92 of the 458 businesses that indicated through a response to a separate survey question that they would be willing to participate in the second phase of this study; 3) 24 of the 92 businesses that indicated through a follow-up telephone interview that they would be willing to participate on a sustained basis in the second phase of the study; 4) 8 of the 24 businesses in which preliminary archival analysis indicated sufficient data for participation in the study; and 5) 4 of the 8 businesses that agreed to provide full ADR archives and selected executive interviewees.
5. Because the participating companies are business units of large companies, the title General Manager (GM) is used to denote the top executive in these units. In practice, two of the four business units use the title Chief Executive Officer (CEO) for this position, one uses President, and one uses General Manager.
6. The identification of ADR benefits and costs for the purpose of conducting the second round of executive interviews was based on factor analysis of the employee survey data. Each of the benefits and costs that were shown by the factor analysis to be independent dimensions (constructs) was included in the interviews.
7. Factor analysis of these data indicated three separate, independent constructs, namely, problem identification, threat avoidance, and policy clarification. Given the emphasis on mutual gains in this paper, however, attention will continue to be paid to the ten ADR system benefits identified by interviewed executives, especially in relation to the ten ADR system benefits identified by employees (see below).

8. For evidence that human resource executives with strictly human resource management backgrounds differ significantly from human resource executives with financial management backgrounds when it comes to assessing the benefits and costs of particular human resource policies/practices, see Briscoe et al. (2005).

9. Factor analysis of these data indicated three separate, independent constructs, namely, redressing ineffective supervision/management, working conditions improvement, and fairness of HR policies. The main purpose here, however, is to compare the larger set of ADR system benefits identified by employees with those identified by the top executives in these four companies (see note 4).

10. The survey included specific questions about costs to the firm and costs to employees.

11. See Boroff and Lewin (1997); Lewin and Boroff (1996).

12. In order to preserve confidentially assurances provided to the companies that participated in this phase of the study, the specific names (acronyms) of their respective ADR systems are not identified. Instead, each such system is referred to as an 'ADR system'. In addition, certain clarifying comments inserted by the author into some of these examples are indicated by [ ].

13. Some industrial relations scholars are not at all shy when it comes to generalizing about the (presumed) lack of employee voice and mutual gains in the non-union sector. See, for example, Freeman and Medoff (1984) and the critiques of their work included in Bennett and Kaufman (2007), especially Lewin (2007).

14. See, for example, Cutcher-Gershenfeld et al. (2006).

References

ADLER, P. S. (1993) The Learning Bureaucracy: New United Motor Manufacturing, Inc., in B. M. Staw and L. L. Cummings, (eds)., *Research in Organizational Behavior*, 15: 111–94. Greenwich, CT: JAI Press.

BACON, N. and BLYTON, P. (2006) The Effect of Co-operating or Conflicting Over Work Restructuring: Evidence from Employees. *Sociological Review*, 54(1): 1–19.

BENNETT, J. T. and KAUFMAN, B. E. (eds) (2007) *What do Unions Do? A Twenty-Year Perspective*. New Brunswick, NJ: Transaction Publishers.

BOROFF, K. E. and LEWIN, D. (1997) Loyalty, Voice, and Intent to Exit a Union Firm: A Conceptual and Empirical Analysis. *Industrial and Labor Relations Review*, 51(1): 50–63.

BRISCOE, F., MAXWELL, J., and TEMIN, P. (2005) H. R. Versus Finance: Who Controls Corporate Health Care Decisions and Does it Matter? in D. Lewin, and B. E. Kaufman, (eds), *Advances in Industrial and Labor Relations*, 14: 1–32. London: Elsevier.

BUDD, J. W. (2005) *Labor Relations: Striking a Balance*. New York: McGraw-Hill/Irwin.

COLVIN, A. J. S. (2003) Institutional Pressures, Human Resources Strategies, and the Rise of Nonunion Dispute Resolution Procedures. *Industrial and Labor Relations Review*, 56(3): 375–92.

—— (2004). Adoption and Use of Dispute Resolution Procedures in the Nonunion Workplace, in D. Lewin, and B. E. Kaufman (eds), *Advances in Industrial and Labor Relations*, 13: 69–95. London, UK: Elsevier.

CUTCHER-GERSHENFELD, J., SLEIGH, S. R., and PIL, F. K. (2006) Collective Bargaining: Keeping Score on a Great American Institution, in D. Lewin, (ed), *Contemporary Issues in Employment Relations*, pp. 39–67 Champaign, IL: Labor and Employment Relations Association.

DEAKIN, S., HOBBS, R., KONZELMANN, S., and WILKINSON, F. (2002) Partnership, Ownership and Control: The Impact of Corporate Governance on Employment Relations. *Employee Relations*, 24(3): 335–52.

DELANEY, J. T., LEWIN, D., and ICHNIOWSKI, C. (1989) *Human Resource Policies and Practices in American Firms*, p. 137 Washington, D.C.: U.S. Department of Labor, BLMR.

EATON, S. C., RUBENSTEIN, S. A., and McKERSIE, R. B. (2004) Building and Sustaining Labor Management Partnerships: Recent Experiences in the U.S. in D. Lewin and B. E. Kaufman (eds), *Advances in Industrial and Labor Relations*, 13: 139–159. London: Elsevier.

FEUILLE, P. and CHACHERE, D. R. (1995) Looking Fair or Being Fair: Remedial Voice Procedures in Nonunion Workplaces. *Journal of Management*, 21(1): 27–42.

—— and DELANEY, J. T. (1992) The Individual Pursuit of Organizational Justice: Grievance Procedures in Nonunion Workplaces, in G. R. Ferris, and K. D. Rowland (eds), *Research in Personnel and Human Resource Management*, 10: 187–232. Greenwich, CT: JAI Press.

FISHER, R. and URY, W. (1981) *Getting to Yes*. Boston, MA: Houghton Mifflin.

FREEMAN, R. B. (1980) The Exit-Voice Tradeoff in the Labor Market: Unionism, Job Tenure, Quits, and Separations. *Quarterly Journal of Economics*, 94: (September): 643–73.

—— and MEDOFF, J. L. (1984) *What do Unions Do?* New York: Basic Books.

HIRSCHMAN, A. O. (1970) *Exit, Voice and Loyalty: Responses to Decline in Firms, Organizations and States*. Cambridge, MA: Harvard University Press.

ICHNIOWSKI, C., DELANEY, J. T., and LEWIN, D. (1989) The New Human Resource Management in US Workplaces: Is it Really New and is it Only Nonunion? *Relations Industrielles/Industrial Relations*, 44: 97–123.

LEWIN, D. (1997) Workplace Dispute Resolution, in D. Lewin, D. J. B. Mitchell, and M. Zaidi, (eds), *The Human Resource Management Handbook*, Part II, pp. 197–218. Greenwich, CT: JAI Press.

—— (1999) Theoretical and Empirical Research on the Grievance Procedure and Arbitration: A Critical Review, in J. H. Keefe and A. E. Eaton (eds), *Employment Dispute Resolution and Worker Rights in the Changing Workplace*, pp. 137–86. Madison, WI: Industrial Relations Research Association.

—— (2005) Unionism and Employment Conflict Resolution: Rethinking Collective Voice and its Consequences. *Journal of Labor Research* 26(Spring): 209–39.

—— (2007) Unionism and Employment Conflict Resolution: Rethinking Collective Voice and its Consequences, in J. T. Bennett and B. E. Kaufman (eds), *What do Unions Do? A Twenty-Year Perspective*, pp. 313–45. New Brunswick, NJ: Transaction Publishers.

—— (2008a) Resolving Conflict, in P. Blyton, N. Bacon, J. Fiorito, and E. Heery, (eds), *The Sage Handbook of Industrial Relations*, pp. 447–468. London, UK: Sage.

—— (2008b) Workplace ADR: What's New and What Matters? in S. E. Befort and P. Halter, (eds), *Workplace Justice for a Changing Environment: Proceedings of the Sixtieth Annual Meeting, National Academy of Arbitrators*, pp. 23–29. Washington, DC: Bureau of National Affairs.

—— and BOROFF, K. E. (1996) The Role of Loyalty in Exit and Voice: A Conceptual and Empirical Analysis, in D. Lewin, and B. E. Kaufman (eds), *Advances in Industrial and Labor Relations*, 7: 69–96. Greenwich, CT: JAI Press.

Lewin, D. and Peterson, R. B. (1988) *The Modern Grievance Procedure in the United States.* Westport, CT: Quorum.

Lipsky, D. B., Seeber, R. L., and Fincher, R. D. (2003) *Emerging Systems for Managing Workplace Conflict.* San Francisco, CA: Jossey-Bass.

McCabe, D. (1988) *Corporate Nonunion Complaint Procedures and Systems.* New York: Praeger.

McKersie, R. B., Sharpe, T., Kochan, T. A., Eaton, A. E., Strauss, G., and Morgenstern, M. (2008) Bargaining Theory Meets Interest-Based Negotiations. *Industrial Relations,* 47(1): 66–96.

Rubenstein, S. A. (2003) Partnerships of Steel? Forging High-Involvement Work Systems in the U.S. Steel Industry: A View from the Local Unions, in D. Lewin, and B. E. Kaufman, (eds), *Advances in Industrial and Labor Relations,* 12: 115–144. London, UK. Elsevier.

—— and Kochan, T. A. (2001) *Learning from Saturn: Possibilities for Corporate Governance and Employee Relations.* Ithaca, NY: Cornell University Press.

Rusbelt, C. E., Farrell, D., Rogers, G., and Mainous, A. G., III. (1988) Impact of Variables on Exit, Voice, Loyalty and Neglect: An Integrative Model of Responses to Declining Job Satisfaction. *Academy of Management Journal,* 31(September): 599–627.

Walton, R. E. and McKersie, R. B. (1965) *A Behavioral Theory of Labor Negotiations.* New York: McGraw-Hill.

Westin, A. F. and Felieu, A. G. (1988) *Resolving Employment Disputes without Litigation.* Washington, DC: Bureau of National Affairs.

PART V

POLICY AND COMPARATIVE ISSUES

CHAPTER 19

PARTICIPATION ACROSS ORGANIZATIONAL BOUNDARIES

MICK MARCHINGTON
ANDREW R. TIMMING

INTRODUCTION: CONCEPTUALIZING PARTICIPATION IN A MULTI-EMPLOYER CONTEXT

MUCH has been written about participation over the years. Different terms have been used, ranging from 'industrial democracy', with its connotations of justice and worker rights, through 'employee involvement', where the assumption is that participation is something that employers facilitate solely in the pursuit of greater organizational efficiency (Cotton, 1993; Harley et al., 2005; Heller et al., 1998; Marchington et al., 1992; Strauss, 2006). In addition, the term 'voice' has also been used from time to time (Boroff and Lewin, 1997; Bryson, 2004; Marchington et al., 2001), drawing on Hirschmann (1970). The distinctions between these terms are not always clear, but it could be argued that, while participation tends to focus more on processes, voice implicitly refers to outcomes and the impact that participatory processes might have on worker attitudes, their influence over decision making, and on performance.

In this chapter, we distinguish between direct and indirect participation as our organizing framework. *Direct participation* refers to the opportunity for individuals to be directly involved in, and have a say about, what goes on at workplace level. It includes practices like downward communication via team briefing and newsletters, upward problem solving through suggestion schemes and quality circles and grievance raising (Marchington, 2007). *Indirect participation*, on the other hand, refers to employee involvement via workers' representation structures. These include institutions such as trade unions, works councils (Streeck and Rogers, 1995) and joint consultative committees (JCCs) (Brewster et al., 2007; Marchington, 1987; Sako, 1998).

The lion's share of extant research on employee voice, broadly conceived, assumes that participation takes place *within* the context of a single, coherent organization, one in which everyday contact is between managers and employees (or their representatives) working under the umbrella of the *same* employer. While existing literature addresses major issues concerning the sources of authority, imbalances in power and attempts to develop trust at work, it is generally restricted to analyses of how the employment contract is managed within a single organizational hierarchy. Several recent overview papers or collections of work by leading authorities on the subject (Freeman et al., 2007; Gollan and Wilkinson, 2007; Strauss, 2006) do not examine at all the question of participation across organizational boundaries at multi-employer workplaces.

This is a major shortcoming given that the dominant model of the single employer, operating via employment contracts between employer and employee, is increasingly being challenged as outdated and unrealistic. A growing number of people now work across organizational boundaries, typically at the workplace of another employer, through organizational forms such as private–public contracts, joint ventures, franchises, and outsourcing arrangements. The use of agency workers in a wide range of workplaces also casts serious doubt upon the viability of continuing to view HRM and industrial relations, and also participation more specifically, through the lens of the single employer–employee relationship. This clearly has an impact upon the manner in which participation systems are developed, implemented and perceived by those that are subject to them, and it also raises questions about what this means for managers and workers employed by different organizations at the same workplace.

For example, it is difficult, if not impossible, to see how systems of management based upon control through the organizational hierarchy can function in multi-employer workplaces when authority is diffused through commercial contracts between employers as well as through employment contracts across several organizations (Gallagher and McLean Parks, 2001; Marchington et al., 2005a; Truss, 2004).

Of course, we are not suggesting that traditional employment contracts are now a thing of the past, far from it. But we are concerned that hardly any theoretical or empirical attention has been paid to participation in a multi-employer context.

This sets the scene for the remainder of the chapter where we analyse how direct and indirect participation operate across organizational boundaries at multi-employer workplaces. We recognize that participation raises sizeable questions about authority, power, and trust within the confines of a single organization, but it is clear that added layers of organizational subcontracting and multi-employer contracts further complicate these notions substantially. We conclude that workers employed by organizations other than those that dominate a particular workplace enjoy less participation than their colleagues who work for the dominant employer. In short, 'non-citizen' workers in these contexts experience a double whammy. They suffer not just from the usual hazards that arise from being the weaker party to a traditional employment contract, but also from the additional risks of having their work governed by commercial contracts over which they have no influence and whose systems offer them little or no opportunity to participate.

The next section offers a brief discussion of how subcontracting within multi-employer sites has blurred boundaries and disordered hierarchies within and between organizations that work together on a commercial contract at the same workplace. The bulk of the chapter then examines direct and indirect participation in the context of these organizational forms. We then extend the analysis, somewhat speculatively, to consider how the fragmentation of participation across organizational boundaries can be further complicated in both international and comparative contexts. Finally, we summarize with a brief discussion of the implications of these issues for future research.

UNDERSTANDING EMPLOYMENT AT THE MULTI-EMPLOYER WORKPLACE

In order to analyse participation, we need to appreciate the various employment contexts within which it operates. First, in the traditional organization, the so-called 'standard' employment contract rests upon a legal relationship between a single employer and an employee and is governed by a clear chain of command and generally accepted lines of authority. This is buttressed by the institutions of employment law, and even though there may be occasions when workers challenge this overriding authority (for example, in strike action), this is typically seen as temporary, rather than as an assault on the fundamentals of capitalist society. Within this framework, employers seek worker commitment to organizational goals, both in terms of getting work done according to agreed schedules and increasingly expecting workers to show evidence of loyalty to the corporate brand. Much of the debate about the psychological contract (Guest, 2007) is predicated on the assumption that managers must work hard to gain commitment while at the same time recognizing that they owe an obligation to people who are employed by the organization. Connected with this is the view that employers should try to provide consistency in their HR policies such that workers are treated fairly and equitably, if not equally; this can be seen in issues, such as pay comparability, the universal provision of grievance and discipline procedures, holiday entitlements, work–life balance policies, and consistency in the implementation of redundancies.

An increasing number of organizations do not fit with this relatively simple form, and a couple of examples may help to illustrate this phenomenon. A simple case is where a host organization uses the services of agency workers alongside its own permanent or temporary staff. Agency workers are not employed by the host organization, but they spend most of their working time in it. A slightly more complex relationship is at play in a joint venture or partnership between two or more organizations. These can be solely in the private sector or in the public sector as well. A large proportion of partnership contracts run across the two sectors so that workers may end up owing allegiance to either or both of these employers. Similarly, components of HRM, such as performance appraisals, might be undertaken by managers from the host organization as part of an attempt to achieve consistency and integration within multi-employer teams. Further yet, some workers might have the opportunity to develop their careers within either of the organizations. But in a multi-employer environment, none of the principles underpinning the 'standard' employment contract can be taken for granted or even expected (Rubery et al., 2009).

A major implication of such forms of contracting is that people working for the weaker party to the commercial contract between employers are likely to receive worse terms and conditions than their colleagues working for the stronger party. Indeed, the original purpose of contracting-out work to another employer may well have been to avoid paying costly supplements to the existing workforce or to remove the potential problem of what to do in the event of a market downturn. Thus, rather than attempting to achieve consistency and integration across all workers at a single workplace, in the multi-employer environment it is reasonable to expect the opposite—a range of different pay structures and levels, variable levels of employment security, and contrasting employer views about training, fair treatment, benefits, and voice provisions.

Consequently, rather than attempt to seek wholesale worker commitment to organizational goals at a particular workplace, HRM in a multi-employer environment can take widely disparate forms (Nesheim et al., 2007). For some workers, for example, those employed by agencies or by 'low-road' employers, little organizational benefit might be gained in trying to enlist their commitment because it may not contribute that much to improved organizational performance. This is especially the case where workers are on short-term contracts and owe little or no allegiance to the workplace to which they are deployed. The case of public–private partnerships is particularly interesting given the differing organizational objectives and worker expectations in the two sectors. If public sector workers are transferred to the private sector and continue providing support to the same client group as before, they may face difficulties in accepting private sector goals of profit, as opposed to the traditional public sector values of offering support to the weakest groups in society. The nationalized health services across much of Europe and Canada are cases in point.

Agency workers are also in a precarious position in relation to training and career development, two features of the 'high-road' employment relationship that form, along with participation, a bundle of HR practices. Agency staff may well have skills that have been acquired through training in previous work, for example, as a teacher or a nurse, but now have to keep up-to-date personally or via the agency. Their training and career development are both less extensive and systematic than what is typically provided in a 'standard' employment contract. The situation for long-term career development is especially acute because the short-term contractual relations that characterize most agency work offer very little or no opportunity to build a career. Without any expectation of long-term employment, it is hardly surprising that agency workers gain little from taking part in briefing sessions even if they were invited, or from attempting to run for a position as a union representative even if they were eligible.

If the situation at a multi-employer workplace with two different employers adds complexity, confusion, and ambiguity to employment relationships, this is further exacerbated where workers employed by several organizations operate alongside each other in teams. At an airport, for example, check-in staff may be employed by the airline itself, by a baggage handling firm, or supplied by an agency on a short-term basis to cover during peak periods (Rubery et al., 2003). All of the staff may wear the same uniform, but to whom these different groups of workers owe their allegiance is a moot question: the airline, the baggage handling firm, or the agency? All are expected to provide a similar style of service so that customers are unable to differentiate between them, so in this respect it is important for the airline (in this instance) to engender their commitment, at a base level at least, to customer service and to make sure they use the same terminology. A similar situation could occur in a call centre, but with even more immediate effects if the employer is hoping to extract maximum value by employing agency workers across a number of contracts. Although such workers are not seen by customers, they have to be able to switch between the styles required by different clients potentially each time the telephone rings (Baldry et al., 2007; Walsh and Deery, 2006). Each of the clients might expect different levels of customer service and each employer might utilize different models of HRM with potentially significant room for errors.

As articulated in the next two sections, the implications for direct and indirect participation are significant. Major questions arise about the relationship, if any, between employers and trade unions in different organizations, about the opportunity to include representatives from different contractors on the same JCC, say, or indeed even of guaranteeing access to workers from different organizations at the same team briefings. The likelihood is that, rather than providing a consistent message to all workers, rumours and inconsistencies will occur in a multi-employer context. Moreover, given the multiple influences on HRM and participation across the network— from customers, clients, and agencies, for example— authority relations and organizational hierarchies are likely to be disordered, blurred, and confused.

DIRECT PARTICIPATION ACROSS ORGANIZATIONAL BOUNDARIES

A range of studies shows that direct participation is now widespread in organizations, and some forms, like team briefing, are more or less universally adopted as an integral part of HRM in large firms (Freeman et al., 2007; Kersley et al., 2006). The extent to which they operate at the workplace or are embedded into organizational routines is less certain (Cox et al., 2006). In the remainder of this section we focus on the different categories of direct participation outlined in the Introduction.

A key purpose of downward communication is the transmission of information throughout the organizational hierarchy, for example, about new products, working routines, or changes that are about to take place. Underpinning this transmission is a desire on the part of managers to communicate the 'brand' of the organization and generate worker enthusiasm and commitment to the attainment of high levels of product quality or customer service (Bartel, 2001; Gallagher and McLean Parks, 2001). This is all very well for those employed by the host organization, but it is rather different for those employed by an agency firm, a contractor or a partner because such workers might be expected to have allegiances to their own employer instead of, or in addition to, the client at whose workplace they are located. This is more likely to be the case where workers are employed for relatively short periods of time at a particular site, such as an agency supply teacher (or, as referred to in the US, a substitute teacher) who is filling in for someone for a day or two. In many cases, they may then move on to a different establishment for their next placement, consequently feeling little identification with the host organization.

This can be problematic, however, not just for their role in work teams, but also in terms of service delivery. Failure to be involved in decisions or to receive information can be potentially damaging for quality, for example, if a temporary or contracted worker does not know working protocols in a hospital or teaches the wrong lessons to school students. Research by Boaden et al. (2008: 34) and Gittell and Weiss (2004: 142) illustrate this point with reference to health care provision in the UK and the US, respectively. In the case of the former, so-called integrated teams of social workers and community nurses were found to have received variable levels of information because they worked for different employers. Specifically, those employed by the local city council could not access the hospital intranet, which provided necessary, but sensitive, patient information. Similarly, in the case of the latter study, it was found that confidentiality constraints prohibited the unfettered flow of patient records across organizational boundaries, so downstream service providers were hampered in doing their job.

The situation is even starker when the proportion of contracted workers is small since they can easily be overlooked or not regarded as important enough to be included in communications machinery available to employees at the host organization. Moreover, if there is resentment to this group of 'external' workers, perhaps because they are employed on lower rates of pay or are felt to have taken jobs from 'internal' workers, the chances of them being included in participation schemes is again reduced, both within formal and informal communications (Marchington et al., 2005a: 245). Humphreys and Hoque (2007: 1207), in their study of further education, point to a lack of camaraderie between permanent and temporary agency workers as well as a lack of interest from temporary staff, both of which undermined any attempts to develop an integrated participation scheme.

This is not inevitable, however. Some studies demonstrate that it is possible for contract workers or those who are not employed by the host organization to develop commitment to more than one employer—the one that pays their wages and the one on whose premises they work (Coyle-Shapiro et al., 2006). Much depends on the extent to which they receive organizational and supervisory support from both employers, and it is sometimes the case that temporary agency staff identify more closely with the host organization than they do with their own employer, the agency. As Benson (1998: 369) notes, 'for these workers loyalty to the firm may be determined more by their workgroup and less by their legal employer' given they have little to do with the latter. Workers may identify more with the client than with their employer if the former is seen to be more prestigious and offer greater chances for interesting work and better HR outcomes (Cooke et al., 2004). Accordingly, access to forms of participation—formal and informal—is likely to vary between workplaces due to specific HR factors, but it is also likely to depend upon the nature of the commercial contracts between employers. For example, what happens if the contract is predicated on differentiation between workers? Although participation across organizational boundaries might appeal from the perspective of integration, in this situation it is probably the last thing the host employer and client actually wants!

Upward problem solving via project teams that operate across organizational boundaries is well established in joint ventures and other situations where it is critical that a joint solution is found (Marchington et al., 2005a). It is anticipated that learning can take place across the team to the ultimate benefit of customers, although there are also rigidities which can prevent this from happening as intended because both parties hold on to information in order to protect their own employer's position. There are also examples whereby agency or outsourced workers do not fulfil 'intelligence gathering roles' to the same extent as those employed by the host organization. In their comparison of in-house and outsourced airline establishments, Walsh and Deery (2006: 575) found that customer complaints made to the outsourced call centre were not transmitted to the airline with deleterious results because there was no financial inducement to do so. In addition, the agency workers probably did not feel it was in their best interests to convey information that might be used to terminate their contracts.

Workers not employed by the host organization also miss out on more formal opportunities to participate through suggestion schemes, quality improvement teams, and attitude surveys. On some occasions they are excluded because this is open solely to those employed by the host organization, as is the case with suggestion schemes that offer financial inducements. The transient nature of their work and the relatively short-time periods for which temporary staff may work at a particular location also reduces the opportunity to become part of these teams, especially if they are ongoing. Moreover, the information provided to quality improvement teams may be confidential, so managers are not prepared to take the risk of this getting into the hands of people that have little commitment to the host employer or are not likely to work there for long. Much the same happens with attitude surveys, which are developed with notions of commitment and attachment to the host organization in mind; either people working for agencies or other employers are not included, or if they are, no distinction is made between different types of worker in the analyses. This could be potentially serious for large public sector organizations, such as in Britain's National Health Service, if contracted workers that are in direct contact with patients are excluded from surveys. After all, they have a strong influence on the quality of care (Boaden et al., 2008).

As mentioned above, in addition to contributing to management decisions, workers can also participate by voicing their concerns about current conditions via grievance raising (Marchington, 2007). While this concept has been well researched within the context of the single employer workplace, it has not been examined directly across organizational boundaries even though it is particularly problematic in such an environment. Workers employed by an agency are presumably meant to voice their concerns to that organization, but given that they work away from the site of their employer, this can be difficult. Moreover, while there may be some issues with the agency and how it treats them, many more are likely to arise at the workplace of the host organization given that is where they physically spend their time, often working alongside people employed by that employer. Issues to do with work organization and working conditions, patterns of work and management-style are all under the control of the host employer, and their resolution depends on management at the workplace, rather than at the agency. But agency and other non-citizen workers are effectively precluded from voicing these concerns within the host organization either because there are no procedures for doing so or because they feel unable to raise them with managers at the workplace for fear of reprisal. Perhaps they will get a reputation for griping, with the consequence that they will not be sent to that workplace again or the agency will be informed and give them the worst jobs on their books.

Grimshaw et al. (2003) examined this issue as part of their research on teachers, finding widespread evidence of the precarious nature of agency work in this sector. Supply (substitute) teachers were effectively precluded from raising concerns: one, with the agency because they were beyond its control; two, with the host organization (school) because they worried that it would result in being blacklisted in future; and three, with other teachers because they had different grievances from the temporary staff; moreover, many resented the substitutes. Moving around frequently from one school to another also meant it was hard to establish ties and build close relationships with colleagues and with senior teachers (Marchington et al., 2005a: 246–7). All these factors combined to make it very hard, if not impossible, for agency staff to create a platform for any form of direct participation in their immediate workplace.

In short, while direct participation has become more extensive at workplaces in developed countries, it remains elusive for the growing workforce employed by organizations other than the host employer. Some of the problems are caused by the lack of structural opportunities to get involved at their own organization or that of the host employer, some by an inability to develop a strong presence at any one workplace because of the transient nature of their work and yet others because the initial rationale for outsourcing effectively denies them any form of participation.

INDIRECT PARTICIPATION ACROSS ORGANIZATIONAL BOUNDARIES

It was argued in the previous section that multi-employer workplaces, joint ventures and other such forms of horizontal employment relations can have a fragmenting effect on the prospects for establishing *direct* participation across organizational boundaries. Consistent with the findings of an emerging body of research on participation and voice in the context of inter-organizational contracting (Marchington and Rubery, 2004; Marchington et al., 2004; Marchington et al., 2005b, among others), we have argued that a growing labour force of contingent, flexible and, broadly speaking, non-citizen workers on the periphery of the employment relation struggles to make its frequently marginalized voice heard by a legally elusive employer (Earnshaw et al., 2002; Erickson et al., 2002). This fragmentation of voice thesis equally holds water in the case of *indirect* forms of participation for non-citizen workers. Although rates of indirect participation in, for example, Britain have declined over recent decades (Kersley et al., 2006), the implementation of statutory information and consultation arrangements from the late 1990s has reinvigorated interest in collective forms of voice in the workplace.

The most common structures of indirect (representative) participation include: European-style works councils (Streeck and Rogers, 1995), UK-style JCCs (Brewster et al., 2007) and, increasingly, non-union employee representation bodies (Butler, 2005; Dundon et al., 2005; Haynes et al., 2005; Markey, 2007; Taras and Kaufman, 2006). Each of these institutions enables workers' representatives to have some degree of 'say' in terms of how their organizations are managed (Marchington, 2007: 231). In the context of inter-organizational contracting, however, workers on the periphery of the employment relationship, we argue, suffer from a lower level of access to these institutions than core employees contracted directly with the host organization. In the case of statutory works councils, flexible workers have no legal recourse to collective representation; similarly in terms of outcome, in the case of JCCs and other voluntarist non-union representation fora in the UK and elsewhere, the non-citizen workforce is often proactively excluded by managers, core employees or both.

The example of agency workers, and their lack of access to works councils, offers a useful illustration of the fundamental problem of establishing indirect participation across organizational boundaries. A legalistic distinction within the framework of British labour law is frequently drawn between agency 'workers' and core 'employees' based at the 'user' firm (Deakin and Morris, 2005: 172–6). Although the user firm is obligated, by precedent, to treat flexibly contracted workers as though they were in-house employees in respect to non-discrimination legislation and the protection of health and safety at the workplace (Deakin and Morris, 2005: 172–6), it is under no parallel legal obligation at present to involve the representatives of agency workers in any of its mandated information and consultation arrangements. In contrast, core employees enjoy legally enshrined access to the regulations on the establishment of European works councils (Carley and Hall, 2000) and national works councils (Hall, 2005). German firms, too, have been found to resort to agency workers in order to circumvent works councils legislation (Mitlacher, 2007: 595). It would thus seem that not all workers are equal before the letter of the law.

If flexible workers on the periphery cannot, as yet, fall back on legal regulation to ensure that their voices are heard within the workplace, to what extent can they rely on trade unions to serve as a representative channel through which to establish indirect participation with non-employers in the host organization? The answer to this question depends on two factors. First, there is some evidence, especially in respect to agency workers, that trade unions have sought to exclude and subordinate the non-standard workforce (Heery et al., 2004). To the extent that such proactive exclusion and subordination is taking place, the collective voice of flexible workers is effectively stifled. Second, even in the case of successful union engagement with the contingent workforce (Simms and Dean, 2007), it is nevertheless a reality that, in many countries, trade unions are losing power and influence generally (Howell, 1999), and on JCCs specifically. For example, Kersley et al. (2006: 131) report that only 11 per cent of JCCs in the UK consist wholly of trade union representatives, in comparison to 67 per cent that consist wholly of non-union representatives (the remainder of which are of mixed constituency). In this light, there are two barriers that can obstruct the development of union-based voice for workers on the periphery of the employment relation: one, securing trade union support in the first instance and, on the condition that support is secured; and two, the declining significance of unions, broadly speaking.

Coterminous with the waning power of trade unions has been an increase in attention paid recently to non-union employee representation structures. A corresponding and emerging emphasis on non-union collective voice (for example, Gollan, 2001, 2003, among others) should not be surprising in the light of the fact that, as reported, roughly two-thirds of consultative committees in the UK do not have trade union representation at all (Kersley et al., 2006: 131). Precisely what this paradigm shift means for the flexible workforce depends, once again, on the issue of workers' access to indirect representation structures. In effect, there are two ways in which a worker can gain representation in non-union voice channels: election or appointment. In either case, the scenario for non-citizen workers looks bleak at best.

First, non-union employee representatives are commonly elected in democratic fashion by the broader workforce. As with any political decision process, the elected official must fulfil at least two criteria. Electable candidates must: one, represent the interests of the constituency; and two, hold popular sway over a majority of the voters. On both points, non-citizen workers are dubiously positioned. In respect to one, the contingent workforce can be considered an object of analysis *sui generis* a la Durkheim (1995). Alternatively stated, the material reality of non-citizen workers is qualitatively different from that of core employees. Moreover, the manner by which each group experiences and 'makes senses of' the employment relationship across organizational boundaries is, in some measure, unique (Cooke et al., 2005). In the light of the distinctive realities and needs of flexible workers and core employees, the former cannot represent unambiguously the collective interests of the latter. In respect to two, the popularity (and hence the electability) of temporary workers is dampened by the fact that they are, in great measure, viewed as competitors by core employees (Heery et al., 2004). The comparatively weaker terms and conditions associated with most flexible and outsourced work are perceived as a potential threat to the permanent employment contract. As such, non-citizen workers are unlikely to hold a sufficient level of popular sway in order to win a workplace election.

Second, an alternative mechanism by which to become a non-union worker representative is through managerial appointment. Kersley et al. (2006: 131) report that in 10 per cent of JCCs in Britain, the representatives were selected directly by managers. However, the likelihood that, for example, outsourced or agency workers gain collective representation via direct managerial appointment is limited for reasons that closely parallel those outlined in the preceding paragraph. Because, strictly speaking, agency and other types of temporary workers are not legal employees of the host organization, the flexible workforce lacks sufficient legitimacy to represent the collective interests of the broader core workforce. Not only that, but managerial appointment of non-citizen workers to the JCC could potentially result in a backlash on the part of core employees claiming to suffer from what might be called reverse disenfranchisement (Marchington et al., 2005b: 244–5). Thus, the costs of appointment of temporary workers can be potentially deleterious from the point of view of employee relations.

To summarize, the common thread throughout this section, and indeed across this entire chapter, is that the blurring of organizational boundaries is associated with a two-tier workforce. The dominant tier is characterized by legal recognition, legitimacy, and superior levels of collective organization and base support, and the subordinate tier is characterized by fracture, disenfranchisement, a deficiency of parallel regulatory support, and a poorly organized power base that often struggles to make its voice heard in the host organization. The effects of this bifurcation were illustrated in reference to three institutions of indirect participation, namely, work councils, trade unions, and consultative committees. The fundamental problem, we argue, centres around the extent of the disproportionality of access to these institutions. In other words, non-citizen workers must cope with a unique set of obstacles to representative voice that are not applicable to core employees. All of this amounts to an institutionalized marginalization of, and *de facto* discrimination against, an emerging army of temporary and agency workers.

In the light of the current trends towards outsourcing and the flexibilization of work, it is perhaps only a matter of time before the non-citizen workforce reaches a critical mass, at which point it may begin to challenge more effectively the barriers to indirect participation at the workplace.

PARTICIPATION ACROSS ORGANIZATIONAL AND NATIONAL BOUNDARIES

The nature and scope of employee voice at the intersection of organizational and national boundaries remains largely unexplored terrain. The extant strands of literature on the fragmentation of work are composed primarily of case studies of British firms (Marchington et al., 2005a), but beyond this context there seems to be something of a 'black hole'. In the light of this gap in the literature, the present section seeks to outline a speculative theoretical framework within which the voice of the non-citizen workforce can be analysed in a cross-national context.

Most studies in the field of comparative employment relations are framed in terms of both variable cultural values (Hofstede, 2001; Trompenaars and Hampden-Turner, 1997) and institutional arrangements (Hall and Soskice, 2001). The underlying thrust of these arguments is that the outcomes of employment across societies are moderated by a country's cultural and institutional specificities. It follows that the organization of work can be expected to vary between nation states (Rubery and Grimshaw, 2003). Approaches such as these serve as an appropriate starting point for the comparative study of participation across organizational boundaries. By this, we are referring to the between country variations in the breadth and depth of the voice of non-citizen workers at multi-employer workplaces. In accordance with the structure of this chapter, participation at the intersection of organizational and national boundaries is framed in this section along two streams (direct and indirect participation) and from two perspectives (comparative and international).

First, a comparative, cross-national approach to the study of direct participation across organizational boundaries would seek to explain how different cultural values, as well as legal institutional forces, afford non-citizen workers on the periphery of the employment relationship with variable levels of direct voice across national boundaries. The underlying assumption is that the nature of a societal regime, or business system (Whitley, 2007), should have at least some degree of influence over the extent to which flexible workers are provided with the opportunity to engage with management in, for example, team briefings, quality circles, employee suggestion schemes, problem-solving groups, team working or other such direct forms of voice (Marchington, 2007; Marchington and Cox, 2007). Cross-national variations in terms of access to direct voice procedures on the part of the flexibly employed workforce, at least in theory, should be explicable by pointing to the atmospheric favourability of one national business system vis-à-vis another. In other words, the distance between core employees and non-citizen workers, or the extent of the marginalization of the latter group in reference to the former, can be expected to vary across societies as a result of the fact that some business systems are more favourable than others in the provision of support structures for workers on the periphery of the employment relation.

Second, a comparative, cross-national study of indirect participation across organizational boundaries could be structured along similar lines. The assumption, again, is that non-citizen workers' level of access to representative voice structures should vary between societal employment systems or regimes, some of which may be culturally and institutionally more supportive of non-citizen workers on the periphery than others. For example, one avenue of this line of research that could be pursued would involve a comparison between countries of agency workers' degree of presence, or influence, on works councils or JCCs. The comparison could be framed in terms of the division between liberal market economies and coordinated market economies (Hall and Soskice, 2001). It might be argued that agency workers in coordinated market economies like Germany are more likely to benefit from 'access spillover' as a result of the combination of the density of network relations and legal voice imperatives prevalent there (although this seems less likely to be the case following the Hartz reform of the German Personnel Leasing Act (see Mitlacher, 2007: 584–6)). But there is, as yet, no clear cut answer to this question because of the lack of comparative empirical research on the matter.

As such, there is scope for further development of the comparative study of participation across organizational boundaries along at least two fronts, one of which is conceptual and the other methodological. First, the business systems literature (Hall and Soskice, 2001; Whitely, 2000, 2007, among others) needs to be integrated into the organizational boundaries literature (Marchington et al., 2005a, among others) in order to explain *why* there should be variations between countries in relation to the degree of marginalization of non-citizen workers. In other words, there needs to be a stronger theoretical grounding upon which to construct a set of hypotheses about the nature of cross-national variations. Second, and interrelatedly, the organizational boundaries literature needs to be developed empirically beyond the context of the UK and the US, where the lion's share of the research is based. Only when there is a critical mass of cross-national empirical research on the fragmentation of voice across organizational boundaries can a truly comparative framework emerge.

The central unit of analysis in most comparative studies of employment systems is the nation state (Bamber et al., 2004; Ferner and Hyman, 1998; van Ruysseveldt and Visser, 1996;). An alternative approach, one that fits under the rubric of international HRM, places the MNC at centre stage of the analysis (Edwards and Rees, 2006; Harzing and van Ruysseveldt, 2004; Sparrow et al., 2004). Multinational firms, however, are not stand-alone institutions. Rather, they are more appropriately thought of as central nodes in a multi-scalar, cross-national network involving myriad lower-tier firms that serve both outsourcing (Domberger, 1998; McIvor, 2005; Sahay et al., 2003) and supplier (Akkermans et al., 1999; Er and MacCarthy, 2006; Lane and Bachmann, 1997) functions. The network is also frequently muddled by strategic acquisitions (Child et al., 2001) and joint ventures (Child and Faulkner, 1998), both of which add further layers of complexity to the relational form. Because of these dense horizontal complexities, worker participation within the inter-organizational matrix of the MNC is often fractured on multiple levels.

The case of Nike, a US-based athletics apparel firm, serves as a useful illustration of the fragmentation of participation across the multinational value chain. The company is an internationally recognized brand with yearly revenue as recent as 2007 of $16.3 billion, yet it only employs roughly 30,000 people worldwide. Over and above this core workforce, however, it draws from almost 700 factories across some 52 countries to produce its line. Its total outsourced workforce reaches nearly 800,000 workers worldwide (Nike, 2008). But these non-citizen workers have little or no scope for influencing operations and strategic business decisions taken at the centre. As a rule of thumb, the greater the distance from the core, the more fragmented and disconnected a worker's voice becomes across the broader production network. This distance-based marginalization of voice is problematic because corporate decision making affects concomitantly core employees and non-citizen workers. In effect, in large MNCs, there is potentially a serious 'participation deficit' for the majority of the workers engaged in production of goods.

In parallel with its comparative counterpart, the international (i.e., MNC-centred) approach to the study of participation across the multinational value chain is in dire need of conceptual and empirical development. The focus of conceptual development should centre around the analysis of workers on the periphery of the broad ambit of the MNC and its complex network of inter-organizational relations. This development would entail a multinational extension of the extant body of literature on organizational boundaries and the fragmentation of work. In terms of empirical and methodological development, there is clearly scope for what would most likely take the form of case-based research aimed at unpacking the extent of the marginalization of participation on the margins of multinational production networks. The horizons for this line of research promise to yield novel insights into the evolution of the employment relation.

To summarize, the intersection of organizational and national boundaries is, in great measure, uncharted territory. Accordingly, the comparative and international frameworks articulated in this section raised many more questions than they could possibly answer. What is clear from the discussion is that within country inter-organizational contracting, itself a phenomenon of incredible complexity, only scratches the surface in terms of coming to grips with the broader implications of participation across organizational boundaries. In a cross-national context, a whole new set of analytical complications arise. For example, it has yet to be explained whether, why, and to what extent there are systematic variations between countries in relation to the marginalization of the voice of non-standard workers. There are also unanswered questions regarding the variations in the level of participation across the multinational value chain. This section does not pretend to have been able to address definitively such lacunae. Instead, it has sought to spell out new opportunities for the next generation of employment researchers.

Conclusions and Implications

The recent growth of inter-organizational contracting, whether in the form of a public—private partnership, joint venture, agency work or outsourced production, poses a significant threat to the traditional conception of employment. Where organizational boundaries overlap, it no longer makes sense to think of the employment relationship as a contract between a single employer and an employee. In this chapter, we have sought to articulate the implications of this paradigm shift from the perspective of participation in organizations. Looking at the 'big picture', it is concluded that those workers employed by the weaker party to a commercial contract have less scope for both direct and indirect participation as compared to core employees. Non-citizen workers, as we have called them, face a set of unparalleled obstacles to participation that effectively dampens their ability to influence decision making and have their 'say'.

Furthermore, the trend toward inter-organizational contracting shows no sign of abating. The harsh exigencies of market competition are placing greater demands on firms, both multinational and domestic, to be flexible (Piore and Sabel, 1984) and more responsive to change. If anything, the blurring of organizational boundaries will become even more pervasive as globalization continues to exert pressure on businesses to cut costs and adapt to changing market conditions.

This latter point feeds directly into a key implication of this chapter. The fact that non-citizen workers suffer from lower levels of participation is not just a *consequence* of being employed by the weaker party to the commercial contract. It might very well be the *reason* underlying the inter-organizational contract in the first instance (Grimshaw et al., 2006). In other words, one of the motivations for bringing non-standard workers into a host organization is so that employers can gain from the differentiation between the two groups. There are limits, in this light, to how far, and indeed whether or not, employers are even interested in creating standardized patterns of participation across organizational boundaries. Non-citizen workers are attractive to the host organization because they can be shed easily and they generally possess inferior terms and conditions. If, for example, agency workers were given the same rights as core employees, then the former would no longer be seen by employers as a key contributor to business performance. From this perspective, it makes sense that some managers may not want agency workers to get too committed to the host organization (Gallagher and McLean Parks, 2001).

In sum, the short-term outlook for non-standard workers does not look bright. The 'participation deficit', as explained in this chapter, shows no immediate sign of abating. In order for non-citizen workers and core employees to find each other on the right level, hypothetically, a number of issues need to be addressed. Following Boaden et al. (2008), in order to develop participation across a multi-employer network, a vital role can be seen for: one, the provision of more institutional support structures on the part of the host organization so as to ensure greater consistency in governance and accountability across boundaries; two, collaboration and trust between senior managers and line managers in both the host and client organizations; three, a mutual agreement to adhere to the basic principles of high commitment HRM; and four, commercial contracts that contain specific guidelines for participation and also a set of procedures for monitoring those guidelines. However, if employers are motivated to use flexible workers because of a decreased fiduciary obligation, the latter's prospects for voice do not look good.

References

AKKERMANS, H., BOGERD, P., and VOS, B. (1999) 'Virtuous and Vicious Cycles on the Road Toward International Supply Chain Management'. *International Journal of Operations and Production Management*, 19(5/6): 565–82.

BALDRY, C., BAIN, P., TAYLOR, P., HYMAN, J., SCHOLARIOS, D., MARKS, A., WATSON, A., GILBERT, K., GALL, G., and BUNZEL, D. (2007) *The Meaning of Work in the New Economy*, Basingstoke: Palgrave Macmillan.

BAMBER, G. J., LANSBURY, R. D., and WAILES, N (eds) (2004) *International and Comparative Employment Relations*, 4th edition. London: Sage.

BARTEL, C. (2001) 'Social Comparison in Boundary-Spanning Work: Effects of Community Outreach on Members' Organizational Identity and Identification'. *Administrative Science Quarterly*, 46(3): 379–413.

BENSON, J. (1998) 'Dual Commitment: Contract Workers in Australian Manufacturing Enterprises'. *Journal of Management Studies*, 35(3): 355–75.

BOADEN, R., MARCHINGTON, M., HYDE, P., HARRIS, C., SPARROW, P., PASS, S., CARROLL, M., and CORTVRIEND, P. (2008) *Improving Health through Human Resource Management: The Process of Engagement and Alignment.* London: Chartered Institute of Personnel and Development.

BOROFF, K. E. and LEWIN, D. (1997) 'Loyalty, Voice and Intent to Exit a Union Firm: A Conceptual and Empirical Analysis'. *Industrial and Labor Relations Review,* 29(2): 50–63.

BREWSTER, C., WOOD, G., CROUCHER, R., and BROOKES, M. (2007) 'Are Works Councils and Joint Consultative Committees a Threat to Trade Unions? A Comparative Analysis'. *Economic and Industrial Democracy,* 28(1): 49–77.

BRYSON, A. (2004) 'Managerial Responsiveness to Union and Non-Union Worker Voice in Britain'. *Industrial Relations,* 43(1): 213–41.

BUTLER, P. (2005) 'Non-Union Employee Representation: Exploring the Efficacy of the Voice Process'. *Employee Relations,* 27(3): 272–88.

CARLEY, M. and HALL, M. (2000) 'The Implementation of the European Works Councils Directive'. *Industrial Law Journal,* 29(2): 103–24.

CHILD, J. and FAULKNER, D. (1998) *Strategies of Co-operation: Managing Alliances, Networks and Joint Ventures.* Oxford: Oxford University Press.

—————— and PITKETHLY, R. (2001) *The Management of International Acquisitions.* Oxford: Oxford University Press.

COOKE, F. L., EARNSHAW, J., MARCHINGTON, M., and RUBERY, J. (2004) 'For Better and for Worse: Transfer of Undertaking and the Reshaping of Employment Relations'. *International Journal of Human Resource Management,* 15(2): 276–94.

—————— HEBSON, G., and CARROLL, M. (2005) 'Commitment and Identity Across Organizational Boundaries', in M. Marchington, D. Grimshaw, J. Rubery, and H. Willmott (eds) *Fragmenting Work: Blurring Organizational Boundaries and Disordering Hierarchies.* Oxford: Oxford University Press.

COTTON, J. L. (1993). *Employee Involvement: Methods for Improving Performance and Work Attitudes.* London: Sage.

COX, A., ZAGELMEYER, S., and MARCHINGTON, M. (2006) 'Embedding of employee involvement and participation at work.' *Human Resource Management Journal,* 16(3): 250–67.

COYLE-SHAPIRO, J. A.-M., MORROW, P. C., and KESSLER, I. (2006) 'Serving Two Organizations: Exploring the Employment Relationship of Contracted Employees'. *Human Resource Management,* 45(4): 561–83.

DEAKIN, S. and MORRIS, G. S. (2005) *Labour Law* (4th edition). Oxford: Hart.

DOMBERGER, S. (1998) *The Contracting Organization: A Strategic Guide to Outsourcing.* Oxford: Oxford University Press.

DUNDON, T., WILKINSON, A., MARCHINGTON, M., and ACKERS, P. (2005) 'The Management of Voice in Non-Union Organisations: Managers' Perspectives'. *Employee Relations,* 27(3): 307–319.

DURKHEIM, E. (1995) *The Elementary Forms of Religious Life* (translated by K. E. Fields). New York: Free Press.

EARNSHAW, J., RUBERY, J., and COOKE, F. L. (2002) *Who is the Employer?* London: The Institute for Employment Rights.

EDWARDS, T. and REES, C. (eds). (2006) *International Human Resource Management: Globalization, National Systems and Multinational Companies.* Harlow: Prentice Hall.

ER, M. and MacCarthy, B. (2006) 'Managing Product Variety in Multinational Corporation Supply Chains'. *Journal of Manufacturing Technology Management*, 17(8): 1117–38.

Erickson, C. L., Fish, C., Milliman, R., Mitchell, D. J. B., and Wong, K. (2002) 'Justice for Janctors in Los Angeles: Lessons from Three Rands of Negotiations'. *British Journal of Industrial Relations*, 40(3): 543–67.

Ferner, A. and Hyman, R. (eds). (1998) *Changing Industrial Relations in Europe*. Oxford: Blackwell.

Freeman, R. B., Boxall, P., and Haynes, P. (ed.) (2007) *What Workers Say: Employee Voice in the Anglo-American Workplace*. Ithaca, NY: ILR Press.

Gallagher, D. G. and McLean Parks, J. (2001) 'I pledge thee my troth . . . contingently: Commitment and the Contingent Work Relationship'. *Human Resource Management Review*, 11: 181–208.

Gittell, J. H. and Weiss, L. (2004) 'Coordination Networks Within and Across Organizations: A Multi-level Framework'. *Journal of Management Studies*, 41(1): 127–53.

Gollan, P. (2001) 'Tunnel Vision: Non-Union Representation at Eurotunnel'. *Employee Relations*, 23(4/5): 376–400.

—— (2003) 'All Talk, but no Voice: Employee Voice at the Eurotunnel Call Centre'. *Economic and Industrial Democracy*, 24(4): 509–41.

—— and Wilkinson, A. (2007) 'Contemporary Developments in Information and Consultation'. *International Journal of Human Resource Management*, 18(7): 1133–44.

Grimshaw, D., Earnshaw, J., and Hebson, G. (2003) 'Private Sector Provision of Supply Teachers: A Case of Legal Swings and Professional Roundabouts'. *Journal of Education Policy*, 18(3): 267–88.

—— Marchington, M., and Rubery, J. (2006) 'The Blurring of Organizational Boundaries and the Fragmentation of Work', in G. Wood and P. James (eds), *Institutions, Production, and Working Life*. Oxford: Oxford University Press.

Guest, D. (2007) 'HRM and the Worker: Towards a New Psychological Contract?' in P. Boxall, J. Purcell, and P. Wright, (eds), *The Oxford Handbook of Human Resource Management*. Oxford: Oxford University Press.

Hall, M. (2005) 'Assessing the Information and Consultation of Employees Regulation'. *Industrial Law Journal*, 34(2): 103–26.

Hall, P. A. and Soskice, D. (eds) (2001) *Varieties of Capitalism: The Institutional Foundations of Comparative Advantage*. Oxford: Oxford University Press.

Harley, B., Hyman J., and Thompson, P. (eds) (2005) *Participation and Democracy at Work*. Basingstoke: Palgrave Macmillan.

Harzing, A. W. and van Ruysseveldt, J. (eds) (2004) *International Human Resource Management* (2nd edition). London: Sage.

Haynes, P., Boxall, P., and Macky, K. (2005) 'Non-Union Voice and the Effectiveness of Joint Consultation in New Zealand'. *Economic and Industrial Democracy*, 26(2): 225–52.

Heckscher, C. and Carre, F. (2006) 'Strength in Networks: Employment Rights Organizations and the Problem of Co-Ordination'. *British Journal of Industial Relations*, 44(4): 605–28.

Heery, E., Conley, H., Delbridge, R., Simms, M., and Stewart, P. (2004) 'Trade Union Responses to Non-standard Work', in G. Healy, E. Heery, P. Taylor and W. Brown (eds), *The Future of Worker Representation*. Houndmills: Palgrave Macmillan.

Heller, F., Pusic, E., Strauss, G., and Wilpert, B. (1998) *Organizational Participation: Myth and Reality*. Oxford: Oxford University Press.

HIRSCHMANN, A. O. (1970). *Exit, Voice, and Loyalty: Responses to Decline in Firms, Organizations, and States*. Cambirdge, MA: Harvard University Press.

HOFSTEDE, G. (2001) *Culture's Consequences: Comparing Values, Behaviors, Institutions, and Organizations Across Nations* (2nd Edition). Thousand Oaks: Sage.

HOWELL, C. (1999) 'Unforgiven: British Trade Unionism in Crisis', in A. Martin and G. Ross (eds), *The Brave New World of European Labor*. New York: Berghahn.

HUMPHREYS, M. and HOQUE, K. (2007) 'Have the Lecturers Lost their Voice? Involvement and Participation in the Devolved Further Education Sector'. *International Journal of Human Resource Management*, 18(7): 1199–213.

KERSLEY, B., ALPIN, C., FORTH, J., BRYSON, A., BEWLEY, H., DIX, G., and OXENBRIDGE, S. (2006) *Inside the Workplace: Findings from the 2004 Workplace Employment Relations Survey*. London: Routledge.

LANE, C. and BACHMANN, R. (1997) 'Co-operation in Inter-firm Relations in Britain and Germany: The Role of Social Institutions'. *British Journal of Sociology*, 48(2): 226–54.

McIVOR, R. (2005) *The Outsourcing Process: Strategies for Evaluation and Management*. Cambridge: Cambridge University Press.

MARCHINGTON, M. (1987) 'A Review and Critique of Research into Developments in Joint Consultation'. *British Journal of Industrial Relations*, 25: 339–52.

—— (2007) 'Employee Voice Systems', in P. Boxall, J. Purcell, and P. Wright (eds), *Oxford Handbook of Human Resource Management*. Oxford: Oxford University Press.

—— and COX, A. (2007) 'Employee Involvement and Participation: Structures, Processes and Outcomes', in J. Storey (ed.), *Human Resource Management: A Critical Text*, 3rd edition. London: Thomson.

—— GOODMAN, J., WILKINSON, A., and ACKERS, P. (1992) 'New Developments in Employee Involvement'. Sheffield: Employment Department Research Series no. 2.

—— GRIMSHAW, D., RUBERY, J., and WILLMOTT, H. (eds) (2005a) *Fragmenting Work: Blurring Organizational Boundaries and Disordering Hierarchies*. Oxford: Oxford University Press.

—— and RUBERY, J. (2004) 'Worker Voice across Organizational Boundaries'. *Human Resources and Employment Review*, 2(4): 210–15.

—— —— and COOKE, F. L. (2004) 'Worker Representation Within and Across Organisational Boundaries: A Case Study of Worker Voice in a Multi-agency Environment', in G. Healy, E. Heery, P. Taylor, and W. Brown (eds), *The Future of Worker Representation*. Houndmills: Palgrave Macmillan.

—— —— —— (2005b) 'Prospects for Worker Voice Across Organizational Boundaries', in M. Marchington, D. Grimshaw, J. Rubery, and H. Willmott (eds), *Fragmenting Work: Blurring Organizational Boundaries and Disordering Hierarchies*. Oxford: Oxford University Press.

—— WILKINSON, A., ACKERS, P., and DUNDON, T. (2001) *Management Choice and Employee Voice*. London: Chartered Institute of Personnel and Development.

MARKEY, R. (2007) 'Non-Union Employee Representation in Australia: A Case Study of the Suncorp Metway Employee Council Inc. (SMEC)'. *Journal of Industrial Relations*, 49(2): 187–209.

MITLACHER, L. W. (2007) 'The Role of Temporary Agency Work in Different Industrial Relations Systems—A Comparison between Germany and the USA'. *British Journal of Industrial Relations*, 45(3): 581–606.

NESHEIM, T., OLSON, K. M., and KALLEBERG, A. L. (2007) 'Externalizing the Core: Firms' Use of Employment Intermediaries in the Information and Communication Technology Industries'. *Human Resource Management*, 46(2): 247–64.

NIKE. (2008) 'Company Overview'. www.nikebiz.com/company_overview/fact.html. (Accessed 8 March 2008).

OSTERMAN, P. (2006) 'Community Organization and Employee Representation'. *British Journal of Industrial Relations*, 44(4): 629–49.

PIORE, M. and SABEL, C. (1984) *The Second Industrial Divide: Possibilities for Prosperity*. New York: Basic Books.

RAMSAY, H. (1997) 'Fool's gold? European Works Councils and Workplace Democracy'. *Industrial Relations Journal*, 28(4): 314–22.

RUBERY, J., COOKE, F. L., EARNSHAW, J. and MARCHINGTON, M. (2003) 'Inter-Organizational Relations and Employment in a Multi-Employer Environment'. *British Journal of Industrial Relations*, 41(2): 265–89.

——and GRIMSHAW. D., (2003) *The Organization of Employment: An International Perspective*. Houndmills: Palgrave Macmillan.

——MARCHINGTON, M., GRIMSHAW, D., CARRLL, M., and PASS, S. (2009) 'Employed under different rules: the complexities of working across organizational boundaries.' *Cambridge Journal of Regions, Economy and Society*, 1(1): 1–15.

SAHAY, S., NICHOLSON, B., and KRISHNA, S. (2003) *Global IT Outsourcing: Software Development across Borders*. Cambridge: Cambridge University Press.

SAKO, M. (1998) 'The Nature and Impact of Employee "Voice" in the European Car Components Industry'. *Human Resource Management Journal*, 8(2): 5–13.

SIMMS, M. and DEAN, D. (2007) 'Mobilising Contingent Workers: An Analysis of Two Successful Cases'. Paper presented at the *International Industrial Relations Association European Congress*: University of Manchester, UK.

SPARROW, P., BREWSTER, C., and HARRIS, H. (2004) *Globalizing Human Resource Management*. London: Routledge.

STRAUSS, G. (2006) 'Worker Participation—Some Under-Considered Issues'. *Industrial Relations*, 45(4): 778–803.

STREECK, W. and ROGERS, J. (eds). (1995) *Works Councils: Consultation, Representation, and Cooperation in Industrial Relations*. Chicago: University of Chicago Press.

TARAS, D. G. and KAUFMAN, B. E. (2006) 'Non-Union Employee Representation in North America: Diversity, Controversy and Uncertain Future'. *Industrial Relations Journal*, 37 (5): 513–42.

TROMPENAARS, A. and HAMPDEN-TURNER, C. (1997) *Riding the Waves of Culture: Understanding Cultural Diversity in Business* (2nd edition). London: Nicholas Brealey.

TRUSS, C. (2004) 'Who's in the Driving Seat? Managing Human Resources in a Franchise Firm'. *Human Resource Management Journal*, 14(4): 57–75.

VAN RUYSSEVELDT, J. and VISSER, J. (eds) (1996) *Industrial Relations in Europe: Traditions and Transitions*. London: Sage.

WALSH, J. and DEERY, S. (2006) 'Refashioning Organizational Boundaries: Outsourcing Customer Service Work'. *Journal of Management Studies*, 43(3): 557–82.

WHITLEY, R. (2000) *Divergent Capitalisms: The Social Structuring and Change of Business systems*. Oxford: Oxford University Press.

——(2007) *Business Systems and Organizational Capabilities: The Institutional Structuring of Competitive Competencies*. Oxford: Oxford University Press.

....

CHAPTER 20

PUBLIC POLICY AND EMPLOYEE PARTICIPATION

....

JOHN W. BUDD
STEFAN ZAGELMEYER

'A conversation between a cat and a mouse is not a conversation.'

Anonymous

INTRODUCTION

....

EMPLOYEE participation is frequently seen as a private issue for organizations and their employees. Employers that believe it is in their self-interest to provide vehicles for employee participation will do so; others will not. If organizations with employee participation have a competitive advantage, the invisible hand of competitive markets will push others to adopt similar policies. Similarly, competitive pressures will drive out participation programmes that are not cost-effective. But as this Handbook reveals, employee participation involves much more than employee contributions to business decision making; rather, individual control over daily working conditions, workplace consultation on employment policies, and collective bargaining over compensation are all part of employee participation. Employee participation efforts therefore reach far beyond competitiveness and profitability to also shape the psychological and economic well-being of individuals, the physical and emotional health of a community's families, and the quality of a country's democracy.

In other words, employee participation programmes can generate positive externalities with benefits for more than the corporate bottom line; similarly, the lack or repression of various forms of employee participation can cause harm through negative externalities that spillover into families, communities, and nations. When seen in this light, it becomes clear that employee participation is more than a private affair. Rather, employee participation raises important issues for public policy through governmental regulation of the employment relationship. In fact, the government of any country plays a critical role in determining the nature of that country's employment relations system by shaping the economic, political, social, and legal contexts for the employment relationship. The diversity of employment relations systems across countries can, to a certain extent, be explained by variations in the degree, method, and content of government regulation (Van Waarden, 1995: 110). Many of these elements ultimately pertain to forms of employee participation. This chapter therefore discusses the rationales for public policy interventions in the domain of employee participation and describes various policies that policymakers in Europe, the United States, and elsewhere are using or can use to promote forms of employee participation that benefit not only organizations, but also workers and their families, and communities.

Regulating the Employment Relationship

The rationale for government regulation of any market-based activity is rooted in both the objectives and operation of that activity. For employment-related issues, then, differing views on government intervention depend on beliefs about the goals of the employment relationship and how the employment relationship works. These differing views can be captured by four key models—the egoist, unitarist, pluralist, and critical employment relationships—which are distinguished by their assumptions about employment relationship objectives, the compatibility of these objectives across agents, and the structural context in which these objectives are pursued (Budd and Bhave, 2008). A quick review of these four models serves as an essential foundation for considering public policies on employee participation (see Table 20.1).

Table 20.1 Models of the employment relationship and government regulation

Model	Employment relationship objectives	Compatibility of objectives	Structural context	View of government regulation
Egoist	Efficiency is paramount. Equity is market transactions being fair. Voice is the ability to freely initiate and quit transactions	Employers and employees have self-interest. Exchanges are consummated when self-interests align	Competitive labour markets. Labour as a commodity	Minimal. Fix market failures only when regulation does not do more harm than good
Unitarist	Efficiency is very important. Equity and voice are necessary for psychological satisfaction and individual productivity	Employers and employees primarily have shared interests	Imperfect labour markets. Labour as psychological beings	Low. Promote cooperation and prevent destructive competition
Pluralist	Efficiency, equity, and voice are all important. Equity and voice are necessary for human dignity and freedom	Employers and employees have some shared interests and some conflicting interests	Imperfect labour markets. Labour as economic and psychological beings and democratic citizens	Essential. Establish safety nets and equalize bargaining power to balance efficiency, equity, and voice
Critical	Equity and voice are paramount. Equity and voice are necessary for human dignity and freedom	Employers and employees have inherent, antagonistic conflicts of interest	Employment inequalities embedded in pervasive inequalities throughout society. Labour as economic and psychological beings and democratic citizens	Mixed. Important for protecting employees. Inadequate because of systemic imbalances inherent in capitalism

The objectives of the employment relationship can be summarized as efficiency, equity, and voice (Budd, 2004). Efficiency captures diverse issues pertaining to productivity and competitiveness, equity includes various conceptions of fairness, and voice is a shorthand for participation in decision making. In the egoist model, efficiency is paramount. Employers and employees pursue their self-interest (hence the 'egoist' label) in labour markets. These labour markets are typically assumed to be perfectly competitive by advocates of the egoist model which means that individual self-interest maximizes efficiency. This is a key result of neoclassical economic analysis. In the egoist model, labour is further seen as simply a commodity pursuing income while equity and voice are conveniently conceptualized in market-based terms: voluntary transactions are equitable because they are not coerced; voice occurs through individual choice of what transactions to engage in. These narrow views of equity and voice leave little room for government regulation to target anything but market failures that reduce efficiency. But a wide embrace of competitive markets means that market failures are rare, and even then the case for government intervention is only made if regulation is doing less harm than good. So there is a minimal role for government intervention in the egoist employment relationship; neoclassical economists and other devotees of the liberal market model largely oppose work-related public policies (Reynolds, 1996; Troy, 1999). In the literature on comparative regulatory approaches to employment relations (Crouch, 1982; Gospel and Palmer, 1993; Van Waarden, 1995), this is seen as a market or liberal individualism approach that emphasizes the state's role in protecting property rights, economic exchange, and individual contracts in a freely operating and (supposedly) competitive market system.

The unitarist model rejects the narrow conception of labour as a commodity and instead largely embraces a psychological conception of the human agent. As such, equity and voice are tied to individual perceptions of fairness, justice, and input into decision making, especially in the form of distributive and procedural justice (Folger and Cropanzano, 1998). The other key feature of the unitarist model is the assumption that the interests of employers and employees can be aligned with the correct human resource management policies (Bacon, 2003; Fox, 1974; Lewin, 2001). Efficiency is very important in the unitarist model, but because of universally-shared employer–employee interests, efficiency, equity, and voice support each other. For this reason, employer-promulgated human resource management practices are key. In an ideal unitarist state, government regulations are largely unnecessary, but if some employers are misinformed or misguided, then there can be a role for public policies to encourage cooperative rather than competitive relations between employers and employees, and in the extreme, to prevent destructive competition that might come from ignorant, short-sighted, rogue employers.

The pluralist model of the employment relationship further enriches the conception of employees by also seeing them as human beings with rights in a democratic society. As such, equity goes beyond perceptions of individual fairness to include minimum standards, such as living wages, that all human beings should be entitled to; voice goes beyond narrow task-related input to include industrial democracy—the right of human beings to widely participate in informed decision making (Budd, 2004). Moreover, the nature of employment relationship conflict is more nuanced: employers and employees are assumed to have a mix of shared and conflicting interests (Clegg, 1975; Fox, 1974). With this, efficiency, equity, and voice should be balanced (Budd, 2004). Human resource management policies are therefore important in promoting shared interests, such as an employer's financial viability, but because of inherent conflicts of interests, for example, between profits and wages, it is unwise to rely solely on employer self-interest to look out for workers' interests (Kaufman, 1997). The pluralist industrial relations model also assumes that because of market imperfections, employers have greater bargaining power than individual employees so unlike in the egoist model, competitive markets do not serve as an effective check on abusive employers.

Putting all of these assumptions together, then, yields an essential role for government policies to create minimum labour standards and social safety nets while also promoting unionization in order to balance efficiency, equity, and voice (Befort and Budd, 2009; Budd et al., 2004). In practice, this pluralist approach is typically pursued in one of two ways and such states are characterized as either liberal collectivist (or liberal pluralist) or corporatist (Crouch, 1982; Gospel and Palmer, 1993; Van Waarden, 1995). The former approach involves creating basic legal frameworks within which employees and employers, and their respective collective bodies can balance their legitimate and potentially conflicting interests by negotiating individual and collective agreements. More interventionist state approaches involve various forms of corporatism. Neo-corporatism, for example, (also referred to as 'bargained corporatism' or 'societal corporatism') is character-ized by active state involvement in employment relations above and beyond creating a legal framework for balancing competing interests to also include consultation with trade unions and employers and other mechanisms for involving these actors in economic and social policy making (Van Waarden, 1995: 110).

The critical approach sees employee equity and voice as paramount and as having a fundamental clash with employers' profit maximizing objectives. More-over, this inherent conflict of interests is embedded in a broad context of socio-political conflict between competing groups (Kelly, 1998). The Marxist perspective within this critical view assumes that employer–employee conflict is one element of unequal socio-political power relations between the capitalist and working classes (Hyman, 1975, 2006), the feminist perspective emphasizes unequal power relations between men and women (Amott and Matthaei, 1996; Gottfried, 2006), and the critical race perspective centers on conflict, segregation, and control along racial lines (Amott and Matthaei, 1996; Lustig, 2004). Unlike in the egoist employment relationship, the labour market is not seen as a neutral forum for matching self-interested workers with self-interested firms, but instead is viewed as a socially-based instrument of power and control (Hyman, 1975). Human resource management practices are not seen as methods for aligning employer–employee interests, but as disguised rhetoric that perpetuate corporate control (Thompson and McHugh, 2002; Townley, 1994). As a result, government regulation is needed to protect employees. But unlike the pluralist view in which government regulation can balance efficiency, equity, and voice because employer–employee conflict is confined to the employment relationship, the role of government regulation in the critical model is ultimately insufficient to advance workers' interests, and in many cases is viewed as another tool that the stronger group uses to perpetuate its dominance. Poole's (1986) state corporatism in which the functional interests of social groups are suppressed, subordinated, or incorporated into the political system fits within this perspective.

This framework allows for different conceptualizations of state action. The egoist and unitarist perspectives typically see states as promoters of the public interest, especially with respect to economic prosperity. The pluralist perspective is consistent with a pluralist political theory in which state action balances the political power of competing interest groups. The critical perspective largely sees the state as reflecting the socio-political power of the dominant interest group. Each of these models of state action are important for thinking about the intellectual bases of public policies on employee participation.

RATIONALES FOR PUBLIC POLICIES ON EMPLOYEE PARTICIPATION

The chapters in this Handbook present a number of different forms of employee participation. With respect to public policies, it is instructive to group these diverse forms into four categories along the lines of a combination of the typologies of Befort and Budd (2009) and Dundon et al. (2004):

1. Employee Involvement and Financial Participation.
2. Individual Self-Determination.
3. Information and Consultation.
4. Countervailing Collective Power.

As shown in Table 20.2, these forms of employee participation in organizations differ along two dimensions—whether they promote employer–employee cooperation or employee rights, and whether participation is individual or collective.

In this section, we describe possible arguments that can be used to justify public policies to regulate or promote each type of employee participation programme. In each case, the egoist or laissez-faire liberal market model stands in opposition to public policy intervention on the basis that markets are generally competitive (so regulation is welfare reducing), that the appropriate definitions of equity and voice are market-based (so there is not a need for regulation to promote non-economic goals), and that individual freedom is paramount (so regulation is an unwarranted violation of property rights). This perspective provides an important foil for the

Table 20.2 Employee participation in organizations

Structure	Objective	
	Promoting cooperation	Promoting employee rights
Individual	Employee involvement and financial participation	Individual self-determination
Collective	Information and consultation	Countervailing collective power

rationales developed below. In all of this, it is critical for the reader to recognize that these differing perspectives are rooted in differing models of how the employment relationship works and varied conceptions of efficiency, equity, and voice as described in the previous section. We start by discussing individual forms of employee participation and then move to collective forms.

Employee Involvement and Financial Participation

The first dimension of employee participation consists of human resource management efforts to improve efficiency and economic performance by providing opportunities or incentives for workers to be actively involved in deciding how to carry out their daily job tasks and in sharing their employers' financial risks and rewards. Such participation can take many forms: employee suggestion programmes, quality circles, and self-directed work teams for involving employees in process-improvement decisions; pay for performance, gain sharing, and employee stock ownership programmes for involving employees' in the financial side. These forms of employee participation are focused on improving information flows from employees to management, aligning employees' interests with the goals and objectives of management, improving operations-related decision making, and are thus meant to improve coordination and motivation and ultimately productivity and organizational performance. As a consequence, many would object to the need for, and wisdom of, government supports. Organizations that find that such forms of participation enhance performance to a degree sufficient to offset any additional costs will adopt these participatory mechanisms; organizations that do not, will not. The invisible hand of the free market is the preferred guide.

Levine (1995), however, argues that there are market failures that undermine the adoption of these participatory mechanisms. In particular, it is difficult for just a few employers to adopt an employee participation strategy if suppliers are oriented towards a different production model, unemployment is high, wage differentials are high, and unfair dismissal policies are rare. Each of these scenarios reduces the competitive advantage of a participatory firm so firms acting alone have trouble adopting employee participation schemes. Public policies can help solve this coordination failure and promote a broad-based movement to employee participation which would have benefits for all (Levine, 1995). The unitarist model also relies on employers understanding the mutual benefits of progressive human resource management policies so another rationale for government supports or mandates of employee participation is the promotion of mutually-beneficial human resources practices when employers do not fully appreciate their benefits. Similar arguments can be made for financial participation as it relates to promoting the competitiveness of a country's companies. Moreover, financial participation may be used to promote a wider distribution of wealth (Pendleton and Poutsma, 2004).

Individual Self-Determination

The most basic dimension of employee participation is individual self-determination which involves making decisions about one's own work. Industrial and organizational psychologists frequently describe this as autonomy: 'substantial freedom, independence, and discretion to the individual in scheduling the work and in determining the procedures to be used in carrying it out' (Hackman and Oldham, 1980: 79). This can include prioritizing one's own tasks, troubleshooting problems, evaluating the quality of one's own work, having input into scheduling one's work time, the authority to refuse unsafe work, and the ability to freely voice concerns and complaints.

There are several rationales for public policy interventions to support the individual self-determination form of employee participation. The most general rationale is to promote the healthy, psychological development of adult human beings. Self-determination can be argued to be a basic or fundamental human need; its opposite (being controlled) contradicts what it means to be a healthy adult and undermines our psychological well-being and development (Argyris, 1957; Ryan and Deci, 2002). The sociological giants Karl Marx, Emile Durkheim, and Max Weber similarly emphasized the loss of human dignity that accompanies excessive workplace control (Hodson, 2001). Other arguments for legal supports for self-determination rest on the promotion of physical health (in the case of refusals of unsafe work), families (in the case of control over working time), and political discourse (in the case of free speech). In sum, a key feature of modern employment is the sacrificing of some autonomy in return for pay, but the effects on the individual and society are too corrosive to allow all autonomy to be sacrificed; these negative externalities provide the basis for government policies to support individual self-determination for workers (Befort and Budd, 2009).

Information and Consultation

This category includes collective employee rights to obtain information from the employer, to be consulted by the employer and to voice concerns and suggestions. Workplace information and consultation include varied forms of collective voice that involve exchanges of information and views between employers and employees on business- and employment-related issues that stop short of formal codetermination or bargaining. Such consultations might occur through the inclusion of employee representatives on a corporation's board of directors, or through participate structures, such as joint consultation committees or works councils.

In the unitarist model, public policies to promote information exchange and consultation are seen as beneficial because they can help employers and employees see that cooperative rather than competitive relations are better for all concerned. In the pluralist and critical models, there are instrumental and non-instrumental rationales for government intervention that promote employee consultation. Consultative participatory mechanisms serve as training grounds for political democracies by creating citizens who value participation (Pateman, 1970) and respect diverse viewpoints (Estlund, 2003). A second instrumental reason is that these forms of collective participation can be critical for implementing and enforcing legislated labour standards, such as working time regulations, safety standards, and non-discrimination principles. In fact, transparency and self-regulation are increasingly seen as the preferred methods for enforcement of diverse government regulations, but relying on information disclosure and self-monitoring by employers is largely ineffective for enforcing workplace laws without strong supports for employees that are at least partially independent of their employers (Rogers and Streeck, 1995; Weil et al., 2006). With the right legal supports, workplace-centered committees can provide the needed monitoring mechanism to enhance enforcement of diverse government regulations, while also helping to tailor these regulations to the needs of particular workplaces (Rogers, 1995; Weil, 2005). A third instrumental reason for public policy to promote consultation mechanisms is that employers typically have private information that makes it difficult for employees to make informed decisions about important life events. For example, in the absence of regulatory requirements, employers may hide information about impending layoffs from employees, but mandatory consultation can help employees receive information and act accordingly.

The non-instrumental rationale for employee consultation parallels the support of democracy in the political arena: the inherent belief in the value of self-rule because an essential part of being human and being free is being able to effect one's own destiny (Adams, 1991). In sum, instrumental and non-instrumental aspects of employee consultation posit that such forms of employee participation ultimately support the health of a country's populace and democracy. As such, these arguments are frequently characterized as calls for industrial democracy (Derber, 1970). Industrial democracy is not typically produced naturally in the autocratic employment relationship, so if autocratic policies produce negative externalities through harmful effects on democracy, then there can be a productive role for state action to promote industrial democracy.

Countervailing Collective Power

The fourth and final dimension of employee participation in organizations seeks to promote employee rights through collective participatory structures. Fundamentally, these initiatives promote the collective power of employees as a counterweight to the power of corporations. There are two primary forms of this aspect of employee participation—codetermination and collective bargaining.

Codetermination means the sharing of decision making rights between management and workforce as well as veto power for workforce representatives in the company's decision-making process. In practice, codetermination rights are generally granted by legislation to works councils. Such legislation typically also gives works councils information and consultation rights, but the information and consultation aspects of works councils do not touch upon the employers' ultimate power and authority to make business decisions. Codetermination goes beyond consultation and is included here as a mechanism for countervailing power because the veto aspects of codetermination are intended to redress the power imbalance between employers and unorganized workforces.

The other common employee participation method for redressing this power imbalance involves participation in the determination of wages and working conditions through union representation and collective bargaining. Collective bargaining around the world takes many forms, from decentralized negotiations for just a few workers to centralized bargaining that ultimately covers workers in an entire sector, or from producing skeletal agreements that outline minimum conditions to lengthy contracts that spell out terms and conditions in great detail and prohibit any deviations. But the function is always the same: to give workers a powerful collective voice to obtain a larger share of the economic pie for workers and promote the respectful treatment of workers.

In the egoist model described earlier, codetermination and collective bargaining are largely viewed negatively because they interfere with free markets while also limiting and restricting the unilateral prerogative of management and thereby causing economic inefficiencies. In fact, works councils and unions are seen as labour market monopolies that can abuse their monopoly power by opportunistically exploiting weak employers, distinguishing too sharply between insiders and outsiders, harming workers not represented, lobbying to capture economic rents, or even violating individual rights (Freeman and Rogers, 1993: 26). In the unitarist model, codetermination and collective bargaining are unnecessary because employers will take care of their employees. Information sharing and consultation might promote cooperation, but the additional codetermination or bargaining rights are seen as adversarial and unnecessary since, by assumption, employers and employees have shared interests.

In the pluralist model, in contrast, codetermination and collective bargaining are seen as essential checks and balances against excessive corporate power (recall the key pluralist assumptions of the existence of at least some conflicts of interest and of unequal bargaining power in imperfect labour markets). Works councils with veto rights and labour unions therefore can help correct market failures that undermine worker welfare. And by giving workers a strong voice in the workplace that is independent of management, works councils and unions can also be seen as key supporters of industrial democracy. For both of these reasons, then, subscribers to the pluralist model of the employment relationship argue that government regulations should promote strong works councils and unions, and foster collective bargaining (Budd, 2004, 2005). Certain types of collective bargaining, for example, multi-employer collective bargaining, can also be used by employers to improve their relative power position vis-à-vis a strong trade union (Zagelmeyer, 2007). It should be noted, however, that some subscribers to the pluralist model see works councils as subject to manipulation by employers and therefore argue that true employee power and industrial democracy can only come from labour unions that have the power to strike and are independent of management (Harper, 2001).

Views of works councils, labour unions, and the associated public policies in the critical model are more equivocal. The critical model is supportive of such initiatives to the extent that works councils can represent a welcome shift in the frontier of control in favour of labour while militant unions can protect workers against the abuses of capitalism. On the other hand, the critical approach also sees co-determination and collective bargaining as inadequate because they stabilize the capitalist system and fail to provide workers with full control of the labour process. In other words, codetermination and collective bargaining are ultimately seen as addressing the symptoms rather than causes of the root problems in the critical employment relationship; as such, participatory structures that leave the broader power structure intact are seen as insufficient. Government regulation of works councils and unions are further seen in a negative light to the extent that such regulations are seen as capitalist tools for capping worker discontent and power.

Public Policies in Practice

The previous section demonstrates how employee participation is not strictly a private affair. If one steps outside of the egoist liberal market model that dominates today's

Table 20.3 Public policies on employee participation: rationales and examples

Form of participation	Possible rationales for public policy support	Examples of existing policies
Employee involvement and financial participation	Correcting market failures that undermine organizational performance. Promoting employer–employee cooperation	Europe: Promotion and regulation of various stock ownership and profit sharing plans. US: Tax incentives and non-discrimination requirements for employee stock ownership plans
Individual self-determination	Promoting psychological well-being plus healthy families and communities	Europe: Unjust dismissal and privacy protections. Mandated family leave. US: Unpaid family leave
Information and consultation	Providing information for decision making about life events and promoting transparency and self-regulation. Promoting employer–employee cooperation	Europe: Mandated information sharing and consultation with works councils. US: Advance notice of mass layoffs
Countervailing collective power	Correcting market imperfections that undermine workers' psychological, economic, and political welfare	Europe: Codetermination rights for works councils. Provisions for extending collective bargaining agreements. US: NLRA protection of unionization attempts and requirements for good faith bargaining

popular discourse, there are various reasons why public policies can improve individual and aggregate welfare by regulating and promoting various forms of employee participation. As such, individual countries as well as transnational authorities like the European Union (EU) have enacted a variety of public policies pertaining to employee participation; where such policies are lacking, scholars and activists have crafted a number of proposals to fill this perceived void. This section outlines notable public policy approaches to regulating employee participation programmes. The experience of Europe and the United States are described for each of the four types of employee participation programs as these two regions generally represent the two extremes. Notable public policies from some other countries are also used as examples where appropriate. Throughout this discussion it is essential to remember the rationales for government intervention in each category of employee participation (see Table 20.3).

Employee Involvement and Financial Participation

Laws that promote employee involvement in day-to-day operational decision making are rare, if not non-existent. This is because employee involvement is widely seen as a private rather than public issue. The area of financial participation—profit sharing, employee share ownership, and employee stock options—is somewhat different. Mexican and Ecuadorian labour law mandate profit sharing as companies are required to pay out 10–15 per cent of their profits to their employees every year. American and European public policies, in contrast, typically see the decision of whether to adopt financial forms of participation as private decision for each employer to make. But American and European policies encourage companies to adopt participatory financial mechanisms and also establish the regulatory framework for such plans. For example, the US tax code provides incentives for firms to adopt 401(k) retirement plans and employee stock ownership plans; and if a company chooses to implement such plans, there are non-discrimination requirements that must be followed to enjoy the tax benefits.

Similarly, financial participation has been an increasingly important policy issue in the European Union and its Member States for many years. At the EU level, there have been the two PEPPER (Promotion of Employee Participation in Profit and Enterprise Results) reports in 1991 and 1996, a Commission Communication ('On a framework for the promotion of employee financial participation') in 2002 and further activities by the European Economic and Social Committee and the European Parliament (Pendleton and Poutsma, 2004). As such, while financial participation is typically not mandated, European public policy is nevertheless a key influence on the nature and extent of financial participation in Europe (European Commission, 1996; Poutsma, 2001; Uvalic, 1993; Vaughan-Whitehead et al., 1995). The United Kingdom, for example, has a long tradition of financial participation and, as a result of legislation introduced since 1978 to promote employee share-ownership schemes, now has the highest incidence of share-based financial participation schemes in the EU. Employee share ownership in France has also been boosted by recent legal changes, including a new requirement that profit sharing and savings plan arrangements must be included on the agenda of obligatory annual negotiations with employee representatives. Other national approaches to financial participation are described by Pendleton and Poutsma (2004).

Individual Self-Determination

Public policy can support individual self-determination by empowering employees to express themselves, protect their privacy, control their work schedules, and refuse unsafe work. Only a few such policies exist in the United States. There is a general lack of free speech protections so workers can be and are fired for expressing themselves and complaining (Befort and Budd, 2009). US public policy also allows employers to aggressively monitor their employees (Rosenberg, 2005). The Occupational Safety and Health Act (OSHA) includes a right to know provision which gives workers the right to know about hazardous chemicals in their workplace, but more generally, the protections for refusing unsafe work are quite weak (Klaff, 2005). The Family and Medical Leave Act (FMLA) gives workers the right to take twelve weeks of leave to care for themselves or family members with serious health conditions; this weakly promotes control over one's work schedule because this leave is unpaid. Moreover, with the exception of a handful of state laws that generally focus only on nurses, employee control over working time to promote a healthier work–family balance is undermined by employers' legal authority to require mandatory overtime (Golden and Jorgensen, 2002).

In Europe, there are stronger public policy supports for individual self-determination in the workplace. Laws in Belgium, France, Italy, Germany, Great Britain, and Spain protect permanent workers from being dismissed except for poor performance or economic necessity (Wheeler and Rojot, 1992). This protects freedom of expression and other aspects of individual autonomy. With respect to privacy, the Council of Europe's Convention for the Protection of Human Rights and Fundamental Freedoms, which has been ratified by all EU Member States, states that everyone has the right to respect for his private and family life, his home, and his correspondence. This right was extended by case law in the European Court of Human Rights to 'professional or business activities'. The Charter of Fundamental Rights of the European Union signed in 2000 includes an equivalent provision. While these provisions are rather general, there are more specific provisions on the right to respect for privacy and to the protection of personal data, such as the European Parliament and Council Directive (95/46/EC) 'on the protection of individuals with regard to the processing of personal data and on the free movement of such data'. Among others the Directive states that personal data must be: processed fairly and lawfully; collected for specified, explicit, and legitimate purposes, and kept in a form which permits identification of data subjects for no longer than is necessary. The person concerned must be informed about the data processing and of the respective aim, and must have access to the data collected. In August 2001, the European Commission launched a first stage of consultation of the social partners on the protection of workers' personal data (Delbar et al., 2003).

In addition to European legislation, most EU countries have national level labour laws on the protection of privacy in the workplace (with some exceptions, such as Ireland). In the case of Belgium there are collective agreements with the force of law. The French Labour Code prohibits restrictions of workers' rights and freedoms except where justified. The Italian Workers' Statute regulates a number of privacy matters, while Portugal's Labour Code provides for privacy in areas related to workers' personal lives. The specific issue of monitoring and video surveillance at the workplace is made subject to various conditions by legislation in countries such as Belgium (a national collective agreement), Denmark, and France. In some countries, bodies of workplace representation or employee representatives have specific rights with respect to the introduction and/ or use of equipment for monitoring employees' performance and work. This may range from information and consultation rights in Belgium, Finland, or Spain to codetermination in Austria, Germany, Luxembourg, and the Netherlands. In Sweden, the codetermination rights of local unions include matters related to personal integrity (Delbar et al., 2003).

Individual self-determination among European workers is also supported by policies establishing working time flexibility and various opportunities for family-related leave that are part of the broader effort to promote work–life balance and gender equity in Europe. At the EU level, the maternity Directive (92/85/EEC of 19 October 1992) and parental leave Directive (96/34/EC of 3 June 1996) stipulate employment protection and time off for working parents. As the implementation of EU directives is left to individual countries, there is a large variety of mandated leaves—maternity leave, paternity leave, parental leave, and leave for urgent family reasons—that range from short to long periods of time and from unpaid to paid arrangements, that differ widely in terms of eligibility, administrative criteria (means-tested or other criteria, such as number of children and/or previous employment) and administrative processes (calculation of amount of transfer). Nevertheless, legal provisions for parental leave across the EU countries are widespread (Math and Meilland, 2004).

Family-friendly public policies are not typically seen as part of the domain of employee participation, but they do, in fact, promote the individual self-determination aspect of employee participation by increasing employees' abilities to control their work schedules in the face of family responsibilities. This is further illustrated by the working time flexibility of European family leave laws. Statutory parental leave may be divided into a number of separate blocks or staggered in most EU countries, apart from Ireland, Luxembourg, and Greece. In Sweden, parental leave of 480 days, of which 60 are reserved for each of the parents, may be distributed between the two parents and taken in blocks of as little as one hour until the child reaches the age of eight. Flexibility may also be achieved by permitting employees taking statutory leave to work part-time, or by entitling parents to reduced working hours or a reorganized work schedule. In Austria, combining parental leave and part-time employment is a right for employees with at least three-years' service in companies with a workforce of at least twenty-one. Similar rights exist in Belgium, Denmark, Finland, France, the Netherlands, Norway, Portugal, Slovakia, Spain, and Sweden. In Germany and the United Kingdom, employees are entitled to request specific work schedules (Math and Meilland, 2004).

Occupational safety and health laws can also promote workplace self-determination. Under the Swedish Work Environment Act, employee-appointed safety delegates have the right to stop hazardous work (Klaff, 2005). The British Employment Rights Act protects workers against reprisals for taking appropriate steps to protect themselves when the work is believed to pose a 'serious and imminent' danger. State-level legislation in Australia and provincial-level legislation in Canada also grant workers the right to refuse unsafe work.

Information and Consultation

In the European Union, public policies that support information and consultation rights are quite extensive with respect to both the structure of the consultative bodies and the issues covered. While the operational details vary across the countries of the EU, the primary mechanisms for workplace information and consultation are works councils and board-level employee representation. In some countries, works councils might also have veto power over certain proposed changes to the employment relationship; this codetermination aspect of works councils goes beyond promoting cooperation and understanding and will be addressed in the next section. The concern in the present section is with the consultation and information sharing aspects of works councils and related bodies.

Works Councils in Europe

Government legislation on works councils varies across the European Union along several dimensions (Rogers and Streeck, 1995). The *creation of works councils* is usually not mandatory, but requires a certain level of initiative by the workforce or the union(s), and non-interference by employers. As far as *election procedures* are concerned, most countries regulate the voting procedure, the nomination of union and non-union candidates, and the lengths of terms of service of councillors. In all countries, employers must bear the *costs of councils*. Legislation regulates the number of paid hours councilors can spend on works council work, employment protection, training of councillors, and the required office facilities.

Regulation differs perhaps most widely in terms of *legal rights and obligations* of works councils. Rights may be related to access to information, consultation (including rationalization and collective redundancy), and codetermination, for instance, joint decision making with veto power for the council on a range of human resource management issues (such as working hours, payment systems, health and safety, staff assessment, and vocational training, etc.). Works councils have monitoring rights concerning the implementation of the labour laws, social security, employment and health and safety regulations, and conditions of work established by agreements, customs, or practice. Councils also have the right to take (legal) action where the employer does not comply with the rules. The council may be legally obliged to preserve confidentiality, to observe industrial peace, and to cooperate with the employer in good faith (Rogers and Streeck, 1995; Salamon, 2000).

As far as information rights are concerned, works councils in almost all countries are entitled to receive regular information from management on matters such as recruitment, promotion, pay policies, health and safety, working time, equality, training, and financial participation. Some countries use a catch-all requirement to inform on all matters likely to seriously affect employees' interests. By its nature, information on structural change in the business is less likely to be provided on a regular basis, being more dependent on events. In almost all cases, information is required on matters such as closures, transfer of production, relocation, mergers, takeovers, and the introduction of new technologies—especially where these are likely to lead to collective redundancies (Carley et al., 2005).

Consultation can generally be regarded as a right to be informed of planned measures in advance and to have an opportunity to express an opinion prior to implementation. The most common issues covered by consultation rights are: changes to the company's legal status; the removal, expansion, or downsizing of all parts of the company installations; the introduction of new technologies; any change in staff structure (increase or decrease of the number of employees, layoffs, subsidized short-time work); the annual budget for the company health and safety measures; the scheduling of overtime exceeding maximum working hours; redundancies and vocational training; the nomination of workplace and safety committee members (if any); and, more rarely, affirmative action for gender equality. In Italy, works councils are also responsible for supplementary negotiations on matters referred to at company-level bargaining by sectoral collective agreements (generally mandated to the trade unions), such as pay increments, union rights, variable parts of wages, etc. (Carley et al., 2005).

Moving from the national to the international or supranational level, there have been initiatives from within the European Union to strengthen, codify, and institutionalize employee participation in organizations that are operating across borders, and to harmonize regulations on employee representation. Initiatives to strengthen representation existed under directives relating to collective redundancies (1975), transfer of undertakings (1976), and the health and safety of workers (1989). Proposals have been made to harmonize policies across EU Member States, for example, a proposal for worker–directors within a two-tier board structure (5th Directive, 1972), or the 1998 proposal for a company works councils. In 1994 the EU adopted the European Works Councils Directive which applies to organizations with more than 1,000 employees including at least 150 employees in operations in two or more Member States and requires them to establish a European-level works council (Salamon, 2000: 377, 403).

Board-Level Representation in Europe

Board-level employee representation involves employee representatives who sit on the supervisory board, board of directors, or similar structures, in companies. These employee representatives are directly elected by the workforce, or appointed in some other way, and may be employees of the companies, officials of organizations representing those employees, or individuals considered to represent the employees' interests. Board-level representation provides employee input into overall company strategic decision making rather than focusing on information and consultation on day-to-day operational matters at the workplace.

Legislation on employee representation on the board of directors (worker–directors) exists in many European countries, although it has been restricted to the public sector in countries such as Greece and Ireland. In the Netherlands, employees can veto the appointment of board members (Salamon, 2000: 393). The issue gained importance in Europe with the discussions around the European company statue. The proposal includes the requirement for management of organizations wishing to be regulated by EU law rather than national law to reach agreement with the workforce and the unions on employee information and consultation, and, where applicable, board-level participation of employees (Salamon, 2000: 394).

Systems of board-level employee representation in different national industrial relations systems vary widely. In most EU countries, employee representatives are in the minority, and board-level participation is associated with the obtaining of information and understanding, and the expression and exchange of opinions, views, and arguments about an enterprise's strategy and direction. In a few cases, however, when employee representatives are equal in number to those of shareholders or other parties, issues of control, veto, and real influence over company strategy—that is, codetermination—come into play (Schulten et al., 1998).

Legal regulation and practice is quite diverse regarding the selection of employee representatives to sit on the board. Elections among the workforce concerned is a basic method of selecting representatives, applying in Denmark, Finland, Germany (except for the parity codetermination system), Greece, Ireland, Norway, and Portugal. In Austria, it is the works council that appoints the board representatives. In France, works councils appoint (non-voting) board representatives in the private sector, while trade unions play a decisive role in the selection of board representatives in the public sector. In Sweden, it is the local branches of the trade unions that appoint the board representatives. In the Netherlands it is the supervisory board that co-opts its own members, with the works council being one of the bodies with nomination rights. With few variations and exceptions, employee representatives enjoy the same rights, responsibilities, and obligations as other board members. In France, works council-appointed representatives have only a consultative role while employee-elected board representatives have the same rights and confidentiality obligations as shareholders' representatives and representatives appointed 'due to their expertise' (Schulten et al., 1998).

In 2001, the EU adopted a statute and directive on the establishment of the European Company (or Societas Europaea, SE), offering Member States to either adopt the laws, regulations, and administrative provisions necessary, or to make sure that the social partners agree on equivalent provisions. As far as employee participation is concerned, management and workforce in each SE are required to agree on standards of information, consultation, and even board-level representation, with a set of backup statutory 'standard rules' where no agreement is reached (Broughton, 2002).

Consultation in the United States

The situation in the United States is very different than in Europe. Employee representation on corporate boards of directors is rare except in employee-owned companies. Employers do not need to meet with employee representatives about changes in wages, hours, and other terms and conditions of employment unless the workers are unionized (in which case the employer must bargain over these proposed changes). And even unions can only compel companies to share financial information in limited circumstances. More generally, US labour law is fairly hostile towards non-union representation for fear that such forms of employee participation can be manipulated by managers in order to prevent the employees from unionizing (Moberly, 2005). As such, US public policy forces workers to choose between individual representation (backed up by the threat of quitting) and full-fledged unionization; there is very little middle ground for consultation with just a few exceptions.

One exception is the Worker Adjustment and Retraining Notification (WARN) Act which requires employers to provide employees with a sixty-day advance notice of a plant closing or mass layoff. While not consultation per se, this advance notice allows workers to better plan and make decisions for their future which is consistent with the goals of industrial democracy. As a second US exception, at least thirteen states mandate health and safety committees which serve as participation vehicles for consultation on workplace safety policies (Finkin, 2002). In non-union workplaces, however, these committees need enhanced supports to be effective (Weil, 1999). A third example occurs in the US federal sector in which unions that represent at least 10 per cent of a set of employees, but less than a majority, are entitled to consultation rights. These consultation rights, however, typically go unnoticed in US industrial relations. As such, there are frequent calls for adopting European works councils in the United States (Befort, 2004; Befort and Budd, 2009; Fairris, 1997; Weiler, 1990). Similar calls have been made for Australia (Gollan et al., 2002).

Countervailing Collective Power

The fourth class of public policies that support employee participation seek to promote the collective power of employees as a counterweight to the power of corporations. The ultimate objective of these policies is not the promotion of employer–employee cooperation, it is a rebalancing of power to promote equitable outcomes and meaningful employee voice. This objective is typically pursued through laws that support codetermination and/or collective bargaining through labour unions.

Codetermination

As described in the previous section on information and consultation rights, there are diverse policy supports for works councils across many European countries. The provisions already described pertaining to the size, formation, and administration of works councils applies here as well. But some countries endow works councils with more than just information and consultation rights. In particular, in several countries such as Austria, Germany, Italy, and Sweden, the rights of employee representation bodies extend into codetermination associated with a right to veto management decisions. Codetermination rights refer to matters that are of material importance for employees and their working conditions, which relate to the activities of the enterprise, such as: substantial investments, changes in systems and methods of production, quality, product development, plans for expansion, reductions, or restructuring. Decisions of this kind are submitted to the council for its opinion before any decision is made (Carley et al., 2005).

In Germany, the works council's codetermination rights cover participation in arrangements on health and safety at work, works rules, working time, the formal adoption of a reconcilement of interests, a 'social plan' in restructuring as well as in deciding on the design of staff application forms, methods of appraisal and guidelines for personnel selection, in-service training, and individual staff measures (engagement, grading and regrading, transfer, dismissal) (Works Constitution Act §§87 ff.). The right of codetermination must be observed even in urgent cases.

It is therefore obligatory for employers to allow employees to participate in matters connected with: works rules; working time in the establishment, including breaks, short-time working, and overtime; the method of payment used for remuneration; the arrangement of general principles on annual holidays and the preparation of the holiday roster; the introduction and use of technical devices for monitoring employees' conduct and performance; accident prevention and health protection; the form, structure, and administration of fringe benefits; the provision and withdrawal of company-owned housing; matters connected with remuneration arrangements in the establishment and principles and methods of remuneration; the fixing of performance-related rates of pay; and the principles underlying the company suggestions scheme for employees' suggestions for improvements. On these matters, the employer cannot take any action without the agreement of the works council (EMIRE without date).

Collective Bargaining

In continental Europe, collective bargaining is largely seen as a complement to works councils. In Germany, for example, industry-wide collective bargaining has traditionally established minimum standards for compensation while works councils address issues of working conditions within individual workplaces. This complementarity is reinforced by the fact that many works councilors are also union members. One of the most important legal supports for collective bargaining in Europe is the extension mechanism. Specifically, most European countries (important exceptions being the UK, Sweden, and Norway) have legal provisions which may extend collective agreements to employers and employees not directly covered by collective negotiations. Traxler and Behrens (2002) distinguish three forms of extension mechanisms:

1) extension in the narrow sense, which makes a collective agreement generally binding within its field of application (typically an industry) by explicitly binding all those employees and employers which are not members of the parties to the agreement;

2) enlargement, which provides for a collective agreement concluded elsewhere to apply in sectors or areas where no union and/or employers' association capable of collective bargaining exists; and

3) functional equivalents, such as compulsory membership of the bargaining parties' organizations or legal provisions requiring government contractors to comply with the terms of a relevant collective agreement. These functional equivalents result in the phenomenon that all employees and firms in the respective area are covered by the terms and conditions without the formal extension of the agreement.

Various kinds of extension in the narrow sense apply to most Western and Central European countries, albeit with differences in terms of whether extension is automatic, applies to entire agreements, and the thresholds to trigger extension. Enlargement procedures are found in Austria, Portugal, and Spain. Examples of the functional equivalents approach are Italy and Slovenia.

Two interesting cases for public policy support for collective bargaining are France and the UK. France has a long tradition of legal support for collective bargaining in the form of several statutes (1919, 1936, 1946, 1950, 1971, and 1982). While the 1971 law supported multi-industry collective bargaining on, among others, vocational training, working conditions, and job security, the 1982 Act introduced compulsory annual collective bargaining on pay and working hours for unionized firms. In 2001, the number of issues covered by compulsory collective bargaining was extended to equal employment rights, sickness benefits, and saving schemes (Goetschy and Jobert, 2004). The UK saw the introduction of a statutory trade union recognition procedure in 2000, through which unions can seek recognition from employers for collective bargaining purposes. The union recognition provisions of the Employment Relations Act 1999 provide that, where union and employer cannot agree on union recognition for collective bargaining purposes, the union may ask the tripartite Central Arbitration Committee (CAC) to decide the issue and to determine the scope of the bargaining unit (Hall, 2000).

US labour law emphasizes collective bargaining, not codetermination, as the route to create a balance of power in the American employment relationship. Specifically, the National Labor Relations Act (NLRA) makes it illegal to fire or otherwise discriminate against employees who try to form unions and also obligates companies to bargain in good faith with unions when they represent a majority of a defined set of workers. But union density in the private sector is less than 10 per cent and union supporters point to many weaknesses in the NLRA framework: exclusive representation, majority support, the legality of permanent strike replacements, restrictions on secondary boycotts, weak penalties and remedies when the law is broken, and the like (Compa, 2004; Fantasia and Voss, 2004; Summers, 1998). As such, reform proposals are common (Befort and Budd, 2009; Craver, 1993; Stone, 2004). Moreover, approximately 25 per cent of US employees are not covered by a protective statute because some private sector occupations and industries are excluded from the NLRA and because a number of states do not have any protective legislation (General Accounting Office, 2002).

CONCLUSION

The rationale for public policy intervention in the employment relationship lies in the intersection of the objectives of the employment relationship and how this relationship works. If the objectives are seen as narrowly defined with a particular emphasis on economic efficiency and if the employment relationship is seen as working largely through voluntary transactions among well-informed, self-interested actors in perfectly competitive markets, then there is little to no productive role for government regulation. From this egoist perspective, employee participation and other important aspects of work are private affairs best left to individual choice and the invisible hand of the market. But if the objectives are more broadly defined to include things like equity and voice for employees, and if the employment relationship is seen as a complex affair in which workers with human needs and possibly democratic rights are not the equals of their employers because of imperfect markets and other real-world complexities, then there is the potential for public policies to improve the workings of the employment relationship. From a unitarist perspective, for example, there can be a beneficial role for government policies in encouraging cooperative relations between employers and employees while also preventing short-sighted employers from starting a vicious cycle of destructive competition. From a pluralist perspective, employee participation is important for workers and their communities, and therefore should be promoted and protected by state action even when employers might be opposed. From a critical perspective, public policies to democratize the workplace through employee participation are also championed, but are ultimately seen as imperfect solutions when power imbalances between employers and employees are deeply embedded in the socio-political system.

The public policies on the four dimensions of employee participation observed in Europe, the United States, and elsewhere reflect these different theoretical perspectives. In the United States, the underlying laissez-faire approach is rooted in an egoist perspective that sees employee participation as a private affair. As such, there are few public policies in the United States that promote or protect employee participation. The main exception to this is the National Labor Relations Act that encourages unionization and collective bargaining; the passage of this act in 1935 reflects the dominance of the pluralist school of thought during the Great Depression. However, the failure to redress the act's weaknesses are rooted in the dominance of the egoist and unitarist perspectives since the 1950s.

In Europe, employee participation is seen more as a public issue than in the United States. At the EU level and in the Member States, there is a multiplicity of legal regulation and public policies concerning all dimensions of participation in organizations except for employee involvement. This generally reflects a pluralist approach to the employment relationship, albeit with different variants across countries and eras. This is not to say that there are not any exceptions—Thatcherite public policy in the UK, for example, is a notable deviation from the pluralist approach—but by and large, European governments have an inclination for establishing legal frameworks that are supportive of various forms of employee participation (excluding employee involvement), with (occasionally) more or less strong neo-corporatist or statist elements.

Beyond the promotion of a deeper understanding of public policies on employee participation, thinking about policy rationales can also help scholars and practitioners analyse the elements and operations of various employee participation schemes. Identifying problem areas that might need legal supports reveals where there is the potential for employee participation mechanisms to be one-sided or manipulated. More specifically, Greenfield and Pleasure (1993: 194) argue that true employee voice requires legitimacy (employee consent to engage in voice or be represented by others) and power (the ability to influence outcomes or decisions); otherwise, 'without power and legitimacy, any individual or collective worker statement can be labelled voice, even if that voice is, in reality, muffled or inaccurate, stifled or distorted'. If efficiency is the sole objective, then legitimacy and power are presumably not a concern. But for participation mechanisms intended to deliver richer forms of employee voice, legitimacy and power are essential concerns. Voice mechanisms that lack legitimacy and power are likely to need government support to provide these critical dimensions.

In sum, employee participation is not necessarily a private affair, and it is not simply about improving economic performance. Understanding various rationales for state intervention in employee participation programmes is necessary for a deep knowledge and understanding of the diverse forms of employee participation and their widespread effects on organizations, employees, families, and communities. Scholars, practitioners, and policymakers should not overlook the public nature of employee participation programmes.

References

Adams, R. J. (1991) 'Universal Joint Regulation: A Moral Imperative', in J. F. Burton (ed.), *Proceedings of the Forty-Third Annual Meeting*, pp. 319–27. Madison, WI: Industrial Relations Research Association.

Amott, T. and Matthaei, J. (eds) (1996) *Race, Gender, and Work: A Multicultural Economic History of Women in the United States* (rev. edition). Boston, MA: South End Press.

Argyris, C. (1957) *Personality and Organization: The Conflict Between System and the Individual.* New York: Harper and Row.

Bacon, N. (2003) 'Human Resource Management and Industrial Relations', in P. Ackers and A. Wilkinson (eds), *Understanding Work and Employment: Industrial Relations in Transition*, pp. 71–88. Oxford: Oxford University Press.

Befort, S. F. (2004) 'A New Voice for the Workplace: A Proposal for an American Works Council Act.' *Missouri Law Review*, 69: 607–51.

—— and Budd, J. W. (2009) *Invisible Hands, Invisible Objectives: Bringing Workplace Law and Public Policy Into Focus.* Stanford, CA: Stanford University Press.

Broughton, A. (2002) 'European Company Statute in Focus', EIROnline at http://www.eurofound.europa.eu/eiro/2002/06/feature/eu0206202f.html.

Budd, J. W. (2004) *Employment with a Human Face: Balancing Efficiency, Equity, and Voice.* Ithaca, NY: Cornell University Press.

—— (2005) *Labor Relations: Striking a Balance.* Boston, MA: McGraw-Hill/Irwin.

—— and Bhave, D. (2008) 'Values, Ideologies, and Frames of Reference in Industrial Relations', in P. Blyton et al. (eds), *Sage Handbook of Industrial Relations*, pp. 92–112. London: Sage.

—— Gomez, R., and Meltz, N. M. (2004) 'Why a Balance is Best: The Pluralist Industrial Relations Paradigm of Balancing Competing Interests', in B. E. Kaufman (ed.), *Theoretical Perspectives on Work and the Employment Relationship*, pp. 195–227. Champaign, IL: Industrial Relations Research Association.

CARLEY, M., BARADEL, A., and WELZ, C. (2005) 'Works Councils—Workplace Representation and Participation Structures', Dublin: European Foundation for the Improvement of Living and Working Conditions.

CLEGG, H. A. (1975) 'Pluralism in Industrial Relations.' *British Journal of Industrial Relations*, 13: 309–16.

COMPA, L. (2004) *Unfair Advantage: Workers' Freedom of Association in the United States under International Human Rights Standards.* Ithaca, NY: Cornell University Press.

CRAVER, C. B. (1993) *Can Unions Survive? The Rejuvenation of the American Labor Movement.* New York: New York University Press.

CROUCH, C. (1982) *The Politics of Industrial Relations* (2nd edition). Manchester: Fontana.

DELBAR, C., MORMONT, M., and SCHOTS, M. (2003) 'New Technology and Respect for Privacy at the Workplace,' EIROnline at http://www.eurofound.europa.eu/eiro/2003/07/study/tn0307101s.html.

DERBER, M. (1970) *The American Idea of Industrial Democracy, 1865–1965.* Urbana, IL: University of Illinois Press.

DUNDON, T., WILKINSON, A., MARCHINGTON, M., and ACKERS, A. (2004) 'The Meanings and Purpose of Employee Voice'. *International Journal of Human Resource Management*, 15: 1149–70.

EMIRE (without date) Germany—Co-Determination Rights of the Works Council. http://www.eurofound.europa.eu/emire/germany/codeterminationrightsoftheworkscouncil-de.html.

ESTLUND, C. (2003) *Working Together: How Workplace Bonds Strengthen a Diverse Democracy.* Oxford: Oxford University Press.

European Commission (1996) Report from the Commission: PEPPER II: Promotion of Participation by Employed Persons in Profits and Enterprise Results (including equity participation) in Member States, COM (96) 697 Final. Brussels.

FAIRRIS, D. (1997) *Shopfloor Matters: Labor-Management Relations in Twentieth-Century American Manufacturing.* London: Routledge.

FANTASIA, R. and VOSS, K. (2004) *Hard Work: Remaking the American Labor Movement.* Berkeley, CA: University of California Press.

FINKIN, M. W. (2002) 'Employee Representation Outside the Labor Act: Thoughts on Arbitral Representation, Group Representation, and Workplace Committees.' *University of Pennsylvania Journal of Labor and Employment Law*, 5: 75–100.

FOLGER, R. and CROPANZANO, R. (1998) *Organizational Justice and Human Resource Management.* Thousand Oaks, CA: Sage.

FOX, A. (1974) *Beyond Contract: Work, Power and Trust Relations.* London: Faber and Faber.

FREEMAN, R. B. and ROGERS, J. (1993) 'Who Speaks for Us? Employee Representation in a Nonunion Labor Market', in B. E. Kaufman and M. M. Kleiner (eds), *Employee Representation: Alternatives and Future Directions.* Madison, WI: Industrial Relations Research Association, pp. 13–80.

General Accounting Office. (2002) *Collective Bargaining Rights: Information on the Number of Workers With and Without Bargaining Rights*, GAO-02-835. Washington, DC: United States General Accounting Office.

GOETSCHY, J. and JOBERT, A. (2004) 'Employment Relations in France', in G. J. Bamber, R. D. Lansbury, and N. Wailes (eds), *International and Comparative Employment Relations* (4th edition), pp. 176–210. London: Sage.

GOLDEN, L. and JORGENSEN, H. (2002) 'Time After Time: Mandatory Overtime in the U.S. Economy.' Washington, DC: Economic Policy Institute Briefing Paper.

GOLLAN, P., MARKEY, R., and ROSS, I. (eds) (2002) *Works Councils in Australia: Future Prospects and Possibilities.* Sydney: Federation Press.

GOSPEL, H. F. and PALMER, G. (1993) *British Industrial Relations* (2nd edition). London: Routledge.

GOTTFRIED, H. (2006) 'Feminist Theories of Work', in M. Korczynski, R. Hodson, and P. Edwards (eds), *Social Theory at Work*, pp. 121–54. Oxford: Oxford University Press.

GREENFIELD, P. A. and PLEASURE, R. J. (1993) 'Representatives of Their Own Choosing: Finding Workers' Voice in the Legitimacy and Power of Their Unions', in B. E. Kaufman and M. M. Kleiner (eds), *Employee Representation: Alternatives and Future Directions*, pp. 169–96. Madison, WI: Industrial Relations Research Association.

HACKMAN, J. R. and OLDHAM, G. R. (1980) *Work Redesign.* Reading, MA: Addison-Wesley.

HALL, M. (2000) 'Statutory Trade Union Recognition Procedure Comes into Force', EIROnline at http://www.eurofound.europa.eu/eiro/2000/07/feature/uk0007183f.html.

HARPER, M. C. (2001) 'A Framework for the Rejuvenation of the American Labor Movement.' *Indiana Law Journal*, 76: 103–33.

HODSON, R. (2001) *Dignity at Work.* Cambridge: Cambridge University Press.

HYMAN, R. (1975) *Industrial Relations: A Marxist Introduction.* London: Macmillan.

——— (2006) 'Marxist Thought and the Analysis of Work', in M. Korczynski, R. Hodson, and P. Edwards (eds), *Social Theory at Work*, pp. 26–55. Oxford: Oxford University Press.

KAUFMAN, B. E. (1997) 'Labor Markets and Employment Regulation: The View of the "Old" Institutionalists', in B. E. Kaufman (ed.), *Government Regulation of the Employment Relationship*, pp. 11–55. Madison, WI: Industrial Relations Research Association.

KELLY, J. (1998) *Rethinking Industrial Relations: Mobilization, Collectivism and Long Waves.* London: Routledge.

KLAFF, D. B. (2005) 'Evaluating Work: Enforcing Occupational Safety and Health Standards in the United States, Canada, and Sweden'. *University of Pennsylvania Journal of Labor and Employment Law*, 7: 613–59.

LEVINE, D. I. (1995) *Reinventing the Workplace: How Business and Employees Can Both Win.* Washington, DC: Brookings.

LEWIN, D. (2001) 'IR and HR Perspectives on Workplace Conflict: What Can Each Learn from the Other?' *Human Resource Management Review*, 11: 453–85.

LUSTIG, J. R. (2004) 'The Tangled Knot of Race and Class in America', in M. Zweig (ed.), *What's Class Got To Do With It? American Society in the Twenty-First Century*, pp. 45–60. Ithaca, NY: Cornell University Press.

MATH, A. and MEILLAND, C. (2004) 'Family-Related Leave and Industrial Relations', EIROnline at http://www.eurofound.europa.eu/eiro/2004/03/study/tn0403101s.html.

MOBERLY, R. S. (2005) 'The Story of *Electromation*: Are Employee Participation Programs a Competitive Necessity or a Wolf in Sheep's Clothing', in L. J. Cooper and C. L. Fisk (eds), *Labor Law Stories*, pp. 315–51. New York: Foundation Press.

PATEMAN, CAROLE. (1970) *Participation and Democratic Theory.* London: Cambridge University Press.

PENDLETON, A. and POUTSMA, E. (2004) 'Financial Participation: The Role of Governments and Social Partners', Dublin: European Foundation for the Improvement of Living and Working Conditions.

POOLE, M. (1986) *Industrial Relations: Origins and Patterns of National Diversity*. London: Routledge and Kegan Paul.

POUTSMA, E. (2001) 'Financial Participation in Europe. Development and Prospects of Employee Participation in Profits and Enterprise Results,' Dublin: European Foundation for the Improvement of Living and Working Conditions.

REYNOLDS, M. (1996) 'A New Paradigm: Deregulating Labor Relations.' *Journal of Labor Research*, 17: 121–28.

ROGERS, J. (1995) 'United States: Lessons from Abroad and Home', in J. ROGERS and W. Streeck (eds), *Works Councils: Consultation, Representation, and Cooperation in Industrial Relations*, pp. 375–410. Chicago, IL: University of Chicago Press.

——and STREECK, W. (1995) 'The Study of Works Councils: Concepts and Problems', in J. Rogers and W. Streeck (eds), *Works Councils: Consultation, Representation, and Cooperation in Industrial Relations*, pp. 3–26. Chicago, IL: University of Chicago Press.

ROSENBERG, R. S. (2005) 'The Technological Assault on Ethics in the Modern Workplace', in J. W. Budd and J. G. Scoville (eds), *The Ethics of Human Resources and Industrial Relations*, pp. 141–71. Champaign, IL: Labor and Employment Relations Association.

RYAN, R. M. and DECI, E. L. (2002) 'An Overview of Self-Determination Theory: An Organismic-Dialectical Perspective', in E. L. Deci and R. M. Ryan (eds), *Handbook of Self-Determination Research*, pp. 3–33. Rochester, NY: University of Rochester Press.

SALAMON, M. (2000) *Industrial Relations: Theory and Practice* (4th edition). London: FT Prentice Hall.

SCHULTEN, T., ZAGELMEYER, S., and CARLEY, M. (1998) 'Board-Level Employee Representation in Europe', EIROnline at http://eurofound.europa.eu/eiro/1998/09/study/tn9809201s.html.

STONE, K. V. W. (2004) *From Widgets to Digits: Employment Regulation for the Changing Workplace*. Cambridge: Cambridge University Press.

SUMMERS, C. W. (1998) 'Questioning the Unquestioned in Collective Labor Law'. *Catholic University Law Review*, 47: 791–823.

THOMPSON, P. and McHUGH, D. (2002) *Work Organisations: A Critical Introduction* (3rd edition). Basingstoke: Palgrave.

TOWNLEY, B. (1994) *Reframing Human Resource Management: Power, Ethics and Subject at Work*. London: Sage.

TRAXLER, F. and BEHRENS, M. (2002) 'Collective Bargaining Coverage and Extension Procedures', EIROnline at http://eurofound.europa.eu/eiro/2002/12/study/TN0212102S.

TROY, L. (1999) *Beyond Unions and Collective Bargaining*. Armonk, NY: M. E. Sharpe.

UVALIC, M. (1993) 'Workers' Financial Participation in the European Community'. *Economic and Industrial Democracy*, 14: 185–94.

VAN WAARDEN, F. (1995) 'Government Intervention in Industrial Relations,' in J. Van Ruysseveldt, R. Huiskamp, and J. Van Hoof (eds), *Comparative Industrial and Employment Relations*, pp. 109–34. Heerlen: Sage.

VAUGHAN-WHITEHEAD, D. et al. (1995) 'Workers' Financial Participation: East-West Experiences,' ILO Labour Management Series no. 80. Geneva: International Labour Office.

WEIL, D. (1999) 'Are Mandated Health and Safety Committees Substitutes for or Supplements to Labor Unions?' *Industrial and Labor Relations Review*, 52: 339–60.

WEIL, D. (2005) 'Individual Rights and Collective Agents: The Role of Old and New Workplace Institutions in the Regulation of Labor Markets', in R. B. Freeman, J. Hersch, and L. Mishel (eds), *Emerging Labor Market Institutions for the Twenty-First Century*, pp. 13–44. Chicago, IL: University of Chicago Press.

——et al. (2006) 'The Effectiveness of Regulatory Disclosure Policies'. *Journal of Policy Analysis and Management*, 25: 155–81.

WEILER, P. C. (1990) *Governing the Workplace: The Future of Labor and Employment Law.* Cambridge: Harvard University Press.

WHEELER, H. N. and ROJOT, J. (eds) (1992) *Workplace Justice: Employment Obligations in International Perspective.* Columbia: University of South Carolina Press.

ZAGELMEYER, S. (2007) 'Determinants of Collective Bargaining Centralization: Evidence from British Establishment Data.' *Journal of Industrial Relations*, 49: 227–45.

....

CORPORATE GOVERNANCE AND EMPLOYEE PARTICIPATION

....

HOWARD GOSPEL
ANDREW PENDLETON

INTRODUCTION

....

IN recent years, there has been a growing interest in corporate governance among the various parties in organizations, governments, and academic commentators. Although corporate governance is widely viewed as being primarily about the relationship between shareholders and managers, it is also highly relevant to employees and their representatives. Clearly, employees will be affected by how their organization is governed. They may also affect the character of governance, especially if they participate directly in it. Two reasons for greater involvement of employees in governance have come to the fore in recent years. First, by investing their human capital in their employing organization, they bear opportunity costs by foregoing alternative employment possibilities. In this way, they can be said to have a legitimate right to protect the returns and guard against the risks arising from this investment (Blair, 1995). Second, workers often invest financial capital

('Labour's Capital') in the corporate sector, either directly in their employer via employee share ownership plans or indirectly in other corporations via their pension contributions. Traditionally, (some) workers protected their interests as employees by bargaining over the distribution of returns to human capital. Increasingly, the agenda for worker action is widening to take more account of their financial investments. Governance regimes affect how they do both of these, while participation in corporate governance institutions affects their returns from these activities.

In this chapter, we examine the role and extent of employee participation in the main areas of corporate governance. It will become apparent that there are considerable differences between countries in governance institutions and practices. Many of these differences hinge on the role of employees in the governance process. In the next section, we provide an overview of the main practitioner and academic perspectives on governance, highlighting differences in the role accorded to employees. In the third section, broad national and comparative perspectives are outlined to provide some context for the subsequent discussion of more specific aspects of employee involvement. In the fourth section, we identify the main elements of corporate governance systems—the involvement of owners, the role of governing boards, information flows and transparency, the remuneration of managers, and the market for corporate control. All these are addressed with reference to the actual and potential participation of employees. In the last section, some broad conclusions are drawn.

Perspectives on Corporate Governance

Corporate governance may be defined narrowly to cover the relationship between the owners and managers of organisations (Shleifer and Vishny, 1997). In the case of public corporations, this definition views corporate governance as being about the alignment of shareholder and managerial interests, and involves issues such as shareholder involvement and influence, company board structure, and the incentivization of senior managers. On the whole, this perspective does not perceive employees as having a legitimate or worthwhile role in governance. An alternative view of corporate governance defines it more broadly to cover the relationships between all the parties who have an interest in the organization, including employees, suppliers, and the wider community. In this perspective, the subject of governance is about the power relations within a firm that determine who allocates resources and receives benefits (Gourevitch and Shinn, 2005: 1–2). Also, this broader view of corporate governance embraces a wide spread of organizations, including public sector bodies, schools and universities, mutuals and cooperatives, clubs and charities, as well as privately and publicly-owned companies.

These definitions correspond to 'principal agent' or 'shareholder value' and stakeholder perspectives on corporate governance. We outline each in turn.

The 'principal agent' or 'shareholder value' is the most influential perspective on the governance of large, publicly listed corporations. According to this view, principals (owners, shareholders) establish governance systems to ensure that agents (managers) run the organization in the best interests of the owners. However, a fundamental argument is that owners and shareholders bear risk from investing in the firm. In return for risk bearing they should possess control rights. The fundamental problem is that owners and managers may have different interests: while the former seek a return on their investment, the latter may have objectives that conflict with this, such as high salaries and a 'quiet life'. Corporate governance is therefore concerned with protecting investors and has a number of goals—the prevention of fraud, wealth protection, and wealth creation. In this view, the primary purpose of the company is making profits (Friedmann, 1970). Corporate governance is about supporting this goal and distributing the returns of this activity to those who bear risk and who have control rights. This perspective is espoused by many owners and managers and has been well articulated by various theorists of corporate governance, in particular by economists (Jensen and Meckling, 1976; Shleifer and Vishny, 1997).

This view of corporate governance has little place for employees. Hansmann and Kraakmann (2000) argue that, unlike the 'contract' between firms and investors, the labour contract is completely specified with no 'grey areas': hence workers bear no uncontracted risk. As a result, governance rights for workers cannot be justified. It is also argued that employee participation in governance is inefficient because of lack of worker expertise, divergent worker interests, and diluted managerial control (Jensen and Meckling, 1979). For these reasons, governance systems characterized by involvement of workers in governance will be gradually superceded by those without employee participation (Hansmann and Kraakmann, 2000).

The 'stakeholder' perspective considers a broader set of organizations, while still having a significant focus on the public corporation. It also tends to view organizations, including firms in the private sector, as public entities rather than the private property of owners. According to this view, organizations comprise a number of stakeholders which include insiders, such as owners, managers, and employees, and outsiders, such as lenders, suppliers, customers, and the broader communities within which organizations operate. The stakeholder perspective identifies a broader purpose of the company than financial returns for shareholders: it is instead about mobilizing resources to enhance the wealth of all stakeholders. Corporate governance is about checks and balances so that the interests of all stakeholders are balanced. This perspective is associated with a variety of interest groups, including trade unions and community groups, as well as some influential academic theorists (Donaldson, 1989; Donaldson and Preston, 1995; Freeman, 1984; Post et al., 2002). The stakeholder view has been criticized on the grounds that reconciling the interests of a potentially highly diverse set of stakeholders is extremely difficult, and is likely to lead to confused corporate objectives and self-serving managers (Easterbrook and Fischel, 1991). Refinements of stakeholder theory have focused on particular groups of stakeholders, workers especially, and the nature of their stake in the company. Blair has argued that, in developing firm-specific human capital, workers make 'relation-specific' investments in their employer, thereby incurring opportunity costs and bearing risk. For this reason, she argues, workers should have governance rights commensurate with those held by financial investors (Blair, 1995).

Attempts have been made to reconcile the two previous perspectives and to formulate a so-called 'enlightened shareholder value' or 'instrumental stakeholder value' model of the firm. According to this view, firms have a variety of stakeholders but the primary purpose of the firm is to deliver returns to their owners. Wise owners and managers recognize that stakeholder interests have to be taken into account so as to meet corporate objectives. Thus, an enlightened organization will pursue policies that accept labour has legitimate interests because a well-motivated workforce will be good for profits. For their part, stakeholders, such as employees, must recognize that the survival and prosperity of the organization depends on their acceptance of certain goals and objectives, including management's key role in running the organization. This view also overlaps with what has sometimes been referred to as the 'stewardship' theory of governance. This suggests that managers are stewards for all stakeholders and their role is to balance their short- and long-term interests (Davis et al., 1997; Kay, 1997; Kay and Silberson, 1995; Porter, 1992). In this perspective employee participation on governance is on grounds of efficiency rather than rights: giving workers voice in governance assists in exchanging production-relevant information, motivates workers, and enables managers to respond to employee concerns and grievances before they have serious adverse effects.

TYPES OF GOVERNANCE SYSTEMS

Alongside the development of philosophical, ideological, and theoretical perspectives on corporate governance, much of the literature has tried to classify types of governance system. Several distinct types of system have been discerned, and some of these correspond quite closely to the normative perspectives on corporate governance and the function and nature of the company identified above (Allen and Gale, 2000; Amable, 2004; Gourevitch and Shinn, 2005; Hopt et al., 1998; McCahery et al., 2002; O'Sullivan, 2000).

One body of literature has distinguished broad differences between national systems in terms of 'market-outsider' and 'relational-insider' arrangements (Franks and Mayer, 1997; Gospel and Pendleton, 2003). Market-outsider systems tend to have large stock markets with a relatively large number of stock market listed firms. They also tend to be dominated by institutional investors with wide portfolios of relatively small shareholdings in a large number of firms. Because ownership is dispersed, governance takes a market or outsider form. For a variety of reasons relating to the costs of monitoring, it is more efficient for investors to discipline managers by buying and selling shares rather than taking a direct voice in the governance of firms. This means that firms can be at the mercy of the 'market for corporate control' (mergers and acquisitions). The need to maintain stock price to protect the firm or to facilitate takeovers is said to provide strong market-based governance discipline on managers. Since governance is marketized, it is believed that there is little or no need for employee involvement in governance. The US and UK are usually said to exemplify systems of this type.

By contrast, relational-insider systems are those where firms are said to have relied rather less on equity markets for raising capital or restructuring transactions and more on relational borrowing from banks and other firms, and where ownership is more concentrated in a few large blockholders (families, banks, other companies). In these systems, there tend to be fewer listed firms, and stock markets are typically smaller and with lower turnover of shares. This means that the market for corporate control is much less developed, and hostile takeovers are rare. Governance takes a very different form to that found in market-outsider systems. Because owners typically have a large ownership stake, it is worthwhile becoming directly involved in governance as 'insiders'. Germany is typically seen as the exemplar of this kind of system. As discussed below, this has implications for employees who may also be part of this insider governance.

Another body of literature has similarly identified two main types of capitalism—'liberal market' and 'coordinated market' economies. In the former, coordination between economic actors is achieved through market mechanisms and corporate governance always has the backup of the external market for corporate control. Employees have predominantly market relationships with the firm (i.e., there is a strong reliance on external rather than internal labour markets) so employee interests are assumed to be expressed through market mechanisms. Hence there is little or no role for employees in corporate governance. By contrast, in coordinated market economies, where ownership is typically more concentrated, the firm's operations are substantially coordinated through cooperative relationships between actors. This implies that labour should have a voice in the governance of the firm, and these systems tend to be characterized by forms of board representation and works councils and support for this is underpinned by employers' organizations and trade unions (Hall and Soskice, 2001). In some instances, employee participation may take the form of formal involvement of employee representatives in company boards, as in German codetermination, while in others employee voice is achieved via managerial representation, as in Japan.

The broad typologies identified above have some intuitive plausibility but nevertheless are beset by several significant problems. The first is that within-system heterogeneity can be substantial, with the result that the implicit uniformity found in these perspectives may be misleading. There are typically several types of organizations within countries, with quite different governance characteristics. These include private firms, publicly-quoted firms, public sector organizations, cooperatives, mutuals, social enterprises, and charities. Within the listed sector there can be significant differences in ownership and governance. A second problem is that such typologies essentially offer a bipolar view of the world. They leave out differences within broad governance systems, such as the differences between Anglo-Saxon countries and between continental European countries. Moreover, they have even less to say about corporate governance arrangements in Asian countries (with the exception of Japan), transition economies, and developing countries. Recent accounts have typically identified several governance systems and business systems (Amable, 2004; Gourevitch and Shinn, 2005; Whitley, 1999). Finally, the distinction between markets and relationships common to binary classifications tends to ignore the role of social relationships in regulating markets, thereby providing an oversimplified view of the governance world.

There are a variety of explanations for the development of corporate governance systems. One influential perspective has been the 'law and finance' view associated with La Porta et al (1998). This view claims that legal traditions have had a major influence on the development of ownership and governance, with 'case law' countries, such as the UK, providing greater protection to minority investors than European 'civil law' countries. This explains the dispersion of ownership, and associated governance features, in market-outsider countries. However, this view has been criticized on the grounds that minority investor protection pre-dated legal regulation in the UK (Franks et al., 2003) and also that legal change has had little impact on stock market development (Armour et al., 2007).

Others have emphasized political factors. For instance, popular movements against the power of finance capital in the US in the early twentieth century led to legal prohibition of corporate ownership by banks and discouragement of concentrated ownership. This contributed to the spread of dispersed ownership in the US, and hence the marketized system of corporate governance. By contrast, in those countries where labour has been strongly organized as a class political interest, stakeholder models of the firm have tended to emerge (Roe, 2003). It has also been argued that strong labour rights in corporate governance have tended to discourage dispersed ownership because minority investors fear expropriation by strong labour (Pistor, 1999; Roe, 1999). In this reckoning, the pattern of labour representation helps to determine ownership structure and governance rather than vice versa.

A further set of arguments has suggested that 'workers' capital' has influenced the development of ownership and governance systems. In those countries where pension provision has been substantially funded by regular worker and company contributions to pension schemes (rather than state provided schemes funded by taxation), very large pools of capital have been generated and then invested mainly in the listed company sector by institutional investors, such as pension funds and mutual funds. Clark (2000) calls this 'pension fund capitalism' (Drucker (1976) earlier referred to it as 'pension fund socialism'). This capital has driven the expansion of stock markets, encouraged dispersed ownership (because these funds typically diversify over a large number of companies), and encouraged an emphasis on financial returns (Jackson and Vitols, 2001). Thus, perhaps paradoxically, 'workers' capital' can be said to have contributed to the development of governance systems which are often viewed as operating against labour's interests by encouraging firms to prioritize short-term profits and facilitating takeovers (Hutton, 1996). This may have been accentuated recently with the growth of private equity houses (increasingly invested in by pension funds) and hedge funds (which borrow shares from institutional investors to 'short sell'). While the former is often said to extract value from companies at labour's expense (Clark, 2009), the latter can destabilize companies by driving down share prices.

KEY COMPONENTS AND DIMENSIONS OF CORPORATE GOVERNANCE

Here we identify a number of key components or dimensions of corporate governance such as are to be found in most national systems and such as are considered in the academic literature (Filatochev et al., 2007). These components are: owner or shareholder involvement; the structure and composition of boards and other governing bodies; transparency and information disclosure; incentives and alignment of interests; and the market for corporate control. Below we consider each of these in turn, outlining their function, describing their operation, and considering the role of employee voice within them. For the most part we focus on the governance arrangements found in the USA and UK, though we also refer to countries with different governance systems such as Germany and Japan.

Ownership and Shareholder Involvement

As outlined above, the ownership of the organization must be seen as an important aspect of its governance, resulting from the legal property rights and subsequent power implications they confer. It might be expected that shareholders seek to exercise their ownership and governance rights by extensive involvement in the management and direction of the company. While this may be the case in small, unlisted companies, and exemplified in owner-managed companies, it is rarely the case in large US and UK listed firms with dispersed ownership (major corporate crises are an exception) (Thomsen and Pedersen, 2000). By contrast, active involvement of major owners tends to be greater in those systems where ownership is more concentrated.

There are a variety of reasons for limited involvement in the US and UK. Corporate law in many countries limits the involvement of shareholders. This is especially the case in the US where historically political campaigns to limit the power of finance capitalism resulted in extensive legislation on this issue (Roe, 1994). There is a danger that extensive shareholder involvement might result in investors falling foul of the 'insider trading' regulations found in many advanced countries. Further, where ownership is dispersed there is a free-rider problem facing those who choose active involvement in governance: they bear the costs but share the benefits with all other shareholders. Finally, many institutional investors experience conflicts of interest emanating from the trend towards integrated investment banking. For instance, many pension fund managers provide a range of other corporate services (many of which have higher margins than fund management), and they are reluctant to engage in active monitoring of investee companies for fear of losing other corporate business (Davis and Han Kim, 2007). For these reasons, investor quiescence pervades the governance relationship in listed companies (at least in public), and portfolio investors are said to prefer exit, rather than voice, as the primary means to monitor and discipline managers (the so-called 'Wall Street Walk').

Nevertheless, corporate law typically provides shareholders with certain rights and obligations. These include the right to attend certain meetings, the right to put forward and vote on resolutions, and the right to appoint the board of directors. However, there is great deal of variety in the specific nature of these provisions, and shareholder rights in these areas are usually hedged with restrictions (for instance, minimum numbers of signatories are required to table resolutions). In practice, in most countries and most public companies, the role of shareholder meetings and voting tends to be somewhat limited, for the reasons outlined above. Nevertheless, in recent years, this has gradually been changing due to a growing concentration of ownership, thereby favouring voice over exit, and regulatory reform. For instance, in the UK corporate law now permits an advisory vote at the AGM on the remuneration report of the company. This has provided a focus for recent shareholder protests about executive pay packages (see below). Despite this, informal influence by big shareholders is as, or more, important than formal involvement as described above, both in liberal and coordinated market economies. This often takes place outside the public gaze with the result that it is difficult to assess the activities of major shareholders in governance (Pendleton and Gospel, 2005). However, it is clearly an important process. Major UK investors hold a large number of informal meetings with investee companies each year, and senior company managers spend a substantial proportion of their time on this activity (Pye, 2001).

How might employees participate in and influence these aspects of governance, and why should they want to do so? Employee action might focus on labour standards, terms and conditions, and policies in their own company (e.g., pay levels, union recognition, pension provision, etc.), or on encouraging investors to pressurize a range of other companies, possibly in their own employer's supply chain (e.g., child labour in developing countries). There are several ways in which they may do so, either directly or indirectly via their representatives.

First, they can try to lobby shareholders and influence their decisions, either publicly at shareholder meetings or privately at bilateral meetings (Anderson et al., 2007). There is little evidence on the incidence or success of either, though there are occasionally well-publicized examples of the former. For instance, in Germany, this kind of lobbying (accompanied by other forms of representation discussed below) has influenced decision making in large companies (Jackson et al., 2005). When workers mount protests at the AGM they attempt to influence shareholders and to embarrass managers. The limitation of this tactic is that the AGM is rarely the key site of corporate governance. However, it can be a useful means of publicizing grievances as part of a wider campaign. In the US shareholder resolutions are increasingly being accompanied by publicity campaigns by shareholder groups (Gillen and Starks, 2007).

Second, employees may be shareholders themselves. Employee share ownership is common among large companies in most liberal market economies and increasingly in other countries (Kaarsemaker et al. Chapter 13). In principle, employee share ownership provides participating employees with governance rights as owners. For the most part, however, this has not provided a vehicle for either a widespread or effective role in corporate governance. In most listed companies, the combined ownership stakes of employees is relatively small (under 5 per cent). In any case, mobilizing the interests of employee shareholders to exert such an ownership bloc is difficult and rarely occurs, though there are employee shareholder associations in some European companies. In addition, employee shareholders may have conflicting interests between their role as employees and owners. Furthermore, in most cases employees' orientations to share ownership plans appear to be predominantly financial, and companies 'market' share plans to their workforces on this basis (rather than as a means of gaining control) (Pendleton, 1997). A tiny number of employees actually attend AGMs: in a recent survey conducted by one of the authors just over 1 per cent of employee shareholders were regular attendees. However, employee shareholder rights can be a useful tool in wider employee/union campaigns.

Third, employees can also potentially influence companies through their pension funds. In most liberal market economies, a substantial proportion of private sector employees subscribe to funded pensions in addition to state provided pensions. There are also some public sector pension funds, such as CALPERS in the US. The provision of funded pensions (i.e., financed by employee and company contributions rather than by taxation) has led to the accumulation of very substantial pools of capital ('workers' capital'), which have underwritten the steady expansion of stock markets in these countries. There is considerable scope for employee participation in the management of these funds. In the UK, up to one-third of fund trustees are nominated by members, while American Taft-Hartley multi-company pension funds and Australian industry superannuation funds are jointly managed by employers and unions. Since these funds typically invest substantially in equity, and because pension funds between them own very substantial proportions of listed companies, trustees have the capacity to exert significant influence on investee companies should they choose to do so. In recent years, trade unions in countries such as the US, UK, and Australia have attempted to mobilize 'Workers' Capital' by building networks of fund trustees and by tabling shareholder resolutions at company AGMs (Williamson, 2003). In the US, union-mounted campaigns are the fastest growing variant of this form of shareholder activism and around 40 per cent of shareholder resolutions come from 'union funds'. A key focus in recent campaigns in the US has been executive pay (Gillen and Starks, 2007). Again, however, in practice the impact of this representation can be highly constrained by fiduciary responsibilities, ambiguous interests, and lack of expertise, though US evidence suggests this need not be the case if union pension funds choose 'orthodox' corporate governance issues for their activism (Schwab and Thomas, 1998).

Boards and Governing Bodies

For the most part, of course, owners and shareholders cannot be involved in the actual oversight of strategy and the operational management of the company. It is for this reason that boards and other governing bodies are created and are charged with responsibility for matters, such as approval of strategy, appointment, and remuneration of senior managers, and the financial propriety and audit of the firm. As a consequence, the structure and composition of the board is, and should be, of interest to employees.

Boards vary considerably. US companies have a single (unitary) board which is often quite large and which has substantial representation of shareholder interests (though usually not shareholders themselves). In the UK, boards are also unitary, but tend to be smaller and to have smaller external representation or non-executive representation. By contrast, in Germany and to varying degrees in some other continental European countries, boards are or may be binary in the sense that there is an upper tier supervisory board and a lower tier management board. Shareholder and worker representatives sit on the upper board (*Aufsichtsrat*) while executive managers make up the management board (*Vorstand*). In Japan, boards are unitary and tend to be larger than in the US. They are notable for the high proportion of 'insiders': most board members are promoted from within, while the remainder tend to be appointed from companies who are affiliated with the company (Araki, 2005).

Much of the research on company boards in the US and UK has been concerned with the relationship between board composition and company performance, with the primary argument being that strong outsiders inhibit the potential for entrenchment and self-enrichment by insiders. Research findings have been inconclusive on this issue, but it is apparent that powerful insiders are often able to dominate external members of boards, partly because of their central role in the board appointment process (Filatotchev et al., 2007). This might work to the advantage of employees in so far as insider board members may advance the interests of all insiders. Pagano and Volpin (2005) argue that managers may develop employment policies that are favourable to labour to provide a 'shark repellent' against unwanted takeovers. Recent research indicates that boards with a greater proportion of outside directors are more likely to resort to layoffs during performance decline (Yawson, 2006). Protection of the interests of insiders is found in the Japanese corporate governance system where an important function of the board is to protect employee interests, and where external board members are usually quiescent. It is also often argued that employees have a *de facto* voice in governance through the promotion of long-service managers to the company board (Aoki et al., 2008; Araki, 2005; Inagami and Whittaker, 2005). In countries like the US and UK, however, it is argued that top managers have become increasingly divorced from other employees in large corporations and have pursued their own interests without reference to other groups in the company. This is said to be exemplified by steep rises in executive pay in these countries (Froud et al., 2006; Lazonick and O'Sullivan, 2000).

Employees may gain a voice in corporate governance through representation on company boards. This is legally mandated in a sizeable number of OECD countries (mainly in continental Europe). There is now also provision for European companies to incorporate as a European Company (SE), which includes board representation on German lines, though few companies have done so. There are no legal requirements to have employee directors in the major liberal or outsider market economies though a very small numbers of firms do have workers on the board. These have included major firms in the steel industry in the United States.

Advocates of board-level representation argue that companies will benefit from greater information flows and worker consent, while workers will gain from greater understanding and access to the key decision-making forum in the company (Commission on Codetermination, 1998). Critics claim that board-level representation will 'dilute' the pursuit of profit, thereby promoting managerial confusion and economic inefficiency (Jensen and Meckling, 1979).

For a time in the mid-1970s, there was active consideration of proposals for worker directors in the UK and there was an experiment with board-level representation in the Post Office (Batstone et al., 1983). Research in the US and UK indicated that worker directors tended to be most involved and effective on labour management and industrial relations decisions (Batstone et al., 1983; Brannen et al., 1976; Hammer et al., 1991; Towers et al., 1985). This research also indicated that worker directors needed to be closely linked to unions to be effective, though the downside was that this reduced their legitimacy with other directors.

Subsequently, research into board-level representation has focused on the German and Scandinavian countries, where the practice is widespread. In Germany, a series of laws on codetermination from the 1950s to 1970s provide 50 per cent employee representation in firms with 2000 or more employees and one-third representation in public companies with 500–2000 employees. Approximately five million German workers work in companies with board-level representation (Commission on Codetermination, 1998). In terms of effects, there has been considerable debate. Recent studies by Schmid and Seger (1998) and Gorton and Schmid (2000) find that parity codetermination caused a 21–25 per cent decrease in share price relative to companies with one-third codetermination. However, Baums and Frick (1998) find no negative effect on share price following on the introduction of parity codetermination and significant court decisions. Kraft and Stank (2004) and Fitzroy and Kraft (2005) show a small positive effect of codetermination on the innovation and on productivity. However, German evidence also suggests two further considerations. First, representation through legally constituted works councils gives workers more say and has more positive benefits. Second, board representation would seem to require the support of works councils and trade unions for it to be effective (Frick and Lehman, 2005; Muller Jentsch, 2003; Vitols, 2004), though some research indicates that involvement of union representatives or outsiders removes any positive economic effects of codetermination (Fauver and Fuerst, 2006).

Transparency and Information Disclosure

The quality and flow of information is usually seen as an essential part of corporate governance. Here information flows are of various kinds: there is the flow of information from company directors and managers to shareholders; there is the flow of information from managers to board directors, especially non-executive directors; there is also the flow of information to other stakeholders, including employees. Timely flows of high-quality information, be they legally mandated or beyond those required by law, are seen as desirable in terms of preventing fraud, raising funds, and facilitating checks on participants in the firm. The reduction of informational asymmetries should also reduce power imbalances between those with an interest in the firm, thereby making for a more effective system of checks and balances.

There are significant differences between countries in the amount and type of information which is provided. Companies in the US, UK, and other Anglo-Saxon countries are generally reckoned to be good providers of information, at least to shareholders and debt holders. The same also applies to Germany, the Scandinavian countries, and Japan. By contrast companies in Southern Europe are required to, and in reality provide, less information to shareholders and other parties. The provision of information in other parts of the world can be very limited (Filatotchev et al., 2007; La Porta et al., 1998).

In some countries, the disclosure of information by managers to employees is mandated by law. This applies in particular in Germany, the Netherlands, France, and other continental European countries. It is also more widely mandated in the EU in specific circumstances, such as where there are transfers of undertakings, M&As, collective layoffs, and where joint councils have been established. However, such legal rights are often minimal, restricted to information which is operational rather than strategic, and often backward-looking. It is often no better than the basic information formally provided to all shareholders (Gospel and Willman, 2005).

There have been a number of studies of information provision within different countries. These suggest that *de jure* rights to information matter and make for higher *de facto* levels of information provision, as in continental Europe. We also know that, over and above the law, information is likely to be provided to employees where managements pursue more sophisticated human resource policies, where there is some financial distress, and where there is a trade union or works councils. The evidence suggests some positive effects of information sharing on climate and performance (Kleiner and Bouillon, 1988; Morishima, 1989, 1991; Peccei et al., 2008).

Incentives and Alignment of Interests

In the literature on corporate governance, substantial consideration is given to how the interests of senior managers are aligned with those of shareholders, when there is a separation of ownership and control (Fama, 1980; Shleifer and Vishny, 1997). This in turn revolves in large part around executive pay, bonuses, and share options. In countries, such as the US, UK, and Australia, there has been considerable growth in the use of stock-based remuneration and stock options in recent years, and a correspondingly large literature has developed around this (Muurling and Lehnert, 2004). However, firms in other countries, including France, Japan, and Germany, have also made increasing use of stock-based remuneration for top managers. 'Base pay' (i.e., core salary before bonuses and stock awards) has also been growing, relative to average worker pay. In the US, average CEO pay in Fortune 500 companies has risen from being 42 times average worker pay in 1980 to 364 times in 2007 (Institute for Policy Studies, 2007). Some of the rise in executive pay is attributed to corporate governance reforms. The use of remuneration committees, supported by remuneration consultants, coupled with greater disclosure of executive pay, is thought to have 'ratcheted up' top executive pay by setting a 'going rate' based on the highest paying firms (Clarke et al., 1998).

Employees may have an interest in executive pay for various reasons. Given the governance rationale for stock-based remuneration, executive pay ought to be associated with company performance. The broad consensus from the research is that, at low levels of managerial stock ownership, managers' interests will be insufficiently aligned with those of shareholders, but that alignment will grow as ownership rises. However, beyond a certain point, managers will become entrenched as major owners and may extract private benefits from control, possibly at the expense of minority shareholders (Davies et al., 2005; Morck et al., 1988). In general terms, alignment with shareholder interests may have adverse effects for labour if shareholder objectives focus on redistribution of earnings away from other stakeholders. Among critical commentators, 'shareholder value' strategies have been characterized as 'downsize and distribute', with labour being a significant loser in this process (Lazonick and O'Sullivan, 2000).

Most of the attention recently, however, has focused on stock options and the adverse effects these may have for other stakeholders. The key characteristic of options is that they have little downside risk. Coupled with the large size of many recent option awards, there is the possibility that options encourage top executives to take risky decisions. In the executive compensation literature this is generally viewed favourably as it means that executives will do more than focus on a quiet life and job security. However, option awards may encourage excessively risky behaviour, a shortening of time horizons, a decline in research and development expenditure (DeFusco et al., 1991), and in the worst cases accounting misreporting and fraud (Ericksen et al., 2006).

A further concern about the contingent elements of executive pay is that the performance targets on which they are typically based are insufficiently challenging. It has been argued that executive pay is often about 'rent extraction' rather than 'optimal contracts' (Bebchuk and Fried, 2004), with executives in effect controlling the timing, size, and triggers for contingent pay awards. Executive pay has become a major focus of shareholder activism in both the US and UK.

Therefore, it is not surprising that unions are becoming increasingly active on the topic of executive pay, partly on equity grounds, partly because of fears about perverse incentives. It is possible that greater employee involvement and participation in AGMs, on boards, and in works councils will constrain somewhat the growth in executive pay; though, to date, there is little firm evidence on this issue. It is noticeable, however, that in those European countries with extensive codetermination arrangements, executive pay has risen more slowly than in the liberal market economies. Studies of CEO compensation and union presence find that union presence is associated with lower levels of total compensation, and higher proportions of base pay (Gomez and Tzioumis, 2006; Jackson et al., 2005).

The Market for Corporate Control

The market for corporate control is usually seen as a core feature of corporate governance systems, though it is especially important as a governance device in market/outsider systems, such as the UK and USA. The argument is that takeovers discipline poor performing managements by threatening them with displacement. Where a firm is taken over by another, or where ownership of the firm changes, the new owners often replace the incumbent management. The corporate governance literature has argued that poor performing firms will be especially vulnerable to this form of restructuring (Manne, 1965). A further form of discipline on poor performing managers, often operating in tandem with the market for corporate control, is the managerial labour market: poor performing managers displaced by takeovers may find it difficult to secure alternative employment (Fama and Jensen, 1983).

In practice, we know that the market for corporate control operates in different ways in different countries. In the UK, it has been particularly active, and the British model of takeover regulation is coming to provide something of a model for the EU and other countries (Deakin et al., 2003). The hostile takeover is especially associated with liberal market economies, such as the UK, though the actual numbers of such takeovers are relatively small (Deakin and Slinger, 1997). The US also has an active takeover market but there are many obstacles to hostile takeovers, such as so-called 'poison pills' (existing shareholders acquire additional rights triggered by hostile takeovers) and state-level legal restrictions. In Germany and Japan, the takeover market is less active and, to date, this has been a less significant factor influencing governance.

Takeovers are widely seen as having negative implications for employees, though it is not always the case that they are harmful to labour interests or that labour always opposes them. The expectation that takeovers will be bad for employees is encapsulated in the 'breach of contracts' perspective: takeovers enable new managers to break the implicit contracts reached between workers and the previous management and to redistribute wealth from workers to shareholders (Shleifer and Summers, 1988). Other accounts suggest that new owners reduce labour costs to recoup the premiums that are paid when takeovers are mounted. There is substantial evidence that employment falls post-takeover (Conyon et al., 2002b; Deakin et al., 2003), and some evidence that wage growth may be reduced (Brown and Medoff, 1988; Lichtenberg and Siegel, 1990). Employment reductions are most likely when takeovers are hostile or where target companies have similar activities to the bidder (Conyon et al., 2001a). There is little systematic evidence on the implications for employee representation though there are anecdotal accounts of withdrawal of union recognition and reductions in other forms of employee voice. Recently, the labour implications of ownership change has attracted considerable attention because of the activities of private equity investors. Concern has been widely expressed that public-to-private transactions and other large private equity-backed buyouts have led to job losses and reductions in union voice (Clark, 2009), though other accounts have pointed to a more complex set of effects (Wright et al., 2009).

An important policy issue concerns the rights of employees to information and consultation during takeovers and other ownership restructuring. In Europe, employees have rights to information and protection of their employment status when their employment is transferred, deriving from the Acquired Rights Directive. Since 2004 the Thirteenth Company Law Directive has required company boards to inform employees of takeover bids and has given the right to employees or their representatives to express an opinion on the bid (Pendleton and Deakin, 2007). Employees also have rights to information and consultation on any significant changes to employment, including redundancies, which may occur once takeovers have been affected. However, employment protection rights do not apply to takeovers involving share transfers, as is the case in many takeovers of listed firms. This has been a particular issue in private equity buyouts. In the US, state-level takeover legislation has provided opportunities for firms to consult with stakeholders, including employees, during takeovers, but this legislation has not been effective in giving employees voice and, ironically, union shareholder campaigns have often lobbied for these obligations to be removed (on the grounds that they are bad for governance) (O'Connor, 2000). In countries where workers are represented on company boards there are more opportunities for worker voice in takeovers and workers may ally with shareholders in supporting takeovers (Jackson et al., 2005).

An obstacle to effective exercise of employee voice during takeovers in liberal market economies is that managers are responsible primarily to shareholders, unlike other areas of corporate law and regulation where managers are responsible to the *company* (Deakin et al., 2003). However, on some occasions managers and employees form alliances to fight takeovers. Workers and their representatives may be able to mobilize public sympathy and political support that are unavailable to managers. It has also been argued that some managers pay high wages and provide extensive employee voice to deter takeover activity ('shark repellents'). These raise the costs of takeovers for acquiring companies (Pagano and Volpin, 2005).

Conclusions

The linkages between employee participation and corporate governance are complex. Although at first sight there seems to be little direct link between them in some countries, on closer examination there are a variety of linkages even though labour may have little or no formal role in governance. In other countries, of course, employee involvement in governance is far more apparent. In countries where employees have little direct role in formal governance, they have the potential for involvement via their ownership of company shares and their participation in funded pension schemes. Clearly, these forms of involvement are growing, though there are many obstacles to effective labour representation in these areas. The chapter has shown how employee participation and representation may impact on various aspects of 'mainstream' corporate governance, such as executive pay, even where there is little direct role. If corporate governance is defined in broader terms than the conventional way found in most policy discussions, the role for labour should be greater. Much also depends on the perceived purpose of the company. If wider definitions of corporate purpose and corporate governance are subscribed to, it becomes clear that the main actors are owners/shareholders, managers, and employees. There are several potential configurations and alliances of these actors, and these have led to a rich variety of governance systems and practices in various political and economic environments (Gourevitch and Shinn, 2005; Jackson, 2005; Jackson et al., 2005).

References

Allen, F. and Gale, D. (2000) *Comparing Financial Systems*. Cambridge, MA: MIT Press.

Amable, B. (2004) *The Diversity of Modern Capitalism*. Oxford: Oxford University Press.

Anderson, K., Ramsay, I., Marshall, S., and Mitchell, R. (2007) 'Union Shareholder Activism in the Context of Declining Labour Law Protection: Four Australian Case Studies'. *Corporate Governance: An International Review*, 15(1): 45–56.

Aoki, M., Jackson, G., and Miyajima, H. (2008) *Corporate Governance in Japan*. Oxford: OUP.

Araki, T. (2005) 'Corporate Governance, Labour, and Employment Relations in Japan: The Future of the Stakeholder Model', in H. Gospel and A. Pendleton, *Corporate Governance and Labour Management: An International Comparison*. Oxford: Oxford University Press.

Armour, J., Deakin, S., Sarkar, P., Siems, M., and Singh, A. (2007) *Shareholder Protection and Stock Market Development: An Empirical Test of the Legal Origins Hypothesis*. Cambridge: Centre for Business Research, Working Paper.

BATSTONE, E., FERNER, A., and TERRY, M. (1983) *Unions on the Board: An Experiment in Industrial Democracy.* Oxford: Blackwell.

BAUMS, T. and FRICK, B. (1998) Codetermination in Germany: The Impact of Court Decisions on the Market Value of the Firm. *Economic Analysis,* 1(2): 143–61.

BEBCHUK, L. and FRIED, J. (2004) *Pay Without Performance: The Unfulfilled Promise of Executive Compensation.* Cambridge, MA: Harvard University Press.

BLAIR, M. (1995) *Ownership and Control: Rethinking Corporate Governance for the Twenty First Century.* Washington, DC: Brookings Institution.

BRANNEN, P., BATSTONE, E., FATCHETT, D., and WHITE, P. (1976) *The Worker Directors.* London: Hutchinson.

BROWN, C. and MEDOFF, J. (1988) 'The Impact of Firm Acquisitions on Labor', in A. Auerbach (ed.), *Corporate Takeovers: Causes and Consequences.* Chicago, IL; University of Chicago Press.

CLARK, G. (2000) *Pension Fund Capitalism.* Oxford: Oxford University Press.

CLARK, I. (2009) 'Private Equity in the UK: Job Regulation and Trade Unions'. *Journal of Industrial Relations,* forthcoming.

CLARKE, R., CONYON, M., and PECK, S. (1998) 'Corporate Governance and Directors' Remuneration'. *Business Strategy Review,* 9(4): 21–30.

Commission on Codetermination (1998) *The German Model of Codetermination and Cooperative Governance.* Gutersloh: Bertelsmann Foundation Publishers.

CONYON, M., GIRMA, S., THOMPSON, S., and WRIGHT, P. (2001a) 'Do Hostile Mergers Destroy Jobs?' *Journal of Economic Behaviour and Organisation,* 45(4): 427–40.

——————————(2001b) 'The Impact of Mergers and Acquisitions on Company Employment in the United Kingdom.' *European Economic Review,* 46: 31–49.

DAVIES, J., HILLIER, D., and McCOLGAN, P. (2005) 'Ownership Structure, Managerial Behaviour, and Corporate Value.' *Journal of Corporate Finance,* 11: 645–60.

DAVIS, G. and HAN KIM, E. (2007) 'Business Ties and Proxy Voting by Mutual Funds.' *Journal of Financial Economics,* 85: 552–70.

DAVIS, J. H., SHOORMAN, F. D., and DONALDSON, L. (1997) 'Toward a Stewardship Theory of Management', *Academy of Management Review,* 20: 20–47.

DEAKIN, S., HOBBS, R., NASH, D., and SLINGER, G. (2003) 'Implicit Contracts: The Impact of the City Code on Takeovers and Mergers', in D. Campbell and H. Collins (eds), *Implicit Dimensions of Contracts.* Oxford: Hart.

—— and SLINGER, G. (1997) 'Hostile Takeovers, Corporate Law, and the Theory of the Firm'. *Journal of Law and Society,* 24: 124–50.

DEFUSCO, R., ZORN, T., and JOHNSON, R. (1991) 'The Association between Executive Stock Option Plan Changes and Managerial Decision-Making'. *Financial Management,* 20: 36–43.

DONALDSON, T. (1989) *The Ethics of International Business.* Oxford: Oxford University Press.

—— and PRESTON, L. (1995) 'The Stakeholder Theory of the Corporation: Concepts, Evidence, and Implications'. *Academy of Management Review,* 20: 65–91.

DRUCKER, P. (1976) *The Unseen Revolution: How Pension Fund Capitalism Came to America .* London: Heinemann.

—— (1993) *Post-Capitalism Society.* Oxford: Butterworth-Heinemann.

EASTERBROOK, F. and FISCHEL, D. (1991) *The Economic Structure of Corporate Law.* Cambridge, MA: Harvard University Press.

ERICKSEN, M., HANLON, M., and MAYDEW, E. (2006) 'Is there a link between Executive Compensation and Accounting Fraud?' *Journal of Accounting Research,* 44(1): 113–43.

FAMA, E. (1980) 'Agency Problems and the Theory of the Firm'. *Journal of Political Economy*, 88: 288–307.

——and JENSEN, M. (1983) 'Separation of Ownership and Control'. *Journal of Law and Economics*, 26: 301–25.

FAUVER, L. and FUERST, M. (2006) 'Does Corporate Governance Include Employee Representation? Evidence from German Corporate Boards.' *Journal of Financial Economics*, 82: 673–710.

FILATOTCHEV, I., JACKSON, G., GOSPEL, H., and ALLCOCK, D. (2007) *Identifying the Key Drivers of 'Good' Corporate Governance and the Appropriateness of Policy Responses.* DTI Economics Paper, 1–227, URN 07/581/.

FITZROY, F. R. and KRAFT, K. (2005) 'Codetermination, Efficiency, and Productivity'. *British Journal of Industrial Relations*, 43(2): 233–47.

FRANKS, J. and MAYER, C. (1997) 'Corporate Ownership and Control in the U.K., Germany, and the U.S.', in D. Chew (ed.), *Studies in International Corporate Finance and Governance Systems.* New York: Oxford University Press.

————and ROSSI, S. (2003) *The Origination and Evolution of Ownership and Control.* London: Centre for Economic Policy Research, Paper 3822.

FREEMAN, R. (1984) *Strategic Management: A Stakeholder Approach.* Boston, MA: Pitman.

FRICK, B. and LEHMANN, E. (2005) 'Corporate Governance in Germany: Ownership, Codetermination, and Firm Performance in a Stakeholder Economy', in H. Gospel and A. Pendleton (eds), *Corporate Governance and Labour Management.* Oxford: Oxford University Press.

FRIEDMANN, M. (1970) 'The Social Responsibility of Business is to Increase its Profits.' *New York Times Magazine*, 13 September.

FROUD, J., JOHAL, S., LEAVER, A., and WILLIAMS, K. (2006) *Financialization and Strategy: Narrative and Numbers.* London: Routledge.

GHILARDUCCI, T., HAWLEY, J., and WILLIAMS, A. (1997) 'Labour's Paradoxical Interests and the Evolution of Corporate Finance'. *Journal of Law and Society*, 24(1): 26–43.

GILLEN, S. and STARKS, L. (2000) 'Corporate Governance Proposals and Shareholder Activism: The Role of Institutional Investors'. *Journal of Financial Economics*, 57: 275–305.

————(2007) 'The Evolution of Shareholder Activism in the United States'. *Journal of Applied Corporate Finance*, 19(1): 55–73.

GOMEZ, R. and TZIOUMIS, K. (2006) 'What do Unions do to CEO Compensation?'. CEP Discussion Paper 720. London: Centre for Economic Performance, London School of Economics.

GORTON, G. and SCHMID, F. (2000) *Class Struggle inside the Firm: A Study of German Codetermination.* Federal Reserve Bank of St Louis, Working Paper 2000–25.

GOSPEL, H. and JACKSON, G. (2008) 'Corporate Governance and Employee Voice: An EU Perspective', King's College London, mimeo.

——and WILLMAN, P. (2005) 'Statutory Information Disclosure for Consultation and Bargaining: A German, French, British Comparison', in J. Storey (ed.), *Adding Value through Information and Consultation*, pp. 219–37. London: Palgrave.

GOUREVITCH, P. and SHINN, J. (2005) *Political Power and Corporate Control: The New Global Politics of Corporate Governance.* Princeton, NJ: Princeton University Press.

HALL, P. and SOSKICE, D. (eds) (2001) *Varieties of Capitalism: The Institutional Foundations of Comparative Advantage.* Oxford: Oxford University Press.

HAMMER, T., CURALL, S., and STERN, R. (1991) 'worker representation on boards of directors: a study of competing roles.' *Industrial and Labor Regulations Review*, 44(4): 661–80.

HANSMANN, H. and KRAAKMAN, R. (2000) 'The End of History for Corporate Law.' Newhaven, CT: Yale University, Law and Economics Working Paper 235.

HOPT, K. J., KANDA, H., ROE, M., WYMEERSCH, E., and PRIGGE, S. (1998) *Comparative Corporate Governance*. Oxford: Oxford University Press.

HUTTON, W. (1996) *The State We're In*. London: Routledge.

INAGAMI, T. and WHITTAKER, D. H. (2005) *The New Community Firm. Employment, Governance and Management Reform in Japan*. Cambridge: Cambridge University Press.

Institute for Policy Studies (2007) *Executive Excess 2007*. Washington, DC: Institute for Policy Studies.

JACKSON, G. (2005) 'Towards a Comparative Perspective on Corporate Governance and Labour Management: Enterprise Coalitions and National Trajectories', in H. Gospel and A. Pendleton (eds), *Corporate Governance and Labour Management*. Oxford: Oxford University Press.

——HOPNER, M., KURDELBUSCH, A. (2005) 'Corporate Governance and Employees in Germany', in H. Gospel and A. Pendleton (eds), *Corporate Governance and Labour Management*. Oxford: Oxford University Press.

——and VITOLS, S. (2001) 'Between Financial Commitment, Market Liquidity and Corporate Governance. Occupational Pensions in Britain, Germany, Japan and the USA', in B. Ebbinghaus and P. Manow (eds), *Comparing Welfare Capitalism: Social Policy and Political Economy in Europe, Japan, and the USA*. London: Routledge.

JENSEN, M. and MECKLING, W. (1976) 'Theory of the Firm: Managerial Behavior, Agency Costs and Ownership Structure.' *Journal of Financial Economics*, 3: 305–60.

————(1979) 'Rights and Production Functions: An Application to Labor-Managed Firms and Codetermination'. *Journal of Business*, 52: 469–506.

KAY, J. (1997) 'The Stakeholder Corporation', in G. Kelly et al. (eds), *Stakeholder Capitalism*. London: Macmillan.

——and SILBERSTON, A. (1995) 'Corporate Governance'. *National Institute for Economic and Social Research*, 84: 84–97.

KLEINER, M. and BOUILLON, M. (1988) 'Providing Business Information to Production Workers: Correlates of Compensation and Profitability'. *Industrial and Labor Relations Review*, 41: 605–17.

KRAFT, K. and STANK, J. (2004) 'Die Auswirkungen der Gesetzlichen Mitbestimmung auf die Innovationsaktivitaten Deutscher Unternehmen'. *Schmollers Jahrbuch*, 124: 421–49.

LA PORTA, R., LOPEZ-DE-SILANES, F., SCHLEIFER, A., and VISHNY, R. W. (1998) 'Law and Finance'. *Journal of Political Economy*, 106: 1113–55.

LAZONICK, W. and O'SULLIVAN, M. (2000) 'Maximising Shareholder Value: A New Ideology for Corporate Governance.' *Economy and Society*, 29: 13–35.

LICHTENBERG, F. and SIEGEL, D. (1990) 'The Effects of Ownership Changes on the Employment and Wages of Central Office and other Personnel'. *Journal of Law and Economics*, 33: 383–408.

MANNE, H. (1965) 'Mergers and the Market for Corporate Control'. *Journal of Political Economy*, 73: 110–20.

McCAHERY, J. A., MOERLAND, P., RAAIJMAKERS, T., RENNEBOOG, L. (2002) *Corporate Governance Regimes: Convergence and Diversity*. Oxford: Oxford University Press.

MORCK, R., SHLEIFER, A., and VISHNY, R. (1988) 'Management Ownership and Market Valuation: An Empirical Analysis'. *Journal of Financial Economics*, 20: 293–315.

MORISHIMA, M. (1989) 'Information Sharing and Firm Performance in Japan'. *Industrial Relations*, 30: 37–61.

MORISHIMA, M. (1991) 'Information Sharing and Collective Bargaining in Japan: Effects on Wage Negotiations'. *Industrial and Labor Relations Review*, 44: 469–85.

MULLER JENTSCH, W. (2003) 'Reassessing Co-determination,' in W. Muller Jentsch and H. Weitbrecht (eds), *The Changing Contours of German Industrial Relations*. Munich: Rainer Hampp Verlag.

MUURLING, R. and LEHNERT, T. (2004) 'Option-Based Compensation: A Survey' *International Journal of Accounting*, 39: 365–401.

O'CONNOR, M. (2000) 'Labor's Role in the American Corporate Governance Structure'. *Comparative Labor Law and Policy Journal*, 22(1): 97–134.

O'SULLIVAN, M. (2000) *Contests for Corporate Control. Corporate Governance and Economic Performance in the United States and Germany*. Oxford: Oxford University Press.

PAGANO, M. and VOLPIN, P. (2005) 'Managers, Workers, and Corporate Control'. *Journal of Finance*, 60: 841–68.

PECCEI, R., BEWLEY, H., GOSPEL, H., and WILLMAN, P. (2008) 'Look Who's Talking: Sources of Variation in Information Disclosure in the UK'. *British Journal of Industrial Relations*, 46(2): 346–66.

PENDLETON, A. (1997) 'Stakeholders as Shareholders: The Role of Employee Share Ownership', in G. Kelly, D. Kelly, and A. Gamble (eds), *Stakeholder Capitalism*. Basingstoke: Macmillan.

——— and DEAKIN, S. (2007) 'Corporate Governance and Workplace Employment Relations: The Potential of WERS 2004.' *Industrial Relations Journal*, 38(4): 338–55.

——— and GOSPEL, H. (2005) 'Markets and Relationships: Finance, Governance, and Labour in the UK', in H. Gospel and A. Pendleton (eds), *Corporate Governance and Labour Management*. Oxford: Oxford University Press.

PISTOR, K. (1999) 'Codetermination: A Socio-Political Model with Governance Externalities', in M. Blair and M. Roe (eds), *Employees and Corporate Governance*. Washington, DC: Brookings Institution.

PORTER, M. (1992) *Capital Choices. Changing the Way America Invests in Industry*. Boston, MA: Harvard Business School and Council on Competitiveness.

POST, J., PRESTON, L., and SACHS, S. (2002) *Redefining the Corporation: Stakeholder Management and Organizational Wealth*. Stanford, CA: Stanford University Press.

PYE, A. J. (2001) 'A study in studying corporate boards over time: looking backwards to move forwards.' *British Journal of Management*, 12: 33–46.

ROE, M. (1994) *Strong Managers, Weak Owners: The Political Roots of American Corporate Finance*, Princeton NJ: Princeton University Press.

——— (2003) *Political Determinants of Corporate Governance: Political Context, Corporate Impact*. Oxford: Oxford University Press.

SCHMID, F. A. and SEGER, F. (1998) 'Arbeitnehmerbestimmung, Allokation von Entscheidungsrechten, und Shareholder Value'. *Zeitschrift fur Betriebswirtschaft*, 69(5): 453–73.

SCHWAB, S. and THOMAS, R. (1998) 'Realigning Corporate Governance: Shareholder Activism by Labor Unions.' *Michigan Law Review*, 96(4): 1018–94.

SHLEIFER, A. and SUMMERS, L. (1988) 'Breaches of Trust in Hostile Takeovers', in A. Auerbach (ed.), *Corporate Takeovers: Causes and Consequences*. Chicago, IL: University of Chicago Press.

——— and VISHNY, R. (1997) 'A Survey of Corporate Governance'. *Journal of Finance*, 52: 737–783.

THOMSEN, S. and PEDERSEN, T. (2000) 'Ownership Structure and Economic Performance in the Largest European Companies'. *Strategic Management Journal*, 21: 689–705.

TOWERS, B., COX, D., and CHELL, E. (1985) *Worker Directors in Private Manufacturing Industry in Great Britain*. London: Department of Employment, Research Paper 29.

VITOLS, S. (2004) 'Continuity and Change: Making Sense of the German Model'. *Competition and Change*, 8(4): 331–8.

WHITLEY, R. (1999) *Divergent Capitalisms. The Social Structuring and Change of Business Systems*. Oxford: Oxford University Press.

WILLIAMSON, J. (2003) 'A Trade Union Congress Perspective on the Company Law Review and Corporate Governance Reform'. *British Journal of Industrial Relations*, 41(3): 511–30.

WRIGHT, M., BACON, N., and AMESS, K. (2009) 'The Impact of Private Equity and Buyouts on Employment, Remuneration, and other HRM Practices'. *Journal of Industrial Relations*, forthcoming.

YAWSON, A. (2006) 'Evaluating the Characteristics of Corporate Boards Associated with Lay-off Decisions'. *Corporate Governance: An International Review*, 14(2): 75–84.

....

CHAPTER 22

CROSS-NATIONAL VARIATION IN REPRESENTATION RIGHTS AND GOVERNANCE AT WORK

....

CAROLA FREGE
JOHN GODARD

In its purest form, the capitalist employment relation is a relationship of subordination, in which employees have no a priori rights of participation or representation and take on the status of resources to be employed in accordance with the interests of capital. The structure of this relation should, according to neoliberal theory, give rise to superior levels of economic performance, because employees have little choice but to accept and comply with employer objectives, and there are few restrictions on the exercise of employer authority. But it can serve as an underlying source of conflict and employee distrust, because the interests of those over whom authority is exercised are subordinated to, and hence always potentially sacrificed in favour of, those of capital. It can also stifle forms of employee input that are potentially conducive to both employee consent and economic performance. Moreover, it is contrary to basic democratic values underpinning liberal democracies, potentially creating problems of legitimacy within the economy at large and the workplace in particular. Ultimately, it can give rise to widespread economic unrest, and this unrest can spill over into the social and political spheres.

The extent to which these problems actually become manifest, and the ways in which they do, vary in accordance with a variety of considerations, including the design of organizational governance structures and hence the extent to which the interests of capital indeed dominate, and, more generally, predominant norms and the broader institutional environment within which the parties act (Poole, 1986). But their realization, or the threat thereof, has provided perhaps the primary impetus for the formal establishment of representational rights in developed capitalist economies (Adams, 1995).

Historically, the design and strength of these rights has varied considerably, with potentially important implications for organizational governance and ultimately for national economic and social outcomes. As a number of preceding chapters in this book reveal, this variation has persisted and possibly even increased over the past few decades despite various pressures for economies to converge towards a neoliberal model. As a result, there continues to be considerable cross-national diversity in both the institutional context of the employment relation and the way in which conflicts are resolved given this context.

The contribution of this chapter, is to address the reasons for this variation and why it persists in view of such pressures. We begin by briefly describing cross-national differences in representational rights and in organizational governance structures associated with these rights (or lack thereof). We then address various explanations that have or can be advanced to explain this variation and why it persists. Next, based on these explanations we adopt a historical institutionalist perspective to explore the historical basis of this variation. Throughout, we focus on the United States and Germany, because they are commonly identified as exemplars of distinctive varieties of capitalism, with markedly different participation and representation rights. However, we also refer to other countries where relevant.

For the purposes of this chapter, we define representational rights to include a variety of institutional systems that give employees some form of participation in managerial decision making or corporate governance, especially works councils, representatives on supervisory boards, or union-led collective bargaining. This definition includes voluntaristic as well as legal systems of rights, provided that these systems are institutionalized through widely held normative rules and understandings as to employee representation rights (e.g., the post-Second World War British system). It generally excludes systems of 'direct' participation, such as autonomous work teams, and indirect systems initiated and controlled by employers, such as company unions. Although both may provide workers with meaningful opportunities for participation and representation, both also exist at the behest of the employer and are generally implemented to serve employer interests. Neither can be considered to provide workers with rights in any meaningful sense of this term. Thus, while we refer to such systems where relevant, they generally fall outside of the main purposes of this chapter.

VARIATION

Although there has always been variation in representation rights at work, this variation became especially apparent in the 1950s, in reflection of different post-war 'accords' between labour and capital. Yet during the 1950s there also emerged a widespread belief that, as nations become more economically and technologically developed and integrated, their standards of living can be expected to converge, and so can their institutions and the compromises on which they are based. This convergence would be towards a pluralist model, in which employers sought to balance off competing imperatives rather than privileging the interests of capital, and in which unions and collective bargaining would serve as the primary source of participation and representation rights for workers (Kerr et al., 1960).

More recently, a new, neoliberal convergence thesis has emerged, one in which globalization has rendered international competitive forces so strong and capital so mobile that national governments and their populations have no choice but to effectively accept neoliberal reforms or risk national economic decline and possibly destitution (OECD, 1994). Under this model, unions and collective bargaining, and participatory rights in general, serve as impediments to economic growth and prosperity unless they effectively become tools of management. Where the pluralist convergence thesis suggests a shift in direction away from a 'pure capitalist' employment relation, the neoliberal thesis suggests a shift back.

It is arguable that both of these theses contain some merit. For example, it may be argued that economic and technological development has historically tended to be associated with the adoption of representation rights in some form, even if these rights have varied considerably and have often been resisted by employers. It may also be argued that globalization pressures have had important implications not only for representation rights and organizational governance laws (Gospel and Pendelton, 2005), but also for the way in which these rights and laws are practiced. Yet even if one attempts to give these theses their due, there can be little question that substantial variation in these laws and, more generally, the institutional environments that support them, persists and may even have increased in recent decades (Godard, 2004a).

To illustrate, union representation remains the only system of legal workplace representation in the United States, and laws in support of it have been so badly weakened that it now accounts for only one in eight workers. Moreover, despite recent hopes that a resource-based 'stakeholder' model may be emerging (Jacoby, 2005a: 10), management in the private sector remains accountable only to capital, a relationship strengthened by recent financial system reforms (Jacoby, 2005b: 49–50). In contrast, there are three systems of institutional or indirect representation in Germany, by unions, by works councils, and by representation on supervisory boards. Although these systems are often absent in small employers and may have undergone some decline in coverage over the past decade or more (Hassel, 1999), they can be found in some combination in the large majority of medium and large workplaces, and remain central to organizational governance systems (Ellguth and Kohaut, 2004; Stettes, 2007). They are also complemented by ownership arrangements and traditions that, despite some recent reforms, are generally conducive to a partnership model (Thelen, 2004).

These two examples in many respects represent extremes. Yet within these extremes there continues to be substantial cross-national variation in representation rights and governance systems within advanced democracies. Canada, for example, has similar organizational governance systems to those of the United States, but two-and-a-half times the level of union representation. Britain also has similar governance systems, and roughly the same coverage level as Canada, yet unions appear to play a much more collaborative role, and workers also enjoy limited information sharing and consultation rights (even if largely in response to European Union directives). In Sweden, nine in ten workers are represented by a union, and unions play a much stronger role in the workplace, in many respects similar to that of works councils in Germany; workers also have elected representatives on company boards. Japan has relatively weak representation rights at law, with unions representing only one in five workers and appearing to serve a largely integrative function, yet corporate governance systems and norms have traditionally meant that employees are in most medium- and large- sized corporations considered to be major if not primary stakeholders and are able to exercise voice through consultation councils (Tackney, 2000).

Representation systems within these nations have by no means remained static. There has been some weakening of, or at least reform to, these systems and most of their counterparts within the developed world. However, these changes have been more complex than can be accounted for by the neoliberal convergence thesis, and fundamental institutional differences remain. This raises the question not only of why nation states have been characterized by such differences in representation rights at work, but also of why these differences persist. The remainder of this chapter addresses these questions.

Understanding Variation

Cross-national variation in participation rights and the predominant organizational governance system with which these rights are associated may ultimately be viewed as the product of national choices. There is an extensive body of literature on how such choices are made and why they appear to persist over time. In an analysis of the politics of the welfare state, Olsen (2002) identifies six perspectives, all of which may be viewed as having some relevance to analysis of variation in representation rights and governance systems: structural functionalist, cultural/ideological, pluralist, power resource, instrumentalist (Marxist), and polity-centred. Where a structural functionalist explanation might explain cross-national differences as arising and persisting due to different functional needs within national economies, a cultural/ideological explanation would attribute them to different national values, a pluralist explanation to differences in interest group preferences and pressures, a power resource explanation to differences in the relative power of labour and capital, an instrumentalist explanation to differences in the interests of capital, and a polity-centred explanation to differences in dominant state paradigms and the traditions associated with them.

Each of these explanations could likely be applied to the study of participation and representation rights. Yet although doing so might help to illustrate each, it would in the present context represent little more than an exercise in theoretical relativism and as such do little to advance our understanding of variation. In order to understand this variation, there is need of a more coherent perspective, one that combines elements of each to the extent possible yet avoids the relativist trap. The 'new institutionalism' in socio-economics and political studies, particularly the 'varieties of capitalism' (VofC) and the historical institutionalist literature, provides a starting point for developing such a perspective.

The VofC literature is useful within the present context primarily because it points to the importance of the institutional environments, including legal systems, state structures, policies, and paradigms, business system characteristics (e.g., firm governance, training regimes, and market structures), and various understandings and expectations that support established institutional arrangements (Godard, 2002). Under the VofC approach, in particular, these environments consist of coherent institutional configurations, in which there are complementarities between specific institutions. By implication, this environment is likely to be hostile to institutions and institutional designs that do not 'fit', thereby lowering their likelihood of success unless adapted accordingly.

It follows that variation in participation and representation systems may be attributed to variation in the broader institutional environments of which they are part. In this regard, the most developed formulation of the VofC thesis, as advanced by Hall and Soskice (2001), distinguishes between 'liberal' and 'coordinated' market economies. The former, which are most exemplified by the United States, rely on highly competitive capital, labour, and product markets, and require maximum flexibility. Within this environment, there is little positive economic role for unions and participatory rights in general. They simply lack 'fit' with the broader institutional environment. The latter, which are most exemplified by Germany, rely on coordinated capital, labour, and product markets, and require high levels of cooperation or 'partnership'. Unions and participatory rights may be seen in this regard to play a critically important role, as unions coordinate labour markets and both works councils and board representation help to ensure high levels of cooperation.

Although this literature is of value for helping to understand why particular participation and representation rights might be expected to function effectively in some environments but not others, the Hall and Soskice formulation implies an unduly functionalist conception of institutional design, failing to address how it is that particular institutional configurations come about. It also assumes a purely economic rationale for institutions, thereby ignoring the role of social and political forces both in shaping institutions and in determining their apparent fit within the broader economy and society.

Historical institutionalism provides a basis for addressing these limitations. It essentially finds that institutions and configurations thereof are path dependent, moving along a historical trajectory, and that deviations from this trajectory tend to be relatively minor (Pierson, 2004; Sewell, 1996). Although there is room for agency in shaping how this trajectory unfolds and even a possibility of transformational change over time (Streeck and Thelen, 2004), most accounts of institutional change in this literature argue that agency matters most in periods of crisis, which serve as 'critical junctures' for institutional transformation (Krasner, 1988; Lehmbruch 2001; Mahoney, 2000; Pempel, 1998).

A key problem for historical institutionalist analysis has been to explain why institutions appear to be path dependent. A variety of explanations have been proposed, many of which parallel those identified by Olsen for welfare state policies (Mahoney, 2000: 515–26). One suggests that institutions represent institutionalized power relations, and that these relations become increasingly entrenched over time, alterable only during some form of major shock or crisis (Thelen, 1999). Another argues that institutions become self-reinforcing, perpetuated through various forms of investment and positive feedback which generally render the costs of transformation greater than the benefits (Pierson, 2000, 2004). Yet another argues that institutional reproduction occurs because it reinforces subjective orientations and beliefs about what is morally legitimate and so actors voluntarily opt for its reproduction (Mahoney, 2000: 524). A further explanation, one that is consistent with the VofC thesis (also see Mahoney, 2000: 519), is that institutions persist because they complement other institutions and, conceivably, evolve in ways that maintain this fit.

All of these explanations can be seen to contribute to our understanding of why institutional differences persist, suggesting that differences in participation and representation systems (or a lack thereof) are embedded in (and in this sense constrained by) broader institutional environments and that these environments tend to be deeply rooted and path dependent. But historical institutionalists have often failed to adequately theorize the initial design or foundations of institutions. What, for example, accounts for the particular form of representation (collective bargaining) rights that came to predominate in the United States? What accounts for the more elaborate system of rights that came to predominate in Germany? To simply argue that these tend to be rooted in historical differences leaves open the question of why and how these differences initially came about.

One reading of the historical record that would be consistent with the historical institutionalist literature (and with strategic choice theory in industrial relations) suggests that participation and representation rights within developed economies have tended to become established at specific historical junctures, and that they have reflected choices of key actors made in response to unique combinations of economic, social, and political conditions. Under this explanation, for example, the adoption of the US 'Wagner model' of union representation in the 1930s can be attributed to the crisis created by the Great Depression and a belief that the provision of positive collective bargaining rights would boost worker spending power, thereby helping to regenerate the economy (Kaufman, 1996). It can also be attributed to militancy in the labour movement, particularly as reflected in the growth of industrial unionism and formation of the Congress of Industrial Organization. By comparison, the adoption of the German system of codetermination after the Second World War may be attributed to a desire to ensure dispersed economic and political power and hence help avoid a return to fascism and to foster levels of labour cooperation needed to rebuild the German economy.

Although such a reading is plausible, we believe it to be inadequate. As we demonstrate below, a more careful reading of history suggests that the representation systems selected within each country can be traced to traditions that long pre-date the historic junctures in which they were formally established. To an extent, they may in this respect reflect earlier historic junctures and the developments associated with them.[1] But while historic junctures may matter, we believe that representation systems and the traditions underpinning them are ultimately rooted in formative economic, social, and political conditions and developments within a nation's history and the dominant discourses associated with them. Formative conditions and discourses do not just shape institutional choices at key junctures in history, they also come to be reflected in deeply held institutional norms, or beliefs, values, and principles as to the role, rationale for, and legitimacy of established institutions (Godard, 2009). These norms essentially restrict the range over which subsequent political discourse and the institutional (re)designs that follow from it are likely to gain and maintain legitimacy, in effect institutionalizing the implications of formative conditions and explaining long-term institutional continuity. Although they may allow considerable scope for interpretation and hence for politics (e.g., Jackson, 2005), they therefore give rise to biases that privilege one or more institutional alternatives over others (e.g., Bachrach and Baratz, 1962; Lukes, 1974). These biases become not just structurally embedded, in the way institutions are designed and the distribution of power resources, but also cognitively embedded, in the way actors think about institutions and the ideologies around them.

Our essential argument, therefore, is that cross-national variation in representation rights reflects deeply embedded historical trajectories, and may ultimately be explained in terms of deeply held institutional norms that can be traced to formative economic, social, and political conditions and the political discourses around them. We believe that this approach offers at least three advantages. First, the concept of institutional norms addresses the problem of historical continuity or paths, while allowing for politics and hence variation along (and in some cases, deviations from) these paths. Second, it helps to account for institutional configurations or 'varieties of capitalism', suggesting that institutional fit occurs because of underlying norms that tend to be shared across institutions.[2] Third, it allows us to consider the importance of history and the role of ideas in history without adopting an unduly idealist or culturalist approach, in which institutional change is simply a matter of changing minds. Within the present context, this third insight is especially useful as it provides the basis for understanding the historical and ideational roots of representation rights within individual states and why these rights continue to vary. Below, we demonstrate the value of this approach by comparing the development of institutional norms and representation rights in the United States to that of Germany.

THE CASE OF TWO NATIONS: THE UNITED STATES AND GERMANY

The differences between the representation rights found in the United States and Germany are stark. The United States is known for its highly voluntarist approach to participation, originally comprising a pluralistic notion of free collective bargaining which over time got eroded and substituted by voluntarist forms of firm-specific direct employee participation. In contrast, Germany is known for a more corporatist approach to participation and is usually regarded as the prototype of legalistic participation regimes, having achieved workers' participation in managerial decision making through legal rights for works councils and workers' representatives at companies' supervisory boards, as well as free collective bargaining. These differences are, as earlier suggested, in part explained by functional requirements associated with the broader institutional environments of each nation. But they also represent deeply rooted historical differences and institutional norms. This is the focus of the present section.

The United States[3]

The United States is characterized by a strong distinction between the political sphere, where democratic rights are viewed as of central importance, and the economic sphere, where property rights and the unfettered pursuit of 'life, liberty, and happiness' are viewed as of central importance (Kiloh, 1986: 17). This distinction has been reflected in labour and employment law. Until the early twentieth century, the dominant legal doctrine, as repeatedly affirmed in Supreme Court decisions, was one of freedom to contract, based on the assumption that workers as individuals are on equal footing with their employers, and that the absence of representation rights reflects their consent (Hattam, 1993). It therefore allowed virtually no legal basis for collective voice or representation at work. This changed in the New Deal era, when workers were provided with the right to collective bargaining. But although many proponents of this right saw it primarily as a democratic one (Barenberg, 1993; Dubofsky, 1994), it was justified primarily on the grounds that it would boost spending power and hence be good for the economy (Kaufman, 1996; Pope, 2002; Tomlins, 1985), not on the grounds that it would introduce democracy into the workplace. Since then, the ability of workers to gain even the basic representation rights associated with collective bargaining has been substantially eroded (Godard, 2003).

The limited representation rights and role of unions in the United States may be seen to reflect a number of formative conditions and the discourses surrounding these conditions. The United States was characterized by a history of individualist, frontier development, one in which the state played a limited role. It was initially settled by Puritans fleeing persecution in Britain and subsequently borne out of a revolt against the British state's taxation of the American colonies and refusal to provide them with democratic representation rights. These stylized conditions are commonly argued to have given rise to a number of dominant norms and values (Hartz, 1955; Hutton, 2002; Jacoby, 1991; Lipset, 1963, 1964; Lipset and Meltz, 1998; Perlman, 1949 [1928]; Tocqueville, 1998 [1835];). The United States, even more than other liberal democracies, is known for its 'possessive individualism', its strong, Lockean conception of the sanctity of property and of ownership rights deriving from property, a belief that property and wealth are attributable to the achievements of the individual and so do not carry with them the same duties or obligations as would be the case if they derived from inherited status (Hutton, 2002), a corresponding belief that authority deriving from property rights should not be interfered with and entails few if any obligations to either workers or society, a distrust of centralized state power and hence administrative law, an emphasis in law on freedom of contract and hence both 'free' labour and 'free' product markets, and a comparatively conservative and weak working class.

In particular, a liberal conception of society and state, derived from the writings of Hobbes and Locke, and embedded in the US constitution by its framers, has been predominant. This conception emphasizes a state–society distinction, under which the state is viewed as an instrument of society rather than a higher, ideational good. As Dyson (1980) convincingly shows, this 'mechanic view' of the state goes hand in hand with an individualistic, positivist conception of society. Society is perceived as a composition of a multitude of autonomous individuals who possess and express their free will. A high value is placed on individual freedom, which is defined as being free from any superior power, such as the state. The source of all law and state action is the individual, who is the only real, free, and responsible being. The rights of the individual are prior and superior to the state, whose only absolute value is the liberty of the individual.

This conception has been antithetical to any notion that workers should be provided with meaningful co-decision rights at work or that the state should intrude into the economic sphere in order to mandate such rights. This is not to suggest that there has been no support for democratic forms of work (Derber, 1970).[4] But these forms have had little chance against a dominant liberal reading that centres on the explicit separation of the 'private' economic and 'public' political spheres and which emphasizes both employer proprietary rights and the freedom of parties to establish their own contracts.

The result has been a variant of capitalism more hostile to independent workplace representation than perhaps any other. Where in Europe employers may have been subject to strong pressures to accept the passage of strong representational rights for workers or face substantial unrest and possibly socialization of their property, US employers have been notorious for the intensity with which they have resisted such rights, and union representation rights in particular. While workplace or employer-level representation systems have been established by employers, they have historically tended to be management dominated and designed to supplant unions, rarely providing workers with meaningful rights. For this reason they were sharply constrained under the 1935 Wagner Act. More recently, so-called 'high performance' work practices, which in theory include autonomous (and hence participative) teams, information sharing, and financial participation have generally failed to provide workers with any meaningful say in managerial decision making (Strauss, 2006). US employers are typically not opposed to participation or even representation, provided that they serve employer objectives, do not interfere with managerial decision prerogatives, and exist at the employer's behest. But they strongly oppose any system that does not meet these three criteria, especially where it entails legal *rights* to either participation or representation.

Within this context, labour unions have historically had little effective choice but to adopt a narrow, economistic orientation, one that minimizes challenges to employer property rights and authority and as such displays little interest in obtaining meaningful co-decision rights or social reforms for workers. Although there were substantial debates and disagreements within the US labour movement throughout the nineteenth century, the combination of a conservative working class, hostile employers, a hostile legal system, and a weak state meant that, by the end of that century, dominant labour leaders had determined that they would have little chance of success unless they eschewed a strong role for the state and limited their role to the negotiation of improved terms and conditions of employment for their members through 'free' collective bargaining at the workplace and employer level. Collective bargaining subsequently came to be largely equated with the term 'industrial democracy,' and alternative forms of industrial democracy came to be largely excluded from mainstream discourse in both labour and academic/policy circles (Derber, 1970).[5] Although collective bargaining may have offered some potential for greater control over managerial decision making (Chamberlain, 1948) and hence the attainment of real industrial democracy, it developed into a narrow, 'workplace contractualism' under which democratic goals were subordinated to the maintenance of industrial stability (Lichtenstein, 1993; Stone, 1981). In C. Wright Mills' (1948) famous phrasing, union leaders became little more than 'managers of discontent'.

The result has not only been a nation in which unions represent the only channel through which workers can obtain independent representation, but also one in which this channel has been a narrow one, limited to the terms and conditions of employment and allowing workers few if any meaningful consultation or co-decision rights. Indeed, US labour law effectively excludes such rights from the realm of collective bargaining, labelling these as 'permissive' issues over which employers are not required to bargain and unions not allowed to strike.

Even with this limited role, unions have been subject to substantial institutional biases. These have included a widespread public distrust of strong unions (despite widespread support for the right to join a union; see Bok and Dunlop, 1970: 10–12),[6] an ineffectual labour law regime (Godard, 2004c; Gould, 1993; Human Rights Watch, 2000), and an economic environment increasingly hostile to collective bargaining (Slaughter, 2007). Part of the labour movement's problem may have been that, in the United States in particular, unions substantially increases labour costs yet serve little positive function for employers (Freeman, 2007). This in turn reflects the realities of a liberal market economy and a concomitant rejection of corporatism in any form by employers and the state (Schatz, 1993). But more important may be the poor fit between US institutional norms and New Deal legislation providing the framework for union representation rights.

Despite attempts to sell the Wagner Act on economic grounds and to draft it in a way that defined labour rights largely in terms of individual rights and 'liberty of contract' (Woodiwiss, 1990: 162–4), it was widely considered to represent an unconstitutional intrusion of state power into economic affairs. A 1937 Supreme Court decision upholding its constitutionality was unexpected, and may have reflected in part both public pressures and President Roosevelt's threat to 'pack' the court by expanding it with his own appointees (Pope, 2002). Even with this ruling, however, political support for labour rights pretty much died within two years (Harris, 1982: 37), and the act was substantially weakened over the ensuing decade.

The provisions necessary for the effective functioning of the Wagner Act have been so alien to US legal traditions and institutional norms that opponents have had little trouble obtaining rulings and legal reforms to hobble it (Godard, 2009). A tradition of formal democratic processes has made it possible for employers to obtain a recognition system that requires a formal campaign period and ballot, thereby providing them extensive opportunities to discourage unionization. Norms that privilege property rights over labour rights have yielded rulings that enable employers to deny unions access during a recognition campaign and to hire permanent striker replacements where a union is recognized. Norms of free speech have allowed employers to obtain substantial latitude in what they communicate to workers during a recognition campaign, even allowing them to 'predict' that the workplace will no longer be viable and hence will be closed should a union be recognized. Norms against state intervention have meant that the National Labor Relations Board (charged with enforcing the Act) has been given only weak enforcement powers, so that even where the employer may be deemed to have engaged in illegal firings, threats, or intimidation, the remedies are weak and often subject to lengthy appeal processes; board decisions to recognize a union can also be subject to lengthy appeals, delaying the start of bargaining by months and even years. Norms supporting 'free' markets and 'free' contracts have meant weak provisions in the law for good faith bargaining, which, in combination with the right to hire permanent striker replacements, makes it relatively easy for an employer to undermine a union should it actually become recognized. The overall result is a system that can be characterized as neither 'free' nor 'fair' (Lafer, 2008).

As a consequence, even the narrow conception of industrial democracy and representation rights associated with collective bargaining has largely failed, leaving the overwhelming majority of workers in the United States with no independent representation at work, and the small and shrinking minority that do have representation with little or no meaningful input to employer decision making. Indeed, by the late twentieth century the very term 'industrial democracy' had been replaced by the more sanitized terms 'voice' in industrial relations circles and 'empowerment' in management circles. Where the former increasingly seems to have referred to grievance and managerial-initiated internal 'justice' systems (an exception is Budd, 2004), the latter has been employed primarily to refer to job design. In turn, the term 'employee ownership' which had initially referred to worker-owned firms, came increasingly to refer to managerial controlled stock option plans, advocated as a means of enhancing economic performance but not democracy.

As of the early twenty-first century, there has continued to be substantial support for labour unions and collective bargaining within the American public, likely in reflection of norms favouring collective self-help (see note 6). There have also been continuing efforts to revitalize the US labour movement. Most noteworthy in this context has been the introduction of the Employee Free Choice Act (2006), designed to make it easier for unions to organize and obtain first agreements. So, support for limited representation rights, in the form of collective bargaining, remain. But it is still largely excluded from the dominant discourse, and political support has come to be couched largely in terms of reducing poverty and inequality rather than of introducing democratic rights. As in the 1930s, this in part reflects dominant institutional (especially legal) norms. Legal reforms needed to ensure unfettered access to union representation (including those proposed under the Employee Free Choice Act) are alien to these norms and, even if passed, would likely be soon undermined by employer groups.

The prospects for alternative forms of representation rights and democracy would seem to be even bleaker. There was some experimentation with worker cooperatives in the 1970s and 1980s (Russell, 1988: 384–7), and some subsequent support for works councils among a few prominent IR scholars (Kochan and Osterman, 1994: 204–207; Weiler and Mundlak, 1993). But neither these nor alternative forms of representation rights at work have gained support even within academic circles. They would seem to be too alien to US institutional norms to ever stand much of a chance.

In short, the historical trajectory of the United States may have become somewhat more favourable to representation rights at work during the New Deal era, but this was only temporary and may even have been an aberration. The problem has not so much been with employer power within the political system per se as it has been with institutional norms and traditions that both support this power and enable employers to mount successful appeals to policy makers, the judiciary, and the general public. These norms can be traced to the conditions under which the United States was founded, and although they have no doubt evolved over time, this evolution has been part of a trajectory under which the institutional bias against representation rights has, if anything, been strengthened. The developments of the New Deal era suggest that these biases may not completely rule out the future attainment of enhanced rights. Yet these developments, and the subsequent undermining of the Wagner model, also suggest that they may substantially limit both the prospects for such rights in future and the likely success of these rights should they become established.

Germany

In contrast to the United States, Germany has a long tradition of support for expanding democracy throughout all spheres of public life, including the economic arena. This tradition became the dominant paradigm of state-led social and industrial reforms during the end of the nineteenth and the beginning of the twentieth centuries (e.g., Bismarck's welfare legislation), at the very time that the meaning of industrial democracy was coming to be equated with a narrow conception of collective bargaining in the United States. Again in contrast to the United States, norms and laws favouring participation rights at work were well established by the early twentieth century (during the Weimar Republic). They were undermined during the Nazi era, the very period in which collective bargaining rights were established in the United States. But they were re-institutionalized and further expanded after the Second World War, and underwent further strengthening in the 1970s and again in 2001. The German experience would, therefore, appear to be the mirror image of its US counterpart. But as for the United States, it is deeply rooted in institutional norms that may ultimately be attributed to the conditions and developments under which the German nation was formed.

Unlike its US counterpart, the modern German nation emerged not out of revolution against state power in the late eighteenth century, but rather out of an exercise in state building a century later, as Bismarck achieved the unification of the German states. Because Germany developed out of a feudal system, status and the property attaching to it were inherited rather than accumulated, contrary to the United States. Despite being the home of the Reformation, Germany also retained a strong and influential social Catholic tradition (Lehmbruch, 2001: 56–8), in contrast to the strong Calvinist tradition in the United States (Weber, 1930 [1905]). Moreover, there was no frontier 'safety valve' for discontent, as in the US, with the result that working-class radicalism was more prevalent. Finally, in contrast to the United States, the state played a major role in Germany's industrial development in the late nineteenth century, establishing state-owned banks to finance firms and providing the impetus for what came to be referred to as 'banker's capitalism'. Yet it also had to be mindful of power centres within the newly formed German Federation, leading it to adopt a decentralized model, one in which the central government set laws and policies, but delegated their implementation and administration to Member States and corporate interest associations encouraged by the state and which included a role for labour.

These conditions both gave rise to and reflected a very different system of norms and values than in the United States. In a nation where there was a scarcity of land

and strict status hierarchies, there was little support for a Lockean justification of absolute property rights or for the belief that an individual's success or failure was a reflection of his or her worth. Instead property and status were considered to carry moral obligations towards society (including workers), and ownership or control of economic enterprises did not confer the same absolute prerogatives as in the United States. Major firms and banks came to be viewed as social institutions, with concomitant obligations to society and, more narrowly, workers. There was also a much greater trust of the state and a perception that the state had an important role to play in the development and regulation of the economy, even if indirectly, through the social partners. This also came to be the case for labour unions, which have played a critical role in the German social partnership model.

These norms were embodied by a long-standing intellectual craving for extending democratic ideas to all societal areas including the economy. The distressing British experiences of the 'labour problem' during the period of 'Manchester capitalism' provided an incentive for German intellectuals and policymakers to seek alternative routes, and the combination of the French Revolution and Enlightenment with a fragmented political, social, and religious structure encouraged them to look for alternative ideals more consistent with German traditions than those associated with Manchester capitalism (Frege, 2007).

German thinkers, such as Herder and Hegel, sought to repair the social fragmentation caused by capitalism by creating an integrated, cohesive political community in which the state is both a cultural and moral authority and an integrated system of institutions. Their conception of the modern nation state was therefore a theory of social relations in a broad sense and created a German concern for the state as a cultural and moral authority in contrast to the Anglophone positivist tradition which was leaning towards the state as a rational, mechanic, morally neutral organization. In other words, the state was conceived as an integrated system of institutions, rather than, as Hobbes and the Anglophone tradition which followed him had seen it, as an aggregation of individuals acting in consort to satisfy individual interests (Manicas, 1987: 94). This conception was linked with a concern about the enervating effects of social fragmentation on the individual, caused by a growing capitalist economy and technical rationality models of state and society (Dyson, 1980: 151), and to both the increasing labour problem (the 'social question') of early industrialization and the growing force of socialist parties and trade unions.

Although Germany was still a largely agrarian society, political elites had by the mid-nineteenth century already begun to settle on the development of an encompassing coordinated political economy which contained representation rights for workers. Particularly noteworthy was the 'Berliner Centralverein', founded in 1844 by leading industrialists and Prussian bureaucrats, which promoted industry-based 'factory committees' within each town. This influenced the events of the 1848 democratic revolution and a subsequent White Paper on the factory constitution of the 'Frankfurter Paulskirche', which was to have a new economic order at the macro, industrial, and firm levels that included national chambers of crafts where worker representatives participated, industry-level worker committees, and joint committees with legal participation rights for workers at the factory level.[7]

This legislation never came to pass because parliament was dissolved and the monarchy regained control. But it clearly portended the reforms of the late nineteenth century and the German model of representation rights implemented after the Second World War. It also influenced subsequent discourse supporting state intervention in the economy and the need to make economic institutions compatible with political democracy rather than viewing the economic and political spheres as separate, as in the United States (Bitzer, 1861: 268; Schmoller, 1873). For example, Gustav Schmoller, one of the leading economists of the German monarchy, argued that from a particular size onwards a firm was to be treated like a quasi-public institution and not simply a private matter. The state to him had the right to intervene in workplace relations for the benefit of the whole society. The idea was, therefore, to advocate a corporatist economic order that would fit the vision of an inclusive and encompassing state and society. Representation rights at work and within the economy in general became central to this vision.

Although these arguments were heavily criticized by employer groups and were not to be fully accepted within even the Social Democratic Party until the First World War, they reinforced emergent institutional norms, resulting in a tradition of state mandated representation rights reaching far back into the nineteenth century. In contrast to the United States, where both legislation and legal doctrine remained generally hostile to labour union formation until well into the early twentieth century, workers in Germany were first provided with the right to form unions ('coalitions') in 1869 (Lehmbruch, 2001: 58). In the 1880s, the Bismarck Government made provision for works committees with limited consultation rights (Jackson, 2005: 150; Teuteberg, 1961), and established a system of social insurance that allowed considerable opportunity for labour influence. They also introduced 'industrial chambers' in which unions played a major role in order to promote training needed for German industrialization. These initiatives were ultimately a compromise between the government's aim to check the threat of labour radicalism and foster economic development and the conviction of influential scholars, bureaucrats, and social democrats to promote democratic rights at work. But they reflected a long tradition of intellectual concern for such rights, and embodied institutional norms that were to become increasingly embedded within the German political economy, essentially underpinning the development of Germany's social/coordinated market economy.

These rights were strengthened after the First World War. A central committee consisting of leading representatives of labour and employers and established to coordinate the transition to a peace time economy agreed a first treaty encouraging union recognition and promoting 'social partnership'. Codetermination rights of workers were included in the constitution of the Weimar Republic (1919), and a works council law enacted in 1920 included participation rights works councillors on supervisory boards. Although these arrangements were undermined during the Nazi era, they were again re-established and further strengthened after the Second World War—in part to promote democratic institutions as bulwarks against the political control of the economy through capitalist firms that had marked the Nazi era. The right to union representation was enshrined in the German constitution, and workers were provided not only with the right to works councils, but also with substantial representation on supervisory boards. Within the macroeconomy, unions developed an important role not only in coordinating and regulating wage settlements, but also in the dual training system considered to be central to the German model.

In view of this context, employers have had little real alternative but to accept extensive representation rights for workers, and, given their largely positive role within a coordinated market economy, much less incentive than in the United States to resist such rights. As in virtually all capitalist economies, employers have generally not supported legislation strengthening these rights (Adams, 1995). Yet they have had neither the power nor the inclination to successfully fight against them at either the state or the workplace levels. Instead they have generally accepted and learned to work with employee representatives, so much so that there is now considerable normative support for worker representation rights within the employer community. This is especially true for works councils (Freeman and Rogers, 1993: 51–5; Jacobi et al., 1998: 213), which were strengthened in 2001 in response to the recommendations of a joint labour–employer commission. There has been some recent pressure to weaken supervisory board representation in order to strengthen accountability to the demands of capital, and there have been some cases of overt union avoidance, although these cases remain the exception rather than the rule.

This context has also meant that labour unions have enjoyed a considerable amount of power and influence, especially in comparison to their US counterparts. Although initially anti-capitalist, leading socialist unions came by the late 1880s to adopt a reformist platform, in response to reformist changes in the Social Democratic Party (e.g., from the Bernstein wing) and possibly also in response to various accommodations by the Bismarck Government. Since then, the history of the German labour movement has been pretty much the mirror image of its US counterpart. With the exception of the 1930s and early to mid-1940s (the high point of the US labour movement and lowpoint of its German counterpart), its role in the economy has steadily grown. Not only is it responsible for the negotiation of collective agreements covering two-thirds of German workers (OECD, 2004) it also continues to play a vital role as a 'social partner' in both the establishment and the implementation of social and economic policies.

Harsh economic conditions following German reunification placed consider-able pressure on traditional bargaining arrangements throughout the 1990s, resulting in some decentralization. Union economic and political power would also appear to have declined in recent years as employers and the state have attempted to adopt market based reforms (Bosch et al., 2005). Yet although the German system has been weakened, the institutions of codetermination have remained largely intact (Frege, 2003; Thelen, 2000). Indeed, the 2001 reforms to works council laws were introduced in part to make it easier to form works councils in small workplaces, in the belief that bureaucratic hurdles rather than a lack of demand represent the primary explanation for declining works council coverage.

In sum, the historical trajectory of Germany has generally been a positive one with regard to workplace representation rights, even if there may have been some weakening of the exercise of these rights over the past decade. The German system has no doubt been intended in part to placate workers and to diffuse the power of working-class institutions, which have historically been both more radical and more powerful than their US counterparts. It has also been consistent with the model of an 'enabling state', in which the social partners play a critical role, and with a coordinated market economy, within which worker and labour union consent is more critical. Yet it also reflects the more deeply held institutional norms emergent in the nineteenth century and a response to broader legitimation problems underlying labour radicalism. These norms have historically become embedded within and largely explain the strong representation and governance rights of workers within the German model. Property rights and the interests of capital have been much less dominant than in the United States, allowing much greater 'space' for labour rights and interests. They have also meant that economic democracy has played a much greater role and won much greater acceptance than in the United States.[8] Thus, representation rights have remained strongly entrenched despite pressures associated with globalization and are likely to remain so in future. Indeed, any recent weakening may be temporary, subject to reversal as the German economy strengthens.

BEYOND THE UNITED STATES AND GERMANY?

This chapter has focused on the differences between the United States and Germany. These two nations are viewed as representative of distinctive varieties of capitalism, and they have very different representation rights and institutional norms accounting for these varieties. Yet we believe that the approach we have adopted can be fruitfully applied to other nations as well, including those associated with the same varieties of capitalism.

For example, Britain is regularly identified as a liberal market economy, has intellectual traditions similar to those of the United States, and may be seen to have adopted a similar conception of the state. Yet its monarchical and feudal tradition, coupled with a more socially conscious religious tradition (i.e., the Church of England), have given rise to substantially different institutional norms. The British concept of democracy has historically been one in which the landed classes were to remain dominant within the political sphere, but which also included a feudal concern for the well-being of the lower classes and deeply rooted norms of fairness and legal equality that may ultimately be traced back to the Magna Carta in the thirteenth century. This concept was paralleled in the economic sphere, where the authority of owners was largely unquestioned, but where owners were also expected to adopt a more paternalistic, organic view of their responsibilities than their US counterparts (Jacoby, 1991).

In part in reflection of these norms, British employers have historically been expected to voluntarily recognize unions and have generally conformed to this expectation. Thus, there is a strong tradition of legal voluntarism, under which the state has relied only on 'informal' pressures rather than law to ensure that employers 'play by rules' (Adams, 1994; Davies and Freedland, 1983). Moreover, although the formal role of unions has traditionally been limited to industry-level bargaining over a relatively narrow range of economic issues, there has also been a tradition of strong shop steward representation and 'mutuality' in the workplace.

These traditions were substantially weakened during the Thatcher/Major era. But the level of overt employer resistance to unions remained low, and labour law reforms passed in 1999 have been designed to restore them, providing for state imposed recognition, but only as a last resort (Wood and Godard, 1999). Moreover, the government has recently enacted mild consultation and information sharing laws. Although these are primarily in response to EU directives, they are largely consistent with the British tradition of mutuality, and so may prove to be sufficiently consistent with British institutional norms to function effectively. They would, in any case, never receive the light of day in the United States.

A further example is Canada, which has a number of institutional and historical similarities to the United States. But it was not borne of a revolution, and has a much stronger institutional tradition of elite rule and paternalism, including a stronger traditional role for the state in its economic development (Lipset, 1963). This has translated into norms supporting greater state involvement and acceptance of administrative law, on the one hand, and a greater concern for industrial order and stability, on the other, both of which may be seen to account for

Canada's 'stronger' system of labour laws regulating union recognition and collective bargaining and ultimately union coverage levels that, although low by European standards, are almost two-and-a-half times those of the United States (Godard, 2002, 2007).

As a final example, one might argue that legal representation rights in Sweden are somewhat weaker at the workplace and employer levels than is the case in Germany. Formal works councils are not mandated by law, and supervisory board representation is more limited. But workplaces are highly participative and democratic. This is reflected not only in work design (EPOC, 1997), but also in the tendency to have much more developed joint decision bodies in the workplace; these typically have high levels of union involvement and bear little resemblance to their management initiated counterparts in the United States (Kjellberg, 1998: 105). One might argue that this can ultimately be explained by strong social democratic traditions dating back as far as the fifteenth and sixteenth centuries, when serfs were given the right to own property and provided with the right to elect representatives in parliament (Olsen, 1994).

Each of these examples is undoubtedly over-simplified, especially as they do not take into account important historical conflicts and compromises. But we believe that they help to underscore the basic message of this chapter. Cross-national variation in representation rights, both historically and at present, reflects deeply embedded institutional norms and discourses that can be traced to formative economic, social, and political conditions. These norms and discourses apply not just to representation rights, but to broader institutional configurations. Although they are by no means static and may contain substantial ambiguity (and adaptability), they tend to limit or bias institutional trajectories in ways that enable us to understand not only why representation rights vary, but also why this continues to be the case in the face of global economic and technological developments.

A basic implication is that attempts to prescribe or alter representation rights are not likely to succeed unless they take into account not just the broader institutional environments within which these rights are (or are not) embedded, but also historically rooted institutional norms and traditions. This is a pessimistic message for those who seek to substantially improve representation rights in some nations (e.g., the United States), but an optimistic one for those who worry that globalization will wash these rights away in other nations (e.g., Germany). This does not mean that the former should stop trying or that the latter should stop worrying. Institutional norms do not represent immutable laws, and the biases to which they give rise do not preclude change. But any attempt to explain variation in, or prescribe changes to, representation rights is likely to be unsuccessful if it is not informed by them.

Notes

The authors thank Roy Adams for his comments on an earlier draft of this chapter.

1. In the United States, for example, some identify the adoption of a narrow, economistic form of unionism in the 1880s as a historic juncture; the same could be said of the adoption of Bismarck's reforms and of the German labour movement's shift to reformism in the 1880s.

2. This is not to suggest that these norms are *necessarily* consistent; much of the scope for politics may be due not only to the ambiguity of specific norms but also to contradictions between them, which can also spill over into institutional designs and even various forms of conflict. Yet these tend to be worked out over time, through various compromises and accords. It is beyond the present purpose to address these processes, though it would be interesting to explore if there might be some sort of Marxian dialectic between the development of norms and 'real' (i.e., material) economic and social conditions.

3. For a more complete development of many of the arguments in this section, see Godard, 2009.

4. Throughout much of the nineteenth century, there was some support in the United States for producer cooperatives and communitarian societies emphasizing the virtues of cooperation (Derber, 1970: 37; Perlman, 1949 [1928]: 188–90). But this support did not envision a role for the state in establishing democratic rights at work. Nor did it suggest that such rights should trump property rights. To the contrary, these alternatives were to be based on a model in which authority would continue to derive entirely from property rights. There were subsequent attempts by socialist and religious reformists, in the first two decades of the twentieth century, to argue that this should not be the case, and that the same democratic rights applicable in the political sphere should also extend to the economic sphere (Derber, 1970: 141–61). They met with little success.

5. They did continue to form part of the discourse of the 'left' for a few decades into the twentieth century, primarily among socialists and social Catholics (Derber, 1970: 141–62), but both were largely excluded from mainstream labour academic, or political thought.

6. This apparent contradiction may also be explained by institutional norms. The lack of reliance on the state has meant a tradition of collective self-help, which unions may be seen to epitomize—provided that they operate as 'grass roots' organizations and do not rely unduly on state support or coercion or threaten traditional employer prerogatives.

7. Worker committees were viewed as central to the attainment of this goal. These committees would have equal proportions of employer and worker members and would not only influence internal workplace relations, but also create savings banks for members, provide subsidized housing and education for workers, control child labour, and organizing arbitration for workplace conflicts. An underlying purpose was to avoid Protestant notions of 'self-help' and charity dominant in the United States and Britain in favour of positive rights of equality and codetermination (Schmidt, 1845).

8. Of note, data from the 2001–2002 World Values Survey (Inglehart et al., 2004) reveal that only a third of Germans would follow a command from their employer without asking for an explanation, compared to two-thirds of Americans.

References

ADAMS, R. (1993) 'The North American Model of Employee Representational Participation: A Hollow Mockery.' *Comparative Labor Law Journal*, 15(4): 4–14.

—— (1994) 'Union Certification as an Instrument of Labor Policy: A Comparative Perspective'. in S. Friedman et al. (eds), *Restoring the Promise of American Labor Law*, pp. 260–69. Ithaca, NY: ILR Press.

—— (1995) *Industrial Relations Under Liberal Democracy*. Columbia, SC: University of South Carolina Press.

BACHRACH, P. and BARATZ, M. (1962) 'The Two Faces of Power.' *American Political Science Review*, 56: 947.

BARENBERG, M. (1993) 'The Political Economy of the Wagner Act: Power, Symbol, and Workplace Cooperation'. *Harvard Law Review*, 106: 1379–96.

BEHRENS, M., HAMMAN, K., and HURD, R. (2004) 'Conceptualizing Labour Union Revitalization', in C. Frege and J. Kelly, (eds), *Varieties of Unionism: Strategies for Union Revitalization in a Globalizing Economy*, pp. 11–30. Oxford: Oxford University Press.

BITZER, F. (1861) *Kapital und Arbeit*. Studdgart.

BOK, D. and DUNLOP, J. (1970) *Labor and the American Community*. New York: Simon and Schuster.

BOSCH, G., HAIPETER, T., LATNIAK, E., LEHNDORFF, S., and SCHIEF, S. (2005) 'Changes in the System or Change of System? The National Employment Model of Germany.' Unpublished manuscript, Institute for Work and Technology, Gelsenkirchen, Germany.

BUDD, J. (2004) *Employment with a Human Face*. Ithaca, NY: Cornell University Press.

CHAMBERLAIN, N. (1948) *The Union Challenge to Management Control*. New York: Harper.

DAVIES, P. and FREEDLAND, M. (1983) *Labour Legislation and Public Policy*. London: Clarendon Press.

DERBER, M. (1970) *The American Idea of Industrial Democracy, 1865–1965*. Urbana, IL: Univeristy of Illinois Press.

DOELLGAST, V. and GREER, I. (2007) 'Vertical Disintegration and the Disorganization of German Industrial Relations.' *British Journal of Industrial Relations*, 45(1): 55–76.

DUBOFSKY, M. (1994) *The State and Labor in Modern America*. Chapel Hill, NC: University of North Carolina Press.

DYSON, K. (1980) *The State in Transition in Western Europe*. New York: OUP.

ELLGUTH, P. and KOHAUT, S. (2004) 'Tarifbindung und betriebliche Interessenvertretung: Ergebnisse des IAB-Betriebspanels 2003', *WSI-Mitteilungen*, 57(8): 450–68.

EPOC Research Group, (1997) *New Forms of Work Organization. Can Europe Realize its Potential?* Dublin: European Foundation for the Improvement of Living and Working Conditions.

FREEMAN, R. (2007) *America Works*. New York: Russell Sage Foundation.

—— and ROGERS, J. (1993) 'Who Speaks for Us? Employee Representation in a Nonunion Labor Market', in B. Kaufman and M. M. Kleiner (eds), *Employee Representation*. Madison: WI: Industrial Relations Research Association.

FREGE, C. (2003) 'Transforming German Workplace Relations: Quo Vadis Cooperation?' *Economic and Industrial Democracy*, 24(3): 317–47.

—— (2007) *Employment Research and State Traditions*. Oxford: Oxford University Press.

GODARD, J. (2002) 'Institutional Environments, Employer Practices, and States in Liberal Market Economies: the U.S., Canada, and the U.K.' *Industrial Relations (U.S.)*, April, 41 (2): 249–86.

—— (2003) 'Does Labor Law Matter? The Density Decline and Convergence Thesis Revisited'. *Industrial Relations (US)*, 42–3(July): 458–92.

—— (2004a) 'The New Institutionalism, Capitalist Diversity, and Industrial Relations', in B. Kaufman (ed.), *Theoretical Perspectives on Work and the Employment Relationship*, pp. 229–64. Urbana-Champaign, IL: Industrial Relations Research Association.

—— (2004b) 'A Critical Assessment of the High Performance Paradigm.' *The British Journal of Industrial Relations*, 42–2(June): 349–78.

—— (2004c) *Trade Union Recognition: Statutory Unfair Labour Practice Regimes in the USA and Canada*. London: The Department of Trade and Industry Employment Relations Research Series, #25, UK Government.

—— (2007) 'Institutional Norms and the Survival of the Wagner Model in Canada', Working Paper, University of Manitoba.

—— (2009) 'The Exceptional Decline of the American Labor Movement', *Industrial and Labor Relations Review*, 63(1): forthcoming.

GOSPEL, H. and PENDELTON, A. (2005) 'Corporate Governance and Labour Management: An International Comparison', in H. Gospel and A. Pendelton (eds), *Corporate Governance and Labour Management: An International Comparison*, pp. 1–32. Oxford: OUP.

GOULD, W. B. (1993) *Agenda For Reform. The Future of Employment Relations and the Law*. Cambridge, MA: MIT Press.

HALL, P. A. and SOSKICE, D. (2001) 'An Introduction to Varieties of Capitalism', in P. A. Hall and D. Soskice (eds), *Varieties of Capitalism: The Institutional Foundations of Comparative Advantage*, pp. 1–70. Oxford: Oxford University Press.

HARRIS, H. (1982) *The Right to Manage*. Madison: University of Wisconsin Press.

HARTZ, L. (1955) *The Liberal Tradition in America*. New York: Free Press.

HASSEL, A. (1999) 'The Erosion of the German System of Industrial Relations'. *British Journal of Industrial Relations*, 37(3): 483–505.

HATTAM, V. (1993) *Labor Visions and State Power*. Princeton, NJ: Princeton University Press.

Human Rights Watch (2000) *Unfair Advantage*. New York: Human Rights Watch.

HUTTON, W. (2002) *The State We're In*. London: Little Brown.

INGLEHART, R., BASANEZ, M., DIEZ-MEDRANO, J., HALMAN L., and LUIJKX, R. (2004) *Human Beliefs and Values: A Cross-Cultural Sourcebook Based on the 1999–2002 Values Surveys*. Mexico: Siglo XXI.

JACKSON, G. (2005) 'Contested Boundaries: Ambiguity and Creativity in the Evolution of German Codetermination'. *Beyond Continuity: Institutional Change in Advanced Political Economies*. Oxford: Oxford University Press.

JACOBI, O., KELLER, B., and MULLER-JENTSCH, W. (1998) 'Germany: Facing New Challenges', in A. Ferner and R. Hyman (eds), *Changing Industrial Relations in Europe*, pp. 190–239. Oxford: Blackwell.

JACOBY, S. (1991) 'American Exceptionalism Revisited: The Importance of Managers', in S. Jacoby (ed.), *Masters to Managers: Historical and Comparative Perspectives on American Employers*, pp. 173–200. New York: Columbia University Press.

—— (2005a) *The Embedded Corporation*. Princeton, NJ: Princeton University Press.

JACOBY, S. (2005b) 'Corporate Governance and Employees in the U.S', in H. Gospel, and A. Pendelton (eds), *Corporate Governance and Labour Management: An International Comparison*, pp. 33–58. Oxford: OUP.

KAUFMAN, B. (1996) 'Why the Wagner Act? Re-establishing Contact with its Original Purpose', in D. Lewin, B. Kaufman, and D. Sockell (eds), *Advances in Industrial and Labor Relations*, pp. 15–68. Greenwich, CT: JAI Press.

KERR, C., DUNLOP, J., HARBISON, F., and MYERS, C. (1960) *Industrialism and Industrial Man*. New York: Oxford University Press.

KILOH, M. (1986) 'Industrial Democracy', in D. Held and C. Pollitt (eds), *New Forms of Democracy*. London: Sage.

KJELLBERG, A. (1998) 'Sweden: Restoring the Model?' in A. Ferner and R. Hyman (eds), *Changing Industrial Relations in Europe*. Oxford: Blackwell.

KOCHAN, T. and OSTERMAN, P. (1994) *The Mutual Gains Enterprise*. Boston, MA: Harvard Business School Press.

KRASNER, S. (1988) 'Sovereignty: An Institutional Perspective'. *Comparative Political Studies*, 21(1): 66–94.

LAFER, G. (2008) 'What's More Democratic Than a Secret Ballot? The Case for Majority Sign-up.' *Working USA*, (March): 71–98.

LEHMBRUCH, G. (2001) 'The Institutional Embedding of Market Economies: The German 'Model' and Its Impact on Japan', in W. Streeck and K. Yamamura, (eds), *The Origins of Nonliberal Capitalism: Germany and Japan in Comparison*, pp. 39–93. Ithaca, NY: Cornell University Press.

LICHTENSTEIN, N. (1993) 'Great Expectations: The Promise of Industrial Jurisprudence and its Demise, 1930–1960', in N. Lichtenstein and H. J. Harris (eds), *Industrial Democracy in America*, pp. 113–41. Cambridge: Cambridge University Press.

——(2002) *State of the Union: A Century of American Labor*. Princeton, NJ: Princeton University Press.

LIPSET, S. M. (1963) *The First New Nation: The United States in Historical and Comparative Perspective*. New York: Basic Books.

——(1964) 'Canada and the United States—A Comparative View.' *Canadian Review of Sociology and Anthropology*, 1: 173–85.

——and MELTZ, N. (1998) 'Canadian and American Attitudes Toward Work and Institutions'. *Perspectives on Work*, 1–3: 14–19.

LUKES, S. (1974) *Power: A Radical View*. London: Macmillan.

MAHONEY, J. (2000) 'Path Dependence in Historical Sociology.' *Theory and Society*, 29(4): 507–48.

MANICAS, P. (1987) *A History and Philosophy of the Social Sciences*. New York: Basil Blackwell.

OECD, (1994) *The OECD Jobs Study: Evidence and Implications*. Paris: OECD Publications.

——(2004) *Economic Outlook*. Paris: OECD Publications.

OLSEN, G.(1994) *The Struggle for Economic Democracy in Sweden*. Aldershott: Avebery/Gower.

——(2000) *Politics of the Welfare State*. Toronto: OUP.

——(2002) *The Politics of the Welfare State: Canada, Sweden, and the United States*. Don Mills, ON: Oxford University Press.

PEMPEL, T. J. (1998) *Regime Shift: Comparative Dynamics of the Japanese Political Economy*. Ithaca, NY: Cornell University Press.

PERLMAN, S. (1949 [1928]) *A Theory of the Labor Movement*. New York: Augustus M. Kelley.

PIERSON, P. (2000) 'Increasing Returns, Path Dependence, and the Study of Politics.' *American Political Science Review*, 94(2): 251–67.

——(2004) *Politics in Time*. Princeton, NJ: Princeton University Press.

POOLE, M. (1986) *Industrial Relations: Origins and Patterns of National Diversity*. London: Routledge and Kegan Paul.

POPE, J. G. (2002) 'The Thirteenth Amendment versus the Commerce Clause: Labor and the Shaping of American Constitutional Law, 1921–57.' *Columbia Law Review*, 102(1): 1–121.

RUSSELL, R. (1988) 'Forms and Extent of Employee Participation in the Contemporary United States', *Work and Occupations*, 15: 374–95.

SCHATZ, R. (1993) 'From Commons to Dunlop: Rethinking the Field and Theory of Industrial Relations'. in N. Lichtenstein and H. J. Harris (eds), *Industrial Democracy in America*. Cambridge: Cambridge University Press.

SCHMIDT, A. W. (1845) *Die Zunkunft fer arbeitenden Klassen und die Vereine fuer deren Wohl Eine Mahnung an die Zietgenossen*. Berlin.

SCHMOLLER, (1873) *Grundfragen des Rechtes and der Moral*. Berlin.

SEWELL, W. H. (1996) 'Three Temporalities: Toward an Eventful Sociology', in T. J. McDonald (ed.), *The Historic Turn in the Human Sciences*. Ann Arbor, MI: University of Michigan Press.

SLAUGHTER, M. (2007) 'Globalization and Declining Unionization in the United States'. *Industrial Relations*, 46(2): 329–46.

STETTES, O. (2007) 'Impact of Codetermination at Company Level.' Eironline, 2007-08-20.

STONE, K. (1981) 'The Post-War Paradigm in American Labor Law'. *The Yale Law Review*, vol. 90(7): 1511–80.

STRAUSS, G. (2006) 'Worker Participation—Some Under-Considered Issues'. *Industrial Relations*, 45(4): 778–803.

STREECK, W. and THELEN, K. (2004) 'Introduction: Institutional Change in Advanced Political Economies', in W. Streeck and K. Thelen (eds), *Beyond Continuity: Institutional Change in Advanced Political Economies*. Oxford: Oxford University Press.

TACKNEY, C. T. (2000) 'Changing Approaches to Employment Relations in Japan', in G. Bamber, F. Park, C. Lee, P. Ross, and K. Broadbent (eds), *Employment Relations in the Asia-Pacific: Changing Approaches*. New South Wales: Allen and Unwin.

TARAS, D. (1997) 'Collective Bargaining Regulation in Canada and the United States: Divergent Cultures, Divergent Outcomes', in B. Kaufman, *Government Regulation of the Employment Relationship*, (ed.), pp. 295–342. Madison, WI: IRRA.

TEUTEBERG, H. J. (1961) *Geschichte der industriellen Mitbestimmung in Deutschland*. Tuebingen: J. C. B. Mohr.

THELEN, K. (1999) 'Historical Institutionalism in Comparative Politics'. *The Annual Review of Political Science*, 2: 369–404.

——(2000) 'Why German Employers Cannot Bring Themselves to Dismantle the German Model', in T. Iversen, J. Pontusson, and D. Soskice (eds), *Unions, Employers, and Central Banks*, pp. 138–72. Cambridge: Cambridge University Press.

——(2004) *How Institutions Evolve: The Political Economy of Skills in Germany, Britain, the United States, and Japan*. Cambridge: Cambridge University Press.

TOCQUEVILLE, A. DE (1998 [1835]) *Democracy in America*. Hertfordshire: Wordsworth.

TOMLINS, C. (1985) 'The New Deal, Collective Bargaining, and the Triumph of Industrial Pluralism'. *Industrial and Labor Relations Review*, 39(1): 19–34.

WEBER, M. (1930 [1905]) *The Protestant Ethic and the Spirit of Capitalism* (T. PARSONS, Trans.) New York: Scribner's.

WEILER, P. and MUNDLAK, G. (1993) 'New Directions for the Law of the Workplace.' *The Yale Law Journal*, 102(8): 1907–25.

WOOD, S. and GODARD, J. (1999) 'The Statutory Recognition Procedure in the Employment Relations Bill: A Comparative Analysis', *British Journal of Industrial Relations*, 37(2): 203–45.

WOODIWISS, A. (1990) *Rights vs. Conspiracy: A Sociological Essay on the History of Labor Law in the United States.* New York: Berg.

WRIGHT MILLS, C. (1948) *The New Men of Power.* New York: A. M. Kelley.

CHAPTER 23

EMPLOYEE PARTICIPATION IN DEVELOPING AND EMERGING COUNTRIES

GEOFFREY WOOD

WORK and employment relations vary not only according to individual strategic choices by managers, and actions and responses by employees, but also by the social and economic context. Hence, the nature and extent of participation within organizations is likely not only to vary according to the size of firm, the type of firm, and the industry in which it is located, but also its geographical locale. Development is a complex and multifaceted process of structural transformation, including economic and social changes (Przeworski et al., 2001: 1). While a common distinction is often drawn between the *first* and *third worlds,* that is between nations who have attained a degree of socio-economic development characterized by certain levels of income, productivity, investment, formal employment, technological deployment and a range of human capital indicators (Przeworski et al., 2001), the latter category is an extremely broad one in itself. It may encompass 'emerging market' nations such as Brazil and South Africa, which are characterized by advanced industrial sectors, developed capital and labour markets, and, indeed, pockets of great prosperity, and nations where economic activity centres around the production of unprocessed or semi-processed primary commodities, with only limited downstream industrial development. In this chapter, we primarily focus on this second category, although some attention is also devoted to the case of 'emerging markets'.

Defining Participation in Organizations

There is an extensive literature on participation in organizations; participation in organizations has a variety of meanings, reflecting differences in underlying value systems (Dachler and Wilpert, 1978: 1–2). Participation may range from cautious moves to involve employees in basic operational decisions to the genuine democratization of all aspects of working life (Dachler and Wilpert, 1978). There are two contrasting approaches to participation and involvement. First, participation and involvement may be viewed in moral terms, as a means of promoting fairness and democracy at the workplace; second, it may be viewed as a means of enhancing organizational efficiency (Brewster et al., 2007). The first is most commonly associated with the employment relations literature, and the second with the human relations tradition (Brewster et al., 2007). Although, it has been argued that both these objectives are mutually reconcilable (Kochan and Osterman, 2000), it is worth considering these differing objectives in their own right; hence, this chapter looks at the implications of a relative lack of progress in advancing participation and involvement in the developing world in both fairness and efficiency terms.

Although participation may take place at all levels of the organization, the most decisive changes in organizational mindsets can be brought about when it is broadened at the base of the organization; in other words, when a real redistribution of power takes place within the organization (Kolaja, 1982).

Parnell and Crandall (2001: 52) note, while the jury is out as to the specific productivity effects of participation, participation has the potential to improve employee satisfaction and performance. The latter represents a product of the greater extent to which employees will identify with their tasks (Scott-Ladd and Marshall, 2004: 646). However, the relative effectiveness of such programmes is contingent both on the degree of management buy-in, and the external and internal constraints on the genuine operationalization of such programmes (Scott-Ladd and Marshall, 2004). Meaningful participation is contingent on a viable organizational community, which in turn, depends on a basic degree of shared values and trust (Waddock, 1999: 332).

Participation, of course, varies greatly in scope and depth. Employers may seek to *involve* employees, through regular communication and through soliciting their views on a range of issues, which, however, the employer has no obligation to act on (Brewster et al., 2007). *Participation* would suggest that employees are accorded some say in the running of the enterprise; in other words, they may make decisions which are likely to be implemented—not merely considered—by management. However, the range and scope of these decisions is likely to vary greatly: involvement and participation represent places on a continuous scale, rather than discrete categories.

Employees may participate on an individual and direct basis: in other words, they may express opinions and work to implementing them on an individual basis, personally interacting with the representatives of management. Alternatively, they may participate on an indirect and representative basis as a collective: in other words, they may elect representatives to act on their behalf. On the one hand, this may make the representation of employee views less direct, and place a greater distance between employees and managers. On the other hand, representative and indirect mechanisms protect individual employees from victimization should their opinions not be well received by management, while managers are more likely to take the views of a collective workforce more seriously than those of an individual employee (Harcourt et al., 2004). These

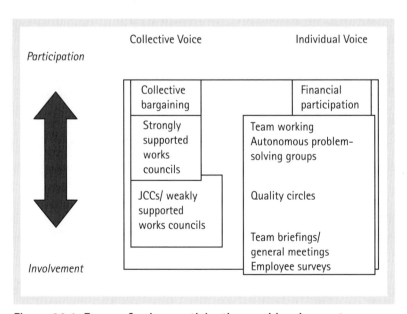

Figure 23.1 Forms of voice, participation, and involvement

Source: Brewster et al., 2007.

relationships are summarized in Figure 23.1, which provides examples of typical forms of participation and involvement.

THE DEVELOPING WORLD CONTEXT

Developing countries have performed highly unevenly over the past two decades. While, the Asian financial crisis notwithstanding, a number of countries in South-East Asia have performed generally well, the performance of most tropical African and many Latin American and central Asian economies has been generally poor.

As Miyho and Schiphorst (2002: 420) note, most African states have faced economic crisis for two decades: problems have included a stagnation and decline of industrial capacity, and a reliance on a few price volatile primary exports; the same can be said to be true for a large number of Latin American and, indeed, a number of South and East Asia countries. Debt crises in the 1980s led to the imposition of structural adjustment programmes by the World Bank and the International Monetary Fund (IMF). These programmes involve the cutting back of protective tariffs, wholesale privatizations, and general cutbacks in government spending (Kanaan, 2000; Rosser and Rosser, 2001). It was held that governments had no business in supporting 'uncompetitive' industries that could not cope with overseas competition, and that much state spending was wasted: indeed, even spending on basic education and health care could constitute the misallocation of economic resources that could otherwise have been retained by the private sector to promote commercial activity (Hanlon, 1996). In practice, these assumptions proved fatally flawed; the imposition of structural adjustment proved devastating to many developing economies, accelerating industrial decline, boosting unemployment, worsening social inequality, and gutting state education and training provisions. This represented the product of two flaws in the underlying logic of such programmes. First, such programmes ignored the human factor: not only did the effects of large-scale unemployment prove devastating for domestic demand and in terms of general quality of life, but they also resulted 'in a crisis of worsening human skills' (Miyho and Schiphorst, 2001: 424; Rosser and Rosser, 2001). Second, such programmes were widely over-optimistic regarding the revenues that could be generated through the export of many primary commodities, and ignored the tendency of developed nations to dump heavily subsidized agricultural surpluses into the developing world (Miyho and Schiphorst, 2001).

Wide scale public service cutbacks and over-hasty privatizations, and the collapse of much indigenous industry have resulted in the informal sector playing an increasingly important role; indeed, the latter plays a central role in economic activity in the developing world.

ALTERNATIVE APPROACHES TO THINKING ABOUT DEVELOPMENT AND PARTICIPATION

Classic Accounts of Development and Participation

The underlying causes of this poor performance have been the subject of intense academic debate. *Modernization* theories held that all societies were subject to a process of evolution from simple to complex forms: in looking at the developing world, modernization theories focused on perceived indigenous barriers to progress, and the role that indigenous elites could play in creating the conditions more conducive to growth (Williams and Wildebank, 2000). Organizations encountered in the developing world would tend to be in an early or transitionary phase en route to a more advanced future; in time, advanced production paradigm—and modes of participation—will gradually disseminate in line with broader social progress. Modernization theories informed Western-sponsored development and aid policies in the 1950s and 1960s, but fell into disrepute as a result of the economic collapse of many developing world economies in the 1970s.

Dependency theories focused on the external relations between developing world states and the metropole: it was held that the latter, assisted by the local bourgeoisie, locked the continent into a junior and subservient trading status through crippling debt (Amsden, 1990). This would involve distorted local economic development, centring on trade and distribution, rather than autonomous and balanced economic development. A major social divide would exist between a 'junior', local elite, and an impoverished majority, engaged in peasant production and other low scale survival-level economic activities. Cheap exports of primary materials would be contingent on high levels of labour repression; local elites discipline and control labour to ensure low cost production of agricultural products and minerals. There is some evidence to support the latter assumptions: structural adjustment programmes have forced developing nations to open up their markets to international competition, while many developing nations continue to heavily protect and subsidize agricultural and other politically sensitive sectors. Hence, there can be no automatic assumption of development either at societal or organizational level. Indeed, the predominance of low-value-added production paradigms would encompass autocratic managerial styles, with little room for autonomy or participation by employees.

Contemporary Institutional Approaches

Later neo-institutionalist *theories of the failure of the state* argued that one of the primary causes of the continent's poor performance was the narrow social base of the state, and the debilitating effects of informal extended networks of support (Hyden, 2002). Again, however, there was an underlying assumption as to a social-political context poorly conducive to economic growth or development.

The Varieties of Capitalism (VofC) literature holds that firms, and the manner in which they are governed, play a central role in defining the broader political economy (Hall and Soskice, 2001: 4). Firms seek to develop their *core competencies* and/or their *dynamic capabilities*; these decisions are moulded by relationships with key stakeholders; the success of the firm is contingent on its ability to coordinate these relationships (Hall and Soskice, 2001: 6). These challenges of coordination are posed at a range of levels. First, there is the employment rela-tionship between employers and employees, in terms of security of tenure, and voice mechanisms. Second, and related to this is the degree of investment in human capital development. Third, there are inter-firm relationships along supply chains, which may be tenuous or stable, more collaborative or on lines of clear subordin-ation and domination. Fourth, there is the issue of corporate governance, includ-ing sources of investment funds, and the nature—and timescale of returns—expected by investors. (Hall and Soskice, 2001: 7). Initial dichotomous theories focused their attention on two clusters of advanced societies, liberal market economies (such as Britain and the United States) and collaborative market economies (such as Germany, Japan, and Scandinavia) (Hall and Soskice, 2001; Lincoln and Kalleberg, 1990). Later multi-variety theories argued that in fact several distinct varieties of capitalism existed, others being encountered in South-ern and Eastern Europe, and parts of the Far East (Amable, 2003; Whitley, 1999). While it may be easy to merely dismiss large areas of the developing world as simply in a transitional phase to liberal or collaborative markets, this cannot explain the fact that many countries in the south remain locked on a distinct trajectory of mediocre performance, lop-sided economic activity, and specific forms of organizational structure and work relations.

Wood and Frynas (2006) argue that tropical African countries can constitute a business system in their own right: the *segmented business system*, defined by 'the central role played by informal networks interpenetrating the indigenous elite, and the concentration of activity in the metropole—both in the hands of a relatively small commercial and industrial class—and TNCs (Transnational Corporations)'. Wood and Frynas (2006) go on to argue that work and employment relations in segmented business systems are dualistic in nature, with a key division being between large organizations, encountered in the MNC and state sectors, and the indigenous sector, the latter dominated by small, family-owned firms. In the former, there may be some elements of pluralism, but these are likely to be constrained by the poor bargaining position of employees, and the tendency for governments to cut back on state spending—and hence, employment in the state sector—in response to pressures from the World Bank and the IMF. In the latter, managerial strategies tend to be highly autocratic, with industrial relations legislation being widely ignored (Wood and Frynas, 2006). Yet, the latter category of employer may have personalized relations of employees, extending to the use of informal credit, and recruitment via informal family networks. In neither context is there much room for meaningful participation, given both the great weakness of employees, and the intense short term competitive pressures faced by employers: as a result, most firms have neither the capability nor the interest in progressing beyond low cost, low-value-added production paradigms, characterized by autocratic management. Any attempt to invest in people—either through significantly higher pay or higher levels of participation—will result in competitors seizing short term cost advantage (Wood and Frynas, 2006). Hence, while participation may be morally desirable, and/ or conducive to higher-value-added production paradigms, firms lack the capacity and incentives to move beyond the low-value-added labour repressive present.

Cultural Accounts

Hofstede (1980, 1991) argued that different cultures are associated with variations in power distance, individualism–collectivism, uncertainty avoidance, and masculinity–femininity. Central to the relative viability of participation is power distance: cultures with a high power distance—such as those of South-East Asia— are associated with autocratic managerial-styles, and centralized powers (Habir and Larasti, 1999: 549; Yukongdi, 2001: 388, 400). More broadly speaking, cross-cultural accounts of HRM in developing countries have drawn attention to the general lack of participatory management, and great power imbalances between employers and employees (Jackson, 2002: 1008); in other words, cultural reasons lie at the base of low levels of participation—and ultimately, poor organizational performance—in many developing world economies. Conversely, countries with a closer power distance—most typically, liberal market economies in the developed world—are, it is assumed, more conducive environments for the greater empowerment of workforces (Habir and Larasti, 1999). Paternalistic authority of management is commonly accepted, and employees are widely accepting of status differences (Habir and Larasti, 1999: 549).

Also of importance is the relative individualism versus collectivism: higher individualism may make employees more likely to make use of individual oppor-tunities for participation, but this may undermine efforts to promote participation on a collective basis; this may offset some of the disadvantages posed by high power distances. This model has informed some of the recent thinking on the 'African renaissance': it is argued that a culture of collectivism ('ubuntu') may advance more communitarian policies within organizations, allowing for closer cooper-ation between a firm and its people (Karsten and Illa, 2005). However, this literature sheds only limited light on the possibilities for squaring cooperation and productivity with equity and the democratization of working life; little atten-tion is given to the abiding inequality that is commonly embedded in the formal employment contract or how this may be offset through latent communitarianism in a manner that accords employees consistent rights.

A more general limitation of cultural accounts is that they presume specific outcomes for particular societies, when complex differences in organizational practices may be encountered within particular social spaces, and over time (Hollingsworth, 2006). Indeed, empirical research has yielded contradictory outcomes regarding the predicted effects of different cultures on organizational practice in this regard (Habir and Larasti, 1999: 549); there is little evidence to suggest that many developing societies can simply be dismissed as infertile grounds for empowerment, especially given changes in both macroeconomic realities and firm level practices over time.

Linear Path Dependence or Evolution?

Both institutionalist accounts and cultural explanations underscore the relative durability of national 'ways of doing things' (Hollingsworth, 2006; Wisman, 1999); there is insufficient evidence to conclude societies are converging on one common model (Lewis et al., 2004). Hence, models of participation that are encountered in developing world settings do not necessarily represent way stations en route towards 'advanced' models of participation and involvement in their own right, but rather systems that are likely to persist and develop on distinct lines. However, such accounts assume path dependence. This is particularly the case with culturalist accounts, whose understanding of culture has departed little from classic functionalism (Bacharach, 1989). At the same time, the ability of national systems—and sets of firm practices—to develop, change, and infuse practices encountered elsewhere does not mean that they are not likely to retain unique features and develop new ones (Hollingsworth, 2006).

REPRESENTATIVE VOICE IN THE
DEVELOPING WORLD

This leads us to the question of the relative effectiveness of representative voice in the developing world: that is participation that is both delegated and representative. Hyman (1997) argues that central aspects of employee representation on a collective basis encompass autonomy, legitimacy, and efficiency. First, the ability to articulate an effective employee voice on a representative basis requires filtering and prioritizing, which in turn, requires a degree of strategic perspective. Second, any representatives have to be legitimate; the latter has to be sustained by delivery, which may be difficult in hard times (Hyman, 1997). Third, there is the question of efficiency, in representatives' ability to encourage and enable their constituents to own policy goals and act effectively; this should be seen as distinct from overall organizational efficiency issues. Two key problems emerge here of particular relevance to the developing world.

First, as noted above, an inability of representatives to deliver on the basic concerns of employees may undermine the entire process (Hyman, 1997). The imposition of neo-liberal structural adjustment programmes in large areas of the developing world has, in the affected countries, forced wholesale job shedding in the formal sector as a result of a reduced role for the state and state-owned enterprises, privatizations, and the cutting back of protective tariffs. In turn, this is likely to undermine the basis of participation, both in terms of the capacity of employers to make meaningful concessions regarding employment security (and hence, for employee representatives to be seen to deliver to their constituents), and the underlying foundations of organizational trust. Second, poor organizational capacity of unions and other employee collectives in many areas of the developing world may make it difficult to adequately filter and articulate employee demands (Hyman, 1997). Again, this is likely to undermine the basis of organizational participation.

Optimistic theories of contemporary empowerment suggest that, as organizations evolve to more complex forms, more advanced forms of participation and involvement are likely to emerge (Scarnati and Scarnati, 2002). On the other hand, it can be argued that more complex organizations are likely to be associated with higher levels of alienation, which, in turn, may prompt employees to take participative mechanisms less seriously (Geyer, 1994: 17). Hence, it cannot be assumed that participation and involvement will naturally expand in both incidence and depth as organizations become more complex in a developing world setting.

DOMINANT MODELS OF PARTICIPATION IN THE DEVELOPING WORLD

Peripheral Fordism Revisited

As Wood and Frynas (2006) argue, both pre-colonial and colonial societies left a legacy of paternalism in the workplace: this has led to the persistence of Taylorist (and pre-Taylorist) work systems, characterized by authoritarianism, fixed divisions of labour, limited and informal training (also a product of weak local training institutions), and low levels of participation and involvement. On the one hand, it could be argued that increased consumer pressures have forced indigenous firms linked to global commodity chains to upgrade their practices. On the other hand, it can be argued that, in the operation of such networks, labour standards continue to receive a low priority when compared to cost or quality concerns (Mellahi and Wood, 2002). Again, insecure tenure has become the norm in most tropical African states, compounded by wholesale job shedding as a result of SAPs.

In an influential account, Lipietz (1987) suggested that, in the face of declining profits, firms intensified efforts from the 1960s onwards to establish manufacturing plants in a selected number of low wage economies, with deregulated labour markets and a lack of institutional restraints on extreme labour repression, employing workers—often women—with little previous work experience (Sum, 2007). Geared towards exports, such activities did little to promote the development of internal markets, and faced the omnipresent threat of even cheaper competition from elsewhere in the developing world (Sum, 2007).

Broad (1990) argues that 'bloody Taylorism' potentially represents neither an aberration nor a transitory phase: super exploitation of labour is inevitable given both intense global competition and uneven regulation. While debt crises, popular backlashes, and rising civil discontent may drive compromises both within and beyond the workplace, it is likely that such processes will be both messy and contested (Broad, 1990). Indeed, there has been rising social inequality in many developing countries, corresponding with worsening conditions of employment and the decline of good work: secure employment under reasonable terms and conditions of service (Soucek, 1993). Indeed, it can be argued that labour repression, rather than simply being inefficient, has proved an effective means for powerful elites to accumulate resources: hence, there are few immediate incentives to move over to higher-value-added production paradigms even if, in the long term, they may be more conducive to sustainable high value added production (Broad, 1990; Wood and Frynas, 2006).

Paternalism

Much of the literature on paternalism treats it as a symptom of early industrialization: highly personalized relationships in relatively small organizations (Fleming, 2004: 1469). Paternalism derives from 'patriarchy', with employees gaining 'fatherly' support in return for loyalty and obedience. Underlying it are dependence, and a demand that subordinates defer to the moral judgement of their seniors, Fleming, 2004: 1470;   (also see Aycan et al., 2006). In much of the developing world, paternalist relations remain common, with family, clan, and community relationships interweaving the employment relationship (Khan and Ackers, 2004: 130).

Smith et al. (2004: 204) point out that paternalism can constitute a non-wage form of retention. It represents a form of corporate integration that goes beyond the wage relationship (Montgomery, quoted in Smith et al., 2004: 394). Contemporary studies on paternalism comparing paternalism in non-Western contexts—most notably China—with earlier Western manifestations, depict it as either a 'throw back' or transitional phase en route to more advanced managerial paradigms (Fleming, 2004: 1470). It has been argued that paternalist authority is eroded by market pressures that force the employer to become ever more focused on the 'bottom line', driving the employment relationship to a strictly contractual model (Warren, 1999: 52). However, there is considerable evidence to suggest that elements of paternalism persist in Western organizations: paternalist ways of doing things may be remarkably durable, especially in relation to historically disadvantaged categories of labour, such as 'women's work' (Fleming, 2004). Paternalism has political and ideological dimensions, reconstituting subordination within and beyond the workplace (Fleming, 2004).

In might seem that an organization characterized by paternalist managerial strategies might accord little room to employee participation. However, while decision-making power—and moral authority—remains vested in the hands of central management, relations between manager and worker are relatively close and personal. This would mean frequent meetings between management and employees, on either formal or informal lines (Webster and Wood, 2005). While the agenda of such meetings is likely to be strictly top down, space would be left for limited employee feedback or dialogue, as a way of cementing the close and personal nature of the relationship (Fleming, 2004; Warren, 1999; Webster and Wood, 2005). A fiction of a 'free and fair' negotiation process is maintained to strengthen the moral foundations of managerial power (Warren, 1999). Nor would such feedback or dialogue be confined to workplace issues: it may concern aspects of the employee's personal life and family circumstances, with the employer's moral judgements regarding personal behaviour being paralleled with moral and financial support. The latter may be expressed through loans and advances on wages, for unexpected expenses, such as weddings and funerals (Wood and Frynas, 2006).

Optimistic accounts have suggested that in a range of different contexts, notions of shared commitment may evolve into more equitable forms of participation (Aycan et al., 2000). However, more critical accounts have suggested that the scope of any dialogue is likely to be focused on the employee's own condition and how he or she may serve the wider organizational family best, rather than making the organization more receptive or accommodating to individual concerns regarding wages and the conditions of work: serious decision making remains firmly in the hands of management (Warren, 1999: 50). While informal credit may alleviate short-term financial hardship, it further serves to lock an employee into a cycle of dependency and commitment without reciprocal concessions from management, and may, at worst, degenerate into debt servitude (Wood and Frynas, 2006).

Hence, any participation within the paternalist model is likely to be closely confined and directly aimed at ensuring that the individual provides adequate 'service' in return for the organization's 'support', rather than a genuine sharing of power. While paternalist relationships are—theoretically speaking at least—about mutual commitment, there is little evidence to suggest that, in practice, organizations characterized by paternalist approaches to management are any less inclined to shed labour in the case of organizational need (Webster and Wood, 2005). Finally, as noted above, paternalist managerial approaches may be remarkably durable, and persist even in mature industrial societies: there is no evidence to suggest that, over time, it will automatically soften into more equitable forms of participation and involvement.

Participation in the Informal Sector

As noted above, the informal sector constitutes a crucially important area of economic activity in the developing world. While optimistic accounts argue that the informal sector can provide a stepping stone for entrepreneurs wishing to enter the formal sector, more realistic explanations have pointed to the insecure and marginal nature of most informal sector activity (Maloney, 1999; Stewart and Berry, 2000). Indeed, informal sector activity has tended to proliferate following the imposition of structural adjustment programmes, which have had the effect of greatly reducing employment in the formal sector (Stewart and Berry, 2000). The informal sector represents a productive system built around the usage of labour on an informal and open-ended basis, generally outside of formal labour law (Nyssens and Van der Linden, 2000). In many instances, it represents a survival strategy of last resort, locking those involved into a vicious circle of social exclusion (Rosser and Rosser, 2001). A very large proportion of the world's population has been forced to turn to the informal sector for survival (Williams and Wildebank, 2000; Wood and Brewster, 2007).

Work in the informal sector tends to be marginal, dangerous, insecure and poorly rewarded: yet, it can be argued that informal sector work represents the *typical employment relationship encountered in Africa* (Wood and Brewster, 2007). Those engaged in informal sector activity are often both workers and owners, and/or with employees being immediate family members: hence boundaries of management and worker may be blurred. This makes any attempt at collective representation via unions extremely difficult: 'politically powerful informal *traders' associations* in many parts of Africa tend to have populist–reformist orientations, and are often closer to political elites than the bulk of those employed in this area' (Wood and Brewster, 2007).

Within informal enterprises, supervision by the owner–entrepreneur is likely to be direct and personal (Rogerson and Preston-Whyte, 1991). Any participation encountered is likely to be individual and ad hoc, representing a response more to limitations in managerial capacity rather than a genuine desire to democratize working life. In practice, this means that employees marketing goods and services in locations remote from the immediate presence of the owner are still closely bound to the latter through relations of extreme dependency, often debt, and, in the case of underground and peripheral areas of the informal sector, even by the threat of physical retaliation in the event of misconduct.

PARTICIPATION IN ORGANIZATIONS IN EMERGING MARKETS

In contrast to much of the third world, a limited number of emerging market economies, most notably India, Brazil, South Africa, and China, have enjoyed robust growth, underpinned by strong performance of export industries in the 1990s and 2000s. There are a very wide range of models of participation encountered in such contexts. This section provides a particular focus on the cases of South Africa and China.

In countries such as South Africa and Brazil, labour movements remain strong, and this has moulded the nature and extent of participation. As Jackson (2002) notes, the developed/developing world dichotomy is a somewhat misleading one, in that it assumes that the former simply represents a way station or a diversion en route to the latter, and, hence, discounts the possibility that developing nations may find new, innovative and/or more equitable HR paradigms than those encountered in the developed world (Khan and Ackers, 2004).

For example, in the case of South Africa, many organizations have shifted from autocratic racial Fordism—Fordist methods combined with a racial division of authority and labour—towards more inclusivist paradigms. Such paradigms include the use of a wide range of participative forums, supplementing robust and inclusive collective bargaining (Jackson, 1999). The key role of the unions in driving the transition forced firms to adopt more pluralist approaches to industrial relations, shifts that preceded the demise of apartheid; the post-apartheid era has seen a shift towards more participative models of management (Templer et al., 1997: 559). Such participative models typically combine the *representative participation of collective bargaining,* with a range of more direct forms of participation and involvement, including quality circles, green areas, and team working. In part, this has been impelled by both the strength of organized labour, and the generally acknowledged need to promote greater equity as a means of redressing some of the wrongs of apartheid (Visagie, 1999: 159). The use of high-value-added production paradigms in manufacturing have greatly boosted productivity, and supplanted the trench warfare industrial relations of late apartheid, contributing to South Africa's robust export performance in manufactured goods, such as motor cars, in the 2000s. Again, more democratic practices at the workplace have helped promote greater equity, eroding the apartheid-era racial division of labour and decision making. However, such advanced production paradigms have yet to penetrate most rural areas and SMEs. Much labour repression persists in both conservative areas of the formal sector, such as large areas of agriculture, and the informal sector; significantly, the trade union movement has failed to make headway in either area.

Jackson (2002: 1011) points to pressures to promote consensus based participation within the *African Renaissance* model, discussed above; this would centre on shared notions of collective responsibility and trust. Indeed, Khan and Ackers (2004: 336) note that personal and community relationships have done much to mitigate the effects of wholesale job cuts: extended personal networks of support have alleviated some of the most adverse consequences of structural adjustment policies.

Following on the 1949 revolution, China sought to adopt a lifelong provision of social services, the 'iron rice bowl' model, centring on employment in state-owned companies: rhetoric of worker rights masked autocracy, mitigated by high levels of employment security. From the 1980s onwards, market-driven reforms have challenged the established paradigm: this has led to the diffusion of Western HR practices, but also to the erosion of the 'iron rice bowl' model (Law et al., 2003; Warner, 2004). While the low wages and low consumption paradigm that characterized it has persisted in many organizations, this has been worsened by rising health, housing, and education costs, and by greatly reduced security of tenure (Warner, 2003: 23, 2004: 632): hence, while some firms have infused aspects of advanced HR systems, others have reverted to a de facto 'bloody Fordist' paradigm that has characterized employment relations in much of the developed world (Gamble et al., 2004). In the latter instance, work organization is fragmented, training rudimentary, and any communications simply top-down and one way: the use of such paradigms would reflect the extent to which many corporations based in the developed world have 'hollowed out' productive activities that lend themselves to routinization, limited HR capacities in host regions, and a lack of institutional restraints on the use of such paradigms (Gamble et al., 2004). Again, autonomous interest in sustaining participation may be weak unless sustained by the wider institutional context: employees may focus on personal concerns related to day-to-day physical survival, and hence have little interest in the wider democratization of work (Tang, 1993: 936). In summary, the Chinese model remains a mixed one, with advanced participative forms of HRM making few gains outside of a few major urban centres and firms.

CONCLUSION

Outside of a few 'islands' of economic activity, characterized by sophisticated production paradigms, the levels of participation and involvement encountered in the developing world are generally low. However, while peripheral Fordist practices are widespread—and have indeed made gains in privatized state enterprises, where unions have been unable to check the wholesale abandonment of pluralist employment relations polices—they are by no means the only paradigm encountered. Within the informal sector, even bleaker forms of labour repression are the norm. While paternalist managerial policies—often encountered in family-owned enterprises—acknowledge some responsibilities towards the employees, they again centre on the concentration of power in the hands of managers. At the same time, the ability of a number of developing societies—such as South Africa—to reform work and social relations challenge notions of path dependence: while the balance of global forces and the concentration of power would seemingly mitigate against the advancement of greater equity within the workplace in most areas of the developing world, the infusion of higher-value-added production paradigms—in the interests of longer term productivity and/or equity—cannot be ruled out. As Hollingsworth (2006) notes, the evolution of both wider regulation and firm practices may assume a non-linear form, allowing for the periodic emergence and diffusion of alternative models, models that will allow employees a greater say in the running of firms for fairness and sustainability.

References

AMABLE, B. (2003) *The Diversity of Modern Capitalism*. Oxford: Oxford University Press.

AMSDEN, A. (1990) 'Third World Industrialization: Global Fordism or a New Model', *New Left Review*, 1: 5–31.

AYCAN, Z., KANUNGO, R., MENDONCA, M., YU, K., DELLER, J., STAHL, G., and KURSHID, A. (2006) 'Impact of Culture on Human Resource Practices: A Ten Country Study', *Applied Psychology: An International Review*, 49(1): 192–221.

BACHARACH, S. (1989) 'Organizational Theories: Some Criteria for Evaluation', *Academy of Management Review*, 14(4): 496–515.

BREWSTER, C., WOOD, G., CROUCHER, R., and BROOKES, M. (2007) 'Collective and Individual Voice: Convergence in Europe?' *International Journal of Human Resource Management* (in print).

BROAD, D. (1990) 'Mirages and Miracles: The Crisis of Global Fordism', *Monthly Review* (March).

DACHLER, P. H. and WILPERT, B. (1978) 'Conceptual Dimensions and Boundaries of Participation in Organizations', *Administrative Science Quarterly*, 23(1): 1–39.

FLEMING, P. (2004) 'Kindergarten Cop: Paternalism and Resistance in a High Commitment Organization', *Journal of Management Studies*, 42(7): 1469–89.

GAMBLE, J., MORRIS, J., and WILKINSON, B. (2004) 'Mass Production is Alive and Well: The Future of Work and Organization in South-East Asia', *International Journal of Human Resource Management*, 15(2): 397–409.

GEYER, F. (1994) 'Alienation, Participation and Increasing Social Complexity', *Kybernetics*, 23(2): 10–34.

HABIR, A. and LARASTI, A. (1999) 'Human Resource Management as Competitive Advantage in the New Millennium', *International Journal of Manpower*, 20(8): 548–62.

HALL, P. and SOSKICE, D. (eds) (2001) *Varieties of Capitalism: The Institutional Foundations of Competitive Advantage*. Oxford: Oxford University Press.

HANLON, J. (1996) *Peace without Profit: How the IMF Blocks Rebuilding in Mozambique*. Oxford: James Currey.

HARCOURT, M., HARCURT, S., and WOOD, G. (2004) 'Do Unions Affect Employer Compliance with the Law?' *British Journal of Industrial Relations*, 42(3): 527–41.

HOFSTEDE, G. (1980) *Culture's Consequences: International Differences in Work-Related Values*. Beverly Hills, CA: Sage.

—— (1991) *Cultures and Organizations*. London: McGraw-Hill.

HOLLINGSWORTH, J. R. (2006) In G. Wood and P. James (eds), *Advancing our Understanding of Capitalism Through Niels Bohr's Thinking about Complementarity, Institutions, Production and Working Life*. Oxford: Oxford University Press.

HYDEN, G. (2002) 'Rethinking the Study of African Politics', in R. Haines and G. Wood, *Postmodernism in Africa*. Port Elizabeth: IPDR.

HYMAN, R. (1997) 'The Future of Employee Representation', *British Journal of Industrial Relations*, 35(3): 309–36.

JACKSON, T. (1999) 'Managing Change in South Africa: Developing People and Organizations', *International Journal of Human Resource Management*, 10(2): 306–26.

—— (2002) 'Reframing Human Resource Management in Africa: A Cross Cultural Perspective', *International Journal of Human Resource Management*, 13(7): 998–1018.

KANAAN, O. (2000) 'Tanzania's Experiment with Trade Liberalization', *Finance and Development*, 37(2): 30–33.

KARSTEN, L. and ILLA, H. (2005) 'Ubuntu as a Key African Management Concept: Contextual Background and Practical Insights for Knowledge Application', *Journal of Managerial Psychology*, 20(7): 607–20.

KHAN, A. and ACKERS, P. (2004) 'Neo-Pluralism as a Theoretical Framework for Understanding HRM in Sub-Saharan Africa', *International Journal of Human Resource Management*, 15(7): 1330–53.

KOCHAN, T. and OSTERMAN, P. (2000) 'The Mutual Gains Enterprise', in C. Mabey, G. Salaman, and J. Storey (eds), *Strategic Human Resource Management*. London: Sage.

KOLAJA, J. (1982) 'Worldwide Interest in Worker Participation in Management', *American Journal of Economics and Sociology*, 41(2): 211–13.

LAW, K., TSE, D., and ZSHOU, N. (2003) 'Does Human Resource Management Matter in a Transitional Economy', *Journal of International Business Studies*, 34(3): 255–65.

LEWIS, D., MACHOLD, S., OXTOBY, D., and AHMED, P. (2004) 'Employee Roles in Governance', *Corporate Governance*, 4(4): 16–28.

LINCOLN, J. and KALLEBERG, A. (1990) *Culture, Control and Commitment: A Study of Work Organization in the United States and Japan*. Cambridge: Cambridge University Press.

LIPIETZ, A. (1987) *Mirages and Miracles*. London: Verso.

MALONEY, W. (1999) 'Does Informality Imply Segmentation in Urban Labor Markets: Evidence from Mexico', *World Bank Economic Review*, 13(2): 275–310.

MELLAHI, K. and WOOD, G. (2002) 'Desparately Seeking Stability: The Remaking of the Saudi Arabian Labour Market', *Competition and Change*, 6(4): 345–62.

MIYHO, P. and SCHIPHORST, F. (2001) 'Africa: A Context of Sharp Economic Decline', in J. Kelly (ed.), *Industrial Relations: Critical Readings in Business and Management—Volume 1*. London: Routledge.

NYSSENS, M. and VAN DER LINDEN, B. (2000) 'Embeddedness, Cooperation and Popular Economic Firms in the Informal Sector', *Journal of Development Economics*, 61(1): 175–204.

PARNELL, J. and CRANDALL, W. (2001) 'Rethinking Participative Decision Making', *Personnel Review*, 31(3): 523–35.

PRZEWORSKI, A., ALVAREZ, M., CHELBUB, J., and LIMONGI, F. (2001) *Democracy and Development*. Cambridge: Cambridge University Press.

ROGERSON, C. and PRESTON-WHYTE, E. (1991) 'South Africa's Informal Economy: Past, Present and Future', in E. Preston-Whyte, and C. Rogerson (eds), *South Africa's Informal Economy*. Cape Town: Oxford University Press.

ROSSER, J. and ROSSER, M. (2001) 'Another Failure of the Washington Consensus', *Challenge*, 44(2): 39–50.

SCARNATI, J. and SCARNATI, B. (2002) 'Empowerment: The Key to Quality', *TQM Magazine*, 14(2): 110–19.

SCOTT-LADD, B. and MARSHALL, V. (2004) 'Participation in Decision-Making: A Matter of Context', *Leadership and Organization Development Journal*, 25(8): 646–52.

SMITH, C., DASKALAKI, M., ELGER, T., and BROWN, D. (2004) 'Labour Turnover and Management Retention Strategies in New Plants', *International Journal of Human Resource Management*, 15(2): 371–96.

SOUCEK, V. (1993) 'Post-Fordist Workplace', Paper presented to the AARE Annual Conference in Fremantle, 21–25 November.

STEWART, F. and BERRY, A. (2000) 'Globalization, Liberalization and Inequality', *Challenge*, 43(1): 44–92.

SUM, N. (2007) 'Theorizing Export-Oriented Economic Development in East Asian Newly-Industrializing Countries: A Regulationist Perspective', Department of Politics, Lancaster University. www.lancs.ac.uk/fss/politics/people/ngailing/exportism.doc.

TANG, W. (1993) 'Workplace Participation in Chinese Local Industries', *American Journal of Political Science*, 37(3): 920–40.

TEMPLER, A., HOFMEYR, K., and RALL, J. (1997) 'An International Comparison of Human Resource Management Objectives and Activities', *International Journal of Human Resource Management*, 8(4): 550–62.

VISAGIE, J. (1999) 'The Influence of Affirmative Action on SMME Culture in South Africa', *Participation and Empowerment: An International Journal*, 7(6): 148–72.

WADDOCK, J. (1999) 'Linking Community and Spirit', *Leadership and Organization Development Journal*, 12(4): 332–47.

WARNER, M. (2003) 'China's HRM Revisited: A Stepwise Path Towards Convergence', *Asia Pacific Business Review*, 9(4): 15–22.

—— (2004) 'Human Resource Management in China: An Introduction', *International Journal of Human Resource Management*, 15(5): 617–34.

WARREN, R. (1999) 'Against Paternalism in Human Resource Management', *Business Ethics: A European Review*, 8(1): 50–59.

WEBSTER, E. and WOOD, G. (2005) 'Human Resource Management Practice and Institutional Constraints', *Employee Relations*, 27(4): 369–85.

WHITLEY, R. (1999) *Divergent Capitalisms*. Oxford: Oxford University Press.

WILLIAMS, C. and WILDEBANK, J. (2000) 'Beyond Employment: An Examination of Modes of Service Provision in a Depressed Neighbourhood', *The Service Industries Journal*, 20(4): 33–46.

WISMAN, J. (1999) 'Should Formerly Socialist Economies Attempt to Leapfrog Classical Capitalism?', *International Journal of Social Economics*, 20(2): 12–26.

WOOD, G. and BREWSTER, C. (2007) 'Introduction: Comprehending Industrial Relations in Africa', in G. Wood, and C. Brewster (eds), *Industrial Relations in Africa*. London: Palgrave.

WOOD, G. and FRYNAS, G. (2006) 'The Institutional Basis of Economic Failure: Anatomy of the Segmented Business System', *Socio-Economic Review*, 4(2): 239–77.

YUKONGDI, V. (2001) 'Teams and TQM: A Comparison between Australia and Thailand', *International Journal of Quality and Reliability Management*, 18(4): 387–403.

....

CHAPTER 24

INTERNATIONAL AND COMPARATIVE PERSPECTIVES ON EMPLOYEE PARTICIPATION

....

NICK WAILES

RUSSELL D. LANSBURY

INTRODUCTION

....

How do we account for similarities and differences in participation patterns across countries and firms? Empirical studies have consistently suggested that there are persistent cross-national differences in patterns of employee participation (Gill and Kreiger, 1995; Poole at al., 2001). This implies that national level factors play an important role in determining the form and incidence of participation and that comparative analysis is likely to provide important insights into some of the key causal drivers of participation. In earlier work, we have argued that a *Varieties of Capitalism* (VofC) approach, based on the work of Hall and Soskice (2001), can be used to explain national differences in the incidence and forms of direct participation. (Lansbury and Wailes, 2007). However, while a VofC approach can help explain differences across countries, closer examination of the empirical evidence on participation suggests a more complex explanatory task. First, while the incidence and nature of participation varies from country to country, there is also evidence of within country diversity in the adoption and effectiveness of these practices. Second, there is growing evidence of an international dimension to employee involvement and participation. Recent research suggests that multinational companies (MNCs) play a role in diffusing participatory practices from their home country operations to their subsidiaries in other countries (Almond and Tempel, 2006). Similarly, the implementation of the European Works Council directive in the European Union has seen the emergence of direct forms of participation in countries where there is no established tradition of this type of worker involvement.

In this chapter we seek to modify and extend the VofC approach in a way that makes it possible for it to account for both within country diversity and the role that international factors play in shaping national patterns of participation. It does so by drawing on recent debates about the VofC approach in general and comparative corporate governance in particular. Both these literatures suggest the need for VofC analysis to adopt a less deterministic view of the role that institutions play in shaping social action, to focus more on the role of agency and interests, and suggest the need to explore the interconnections between countries in more detail. We use this modified VofC framework to examine the extent to which it can help explain recent developments in two countries, the United Kingdom and Germany. The chapter concludes by outlining suggestions for further research.

The Varieties of Capitalism Approach and its Implications for Employee Participation

One of the key tasks of the international and comparative study of employee participation is accounting for cross-national differences. In the aftermath of the collapse of the Soviet bloc and the context of globalization, it was predicted that differences between capitalist economies including labour market regulation and employer–employee relations would erode and that there would be convergence on a free market neoliberal form of capitalism. These predictions of convergence have been met with an increasing number of theories of capitalist diversity. Drawing on empirical evidence of continued, and in some cases, increasing diversity across market economies in the face of common external pressures, these theories argue that there is more than one way to organize a capitalist economy. In this respect these theories are closely related to the rediscovery of the importance of institutions that has occurred across many social sciences over the past two decades.

Arguably the most influential theory of capitalist diversity is Hall and Soskice's (2001) *Varieties of Capitalism* (VofC) approach. Hall and Soskice (2001: 6–9) argue that firms operating in a market economy are faced with a series of coordination problems, both internally and externally. They focus on five spheres of coordination that firms must address: industrial relations; vocational training and education; corporate governance; inter-firm relations and relations with their own employees. Rejecting the idea that there is one best way to organize capitalism, they argue that it is possible to identify at least two institutional equilibria associated with superior economic returns: liberal market economies (LMEs), in which firms rely on markets and hierarchies to resolve coordination problems, and coordinated market economies (CMEs), in which firms are more likely to use non-market mechanisms to coordinate external and internal relationships. LMEs are likely to be characterized by well-developed capital markets and outsider forms of corporate governance; market-based forms of industrial relations with few long-term commitments by employers to workers; and the use of market mechanisms and contracts to coordinate their relations with supplier and buyer firms. CMEs, on the other hand, are more likely to exhibit, among other things, insider forms of corporate governance and 'patient' forms of capital; industrial relations systems based on bargaining and which reflect a longer-term commitment to employees; and the use of non-market mechanisms, such as industry associations, to coordinate relations between firms within and across industries and sectors.

Central to Hall and Soskice's argument, and of particular significance for understanding the implications of this framework for issues of employee involvement and participation, is the concept of *institutional complementarities*. Hall and Soskice (2001: 18) argue that 'nations with a particular type of coordination in one sphere in the economy should tend to develop complementary practices in other spheres as well'. Subsequent studies have found strong empirical associations between corporate governance arrangements and employment relations practices and outcomes (Gospel and Pendleton, 2005; Hall and Gingerich, 2004). As we have argued elsewhere (Lansbury and Wailes, 2007) there are a number of features of the VofC approach that suggest that it is well suited to explaining cross-national differences in patterns of employee participation in the contemporary context. In particular the VofC approach is firm centric and therefore has the potential to explain the relationship between institutional context and management-initiated participation practices.

This suggests that patterns of participation and involvement are likely to vary systematically across varieties of capitalism and to reflect differences in institutional context. In LMEs, where there is a heavy reliance on equity markets for firm finance and outsider forms of corporate governance, labour management practices and production systems tend to be market-based and short term in character. Forms of financial participation, which give workers market-based rewards but limit the long-term commitment of the firm to workers, appear to be more consistent with the institutional matrix of LMEs than other forms of participation and involvement, which are predicated on a longer-term relationship between workers and the firm. In CMEs, which are characterized by patient capital, insider forms of corporate governance and production strategies based on exploiting firm-specific skills developed over long periods of time, forms of participation which build on long-term commitment and elicit worker contribution to decision making and work design are likely to be more common than those which reduce the relationship to short-run, market exchanges. Thus, the VofC approach suggests that long-term direct participation by workers in decision making is likely to be more common in CMEs than is the case for LMEs. Similarly the VofC approach implies that ongoing employee involvement in LMEs is more likely to be concentrated on financial participation, which will be less prevalent in CMEs.

The VofC approach also implies that there are likely to be higher levels of experimentation with different forms of involvement and participation, both direct and financial, in LMEs than in CMEs. It has been widely argued that in CMEs competitive advantages are likely to arise from the development of firm-specific assets associated with the long-term commitment of capital and labour (Aoki, 2000). The institutional matrix of CMEs produces conditions for diversified quality production systems where the main focus is on incremental improvements to existing products and technologies (Streeck, 1991). Lacking certainty in the long-term financial commitment of investors, and unwilling to provide employees with the commitment necessary to encourage investment in firm-specific human capital, the competitiveness of firms in LMEs are less likely to be based on the development of firm-specific assets and more likely to be derived from innovation and experimentation (Jürgens, 2003). This argument can be extended to management practices, including those associated with involvement and participation. Thus, from a VofC perspective LMEs are more likely to be characterized by high levels of experimentation with and abandonment of different forms of employee involvement and participation than is the case in CMEs. Research on the adoption of Japanese-style involvement processes by US and UK companies during the 1980s appears to provide empirical support for this proposition. While US and UK managers eagerly adopted participation based on Japanese quality control systems during the 1980s, the results were disappointing and these schemes were rapidly abandoned (Ackroyd et al. 1988). As Bradley and Hill (1983: 308) put it, this, in part, reflected the fact that Japanese 'management culture and worker behaviour is based on a different set of rules and institutions'.

While the VofC approach may help explain cross-national differences in participation, there are a number of limitations to this framework which suggest the need for a more complex theoretical framework. First the VofC framework makes it difficult to explain diversity in participation practices *within* national systems. Despite evidence which suggests that participation practices vary across countries, there is also evidence of diversity within national systems. Thus, for example, while the use of works councils is relatively widespread within Germany there is a considerable and growing percentage of German companies that do not adopt these practices. Similarly, although the vast majority of US firms avoid providing their employees with opportunities for direct or indirect participation in their firms, there are some notable exceptions to this pattern (Ichniowski et al., 1996). A second problem with the VofC approach is that it has difficulties accounting for developments in participation that are international in origin. Thus, for example, while the institutional context in the UK may not have favoured the development of consultation mechanisms, developments at a European level have resulted in the introduction of legislation designed to give affect to the European Works Council directive. Similarly, there is considerable evidence that MNCs are important sources of innovation in participation practices, often seeking to reproduce all or part of the practices that they adopt in their home country operations in their subsidiaries. These international developments are difficult to accommodate within a traditional VofC framework which tends to treat national systems as closed. These limitations are consistent with broader criticisms of the VofC approach.

RECENT DEVELOPMENTS IN EMPLOYEE PARTICIPATION UNDER DIFFERENT VARIETIES OF CAPITALISM

In order to examine whether the VofC approach provides a useful means of explaining differences in employee participation practices, the experience of Germany (as an example of a coordinated market economy) and the United Kingdom (as an example of a liberal market economy) are examined in the following sections of this chapter.

Germany

The German system of industrial relations and employee participation has long been characterized as a 'dual system of interest representation' that comprises collective bargaining between union and employers at the industry level and codetermination at the level of the enterprise. The autonomy of collective bargaining has been guaranteed by a complex array of laws and regulations, dating back to the end of the Second World War, which determine how conflicts should be negotiated and articulated without direct intervention by the state. Proponents of the German system argue that it has achieved an institutional balance of power between labour and capital that has promoted economic growth and adaptation to changing circumstances (Baethege and Wolf, 1995; Frege, 2003; Haipeter, 2006). Yet the system is under strain for a variety of reasons. The unification between West and East Germany has involved significant economic burdens for the 'new' Germany. There have been increasing levels of unemployment and a waning of union influence in both the political and economic sphere. The locus of collective bargaining has been shifting from the industry to the firm level, where works councils rather than unions tend to assume the primary role in representing workers' interests. Employers have also been increasingly successful in their attempts to deregulate and increase flexibility of employment. They have introduced performance-based pay, more flexible working hours and the contracting-out of various functions (Raess and Burgoon, 2006). Changes in corporate governance have resulted in attempts to introduce 'shareholder value' management-styles into German companies, although some observers argue that this has been more espoused than implemented (Aguilera and Jackson, 2003; Fiss and Zajac, 2004).

Works councils are required in all firms with more than five employees and are governed by the Works Constitution Act 1952, which established works councils as separate, non-union organs for employee representation. Although the 1952 Act was partly an attempt to isolate unions from the workplace level and sought to limit union influence to industry-wide bargaining, the majority of works councillors are union members. Works councils have carefully defined rights and are obligated to maintain labour peace, but they have extensive consultation and information rights on social concerns and human resource issues, such as selection and training, and veto rights over certain matters, such as recruitment, redeployment, and dismissal. However, there are also limitations on the operations and influence of works councils. Firms with less than five employees cover 87 per cent of all employees in Germany and are outside the scope of works councils. Furthermore, while the law permits the election of works councils, it does not stipulate that they have to be formed. Daubler (1989, 1995) notes that there is no legal sanction against firms that refuse to install works councils, even if there is an initiative by the employees to establish one. For smaller firms, with more than five employees, the existence of works councils depends largely on the ability of unions to 'persuade' the owners to establish works councils. Auer (1996) has noted that less than 25 per cent of companies with fewer than 100 employees have works councils, compared with 90 per cent of firms with 100 to 1,000 employees. However, improved conditions of work, shorter hours and wage gains that have been won by unions in larger firms generally have flowed to smaller firms through what Thelen (1991) describes as 'negotiated adjustment', which occurs to a much greater extent in Germany than in many other comparable economies.

Until the past decade or so, there was a general acceptance of works councils by both management and the workforce. Muller-Jentsch (1995) claimed that works councils played a significant role in achieving social consensus at the workplace level in resolving conflict over issues such as adjusting to downsizing the workforce and assisting with organizational innovation. Sorge and Streeck (1988) argued that works councils had been important in forcing employers to follow a high wage/ high skill/labour-valued-added strategy. Wever (1994) argued that works councils were regarded as a basic political right by the majority of Germans. Works councils were also viewed as providing an important instrument for workers achieving a 'collective voice' (in tandem with unions) by aggregating worker preferences and transmitting them to management (Addison et al., 1997). Yet there were growing criticisms of works councils for lacking sufficient autonomy from unions, being focused mainly on traditional sectors, such as manufacturing and heavy industry, and not providing sufficient representation for women and foreign/guest workers. There were also concerns whether the German model was capable of supporting more flexible, decentralized bargaining arrangements at the enterprise and work-place level without endangering the core principles of the industrial relations system. Streeck (1997), for example, predicted the rise of more heterogeneous and conflictual relations in the workplace, which cast doubts over the future stability and cooperative nature of the German system. In a similar vein, Hassel (1999) felt that works councils would become more sectionalist in their demands as they achieved an increased role in the bargaining process. According to Frege (2003), the crucial question is whether the trend towards a more decentralized model of industrial relations in Germany will increase the power and independence of works councils vis-à-vis the union or become increasingly incorporated into the union structure at the workplace level.

Clearly there are changes occurring in the German system which are resulting in a more diverse range of applications of the Works Councils Act. This is supported by the results of a major survey conducted by Frege (2003) of 485 works councillors from two unions: DPG (Deutsche Post Gewerkschaft) covering telecommunications, postal workers, and postal bank employees, and the IG BCE (Industrie-gewerkschaft Bergbau, Chemie und Energie) comprising the chemical, mining, energy and leather industries. The focus of the survey was on the attitudes and role identities of works councillors in order to evaluate the degree to which works councils were undergoing a process of transformation. The survey revealed that although the industries faced extensive external and internal challenges (including privatization, mergers, and increasing globalization), there was no observable tendency for works councillors to become weak and subservient to management. Rather, the cooperative attitudes displayed by the works councillors suggested stability rather than significant changes. Frege concluded that workplace cooperation between works councillors and management was still dependent on day-to-day power relations. The results of Frege's research suggested that although the legal framework underpinning works councils was necessary it was not sufficient by itself to guarantee cooperative workplace relations. Yet a more equal power balance seemed to be a key precondition to ensure cooperation between the parties in the workplace.

Another study of the changing nature of works councils in Germany was undertaken by Haipeter (2006) at Volkswagen (VW). Over the past two decades, there have been radical changes at VW, beginning in the early 1990s when a major crisis resulted in major reorganization of the company. In facing these challenges, the VW works councils changed from a defensive to an offensive strategy which resulted in the establishment of VW's European Works Councils (EWCs). The EWC developed its own concept of organizational development based on three pillars: broad qualifications, innovative work organization and decentralized plant organization. Works councils have supported decentralization on the basis that it will improve the employees' prospects to participate in business policy and strategic decision making. Works councils at VW have established symposia in which they can obtain comprehensive information on procurement decisions and can gain influence over global sourcing strategies. Works councils are also involved in bids for in-house production and the product development process (D'Alessio and Oberbeck, 2000). However, this does not prevent rationalization of industries arising from market pressures. Although it is difficult to generalize from one case study, Haipeter argued that the VW case is an example of applying 'enlightened shareholder value' in which codetermination contributes to business success by protecting the corporation against the negative effects of 'untamed' market control. In another study of decentralized bargaining over working time in the German auto industry, Haipeter and Lehndorff (2005) argued that works councils have been able to prevent 'a headlong flight towards deregulation' by negotiating a form of 'regulated flexibility'.

A less optimistic view of the operation of works councils in Germany is provided by a study of 'fast food bargaining power' under the leadership of McDonald's. Although McDonald's agreed to accept regular collective bargaining rounds with unions, after eighteen years of resistance, Royle (2002: 457) argued that this was largely to improve the company's public image rather than signalling acceptance of unions as a 'pluralist principle'. Furthermore, McDonald's has succeeded in restricting the establishment of works councils to only a small number of its restaurants. According to Royle (2002), the breakdown in sector-wide regional collective agreements has been driven by high levels of unemployment and by employers gaining concessions from works councils at the workplace level. He concedes that despite McDonald's and other firms in the fast food industry success in restricting the impact of works councils on their operations, the system is not on the verge of collapse. However, Anglo-Saxon-based MNCs appear to be more likely to adopt non-union and/or works council avoidance strategies than German firms. Furthermore, by being flexible and adaptable to the needs of employers, works councils may lose credibility with the workers, weaken their power of representation and undermine the terms and conditions of employment.

The impact of globalization and greater economic openness on the operation of works councils in Germany was the subject of a study by Raess and Burgoon (2006). In their survey of eight factories, with varying exposure to globalization flows and threats, Raes and Burgoon found that greater openness, especially to foreign direct investment (FDI), tended to increase concessions by works councils. In one case, Siemens AG threatened to relocate 2,500 jobs to Hungary unless the company was permitted to introduce a 40-hour week, without a wage increase, and to replace Christmas and holiday payments by a performance-related bonus. Daimler Benz followed with similar demands at its Sindelfingen plant and achieved concessions from the works council. In the Netherlands, where the system of works councils is similar to Germany, Looise and Drucker (2003) found that works councillors in MNCs reported a significantly lower influence than those in companies operating on the domestic market. The main conclusions from these studies in both Germany and the Netherlands were that greater foreign investment and trade tended to trigger deeper concessions from works councils.

New forms of production and work organization in German industry have also created new challenges for works councils and unions. Many enterprises, particularly those involved in the automobile sector, have undergone extensive organizational restructuring in order to remain competitive in the international market. According to Auer (1996), German managers adopted 'lean production' with greater enthusiasm arguing that it was necessary to abandon 'inflexible' work practices and to reduce the workforce. German unions were placed in a dilemma. While they welcomed the opportunity for more participative work organization, they opposed rationalization that led to 'downsizing' the workforce (Jürgens, 2007). Although works councils are entitled to be consulted on changes to production and organization, some employers seek to consult workers directly rather than through representative bodies. In any case, works councils are not empowered to refuse change in work organization. Some strategic decisions, such as the location of production factories, have been increasingly centralized, while decisions dealing with work arrangements at particular plants have been decentralized. Regional union representation, which previously served as a counterbalance to management, no longer provided an effective means of influencing decisions that have been moved from middle management's discretion to the responsibility of headquarters' management. New forms of organization have also created problems for works councillors. Management has used group or teamwork, quality circles and the like, to enable workers to influence and directly participate in decision making, effectively bypassing the works councillors (Roth, 1997: 118).

Changes over recent decades, including the reunification of East and West Germany, have placed the post-war German 'model' under considerable strain. Both employers and unions have to adjust to pressures arising from persistent levels of higher unemployment and more conflictual industrial relations that are not easily resolved by either codetermination or collective bargaining. In many small-to medium-scale enterprises, works councils and unions are finding it difficult to provide adequate channels for employee representation. Furthermore, larger-scale MNCs, such as McDonald's, have found ways of either avoiding or incorporating works councils thereby reducing their effectiveness. However, by adapting to new forms of direct participation, the unions and works councils may provide a third tier of participation by individuals at the workplace level to counterbalance unilateral decision making by management.

The United Kingdom

Recent decades have witnessed significant change in British industrial relations as trade union membership declined from 65 per cent in 1980 to 26 per cent in 2004. According to the most recent Workplace Employment Relations Survey (Kersley et al., 2005), only 34 per cent of all employees in workplaces with ten or more employees were union members, while 64 per cent of workplaces had no union members. With this dramatic decline in union density, the traditional notion of collective bargaining providing the primary means of achieving employee voice and participation at work is of questionable validity. This is despite the long-held view, forcefully articulated by Clegg (1960), that only trade unions could reflect the interests of employees (industrial workers) and that the ownership of industry was irrelevant to 'good industrial relations' and, by extension, to the achievement of industrial democracy. With the decline from collective bargaining and the dimin-ished role of unions at the workplace, the 'representation gap' (Towers, 1997) has grown considerably and there is the need to examine a wider range of possible avenues for employee representation at work.

Despite the election of a British Labour Government in 1997, led by Tony Blair, the neoliberalist policies of the Thatcher years have remained very influential in setting the economic and political agenda (Kelly, 1997). The past decade has been marked by an emphasis on market focus as opposed to state intervention in economic activity, an expanded role for individualism rather than collectivism in the employment relationship, a heightened role for law in industrial relations and enhanced managerial decision-making autonomy in the enterprise (Smith and Morton, 2001). While the Blair Labour Government softened the harsher elements of the Thatcher and Major Conservative Governments' policies, they did not revert to the more union-friendly approaches of previous Labour Governments. Never-theless, there were some important changes to the legal framework of industrial relations through the introduction of statutory union recognition procedures (Wood and Godard, 1999) and the establishment of the Low Pay Commission (Brown, 2005). Yet the broader political economy of Britain experienced a continuing shift from manufacturing to service activities and a reduction in the role of the public sector, especially through privatization (Pendelton, 1997). Globalization of product markets continued to affect workplace relations, encouraging the development of a more flexible and productive workforce. As the collective bargaining emphasis of traditional industrial relations declined, there was an appreciable rise of interest in human resource management with an emphasis on individual employee motivation and commitment as a key ingredient in economic success at the level of the firm (Guest, 1997).

While the Blair Government was more positive towards the European Union than its predecessor, they remained cautious and concerned to preserve independence for the UK as far as possible. Following the 1994 European Union (EU) Directive on works councils, there was an increase in the propensity of large multinational corporations (MNCs) in the UK to adopt works councils. By the late 1990s, European Works Councils (EWCs) had been introduced with at least twenty-nine UK MNCs, representing 27 per cent of British firms affected by the new law (Heery, 1997). In the WERS 1998 survey, however, only 19 per cent of workplaces that were part of private sector MNCs appeared to have developed EWCs (Millward et al., 2000). The WERS 2004 findings indicated that only 14 per cent of workplaces with ten or more employees had a joint consultative committee. A further 25 per cent of workplaces did not have a workplace-level committee but had a committee at a higher level within the organization. This revealed a decline over the previous six years, with WERS 1998 equivalent figures of 20 per cent and 25 per cent respectively. In addition, 42 per cent of all employees worked in an enterprise with a joint consultative committee at the workplace level compared with 46 per cent in 1998 (Kersley et al., 2005).

In a number of European countries, it is generally the responsibility of unions to set the structure of works councils. In the UK, however, where joint consultative committees, are more common than works councils, these are frequently initiated by management. Wilkinson et al. (2004) note that for a large majority of firms in the UK, the main aim of collective consultation is to increase information and consultations rather than bargaining. Managers tend to view consultative structures as a means of building mutual cooperation with the workforce and promoting an understanding of company policy. Non-union collective consultation is regarded by management as a more effective channel of communication than working through unions and is seen as a means of increasing company productivity and efficiency. In a study of non-union representation arrangements, Gollan (2006) reported that management usually controlled the structure and agenda at meetings and most of the non-union representative bodies were only given powers of recommendation to management. Unlike collective bargaining, few consultative committees had negotiation and bargaining rights over pay and conditions, and there was a lack of financial, investment and strategic data available to non-union committees. All matters involving conflict resolution or grievance handling were dealt with by local managers or internal dispute resolution mechanisms.

In April 2005, the EU Directive on Informing and Consulting Employees (I and C Directive) came into force in the UK. The purpose of the Directive is to establish a general framework of minimum requirements for the right to information and consultation of employees (European Parliament and Council, 2002). It is estimated that the Directive could cover approximately 60 per cent of employees within the EU and 65 per cent of the UK workforce (Burns, 2000). It potentially has far-reaching consequences for the way in which UK employers inform and consult employees over a wide range of organizational issues. Although it does not make employee representative structures compulsory, this may prove necessary to meet the requirements of the Directive. The Directive requires:

- Information on the recent and probable development of the undertakings' or the establishments' activities and economic situation;
- Information and consultation on the situation, structure, and possible development of employment and on any anticipatory measures envisaged, in particular, where there is a threat to employment; and
- Information and consultation with a view to reaching an agreement, on decisions likely to lead to substantial changes in work organizations' contractual relations.

The UK and Eire are affected by the Directive more than most other EU Member States because they currently do not have any general permanent and statutory system of information and consultation (Hall et al., 2002). However, opinion is divided over whether the Directive is likely to lead to fundamental change in how British employers involve and engage their employees. For some, according to Sisson (2002: 13), the Directive represents the 'opportunity to improve the quality of UK industrial relations with the potential for widespread general gains that have come to be associated with the concept of partnership'. Furthermore, research by the Chartered Institute of Personnel and Development (CIPD) into employee attitudes shows that organizations that involve and engage their employees in matters that affect their employment experience are likely to gain significant benefits (CIPD, 2005). Yet Hall (2005) believes that 'legislatively promoted voluntarism' may not be sufficient to provide a 'platform for fundamental change in employment relations'. Similarly Gollan's research on the Euro tunnel case suggests that employees may not regard the Directive as addressing their key concerns and will thus see it as impotent and ineffective (Gollan, 2001). From a study of the initial impact of the ICE regulation, Hall (2006) has concluded that few firms have introduced pre-existing agreements to meet the legislative requirements. Indeed, rather than the ICE regulation bringing the UK closer to the 'European social model', the flexibility built into the regulations may provide employers with a tool for continued 'British exceptionalism' (Bercusson, 2002). This latter outcome appears to be more likely than the former in the context of a generally cautious approach by employers and a defensive attitude exhibited by many unions.

While there is mixed evidence regarding the past and likely future success of indirect or representative forms of participation in the UK, there has been a rise in the prevalence of direct forms of participation from involvement of employees in decision making at the workplace to employee shareholding and profit sharing schemes (Bryson, 2000; Cully et al., 1999). Evidence from the European Foundation for the Improvement of Living and Working Conditions (EPOC) survey of 1996 revealed that 52 per cent of firms in the UK had individual consultation ('face-to-face'), 40 per cent had individual consultation ('arm's length'), 33 per cent had group consultation ('temporary groups'), while 41 per cent had group consultation ('permanent groups') (Gill and Kreiger, 1995: 530).

In an IRS survey of trends in employee involvement, all organizations claimed to use at least two forms of communication, with team meetings being reported in 92 per cent of cases, suggestion schemes in 42 per cent of firms, and quality initiatives in 39 per cent of organizations (IRS, 1999). WERS 2004 reported that 82 per cent of managers in the private sector held meetings with their entire workforce or team briefings in 1998 compared with 90 per cent in 2004. There was little change in the public sector during this period (Kersley et al., 2005).

Another important development in the UK since the mid-1980s has been the growth of employee shareholdings and profit sharing schemes. These were boosted originally by various parliamentary Finance Acts that ensured tax advantages to firms that introduced schemes which met the guidelines of the Inland Revenue. By the end of the 1990s, more than 1,300 employee share schemes had been approved. According to WERS 1998, at least 30 per cent of workplaces in the UK had profit sharing schemes for non-managerial employees (Millward et al., 2000). The continuing debate about the impact of financial participation schemes, however, is whether they actually enhance the degree of participation and involvement of employees in decision making within both the workplace and enterprise. Evidence from the US, where employee stock owner-ship plans (ESOPs) are more widespread than in the UK, suggests that financial participation alone is unlikely to stimulate employee commitment and involve-ment in the enterprise. Meaningful employee participation occurs only when appropriate structures are in place to provide the vehicle for participation (Eaton, 1993; Strauss, 1996).

In summary, recent evidence from the UK reveals a growing diversity of ap-proaches to employee participation compared with the past when employee voice in the workplace was mainly expressed through unions in collective bargaining. The restructuring of the economy away from manufacturing and public sector employ-ment, where unions were strong, to the service sector, where unions are weaker, provides part of the explanation for the decline of union-led collective bargaining. The neoliberalist and anti-collectivist ideologies of the Thatcher Government have also remained influential, despite more than a decade of Labour Government which has been more union-friendly. EU initiatives have begun to have impact, at least on some of the larger MNCs that operate across Europe, and have encouraged the expansion of European Works Councils and similar workplace committees in Britain. The EU Directive on Informing and Consulting Employees, which came into force in the UK in 2005, is likely to strengthen formal mechanisms for employee participation in the workplace. Yet direct forms of participation, which do not involve representative structures and are initiated by management, are likely to extend their coverage of the workforce despite pressures from the EU and unions for more representative forms of participation. However, the sustainability of direct forms of participation are likely to be less certain in the future if there is not strong institutional and government support for a wide range of genuine participative practices.

CONCLUSIONS

Recent decades have witnessed renewed interest in employee participation and its contribution both to improved productivity and increased flexibility in increasingly competitive markets. Despite an increase in the number of management-initiated participation and involvement schemes in many countries, empirical evidence suggests that there continues to be considerable diversity in patterns of participation at the national level. The previous section provided an analysis of patterns of participation in two countries: Germany as an example of a coordinated market economy and the United Kingdom as an example of a liberal market economy. As these examples indicate, the relationship between varieties of capitalism and employee participation is complex. It is apparent that labour market institutions play an important role, as does historical experience. Countries do not remain rigidly fixed within one paradigm and are constantly changing.

These findings are consistent with the view, advanced by Gospel and Pendleton (2005: 9) among others, that the VofC approach is too formal and simplistic to capture all of the factors that produce differences between and change within national patterns of labour management. Despite these limitations, the empirical evidence presented in this chapter is broadly consistent with the propositions drawn from the VofC framework and suggests that the national institutional matrix has a significant impact on the adoption and sustainability of different forms of employee participation. Furthermore, our examination of employee participation in the two countries studied has revealed that where the conjunction of historical and institutional factors are favourable, employee participation practices are more likely to be sustainable. In the past, this has characterized coordinated market economies, such as Germany, more than liberal market economies, such as the UK.

However, if labour market institutions continue to be weakened in Germany and corporate governance reforms mean that managers in this country become more susceptible to short-term investor pressure, they are likely to become less distinguishable from a liberal market economy like the UK. Hence, the sustainability of employee participative practices in the workplace in either a coordinated or liberal market economy will be less certain in the future unless there is stronger institutional support for their continuation and further development.

Further research is needed to test the applicability of the VofC approach to developments in employee participation across a wider range of countries representing both liberal and market economies. It is also necessary to extend research to emerging economies, such as South Korea, which cannot readily be assigned to one of these categories but where new forms of employee participation are being used. Recent studies of employment practices in newly industrializing Asian countries reveal dynamic changes which are creating different patterns of labour–management relations from more established economies. This is particularly the case in countries, such as China and Vietnam, which are undergoing transition from state-controlled economies to quasi-liberal market economies but with strong coordination and direction from government. As labour market institutions change and develop in these countries, as a result of economic and political pressures, new forms of employee participation are likely to emerge in order to satisfy growing demands for voice and representation by workers. The role of multinational corporations is important in this process of change as they transmit new forms of employment relations into host countries and industries in which they operate. Research on MNCs, however, indicates that the process of transfer and diffusion of policies and practices, such as employee participation, is a complex and contested one. Important factors in this process include the significance of the subsidiary to the firm's global operations and the origin and resources of local managers. Similarly, at a national level, government policies on employee participation may be influenced by the advice and support provided by major international bodies, such as the International Labour Organisation, the World Bank, and the World Trade Organization.

Future research on employee participation will be enriched by greater attention being given to comparative employment relations scholarship and the means by which the international dimension is integrated into the analysis. Simplistic predictions that globalization would completely erode national differences in the organization and regulation of employment relations have proven to be false. National institutional arrangements have continued to shape distinct patterns of employee participation in different countries. A theoretical framework, such as the VofC approach, is useful in explaining how globalization has differential effects across countries, particularly in advanced industrial economies However, a more comprehensive approach is needed to analyse a wider range of emerging economies and the conditions under which new forms of employee participation are likely to be sustainable.

REFERENCES

ACKROYD, S., BURRELL, G., HUGHES, M., and WHITACKER, A. (1988) 'The Japanisation of British industry?' *Industrial Relations Journal*, 19(1): 11–23.

ADDISON, J. T., SCHNABEL, C., and WAGNER, J. (1997) 'On the determinants of mandatory works councils in Germany', *Industrial Relations*, 36: 419–45.

AGUILERA, R. V. and JACKSON, G. (2003) 'The cross-national diversity of corporate governance: Dimensions and determinants', *Academy of Management Review*, 28(3): 447–65.

ALLEN, M. (2004) 'The varieties of capitalism paradigm: not enough variety?' *Socio-Economic Review*, 2: 87–107.

ALMOND, P. and FERNER, A. (eds) (2006) *American Multinationals in Europe: Managing Employment Relations Across National Borders*. Oxford: Oxford University Press.

—— and TEMPEL, A. (2006) 'Multinationals and national business systems: A 'power and institutions perspective', in P. Almond and A. Ferner (eds) *American Multinationals in Europe: Managing Employment Relations Across National Borders*. Oxford: Oxford University Press.

AMABLE, B. (2003) *The Diversity of Modern Capitalism*. New York: Oxford University Press.

AOKI, M. (2000) *Information, Corporate Governance and Institutional Diversity: Competitiveness in Japan, the USA and the Transitional Economies*. Oxford: Oxford University Press.

AUER, P. (1996) 'Co-determination in Germany: Institutional stability in a changing environment', in E. Davis and R. D. Lansbury (eds), *Managing Together: Consultation and Participation in the Workplace*, pp. 160–72. Melbourne: Addison–Wesley Longman.

BAETHEGE, M. and WOLF, H. (1995) 'Continuity and change in the 'German model' of industrial relations', in R. M. Locke, T. Kochan, and M. Piore (eds), *Employment Relations in a Changing World Economy*, pp. 231–561. Cambridge, MA: MIT Press.

BERCUSSON, B. (2002) 'The European social model comes to Britain', *Industrial Law Journal*, 31(3): 209–44.

BRADLEY, K. and HILL, S. (1983) ' "After Japan": The quality circle transplant and productive efficiency', *British Journal of Industrial Relations*, 21(3): 291–311.

BROWN, W. (2005) 'Third party labour market intervention in open economies', in J. Isaac and R. D. Lansbury (eds), *Labour Market Deregulation Rewriting the Rules: Essays in Honour of Keith Hancock*, pp. 191–203. Sydney: The Federation Press.

BRYSON, A. (2000) 'Have British workers lost their voice, or have they gained a new one?' Policy Studies Institute, mimeo, July.

BURNS, P. (2000) *The Silent Stakeholder: Reforming Workplace Consultation Law*. Policy Paper. London: The Industrial Society.

CASSON, M. and LUNDAN, S. (1999) 'Explaining international differences in economic institutions: A critique of the 'national business system' as an analytical tool', *International Studies in Management and Organisation*, 29(2): 25–42.

Chartered Institute of Personnel and Development (CIPD) (2005) *The Information and Consultation Regulations: A Guide*. London: CIPD.

CLEGG, H. A. (1960) *A New Approach at Work*. Boston, MA: Harvard Business School Press.

CROUCH, C. (2005) *Capitalist Diversity and Change: Recombinant Governance and Institutional Entrepreneurs*. Oxford: Oxford University Press.

CROUCH, C., STREECK, W., BOYER, R., AMABLE, B., HALL, P., and JACKSON, G. (2005) 'Dialogue on 'institutional complementarity and political economy', *Socio-Economic Review*, 3: 359–82.

CULLY, M., WOODLAND, S., O'REILLY, A., and DIX, G. (1999) *Britain at Work*. London: Routledge.

D'ALESSIO, N. and OBERBECK, H. (2000) *Rationalisierung in Eigenregie. Ansatzpunkte fur den Bruch mit dem Taylorismus bei VW*. VSA: Hamburg.

DAUBLER, W. (1989) 'The individual and the collective: No problem for German labor law?' *Comparative Labor Law Journal*, 10: 180–95.

——— (1995) *Das Grundrecht auf Mitbestimmung*. Frankfurt-Main: Europeaishe Verlagsonstalt.

EATON, A. (1993) 'Factors contributing to the survival of employee participation programs in unionized settings', *Industrial and Labor Relations Review*, 47: 371–89.

EDWARDS, T., COLLING, T., and FERNER, A. (2007) 'Conceptual approaches to the transfer of employment practices in multinational companies: an integrated approach', *Human Resource Management Journal*, 17(3): 201–17.

European Parliament and Council (2002) *A General Framework for Information and Consulting Employees*. Council Directive 2002/14/EC, 2002 OJ (L 080).

FISS, P. C. and ZAJAC, E. J. (2004) 'The diffusion of ideas over contested terrain: The (non) adoption of a shareholder value orientation among German firms', *Administrative Science Quarterly*, 49(4): 501–34.

FREGE, C. M. (2003) 'Transforming German workplace relations: Quo vadis cooperation?' *Economic and Industrial Democracy*, 24(3): 317–47.

GILL, C. and KREIGER, H. (1995) 'Direct and representative participation in Europe: Recent survey evidence', *International Journal of Human Resource Management*, 10(1): 572–91.

GOLLAN, P. J. (2001) 'Tunnel vision: Non-union employee representation at Eurotunnel', *Employee Relations*, 23(4): 376–400.

——— (2006) 'The changing dynamics of employee voice and non-union and union representation in the new workplace, *Industrial Relations Journal*, 37(5): 428–37.

GOSPEL, and PENDLETON, A. (2005) Corporate governance and labour management: An international comparison. Oxford: Oxford University Press.

GUEST, D. (1997) 'Human resource management and performance: A review and research agenda', *International Journal of Human Resource Management*, 8(3): 263–76.

HAIPETER, T. (2006) 'Recent developments in co-determination at Volkswagen: Challenges and changes', *Journal of Industrial Relations*, 48(4): 541–7.

——— and LEHNDORFF, S. (2005) 'Decentralised bargaining of working time in the German automotive industry', *Industrial Relations Journal*, 36(2): 140–56.

HALL, M. (2005) 'How are employers and unions responding to the information and consultation of employee regulations', *Warwick Papers in Industrial Relations*, no. 77. Warwick University.

——— (2006) 'A cool response to the UK ICE regulations? Employer and trade union strategies under the new legal framework for information and consultation', *Industrial Relations Journal*, 37(5): 456–72.

——— BROUGHTON, A., CARLEY, M., and SISSON, K. (2002) *Works Councils for the UK? Assessing the Impact of the UK Employee Consultation Directive*. London: Industrial Relations Services/Industrial Relations Research Unit.

HALL, P. and GINGRICH, D. (2004) 'Varieties of capitalism and institutional complementarities in the macroeconomy: An empirical analysis', *Max Planck Institute for the Study of Societies Discussion Paper*, 04/5.

HALL, P. and SOSKICE, D. (2001) 'An introduction to varieties of capitalism', in P. Hall and D. Soskice (eds), *Varieties of Capitalism: The Institutional Foundations of Comparative Advantage*, pp. 1–69. New York: Oxford University Press.

HASSEL, A. (1999) 'The erosion of the German system of industrial relations', *British Journal of Industrial Relations*, 37(3): 483–505.

HEERY, E. (1997) 'Annual review article 1996', *British Journal of Industrial Relations*, 35(1): 87–109.

HOWELL, C. (2003) 'Varieties of capitalism: and then there was one?' *Comparative Politics*, 36: 90–110.

HYMAN, R. (1996) 'Is there a case for statutory works councils in Britain?', in A. McColgan (ed.), *The Future of Labour Law*, pp. 64–84. London: Mansell.

—— (1997) 'The future of employee representation', *British Journal of Industrial Relations*, 35(3): 309–36.

ICHNIOWSKI, C., KOCHAN, T., LEVINE, D., OLSON, C., and STRAUSS, G. (1996) 'What works at work', *Industrial Relations*, 35: 299–333.

Industrial Relations Services (IRS) (1999) 'Trends in employee involvement', *IRS Employment Review*, 83(July): 6–16.

JACKSON, G. and DEEG, R. (2005) 'How many varieties of capitalism? Comparing the comparative institutional analyses of capitalist diversity', *Max Planck Institute for the Study of Societies Discussion Paper*, 06/2.

JÜRGENS, U. (2003) 'Transformation and interaction: Japanese, US and German production models in the 1990s', in W. Streeck and K. Yamamura (eds), *The End of Diversity? Prospects for German and Japanese Capitalism*, pp. 212–39. Ithaca, NY: Cornell University Press.

—— (2007) 'Germany: Implementing lean production', in T. A. Kochan, R. D. Lansbury and J. P. MacDuffie (eds), *After Lean Production: Evolving Employment Practices in the World Auto Industry*, pp. 109–16. Ithaca, NY: Cornell University Press.

KELLY, J. (1997) 'Industrial relations: Looking to the future', *British Journal of Industrial Relations*, 35(3): 393–8.

KERSLEY, B., ALPIN, C., FORTH, J., BRYSON, A., BEWLEY, H., DIX, G., and OXENBRIDGE, S. (2005) *Inside the Workplace: First Findings from the 2004 Workplace Employment Relations Survey*. London: Department of Trade and Industry.

LANSBURY, R. D. and WAILES, N. (2007) 'Direct Participation', in P. Blyton, N. Bacon, J. Fiorito and E. Heery (eds), *The Sage Handbook of Industrial Relations*, pp. 434–46. London: Sage.

LOOISE, J. K. and DRUCKER, M. (2003) 'Dutch works councils in times of transition: The effects of changes on society, organizations and work on the positions of works councils', *Economic and Industrial Democracy*, 24(3): 379–409.

MILLWARD, N., BRYSON, A., and FORTH, J. (2000) *All Changes at Work?* London: Routledge.

MORGAN, G. (2007) 'National business systems research: progress and prospects', *Scandinavian Journal of Management*, 23(2): 127–45.

MULLER-JENTSCH, W. (1995) 'Germany: From collective voice to co-management', in J. Rogers and W. Streeck (eds), *Works Councils: Consultation, Representation and Cooperation in Industrial Relations*, pp. 53–78. Chicago, IL: University of Chicago Press.

PENDELTON, A. (1997) 'The evolution of industrial relations in the U.K. nationalized industries', *British Journal of Industrial Relations*, 35(2): 145–72.

PONTUSSON, J. (1995) 'From comparative public policy to political economy: Putting political institutions in their place and taking interests seriously', *Comparative Political Studies*, 28(1): 117–48.

—— (2005) 'Varieties and commonalities of capitalism', in D. Coates (ed.), *Varieties of Capitalism, Varieties of Approaches*, pp. 163–88. London: Palgrave McMillian.

POOLE, M., LANSBURY, R. D., and WAILES, N. (2001) 'A comparative analysis of developments in industrial democracy', *Industrial Relations*, 40(3): 490–525.

RAESS, D. and BURGOON, B. (2006) 'The dogs that sometimes bark: Globalization and works council bargaining in Germany', *European Journal of Industrial Relations*, 12(3): 287–309.

ROTH, S. (1997) 'Germany: Labor's perspective on lean production', in T. A. Kochan, R. D. Lansbury and J. P. MacDuffie (eds), *After Lean Production: Evolving Employment Practices in the World Auto Industry*, pp. 117–36. Ithaca, NY: Cornell University Press.

ROYLE, T. (2002) 'Multinational corporations, employers associations and trade union exclusion strategies in the German fast food industry', *Employee Relations*, 24(4): 437–60.

SISSON, K. (2002) 'The information and consultation directive: Unnecessary 'regulation' or an opportunity to promote 'partnership'?', *Warwick Papers in Industrial Relations, no. 67*. Coventry: Industrial Relations Research Unit (IRRU), Warwick University.

SMITH, C. (2005) 'Beyond convergence and divergence: Explaining variations in organizational practices and forms', in S. Ackroyd, R. Batt, P. Thompson and P. Tolbert (eds), *The Oxford Handbook of Work and Organization*, pp. 602–25. Oxford: Oxford University Press.

—— and MEISKINS, P. (1995) 'System, society and dominance effects in cross-national organisational analysis', *Work, Employment and Society*, 9(2): 241–67.

SMITH, P. and MORTON, G. (2001) 'New Labour's reform of Britain's employment law: The devil is not only in the detail but in the values and policy too', *British Journal of Industrial Relations*, 39(1): 119–38.

SORGE, A. and STREECK, W. (1988) 'Industrial relations and technological change: The case for an extended perspective', in R. Hyman and W. Streeck (eds), *New Technology and Industrial Relations*, pp. 19–47. London: Basil Blackwell.

STRAUSS, G. (1996) 'Participation in the United States: Progress and barriers', in E. M. Davis and R. D. Lansbury (eds), *Managing Together: Consultation and Participation in the Workplace*, pp. 173–92. Melbourne: Longman.

STREECK, W. (1991) 'On the institutional conditions for diversified quality production', in E. Matzner and W. Streeck (eds), *Beyond Keynesianism: The Socio-Economics of Production and Full Employment*, pp. 21–61. Brookfield: Elgar.

—— (1997) 'German Capitalism: Does it exist? Can it survive?' *New Political Economy*, 2: 237–56.

THELEN, K. A. (1991) *Union of Parts: Labor Politics in Postwar Germany*. Ithaca, NY: Cornell University Press.

TOWERS, B. (1997) *The Representative Gap*. Oxford: Oxford University Press.

WAILES, N. (2007) 'Globalisation, varieties of capitalism and employment relations in retail banking', *Bulletin of Comparative Labour Relations*, 63: 1–11.

—— RAMIA, G. and LANSBURY, R. D. (2003) 'Interests, institutions and industrial relations', *British Journal of Industrial Relations*, 41(4): 617–37.

WEVER, K. (1994) 'Learning from works councils: Five unspectacular cases from Germany', *Industrial Relations*, 33: 467–81.

WHITLEY, R. (1992) *Business Systems in East Asia: Firms, Markets and Societies*. London: Sage.

—— (1998) 'Internationalisation and varieties of capitalism: the limited effects of cross-national coordination of economic activities on the nature of business systems', *Review of International Political Economy*, 5(3): 445–81.

—— (1999) *Divergent Capitalisms: The social structuring and change of national business systems*. Oxford: Oxford University Press.

WILKINSON, A., DUNDON, T., MARCHINGTON, M., and ACKERS, P. (2004) 'Changing patterns of employee voice', *Journal of Industrial Relations*, 46(3): 298–322.

WOOD, S. and GODARD, J. (1999) 'The statutory union recognition procedure in the employment relations bill: A comparative analysis', *British Journal of Industrial Relations*, 37(June): 203–44.

CHAPTER 25

FREEDOM, DEMOCRACY, AND CAPITALISM:

ETHICS AND EMPLOYEE PARTICIPATION

ROBIN ARCHER

EVER since the Enlightenment, if not before, the idea of individual freedom or individual liberty has provided a basic ethical reference point against which the legitimacy of social and political institutions has been judged. There are, of course, many different ideas of what an adequate conception of freedom entails. Here, I want to appeal to just one idea which is often thought to be a necessary element of the concept of freedom and which has a strong intuitive appeal. The idea I have in mind is the idea that an individual can only be free to the extent that his or her choices govern (or determine) his or her actions.[1]

This idea underpins one of the principle arguments for democracy. In this chapter I will set out the basic features of this argument. I will then seek to show that it applies not just to political institutions but also to many other kinds of associations and, in particular, to economic enterprises. I propose to show that the same basic ethical commitments that lead us to promote political democracy should lead us to promote economic democracy, where, by economic democracy,

I mean a system in which enterprises operate in a market economy but are governed by those who work for them.[2]

Freedom and Authority

Some human goals are best pursued individually. Others are best pursued by forming organizations or associations. Indeed some can only be pursued in this way. Forming associations enables cooperating individuals to coordinate their activities, but to do this, these associations must be able to make choices and act on them. How can these collective choices be made in a way that is compatible with the value of individual freedom? In particular, given the idea of freedom suggested above, how can they be made so as to maximize the extent to which an individual's choices govern his or her actions?

The decisions of an association, or rather the actions that result from these decisions, will affect various individuals. If I am one of these individuals then the only way that I can maximize my freedom is to ensure that the choices, and hence the actions, of the association are in accord with my own choices. And the only way to ensure that is to control the association's decision-making process. In order to control an association's decision-making process I must ensure that nobody who disagrees with me can affect the outcome of that process. Setting myself up as a dictator would be one way of achieving this. Ensuring that I was part of a permanent majority would be another. Either way I would guarantee that I had the maximum individual freedom, but only by denying a similar freedom to other individuals.

But proponents of liberty typically argue that all individuals are equally entitled to be free: at least to the extent that this is compatible with a similar freedom for others. This principle—the principle of equal liberty—means that each affected individual must be prepared to accept less than maximum individual freedom, since (except in the special case in which there is always unanimity) it is not possible for each individual who is affected by an association simultaneously to exercise complete control over it. If the freedom we gain from controlling an association's decision-making process is to be compatible with an equal freedom for every other individual who is affected by that process, then that control can only be partial and must be shared with every other affected individual. In other words: all individuals whose ability to make choices and act on them is affected by the decisions of an association should share control over the process by which those decisions are made. I will call this the 'all-affected principle'.

Versions of the all-affected principle can be found in the work of Bacharach (1969: 74, 95, 98), Budd (2004: 26, 28), Cole (1920: 33–5), Gross (1999: 70), Holmes (1988: 235) and Lindsay (1962: 231). Especially influential has been the work of Dahl (1970). Dahl formulates his version of the all-affected principle as follows: 'Everyone who is affected by the decisions of a government should have the right to participate in that government' (1970: 64), where by government he means the government of any association; not just that of the state.[3]

The all-affected principle provides an answer to the most fundamental question that confronts any democratic theory. Democracy is, by definition, rule by the people. A theory of democracy must specify how the people will rule—whether by direct participation, elected representatives, referendum, or some other means. But before it can do this, it must first specify who the people are. The all-affected principle provides an answer to this question. Every association, whether it be a state or a shoe factory, should be controlled by a group consisting of all individuals who are affected by its decisions.

However, any attempt to operationalize the all-affected principle, or even just to give it greater specificity, runs into theoretical and practical difficulties. For example, it is unclear whether the all-affected principle really is able to specify meaningfully which group of individuals should share control over the decisions of an association. After all, many decisions ultimately have some effect on every individual. This suggests that the all-affected principle is only workable if we can specify a degree of effect above which an individual qualifies for a share of control.

An apparently still more intractable problem emerges wherever it is possible to exercise more than one kind of control over an association. Yet typically this is the case. For example, votes are not the only kind of control over national governments. Those with property have a separate kind of control (Lindblom, 1977: 170–88). Now if each of these sources of control is distributed in the same proportions, as recommended, for example, by Thomas Jefferson (Dahl, 1985: 3, 70, 103), this does not present a problem. But, leaving aside whether this is desirable, it is not always possible. Consider, for example, another source of control over a national government: the power exerted by foreign governments. It is hard to see how this could be parcelled out according to the Jeffersonian formula. But how, then, are the various kinds of control to be distributed among the various affected individuals? Finding a solution to this problem leads to the development of a second fundamental principle of democracy.

In order to find this solution, we need to recognize that there is an important distinction between two different ways in which control can be exercised over an association (Ellerman, 1990: 46). On the one hand, control can be exercised directly by making decisions: that is, by choosing from the options allowed for by a set of given constraints. On the other hand, control can be exercised indirectly by setting those constraints in place. In the example above, property owners and foreign powers place constraints on a national government (by, for example, refusing to invest or imposing tariffs), while voters, or rather their representatives, make decisions within those constraints.

The distinction between these two ways in which control can be exercised over an association, corresponds to another distinction between two ways in which individuals can be affected by an association. On the one hand, there are individuals who are affected in the sense that they are subject to the authority of an association. On the other hand, there are individuals who are affected by an association without being subject to its authority. Typically the distinction between subjects and affected non-subjects is the same as the distinction between members and affected non-members. Now I want to suggest that direct control is the appropriate form of control for subjects and that indirect control is the appropriate form for affected non-subjects. But to see why this should be so we will have to clarify what it means for an association to have authority over an individual.

To begin with two conceptual points need to be clarified. First, 'authority' is being used here to refer to all effective or *de facto* authority and not just to legitimate or *de jure* authority. Second, 'authority' here refers to 'practical authority' as opposed to 'theoretical authority'. Practical authority is exercised by someone who is 'in authority' (like a policeman). Theoretical authority is exercised by someone who is 'an authority' (like a doctor), and when it is exercised it is really a form of advice. These two forms of authority are distinct because while we are bound to comply with the decisions of a practical authority to which we are subject, we are not bound to follow the advice of a theoretical authority, although it may be foolish not to (Green, 1988: 27; Soper, 1989: 219). Unlike when a doctor suggests a course of action, when a policeman tell you to do something, you cannot ask for a second opinion. But while being bound to comply is a necessary characteristic of (practical) authority, it is not sufficient to define it. A promise, for example, often shares this characteristic. If I promise to help you I am bound to do so. What is distinctive about being subject to authority is that, at least partially, and often fully, I am bound, not by my own decision (as in the case of a promise), but by the decision of someone else (Green, 1988: 40).

Several people have tried to capture what is at stake here by arguing that being subject to authority involves a 'surrender of judgement' (Friedman, 1973: 129). According to this interpretation, when I enter an authority relationship as a subject I surrender my judgement over a certain range of matters to somebody else. I may, for example, surrender it to an individual, such as a king or to a collective body in which I may or may not participate. However, to talk of a surrender of judgement can be misleading. It is not meant to imply that when an authority requires me to do something I must surrender my right to make a judgement about the requirement. Rather, it means that I must surrender my right to act in accordance with my judgement. How I act, not how I think, is what matters to those in authority (Raz, 1986: 39). Since my choices are the outcome of my judgements, surrendering my right to act in accordance with my judgements entails surrendering my right to act

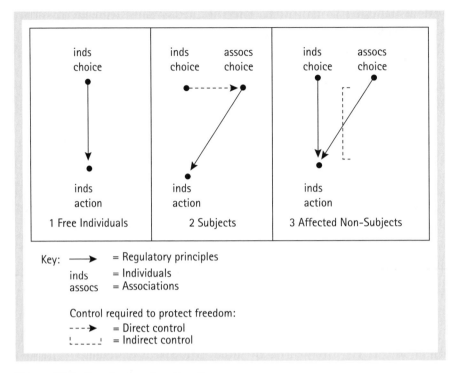

Figure 25.1 Freedom and authority

in accordance with my choices. Thus whenever I am subject to an authority, my choices are *excluded* from playing a role in the regulation of my actions, and are replaced in this role by the choices of the authority (Green, 1988: 38, 42; Raz, 1986: 46, 1987: 79). This exclusion and replacement of one person's choices by another's is the defining feature of an authority relationship.

We are now in a position to see why direct control is the appropriate form of control for subjects and indirect control is the appropriate form for affected non-subjects. Figure 25.1 may help to illustrate the argument of the next couple of paragraphs. Recall, before we begin, that I am assuming that the principle that my actions should be governed (or determined) by my choices is the basic regulatory principle that lies at the heart of the concept of freedom.

In cases where I am subject to the authority of an association this basic regulatory principle is replaced by another regulatory principle. In place of my own choices those of the association determine my actions. Thus, so long as this alternative principle remains in force, the only way to ensure that my freedom is protected is to ensure that the association makes choices that are identical to mine. Since regulation by my choice has been replaced by regulation by the association's choice, the association's choice must be replaced by my choice. And the only way to ensure this is to make the association's choices myself: in other words, to exercise direct control over its decision-making process. Of course, according to the principle of equal liberty, I must consider not just my own freedom but also that of all the association's other subjects. But if the freedom that each subject gains from directly controlling an association's decision-making process is to be compatible with an equal freedom for every other individual who is subject to that association, then each subject's direct control can only be partial and must be shared with every other subjected individual. In other words: all individuals who are subjected to the authority of an association should share direct control over the decisions of that association. I will call this the 'all-subjected principle'. If the range of matters over which the association has authority is the same for all subjects, then each subject is entitled to an equal share of control over the association's decision-making process.

In cases where I am not subject to the authority of an association but am nevertheless affected by it the basic regulatory principle is not replaced. It is, however, added to. The association's choices become an additional factor that must be weighed in alongside my own choices before I can act. To ensure that my freedom is protected in these circumstances, I need only constrain the association from making choices which would lead to this additional effect: in other words, I need to be able to exercise indirect control over the association. There are various forms of indirect control or constraint. The most complete form is a personal veto. Note, however, that the veto which is required is not a veto over the association's decisions *per se*, but a veto over the ability of the association's decisions to affect me.[4] Again, of course, I must share these various forms of indirect control with all the other non-subjects who are affected by the association. This may or may not involve weakening my personal indirect control.[5]

As an affected non-subject, I could also protect my freedom by securing direct control over the relevant association. However, to do so would be both unnecessary and unjustified. It would be unnecessary because, as we have just seen, I only need to exercise indirect control in order to protect my freedom. And it would be unjustified because I would then be making decisions which bound others (namely the association's subjects) but which did not bind me and which I did not have to obey. Therefore non-subjects should be limited to exercising indirect control, reserving direct control for subjects.

The idea that it is only the subjects or members of an association who should exercise direct control over its decision-making process is explicitly endorsed by Dahl (1979: 99, 125). Other versions can be found in Gould (1988: 85, 144), Norman (1987: 91–9), and Walzer (1983: 292). But it is important to make clear that unlike some of these latter authors I am not suggesting that non-subjects should have no control, only that the appropriate control for non-subjects to exercise is of a different sort. Unless it is possible to establish that non-subjects are only negligibly affected by an association, it would be morally arbitrary from the point of view of the principle of equal liberty to deny non-subjects any control over its decision-making process.

The most familiar example of an association to which the all-subjected principle is applied is the democratic state. Since each member of the state is subject to its authority, each member shares direct control over it. Furthermore, since each member is subject to the state's authority over the same range of matters, each has an equal share of direct control over it: an equally valuable vote. Even if in practice there are numerous difficulties, this is the fundamental rationale underpinning the democratic state. Its members are simultaneously authority bearing subjects and direct control exercising citizens. Non-subjects, however, are not citizens, even though they may be affected by the decisions and activities of the state. This does not mean that they have no control over the state—they may, for example, impose tariff barriers against the state's produce—but their control is indirect.

To summarize, given an ethical commitment to the principle of equal liberty, there are good reasons to govern associations according to the all-affected principle and the all-subjected principle, which are both fundamental principles of democracy.

Economic Democracy

In this section I want to consider whether enterprises (or firms) in a capitalist economy live up to these democratic principles. In the process of doing this I will begin to develop a model of economic democracy. The model will not propose change for the sake of change. Where existing capitalist practices live up to democratic principles they will be incorporated into the model unchanged. But where they do not, something new will be required.

Like all other associations, enterprises ought to be governed in accordance with the all-affected principle. In a capitalist economy there are many groups of individuals, or stakeholders, who are affected by the activities of a firm. They include, among others: employees or workers; consumers; shareholders or capitalists; suppliers of raw materials and producer goods; banks and other financial institutions; and local residents. According to the all-affected principle, each of these stakeholders should exercise some control over the firm.

As we noted in the last section, there are two distinct ways in which individuals can exercise control over an association. They can exercise control directly, by participating in its decision-making process, or they can exercise control indirectly, by setting constraints on the decisions that can emerge. Those who are subject to the association's authority should exercise control directly. Those who are not subject to its authority should exercise control indirectly.

In a capitalist economy, indirect control is available to each of the stakeholders. Indirect control over firms falls into two subcategories: 'government regulation'

(Dahl, 1970: 121) and 'exit control' (Hirschman, 1970: 4). Exit is a particularly desirable form of indirect control because it allows each individual to simultaneously exercise the maximum possible indirect control by completely blocking the effect which a firm's decisions would otherwise have on them. However, exit is only effective if (a) there is a competitive market and (b) the costs of exit are low. Wherever either of these conditions does not pertain, stakeholders must supplement or replace exit control with government regulation. For most stakeholders a mixture of both is needed, even for those stakeholders for whom exit control is paradigmatically advantageous.

Consider the case of consumers. In a competitive market economy exit is a particularly appropriate way for consumers to exercise control over a firm because it enables all those and only those consumers who are affected to exercise control, and because it enables these consumers to better satisfy their choices (i.e., their 'demand') both in the short term, by getting a better deal elsewhere, and in the long term, by forcing improvements on wayward firms. The mechanism is simple enough. If the quality of a firm's product deteriorates or if its price rises then customers will cease to buy that firm's product (that is, they will 'exit' from their relationship with that firm) and will instead buy what they want from a competitor. Falling revenue will alert the firm's management to customer dissatisfaction and force the firm to make alterations if it wants to stay in business.[6] In this way, exit control allows the consumer to constrain a wayward firm.

There are times, however, when exit control alone is not enough for consumers and must be supplemented by, or even predicated on, government regulation. For example, government regulation is needed where there is monopoly control over a product, especially where the product is a staple, since in these cases exit control becomes ineffectual. Government regulation is also needed where consumers lack the relevant information or expertise, or where the cost of acquiring these is too great (Hirschman, 1981: 219–20). And it is needed wherever consumer safety is an issue, since exit control would have to rely on people actually being injured in order to come into effect.

Nevertheless, it remains the case that consumer control over firms should predominantly be exercised by exit. The experience of attempts to rely predominantly on government regulations to exercise control on behalf of consumers reinforces this conclusion. In traditional Soviet-style economies these attempts seriously weakened the position of consumers vis-à-vis firms (Nove, 1983: 71) and led to chronic shortages of consumer goods (Kornai, 1986: 9). Thus, as in a capitalist economy, in an economy based on economic democracy, consumer control would predominantly be exercised by exit. And this implies that the economy must be a market economy, at least to the extent of having a competitive market in consumer goods.

Various combinations of exit control and government regulation are available to each of the other stakeholders. Exit control can play a prominent role wherever a competitive market can be established between the stakeholder and the firm. Thus labour markets, stock markets, financial markets, and markets for suppliers of raw materials and producer goods all facilitate exit control. Only in the case of residents is a prominent role for exit difficult to envisage. But in that case government regulation can play an important role.

The basic point to note is that capitalism *does* provide adequate mechanisms of *indirect* control to each stakeholder. Thus, in an economy based on the principles of democracy, indirect control would look much the same as in a capitalist economy. No doubt some significant changes would be needed, but the basic mechanisms through which stakeholders gain indirect control would be the same.

It is only when we begin to consider who should have direct control over a firm that the fundamental difference between economic democracy and capitalism becomes clear. Following Hirschman (1970: 19) I will sometimes refer to direct control as 'voice' control. This serves to highlight the distinction between the non-market, 'political' character of direct control and the market-based, 'economic' character of exit control.[7] To see the difference between capitalism and economic democracy we need only focus on the position of the traditional industrial antagonists: capital (the shareholders) and labour (the employees). For under capitalism, direct 'voice' control is exercised by capital. But, I will argue, in an economic democracy, it must by exercised by labour.

It is possible to make this argument on the grounds that capital is intrinsically more mobile than labour. Some reasons for thinking that capital is more mobile are discussed by Offe (1985: 178) and Archer (1995: 92–4). Mobility is relevant because it is a necessary condition for the effective use of exit control. If exit control were the only form of control available, then capital's effective control would be greater than labour's because of its greater intrinsic mobility. Thus an argument can be made that labour should be given greater direct voice control in order to compensate for its inability to effectively exercise full exit control. This, however, is not the argument that I want to pursue here. Rather, I will argue that direct voice control should be exercised by labour because the employees who sell this labour are the only human individuals subject to the authority of the firm.

In capitalist societies labour is defined by its role in the employment contract. Indeed, it is arguable that the employment contract is capitalism's most characteristic feature (Offe, 1985: 52). According to the standard neoclassical interpretation, the employers and employees who are party to an employment contract are simply buying and selling a commodity like any other. The employee sells a certain amount of his or her labour to the employer in exchange for a wage. But labour is not a commodity like any other. It is a 'fictitious' commodity (Polanyi, 1957: 72). When a genuine commodity (such as a piece of machinery) is exchanged, it is transferred from the seller to the buyer along with the exclusive right to decide what to do with it. But when labour is exchanged it remains physically attached to its seller. For there is no separate or detachable entity 'labour' which the labourer can hand over to an employing firm. 'Labour is only another name for a human activity which goes with life itself' (Polanyi, 1957: 72). Thus a firm can only gain its exclusive right to decide what it will do with the labour it buys if it gains an exclusive right to decide what the labourers themselves will do. And a firm can only gain an exclusive right to decide what the labourers will do if its decisions about what they will do exclude and replace those of the labourers. But the exclusion and replacement of choice is the defining feature of an authority relationship. Thus, when labourers sell their labour to a firm, they themselves become subject to the authority of that firm.

Moreover, the firm will have a powerful incentive to actually exercise this authority over its workers. This is because there is a gap between what the firm acquires under the contract of employment and what it wants from that contract. The gap exists because the 'commodity' that the labourer sells is not labour itself, but what Marx calls 'labour power' or 'the capacity for labour' (Marx, 1976: 270). The firm buys this capacity for a certain period of time. In doing so it only acquires the potential for labour (labour power) as opposed to its actual per-formance (labour). Clearly this potential labour is of no use to the employer unless it is turned into actually performed labour. But the actual labour that can be acquired from a given amount of labour power is variable and remains unspecified in the employment contract. This variability leads to a conflict of interest between workers and capitalists. Since the cost of the labour has already been set, the more labour the capitalists can get the labourer to perform, the more profit they stand to gain. Thus, if the firm is to maximize its profits, it may be imperative for it to exercise authority over the labour power that it has bought.[8]

It seems, then, that the employment of labour involves the worker not just in the initial exchange relationship, but also in a subsequent authority relationship with the firm. According to Marx the first relationship is 'a very Eden of the innate rights of man' (1976: 280), but, once inside 'the hidden abode of production' (p. 279), the second relationship takes over. Here 'the capitalist formulates his autocratic power over his workers like a private legislator ... unaccompanied by either that division of responsibility otherwise so much approved of by the bourgeoisie, or the still more approved representative system' (pp. 549–50).

It is this latter authority relationship that does not live up to the democratic principles discussed in the last section. For although it is the workers who are subject to the authority of the firm, it is, under a capitalist regime, the capitalists (i.e., the shareholders) who have direct 'voice' control over the firm. Thus, in an economic democracy, direct 'voice' control over a firm must be transferred to those who work in that firm. Note that this does not imply either that labour has no control under capitalism, or that capital has no control under economic democ-racy. On the contrary, both continue to exercise indirect 'exit' control under both systems. In brief, then, capitalism is a system where capital can exercise both exit and voice control while labour can exercise only exit, whereas economic democracy is a system where labour can exercise both exit and voice control while capital can exercise only exit. I will call this the basic model of economic democracy.

THREE OBJECTIONS

I now want to consider three fundamental objections to this basic model of economic democracy. According to the *first*, the employees are not subject to the authority of the firm. According to the *second*, it is the shareholders who are subject. And according to the *third*, the firm need not have any subjects at all.

Recall that a person who is subject to authority is bound to comply with the decisions of that authority in the sense that their choices are excluded and replaced by those of the authority. The first objection argues that workers are not bound in this way because they can leave the firm whenever they want to (Alcian and Demsetz, 1986: 111–12). There are a number of ways to answer this objection.

For one thing, it is usually not true that workers can leave a firm whenever they want to. Employment contracts typically specify a period of 'notice' (usually some number of weeks) which must be served before an employee can leave. This means that, at least for that period, employees certainly are bound to obey their employers. Under these conditions, hiring a worker is a bit like renting a house: neither the worker nor the landlord can regain authority over what they have rented out until a certain time has elapsed.

But even if we set aside the question of notice it is still possible to argue that workers are bound to obey the firm that employs them. Dahl suggests we compare the relationship between a worker and his firm with the relationship between a citizen and his municipality or even with the relationship between a citizen and his state. It may be true that a worker who does not want to obey a management directive can leave a firm. But, similarly, a citizen who does not want to obey an ordinance can leave her municipality and (in many countries) a citizen who does not want to obey the laws of her state can leave that state. However, in all three cases, despite the fact that membership appears to be voluntary, the cost of leaving is so high that it is for all practical purposes compulsory (Dahl, 1985: 114–15).

Both of the responses we have considered so far share an assumption with the objection that they are answering. They assume that being bound involves an unconditional compulsion: to be bound to do something is to be compelled to do it 'no matter what'. But it is also possible to answer the objection by rejecting this assumption. Indeed, I think that this is the lesson that should be drawn from the example of municipal and state authority. If, as Dahl suggests, it is only because of the high cost of departure that citizens are bound to obey municipal or state laws, then a great many citizens are not bound at all. In some countries large groups of people move between municipalities at little or no cost, and the same is true for smaller groups of people who move between states. But we still think of these people as being subject to the authority of a municipality or a state and as being bound to obey their laws. Indeed, the authority of a state over its citizens is the paradigmatic example of authority. If states do not have authority it is hard to imagine who does.

This suggests that rather than denying the authority of the state we should reconsider what it means to say that a subject is 'bound'. Rather than defining someone as bound if they are unconditionally compelled to obey an association, we should define someone as bound if they are compelled to obey an association *so long as they are a member* of it. This means that questions about the nature of authority relations within an association can be posed independently of questions about whether membership of that association is compulsory or voluntary. This is as it should be. Clearly it is important to distinguish subjects who cannot exit (such as serfs) from subjects who can exit (such as workers). But it is equally important to distinguish between the different kinds of authority to which those who can exit are subject. A dictatorial and a democratic state do not become identical simply because the members of each are able to exit. The fundamental problem with the first objection is that it depends on a definition of boundness which reduces questions about authority to questions about exit rights. In summary then, even if workers can leave a firm, they are still subject to its authority while they work for it. For the duration of their employment they are bound to comply with certain decisions of the firm and it is this which justifies their claim to direct control.[9]

According to the second objection to the basic model of economic democracy, shareholders are subject to the authority of the firm and hence should share direct control over it. The trouble with this objection is that it confuses an exclusive right to decide what to do with certain commodities with authority over persons. Certainly a firm has an exclusive right to decide what to do with the capital which capitalists invest in it. But this does not mean that the capitalists themselves are subject to the firm's authority. For unlike labour, capital is not a fictitious commodity because it can be exchanged without remaining attached to the capitalist who sells or rents it. Consider the different ways in which the owners of capital and the owners of labour are affected by contracts to let third parties use their respective 'commodities'. While I am using your capital you can do something else, but while I am using your labour power you cannot. Since capital can be separated from the capitalist, the firm's authority does not extend to the capitalist. The firm can issue orders about how its capital will be utilized but it cannot tell the capitalists themselves what to do. Who has ever heard a company manager yelling at the shareholders to 'invest harder'? Since the shareholders are not subject to the authority of the firm they should not have direct control over it.

In this respect it is useful to compare the position of shareholders with that of banks and other financial institutions. Both provide the firm with the same commodity (capital); and both gain a return for undertaking this risk (dividends in the case of equity, and interest in the case of debt). But nobody thinks of banks as subject to the authority of the firms to which they lend, and, at least in the Anglo-Saxon world, nobody suggests that it is wrong that under capitalism banks do not exercise direct control over these firms. Why, then, should shareholders be thought of as subjects entitled to exercise direct control?

To deny that shareholders are subject to the authority of the firm in which they invest is not to deny that they are affected by the decisions of that firm and hence should exercise control over it. But, under the basic model of economic democracy, shareholders *do* exercise control over the firms in which they invest: they exercise indirect control through their power to 'exit'. As with the analogous control exercised by banks, this 'exit' control depends on the existence of a market: a capital market in the case of banks and a stock market in the case of shareholders. And it is clear from the experience of capitalist societies that the control which these markets give both to banks and to shareholders can be very substantial.

Indeed, even though shareholders in capitalist societies nominally have direct control over their firms, it is arguable that, for some time, indirect control exercised through their power to 'exit' has been by far the most important source of control available to them. This argument is closely related to Berle and Means' (1932) thesis that in the modern corporation ownership and (direct) control have become separated. The shareholders still own the firm, but (direct) control has passed into the hands of a managerial elite. As a result it has become a 'Wall Street rule' that 'if you do not like the management you should sell your stock' (Hirschman, 1970: 46).

According to the third objection to the basic model of economic democracy there need not be any subjects at all. The fact that capitalism makes workers subject to the authority of a firm does not mean that other systems must do likewise. On the contrary, according to this objection, it is possible to organize work in such a way that no individual is subject to an authority relationship. This can be done, it is suggested, by making every worker into an independent contractor. We know from our experience of capitalism that it is possible for independent contractors to perform certain kinds of work. But is it possible to universalize this form of coordination, thereby eliminating authority relations from the economy and establishing a kind of 'contract-socialism' (Pateman, 1988: 152)? Work by 'transaction cost' economists suggests that the answer is 'no'.

Some of the most influential work on transaction costs has been done by Oliver Williamson. Building on the seminal work of Ronald Coase (1986) and others, Williamson argues that to eliminate authority relations from the organization of work would be prohibitively costly. Williamson (1985: 229) compares various modes of organizing a typical manufacturing task—Adam Smith's often discussed example of the pin manufacturers—and finds that all modes which rely solely on contracts are decidedly less efficient than modes that rely on an authority relation.

The question of costs arises because we live in a 'changing world' which requires individuals and their transactions to constantly adjust to new circumstances (Hayek, 1986: 69). Transactions that are solely contractual can meet this requirement in one of two ways. Either the contract must include terms which enable the relevant adjustments to be made, or the contract must be renegotiated; in effect, that is, a new contract must be made. The first option requires a contingent claims contract. The second option requires sequential spot contracting.

Williamson explains his findings about the inefficiency of contract-only modes of work organization by appealing to two reasonable-sounding 'behavioural assumptions' about human individuals. He calls the first 'bounded rationality' and the second 'opportunism'.

Bounded rationality is an assumption about the cognitive competence of individuals (Simon, 1983: 19; Williamson, 1985: 45). According to this assumption, individuals have only a limited ability to predict the consequences of their actions. In part, at least, this is because individuals have limited access to information and limited capacity to process it (Arrow, 1974: 37, 39). Because of these limits, cognitive competence is a scarce resource, and hence like any other scarce resource, the more of it we have to use in order to achieve a goal, the more expensive the achievement of that goal becomes. This means that drawing up a contingent claims contract will be expensive. A fully-specified contingent claims contract is a contract that sets out the obligations of each party in every possible contingency. The more contingencies and their concomitant obligations we attempt to specify, the more cognitive competence we will have to use and the more costly the contract will become.

Opportunism is an assumption about the motivation of individuals who engage in transactions (Williamson, 1985: 47). It is a strong version of the assumption that individuals are self-interest seeking. Opportunist individuals are prepared to seek their self-interest with guile, and Williamson assumes that at least some individuals are prepared to act in this way. Typical examples of opportunism include providing false or misleading information to those with whom one is entering into a contract, and violating the terms of a contract after one has entered into it whenever it is convenient to do so. Opportunism takes on its greatest significance in a context of 'asset specificity'. Asset specificity refers to the fact that the value of certain assets is specific to a particular transaction. For example, if I agree to build a plant for you on a particular site, then the more it would cost to relocate the plant, the more its value will be specific to our particular transaction (Williamson, 1985: 95). Labour also often manifests asset-specificity resulting, for example, from task-specific training.[10] In each case the result is a 'lock-in effect' (p. 53). Once such an asset has been invested, one or both of the parties to the investment contract will have a monopoly power, which, assuming opportunism, they can exploit to their own advantage each time that the contract is renegotiated. This means that sequential spot contracting will be expensive. Pure sequential spot contracting involves a series of one-off, task-specific deals, such as those between a customer and his or her grocer (Williamson et al., 1986: 144). The more frequently renegotiations take place, the more scope there will be for utilizing the power of asset-specific investments and the more costly the contracting process will become (Williamson, 1985: 78).

Thus it is clear that, if we accept Williamson's two behavioural assumptions, any attempt to coordinate the relationship between firms and labourers solely by contracts would be extremely costly. Bounded rationality makes contingent claims contracts costly, and opportunism does the same for sequential spot contracting. Authority relations, on the other hand, can reduce these costs. By establishing a long-term relationship the expenses associated with renegotiations are curtailed, but at the same time the need for expensive contingency planning is avoided. Thus there is no way of efficiently organizing some forms of work without subjecting individuals to an authority relationship (Arrow, 1974: 69). In the real world of the advanced capitalist countries this will be enough to ensure that these forms of work continue to be organized in such a way that workers are subject to the authority of their firm.

Nevertheless, a proponent of the objection that we are considering may continue to argue that while it would certainly be very costly to eliminate economic subjects it is still *possible*. However, there are good reasons to think that even this is not so. Remember that since the organization of work will have to adapt over time, contract-only coordination must take one of two forms: contingent claims contracting or sequential spot contracting.

A contingent claims contract is a fully-specified contract that sets out the obligations of each party in every possible contingency. We have already seen how Williamson argues that such contracts can be very expensive because of bounded rationality. In fact, however, he can and does make the stronger claim that, for any reasonably complex transaction, bounded rationality makes a fully-specified contingent claims contract impossible. There are just too many possible alternatives and it is not possible to estimate the consequences of each (Williamson et al., 1986: 142–3). Furthermore, unlike in, say, chess, there is no way of even specifying all the alternatives. A fully-specified contingent claims contract is impossible because of uncertainty about the future.

Sequential spot contracting avoids this problem by adapting to the future only when it is reached. No attempt is made to foreshadow future changes within the framework of any one contract (as in contingent claims contracting). Rather, the contract itself is continually renegotiated to meet these changes as they arise. But this procedure can also fall prey to uncertainty: not in the future, but in the present. Consider a complex, rapidly changing production process that requires each of a large number of workers to simultaneously perform different but interrelated functions. Given the bounds of human rationality there is no way that all the individuals whose actions must be coordinated can renegotiate their contracts either quickly enough or often enough without overloading their cognitive competence. The problems posed by bounded rationality will be further exacerbated in such a situation by the interdependence of the various renegotiations. Each contractor will need to consider each of the possible deals which the other contractors may reach before being able to make his or her own deals. This seems to lead back to another kind of contingent claims contracting. In this case the contingent claims contract would have to specify all the various contracts that the contractor is prepared to enter into as a function of each of the other possible contracts which may be agreed between third parties.[11]

Thus, at least for certain forms of work, it is simply not possible for contract-only coordination to displace authority relations between a firm and its workers.

So each of the three objections to the basic model of economic democracy fails. According to the first objection employees are not subject to the authority of their firm. This objection fails because it mistakenly conflates questions about authority with questions about exit rights. According to the second objection capitalists are subject to the authority of their firm. This objection fails because it mistakenly conflates exclusive rights over capital with authority over capitalists. Finally, according to the third objection the firm need not have any subjects at all. But this objection also fails because it makes unrealistic assumptions that ignore human bounded rationality and opportunism.

Conclusion

If individual freedom—freedom for all—is the basic ethical reference point against which the legitimacy of our social and political institutions should be judeged, then direct voice control over an enterprise should be transferred from the capitalists who own that enterprise to the workers who are employed by it. Note, however, that this model of economic democracy does not object *per se* to the separate existence of capitalists (who are owners) and workers (who are employees). Rather, it objects to the relationship between the two, and, in particular, to the fact that those who are employed become subject to the authority of those who own. This means that, unlike in some other models of economic democracy, worker ownership is not a necessary characteristic. While it may be possible in certain circumstances to use worker ownership as a vehicle to achieve worker self-government, it is the system of government and not the system of ownership that defines an economic democracy.

As I have argued elsewhere, the introduction of economic democracy need not be an all or nothing affair (Archer, 1995). It can involve, and often has invovled, incremental reforms and gradual step-by-step transfers of direct control. Surges of interest in economic democracy and movements seeking to pursue it, have occurred at repeated intervals since the emergence of industrial capitalism. In important surges of interest occurred in the early twentieth century, notably in the work of the Webbs (1898), Cole (1920), and Tawney (1964); in the post-war reforms in the middle of the century, such as those in Germany (Thelen, 1991) and France (Steinhouse, 2001); and in the 1970s and 1980s, when reforms in Sweden and Germany where followed by interest in the English speaking world (Poole et al., 2001).

For the most part, however, the last decade or two have not been marked by any such surge of interest. Yet, during this time, rarely has a year gone by in which we have not been reminded of the virtues of democracy and the fundamental importance of freedom. In much of the advanced capitalist world these values have become touchstones for the legitmacy of all sorts of polices. Indeed so great are their virtues thought to be that they have increasingly been used to justify large-scale interventions in the affairs of other states. But, as we have seen, these same values raise fundamental questions about the legitimacy of basic economic institutions in the advanced capitalist countries themselves.

Notes

1. For the case for this conception of liberty see Archer (1995: 13–23).
2. To do this I will draw on a number of arguments first set out in an earlier work (Archer, 1995). Interested readers can find a fuller version of some of these arguments there.
3. For a discussion of whether there is a trade-off between this liberty-based principle and other values like competence and economy (Dahl, 1970) or efficiency and equity (Budd, 2004), see Archer (1995: 27).
4. For example, in a competitive market, a consumer has a veto over a firm's ability to affect him because he can take his custom elsewhere, but he does not have a veto over the firm's decisions themselves.
5. For example, consumers can share the indirect control that they exercise through the market without weakening their personal indirect control. On the other hand, residents exercising indirect control through the regulatory powers of a local government will weaken their personal indirect control by sharing these powers with others.
6. Note, however, that where both prices rise and quality deteriorates, the price rise can shield a certain number of exits (Hirschman, 1970: 23). This illustrates the more general problem that exit control is sometimes ineffective because the information it conveys is rich enough in detail.

7. Note, however, that I am using 'voice' more narrowly than Hirschman (1970: 30) does. Compare with Archer (1995: 41–2, note 5).

8. See Bowles (1986: 334); Edwards (1986: 280); Offe (1985: 57).

9. In the English common law tradition the existence of an authority relationship has long been considered the single most important, if not the only, defining feature of the relationship between an employer and employee or, in the language of this law, a master and servant (Rideout and Dyson, 1983: 4–6).

10. Even in unskilled jobs there is usually a certain amount of on-the-job learning as well as efficiencies that result from personal relations with co-workers. Simply by working for a particular firm your labour will come to manifest some degree of asset-specificity. Williamson (1985: 61) refers to this as the 'fundamental transformation'.

11. In addition there are likely to be multiple 'coordination problems' in the game theoretic sense (Schelling, 1960: 89). These would exist even in the absence of bounded rationality.

References

ALCIAN, A. and DEMSETZ, H. (1986) 'Production, Information Costs and Economic Organisation', in Putterman, (ed.) (1986).

ARCHER, R. (1995) *Economic Democracy: The Politics of Feasible Socialism*, Oxford: Oxford University Press.

ARNESON, R. (1993) 'Democratic Rights and National and Workplace Levels', in D. Copp et al., (eds), *The Idea of Democracy*. Cambridge: Cambridge University Press.

ARROW, K. J. (1974) *The Limits of Organization*. New York: Norton.

BACHARACH, P. (1969) *The Theory of Democratic Elitism*. London: University of London Press.

BERLE, A. and MEANS, G. (1932) *The Modern Corporation and Private Property*. New York: Commerce Clearing House.

BOWLES, S. (1986) 'The Production Process in a Competitive Economy', in Putterman, (ed.) (1986).

BUDD, J. W. (2004) *Employment with a Human Face*. Ithaca, NY: Cornell University Press.

COASE, R. (1986) 'The Nature of the Firm', in Putterman, (ed.) (1986).

COLE, G. D. H. (1920) *Guild Socialism Restated*. London: George Allen and Unwin.

DAHL, R. A. (1970) *After the Revolution*. New Haven, CT: Yale University Press.

—— (1979) 'Procedural Democracy', in P. Laslett and J. Fishkin, (eds), *Philosophy, Politics and Society*, 5th series. New Haven, CT: Yale University Press.

—— (1985) *A Preface to Economic Democracy*. Cambridge: Polity.

EDWARDS, R. (1986) 'From *Contested Terrain*', in Putterman, (ed.) (1986).

ELLERMAN, D. (1990) *The Democratic Worker-Owned Firm*. Boston, MA: Unwin Hyman.

FRIEDMAN, R. (1973) 'On the Concept of Authority in Political Theory', in R. E. Flathman, (ed.), *Concepts in Social and Political Philosophy*. New York: Macmillan.

GOULD, C. C. (1988) *Rethinking Democracy*. Cambridge: Cambridge University Press.

GREEN, L. (1988) *The Authority of the State*. Oxford: Oxford University Press.

GROSS, J. A. (1999) 'A Human Rights Perspective on U.S. Labor Relations Law', *Employee Rights and Employee Policy Journal*, vol. 3.

HAYEK, F. A. (1986) 'The Use of Knowledge in Society', in Putterman, (ed.) (1986).

HIRSCHMAN, A. O. (1970) *Exit, Voice and Loyalty*. Cambridge, MA: Harvard University Press.

—— (1981) *Essay in Trespassing*. Cambridge: Cambridge University Press.

HOLMES, S. (1988) 'Precommitment and Paradox of Democracy', in J. Elster and R. Stagstad, (eds), *Constitutionalism and Democracy*. Cambridge: Cambridge University Press.

KORNAI, J. (1986) *Contradictions and Dilemmas*. Cambridge, MA: MIT Press.

KORPI, W. (1978) *The Working Class in Welfare Capitalism*. London: Routledge.

LINDBLOM, C. E. (1977) *Politics and Markets*. New York: Basic Books.

LINDSAY, A. D. (1962) *The Modern Democratic State*. Oxford: Oxford University Press.

MARX, K. (1976) *Capital*, vol. 1. Harmondsworth: Penguin.

McPHERSON, M. (1983) 'Efficiency and Liberty in the Productive Enterprise', *Philosophy and Public Affairs*, 12(4) Fall.

MUELLER, D. C. (1970) *Public Choice*. Cambridge: Cambridge University Press.

NORMAN, R. (1987) *Free and Equal*. Oxford: Oxford University Press.

NOVE, A. (1983) *The Economics of Feasible Socialism*. London: George Allen and Unwin.

OFFE, C. (1985) *Disorganised Capitalism*. Cambridge: Polity.

PATEMAN, C. (1988) *The Sexual Contract*. Cambridge: Polity.

POLYANI, K. (1957) *The Great Transformation*. Boston, MA: Beacon.

POOLE, M., LANSBURY R., and WAILES N. (2001) 'A Comparative Analysis of Developments in Industrial Democracy', *Industrial Relations*, 40(3) July.

PUTTERMAN, L. (ed.) (1986) *The Economic Nature of the Firm*. Cambridge: Cambridge University Press.

RAZ, J. (1986) *The Morality of Freedom*. Oxford: Oxford University Press.

—— (1987) 'Government by Consent', in J. W. Pennock and J. R. Chapman, (eds), 'Authority Revisited', *Nomos*, 29. New York: New York University Press.

RIDEOUT, R. W. and DYSON, J. (1983) *Rideout's Principles of Labour Law*, 4th edition. London: Sweet and Maxwell.

SCHELLING, T. C. (1960) *The Strategy of Conflict*. Cambridge, MA: Harvard University Press.

SIMON, H. (1983) *Reason in Human Affairs*. Oxford: Blackwell.

SOPER, P. (1989) 'Legal Theory and the Claim of Authority', *Philosophy and Public Affairs*, 18(3) summer.

STEINHOUSE, A. (2001) *Workers Participation in Post-Liberation France*. Lanham, MD: Lexington Books.

TAWNEY, R. H. (1964) *The Radical Tradition*. London: George Allen and Unwin.

THELEN, K. (1991) *Union of Parts: Labor Politics in Postwar Germany*. Ithaca, NY: Cornell University Press.

WALTZER, M. (1983) *Spheres of Justice*. Oxford: Martin Robertson.

WEBB, S. and WEBB, B. (1898) *Industrial Democracy*. London: Longmans, Green.

WILLIAMSON, O. (1985) *The Economic Institutions of Capitalism*. New York: The Free Press.

—— WACHTER, M., and HARRIS, J. (1986) 'Understanding the Employment Relation' in Putterman, (ed.) (1986).

Index